Understanding Leisure and Recreation:
Mapping the Past, Charting the Future

Understanding Leisure and Recreation:

Mapping the Past, Charting the Future

Edgar L. Jackson

Department of Geography,
University of Alberta

Thomas L. Burton

Department of Recreation and Leisure Studies,
University of Alberta

Venture Publishing, Inc.
State College, PA 16803

Cover Design by Sandra Sikorski
Design by Susan McDade
Production Supervisor Bonnie Godbey
Library of Congress Catalogue Number 89-51384
ISBN 0-910251-34-7

distributed outside North America
by E & F N Spon. Ltd.
11 New Fetter Lane
London, England EC4P 4EE

The *Spatial Perspective* on page 326 is adapted from S.L.J. Smith. *Recreation Geography*. London: Longman, 1983, p189

For

Patrick and Nicholas Jackson

and

Julian Dale-Burton

UNDERSTANDING LEISURE AND RECREATION: MAPPING THE PAST, CHARTING THE FUTURE

PREFACE

PART ONE: THE PAST

PART TWO: CONCEPTS AND CONCEPTIONS

PART FIVE: THE FUTURE

APPENDIX

Preface

It would be foolhardy to embark on a long journey into uncharted territory without knowledge of the terrain already traversed and some sense of the land that lies ahead. We believe that the social scientific study of leisure and recreation is now in the midst of a long and difficult exploration: hence the cartographic metaphor embodied in the sub-title of this book — *Mapping the Past, Charting the Future* — and in the titles of our opening and closing chapters.

By now, some two decades after the publication of the first edition of the *Journal of Leisure Research* — one of the most important milestones in the brief history of leisure studies — the essential topography of leisure and recreation has been mapped in great detail; we know the nature, location, and importance of many of its landmarks (although the interpretation of the landscape as an entity still varies greatly). But, without a clear sense of the destination towards which we can and should be moving in the future, and of the opportunities and obstacles to come — a chart, in effect — leisure studies and leisure researchers run the serious risk of running off in all directions at once.

We both believe that knowledge is enhanced, not only by new discoveries in original research, but also by the consolidation and critical assessment of what has been learned to date. In addition, believing that such consolidation and critical assessment will assist in directing future research efforts, we first agreed on the need for this book in the summer of 1984, when we drew up an initial list of topics, chapters, and contributors. Unfortunately, because of non-coincidental study leaves from the University of Alberta, the idea lay dormant for two years. Then, in the fall of 1986, we revised our list, developed some firm objectives for the book, and wrote to most of the contributors whose chapters appear here. Our belief in the need for the book was substantiated by the immediate and uniformly enthusiastic response of everyone whom we first contacted. At that stage, too, several topics and additional contributors were suggested to us; our invitations to them to write chapters also met with success.

From the outset, we felt that *Understanding Leisure and Recreation* could and should be far more than the typical set of disjointed essays, each with its own merits, perhaps, but with little sense of cohesion or contribution to the book as a whole. Thus, while we urged each author to interpret and address the suggested topics in his or her own special way, we have also made several efforts to integrate and consolidate the chapters, in ways which, we feel, make this book unique.

First, we asked all contributors to prepare a detailed chapter outline; these summaries were circulated to every contributor. Then, all chapters were subjected to several rounds of review. Both of us conducted detailed and independent reviews of each first full chapter draft and developed an integrated response to each author. Next, when almost all the second drafts had been received, a complete set of chapters was sent to all contributors, who were strongly encouraged to cross-reference (and, if necessary, take issue with) their co-contributors.

Then — and most unusual if not unique in endeavors of this kind — we were able to assemble small groups of the contributors on three occasions to discuss the progress of the book and its content. The first such meeting took place at the Fifth Canadian Congress on Leisure Research at Dalhousie University in Halifax, Nova Scotia, in May 1987; this was during the early stages of the book, but the meeting nonetheless gave several of us the opportunity to meet one another for the first time and to explore themes and overall direction. Then, almost exactly a year later, when most of the second drafts had been written, a small meeting took place during the World Congress on Free Time, Culture and Society, convened by the World Leisure and Recreation Association and the Department of Recreation and Leisure Studies, University of Alberta, at Lake Louise, Alberta.

The most important such meeting, however, and the most purposeful and productive one, occurred when more than half the authors met in Edmonton towards the end of August, 1988, spending four intensive days reviewing and discussing each chapter, the overall contents of the book, and the best way to structure and sequence the contributions. After the seminar, all participants rewrote their chapters as necessary and appropriate, while detailed comments were forwarded to the remaining authors, whom our finances had prevented us from inviting to Edmonton.

The result, we hope, is a book about leisure and recreation research that is unmatched in its blend of integration and debate. We have not striven for consistency or uniformity in chapter content, nor have we dictated the authors' choice of concepts or approaches — quite the reverse. Although we ourselves provided considerable feedback to all the authors, and while each enjoyed the benefits of the comments from the authors' seminar, our objective has always been to allow the authors to speak for themselves.

Another unique aspect of the book arises from our decision to conduct an international survey of active leisure researchers. This study is described in detail in the opening chapter, and its findings are used extensively in that chapter, as well as in the concluding one. The survey gave us the opportunity to tap the views of an international body of leisure scientists with which to complement, substantiate — and sometimes disagree with — the assessments and ideas of the scholars who have contributed to the book.

Inevitably, in a book with such a wide scope as this one, judgments have had to be made concerning what to include and what to leave out. We did not feel it necessary, for example, to solicit chapters devoted to the contributions of disciplines such as sociology or psychology to the understanding of leisure and recreation. In many respects, these contributions are detailed explicitly, if not necessarily systematically, in the chapters on motivations, satisfaction, leisure styles and elsewhere. We did, however, feel we ought to pay special attention to the contributions of geography (with reference to one important branch of that discipline, spatial analysis) and economics. This is because these important frameworks and approaches have become somewhat isolated from the mainstream of leisure studies, at least as evidenced by recent editions of the major leisure studies journals.

Needless to say, in structure, form, and content, *Understanding Leisure and Recreation* has departed radically from the rudimentary outline with which we began almost five years ago. The result is a cohesive set of essays that begin with basic concepts and conceptions, proceed through a set of building blocks and substantive issues, and culminate in the discussion of applications.

Understanding Leisure and Recreation, then, is far more than what we had originally hoped for or expected. For this, we thank, first and foremost, all of the contributors, not only for actually writing their chapters, but (in most cases!) doing so within our deadlines. Probably none of them expected such a rigorous and extensive round of reviews and feedback, but everyone took these in good part and quickly adopted our view of the book's principal purposes and potential.

We should also like to single out the nine people — Leslie Bella, Sue Glyptis, Geof Godbey, Tom Goodale, Jack Kelly, Steve McCool, Steve Smith, Geoff Wall, and Peter Witt — who made the trip to Edmonton for the authors' seminar, and whose contribution to the integration of the book's chapters is immeasurable. As well, the two authors from the University of Alberta, Wes Cooper and Guy Swinnerton, took part in the seminar, along with ourselves.

We also wish to express our gratitude to the sources of funding for the authors' seminar. We received substantial financial support from the Social Sciences and Humanities Research Council of Canada, the University of Alberta Conference Fund, and the Alberta Department of Recreation and Parks. In this last instance, we must make special mention of Rick Curtis, at that time Director of the Department's Planning Secretariat, whose support and encouragement were crucial to the seminar's success. A generous advance from Venture Publishing also helped us to bring more people to Edmonton than would otherwise have been possible.

The international survey of leisure scholars was financed through a grant from the University of Alberta General Research Fund.

Our two Departments (Geography, and Recreation and Leisure Studies) provided much support in the form of secretarial and other assistance. We wish to thank, especially, Tana MacNab, Fran Metcalfe, Sherry Allenson, and Liz Bruce, who typed considerable portions of the manuscript and correspondence. Wendy Molnar, Donna Macbeth, and Wang Shuguang provided invaluable research assistance at various stages of the project, in particular during the survey of leisure researchers. And special thanks are due to Judy Sefton, who assisted in the preparation of several research grant applications for the conduct of the international survey of active leisure scholars.

Finally, we should like to acknowledge the continual support of, and intellectual debate with our wives, Linda Jackson and Lynne Dale.

It has been a privilege to edit this book. We have enjoyed a unique opportunity to be the first to read the most up-to-date thinking of many of the leading authorities in leisure studies around the world, and to gain a sense of what has been achieved, where the field is, and where it should be going. Moreover, we have learned a great deal from each other while cooperating in the editing of the book. While retaining our own disciplinary perspectives (geography and political economy/planning), we have constantly endeavored to view leisure studies as a broadly based and vigorous field that will only achieve success if members of the various disciplines cooperate in an open, critically constructive way, characterized by mutual respect. In large part, and as we argue in the last chapter, this is the essential message of *Understanding Leisure and Recreation*.

Edgar L. Jackson
Thomas L. Burton
University of Alberta

PART ONE

The Past

There is an old saying to the effect that those who do not heed the lessons of history are condemned to repeat them. With this somber thought in mind, we chose to begin this book about the state of recreation and leisure research, its strengths and limitations, and its future potential by considering its past. In one sense, of course, this entire book is historical; for, in attempting to assess the state of the art in particular areas and streams of recreation and leisure research, each author has necessarily begun by examining the past.

The two chapters in this first part of the book are different, however, in that they attempt to map the past broadly — by reference not to a particular topic or theme, but across the spectrum of substance, methodology, and organization. The purpose is to paint a broad canvas, a backcloth against which the reader may set the particular contributions offered in the twenty chapters to be found in Parts Two, Three, and Four.

Our own chapter, "Mapping the Past," offers an assessment of recreation and leisure research as a whole during the past two decades through three principal means. The development of concepts and theories, the evolution of research methods and techniques, the ebb and flow of particular topics, and the growth of specialized recreation and leisure research organizations and journals are traced, first, through an analysis of a wide range of state-of-the-art reviews that have been written during the past decade or so, and, second, by means of an international survey of active leisure research scholars carried out in the Fall of 1987. The information from these two sources is then judged in the context of a simple descriptive model devised for the purpose. We conclude that there is a significant discrepancy between the current state of recreation and leisure studies and what researchers and scholars in the field — and we ourselves — believe that state ought to be.

On the positive side, leisure studies has established a strong sense of scholarly legitimacy for itself; there has been an outpouring of publications and unpublished reports outlining the findings of research, as well as a significant increase in the numbers of organizations and forums that exist for the exchange of these findings; in particular, the number of scholarly journals devoted exclusively to recreation and leisure studies has grown dramatically; and, most evident, the field has broadened its scope over the years to encompass a wide array of diverse topics, issues, and themes relevant to the notions of recreation and leisure.

On the negative side, there is a widespread belief among recreation and leisure scholars that the quality of research has not kept pace with its quantity. There is a sense of frustration with the apparent lack of progress toward the development of a coherent and consistent body of theory, allied to a feeling that the field has become excessively fragmented; and, to some, most important of all, there is a disquieting sense of concern about the dominance of logical positivist research approaches and methods.

The chapter by Burdge is, at once, less broadly conceived in its scope and yet covers a much greater number of writers and scholars in recreation and leisure studies — 1,148 in all! The chapter traces the evolution of leisure research in disciplinary, multidisciplinary, and interdisciplinary terms. Data about the scholarly backgrounds and institutional affiliations of those who have published papers and articles in the *Journal of Leisure Research* and *Leisure Sciences* during various stages in the evolution of these journals are employed to support the argument that recreation and leisure studies as a field of inquiry has moved from being principally the domain of discipline-based scholars to a point at which it is poised to achieve recognized interdisciplinary status.

Taken together, the two chapters are cause for both optimism and concern. Recreation and leisure studies is a vibrant and growing field of scholarly inquiry, with a high level of consensus among its members about the principal issues that need to be addressed in the immediate future. It is also one in which scholars have significant collective doubts about current research directions and themes. In this environment, the chapters that follow seem to us not only to be valuable but also essential if we are to move confidently into the future.

E. L. J.
T. L. B.

MAPPING THE PAST

Edgar L. Jackson and Thomas L. Burton

Two decades have passed since the publication of the inaugural edition of the *Journal of Leisure Research*, the appearance of which marked a major turning-point in the vigor, quality, and academic respectability of leisure and recreation studies, both in North America and around the world. While the appearance of the *Journal of Leisure Research* did not represent the beginning of systematic research on leisure and recreation, it was an important milestone. For the first time, a single journal provided a focus and a forum for leisure scholars working within a variety of disciplines, and an opportunity to disseminate their research results following the conventional procedures of scholarly evaluation.

The ensuing years have been characterized by a large and growing output of theoretically and practically oriented research. The volume of research, at least, is evidenced by the number of journals that are now dedicated to leisure and recreation themes (Burdge 1983), both of a general nature as well as specific branches of the field (e.g. management; therapeutic recreation; tourism and recreational travel). Social scientists from several disciplines and many countries have contributed to this body of knowledge.

At the same time, however, many commentators, especially in the last ten years, have expressed their concern about the lack of theoretical and conceptual integration and the degree of disciplinary fragmentation in leisure studies, despite the widespread recognition of the need for broadly-based, holistic, and interdisciplinary research. One way to enhance communication, and ultimately to break down barriers to the development of a common purpose in leisure studies, is to carry out periodic retrospective and prospective assessments of the field. That is the purpose of this book.

Assessments of a relatively young field of scholarship such as leisure studies are not only desirable but necessary. They serve to consolidate what has been learned (and why), to clarify concepts and theories (if they exist), to encourage their development (if they do not), and to provide both a focus and (sometimes) a prescription for the future. Without such reviews, leisure studies will likely remain as it was in the 1960s, once described as "in a situation not unlike that of Columbus during his fifteenth century voyages to the New World.

When he set out, he didn't know where he was going; when he arrived, he didn't know where he was; and when he returned, he didn't know where he had been" (Burton 1980: 380).

More specifically, the following benefits frequently accrue from occasional assessments:

- They show how changes in the social sciences as a whole have influenced conceptualization and methodological development in the field (even if this has sometimes occurred only implicitly and, perhaps, inadvertently). Critical reviews can serve to re-interpret and make explicit the trends that are occurring in a discipline or field of study, and the reasons why these trends are developing.
- They indicate how scholars can take advantage of, and perhaps adapt, more general changes in the social sciences, thus ensuring that the specific discipline or field of interest maintains it status at the "leading edge."
- They help to consolidate conceptualization and to enhance the development of a common language.
- They may simply provide information, by creating an awareness of what has already been accomplished in a given area. As Butler (1981, and in this volume) points out, it frequently happens that scholars in a particular discipline, working on a particular issue, are spectacularly ignorant of the contributions that might already have been made in cognate disciplines.
- They may serve to enhance and encourage multidisciplinary and interdisciplinary perspectives and approaches.
- They may indicate issues and concepts with respect to which the greatest contributions to knowledge are most likely to happen.

In addition, assessments may help to divert attention away from esoteric topics that are unlikely to have wide appeal or potential in the research community, and to identify likely research "dead-ends" that are probably best abandoned. They may also encourage scholars to develop a respect for the members of other disciplines and their work, thus serving to break down artificial disciplinary boundaries and discourage reductionist thinking. Finally, and consistent with a point made by Driver in his chapter on the practical applications of research later in this book, assessments may provide researchers with the sense of accomplishment and professional pride that comes from being associated with a wider community of successful and productive scholars.

We can identify at least three types of assessments, each of which can stand alone or can be amalgamated with one or both of the others. First are literature reviews, designed to describe and evaluate published work in the field. These range from journal articles and other papers to books (e.g. Manning 1986;

Smith 1983). Second are research projects which set out to ascertain the opinions of relevant populations concerning the state of the field (Crandall and Lewko 1976). Third are commissioned papers or essays, prepared by recognized scholars in the field, which offer an authoritative view of its state of development: Goodale and Witt's (1980, revised 1985) *Recreation and Leisure: Issues in an Era of Change* is an excellent recent case in point.

Of course, the three types are not mutually exclusive. In particular, authoritative essays often incorporate reviews of published works. Nevertheless, the three approaches are sufficiently distinct that they can be classified as separate types. What makes our present assessment of the state of leisure studies unusual and, perhaps, unique, is that it encompasses all three types of assessment. We begin, in this chapter, with a summary of a wide and diverse array of reviews of scholarly works. Our own assessment of the state of leisure studies is then incorporated with the results of an international survey of active leisure scholars. Finally, the main body of the book consists of a series of commissioned chapters prepared by authoritative scholars whose own research has focused on the particular topics and issues that each addresses.

REVIEWS OF LEISURE STUDIES

During the last two decades, many reviews of leisure and recreation research have become available. They have varied in length and formality (e.g. reflective essays versus rigorous content analyses of journals), and they often include a blend of description and prescription. Frequently, reviews appear in the scholarly research journals; occasionally, however, other forums are used, such as conference plenary addresses (e.g. Roberts 1987). Also, as is common scholarly practice, most empirical research papers include a review of the literature that is most relevant to the specific topic under investigation.

Although there is a certain amount of overlap among categories, and while individual pieces usually encompass more than one theme, the following types of reviews may be distinguished:

- Reflective essays about leisure studies as a whole. Often, these are produced by editors of journals (e.g. Burdge 1974, 1983; Hendricks and Burdge 1972; Iso-Ahola 1984, 1986a; Smith 1982). Other reviews in this category include the annual assessments of leisure research that have appeared in the British journal *Progress in Human Geography* (e.g. Collins and Patmore 1982; Patmore and Collins 1980), and statements about desirable future directions for research (e.g. Bregha 1979; Burton 1979, 1980, 1981; Social Science Research Council/Sports Council 1978; Smith 1975; Smith and Haley 1979; Smith and Ng 1983).

- Content analyses of journals (e.g. Burdge 1983; Riddick, DeSchriver, and Weissinger 1984; Van Doren and Heit 1973; Van Doren, Holland, and Crompton 1984).
- Reviews of specific substantive topics and issues, e.g. Crandall (1980) on motivations, Converse and Machlis (1986) on recreation and energy, Ewing (1980) on recreational travel, Crawford and Godbey (1987) and Jackson (1988) on barriers to leisure, Mercer (1970) on perceptions, and the special issue of *Leisure Sciences* (Vol. 6, No. 4, 1984), which included several reviews of social carrying capacity research.
- Reviews of disciplinary contributions, e.g. Butler (1981), Coppock (1982), Mitchell (1969), Smith (1983), and Wolfe (1974) on geography, Gray (1973) and Parry (1983) on sociology, Vickerman (1983) on economics, and Ingham (1986), Mannell (1979), and Neulinger and Crandall (1976) on psychology.
- Methodological reviews (e.g. Burdge and Field 1972; Dawson 1984; Rojek 1985; Stockdale 1987). These reviews also include assessments of disciplinary, multidisciplinary, and interdisciplinary approaches (e.g. Butler 1981; D'Amours 1984), and papers such as those by Howe (1985) and Kelly (1980) on quantitative and qualitative research.
- Conceptual reviews, in which the author reflects on, and frequently re-evaluates, the meaning of basic concepts, such as freedom and leisure (e.g. Harper 1981) or the relationship between work and leisure (e.g. Parker 1983).
- Efforts to develop specific theory (e.g. Iso-Ahola 1986b).
- Assessments of the impact of social changes on leisure and recreation. Some reviews of this type encompass a broad range of social changes (e.g. Cherry 1986; Roberts 1987), while others focus on more specific issues, such as feminism (e.g. Deem 1986; Green, Hebron, and Woodward 1987) or unemployment (e.g. Fryer and Ullah 1987; Glyptis 1983; Kelvin and Jarrett 1985).
- Exhortations to conduct applied research (e.g. Beaman 1979; Brown, Dyer, and Whaley 1973).

This section has served to outline the wide range of different types of reviews of leisure studies that have been carried out during the past twenty years — and, most noticeably, during the past decade. The principal findings of these reviews will not be discussed here; rather, they will be integrated within the section that examines the present state of leisure studies later in the chapter.

THE SURVEY OF LEISURE RESEARCHERS

We know of only one previous attempt to survey systematically the views and judgments of leisure and recreation researchers themselves — and that was conducted more than a decade ago (Crandall and Lewko 1976). Thus, as part of our effort to review the past, present, and future of leisure and recreation research, we believed it desirable to solicit anew the opinions and judgments of scholars who have contributed to the development of leisure studies in the past two decades. Accordingly, we conducted an international survey mailed to several hundred active researchers. The survey was designed to assess the impact of the various social science disciplines on the nature, form, and findings of leisure studies, and to identify the most pressing tasks for the coming decade. Like the broader effort of which it was a part, our survey was both retrospective and prospective in nature.

We believe that our study canvasses the views of those individuals who have been most responsible for the initiation and evolution of leisure studies. We also contend that the scholars who responded to our survey are likely to be the most active members of the recreation and leisure research community, and thus are among those who will make the most significant contributions to leisure studies in the coming decade.

The survey was conducted among all persons who had ever published a paper in one or more of six major leisure and recreation research journals since their inception. The six journals were: the *Journal of Leisure Research* (first published in 1969); *Society and Leisure* (Old Series ran from 1969 to 1976; New Series began in 1978); *Leisure Sciences* (begun in 1977); *Leisure Studies* (begun in 1982); *Recreation Research Review* (begun in 1976); and the *Journal of Park and Recreation Administration* (begun in 1983).

The objectives of the survey were:

- to assess active researchers' views concerning the principal social science disciplines, as well as multidisciplinary and interdisciplinary fields of study, that have contributed to the development of leisure studies over the past two decades;
- to identify what are perceived to have been the dominant themes in leisure studies during this time;
- to determine the relative contributions of disciplinary, multidisciplinary, and interdisciplinary methods and approaches to leisure studies;
- to assess the extent to which active researchers believe that leisure studies has been characterized primarily by unity, coherence, or fragmentation; and
- to identify what the respondents judge to be the principal issues that must be addressed by leisure researchers during the coming decade.

A short questionnaire, consisting of only six questions, was designed to fulfill these objectives. In all, 696 questionnaires were mailed to research scholars in 20 countries in the Fall of 1987. Not surprisingly, in light of the places of publication of these journals, just over 90 percent of the researchers were located in three countries — the United States, Canada, and the United Kingdom (see Burton and Jackson, 1989, for data and more detail about this and other aspects of the survey).

As expected, many of the questionnaires were returned undelivered. After all, in the case of two of the journals, the list of names went back 20 years! Also, it is likely that many other questionnaires did not reach the addressee, but were simply not returned to the Postal Authorities. Notwithstanding this, 143 completed questionnaires were returned, one-fifth of those originally mailed and almost one-quarter of the maximum effective sample (the original sample minus those returned as undelivered). In comparison with the sample, respondents from the United States were under-represented, those from Canada over-represented, while the proportion of British respondents roughly matched those to whom the questionnaire was mailed (Table 1).

Table 1
The Survey of Active Scholars in Recreation and Leisure Studies: The Countries of Origin of the Respondents
(n = 143)

Country	Respondents	
	n	%
United States of America	69	48.2
Canada: Francophone	3	2.1
Canada: Anglophone	41	28.7
United Kingdom	18	12.6
Australia	4	2.8
France	2	1.4
German Federal Republic	1	0.7
Greece	1	0.7
Unknown	4	2.8

Note:
While the individual questionnaires were not identified, it was possible to determine country of origin in most cases by the following means: (1) about half the responses were signed; (2) the remainder were attributed by indicators such as origin of return envelope, allusions in the questionnaire to particular situations, spelling of words (i.e., American English), and so on.

As far as returns from the various disciplines and fields of study of the respondents are concerned, the largest single group consisted of Sociologists (24.5%), followed by Geographers (21.0%), scholars with backgrounds in Recreation and Leisure Studies (14.7%), persons in Economics, Political Science, Business, and Management Studies (12.6%), those from Interdisciplinary and Environmental Studies (9.1%), Psychologists and Social Psychologists (9.1%), and a group of others from disparate disciplines (9.1%). Except for the conspicuous under-representation of the discipline of Forestry in our survey (the low returns from which had to be included in the "Other" category), this breakdown bears a remarkable resemblance to that reported by Burdge, in the next chapter, for the authors of papers published in the *Journal of Leisure Research* and *Leisure Sciences.*

CHANGES IN LEISURE STUDIES

As an aid to examining the present state of leisure studies, we now briefly consider some of the factors that lead to change in any field of study. We do this using a descriptive model as an organizational framework (Figure 1). The model shows two key components of leisure studies, three sets of factors that effect change in leisure studies, and the relationships (influences) among them. The two key components of leisure studies shown are concepts and methodologies — specific substantive topics and issues are best excluded at this level of commentary. Concepts include new ideas about the nature of leisure, perceived freedom, constraints and barriers, the work-leisure relationship, the meaning of activities, and so on (all of these issues are addressed in one way or another by the authors elsewhere in this book). Here, "methods" are broadly defined to include not only the mechanisms and instruments of research, but also overall, general approaches. Thus, "methods" encompass both the collection and analysis of data and the broader investigative framework employed, giving rise to the debate about matters such as quantitative versus qualitative approaches and analysis, and large-scale surveys versus small-scale, ethnographic research.

   The conceptual and methodological components of leisure studies are interrelated with each other. For example, the re-evaluation of concepts has led some leisure scholars to question the ability of large-scale, survey-based, quantitative research to capture the meaning of leisure for many; this is particularly the case in feminist writing on leisure (see Bella's chapter, for instance). Others argue that a cognitive-behavioral approach to understanding recreational activity choice ignores the social context of leisure, which in turn throws into question the very nature of the construct of leisure itself; what this ultimately requires, then, is the development and adoption of new methods of inquiry. Conversely, as new methods are adopted by leisure researchers (e.g. ethnographic techniques), a re-evaluation of concepts and assumptions is sure to emerge.

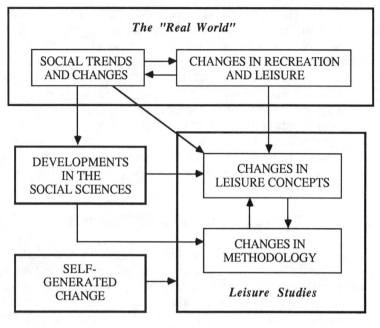

Figure 1
Components of and Influences upon Leisure Studies

Turning now to the three main influences on the development of leisure studies, these are identified in the model as the "real world", the social sciences, and self-generated change. As far as the first is concerned, leisure studies does not take place in a social vacuum. Rather, it is strongly influenced by the real world, which may itself be divided into two elements, also shown in the model, namely recreation and leisure, and the broader social context. Key aspects of recreation and leisure include the emergence of new activities, declines in others, and changes in location, social relations, the amount of time available, and the timing of engagements. The broader social context encompasses changes in a wide range of social, economic, technological, political, attitudinal, and environmental conditions, each having important implications, both for leisure studies and for leisure itself. Examples might include the feminist movement, unemployment, delayed parenting, the ageing of the population, innovations in the electronic media (especially videocassette recorders), the privatization of public services, and even such major epidemics as AIDS.

These two elements (recreation and leisure, and the broader social context) are obviously interconnected. The broad social factors clearly cause changes in patterns of recreation and leisure. For example, as Glyptis shows in her chapter, changes in the form and structure of unemployment have had profound effects, not only on leisure behavior but also upon its very meaning for the unemployed. Conversely, although the influence is probably less strong in the opposite direction, it may well be that changes in recreation and leisure patterns bring about social changes: it has been claimed, for example, that the popularity of video games, in their early years, fundamentally altered societal attitudes towards computers in general (Burton 1983).

Both of these elements of the real world shape the content and form of leisure studies. The greater of the two effects comes from researchers' observations of changes in recreation and leisure itself; the effect of social changes that are more broadly defined than leisure alone has been less direct and immediate. For example, leisure studies has moved rapidly to address issues directly connected to recreation and leisure that derive from the ageing of the North American population, in the form of improved programs, facilities, and services for the elderly. It has been less responsive to issues deriving from this major societal change that do not, at first glance, relate directly to leisure and recreation, such as changes in transportation needs, relative purchasing power, and family structure.

Turning now to the second influence, developments in the social sciences affect leisure studies in terms of both concepts and methodology, although the latter is probably the main effect. This is evident in the fact that the great majority of concepts and methods currently used in leisure studies have been borrowed, usually with no adaptation, directly from appropriate disciplines in the social sciences. Thus, for example, much research in leisure studies has attempted to explain the meaning of leisure by reference to competing theories (see Rojek's chapter). But, once having borrowed initial concepts, leisure studies has been surprisingly reluctant to adopt new concepts and methods developed within these same disciplines — perhaps because, having "migrated" from their original disciplines, scholars may fail to keep abreast of mainstream developments within them.

Furthermore, changes in leisure studies have had very little, if any, reciprocal influence on the social sciences. This is due to three reasons: (1) non-leisure scientists' perceptions of the peripheral nature of leisure; (2) the rather low esteem that leisure studies has enjoyed within the social sciences in general and within the component disciplines; and (3) the emergence of specialist leisure studies journals (that is, papers in leisure studies now rarely appear in the mainstream disciplinary journals).

The third key influence on leisure studies shown in the model consists of self-generated change, i.e. that which happens without reference to real-world changes or to developments in the social sciences. Self-generated change comes about mainly because leisure researchers begin to sense inadequacies in their concepts and methods, which thus inhibit the investigation of the phenomena that interest them. Ethnographic studies of leisure are a case in point. While much self-generated re-evaluation occurs for what might broadly be termed "theoretical" reasons (recognition of the limitations of previous concepts, methods, and explanations), we suspect that much also comes about because of problems experienced in applying previous research results to practical situations (e.g. recent developments in the concept of carrying capacity, and the growing recognition of the importance of constraints on leisure).

The three main influences on leisure studies discussed above are not mutually exclusive — they overlap. Nor are they of equal strength. The interaction among them is particularly evident for the relative effects of social trends, leisure trends, and changes in the social sciences. To try to separate out specific effects would be pointless; rather, the model is a matter of convenience to indicate what are some of the broad influences. With respect to the strength of their effects, we contend that changes in leisure and recreation have been the most powerful influences on the past evolution of leisure studies, followed in rank-order by self-generated change, social change, and developments in the social sciences.

In concluding this discussion of the model, some important qualifications should be made. First, neither changes in the real world nor developments in the social sciences will necessarily lead to changes in leisure studies. They present opportunities, but whether or not these are taken up will depend on other factors, some of which may lie beyond the control of researchers (e.g. the availability of research funds).

Second, none of these influences, either separately or in combination, has had or will have a uniform or universal effect on leisure studies. Some researchers, some topics, and some papers are in the forefront of change. Others are, for want of a better word, more antiquated. Furthermore, there is a good deal of evidence that leisure studies is overly inward looking, in that many of the people who do leisure research neither know nor care about, for example, theoretical and conceptual developments in the social sciences, generally. In like vein, others will never be persuaded of the limitations of multivariate quantitative methods or of the opportunities offered by qualitative and ethnographic techniques.

Third, at this stage in its development, the model is principally a descriptive one. We do not argue that leisure studies should jump on every methodological or conceptual bandwagon emerging from these influences. Indeed, we advocate a certain amount of conservatism, and even healthy skepticism, in the adoption of new ideas and approaches.

Last, the excessive tendency to look inwards, noted above, seems to be associated with frequent calls for the development of unique leisure theory. This preoccupation, we believe, is detrimental to forging links between leisure studies and the social sciences. The central questions, raised by Burdge (1983 and in this volume), are: does leisure studies develop new methods, concepts, and theories, or does it adapt them from elsewhere? Should it? What are the costs and benefits? These pivotal questions are addressed explicitly, if not systematically, throughout this book.

THE PRESENT STATE OF LEISURE STUDIES

The model just discussed provides a backcloth against which we can now present a broadly-based assessment of the current state of leisure studies. This assessment will not employ the model directly to explain the current state of affairs or how the various developments over the past two decades occurred. Such an analysis would be a major research study in its own right (one which may well be tempting to a Ph.D. student looking for a worthy study!). Rather, as we have noted, the model provides a context for our commentary on the present state of leisure studies. The assessment, itself, does not attempt to address, let alone resolve, all of the themes and issues that have been mentioned thus far. However, it will elaborate and complement some of the key points that have emerged.

Characteristics of Leisure Studies

One of the most important characteristics of leisure studies today is that it is no longer necessary to be defensive about it, or to have to argue the case for its legitimacy. If any doubts on this issue still remain, they should surely be put to rest, once and for all, by the opening comments of Cooper's chapter. Indeed, we contend that leisure studies is a vibrant field, showing signs of healthy debate, and of methodological, theoretical, and conceptual pluralism, rather than exhibiting a single dominant paradigm. Three other attributes of leisure studies over the past decade also stand out: growth in the quantity of research; diversity of disciplinary contributions; and breadth of issues and topics.

Growth in the quantity of research

As mentioned at the outset of this chapter and reflected in the many reviews discussed earlier, there has been a dramatic growth in the quantity of research. While none of the studies and reviews has documented this development through the tedious process of counting the numbers of journal articles and research papers that have been published, all have demonstrated the large quantitative growth in other ways. The more recent reviews, for example, have inevitably drawn upon a wider range and greater number of sources than the earlier ones. Additional objective evidence of growth in the quantity of leisure research is also to be found in the increase in the number of specialist journals in leisure studies between 1969 and the present (from 2 to at least 9); in the emergence of organizations like the (British) Leisure Studies Association and the Canadian Association for Leisure Studies; in the establishment of recurring conferences on leisure studies, such as the triennial Canadian Congress on Leisure Research (begun in 1975), the international conferences of the Leisure

Studies Association (begun in 1984 after close to a decade of annual national conferences), and the meetings of the Research Commission of the World Leisure and Recreation Association (of which there have been three since the inaugural meeting in 1980); and in the numbers of specialty groups on leisure that have been established within particular disciplinary organizations. These include the Committee on Leisure of the International Sociological Association, and the Parks, Recreation and Tourism Working Group of the Canadian Association of Geographers. All of these are indicators of the spectacular growth in the quantity of leisure research during the past two decades — though none says anything, explicitly, about the quality of this research.

Disciplinary contributions

Second, virtually all of the social science disciplines have been involved in the development of leisure studies. Not all, however, have contributed equally. As our survey results indicate (Table 2), the greatest disciplinary contributions were perceived to have come from Sociologists (72.0% of respondents said that they had made a major contribution). Next in perceived contribution were Psychologists (58.7%), followed by Geographers (42.0%) and Economists (36.4%). In contrast, only 3.5 percent believed that a major contribution had been made by Anthropologists, with corresponding figures of 5.6 percent for Political Scientists and 6.3 percent for Historians.

Interestingly, the contributions of multidisciplinary, interdisciplinary, and professional fields were also perceived to cover a very wide range. Persons in Recreation and Leisure Studies were perceived to have made the greatest contribution of all (75.5% of respondents said that they had made a major contribution). Other fields with major contributions included persons in Environmental Studies (32.9%) and Physical Educators (27.3%). At the other end of the spectrum were Lawyers (3.5%).

The survey also examined how sub-groups of the sample viewed the contributions of their own and other disciplines and fields of study. We analyzed the results from two perspectives: first with respect to each group's perception of the contributions of all disciplines and fields of study; and second in terms of the perceptions of their own and other disciplines expressed by the representatives of each of the disciplines and fields of study who responded to the survey.

As far as the first perspective is concerned, there was a reasonably uniform, high rating of the contributions of both Sociology and Recreation and Leisure Studies across all sub-groups. The results for Economics and Psychology, however, were rather more variable. Economics received high ratings from the Economics and Interdisciplinary sub-groups, a moderate rating from Geographers, and low ratings from Sociologists and Psychologists. In contrast Geography, with the exception of members of that discipline, received relatively low ratings, especially from representatives of the Economics group.

Table 2
The Perceived Significance of the Contributions of Selected Disciplines and Fields of Study to the Development of Leisure and Recreation Research
(n = 143)

Discipline/Field of Study	Significance of Contribution			
	Minor %	Some %	Major %	No Opinion %
Anthropology	60.1	29.4	3.5	7.0
Business	46.8	39.2	7.0	7.0
Demography	45.4	35.0	11.9	7.7
Economics	11.2	48.9	36.4	3.5
Education	41.2	39.9	13.3	5.6
Environmental Studies	14.0	48.2	32.9	4.9
Geography	14.7	38.4	42.0	4.9
History	60.8	28.0	6.3	4.9
Law	69.9	21.0	1.4	7.7
Philosophy	58.0	26.6	7.7	7.7
Physical Education	16.8	49.6	27.3	6.3
Political Science	57.3	32.9	5.6	4.2
Psychology	7.7	28.0	58.7	5.6
Recreation	1.4	15.4	75.5	7.7
Sociology	1.4	22.4	72.0	4.2
Urban & Regional Studies	19.6	59.4	15.4	5.6
Other	3.5	9.1	6.3	81.1

The main finding to emerge from the alternative perspective was that the representatives of a discipline or field of study tended to reserve their highest or second highest ratings for the contributions of their own disciplines or fields of study. Furthermore, to the extent that the results can be taken as a surrogate indicator of communication between disciplines, there was little indication of a "two-way street." Thus, for example, over 80 percent of the Economics group felt that Sociologists had made a major contribution to leisure studies, whereas only 23 percent of Sociologists evaluated the contribution of Economics as "major". This pattern was repeated for the reciprocal views of the Geography and Economics representatives, the Geographers and Psychologists, and the Psychologists and Economists. In this regard, it is captivating to ponder on the mysterious comment of one geographer who noted that the discipline of Economics had made a major contribution to the development of leisure studies over the past twenty years, but that this contribution had been made "largely by non-economists!"

Issues and topics

The third characteristic of leisure studies in recent years has been the great diversity of the issues and topics that have been investigated. The various state-of-the-art reviews reflect this in exemplary fashion, showing that, among others, the writings in the field have focussed on motivations (e.g. Crandall 1980); energy (e.g. Converse and Machlis 1986); travel (e.g. Ewing 1980); barriers to leisure (e.g. Jackson 1988); perceptions (e.g. Mercer 1970); and social carrying capacity (*Leisure Sciences*, 1984).

Again, the survey results also provide some perspective on the breadth and relative importance of research topics (Table 3). When asked to indicate what had been the dominant themes in leisure studies over the last twenty years, the respondents placed attitudinal research, including studies of motivations, preferences, satisfactions, and values at the top of the list: 85.3 percent said that this was a dominant theme. Close behind came demand analyses, including studies of participation, involvement, activity, and behavior (83.9%). Also significant were tourism studies (67.1%), studies of carrying capacity (65.0%), studies of parks and reserves (53.1%), and water-oriented research (42.7%). At the other end of the spectrum were: studies of voluntarism (only 7.7%), studies of home-based leisure (13.3%), open space studies (14.0%), facility management research (15.4%), cultural studies (16.8%), historical studies (18.2%), and studies of professionalism and practice (20.3%).

As might be expected, there were differences among the various groups of scholars on these topics. For example, the Interdisciplinary Studies and Geography groups considered tourism studies to have been much more dominant in research over the past twenty years than did the Sociologists and Psychologists. In contrast, sport was more frequently identified as a dominant theme by the Sociologists and Psychologists than by most others. And Recreation and Leisure Studies scholars saw professionalism and research into the needs of special populations as much more dominant than did any other group. But, for all the differences, there was a surprising amount of agreement among the respondents, especially regarding issues such as attitudes and demand (Figure 2).

Some respondents also noted that the dominance of particular themes had changed during the twenty-year period. Several, for example, commented that while attitudinal research has been a dominant theme, this has primarily occurred during the latter half of the period. Others, in contrast, remarked that the dominance of demand analyses was most evident during the first decade but had tapered off considerably in recent years. There were also comments that reflected different emphases in the various countries encompassed by the survey. One British scholar remarked that attitudinal research had, indeed, been a dominant theme, "but not in the United Kingdom." The same person also noted that Parks and Reserves had been dominant, "especially in North America."

Table 3
The Perceived Dominant Themes in Leisure and Recreation Research
(n = 143)

Theme	Respondents	
	n	%
Attitudinal Research	122	85.3
Demand Analysis	120	83.9
Tourism Research	96	67.1
Carrying Capacity	93	65.0
Parks and Reserves	76	53.1
Water-Oriented Research	61	42.7
Special Populations	57	39.9
Sport and Sports	56	39.2
Concepts and Theories	56	39.2
Planning, Policy, and Evaluation	46	32.2
Delivery Systems	45	31.5
Model Building	44	30.8
Time Budget Analyses	43	30.1
Professionalism and Practice	29	20.3
Historical Research	26	18.2
Cultural Studies	24	16.8
Facility Management Research	22	15.4
Open Space	20	14.0
Home-Based Leisure and Recreation	19	13.3
Voluntarism	11	7.7
Other	23	16.1

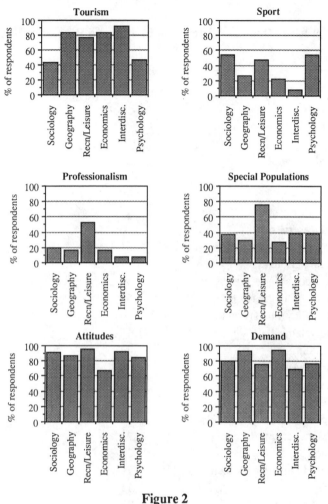

Figure 2
Selected Dominant Themes by Discipline/Field of Study

Finally, there were statements which went beyond an assessment of what had been dominant to comment upon the desirability of particular themes. Thus, one respondent noted that carrying capacity had been a dominant theme — "too much so"; another remarked that while there had been some cultural and cross-cultural studies, there was clearly "not enough."

Limitations of Leisure Studies

Despite the fact that leisure studies has grown considerably in the volume of research output during the past twenty years, there is a consensus that this

growth has not been uniformly matched by improvements in quality. Many of
the state-of-the-art reviews discussed earlier have drawn attention to the piecemeal nature of much of the research, the failure to develop a consistent body of
theory, inadequate conceptual and theoretical foundations, the absence of a
common language, and a reluctance to employ research methods and techniques
other than the relatively simplistic survey questionnaire (Burton 1980; Iso-Ahola
1984; Patmore and Collins 1980; Riddick *et al.* 1984; Social Science Research
Council/Sports Council 1978; Stockdale 1987).

These characteristics, labeled by Burton (1980) as problems *of* leisure
research, have severely restricted the intellectual development of the field.
Indeed, they appear to have created something of a "crisis of confidence" among
researchers in leisure studies. By far the greatest need for research in the coming
decade that was identified by respondents to the survey of active leisure scholars
(see the last chapter for further discussion) was for the development of a
consistent and coherent body of theory (30.8% of respondents identified this
need). This statistical picture was further reinforced by unsolicited comments
made by many respondents. One British scholar remarked: "My general impression of the field is that it is potentially extremely important, but that it lacks
coherence, is badly under-theorized, and dominated by relatively unsophisticated policy-oriented research of the simple fact-gathering variety. This is a
harsh judgment and I say it with some regret; but I feel it needs to be said,
because some change is long overdue." This sentiment was echoed by many
other respondents, although, perhaps, not quite as eloquently.

A related characteristic of leisure studies is its considerable fragmentation, a lack of integration, and a virtual absence of intellectual coordination. Respondents to the survey were asked whether, overall, "recreation and leisure
research has been characterized by unity, coherence, or fragmentation during the
past two decades." Unity was defined as consisting of "conceptual and methodological harmony, common terminology, synthesis, and broad intellectual
agreement." Coherence was defined as displaying "logical connections in
conceptual and methodological development, relative consistency in terminology, integration, and a sense of intellectual common interest." Fragmentation
was defined as consisting of "disparate, and even conflicting, conceptual and
methodological development, inconsistent terminology, disconnected themes,
and intellectual disharmony."

Only two of the 143 respondents considered that leisure studies has
been characterized by unity — and for one of these, at least, this carried a
negative connotation, since there was an additional comment to the effect that:
"The field has been dominated (mistakenly) by the language and methodologies
of a positivist tradition." More significantly, fully three-fifths (61.5%) of the respondents noted that leisure studies has been characterized by fragmentation.
A few of these took a positive view of this, remarking that: "Fragmented
approaches are not unhealthy for a field of study" and "There is no one absolute
truth; the debate, discussion, and differences of opinion that derive from

fragmentation are healthy." There is little doubt, however, that, for the great majority, fragmentation is an undesirable state, indicating disintegration rather than pluralism. This is not to deny the importance of debate and discussion, but rather to argue the need for a coherent framework in which scholars have at least a relatively consistent language and a sense of intellectual common interest.

About one-third (35.0%) of the respondents felt that coherence has been generally achieved, but, for the majority who did not, it was evident that it is the desirable state. One Canadian scholar remarked that "fragmentation is too harsh, but it is nearer the truth than anything else." Another noted that "we have a real splintering problem." But, perhaps, the most poignant observation on this topic came from the American scholar who commented that "the problem with leisure research is that it has persistently failed to be cumulative, to build on what went before, and to offer paradigms for meaningful further research. Carrying capacity sustained us for many years, but the horizons are too large to be limited by such a narrow metaphor."

A further criticism of leisure studies that has recently surfaced is that it has failed to move far from its disciplinary roots to embrace multidisciplinary and interdisciplinary methods and approaches. This complaint has been voiced in several of the state-of-the-art reviews, and was a subject addressed in the survey of active researchers. In this case, respondents were asked to state their views on the relative contributions of disciplinary, multidisciplinary, and interdisciplinary methods and approaches to the development of knowledge and understanding in recreation and leisure during the past twenty years. Disciplinary methods and approaches were defined as being "drawn from and applied in a single discipline." Multidisciplinary methods and approaches were defined as being "drawn from individual disciplines and applied separately, but as part of the same project or study." Interdisciplinary methods and approaches were defined as "implying the transfer of methods and approaches across disciplines."

The respondents were clearly divided on this question (Table 4). Slightly fewer than half ranked interdisciplinary methods and approaches as having made the greatest contribution, with a further one-third ranking disciplinary methods and approaches first. This is in direct contradiction to the oft-cited comments appearing in various state-of-the-art reviews. It is, however, partly reinforced by the responses to the first question in the survey, summarized above, which asked subjects to rate the extent of the contributions of each of the social science disciplines to the development of recreation and leisure research over the last twenty years.

It is difficult to draw any obvious conclusions from the apparent contradictions between the state-of-the-art reviews and the survey of active researchers on this question. But, perhaps, the most valuable point that can be made is that, notwithstanding the majority view in the survey, both the reviews and the survey results display evident concerns about the quality and

Table 4
The Perceived Relative Contributions of Alternative Research Methods and
Approaches to the Development of Recreation and Leisure Research
(n = 143)

Methods and Approaches	Ranked Contribution					
	1st		2nd		3rd	
	n	%	n	%	n	%
Disciplinary Methods and Approaches (drawn from and applied in a single discipline)	50	35.0	20	14.0	64	44.6
Multidisciplinary Methods and Approaches (drawn from individual disciplines and applied separately, but as part of the same project or study)	21	14.7	82	57.3	30	21.0
Interdisciplinary Methods and Approaches (drawn from individual disciplines, but applied jointly as part of the same project or study, i.e., implies the transfer of methods and approaches across disciplines)	69	48.3	29	20.3	36	25.2
No Response	3	2.1	12	8.4	13	9.1

appropriateness of the bundle of research methods and approaches currently being employed in leisure studies, in particular its heavy dependence upon quantitative research methods tied very closely to those employed in the parent disciplines.

While the survey did not explicitly address the issue of the adequacy of research methods and approaches in leisure studies, the issue surfaced repeatedly in responses to the question which asked subjects to identify the three principal issues or needs to be addressed during the next decade or so. We noted earlier that the single greatest need that was identified was for the development of concepts and theories. Second to this was the need for the development of appropriate and relevant methods and techniques (23.1%). These answers assume even greater significance when it is recognized that they were given in response to an open-ended question — that is, there was no predetermined checklist of possible responses. Furthermore, in some instances, they were reinforced by the general comments made by respondents elsewhere in the questionnaire. One American scholar remarked that: "Many researchers seem to be a bit frustrated with progress in leisure research and are somehow seeking new 'paradigms' as the answer. I concur that we are in a period of stagflation or whatever. I attribute this primarily to a shortage of quality researchers tackling substantive problems." Another leading British scholar put the matter more succinctly and with a tinge of sadness: "Interdisciplinary research promises so much, but has failed to deliver."

THE VIEW FROM THE ROAD

In conclusion, we suggest that there is a significant discrepancy between the actual state of leisure studies and what researchers and scholars in the field believe that state ought to be. First and foremost, leisure studies has, over the past two decades, established a strong sense of legitimacy for itself within the academic domain. During this time, the field has grown dramatically in the volume of research being carried out, in the number of specialist outlets for the findings of research studies, in the numbers of organizations and forums that exist for the exchange of ideas, methods, and results in leisure research, and in the number and range of social science disciplines and interdisciplinary, multidisciplinary, and professional fields of study that are engaged in, and are contributing to, the development of leisure studies. It has also thrown its net widely, investigating a diverse set of topics, issues, and themes, ranging from theoretical explanations of the nature of leisure to practical problems in the delivery and management of recreation services, from motivations to satisfactions, from home-based activity to tourism and travel, and from the social-psychological determinants of behavior to barriers to involvement.

On the other side of the coin, there is the widespread belief among leisure scholars that the quality of leisure studies has not advanced in a manner fully commensurate with its quantity. There is a sense of frustration with the progress that has been made in developing a coherent and consistent body of theory, a feeling that the field is excessively fragmented, and a perception that it has been unduly conservative — rigid, even — in its methodological progress. In short, leisure studies has come a significant distance, but it has not moved as far forward as many thought it would do twenty, and even ten, years ago. The gap is between the actual and the expected rate of progress.

Despite all this, several signs of change give cause for optimism. First, both the state-of-the-art reviews and the international survey of active leisure scholars show that there is a high degree of consensus about the principal issues that must be addressed by leisure studies in the immediate future. Second, there appears to be a growing recognition and acceptance of the relevance and utility of alternative research methods to the quantitative survey, such as ethnographic studies, phenomenological approaches, and other qualitative methods. Third, there is evidence that conceptualization and theory development is not only seen as a priority for future research, but is also actually being addressed (as many of the chapters in this book will show). In closing, therefore, we prefer to adopt the view of one of the respondents to the survey of active leisure scholars who, in response to the question asking whether leisure research had been characterized by unity, coherence, or fragmentation during the past two decades, replied: "Coherence — I'm feeling optimistic today."

References

Beaman, J. 1979. "Leisure research and its lack of relevance to planning, management, and policy formulation: A problem of major proportions." In *Contemporary Leisure Research: Proceedings of the Second Canadian Congress on Leisure Research,* pp. 250-255. Toronto: Ontario Research Council on Leisure.

Bregha, F.J. 1979. "Future directions of leisure research." In *Contemporary Leisure Research: Proceedings of the Second Canadian Congress on Leisure Research,* pp. 578-581. Toronto: Ontario Research Council on Leisure.

Brown, P.J., A. Dyer, and R.S. Whaley. 1973. "Recreation research — so what." *Journal of Leisure Research 5:* 16-24.

Burdge, R.J. 1974. "The state of leisure research as reflected in the Journal of Leisure Research." *Journal of Leisure Research 6:* 312-317.

Burdge, R.J. 1983. "Making leisure and recreation research a scholarly topic: Views of a journal editor, 1972-1982." *Leisure Sciences 6:* 99-126.

Burdge, R.J. and D.R. Field. 1972. "Methodological perspectives for the study of outdoor recreation." *Journal of Leisure Research 4:* 63-72.

Burton, T.L. 1979. "The development of leisure research in Canada: An analogical tale." *Loisir et Société* 2: 33-34.

Burton, T.L. 1980. "The maturation of leisure research." In *Recreation and Leisure: Issues in an Era of Change,* eds. T.L. Goodale and P.A. Witt, pp. 373-385. State College, PA: Venture Publishing.

Burton, T.L. 1981. "You can't get there from here: A personal perspective on recreation forecasting in Canada." *Recreation Research Review 9:* 38-43.

Burton, T.L. 1983. "Video games: Social menace or moral panic?" In *Games People Play,* pp. 6-15. Edmonton: University of Alberta.

Burton, T.L. and E.L. Jackson. 1989. "Leisure research and the social sciences: An exploratory study of active researchers." *Leisure Studies* (in press).

Butler, R.W. 1981. "Geographical research on leisure: Reflections and anticipations on Accrington Stanley and fire hydrants." Paper presented at the Colloquium on Leisure Research, University of Waterloo, Waterloo, ON.

Cherry, G.E. 1986. "The future of leisure in an urbanising world." Public lecture delivered at the University of Alberta, Edmonton, AB.

Collins, M.F. and J.A. Patmore. 1982. "Recreation and leisure." *Progress in Human Geography 6:* 254-259.

Converse, R.S. and G.E. Machlis. 1986. "Energy and outdoor recreation: A review and assessment of the literature." *Leisure Sciences 8:* 391-416.

Coppock, J.T. 1982. "Geographical contributions to the study of leisure." *Leisure Studies 1:* 1-28.

Crandall, R. 1980. "Motivations for leisure." *Journal of Leisure Research 12:* 45-54.

Crandall, R. and J. Lewko. 1976. "Leisure research, present and future: Who, what, where." *Journal of Leisure Research 8:* 150-159.

Crawford, D. and G. Godbey. 1987. "Reconceptualizing barriers to family recreation." *Leisure Sciences 9:* 119-127.

D'Amours, M.C. 1984. "Leisure sciences and leisure studies: Indicators of interdisciplinarity?" *Leisure Sciences 6:* 359-373.

Dawson, D. 1984. "Phenomenological approaches to leisure research." *Leisure Sciences 11:* 18-23.

Deem, R. 1986. *All Work and No Play? The Sociology of Women and Leisure.* Milton Keynes: Open University Press.

Ewing, G. 1980. "Progress and problems in the development of recreational trip generation and trip distribution models." *Leisure Sciences 3:* 1-24.

Fryer, D. and P. Ullah. 1987. *Unemployed People.* Milton Keynes: Open University Press.

Glyptis, S. 1983. "Business as usual? Leisure provision for the unemployed." *Leisure Studies 2:* 287-300.

Goodale, T.L. and P.A. Witt (eds.). 1980. *Recreation and Leisure: Issues in an Era of Change.* State College, PA: Venture Publishing.

Gray, G.A. 1973. "Leisure studies: An area of research for sociologists?" *Society and Leisure 5:* 181-188.

Green, E., S. Hebron, and D. Woodward. 1987. *Leisure and Gender: A Study of Sheffield Women's Leisure Experiences.* London: Sports Council/ Economic and Social Science Research Council Joint Panel on Leisure and Recreation Research.

Harper, W. 1981. "The experience of leisure." *Leisure Sciences 4:* 113-126.

Hendricks, J. and R.J. Burdge. 1972. "A comment on the sociological direction of research on leisure." *Society and Leisure 5:* 159-163.

Howe, C.Z. 1985. "Possibilities for using a qualitative research approach in the sociological study of leisure." *Journal of Leisure Research 17:* 212-224.

Ingham, R. 1986. "Psychological contributions to the study of leisure." *Leisure Studies 5:* 255-279.

Iso-Ahola, S.E. 1984. "What is appropriate for publication?" *Journal of Leisure Research 16(4):* iv-v.

Iso-Ahola, S.E. 1986a. "Concerns and thoughts about leisure research." *Journal of Leisure Research 18(3):* iv-x.

Iso-Ahola, S.E. 1986b. "A theory of substitutability of leisure behavior." *Leisure Sciences 8:* 367-389.

Jackson, E.L. 1988. "Leisure constraints: a survey of past research." *Leisure Sciences 10:* 203-215.

Kelly, J.R. 1980. "Outdoor recreation participation: A comparative analysis." *Leisure Sciences 3:* 129-154.

Kelvin, P. and J. Jarrett. 1985. *Unemployment: Its Social-psychological Effects.* Cambridge: Cambridge University Press.

Mannell, R. 1979. "A conceptual and experimental basis for research in the psychology of leisure." *Loisir et Société 2:* 179-194.

Manning, R.E. 1986. *Studies in Outdoor Recreation: Search and Research for Satisfaction*. Corvallis, OR: Oregon State University Press.

Mercer, D.C. 1970. "The role of perception in the recreation experience: A review and discussion." *Journal of Leisure Research 3:* 261-276.

Mitchell, L.S. 1969. "Recreational geography: Evolution and research needs." *The Professional Geographer 21:* 117-119.

Neulinger, J. and R. Crandall. 1976. "The psychology of leisure: 1975." *Journal of Leisure Research 8:* 127-130.

Parker, S. 1983. *Leisure and Work*. London: George Allen and Unwin.

Parry, N.C.A. 1983. "Sociological contributions to the study of leisure." *Leisure Studies 2:* 57-81.

Patmore, J.A. and M.F. Collins. 1980. "Recreation and leisure." *Progress in Human Geography 4:* 91-97.

Riddick, C., M. De Schriver, and F. Weissinger. 1984. "A methodological review of research in Journal of Leisure Research from 1978 to 1982." *Journal of Leisure Research 16:* 136-149.

Roberts, K. 1987. "Leisure and social change in the 1980s." Paper presented at the Fifth Canadian Congress on Leisure Research, Dalhousie University, Halifax, NS.

Rojek, C. 1985. *Capitalism and Leisure Theory*. London: Tavistock.

Smith, S.L.J. 1975. "Toward meta-recreation research." *Journal of Leisure Research 7:* 235-239.

Smith, S.L.J. 1982. "Calling it quits." *Recreation Research Review 9:* 4-6.

Smith, S.L.J. 1983. *Recreation Geography*. London: Longman.

Smith, S.L.J. and A.J. Haley. 1979. "Ratio ex machina: Notes on leisure research." *Journal of Leisure Research 11:* 139-143.

Smith, S.L.J. and D. Ng. 1983. "Leisure research: Future directions and needs." In *Proceedings of the Third Canadian Congress on Leisure Research*, pp 21-42. Edmonton, AB: Canadian Association for Leisure Studies.

Social Science Research Council/Sports Council. 1978. "Report of the Joint Working Party on Recreation Research." London.

Stockdale, J.E. 1987. *Methodological Techniques in Leisure Research*. London: Sports Council/Economic and Social Science Research Council Joint Panel on Leisure and Recreation Research.

Van Doren, C.S. and M.J. Heit. 1973. "Where it's at: A content analysis and appraisal of the Journal of Leisure Research." *Journal of Leisure Research 5:* 67-73.

Van Doren, C.S., S.M. Holland, and J.L. Crompton. 1984. "Publishing in the primary leisure journals: Insight into the structure and boundaries of our research." *Leisure Sciences 6:* 239-256.

Vickerman, R.W. 1983. "The contribution of economics to the study of leisure: A review." *Leisure Studies 2:* 345-364.

Wolfe, R.I. 1974. "Recreation geography." In *Practical Geography,* eds. J.N. Jackson and J. Forrester, pp. 70-89. Toronto: McGraw-Hill Ryerson.

THE EVOLUTION OF LEISURE AND RECREATION RESEARCH FROM MULTIDISCIPLINARY TO INTERDISCIPLINARY

Rabel J. Burdge

I appreciate the opportunity to continue as a participant in the systematic and periodic assessment of the evolution and current state of leisure and recreation research (Burdge 1974, 1983, 1984, 1985a, 1985b; Burdge and Beckers 1984; Burdge and Hendricks 1972, 1973). Most of the observations and experiences reported here and previously stem from having been editor of two of the major leisure and recreation research journals (*Journal of Leisure Research* from 1971 to 1974, and *Leisure Sciences* from 1977 to 1982). These two journals have provided an important and cumulative repository for knowledge in our field — at least for North American scholars. I want to see these and the other leisure and recreation research journals expand in the decades ahead. Moreover, like the authors of other chapters in this book, I have a scholarly commitment to leisure research and am concerned about its future. Therefore, I feel that is important to assess, from time to time, the theoretical and methodological directions of this research area.

This chapter analyzes the evolution of leisure and recreation research from a fledgling intellectual pursuit to a focused scholarly concern. In a period of about two decades, leisure and recreation research has emerged from a concern with outdoor recreation program development, in response to North American land management agencies, to an agenda which covers the breadth of leisure and recreation behavior. Progress toward disciplinary status for this research effort is the major interest of this chapter.

In the first section, I define the terms "disciplinary", "interdisciplinary", and "multidisciplinary". The second portion of the chapter analyzes the disciplinary composition of leisure and recreation research. Next, I discuss the disciplinary roots of the researchers and the research topics associated with leisure and recreation. Then, I explain the unit of analysis and the accumulation of findings in leisure and recreation research. In the final part of the chapter, I advance some tentative conclusions, both about the disciplinary future of leisure and recreation research and about the research units within which it is housed.

WHAT IS MEANT BY DISCIPLINARY RESEARCH?

Disciplinary Research

"Disciplinary" research refers to an identifiable body of knowledge focused around a singular unit of analysis. For example, economics as a discipline focuses on material exchange, and the basic unit of analysis is the expression of monetary units. Cost-benefit analysis is an example of the quantification of basic concepts in economics. Sociology studies individuals in groups and the influence of groups on individual behavior. Investigations of families in leisure, and the influence of work settings on leisure behavior, are commonly reported in the literature. Psychology studies the way in which internal physical and emotional factors affect individual behavior. Satisfaction obtained from outdoor recreation activity is a dominant theme of social-psychology. Geography is the study of spatial relationships. Distance-decay models used to understand travel times to resorts represent a practical application of that methodology.

Similar disciplinary descriptions can be undertaken for the physical sciences (e.g., physics and chemistry) and the biological sciences (botany and zoology, among others). Webster defines a discipline as a branch of knowledge requiring research. The dictionary definition also implies some attempt at order and accumulation. For purposes of this chapter, I refer to the cognate, root, or basic disciplines as ones that have a singular unit of analysis around which knowledge accumulates.

Interdisciplinary Research

The definition in Webster's Dictionary suggests that to be "interdisciplinary" means to be together, to connect, as in to "lace together." An article in the *Chronicle of Higher Education* (October 7, 1987, p.1) defines "interdisciplinary" as the attempt "to combine the knowledge of disparate fields in ways that are most significant." Some scholars, including several in this book, refer to "interdisciplinary" as the application of the research methods of one discipline to that of another. Still others maintain that "interdisciplinary" is understanding and using the research approach of one discipline to study the knowledge base of another. Hence, a university department could claim to be a separate discipline (e.g., statistics), but in fact be applying the research methods of one or more basic disciplines (e.g., mathematics) to an applied problem (*Chronicle of Higher Education*, October 7, 1987: 14-15). Furthermore, a university Department of Business Administration may be thought of as an amalgamation of economics, sociology, and psychology. Researchers in business administration apply the theory and methods of the social sciences to the applied problems that face business organizations. At the same time, some Schools of Business Administration include separate departments of organizational behavior, finance, accounting, public relations, and personnel administration, among others. The same might be said for such amalgamated units as Parks, Recreation, and Leisure Studies departments. Much of the Parks and Recreation administration curriculum comes from research in administration and personal development. Application of research findings from the "administrative sciences" to municipal recreation programs remains, in essence, two steps removed from the basic disciplines of economics, sociology, and psychology.

Multidisciplinary Research

The term "multidisciplinary" research "is used to describe a wide variety of academic research and program efforts that transcend the traditional academic departments and involve faculty members and staff from two or more departments" (Alpert 1985). Multidisciplinary efforts are generally organized around a complex (often applied) problem area or issue that calls for the perspectives and methodologies of a number of disciplines. Examples of multidisciplinary university departments are atmospheric science, library and information science, and computer science. Sometimes, the term "cross-disciplinary" is used, which refers to a union of two disciplines where the methodology of one is used to study the subject matter of the other (e.g., biochemistry, educational psychology, and chemical engineering). Academicians who profess (or confess) to being multidisciplinary deal with problems or research areas that use the approaches of many disciplines. The topic or the problem becomes the focus, not the accumulation of disciplinary knowledge. Computer science is one such example. The research area has become so wide and diverse that any pretense to the basic disciplines of mathematics, physics, and engineering has been blurred.

THE DISCIPLINARY ROOTS OF TRADITIONAL CATEGORIES OF LEISURE AND RECREATION RESEARCH

Leisure Research

Leisure research refers to a study of not only activities, but includes time and attitudes toward time and non-work activities. Leisure is not an isolated sphere remaining after obligatory activities have been completed. It is not an end in itself, nor is it seen as recuperative activity. Leisure, in the holistic orientation, is seen as a complex of multiple relationships involving certain choices which indicate both societal and individual aspirations as well as lifestyles.

Leisure research is defined by the editors of the *Journal of Leisure Research* (Vol. 1, No. 1, 1969, Preface) in terms of the perceived substantive content of the Journal as "a body of knowledge in the leisure field. Its contents (i.e., the journal) will include studies on the philosophical and historical development of leisure phenomena, economic issues involved in programs and services, sociological and psychological factors in leisure behavior, planning and design of equipment and facilities, legal and administrative policies and procedures, and other similar problems of primary concern to the field." Suffice it to say that leisure research was seen broadly, and as either interdisciplinary or multidisciplinary by the founding co-editors. These early scholars did not attempt to put any "side boards" on leisure and recreation research. Perhaps they intended leisure to be all-inclusive — in the hope that they would attract enough papers for a second issue!

In a 1985 *Leisure Sciences* article on the state of leisure research, I attempted to establish some boundaries on leisure research. I quote from that article:

> The core of leisure research should be leisure and recreation behavior, to include play and sport. The theory and methods that guide the enterprise should come from the separate social sciences. The meanings and motives attached to leisure and recreation both separately and as they influence behavior and spatial relationships are important to the extent that they define leisure places and give meaning to the activity. Both the physical and perceptual environment should be studied to the extent that it constrains leisure activity (Burdge 1985: 106).

In the first chapter of this book, Jackson and Burton report the findings from a questionnaire that was sent to all authors who had published in six major leisure and recreation research journals. The tabular material from their analysis helps to understand the major thrusts of leisure and recreation research over the last two decades, as well as these scholars' perceptions of the disciplinary nature of the enterprise. I will cite the Jackson-Burton findings extensively throughout the remainder of this chapter.

Recreation Research

Recreation research deals both with activities and facilities and, therefore, has program implications. As long as recreation research comes under the rubric of leisure research, it must be considered multidisciplinary. The organization of multidisciplinary research groups to deal with practical issues and problems certainly applies in the case of recreation research. The study of outdoor recreation program needs, financed to a large extent by North American land management agencies, has been the greatest success story of recreation research. This judgment is based not only on the amount of journal space devoted to reporting these studies, but also from the data shown in the first chapter. Jackson and Burton found that such multidisciplinary topics as "demand analysis," "carrying capacity," "parks and reserves," and "water-oriented" research were ranked as the most dominant research themes of the last two decades by the respondents to their questionnaire.

Parks Administration Research

Recreation administration is the major curriculum focus within Parks and Recreation type departments, at least in the United States. The practical and needed goal is to train students in how to administer recreation programs in municipal park and private sector settings. Teaching is directed toward obtaining a professional degree — with certification coming from the Society of Parks and Recreation Educators. The knowledge base for a parks administration curriculum is drawn from Departments and Colleges of Commerce and Business Administration. Being a good parks administrator requires many of the same traits as being a good business manager. Hence, a steady diet of courses is needed in administration, finance, and public relations, as well as employee motivation. From the Jackson-Burton findings, we note that few research themes cited by the respondents as "dominant" were related to parks administration. Planning, policy, delivery systems, professionalism and practice, facility management research, and, perhaps, "voluntarism," were all placed at the bottom of the list by respondents.

Therapeutic Recreation Research

In my view, therapeutic recreation, as it has come to be called in North America, bears little resemblance to curricula associated with Departments of Parks and Recreation or Leisure Studies. The goal of therapeutic recreation is rehabilitation of the physically and mentally handicapped based on recreation activity. These rehabilitative procedures come from physical therapy, combined with a positivistic self-help approach to therapy taught in educational psychology. Certainly, the study of mentally and physically handicapped at play or in recreation provides much in the way of programmatic experience for practitioners in this area. However, therapeutic recreation is certainly two, and perhaps three, steps removed from any type of disciplinary roots. We might properly label the field "multidisciplinary," with professional practice being the main goal of undergraduate training. "Special populations" was the only one of twenty leisure and recreation research themes cited by the respondents to the Jackson-Burton study that might be associated with therapeutic recreation.

WHICH DISCIPLINES ARE REPRESENTED BY LEISURE RESEARCHERS?

Approximately 67 percent of the respondents to the Jackson-Burton study identified a basic social science discipline as the area of their degree training (i.e., sociology, geography, economics, political science, or psychology). The remaining one-third reported a degree from an applied or professional department (e.g., recreation and leisure studies, forestry, environmental studies, and urban and regional planning). Leisure and recreation researchers with a disciplinary background dominate leisure research, at least to the extent that the respondents to the Jackson-Burton study are representative. Those respondents were persons that had published in one of six journals: *Leisure Sciences*, *JLR*, and the *Journal of Park and Recreation Administration* published in the U.S.; *Recreation Research Review* and *Society and Leisure* published in Canada; and *Leisure Studies* published in the United Kingdom. Researchers who have published in *JLR*, *Leisure Sciences*, and *Society and Leisure* would dominate the response categories because these journals are older.

In the early years, *Society and Leisure* was sponsored by the Committee for Leisure and Popular Culture of the International Sociological Association, and published by the European Centre for Leisure and Education in Prague, Czechoslovakia. In the late 1970s, the Journal was moved to the Department of Leisure Sciences at Trois-Rivières in Quebec. Although retaining much of its sociological flavor due to the editorship of Gilles Pronovost, the journal now includes articles from other social and administrative sciences. Leisure and recreation research in Canada and the United Kingdom (as well as Australia and New Zealand) is centered more in geography and planning departments. Much of the leisure and recreation research in the U.S. is done in Parks and Recreation type departments or by scientists in state and federal land management agencies. That historical note may explain many of the differences between the Jackson-Burton findings and those from Tables 1 and 2 in this chapter.

Degree Discipline of North American Leisure and Recreation Researchers

Table 1 shows the discipline of highest degree for authors of articles in *JLR* and *Leisure Sciences*. Sociologists published the most articles during the early years of *JLR* (1969-1975), but researchers from all social sciences were well represented.

During the second period of *JLR* (1976-1981), the contributions from sociology and economics diminished sharply, with the Ph.D. training of authors more likely to come from a parks and recreation department. The percentage from psychology doubled, but most of those authorships can be attributed to a flurry of activity by Crandall and Tinsley and their students.

Table 1

Discipline of Highest Degree for Authors, Comparing JLR (1969-1975), JLR (1976-1981), JLR (1982-1987), and Leisure Sciences (1977-1982) and (1983-1987)

Journal and Volume Numbers

Discipline of Highest Degree[a]	JLR (1-7) n	%	JLR (8-13) n	%	JLR (14-19) n	%	LS (1-5)[c] n	%	LS (6-10)[d] n	%	Totals n	%
Rural Sociology/ Sociology	53	21	33	13	40	15	49	28	33	17	208	18
Agricultural Econ./Economics	40	15	25	10	26	9	7	4	10	5	108	9
Forestry	42	16	37	15	40	15	33	19	27	13	179	16
Parks Recreation/ Leisure Studies	26	10	37	15	78	29	40	23	73	37	254	22
Geography	22	9	26	11	16	6	17	10	22	11	103	9
Psychology/ Educ. Psych.	19	8	35	15	32	12	13	7	10	5	109	10
Physical Education	6	2	7	3	4	1	3	2	6	3	26	2
Planning and Architecture	11	4	10	5	3	1	6	3	2	1	32	3
Therapeutic Recreation	4	2	3	1	5	2	-	-	-	-	12	1
Engineering	12	5	-	-	7	2	2	1	4	2	25	2
Business Admin./ Marketing	10	4	24	10	12	4	5	3	2	1	53	5
Other Disciplines[b]	10	4	7	3	11	4	-	-	11	5	38	3
Totals	255	-	244	-	274	-	175	-	200	-	1,148	-

(Partially adapted from Burdge 1982, p. 115.)

[a] "Discipline" = the department that granted the highest degree.

[b] Includes statistics, medicine, philosophy, political science, home economics, biology, environmental studies, and anthropology.

[c] Volume 4, Number 3, of *Leisure Sciences* was not included in the tabulations, because that special issue was not reflective of the normal submission process.

[d] Includes only the first three issues of Volume 10.

During the first period of *JLR* (1969-1975), contributions from persons with degrees in business administration and marketing made up ten percent of the authorships. The traditional social science disciplines made up 53 percent, with 44 percent coming from the applied departments of forestry, parks and recreation, physical education, planning and architecture, therapeutic recreation, and engineering. During the second period of *JLR* (1976-81), the proportions were 49 percent traditional social science, compared to 48 percent applied, showing a minor shift toward authors with degrees from applied and professional departments.

However, it was during the latter period of *JLR* (1982-1987) that the shift in authors was away from persons with degrees in social science disciplines to those with degrees from applied or professional departments. Authors with terminal degrees from Parks and Recreation departments doubled, from 15 percent to 29 percent. Articles from persons with forestry degrees remained stable, with a slight overall drop from those in the social science disciplines. From the second to the third period of *JLR*, authors with degrees from the traditional social sciences dropped from 49 to 42 percent. That compares with a proportion of 53 percent for the first period (1969-1975).

Sociologists have the most authorships in *Leisure Sciences* (about one third of the total for the first period, between 1977 and 1982), followed by parks and recreation, with 25 percent (Table 1). Forestry is the next highest, with 17 percent. The pattern for geography remains much the same as it was for *JLR*. The number of articles published by economists in the two journals has declined steadily since the mid-1970s. Forty authors were economists during the early period of *JLR*, compared with only 25 in each of the last two periods. Many of the economists who did resource recreation research (e.g., Chiccetti, Knetsch, Cesario) have now gone on to other natural resource-related issues.

However, during the second period of *Leisure Sciences* (1983-1987), we see a dramatic shift in the source of the highest degree for authors. As was the case with *JLR*, the authors with degrees from Parks and Recreation type departments increased from 23 to 37 percent of the total authorships. Meanwhile, authors with degrees in sociology or rural sociology dropped from 28 to 17 percent. With the exception of a slight decline in authorships from forestry, the disciplinary mix of authors remained quite stable for *Leisure Sciences* between the two periods.

The degree backgrounds of authors for these two journals reflect the multidisciplinary and applied nature of the field. In the early years, persons from the traditional social science disciplines were dominant. Now, researchers with degrees from parks and recreation and forestry represent the majority of the authors. We may expect the trend to accelerate in the years ahead. Data on the academic training of persons who conduct leisure and recreation research help us understand the disciplinary roots of the enterprise.

Location of Leisure and Recreation Research

The institutional location of persons determines the constraints on their research, how they are rewarded, and the type of research problems they select. Employment opportunities for social scientists were traditionally limited to teaching and the conduct of basic research within their own disciplines. Now, they may accept employment in the unit that most closely mirrors their research interests, whether or not it is in the same academic discipline or area from which they received a degree. Ph.D.s in the applied disciplines of engineering, business administration, forestry, and parks and recreation do not always limit their place of work after graduation to academic settings. At one time, I counted seven different departments and units doing research related to leisure and recreation at the University of Illinois: Leisure Studies, Physical Education, Forestry, Agricultural Economics, The Institute for Environmental Studies, Geography, and Landscape Architecture. Historically, leisure and recreation research has been done by persons from a variety of disciplines located in diverse institutional settings. If leisure and recreation research is increasingly concentrated in one institutional setting, then there is evidence that the field is becoming more discipline-like.

The institutional location of the authors of the articles in *JLR* and *Leisure Sciences* is shown in Table 2. These data indicate that the institutional location of authors is quite variable, particularly for the first period of *JLR* (1969-1975). Although the largest number of authors came from sociology departments, the margin was small, with a good mix of professional and traditional discipline departments. The second period of *JLR* (1976-1981) shows that more authors were located in forestry and parks and recreation departments and fewer from sociology and economics. That trend accelerated during the third period of *JLR* (1982-1987). The numbers of authors from parks and recreation type departments increased from 20 to 39 percent. Authors from U.S. Forest Experiment Stations made up almost 10 percent of the total authorships during this last period of the journal.

The institutional location of authors for *Leisure Sciences* was similar to that found for *JLR*, but with more contributions from persons in applied departments and fewer from those in traditional social science departments. As in the case of *JLR*, the institutional location of authors from Parks and Recreation Departments increased (from 27 to 40 percent). In the last period of *Leisure Sciences* (1983-1987), only twenty percent of the authors reported institutional location in traditional social science departments. Contrast that finding with 33 percent for the first period of *Leisure Sciences* (1977-1982) and 38 percent for the first period of *JLR* (1969-1975).

These data on discipline and institutional location of authors of papers in *JLR* and *Leisure Sciences* suggest two conclusions. First, the research area has traditionally been multidisciplinary, in that so many disciplines were represented

Table 2
Institutional Location of Authors, Comparing JLR (1969-1975), JLR (1976-1981), JLR (1982-1987), and Leisure Sciences (1977-1982) and (1983-1987)

Journal and Volume Numbers

Institutional Location	JLR (1-7) n	%	JLR (8-13) n	%	JLR (14-19) n	%	LS (1-5)[a] n	%	LS (6-10) n	%	Totals n	%
University/College Department												
a. Rural Sociology/ Sociology	42	16	21	9	25	9	29	17	14	7	131	11
b. Agricultural Econ./ Economics	24	9	14	6	10	4	2	16	3	56	5	-
c. Forestry	30	12	31	13	37	14	31	18	30	15	159	14
d. Parks and Rec./ Leisure Studies	35	14	49	20	83	30	48	27	79	40	293	26
e. Geography	15	6	22	9	11	4	15	9	13	6	76	7
f. Psychology	12	7	22	9	21	8	11	68	4	74	6	
g. Business Admin./ Marketing	11	4	21	9	14	5	3	24	2	53	5	
h. Planning/Arch.	7	3	7	3	3	1	4	23	1	25	2	
i. Engineering	10	4	-	-	1	1	2	1	1	1	14	1
j. Physical Educ.	4	2	6	2	5	2	2	1	6	3	23	2
k. Other University Depts.	12	5	17	7	14	5	1	1	8	4	52	4
Federal Agencies (U.S. and Canada)												
a. Forestry Experiment Stations	24	9	12	5	24	9	13	7	11	5	84	7
b. U.S. Park Service	6	2	3	1	2	1	5	3	7	3	23	2
c. Parks Canada	4	1	2	1	-	-	2	1	-	-	8	1
d. Other Departments	4	1	5	2	7	3	3	2	4	2	23	2
State and Local Government	12	5	6	2	6	2	-	-	1	1	25	2
Private-Semiprivate[b]	3	1[c]	6	2[c]	11	4[c]	4	1[c]	5	3	29	3
Totals	255	-	244	-	274	-	175	-	200	-	1,148	-

(Partially adapted from Burdge 1982, p. 117.)

[a] Volume 4, Number 3, was not included in the count, because the papers were drawn from a conference on sociological aspects of park development and management.

[b] Includes Resources for the Future Inc.

[c] Due to rounding errors, numbers do not always add to 100.

in the papers published in these two journals. Secondly, authors located in professional degree-granting departments (Parks and Recreation and Forestry) and in state (or provincial) and federal land management agencies now dominate. Research from government agencies almost always deals with natural resource recreation issues.

Both the location of employment and highest degree of authors in *JLR* and *Leisure Sciences* suggest that the research area has moved from a diffuse, multidisciplinary activity of many social and administrative scientists to one increasingly concentrated in Parks and Recreation (Leisure Studies) and Forestry departments. In forestry, the research focus is natural resource recreation. The bringing together of discipline-trained social scientists with those from applied departments indicates that leisure and recreation is at least becoming interdisciplinary.

We should add that, at least in U.S. universities, *JLR* and *Leisure Sciences* are seen as the "disciplinary" journals for Parks and Recreation and Leisure Studies type departments. Extensive publication in these two journals receives full recognition during tenure and promotion evaluations. Persons from traditional social science departments would receive recognition for publishing in these two journals, but to receive tenure they would also be required to publish in disciplinary outlets.

THE DISCIPLINARY ROOTS OF LEISURE AND RECREATION METHODOLOGY

The survey of leisure and recreation research scholars reported in the first chapter by Jackson and Burton included a question on the relative contributions of disciplinary, multidisciplinary, and interdisciplinary methods and approaches to the development of knowledge and understanding in leisure and recreation during the past 20 years. Disciplinary methods and approaches were defined as being "drawn from and applied in a single discipline." Multidisciplinary methods and approaches were defined as being "drawn from individual disciplines and applied separately, but as part of the same project or study." Interdisciplinary methods and approaches were defined as "implying the transfer of methods and approaches across disciplines."

Jackson and Burton admit to some difficulties in the interpretation of their data on the relative perceived contributions of alternative research methods and approaches to the development of leisure and recreation research. However, if methodological approaches can be seen as an indicator of disciplinary roots, we might suggest that, in rank order, leisure research is, first, interdisciplinary; second, multidisciplinary; and third, disciplinary. If a statistical measure of association had been calculated for responses to that question, the directionality of the relationship would be highly significant.

It should be cautioned that, as phrased, the question dealt with the contribution of research methods, and not the basic units of analysis associated with each social science discipline. For example, survey research has been the major research technique utilized to obtain data for the "outdoor recreation" type studies. Nonetheless, these results do suggest some shared perception of the nature of leisure and recreation research. Almost half of these scholars (48 percent) designate leisure and recreation as "interdisciplinary." Based on the statement of the question, leisure and recreation research becomes interdisciplinary because it has a recognized data base that is analyzed utilizing the methods of different disciplines. However, the responses shown in Table 4 in the preceding chapter also indicate that 57 percent of the respondents counted multidisciplinary methods and approaches as quite high in making a contribution to the development of leisure and recreation research.

WHAT ARE THE DEPENDENT AND INDEPENDENT VARIABLES OF LEISURE RESEARCH?

At the core of each social and administrative science discipline is the "unit of analysis" — the basic dependent variable around which systematic and verifiable research accumulates. The knowledge base around which leisure and recreation accumulates comes from a variety of social science disciplines, each with a different unit of analysis. The unit of analysis (dependent variable) must, however, fit the theoretical background in which the research study is based. Some examples of units of analysis are leisure-related expenditures, location and type of recreation activity, and individual values and attitudes about leisure. All are related to individual and group forms of leisure activity, perceptions, or leisure activity choices. Some deal with decisions regarding the allocation of money for leisure activities, and others with values, beliefs, and attitudes, which in turn influence activity choice. The settings in which people experience leisure and recreation are important, because the external environment shapes and limits the type of leisure and recreation activity.

In the last two decades, leisure and recreation research has produced considerable knowledge about a variety of leisure- and recreation-related activity, organized around recognizable research topics. The fact that Jackson and Burton were able to develop a list of "dominant themes" (see their Table 3) from the sample of leisure and recreation scholars indicates that recognizable sub-categories of research have emerged. The "units of analysis" around which knowledge accumulates come from the traditional social and administrative sciences, but the findings are related to leisure and recreation.

Further evidence of the accumulation of knowledge is the increase in the number of scholarly refereed publications devoted to leisure and recreation research which have appeared since the first issue of *JLR*. Jackson and Burton chose six as indicative of the body of leisure and recreation research. However, they might have included others (Burdge 1983). *Play and Culture* (from the Society for the Anthropological Study of Play) published its first volume in 1988, and the *Journal of Leisurability* is achieving scholarly status. Four journals in tourism have begun publication since 1975. Magazines and newsletters that regularly report leisure and recreation research include the *Leisure Information Quarterly, Leisure Today, Parks and Recreation* magazine and the *Journal of the World Leisure and Recreation Association.*

LEISURE AND RECREATION RESEARCH AND PARKS AND RECREATION CURRICULA

Some time ago, I wrote a short essay about the "Coming Separation of Leisure and Recreation Research from Park and Recreation Education" (Burdge 1985a). My main concern was that doing scholarly research on leisure and recreation was difficult in Parks and Recreation and Forestry departments, where practitioner training directed toward professional certification was emphasized.

I argued that a potential conflict was present if faculty members in recreation and parks departments were required to teach practitioners and also do leisure research. Furthermore, I felt there was little compatibility between the teaching methods of parks and recreation education and the methodology utilized by discipline-based leisure scholars. In essence, one curriculum was taught for undergraduates and a very different one for graduate students (Sapora 1977). I was also concerned that the knowledge base generated by leisure and recreation researchers was not finding its way into the textbooks and teaching materials of the undergraduate curriculum. In short, the knowledge base generated by the research side of the department was not being passed on by the teaching side.

Three persons were asked to respond to my question about leisure research being separated from parks and recreation education (Godbey 1985; Goodale 1985; Smith 1985). Most of what I wrote was an effort to provoke critical internal examination by Parks and Recreation departments. Not surprisingly, I received little support for my position. In general, I was assured that, indeed, leisure and recreation research was benefitting practitioners, and that my view of leisure studies was myopic. However, on several points, I remain unconvinced. I do not see evidence of the research content of the leisure and recreation journals showing up in the textbooks or other materials used in Parks and Recreation curricula. (If you need evidence look at the citations at the end of each chapter in this book). Secondly, I do not see a nationwide scholarly body of leisure and recreation researchers emerging to provide support for faculty in Parks and Recreation and Leisure Studies departments. Furthermore, in the U.S., I see Parks and Recreation departments clinging to a practitioner-oriented curriculum, rather than providing an academic program geared to a more intellectually stimulating, liberal arts, type of degree (Sessoms 1984; Twardzik 1984).

WHAT DO WE CONCLUDE ABOUT LEISURE AND RECREATION RESEARCH?

The study of leisure and recreation began from a multidisciplinary perspective utilizing the methodological approaches of the traditional social and administrative science disciplines. It is a research area with a social problem orientation, i.e., we have too much or too little leisure time, or we do not have sufficient recreation facilities, or they are managed improperly (Kleiber 1983).

In the United States, at least, the persons who carried out leisure and recreation research in the late 1960s and through most of the 1970s generally received their degrees from, and were housed in, traditional social and administrative science departments. In the late 1970s and through the 1980s, the trend was for these authors to have received their degrees from professionally oriented departments (mostly Parks and Recreation and Forestry) and to be housed in research settings that emphasize multidisciplinary approaches to leisure and recreation research.

Individual research articles on leisure and recreation, at least as reflected in the refereed literature, almost always reflect the disciplinary orientation of the authors. Generally, a faculty member and student team up on a paper from a recently completed dissertation. The research generally represents the disciplinary perspective of the thesis advisor.

The emerging set of research findings is decidedly interdisciplinary. Except for one, the twenty dominant themes in leisure and recreation research listed by Jackson and Burton are all interdisciplinary or multidisciplinary. The only disciplinary topic would be "demand analysis." That topic is undoubtedly a reflection of the "demand" for leisure and recreation activities and facilities, and not "demand" in the traditional economic sense of recreation units consumed at different prices. Each of the remaining topics that received at least forty percent of the "votes" was interdisciplinary or multidisciplinary.

There have been some major success stories in the "leisure and recreation research" area, particularly as it applies to management and the development of facilities for recreation users. The ROS (Recreation Opportunity Spectrum) is a resource management device developed by Forest Service recreation researchers for use by land management agencies. This planning tool grew out of the recreation experience preference studies of Driver and his associates (Driver *et al.* 1987), and was formalized by Clark and Stankey (1979). The effort is definitely multidisciplinary and was developed because of an expressed need for a recreation resource management tool.

EXTENSION OF CONCLUSIONS

Some one and a half decades ago, I concluded that leisure and recreation represented important topics of study. As in all policy and programmatic areas, the ultimate partial solution or better understanding of the situation would become better known after continued study, utilizing many disciplinary approaches — in essence multidisciplinary. However, I now conclude that leisure and recreation research can almost be called interdisciplinary.

The accumulation of findings about leisure and recreation over the last two decades has been based to a large degree on the strength of the methodology and the research methods of the social science disciplines. The substantive findings reported in the later chapters of this book represent verified concepts that must be part of the separate disciplines that go together to make up an important knowledge base of the social sciences. However, as Jackson and Burton point out, these parent disciplines are in danger of losing a portion of their reality when they ignore such a fundamental and vast segment of the daily human routine as leisure.

To make a point, I want to take issue with a quotation from one respondent to the Jackson-Burton study, who wrote (with an alleged twinge of sadness): "Interdisciplinary research promises so much, but has produced so little." What the respondent probably meant was that the results of an interdisciplinary research effort may be disappointing in a singular sense. However, the history of science and the accumulation of knowledge has been one of multidisciplinary and interdisciplinary research topics eventually developing into disciplines (with full university status). Each discipline tended to carve out units of analysis that were distinct and separate. In the post-World War II era, the "hyphenated disciplines" and interdisciplinary topics have emerged into recognizable university departments. Once we had biology and zoology. Now we have departments of micro-biology, bio-chemistry, entomology, ecology, ethology, evolution, biological sciences, veterinary bio-sciences — to name but a few.

Urban and regional planning and landscape architecture were once bound up with the design arts. Now, these departments are heavily social science in orientation. Urban planning utilizes models borrowed from economics and geography. Landscape architecture includes work on spatial relationships springing from perceptual and emotional theory in psychology.

The researcher from the United Kingdom, quoted above, failed to see that leisure and recreation research is indeed the evolution of a multidisciplinary topic seeking interdisciplinary recognition as a scholarly university department. In the last decade of the 20th century, leisure and recreation research is on the verge of achieving interdisciplinary status. The editors of refereed publications in this field have made great strides in providing a forum for knowledge accumulation. The name "leisure studies," and even "leisure sciences," is becoming a part of more department labels. These university departments are seen as legitimate places to do leisure and recreation research.

There remain some obstacles to the final recognition of leisure and recreation studies as legitimate interdisciplinary topics. The first is the incorporation of the findings from the journals and research monographs into the textbooks and the curricula of graduate and undergraduate programs. The second follows from the first, namely an agreement on role definition for faculty who are expected to train practitioners and also to do leisure and recreation research. Finally, an American Leisure Studies Association (modeled after European and Canadian examples) must be founded to provide a meeting ground for scholars and researchers representing the breadth of interdisciplinary interest in leisure. Such an association would add legitimacy to leisure and recreation research and provide a meeting ground for researchers both inside and outside university departments.

References

Alpert, D. 1985. "On the organization of interdisciplinary research: Issues relating to the governance and mission of the Beckman Institute for Advanced Science and Technology." Unpublished paper, Center for Advanced Study, University of Illinois, Urbana, IL.

Burdge, R.J. 1974. "The state of leisure research." *Journal of Leisure Research 6:* 312-317.

Burdge, R.J. 1983. "Making leisure and recreation research a scholarly topic: Views of a journal editor, 1972-1982." *Leisure Sciences 6:* 99.

Burdge, R.J. 1984. "Future perspectives and political impact in U.S. recreation planning." In *Proceedings Recreatie Planning in Onzekerheid*, ed. A. van Straten, pp. 39-50. Werk Groep Recreatie, University of Wageningen, The Netherlands.

Burdge, R.J. 1985a. "The coming separation of leisure studies from parks and recreation education." *Journal of Leisure Research 17:* 133-141.

Burdge, R.J. 1985b. "Leisure research and park and recreation education: Compatible or not?" In *Recreation and Leisure: Issues in an Era of Change*, Second edition, eds. T.L. Goodale and P.A. Witt, pp. 343-351. State College, PA: Venture Publishing.

Burdge, R.J. and T.A.M. Beckers. 1984. "Breaking the one-way mirror: The increased isolation of North American leisure research." *World Leisure and Recreation 26:* 11-16.

Burdge, R.J. and J. Hendricks. 1972. "The nature of leisure research: A reflection and comment." *Journal of Leisure Research 4:* 215-217.

Burdge, R.J. and J. Hendricks. 1973. "A comment on the sociological direction of research on leisure." *Society and Leisure 5:* 159-163.

Clark, R.N. and G.H. Stankey. 1979. *The Recreation Opportunity Spectrum: A Framework for Planning, Management and Research.* USDA Forest Service General Technical Report PNN-98. Portland, OR: Pacific Northwest Forest Experiment Station.

Driver, B.L., P.J. Brown, G.H. Stankey and T.C. Gregoire. 1987. "The ROS planning system: Evolution, basic concepts, and research needed." *Leisure Sciences 9:* 201-212.

Godbey, G. 1985. "The coming cross-pollination of leisure studies and recreation and park education: A response." *Journal of Leisure Research 17:* 142-148.

Goodale, T.L. 1985. "Carts before heavy mules: Are competing hypotheses too late?" *Journal of Leisure Research 17:* 149-154.

Kleiber, D. 1983. "A critique of leisure research during the last decade in the USA." Paper presented at the Symposium on International Problems of Leisure Research, University of Bielefeld, West Germany.

Sapora, A.V. 1977. "The emergence of a curriculum model for professional leadership for leisure in institutes of higher education." Paper presented at the World Leisure and Recreation Association Conference, East Lansing, Michigan State University.

Sessoms, H.D. 1984. "Research issues in park and recreation education: An overview." *Leisure Sciences 6:* 327-335.

Smith, S.L.J. 1985. "An alternative perspective on the nature of recreation and leisure studies: A personal response to Rabel Burdge." *Journal of Leisure Research 17:* 155-160.

Twardzik, L.F. 1984. "A case for the study of utilitarian ethics in professional recreation education and practice." *Leisure Sciences 6:* 375-385.

PART TWO

Concepts and Conceptions

Many scholars in recreation and leisure studies have become almost obsessed in recent years with a search for stable concepts and theories about leisure and recreation, and with a professed need for the development of a coherent and consistent body of theory. The call for this has reverberated through journals, addresses, surveys, state-of-the-art reviews, conferences, and other forums. It has amounted, at times, to a veritable clamor. In the midst of this din, it is easy to forget that concepts and theories already exist in the field. Moreover, they exist in significant numbers. Some are partial or incomplete. Others are specific to particular topics and themes and cannot be generalized to the wider field. Some are conflicting or competing theories attempting to explain the same leisure phenomenon. Nevertheless, they *do* exist, and cannot be ignored in any attempt to assess the current state of recreation and leisure studies. This part of the book is devoted, therefore, to an examination of the nature, characteristics, evolution, and current evaluation of various concepts and theories about, or pertinent to, leisure and recreation.

The seven chapters in this section encompass a variety of conceptual and theoretical issues and themes. Cooper's opening chapter is a philosophical treatise which, in essence, addresses the question: "Why study leisure?" In so doing, it offers insights into the notion of what constitutes leisure and tackles the recurring issue of the significance of intrinsic and extrinsic rewards in the conception of leisure. The author concludes that any such conception should surely permit of both instrumental and intrinsic motivation.

The transition from concepts (or generalized notions) to theories (specific testable principles that hypothesize explanations) is, of course, a weighty step. Yet this has been done in leisure studies, as is evident in the chapters by Rojek, Kelly, and Bella. Each of these addresses extant theories, although in very dissimilar ways. There is, however, a common theme. It lies in each author's recognition of the relatively minor attention given to the development and testing of theory in the field in comparison to empirical study. Empiricism, grounded in the methods and tools of the "natural sciences", has dominated recreation and leisure research, often willy-nilly, and thereby has wrought a great disservice to the field. For Rojek, competing sociological theories have been shaped in large measure by the demands of empirical method. For Kelly, the architectural dictum that "form follows function" has been turned on its head in leisure research, so that "design follows methods." This, inevitably, constrains and limits the act of theorizing. And for Bella, a slavish adherence to logical positivist empirical research has contributed, significantly though not exclusively, to conceptualizations and theories of leisure which are inherently androcentric.

For all three authors, the principal limitation of much conceptual and theoretical research in leisure studies has been its failure to come to grips with the issues of "meaning." The pertinent question has to do with the meanings that people ascribe to their leisure experiences. It is a question that has rarely been addressed in the field — and certainly not answered in any comprehensive manner. Here, these authors offer their own tentative (and challenging) answers. Furthermore, implicitly if not explicitly, they raise fundamental questions about the meanings that scholars ascribe to leisure behavior and recreational experiences — usually without reference to the perceptions, values, and attitudes of the participants themselves.

The dominance of the scientific method, as defined in the "natural sciences," is also the principal theme in Burton's chapter on leisure forecasting, policymaking, and planning. The author suggests that the central problem with current attempts at forecasting, policymaking, and planning for recreation and leisure is a fascination with science and the scientific method, coupled with an overwhelming felt need to identify, demonstrate and quantify causality, and a dominating desire to separate "facts" from "values" — with the erroneous presumptions that, not only *can* the two be separated, but also that "scientific facts" are somehow superior, and should form the basis for forecasting, policymaking, and planning for leisure. (This too, of course, is itself a value judgment!)

The concern for meaning which permeates the chapters by Rojek, Kelly, and Bella is also a dominant theme in those by Stockdale and Glyptis. The former argues that an understanding of the ways in which leisure is represented to people, and understood by them, is essential to any explanation of the influence of social and cultural values, beliefs, images, and symbols upon leisure behavior. In the more specific context of leisure and unemployment, Glyptis also addresses the question of meaning. People, she suggests, *expect* to work and, generally, *want* to do so. Leisure is no substitute for this. It plays an important role as part of a balanced lifestyle, but its meaning to people does not mirror that of work; nor, as far as we can tell, is it likely to do so in the future.

In summary, the seven chapters in Part Two of the book appear to be, and are in many respects, diverse and divergent. At times, the authors even take issue with each other! Yet two common themes hold the group of chapters together: a profound concern about the misguided importance ascribed in most recreation and leisure research to the scientific method, and a dominant desire to probe beyond leisure *activity* to understand its *meaning* for people, a meaning which cannot be divorced from the meanings that people attach to the other aspects of their lives. In the final analysis, leisure is a part of life in general, not apart from it.

E. L. J.
T. L. B.

SOME PHILOSOPHICAL ASPECTS OF LEISURE THEORY

W. E. Cooper

Concept and Conception

Most of us share a concept of leisure as free time, but there is considerable disagreement about which conception of this concept is best suited to guide theory. Does unemployment count as free time, and hence leisure? (Glyptis, this volume). Or is the freedom of leisure the absence of causal determination, as an indeterminist philosopher might suggest? (Descartes 1912). Or is it the freedom to exercise one's faculties as one wants, without care for the instrumental value of doing so? (Suits 1981). Does our clock-bound modern existence count as free time, or was true leisure available only in a past Golden Age, prior to the Industrial Revolution, when time for us was cyclical rather than linear, thanks to our being closer to the seasons and other aspects of nature? (De Grazia 1964). Is the freedom of leisure more a reality for men than for women? (Bella, this volume). Is our leisure distorted by class conflict? (Rojek, this volume).

These questions are representative of the many theoretical issues that have been posed by people who have thought seriously about leisure. Any adequate account of this subject must address these issues, and the essays in this volume hold out the promise of collectively approaching such an account. A small but important first step towards this goal is realizing that little is to be gained by focusing intently on the concept of leisure and related concepts like free time, as though a happy Gestalt switch in one's intellectual perception might reveal the true meaning of leisure. Towards taking this first step I shall expand on a distinction between the concept and the conception of a thing.

Briefly, the concept of something — leisure, justice, beauty, and so on — is that which most people would agree upon as what they mean when they talk about that thing, even if they have importantly different beliefs about it. These differing sets of beliefs make up differing conceptions (Dworkin 1977; Rawls 1971). For instance, we share a concept of justice as giving to each his due, but we have different conceptions of what is involved in giving to each his due. Are goods distributed justly only when they are distributed equally, or according to the market value of a person's skills, or according to need, or in some other way? Similarly, there are different conceptions of leisure as free time. Is it simply idleness, or an opportunity for self-fulfillment, or schooling in noble values, or a unique mental state of "flow" or "ecstasy," or something else?

A conception makes a concept determinate. A theoretically useful conception should make a concept determinate in a way that raises important questions and promising avenues for research. In what follows I shall suggest what I take to be a theoretically useful conception of leisure, which identifies it with doing things for their own sake. I shall try to show how this conception can figure in a systematic theory of leisure, by replying to some objections to the very idea of such a theory. I aim to conclude that leisure theory can be a science in the way that other social sciences are, but that its research should also aim at helping people to live authentic, self-expressive lives.

An observer may be somewhat bemused to learn that social scientists are making a serious study of leisure. Kelly was remarking on this type of reaction, perhaps, when he said that "the smiles and smirks that often follow when people say that they are studying leisure suggest that there is something odd about taking fun and games seriously" (Kelly 1982). It is tempting to dismiss this attitude, but it is sufficiently prevalent that it warrants a reply. Let it be articulated therefore in the first objection I shall consider, as follows.

OBJECTION ONE (THE ODDNESS OBJECTION)

The phrase "the serious study of leisure" is an oxymoron, a contradiction in terms. It is, by definition, fun and games, and consequently the antithesis of serious study. Therefore, the very idea of a serious study of leisure, not to mention a science of leisure, is intellectually suspect. Scholars and scientists should concern themselves with the serious things in life, not its diversions.

Reply to Objection One

There are several confusions in The Oddness Objection. At the risk of belaboring the obvious, I shall emphasize two. First, it commits a logical fallacy in attributing the alleged qualities of a subject-matter to the study of the subject-matter. This is an instance of what Ryle calls a "category-mistake," which involves thinking of something that belongs to one logical category as though it belonged to another (Ryle 1949). Among Ryle's examples are the category-mistakes of supposing that team spirit is an extra player on a team, and of supposing that a university is something different from the buildings, students, and staff that go to make it up, and so on. Some further examples: the particles that physicists study are extremely small, but it does not follow that doing physics is extremely small — whatever that might mean. So, too, a philosopher who studies hedonism is not, *ipso facto*, revelling in pleasure instead of taking scholarly pains, and a social scientist studying recidivism need not be a convict about to return to prison. In the same way it is a category-mistake to suppose that leisure research is fun and games. To do so is to treat leisure research as leisure, when in fact it is an intellectual activity which takes leisure as its object of study. A leisure theorist need not do his research only in his free time, and all the more it is not required that he be indulging in "fun and games."

Secondly, the Objection illicitly assumes that leisure must be a mere diversion from serious activity, a matter of fun and games, whereas the only reasonable assumption is that someone's leisure may amount to no more than this. The Objection takes for granted, in effect, a conception of leisure that is really quite contentious, and which I shall be contending against in this essay. If leisure is intrinsically desired activity, and if, as thus understood, it is crucial to fully expressing oneself, then it seems evident that leisure can be an important matter in a human life. This is what I hope to show.

An adequate conception of leisure can only be arrived at by argument and reflection on a variety of considerations, not by appeal to what the word "leisure" means. Anyone who has examined a good dictionary's entry for this word knows that what leisure is "by definition" is a very mixed bag of vague and sometimes conflicting things. Consider an unclothed person, obliged to quake in the cold. Few would view this as leisure activity, yet the Oxford English Dictionary (OED) cites the following passage from Chaucer as exemplifying a sense of the word leisure (Oxford English Dictionary 1971: 1601):

> No more was there
> To clothe her with.
> Gret leyser had she to quake.

I also assume that a conception of leisure can safely ignore the anthropomorphic projection that is apparent in another OED entry, Baxter's sentence "The young blades in the fields have leisure to expand and grow again before the scythe returns to cut them down a second time" (Oxford English Dictionary 1971: 1601). The theoretically central cases of leisure must be activities that people want to do for their own sake. Blades of grass, lacking desires altogether, may be left beyond the pale of leisure theory.

I have suggested that we share a concept of leisure as free time, but this is empty by itself of determinate content. In particular, it is empty of the implication that one's free time is occupied in non-work. Exploring that implication would at least be a start towards developing a respectable conception of leisure, but to bestow truth upon it by appeal to definition is to enjoy the advantages of theft over honest toil. A specimen of honest toil in exploring the implication that leisure is non-work is Aristotle's classic statement, which is sufficiently important to warrant being quoted at length (Aristotle 1953: 303-304):

Finally, it may well be thought that the activity of contemplation is the only one that is praised on its own account, because nothing comes of it beyond the act of contemplation, whereas from practical activities we count on gaining something more or less over and above the mere action. Again, it is commonly believed that, to have happiness, one must have leisure; we occupy ourselves in order that we may have leisure, just as we make war for the sake of peace. Now the practical virtues find opportunity for their exercise in politics and war, but these are occupations which are supposed to leave no room for leisure. Certainly it is true of the trade of war, for no one deliberately chooses to make war for the sake of making it or tries to bring about a war. A man would be regarded as a bloodthirsty monster if he were to make war on a friendly state just to produce battles and slaughter.... Political and military activities, while pre-eminent among good activities in beauty and grandeur, are incompatible with leisure, and are not chosen for their own sake but with a view to some remoter end, whereas the activity of the intellect is felt to excel in the serious use of leisure, taking as it does the form of contemplation, and not to aim at any end beyond itself, and to own a pleasure peculiar to itself, thereby enhancing the activity.

Leisure for Aristotle is activity which is, above all, chosen for its own sake. I think Aristotle is right about this, and the point is echoed in the contemporary literature of leisure by such theorists as Iso-Ahola (this volume), for whom the core of leisure is intrinsically motivated or self-determined behavior.

But Aristotle does not only identify leisure with intrinsically desired activity. He goes on to claim that, ideally, nothing comes of it. This seems to me a very doubtful proposition, but once it is premised, his conclusion that philosophical contemplation excels at the serious use of leisure is quite natural. On the Aristotelian conception of leisure, then, leisure and work (or, more broadly, instrumental activity) are mutually exclusive categories. Suits's Grasshopper presupposes an Aristotelian conception of leisure in this respect, although he thinks that game-playing rather than philosophical contemplation is the more plausible candidate for ideal leisure activity (Suits 1981). Neither proposal is particularly plausible, however. Philosophical contemplation may be an appropriate ideal for a few, but there is no reason to think that only that few are capable of the serious use of leisure. Waltzer (1983: 186) makes the point nicely:

> That the philosopher's thoughts do not taint the idea of leisure, but the artisan's table or vase or statue do, is a thought likely to appeal only to philosophers. From a moral standpoint, it seems more important that human activity be directed from within

than that it have no outside end or material outcome. And if we
focus on self-direction, a wide variety of purposive activities can
be brought within the compass of a life of leisure.

My own sketch here of a conception of leisure is, in large part, an
attempt to focus on self-direction as Walzer suggests. I hope to explain what
might be involved in self-direction and what the implications of that might be
for leisure theory.

As for Grasshopper's conception of leisure as game-playing, it follows
from a premise that he announces as follows: "But the whole burden of my
teaching is that you ought to be idle" (Suits 1981: 7). This premise, in turn,
follows, in effect, from Grasshopper's assuming the validity of Aristotle's
exclusionary principle: leisure and instrumentality are incompatible. So, ideally,
he reasons, we would live lives of perfect non-instrumentality. This is his
Utopia. And in order to have something to do in Utopia, so that boredom won't
set in, Grasshopper envisages it as a place where mightily complex and unfath-
omably entertaining games are played.

Whereas Aristotle's conception of leisure restricted it to a philosophical
few, Grasshopper's Utopia seems to exclude everyone. Although it is hailed as
"a dramatization of the ideal of existence" (Suits 1981: 168), it seems not to be
my or your or any human being's existence. For any human existence would
include instrumental activity, such as breathing and finger movements, which
are not typically indulged in for their own sake. So no human being could be a
Utopian, and, therefore, Grasshopper's Utopian conception of leisure, delightful
though it may be, is not a conception that could be seriously entertained as a
fruitful one for leisure theorists to adopt.

I favor a conception of leisure which does not view it as necessarily
devoid of instrumental value. I shall call this a Platonic conception of leisure,
because it is suggested by an important distinction which Plato draws in *The
Republic*. Glaucon is pressing Socrates to explain his theory of goodness (Plato
1974: 30):

> I want to know how you classify the things we call good. Are
> there not some which we should wish to have, not for their con-
> sequences, but just for their own sake, such as harmless pleasures
> and enjoyments that have no further result beyond the satisfaction of
> the moment?
> Yes, I think there are good things of that description.
> And also some that we value both for their own sake and
> for their consequences — things like knowledge and health and the
> use of our eyes?
> Yes.

And a third class which would include physical training,
medical treatment, earning one's bread as a doctor or otherwise —
useful, but burdensome things, which we want only for the sake of
the profit or other benefit they bring?
Yes, there is that third class. What then?
In which class do you place justice?
I should say, in the highest, as a thing which anyone who is
to gain happiness must value both for itself and for its results.

The Platonic conception of leisure supposes that leisure may belong to
the "highest class" of things which are of value for themselves and for their
results. An implausible form of the Platonic conception would hold that an
activity fails to be leisure if it does not belong to this highest class. I hold rather
that there is no theoretical ban on leisure having instrumental value, as Aristotle
supposed, but, equally, that there is no requirement that it should be instrumental.

If the first main point of the Aristotelian conception of leisure — that
leisure and work are mutually exclusive — be rejected, the second main point
may be more acceptable. This is the idea that leisure must be valuable. It was
not his view that any useless activity is leisure, nor is it enough that useless
activity should be desired for its own sake. Rather, the activity must be *desirable*
for its own sake. Once again it is of secondary importance that he supposed
philosophical contemplation to be supremely valuable. This may be denied yet
the main point affirmed. So I incorporate in the conception being advanced here
an ideal of leisure, that is, a value which renders an intrinsically desired activity
desirable for its own sake. Rather than philosophizing or game-playing, I
propose a more general condition which might be satisfied by a wide variety of
activities: what makes an activity desirable and not merely desired is that an
individual would want to engage in that activity if he were thinking clearly and
were fully informed.

Leisure is ideal when it is motivated by desire which satisfies this
condition, but leisure may be less than ideal. Drinking and driving is a form of
leisure activity because it is something one may wish to do for its own sake, but
it may well be an activity which one would not engage in if one were thinking
clearly. Smoking, hunting, and so on are leisure activities which one might
avoid if one were vividly aware of the consequences of doing so.

Note that ideal leisure, despite being sharply distinguished from what a
person actually wants to do, is tightly connected to desire: it is what a person
would want if he were thinking clearly and knew all relevant facts.

Brandt calls this process "cognitive psychotherapy", because a person's
desires and actions are altered by a non-coercive confrontation between his
beliefs and all relevant available information (Brandt 1979). He illustrates the
idea of cognitive psychotherapy in a simple example:

> Let us suppose small Albert refused to play with the interesting
> small daughter of a neighbor because she is devoted to a pet
> rabbit, and he has an intense aversion to rabbits. Let us suppose
> further that he has an aversion to rabbits because someone once
> produced a loud noise in his vicinity while he was reaching out to
> touch a rabbit. Now suppose that Albert would be disabused of his
> aversion if he repeated to himself, on a number of occasions and
> with utter conviction, some justified statement as 'There is no con-
> nection between rabbits and loud noises; rabbits are just friendly
> little beasts.' In this case his aversion would have been removed by
> cognitive psychotherapy and I shall say his aversion is irrational
> (Brandt 1979: 11-12).

The process is cognitive rather than, say, electro-convulsive or chemical or some other form of therapy, because it is distinguished by the effects of
information on belief, desire, and action. It relies simply upon "reflection on
available information, without influence by prestige of someone, use of evaluative language, or use of artificially induced feeling-states like relaxation"
(Brandt 1979: 113). And the process is a form of psychotherapy because the
person who undergoes it is supposed to be more rational as a consequence: "I
shall pre-empt the term 'rational'," Brandt says, "to refer to actions, desires, or
moral systems which survive maximal criticism and correction by facts and
logic" (Brandt 1979: 10). I follow Brandt in thinking of the process as "value-
free reflection," because it is an entirely open question whether someone who is
thinking clearly and who knows all relevant facts will come to want to pursue
this or that moral ideal or other value. The ideal is not imposed on desire "from
without," so to speak, by reference to some alleged standard of objective value.
It is created rather by the uncoerced choice of any rational, fully informed individual. (The conception of leisure I am presenting, consequently, is one which
assumes that value is subjective; and so it is skeptical about the existence of
things which are valuable quite apart from their being desired).

Desirability is understood as relative to an individual at a time; so what
is desirable for you may not be desirable for me, and what is desirable for a
person at one time may not be desirable for him at another time. No one is cut
off from leisure because he is indifferent to the allegedly objectively valuable
thing. One can be cut off from it only by irrationality or ignorance of fact. Ideal
leisure is what this person would want to do for its own sake at this time, if he
were properly apprised of all relevant facts.

Consider how this conception of ideal leisure might apply in criticism
of Grasshopper's Utopia of non-instrumental activity, such as enjoying pleasant
sensations or, paramountly, playing wonderful games. Recall that Grasshopper's
Utopian conception of leisure was rejected because it excluded everybody, since
merely instrumental activity, such as breathing and moving limbs, belongs in the

life rhythm of everyone. It is an extension of this point to suggest that clear-thinking and well-informed people would want to create worked-at objects in the ideal of their existence, where there is no short-cut such as a magic wand for creating the objects in question. Even if it might be wished that the instrumental aspect of one's activity were quicker or easier, there would be a residue of instrumental activity that would belong to the content of one's intrinsic desires, in the way that a sculptor wants not simply that a sculpture should come into existence, but that it should come into existence as a result of his sculpting.

This is especially clear in connection with instrumental activity that has something important to do with one's conception of oneself, as it might be in the case of the sculptor. For it is, in principle, impossible in this kind of case that there should be a shortcut to the state of affairs desired for its own sake. The relevant kind of case may be described as the kind in which one expresses oneself. I propose to generalize this category in a certain way, following Taylor's lead in developing an "expressivist" view of man, which has its roots in late-eighteenth-century Germany, and especially in the *Sturm und Drang* movement, as a reaction to Enlightenment thought. This expressivist view, according to which, in Taylor's words, "human life unfolded from some central core — a guiding theme or inspiration — or should do so, if it were not so often blocked and distorted," became an important source of what is often called Romanticism (Taylor 1979: 2; see also Cooper 1985).

I shall put a point on this expressivist notion of the unfolding of a human life, as follows: for each human being there is a life which is moulded by what I shall call authentic desires. These are intrinsic desires which one would continue to have, or else acquire, after thinking clearly about all information that was relevant to what one might want to do. Such a life, I shall say, is one in which the subject fully expresses himself. A human life is not necessarily an expressive one. For one's desires may be inauthentic, by virtue of one's not thinking clearly or not being sufficiently informed. This is how I interpret the expressivist idea of a life being blocked or distorted.

Self-expression is closely linked to leisure, as it is understood on the conception being advanced here. For self-expression requires living a life in which intrinsic desires are satisfied; to the extent that life is given over to merely instrumental activity, or drudgery, one's life is not expressive. But leisure is intrinsically desired activity, and a pure science of leisure would focus on this category. Furthermore, ideal leisure on the present conception is just authentic intrinsically desired activity; in short, ideal leisure is expressive of the self.

OBJECTION TWO (THE ARBITRARY LIST OBJECTION)

Leisure studies could not have the unity that one expects of a respectable field of intellectual inquiry, because different people and different cultures take their leisure in such different ways. Consider Kelly's recent sociological survey of what North American respondents took to be the most important leisure activities (Kelly 1982). The survey's list — call it LL — is a mixed bag, comprising the following: marital affection and intimacy, reading for pleasure, family conversation, activities as a couple, family outings, visiting family and friends, playing with children, watching television, outdoor sports, eating out, religious worship, short auto trips, gardening and yard care, home decoration and shop projects, arts or crafts such as ceramics or painting, entertaining at home, hunting and/or fishing, child-centered events such as school events and sports, conversation with friends and neighbors, walking and/or jogging, hobbies such as collecting, and companionship on the job. LL is an arbitrary list, in just the same way that the following list is arbitrary: paper clips, the Waldstein sonata, landlords, New Orleans, Jack Russell terriers, Dr. Seuss, Jack Bush, dangling participles, and allergic reactions. Call this list Paper Clip. Now if someone were to propose to erect a science of Paper Clip and Paper Clip-type phenomena, or to philosophize about it, then (the objection continues) he should expect some smiles and smirks. Why should the student of LL-activities expect anything different? A minimum requirement for a science, surely, is that the objects of its study should have significant similarities with one another, so that law-like regularities can be discovered with respect to them. But Paper Clip is an entirely arbitrary list devoid of salient resemblances. And so is LL, according to the Arbitrary List Objection.

Reply to Objection Two

The Arbitrary List Objection fails because there is, indeed, a theoretically interesting unity in a list like LL. It is unified by the fact that the listed activities are done for their own sake, and not just for some instrumental value they might have. According to the conception of leisure that I recommend, this is its central feature. Leisure as that which is done for its own sake, or the intrinsically desired, is the primary subject matter for leisure theory. This is what a science of leisure theory should be about. Amongst the sciences, then, leisure theory is most closely connected to psychology, and in particular to the branches of psychological theory concerned with desire or "valence." Leisure may be studied scientifically by researchers from many disciplines, but the proprietary subject matter for leisure science is intrinsic desire.

My claim that LL exhibits a theoretically interesting unity must be qualified. For one thing, any activity on such a list can be done solely for its instrumental value. Someone may jog for his health, for example, even though he hates doing it. So we need a distinction between a type of activity and a token of that type. Some tokens of the type, jogging, may be performed for their own sake, and other tokens of that type may have only instrumental motivation. (Sometimes daydreaming is cited as the quintessential leisure activity, but it too may have a leisure-defeating complexity: I may do it to keep my mind off a vexing problem, for instance.)

Then my claim about LL is that it exhibits a theoretically interesting unity when it is understood to pick out tokens of the types listed in LL, activity-tokens which are engaged in for their own sake. I am not saying that the respondents to Kelly's survey were presupposing my conception of leisure. Some of them, for instance, might view instrumentally motivated activity as leisure simply because it occurs during free time, that is, time off from one's paid work and other mundane necessities like doing the dishes, whereas I have argued that leisure, in the most theoretically interesting sense, has a particular motivation. If someone is playing miniature golf at Leisure World Recreation Center simply out of familial duty, he is not at leisure despite the outward appearances. All and only intrinsically desired tokens of LL-type activities exhibit a theoretically significant unity, and they provide leisure science with a distinctive subject matter which can be explored in various ways.

I am not arguing that intrinsic and instrumental motivation are incompatible. As an adherent of the Platonic, non-exclusionary conception of leisure, I believe that one can have both instrumental and intrinsic motivation for leisure. I may golf for the tan as well as for the fun of it, for instance, and this complex motivation is compatible with my golfing at leisure. Leisure science studies intrinsic desire wherever it occurs, and whatever the extent of its contribution to an actor's full motivation. Perhaps only a very small fraction of LL-type activities occurs without some degree of intrinsic motivation, so it would not be misleading in practice to disregard the type/token distinction just introduced. It is also probably true that only a small fraction of LL-type activities occurs without some degree of extrinsic motivation. When I take a novel to the seaside, I read it for pleasure (intrinsic motivation) and also to kill time (extrinsic motivation). Mixed motivation is the rule.

I conclude that the Arbitrary List Objection fails.

OBJECTION THREE
(THE PSUEDO-SCIENCE OBJECTION)

Leisure science is no more a science than Christian Science or Scientific Socialism. Leisure science would be substantially scientific only if it could lay claim to those features of the natural sciences, like physics and chemistry, which make the term "scientific" supremely honorific. At a minimum, one would expect it to discover laws, or at least law-like generalizations: exceptionless, mathematically precise generalizations about leisure from which accurate predictions can be deduced. But the generalizations of leisure theorists are not in this way scientific. The problem is not simply the one to which Veal has drawn attention — that the methods available to leisure theorists have not been capable of producing accurate results because it is difficult to gather the relevant facts. He observes that the demand for leisure is more difficult to determine than the demand for such services as education or housing (Veal 1987: 127-128):

For a given child-population the demand for school places is known and the consequences of not providing that number of places would be all too apparent. In the case of leisure the situation is different. Demand cannot be so precisely determined — the numbers of people who want to play sport, visit the countryside, or take part in arts activities are not known. The consequence of not providing facilities for these activities is that people do something else with their leisure time, such as watching more television.

The problem to which Veal refers is real enough, but there is a more basic problem for scientific leisure theory than the difficulty of gathering facts. The problem is that leisure is a cultural artefact (like books) rather than a natural kind (like diamonds), and, as such, it requires a different sort of understanding than the sort which is characteristic of the natural sciences. This different understanding has to do with grasping the social rules that govern leisure. Just as it is wrongheaded to try to understand chess by discovering regularities in the behavior of chess players instead of learning the rules of chess that they play by, it is wrongheaded to try to understand leisure by discovering regularities in the behavior of leisure consumers.

Consider a typical example which illustrates the wrongheadedness in principle, not just the difficulty in practice, of seeking scientific laws of leisure: Ewing's "Progress and problems in the development of recreational trip generation and trip distribution models" examines the unconstrained gravity model of recreational trip frequency within a population (Ewing 1980). The model is expressed in a formula UGM (as it may be labelled), namely:

$$t\,(i,j) = \frac{k\,P\,(i)\,A\,(j)}{C\,(i,j)}$$

UGM states that the number of trips from an origin i to a destination j — that is, $t(i,j)$ — is a certain function (the power function) of the population P of i, the attractiveness A of j, and the cost C of getting from i to j. As Ewing demonstrates, UGM is woefully inadequate, even as a rule-of-thumb, to be used by leisure managers, such as parks and recreation officials. He makes the point that UGM is insensitive to the number of alternatives available to the population, and he goes on to propose models, different from UGM but motivated by the same aim of uncovering a law of trip distribution, which take into account such points.

If it were legitimate in principle to seek such laws, it should make sense to think of successors to UGM approaching perfect predictive power asymptotically. This is a reasonable hope for the generalizations of the natural sciences, which employ a physico-mathematical vocabulary that is genuinely capable of progressing towards the precision required in a law of nature. But the appearance of precision in UGM-type generalizations is necessarily illusory, since the people who make recreational trips, unlike physical and chemical particles, are following social rules or norms which define, for instance, what counts as an attractive destination in that culture. This makes the variable A in UGM very different from variables, such as length and volume, which occur in natural laws, and for which there is a physico-mathematical metric which submits them to increasingly precise measurement. The variable A is said to be the "measure of the quality or attractiveness of destination j, *or some surrogate measure, such as size...*" (my emphasis) (Ewing 1980: 5). But it is specious to think that size could stand as a surrogate for attractiveness. Tourists can be attracted to small destinations as well as large ones. They might want to visit Europe (a "large" size of destination) or they might want to see a European friend's stamp collection (a "small" destination).

(Other variables in UGM are vulnerable to similar objections. Consider C, or cost. A certain formula about cost might capture the outer limits of what most people would want to spend on recreational travel, but if the formula lays down an absolute limit C, it may turn out that a particularly wealthy person is not deterred by that limit).

Of course one might say "UGM, other things being equal," but the immunity from counter-example gained by attaching this "fudge clause" to UGM negates its claim to the status of a scientific generalization. This status, the Objection runs, requires that a scientific generalization be formulated with mathematical precision in such a way that it can be tested severely, with no possibility of seeking refuge in *ad hoc* hypotheses about why the generalization did not hold true in a particular instance. Any generalization can be held to be true "other things being equal." One need merely insist, when a counter-instance seems to present itself, that other things aren't equal! The requirements for scientific status, the Objection implies, are so extremely demanding that only the natural sciences meet them.

Reply to Objection Three

Some of the minor criticism raised in the Objection are well-founded cautions to leisure theory, but its force turns primarily on the questionable assumption that the status of a field of research is an all-or-nothing affair. I shall challenge this assumption.

Leisure science may be a science to a lesser degree than physics, or display a lesser degree of "scientificity," without losing its claim to be a science. Being a science is a scalar affair. We are indebted to Braybrooke for a "scale of scientificity" which provides a plausible alternative to the all-or-nothing view. The scale involves a list of characteristics, proceeding from the bottom (characteristic 1) to characteristics ever more ambitious. Of any activity or inquiry we may ask (Braybrooke 1987: 43-44):

1. Is it pursued indefinitely rather than taken up and brought to an end within the confines of one practical crisis?
2. Does it aim to decrease the stock or potential stock of false statements describing the real world and to increase the stock or potential stock of true statements?
3. Does it circumscribe a field of research and aim to fill gaps in the literature identified as pertinent to the field?
4. Does it aim to establish by generalization explicitly related sets of true descriptive statements?
5. Does the activity aim to increase the stock of true causal generalizations? (This implies increasing at the same time the stock or potential stock of true singular causal statements and the number of explanations and predictions that can be argued in some approximation to the covering law form).
6. Does it distinguish levels of aggregation such that objects on one level in some sense belong to objects on a higher level and supply facts from which facts about the higher level arise?
7. Does it aim to increase the precision of its statements, general and singular, throughout as much of its field as possible?
8. Does the activity aim to bring its chief general statements together in a unified structure expressed or expressible with formal methods as in axiomatic theory?
9. Does it apply statistical analysis in research designs and in interpreting research findings?
10. Does it use, to achieve greater precision or more powerful theories, mathematics beyond arithmetic, elementary algebra, and graphic analysis as found in elementary statistics or economics?

Now the philosophy of science implied by Braybrooke's scale is only one of many, and even if one shares his general outlook one might wish to add or subtract items from his scale. But disagreements of this sort need not interfere with the value of Braybrooke's scale in the present context, which is to call into question the all-or-nothing conception of science.

In applying the scale to leisure theory I shall be concerned with scientific leisure theory in the normal, broad sense, as opposed to the narrow sense I have distinguished. Normal scientific leisure theory is best defined by example, by pointing to leisure research journals in which authors from various disciplines report their attempts to study leisure scientifically. Although leisure research does not score as high on this scale as the natural sciences do, nonetheless it scores well enough to have some standing as a science.

Consider, first, characteristic 1 ("Is it pursued indefinitely rather than taken up and brought to an end within the confines of one practical crisis?").

Over the past twenty years, leisure theory has been pursued in a regular and systematic manner. There is now a sizable group of enquirers who think of themselves as scientists in this field. They have regular conferences, established periodicals for reporting the results of research, introductory courses and texts, and so forth. Evidently, leisure studies has a high ranking for characteristic 1 of the scale of scientificity.

Consider, next, characteristic 2 ("Does it aim to decrease the stock or potential stock of false statements describing the real world and to increase the stock or potential stock of true statements?") Any volume of a major journal of leisure research will exemplify these aims, in attempts to provide informative descriptions and revealing generalizations. Therefore, leisure research does very well on characteristic 2. Volume 5 of *Leisure Studies* may be cited as an example. An article like Heeley's "Leisure and moral reform," exemplifying the descriptive aspect of leisure theory, explores the ways in which the Victorian and Edwardian philosophy of rational recreation found expression in a variety of reformist campaigns (Heeley 1986). As an example of generalization, Jackson's "Outdoor recreation participation and attitudes to the environment" offers evidence for a strong correlation between participation in appreciative recreational activities and concern for protecting the natural environment (Jackson 1986). The merit of Braybrooke's scale of scientificity is that it properly relates studies like Jackson's to science rather than pseudo-science, religion, superstition, and other categories in the large area of the "non-scientific."

As for characteristic 3 ("Does it circumscribe a field of research and aim to fill gaps in the literature identified as pertinent to the field?"), the institutionalization of leisure research attests to its circumscription of a field of research. The creation of university departments of leisure studies, the proliferation of journals and books devoted to leisure research, and the various aspects of a scientific "paradigm" as noted in connection with characteristic 1, all indicate a high ranking for characteristic 3.

With respect to characteristic 4 ("Does it aim to establish by generalization explicitly related sets of true descriptive statements?"), leisure theory is comparable to many social sciences, such as sociology. In both areas an enormous literature attempts to establish generalizations, such as Jackson's correlation of recreational activity and concern with the environment, and such as the study of gravitational models of the sort that Ewing discusses.

In my judgment, leisure theory does not rank particularly high on characteristic 5 ("Does the activity aim to increase the stock of true causal generalizations?"). Many of its characteristic methods — trend extrapolation, respondent assessment, the Delphi technique, scenario writing, cross-sectional analysis — steer clear of claims about causal connections. On the other hand, if my recommendation for a core subject-matter for leisure science were acted upon, I would think that leisure theory could build upon psychological theory in order to discover significant law-like generalizations about what people would intrinsically desire under different circumstances of environment and upbringing. For this reason alone I think there is considerable room for growth in this area.

But there is a danger in this area too, a danger which is sometimes called scientism. This involves failing to appreciate the differences between the subject matter of the natural and social sciences, and treating man in society as though he were a molecule or an atom. The critique of scientism has been extended to leisure theory by Rojek, for instance, in his *Capitalism and Leisure Theory* (Rojek 1985).

Scientism in the social sciences tends to favor the status quo, by treating regularities in social behavior as though they were as inevitable as gravity. Thus it is that the critique of scientism is often undertaken by those who seek large-scale political and social change. A leisure science which limited itself to describing these regular patterns of leisure behavior would be useful to leisure managers in their efforts to deliver leisure products to leisure consumers, and, consequently, it would help to stabilize and reinforce the regularities it describes. This could be viewed as strengthening the socially and politically conservative illusion that patterns of leisure are as immutable as the motions of basic physical particles.

An example may anchor the point: West's "A nationwide test of the status group dynamics approach to outdoor recreation demand" carefully examines and plausibly qualifies Veblen's insight that demand for particular leisure activities tends to diffuse from higher to lower socio-economic groups (West 1982). He hopes to predict demand shifts more accurately than Veblen-type models permit, by challenging the assumption that participation rates within subgroups remain stable as diffusion occurs. In particular, he draws attention to "status-based withdrawal," the phenomenon of a higher status group's withdrawal from a given activity as diffusion occurs. Such studies as West's are legitimate, but it must always be remembered that the regularities they describe are conditional on choices that may change. This complicates things in comparison to the situation for a natural scientist, because molecules and atoms don't make choices. We know that, unlike protons, people can raise normative questions and act on answers to them that lead in directions quite different from the regularities described by West. The classes he describes could be abolished by political activity, for instance, or status-based withdrawal could be eliminated by educational programs. And perhaps such political or educational choices should be made! It bears repeating that this point does not invalidate such studies as West's, but rather emphasizes the peculiarly conditional character of the regularities they describe. And perhaps the point suggests that a purely descriptive leisure theory would be impoverished in a way that a purely descriptive natural science is not, for the descriptive leisure theory would be failing to study the peculiar conditions which make its subject matter uniquely different from the natural sciences: human choice, belief, rationality, and the scope for normative questions created by these conditions.

Leisure theory distinguishes levels of aggregation in the manner typical of the social sciences. It attempts to discover group-facts (e.g. patterns of demand for recreation facilities) by deriving them from person-facts, such as a person's motivation, his cost of travel, and so on. So with reference to characteristic 6 ("Does it distinguish levels of aggregation such that objects on one level in some sense belong to objects on a higher level and supply facts from which facts about the higher level arise?") it shows well — as well as some other social sciences, though not as well as the natural sciences, where there is an elaborately developed body of theory which "reduces" higher level facts to lower level facts, and ultimately to facts described by physics. There is a view according to which the social sciences should look forward to participating in this reductive hierarchy. But one would not expect leisure science — or any other social science, for that matter — to reduce to physics in the way that chemistry does, if it is sound to argue, as I did earlier, that the subject matter of the social sciences is unique by virtue of the fact that people are rational, have beliefs, raise normative questions, and make choices.

Leisure research aims to increase the precision of its statements, as evidenced by tenacious discussion in the journals, in which experimental results are put forward, interpreted, and criticized. Ewing's discussion of the unconstrained gravity model is a case in point. So, with respect to characteristic 7 ("Does it aim to increase the precision of its statements, general and singular, throughout as much of its field as possible?"), leisure theory may be judged to show very well. But it will be recalled from the earlier discussion of Ewing and the formula UGM that there is a danger of false formalism in leisure science — of imparting to generalizations about leisure a spurious air of mathematical precision. So precision in leisure theory may take a very different form than the physico-mathematical metric of natural laws. In some cases, precision may simply amount to careful and sensitive description of leisure activity, or normatively motivated advocacy of some leisure activity, using the vocabulary of rationality, belief, and choice, which is well-suited to the subject matter of leisure theory, namely people.

With reference to characteristic 8 ("Does the activity aim to bring its chief general statements together in a unified structure expressed or expressible with formal methods as in axiomatic theory?"), leisure science does not show well. This is so, I suspect, because of the eclectic nature of what I have called hybrid leisure science. That is, it draws scientific conjectures from various disciplines, and though these disciplines may themselves have a unified logical structure, this is lacking in the result of their convergence in hybrid leisure science. But it may be that pure leisure theory, devoted to enquiry into the intrinsically desired, might have a highly unified logical structure. This would be so if, as many psychologists and philosophers believe, there are psychological laws pertaining to desire and intrinsic desire. Pure leisure science would gain a unified logical structure by virtue of its subject matter being derivable from such laws. Employing these laws, and employing, too, a conception of rationality and empirical fact, pure leisure theorists might be able to make significant predictions about leisure behavior, and significant recommendations about what sorts of leisure would help us lead authentic, self-expressive lives.

Statistical analysis is widespread in leisure research, so it shows very well on characteristic 9 ("Does it apply statistical analysis in research designs and in interpreting research findings?"). This testifies to the effort of leisure theorists to bring scientific objectivity to their studies, by describing regularities in a detached way through statistical analysis. But at this point it is important to take heed of one of the well-founded criticisms in Objection Three, namely the point that leisure is a cultural artefact, and in order to fully understand it one needs to understand the social norms that create and influence leisure activity. And just as understanding the rules of chess is different from knowing statistical regularities pertaining to the movements of pieces, so too understanding leisure activity — indeed, playing chess, for instance — requires the former kind of understanding. This is not to imply that statistical analysis is out of place in leisure studies. It is to say, rather, that objectifying leisure research, such as statistical analysis, should be complemented by norm-sensitive studies, and these call for a more subjective point of view. The researcher will be articulating something like a participant's understanding of the leisure activity he or she is studying, rather than prescinding from such an understanding in order to gain greater objectivity.

Higher mathematics is not extensively used in leisure theory, so it does not show well on characteristic 10 ("Does it use, to achieve greater precision or more powerful theories, mathematics beyond arithmetic, elementary algebra, and graphic analysis as found in elementary statistics or economics?"). As I have suggested, however, pure leisure theory may be expected to improve in this dimension as its connection with learning theory and other branches of cognitive psychology becomes more fully appreciated. The use of higher mathematics in those areas will be seen to have a direct bearing on questions of leisure theory, as its use will shed light on intrinsic desire and its conditions of formation and satisfaction; and these, of course, are topics of cardinal importance for pure leisure theory. On the other hand, the warning bears repeating that a high ranking on item 10 of the scientificity scale should not be purchased at the cost of false formalism of the sort that was criticized in connection with Ewing's discussion of the Unconstrained Gravity Model of trip distribution.

I am now in a position to reject the Pseudo-Science Objection. It is to be rejected because it focuses too narrowly on the absence of true causal generalizations in leisure theory, and on the absence of the precision of higher mathematics in the descriptions and generalizations of leisure theory. But the scale of scientificity broadens the focus in a salutory way. Adopting the perspective of that scale, Objection Three is seen as dwelling arbitrarily on characteristics 5 and 10, to the exclusion of all the rest. Not only is this arbitrary, but it is dangerous to attempt to make progress in the social sciences by encouraging false formalism and other indicators of scientism. Many social sciences do not show well on characteristics 5 and 10, so if their status as sciences is to be explained, it seems plausible to make reference to the other characteristics on the scale. And with these others in mind, the claim of leisure research to scientific status, or to a social science's degree of "scientificity," looks sound enough. It is not at all necessary to show that this claim has the same strength as that of physics. No social science could show this. So there is no reason here for special skepticism about leisure theory.

The standards of the all-or-nothing conception of science are so high that even the putative laws of physics may not satisfy them. Suppose we knew that events prior to the last Big Bang were not governed by the laws that have governed the universe ever since. Then our physical laws would not be excep-tionless, or they would be exceptionless only by virtue of arbitrarily restricting their temporal scope. Should we say that our laws would not be real laws in this case, and that physics is pseudo-science? If not, here is another reason to reject the Pseudo-Science Objection's standards for scientific status.

I conclude that the Pseudo-Science Objection may be dismissed, finally, as relying on an unacceptable, all-or-nothing, conception of science.

CONCLUSIONS

I have advanced a conception of leisure as activity desired for its own sake (intrinsic desire), in the hope that this conception may be suited to guide theorizing about the subject. If it is indeed so suited, leisure researchers may expect to profit by examining the literature of scientific psychology pertaining to desire. Out of this, one might expect to see a major contribution towards what Burton has called "perhaps the most important step in the drive to maturity" for leisure research, "the establishment of a set of unifying concepts and codes for the field" (Burton 1980: 382; see also Jackson and Burton, this volume).

In the spirit of Plato's recognition of the "highest class" of things, and *pace* Aristotle, I understand leisure to permit of instrumental as well as intrinsic motivation. And in the spirit of the Romantic movement's faith in the genius of the individual, the core of personality which unfolds in a self-expressive way unless blocked or impeded, I understand ideal leisure to be not just intrinsically motivated, but authentically and therefore self-expressively so. One would not be dissuaded from that activity if one were thinking more clearly or were more well informed — the desire would survive criticism by logic and scientific fact.

I have proposed that the scientific status of a field of study is best viewed as a scalar matter rather than all-or-nothing. Measured against Braybrooke's scale of scientificity, leisure theorists can legitimately claim that they are participating in a maturing field of social scientific research.

References

Aristotle. 1953. *The Ethics of Aristotle*. Translated by J.A.K. Thomson. London: George Allen and Unwin.

Brandt, R. 1979. *A Theory of the Good and the Right*. Oxford: Clarendon Press.

Braybrooke, D. 1987. *Philosophy of Social Science*. Englewood Cliffs, NJ: Prentice-Hall.

Burton, T.L. 1980. "The maturation of leisure research." In *Recreation and Leisure: Issues in an Era of Change*, eds. T.L. Goodale and P.A. Witt, pp. 373-385. State College, PA: Venture Publishing.

Cooper, W. 1985. "Is art a form of life?" *Dialogue 24:* 443-453.

De Grazia, S. 1964. *Of Time, Work, and Leisure*. Garden City: Anchor.

Descartes, R. 1912. *Meditations on First Philosophy*. Written in 1641 and translated from the Latin by E. S. Haldane and G.R.T. Ross. Cambridge: Cambridge University Press.

Dworkin, R. 1977. *Taking Rights Seriously*. Cambridge, MA: Harvard University Press.

Ewing, G. 1980. "Progress and problems in the development of recreational trip generation and trip distribution models." *Leisure Sciences 3:* 1-24.

Heeley, J. 1986. "Leisure and moral reform." *Leisure Studies 5:* 57-67.

Jackson, E.L. 1986. "Outdoor recreation participation and attitudes to the environment." *Leisure Studies 5:* 1-23.

Kelly, J.R. 1982. *Leisure*. Englewood Cliffs, NJ: Prentice-Hall.

Oxford English Dictionary. 1971. *The Compact Edition of the Oxford English Dictionary*, Volume I. Oxford: Oxford University Press.

Plato. 1974. *The Republic*. Indianapolis, IN: Hackett.

Rawls, J. 1971. *A Theory of Justice*. Cambridge: Harvard University Press.

Rojek, C. 1985. *Capitalism and Leisure Theory*. London: Tavistock.

Ryle, G. 1949. *The Concept of Mind*. New York: Barnes and Noble.

Suits, B. 1981. *The Grasshopper: Games, Life, and Utopia*. Toronto: University of Toronto Press.

Taylor, C. 1979. *Hegel and Modern Society*. Cambridge: Cambridge University Press.

Veal, A.J. 1987. *Leisure and the Future*. London: George Allen and Unwin.

Walzer, M. 1983. *Spheres of Justice*. New York: Basic Books.

West, P.C. 1982. "A nationwide test of the status group dynamics approach to outdoor recreation demand." *Leisure Sciences 5:* 1-18.

LEISURE AND RECREATION THEORY

Chris Rojek

Few topics in leisure and recreation studies generate so much heat as the question of the importance of theory. It is not simply that competing theories are engaged in a struggle to command the terrain, although this is demonstrably the case (see Rojek 1985). There is also the fact that many teachers and students openly ask whether there is any significant place for theory in leisure and recreation studies at all. The latter group regularly attack leisure and recreation theory for being impractical, impenetrable, and irrelevant. Instead, they define the "real" issues in terms of resource management and the impact of market forces. One might venture to suggest that three main reasons lie behind this hostile attitude to theory.

First, as Jackson and Burton point out in the first chapter of this book, leisure and recreation studies is a relatively recent field of academic inquiry. Most university departments and nearly all of the leading journals were founded in the 1970s and early 1980s. Academics in the field have naturally been concerned to show their relevance to the profession and public- and private-sector funding agencies. Against this, theory often leads the theorist to ask some awkward and critical questions. In a climate of professional take-off, where practitioners in leisure and recreation have struggled to achieve public recognition, criticism is all too easily taken for bad faith or lack of commitment.

Second, it is in the nature of theory not to be confined to a narrow field. For, in thinking theoretically, one makes connections, and this can lead one into areas that seem remote from the initial subject of inquiry. For example, in studying what leisure and recreation mean for people in the present day, theorists have been led to consider questions of meaning, power, and epistemology in fields such as philosophy, history, sociology, and psychology. These questions raise issues that are apt to seem remote from the immediate, concrete, training and policy issues facing students and managers in the field.

Third, work, not leisure, has traditionally been regarded as the most important area of life in modern society. Energy, inventiveness, discipline, conflict, and struggle have been narrowly associated with wealth creation. By contrast, leisure has been viewed as a subordinate area of life that plays second fiddle to relations of production. The work-leisure relation has come under keen scrutiny in recent years (see Clarke and Critcher 1985; Pahl 1984). Many authors have lambasted leisure and recreation studies for assigning the relation a false priority in their investigations, and for contributing to inadequate, highly stereotypical, pictures of what work and leisure are (see, in particular, Moorhouse 1989). This criticism has sent a good few ripples across the pond. As social scientists struggle to reconceptualize the concepts of labor, power, free time, stratification, and lifestyle to fit the new economic and social conditions associated with the new technology, these ripples are likely to grow in force and influence. These things take time, however. For the moment, the leisure and recreation theorist faces an academic community in which the received idea that work is the central life interest for most people is only just beginning to crumble.

All of these factors have combined to make empiricism the dominant climate for teaching, research, and management in leisure and recreation. Empiricism is a philosophy of knowledge that assigns a privileged status to quantitative material in understanding. In leisure and recreation studies, its principal research methods are questionnaires, surveys, and statistical analysis. Empiricists claim to start with the observable facts and to build analytical statements upon the accumulation of facts. They assume that subjective experience is the only basis for knowledge. The questions of what experience is, and what the historical and social context of subjective experience consists of, are dismissed as second-order issues.

Now it is perfectly clear that empiricism has played an historically significant role in adding to our knowledge of the world. However, to say this is very different from saying that empiricism produces more reliable and more accurate forms of knowledge than other methods. On the contrary, philosophers of knowledge have concluded that empiricism is open to fundamental objections. What are these objections? At least four points need to be made.

In the first place, the notion that empiricists simply study the "facts" does not stand up to interrogation. The basic criticism has been well made by MacIntyre (1981: 79). As he remarks, the error rests in supposing that "the observer can confront a fact face-to-face without any theoretical interpretation interposing itself." Facts are not automatically given features of human existence. Rather, they are historically and theoretically organized. It follows that we cannot understand them without studying the historical and theoretical contexts that surround them. Practically speaking, this means looking beyond the "facts" of subjective experience and examining the contexts in which these "facts" were accumulated and disseminated.

This brings me to my second point. In claiming only to study the facts, empiricism gains considerable kudos by appearing to be "value-free." However, this claim is plainly inadequate. For one thing, as I have already noted, "facts" are clearly influenced by their context. To study "life-satisfaction," "freedom," "choice," and "pleasure" is not to study universal categories of experience which have a uniform meaning. Rather, it is to study social values. One can illustrate this by addressing the common empiricist objection that theoretical discussion is, by itself, incapable of producing accurate knowledge. For this is only to make value-laden and highly theoretical propositions about what counts as real knowledge. Even the statement that "all theory is bunk" contains assumptions about what the world is, and how knowledge of the world is generated.

A third criticism of empiricism is that it supports a misleading view of society. It is especially weak in exaggerating the stability and harmony of society. Empiricism produces a notoriously anodyne view of leisure and recreation. Thus, leisure and recreation are said to be the inevitable consequence of the logic of industrialization. Free time is intrinsically associated with freedom, choice, and self-determination (see Parker 1983; Roberts 1970; Kraus 1984). Conflict is rarely mentioned. When it does appear, it tends to be dismissed as the temporary friction between systems or sub-systems in society which are misaligned, rather than the concrete effect of opposed social interests. Empiricism has simply ignored huge areas of the practical, regular leisure and recreation experience of millions of people — notably, the area of deviant leisure, which empiricists pass over in silence. I shall come back to this point in the final section of this chapter.

The fourth and final objection has to do with the realism of empiricist assumptions and methods. Questions of what facts are and how we gain knowledge are both relevant and practical. The attempt to get round them by making a fetish out of method and ignoring qualitative matters is both doctrinaire and ill-considered. These questions will not disappear. Indeed, it is a sign of the maturity of a field of scholarship and professionalism to face them frankly. Here, the potential contribution of social theory to leisure and recreation studies is considerable. For social theorists are heir to a tradition of classification, arbitration, and criticism that reaches back at least to the Enlightenment, and which has helped to clarify our understanding of social relations and the processes of accumulating knowledge. Although my discussion will bear directly and obviously upon the question of epistemology, I shall make no attempt to recount the history or status of the debate on epistemology in the social sciences. Apart from space considerations, my main concern is to give a practical example of how theoretical knowledge from the social sciences can be used to clarify the apparently confusing divisions in writing on leisure and recreation.

CLASSIFYING THEORY: FROM AGENCY TO STRUCTURE

The dichotomy between agency and structure is at the core of classifying theory in the social sciences. *Agency* refers to the actions of social actors in relating to the world and struggling to leave their mark upon it. Theories of agency focus on the thoughts, feelings, and conduct of the actor. They subscribe to a *voluntaristic* model of social action in which freedom, choice, and self determination are attributed to the actor. Moreover, they are associated with a *particularistic* model of society, i.e. society is regarded as a basically stable system in which power is diffused among many competing interests, and in which no single competing interest dominates in the long run. Theories of agency emphasize the interpretive capacities of actors to make sense of the world and their ability to shape it. Conversely, theories of *structure* focus on the social context in which the individual is situated. They endorse a *deterministic* model of personal conduct which emphasizes that individual behavior is influenced by social structures that arise from the interactions of individuals through time, but which are beyond the capacity of any single individual or group of individuals to control. Examples include class, gender, race, bureaucracy, and so on. Finally, structure theories recognize conflict in society, and regard social development to be an outcome of social struggle.

Most post-war theories of leisure and recreation can be studied through the structure/agency dichotomy. Examples of agency-based theories include existentialism, phenomenology, and symbolic interactionism; examples of structure-based theories include Marxism, feminism, and discourse analysis. The main criticism of agency-based theories is that they exaggerate the freedom and power of social actors to act in accordance with their will. As for structure-based theories, their main weakness is held to be an over-deterministic view of the power of social structures to shape the thoughts, feelings, and actions of individuals.

These criticisms are so serious, and so intransigent, that they have led many social theorists to wonder if the dichotomy between agency and structure is not false. Logically, there can be no action without structure and no structure without action. The two do not confront one another in an either/or relationship; rather, they are more properly thought of as two parts of the same whole. For example, individuals can be said to act, but they do so within determinate physical (the body, the natural world) and social (language, culture) structures. Similarly, structures (class, gender, race) influence the behavior of individuals, yet they do not stand outside individual action; on the contrary, they are made up of the countless interactions between individuals through time and space. I will come to where these criticisms are leading in the final section of the chapter, when I discuss process approaches to leisure and recreation. Before reaching that point, however, I want to apply the dichotomy of agency and structure to some positions in leisure and recreation studies. My purpose is to give a concrete set of examples to illustrate the applicability of the dichotomy.

AGENCY

Traditionally, leisure and recreation studies has been preoccupied with matters of agency. Leisure and recreation are associated with choice and self-determination. Moreover, this is contrasted with work, which is characterized as a realm of routine and constraint. "Recreation," write Miller and Robinson (1963: 146) "is free from regimentation and coercion. The free and voluntary character of our recreation is an antidote and a saving grace. In leisure people are free to give play to their imaginative impulses. They may voluntarily choose the activities through which they may pursue happiness."

This passage also reflects another standard feature of traditional leisure and recreation theory. That is, leisure and recreation are associated with positive experience — freedom, learning, creativity, and growth. In the words of Dumazedier (1967: 16-17), leisure is "activity — apart from the obligations of work, family and society — to which the individual turns at will for either relaxation or diversion or broadening his knowledge and his spontaneous social participation, the free exercise of his creative capacity."

Such words are entirely representative of most writing on leisure and recreation in the 1950s and 1960s. To add to the examples would be merely to duplicate them — and little would be gained by doing that. Instead, let me expand upon the question of agency and the nature of traditional theory by subjecting both to critical evaluation. In order to highlight my argument, I will make my points in notational form. In addition, my discussion will incorporate illustrative material from key works of the time, as and when appropriate:

1. Traditional theories of leisure and recreation are profoundly humanist in form and content. That is, they assume that "man" is composed of universal and uniform capacities for pleasure, happiness, and excitement. Leisure space and leisure time are assigned a subordinate role to these capacities. In the words of Kraus (1984: 335), they are the "setting in which human values are established and enriched." However, if one looks at the actual distribution of leisure time and leisure space in society, the humanist case begins to look very shaky. For one thing, the distribution is manifestly unequal, with striking contrasts between social categories, e.g. husbands and wives, professionals and non-professionals, skilled workers and unskilled workers, whites and ethnic minorities, and so on (for more on this, see the chapters by Bella and Glyptis in this book). Moreover, it is by no means clear that leisure and recreation experience can be compared in terms of a common measure. If we all experienced the same pleasure in leisure and recreation settings, the job of leisure and recreation planners would be eased considerably. In fact, of course, individuals respond to leisure and recreation settings in different ways. They are

not passive but active agents who are able to bring new meanings to cultural products (see Kelly, this volume). This brings me to my second point.

2. Traditional theories of leisure and recreation rely heavily on utilitarian principles. Utilitarianism is still the foundation of leisure planning, and it therefore influences the quality of leisure and recreation experience. "Organized leisure," comments Nash (1953: 61), "should aim at the highest common denominator, and in varying degrees and ways bring the average human nature up towards the highest human nature." Again, it should be noted that human nature is not a uniform property. It cannot be compared in terms of a common measure.

So Nash's aim is rather impractical. Furthermore, the burden of bringing "the average human nature" up towards the "the highest human nature" conflicts with what is traditionally said to be one of the fundamental characteristics of leisure in modern society, i.e. its free, voluntaristic character. Nash's utilitarianism may spring from the positive motive of improving the quality of leisure and recreation for all. However, the practical effect is to bring coercion and inflexibility in its wake. For the logical consequence of recognizing that "the average human nature" is deficient is to compel the individual to change. A key role of education, leadership, and planning, therefore, is identified for a new category of welfare professional — the leisure and recreation manager. As Sutherland (1957: 34) comments, "since the average citizen is unable to invent new uses for his leisure, a professional elite shares a heavy responsibility for discovering criteria for new ways of employing leisure and creating enthusiasm for common ends within the moral aims of the community."

3. Traditional theory maintains that a natural balance and exchange exists between work and leisure. In the words of Brightbill (1961: 25), "without work there can be no rewarding leisure and without leisure work cannot be sustained." The work/leisure distinction is indeed at the heart of agency models of leisure and recreation. However, it is now quite clear that this distinction is in crisis (see Moorhouse 1989; Pahl 1984). Work and leisure can no longer be treated as opposites. Although there are many counter-arguments, such as the continued exploitation of the worker under capitalism, it is evident that the basic trend in the post-war period in industry and commerce has been the growth of more "worker-friendly" work environments. This is apparent in a number of areas. For example, health and safety-at-work legislation has served to increase workers' rights and physical security. Similarly, human relations techniques of personnel management have given greater recognition of the need for mental and physical well-being in the worker. This is reflected in the production of more attractive workplace designs, the introduction of flextime, the provision of recreation and rest facilities in the workplace, such as a staff bar and play areas, the provision of creche (day-care) facilities, and so on.

Obviously, one must not over-state the case. For most workers, the workplace is no paradise. Yet the trend remains clear. As for leisure, it is plain that in a number of respects it has become more like work. Specialist pursuits like photography, playing musical instruments, and jogging involve a great deal of discipline, planning, and hard work. Furthermore, many mass leisure pursuits, such as watching television, listening to pop music, reading mass circulation weeklies and periodicals, are highly routinized. In addition, one should mention the vast amount of unregistered labor which people expend in their "free time" on activities, such as housework, gardening, and home improvements (Gershuny 1978). These leisure pursuits can be more taxing in terms of the expenditure of energy than paid employment.

The breakup of the work/leisure distinction has challenged the conventional association of work with restraint and leisure with freedom. Both work and leisure are now seen as areas of social life where some human capacities are opened up and others closed down. This has led to a wider interest in the social forces by which our capacities are generally enabled and constrained.

4. Traditional agency models maintain that the individual has considerable choice and freedom in the pursuit of happiness through leisure and recreation. "To a large extent," remarks Roberts (1970: 18) "the way in which people choose to spend their leisure is unrelated to the other social roles they play." This suggests that people are basically free to develop their personal preferences and inclinations in the leisure market, regardless of their class or market position. Such an argument is plainly inadequate. The housewife, the welfare claimant, the unemployed person, the member of an ethnic minority, are all social roles. A direct and palpable relationship exists between the restricted leisure opportunities of these role players and the nature of their role. To give one concrete example, the leisure of the housewife is drastically limited by her household management and child-care roles. She is restricted in her leisure time and leisure space in ways that have no equivalent in the sphere of male experience (see Bella, this volume, and Glyptis, McInnes, and Patmore 1987).

5. Traditional theory endorses the idea of "normal" behavior in leisure and recreation. This is expressed tangibly in the socio-biological concept of "the life cycle" (Rapoport and Rapoport 1975). Life cycle models of leisure maintain that at different stages in the physical development of the individual, different aspects of life assume importance. For example, when the individual starts a family, there is a high propensity to exchange free time for money; at later stages of the life cycle the reverse may be the case. Life cycle models show the "normal" adult to be propertied, heterosexual, and joined in marriage to a lifelong partner. Moreover, "normal" adult leisure is presented as home-centered, family-oriented, and functioning to recuperate the individual from the cares of work. Paid labor is, of course, typically shown as a male preserve, while unpaid domestic labour is typically assumed to be "women's" work. Socio-

biological models of the life cycle, with their empiricist appeal to the laws of nature, are too narrow to cope with the real diversity of leisure and recreation relations found in society. For example, the logic of a model of leisure which subordinates leisure to work looks increasingly faulty in the context where the advanced countries of the West fail to provide paid employment for up to one-fifth of the working population. Similarly, the women's movement and the campaign for gay rights have challenged conventional notions of "normal," "healthy," and "responsible" adult leisure and recreation.

STRUCTURE

The reaction to theories of agency in leisure and recreation studies has involved questioning the notions that action is voluntaristic and that society is pluralistic. Structure-based theories have emphasized the constraints upon action and experience. "To understand leisure," comments Van Moorst (1982: 164) "we must understand work, and to understand both at this particular time we must understand the mode of production called capitalism." Van Moorst calls for the application of Marxist principles to the analysis of leisure and recreation. In other hands this has led to the denial of freedom in capitalist society. As Marcuse (1967: 104) puts it:

> Advanced industrial society is a society in which the technical apparatus of production and distribution has become a totalitarian political apparatus, coordinating and managing all dimensions of life, free time as well as working time, negative as well as positive thinking. To the victims, beneficiaries, and heirs of such a society, the realm of freedom has lost its classical content, its qualitative difference from the realm of necessity.

Similar arguments can be found in the work of Adorno and Horkheimer (1944) and, more recently, Braverman (1974), Alt (1976), and Gorz (1982).

Marxists and neo-Marxists have become increasingly drawn to questions of leisure and recreation in the post-war period. The main reason for this lies in the absence of a revolutionary class movement in the West. The growth of leisure and the development of consumer culture (especially through advertising, television, popular music, and the lesser media) is said to have played a major part in contributing to working class mystification and subordination. As Brohm (1978: 99) has it, "the leisure pursuits he (the worker) thought he had chosen freely turn out to be just what was on offer on the market, controlled by state policy. Nature and physical leisure activities are colonized by big capital." Brohm's words evoke what might be called a "reproductive" position in

Marxism. That is, a position which attributes a key role theoretically to the leisure industry in forming afresh the cultural and economic subordination of the worker.

Other positions assign a contradictory role to leisure and recreation. For example, Clarke and Critcher (1985: 227), following the thought of Gramsci, argue that "leisure is never wholly free nor totally determined activity. It is always potentially an arena for cultural contestation between dominant and subordinate groups." Hall and Jefferson (1976), Gruneau (1983), and Hargreaves (1986) endorse the same position.

Marxists and neo-Marxists have done the most to apply structure-based explanations of leisure and recreation in the modern world. However, they have no monopoly on the concept, and the narrow identification of structure with class has precipitated criticism in other quarters. Feminist writers, in particular, have accused Marxists of attributing an exaggerated importance to relations of *production* and neglecting relations of *reproduction* in their accounts of leisure and recreation. This is undoubtedly true. The production and reproduction of gendered subjects and the role of the family-household system in perpetuating conventional attitudes of "normal," "healthy," "free time" activity are crucial in explaining modern leisure processes. Yet, with one or two exceptions, notably the interesting work of Hargreaves (1982, 1989), feminist writing on leisure and recreation is dull and uninspired (see, for example, Deem 1986; Scraton 1987). It displays none of the intellectual openness and style that one finds in feminist writers on culture such as Wolff (1981) and Williamson (1984), and still less the boldness and energy that Coward (1984) displays in her thoughtful discussion of the structural conditioning of female desire.

While structure theories have explored leisure and recreation in diverse ways, they do share some general weaknesses. I now propose to examine these weaknesses through critical commentary. As with my discussion of agency theories, I will highlight my argument by adopting the notational form:

1. First and foremost, structure-based theories tend to slip into a deterministic mode of analysis regarding leisure and recreation. The reflexivity and creativity of the actor are pushed back into the periphery, so that the actor appears as the mere automaton of social position. "Everybody must behave," write Adorno and Horkheimer (1944: 123-4), "in accordance with his previously determined and indexed level, and choose the category of mass product turned out for his type.... The man with leisure has to accept what the culture manufacturers offer him." If such rhetoric is difficult to take seriously, it is nonetheless difficult to criticize, for it contains more than a grain of truth. Capitalism *is* a global system of commodity production. It *does* aim to turn "free" time into exchange value. It *does* divide society into a series of target groups with custom-built wants and cravings (e.g. the youth market, the yuppie market, the housewife market). However, it is not a system of total domination. Criticism is possible. Resistance is real. The consumer is a creative actor capable of denying

and bending the meanings which the leisure industry propagates. Hebdige (1979: 103) borrows Lévi-Strauss's notion of *bricolage* to illustrate the point. *Bricolage* involves the use of objects, language, style, and so on, to juxtapose two apparently incompatible realities. The use of the humble household safety pin by the punks as an item of dress symbolizing a threatening group identity is a good example. "More subtly," comments Hebdige (1979: 104-5) of the 1960s British "mod" movement, "the conventional insignia of the business world — the suit, collar and tie, short hair, etc. — were stripped of their original connotations — efficiency, ambition, compliance with authority — and transformed into 'empty' fetishes, objects to be dressed, fondled, and valued for their own right."

2. Structure theories tend to produce one-dimensional views of society. For example, Haug (1986: 105) describes society as "one huge supermarket ... which not only tries to determine the meaning and sensuality of each commodity, but also those of people and their social relationships." Similarly, Deem (1986: 148), commenting from a feminist standpoint, writes, "women have far fewer leisure choices than men because their choices about the whole of their lives are more restricted by men and male patriarchal control." The first statement oversteps the mark between rhetoric and sophistry, with its echo of the vulgar Marxist notion of "the totally commodified society." The second statement is merely tautological. There is no question that women have less leisure time and leisure space than men. But to account for this in terms of the domination of women by men simply repeats the observation in different words, and hardly constitutes a valid explanation. Furthermore, both statements suggest that leisure and recreation experience in society can be measured in terms of a common uniform standard, i.e. capitalist domination or male oppression. I have already noted on several occasions in this chapter that such suggestions are faulty because they ignore the real variety and dynamism of actual leisure wants and experience.

3. Structure theories assume that a direct and palpable relationship exists between language and reality. For example, Marxism purports to be the real "science of society." Structuralism and feminism take issue with this judgment, although each does so on the basis of rather different processes of reasoning. Moreover, each claims to go well beyond Marxism in objectivity and truthful analysis. A long line of Western philosophers, from Nietzsche through to Wittgenstein and contemporary "post-structuralist" writers like Foucault and Derrida, reject the idea that language merely reflects the world. Instead, these writers emphasize the ambiguity of acts of communication and the role of language in making meaning. This identifies language as a distinct form of *power*. What is at stake here is no mere academic point. Marxism and feminism are not simply theoretical models to understand the world; they also constitute practical attempts to raise consciousness and transform existing conditions in society. At the heart of the practice of change is language. It is language which,

in Lenin's phrase, sets down what is to be done. It is language which identifies unhealthy, alienating forms of leisure and recreation. Yet what if language is shown to be ambivalent and not precise in naming things? What if meaning is shown to be pluralistic as opposed to singular, dynamic rather than static? The implications of such questions damage the status of Marxism and feminism to be "scientific" forms of understanding. Instead, they are said to be exposed as competing value positions among many others.

4. The question of language and power raises a further point. Structure theories regularly comment on the objective lack of freedom and alienation that people suffer in their leisure and recreation relations. Yet, at the subjective level of immediate and concrete experience, it is quite clear that people derive considerable satisfaction from existing market-based forms of leisure and recreation, especially those which involve personal competition, trials of strength, and the struggle for domination. Are these enthusiasms to be explained simply as the perversions of humanity caused by capitalism and patriarchy? Are the enthusiasts to be written off as dupes luxuriating in false consciousness?

PROCESS

Questions like this are beginning to be asked not only in the field of leisure and recreation studies, but also in social theory as a whole. Action is no longer seen as autonomous and self determining. Rather, it is seen as contingent and interdependent. Structure is no longer regarded as merely constraining. Rather, it is regarded as both enabling and constraining. Think of language: it conditions how we communicate with each other, but it also acts as a resource for critical departures in communication and action. The reaction against the agency/ structure schema crystallizes in the concept of *process*. Social life is seen as *movement*. The new approach to the study of social relations retains the concepts of action and structure, but situates them indissolubly *in time*.

Giddens' (1984) patient but prolix elaboration of "structuration" theory is a case in point. "Analyzing the structuration of social systems," he writes (1984: 25), "means studying the modes in which such systems, grounded in knowledgeable activities of situated actors who draw upon rules and resources in the diversity of action contexts, are produced and reproduced in interaction." Giddens' ideas are being actively applied in the field of leisure and recreation studies, notably by researchers at the Centre for Leisure Studies in Holland, Bramham (1984) in the UK, and, with rather more selectivity, Gruneau (1983) in North America.

Giddens' antagonism to false dualities (individual/society, agency/ structure, order/change, past/present), and his emphasis on the dynamics and interdependence of human relations, finds its direct parallel in the work of Elias and the figurational school. Figurational sociology rejects the idea that leisure and recreation correspond to free, spontaneous, self-determining activity. Moreover, it disputes the idea that leisure behavior is determined. Instead, figurational sociology examines leisure relations as relations of permissible behavior. That is, the individual is said to find scope for the arousal of feelings of pleasure, but only in socially approved forms. As Elias and Dunning 1986: 99) write:

> Leisure activities are a class of activities where, more than in any other, the routine restraint of emotions can, up to a point, be relaxed publicly and with social approval. Here, an individual can find opportunities for an acute arousal of pleasurable emotions of medium strength without danger to himself or herself and without danger, or lasting commitment, to others.

On the face of it, this looks like a straight re-run of the rather hackneyed functionalist argument that leisure in modern society provides a compensatory function for the deprivations of work (see Parker 1983; Wilensky 1960). Yet rather more is involved than that. Figurational sociology sets the whole idea of the controlled release of aggressive and sexual feelings in leisure in the context of deep historical transformations in personality structure. According to Elias (1978, 1982), mock forms of aggression and sexuality play a prominent part in adult leisure in modern society precisely because the comportment of the body and the organization of the passions is more generally "civilized," i.e. social standards of restraint, moderation, and decorum are more severe. It follows that the scope for liberation in leisure activity must therefore be understood in the context of the "civilized" economy of affects. For Elias, leisure is not free, spontaneous, or self-determining. Rather, it is enmeshed in the web of enabling and constraining structures that make up the civilizing process.

Another interesting example of process-style thinking and research in leisure and recreation studies is Kelly's (1987) theory of "social existentialism." Kelly's writings repay our attention because they run through the whole gamut of agency/structure/process in miniature. His early writing displayed the conventional preoccupation with questions of agency in leisure and recreation activity (Kelly 1976; 1978). The emphasis was on the choice and flexibility of the actor, and leisure was generally associated with positive experience. However, his work gradually embraced concepts like the "situated freedom" of the actor and "alienation" in leisure and recreation experience (see Kelly 1983). The question of the *interaction* between agency and structure comes to occupy the center-stage of his deliberations. The whole trend of his thought moves towards the displacement of the structure/agency schema with a process model of leisure and recreation. Thus, in his theory of social existentialism, Kelly writes (1987: 235):

Leisure ... is process with both existential and social dimensions — sometimes in conflict. Leisure is not either/or: decision or state of being, immediate experience or personal development, relaxed or intense, flow or creation, separate or engaged, problematic or structured. Leisure is act and an environment for action, of the culture and creating the "not yet."

CONCLUSION

Now, it is not my contention that leisure and recreation theory can be thought of as proceeding in an unbroken line from agency to structure to process. Quite obviously, the situation is more complicated than that. All that one can say is that process models do seem capable of avoiding some of the familiar snares associated with agency and structure models. Similarly, I do not maintain that process theory, as it is embodied in the writings of Giddens, Elias, Kelly and their followers, is beyond criticism. Far from it. In some respects, process-type writings on leisure and recreation are open to fundamental objections. For example, as we have seen, Elias and Dunning (1986) argue that leisure and recreation activity allows, "up to a point," relaxation from the web of restraint that exists in the civilizing process. In criticism one wants to know at what point, and why, is relaxation tolerated in some settings yet not in others. Similarly, Kelly's theory of social existentialism contains a luminous recognition of the dynamism of leisure and recreation activity. However, at the same time, the view of leisure and recreation that emerges is exceptionally difficult to key into. Indeed, in the passage quoted above, his description of leisure comes dangerously close to being all things to all people.

To some extent these defects are integral to the entire system of process thinking. After all, process theories *are themselves in process*. The whole purpose is to bring the concepts used in process theory more closely into line with the ways in which people actually behave in their leisure, recreation, and other areas of social life. If we accept that the actions and aims of people change, it seems unreasonable to expect process theories to be unchanging and final.

Let me close this chapter by branching out into speculation on the kinds of issues in leisure and recreation studies that process theories might be expected to pursue in the 1990s and beyond. Again, I will highlight my argument by resorting to the notational form of discussion:

1. The collapse of the work/leisure distinction clears the decks for a wider, more searching, exploration of the historical and social mechanisms of enabling and regulating leisure practice. By privileging the economic base as the key determinant of leisure and recreation, generations of researchers have

obscured the many-sided cultural influences which play on our leisure and recreation opportunities, desires, and choices. Leisure and recreation activity is much more than a reaction to, or spillover from, work. In addition, it draws on social constructs of health and illness, virtue and idleness, propriety and profanity, rationality and irrationality. To understand these influences, we need to examine the processes of class and sexual struggle, state formation, rationalization, civilization, and citizenship. By the same token, we need to get away from monochromatic pictures of leisure and recreation which present these very complicated activities as determined "in the last instance" by systems such as class, gender, race, and bureaucracy. Leisure and recreation experience is not the product of a single system. Rather, it arises from the interaction between systems.

2. An obvious and indisputable fact about leisure in modern society is that many of the most popular activities are illegal. Consider the examples of drug-taking, home taping, unlawful sexual activity, and trespass. These are routine "free-time" pursuits for large numbers of people. Yet agency and structure theories have done little to elucidate them. This is a pity, because the sociology of leisure constitutes a rich and long-standing research tradition in deviant leisure activity which has hardly been touched by students of leisure and recreation. One thinks of Matza and Sykes's (1961) study of leisure values in delinquent sub-cultures, of Becker's (1963) classic work on the marijuana user, of Young's (1971) book on the recreational use of drugs in British society, of Cohen's (1972) study of leisure lifestyles in youth sub-cultures, and of the work of Hughes (1977) and Pearson (1987) on the heroin user. It is not my purpose to suggest that these studies are beyond criticism. On the contrary, the labelling, or social reaction, perspective used by Matza and Sykes, Becker, and Cohen is open to fundamental objections (see Fine 1977). All the same, there are insights, pointers, and concrete research achievements here that might be profitably developed in building up a penetrating tradition of research into deviant practice in leisure and recreation. The topic is intrinsically interesting and might stimulate rather more discussion than the somewhat prosaic studies of leisure and its "associated variables" which choke most editions of the major journals of leisure and recreation research (for a critique of "formalist" research, see Rojek 1985: 91-103). More importantly, the study of deviant leisure practice might throw more light on that most obscure and difficult of subjects — "normal" leisure relations.

3. The question of what is deviant and normal in leisure and recreation carries with it the practical requirement to ascertain the locations in which deviant and normal leisure are defined, challenged, and policed (see Rojek 1988, 1989). Agency theories have assumed that a consensus on the limits of "normal" leisure conduct exists in mature society. They have ignored, therefore, the

mobile and plural forms of conflict and reaction that arise in modern leisure and recreation. For their part, structure theories have acknowledged conflict. However, they have contributed to an over-simplified view of mobility and plurality, by postulating monolithic structures of domination, such as the class struggle, the exploitation of women, or the rule of hegemony. At issue here is not the existence of these structures, but their consistency, gravity, permanence, and meaning. The process approach gives a much higher profile to the ambiguous, changeable nature of power relations. This is expressed tangibly in a far greater concern with the "micro" politics of leisure and recreation. Whereas agency and structure theories tend to gravitate towards propositions that apply to the whole of society, process theories are more at home in empirical inquiries which aim to make sense of local disputes over leisure time and space. My own work on the dispute over the use value of Stonehenge between the official managers of the site and the hippie peace convoy, and the historical and social construction of appropriate leisure and recreation practice on Sundays, may be referred to for more detail (Rojek 1988, 1989). The micro politics of leisure and recreation can obviously be used as the building blocks for more prognostic theories. However, in the 1990s and beyond, this localized and concrete form of analysis, which directly addresses the plurality of values, seems set to become more prominent and influential in leisure and recreation studies.

4. Finally, the *ideology* of leisure is a preoccupation of Marxist, neo-Marxist, and feminist accounts of "free time" activity. A common failing of this work is the suggestion that ideology can be unmasked to produce natural, undistorted relations of leisure and recreation. What this ignores is the quest for escape which one finds in all forms of leisure and recreation. This can be studied directly in the fantasy environments of many of the most popular and distinctive leisure pursuits in our society. One thinks of the use of light, darkness, and sound in the discotheque; the employment of costumed actors to re-create the sights and sounds of the past in heritage centers such as the Henry Ford Museum and Greenfield Village in Dearborn, Michigan, the Plimouth plantation in New England, Beamish and Wigan Pier in Britain; the techniques and effects of cinema. theater, and cabaret shows. However, perhaps the fantasy leisure environment is realized on the most monumental scale in modern theme parks such as Phantasialand in West Germany, De Efteling in Holland, Alton Towers in Britain, and Disneyland and Disney World in the U.S.A. Both Marin (1977) and Eco (1986) have commented that Disneyland is set up as a magic city in which the absolutely fantastic is presented as the absolutely real. What matters is not simply the contrast with the regimented, disenchanted "outside" world, but the "authenticity" of the fantasy experience. As a marketing brochure advertising the attractions of Disneyland (AmEx 1986: 3) puts it:

Let Walt Disney's Magic Kingdom work its spell on you....
Visit Main Street, U.S.A., where you'll enjoy turn-of-the-
century charm with horseless carriages, silent movies and
quaint shops. Cruise through lush jungle landscapes and see a
swashbuckling pirate raid in Adventureland. The rough and
tumble world of our pioneering ancestors is brought vividly to
life in Frontierland. You'll learn about our country's illustri-
ous history in Liberty Square. See favorite childhood charac-
ters like Snow White and Peter Pan and travel 20,000 leagues
under the sea in captain Nemo's ship in Fantasyland. Or be
part of a mission to Mars on a high-speed flight to the stars in
Tomorrowland.

The exploration of the fantasy environment as a site of ideological production and incorporation is a major research task for the process approach. Not
only would it be a corrective to the monolithic view of ideology that abounds in
structure theories, but it would also show more clearly how the ideology of
escape operates in everyday leisure and recreation.

References

Adorno, T. and M. Horkheimer. 1944. *Dialectic of Enlightenment*. London Verso.

Alt, J. 1976. "Beyond class: the decline of industrial labour and leisure." *Telos 28:* 55-80.

American Express. 1986. "Walt Disney World Vacation Kingdom." Atlanta: American Express.

Becker, H. 1963. *Outsiders: Studies in the Sociology of Deviance*. New York: Free Press.

Bramham, P. 1984. "Giddens in goal: Reconstructing the social theory of sport." In *New Directions in Leisure Studies*, eds. P. Bramham, L. Haywood, I. Henry, and F. Kew. Department of Applied and Community Studies, Bradford and Ilkley Community College.

Braverman, H. 1974. *Labour and Monopoly Capital*. New York: Monthly Review Press.

Brightbill, C. 1961. *Man and Leisure*. Englewood Cliffs, NJ: Prentice Hall.

Brohm, J.M. 1978. *Sport: A Prison of Measured Time*. London: Interlinks.

Clarke, J. and C. Critcher. 1985. *The Devil Makes Work*. London: Macmillan.

Cohen, S. 1972. *Folk Devils and Moral Panics*. London: MacGibbon and Kee.

Coward, R. 1984. *Female Desire: Women's Sexuality Today*. London: Paladin.

Deem, R. 1986. *All Work and No Play? The Sociology of Women and Leisure*. Milton Keynes: Open University Press.

Dumazedier, J. 1967. *Towards a Society of Leisure*. London: Collier-Macmillan.

Eco, U. 1986. *Faith in Fakes*. London: Secker and Warburg.

Elias, N. 1978. *The Civilizing Process, Vol. 1: The History of Manners*. Oxford: Blackwell.

Elias, N. 1982. *The Civilizing Process, Vol. 2: State Formation and Civilization*. Oxford: Blackwell.

Elias, N. and E.G. Dunning. 1986. *Quest for Excitement: Sport and Leisure in the Civilizing Process*. Oxford: Blackwell.

Fine, B. 1977. "Labelling theory: An investigation into the sociological critique of deviance." *Economy and Society 6:* 166-193.

Gershuny, J. 1978. *After Industrial Society*. London: Macmillan.

Giddens, A. 1984. *The Constitution of Society*. Oxford: Polity.

Glyptis, S., H. McInnes, and J.A. Patmore. 1987. *Leisure and the Home*. London: Sports Council / Economic and Social Research Council Joint Panel on Leisure and Recreation Research.

Gorz, A. 1982. *Farewell to the Working Class*. London: Pluto Press.

Gruneau, R. 1983. *Class, Sports and Social Development*. Amherst: University of Massachusetts Press.

Hall, S. and T. Jefferson, eds. 1976. *Resistance Through Rituals*. London: Hutchinson.

Hargreaves, J., ed. 1982. *Sport, Culture and Ideology*. London: Routledge and Kegan Paul.

Hargreaves, J. 1986. *Sport, Power and Culture*. Oxford: Polity Press.

Hargreaves, J. 1989. "The promise and problems of women's leisure and sport." In *Leisure for Leisure: Critical Essays*, ed. C. Rojek, pp. 130-149. London: Macmillan.

Haug, W.F. 1986. *Critique of Commodity Aesthetics*. Oxford: Polity.

Hebdige, D. 1979. *Subculture: The Meaning of Style*. London: Methuen.

Hughes, P.H. 1977. *Behind the Wall of Respect*. Chicago: University of Chicago Press.

Kelly, J.R. 1976. "Leisure as compensation for work." *Society and Leisure 83:* 73-82.

Kelly, J.R. 1978. "Situational and social factors in leisure decisions." *Pacific Sociological Review 21:* 313-30.

Kelly, J.R. 1983. *Leisure Identities and Interactions.* London: George Allen and Unwin.

Kelly, J.R. 1987. *Freedom To Be: A New Sociology of Leisure.* New York: Macmillan.

Kraus, R. 1984. *Recreation and Leisure in Modern Society*, 3rd ed. Glenview: Scott Foresman and Co.

MacIntyre, A. 1981. *After Virtue.* London: Duckworth.

Marcuse, H. 1967. "Socialist humanism?" In *Socialist Humanism*, ed. E. Fromm, pp. 97-106. London: Allen Lane.

Marin, L. 1977. "Disneyland: A degenerate Utopia?" *Glyph 1:* 50-66.

Matza, D. and G. Sykes. 1961. "Juvenile delinquency and subterranean values." *American Sociological Review 26:* 712-719.

Miller, N.P. and D.M. Robinson. 1963. *The Leisure Age: Its Challenge to Recreation.* Belmont, CA: Wadsworth.

Moorhouse, H.F. 1989. "Models of work, models of leisure." In *Leisure for Leisure: Critical Essays*, ed. C. Rojek, pp. 15-35. London: Macmillan.

Nash, J. 1953. *Philosophy of Recreation and Leisure.* Dubuque, IA: Brown and Co.

Pahl, R. 1984. *Divisions of Labour.* Oxford: Blackwell.

Parker, S. 1983. *Leisure and Work.* London: George Allen and Unwin.

Pearson, G. 1987. *The New Heroin Users.* Oxford: Blackwell.

Rapoport, R. and R.N. Rapoport. 1975. *Leisure and The Family Life Cycle.* Boston: Routledge and Kegan Paul.

Roberts, K. 1970. *Leisure.* London: Longman.

Rojek, C. 1985. *Capitalism and Leisure Theory.* London: Tavistock.

Rojek, C. 1988. "The convoy of pollution." *Leisure Studies 6:* 21-32.

Rojek, C. 1989. "Leisure time and leisure space." In *Leisure for Leisure: Critical Essays*, ed. C. Rojek, pp. 191-204. London: Macmillan.

Scraton, S. 1987. "Boys muscle in where angels fear to tread." In *Sport, Leisure and Social Relations*, eds. J. Horne, D. Jary, and A. Tomlinson, pp. 160-186. London: Routledge and Kegan Paul.

Sutherland, W.C. 1957. "A philosophy of leisure." *Annals of the American Academy of Political and Social Science 34:* 1-10.

Van Moorst, H. 1982. "Leisure and social theory." *Leisure Studies 2:* 157-169.

Wilensky, H. 1960. "Work, careers and social integration." *International Social Science Journal 4:* 543-560.

Williamson, J. 1984. *Consuming Passions.* London: Marion Boyars.

Wolff, J. 1981. *The Social Production of Art.* London: Macmillan.

Young, J. 1971. *The Drugtakers.* London: MacGibbon and Kee.

LEISURE BEHAVIORS AND STYLES: SOCIAL, ECONOMIC, AND CULTURAL FACTORS

John R. Kelly

In architecture, one dictum has been that "form follows function." Translated into research, such a rule would suggest that methods and strategies would be chosen only after questions and types of data are identified. In leisure studies, however, the rule has often been reversed: "design follows methods." Research methods have been assumed rather than selected and the answers to theoretical questions locked into the kinds of findings amenable to the methods.

For example, the fundamental and persistent question of leisure and recreation research has been "who is doing what?" The question is both management- and market-driven. Agencies managing public resources and those planning investments in recreation businesses want to know the magnitude of their clienteles and the composition of their markets. When they turn to social and behavioral scientists, they receive answers couched in the terms of the common methods and concepts of their disciplines.

First, sociologists took the stage with their familiar surveys and demographic variables. They answered questions about potential markets with breakdowns of current participation by age, income, occupation, gender, and a few other customary factors. When such simplistic analysis was found to be less than successful, they responded with a new technique. Factor analysis was employed to identify bundles of activities that tended to have common participants. These bundles were labeled "styles," which were in part an artifact of the analytical method.

Most recently, social psychologists have succeeded in commanding the stage by answering the question of "who is doing what?" in individual rather than aggregate terms. With their familiar bag of scales and models, they have turned the answer to one of perceived outcomes from types of recreation experiences. Also using factoring techniques, the question has been changed from behaviors to preferences. Now styles are defined in terms of such factors as challenge-seeking, status-symbolizing, and family focus. The nature of the answers is determined by the received methods, in this case those of attitude scales and factor analysis.

Note what has occurred. Sociologists assume that preferences are shaped by socialization, which is indexed by socio-economic variables such as income, occupation, education, ethnicity, and gender. Further, they have measured what is amenable to their methods — self-reports of participation in designated activities. Social psychologists assume that behaviors are shaped by preferences or relatively stable values. Further, they have measured by their familiar methods — scales of attitudes that are abstracted from presumed experience. Running parallel have been the economists studying "demand" with proxies of cost, such as distance, and of resources, such as income. Several disciplines have also adopted time as both a definition and measure of leisure under the assumption that it is quantifiable across settings and even across cultures. Under the rubric of "leisure time," time duration is presumed to measure action and provide an index of valuation as well as of participation.

I am not suggesting that we have learned nothing of value from such approaches or that there is some magic method waiting in the wings to take center stage and annihilate the naive. It is, however, necessary to step back a little from what has been going on in leisure research to re-address the question. The real question is one of explanation. Whether we focus on activity or participation, on markets and resource commitments, or on leisure as a dimension of life and meaning, research methods should follow the formulation. What are the behaviors we call leisure and recreation? Are such behaviors best understood in patterns we may call styles? Do those styles reflect individual orientations as well as cultural values and access to resources?

THE NATURE OF LEISURE: A NON-DEFINITION

It is understandable that we generally define phenomena in terms of our own frameworks. It is also understandable that those frameworks are derived from what we have learned. The "domain assumptions" of the disciplinary and theoretical approaches we have been taught direct us to particular definitions of whatever we are to study as well as to modes of explanation. What is leisure? It is social activity learned in social contexts and employing social resources. It is economic choice conducted in market or quasi-market conditions and measured by economic exchange. It is an individual state of mind or consciousness measured in attitudes and leading to activity and choice. So say the sociologists, economists, and psychologists.

Is it possible to step back enough to examine what each perspective places in its own defining framework? One possibility is that each disciplinary definition presupposes some sort of human action. Whether the focus is on engaging in an activity, making a choice, allocating a resource, or experiencing a state of mind, the individual engages in some sort of action. The action may be physical, intellectual, communicative, contemplative, emotional, or a combination of more than one dimension. Even daydreaming involves action of the imagination. The action may be a context for, as well as content of, the experience. I am aware of no-one who is proposing that leisure is or could be a totally self-contained experience apart from what actors do. Even the most narrow "state-of-mind" definition that asserts that it is the nature of the consciousness that defines leisure presupposes that there is an action context. Something happens in directing attention, processing information, defining meaning, and producing the experience.

If action is integral to leisure — or any other meaningful human engagement — then we can begin at a level prior to the consequences of engaging in specified activity, experiencing an identifiable set of attitudes, making a choice, or even completing a period of time. Prior to all measures and methods is human action, doing something in the most inclusive sense.

Human action, leisure or any other designated by the convention of a name, always has two dimensions or components. Human action is both existential and social. It involves action with meaning and takes place in a social environment of learned symbols as well as opportunities and constraints. Further, the meanings that actors ascribe to actions are learned in social contexts so that the existential and social dimensions of action are related rather than separate.

This is not the place to engage in an extended discussion of the persistent problem of the nature of social action. I have attempted to explore the dialectic of the existential and the social in relation to leisure in the recent book *Freedom to Be: A New Sociology of Leisure* (Kelly 1987a). Here I will only list some dimensions and implications of understanding leisure as human action that is both existential and social.

Leisure is existential as action that produces meaning. Leisure is deciding and doing as well as feeling. The action not only has meaning, but produces meaning. Leisure does more than reflect the cultural meanings attached to symbols and settings. Action does more than process information. It creates meaning whenever decision is real and action carried out. Every action is, in at least an infinitesimal way, novel.

Leisure, then, is action that both has and creates meaning. Actors engage in leisure with multiple and complex anticipations. Along with the immediate experience, there is often a dimension of becoming. In the action, the leisure actor anticipates becoming something more or different from the pre-action condition. Whether or not there is a long-term strategy of personal development, there is some future orientation. The traditional Aristotelian theme of freedom from necessity implies an openness of the future as well as the possibility of focus on the experience itself.

Leisure is existential in the sense that it is action in which the actor becomes something more, in which the action creates novelty. The relative freedom and openness of leisure may enhance the developmental component of meaning, the becoming in the action context (Csikszentmihalyi 1981). For example, a sense of competence and self-creation may be central to the meaning of a leisure episode.

At the same time, leisure is social in both its context and orientations. Leisure is learned behavior, thoroughly ethnic in its adoption of the symbols and constructions of a culture. Leisure, even when solitary, incorporates the meaning forms of a culture learned through its social institutions. Further, leisure may be a context for expressing and creating community.

Leisure forms, interpretations, and aims are learned in a particular society. The resources for leisure, including time and skill-acquisition, are products of the social system. However central the existential elements in leisure, it is also social in its contexts, resources, and learned forms. Leisure always employs the forms of a culture in its symbol systems, institutional role sets, socialization processes, and layers of formal and informal organizations.

This does not mean that leisure is wholly "determined." It is contextual, but may re-shape that context. Insofar as the social system is a construction of human action (Berger and Luckman 1966), leisure is a social domain with the potential for altering that construction. As in the arts we shape resistant materials into something new, so in any social action there is the potential of action upon, as well as in, the society. Admitting social structure to explanations of leisure is not a denial of its element of openness or freedom. In fact, recognizing the social embeddedness of leisure admits leisure's openness and historical relativity when social structure is understood as a creation rather than a given.

Leisure, then, is best understood in a dialectical framework that includes both the existential and the social dimensions. Leisure is situated action. It is contextual but not determined, encultured but not static. It is not existential or social, but both. The relationship is not fixed, but dynamic.

To return to the question of "how do we explain what people are doing?" we will find that there are a number of approaches and models. Each focuses on one aspect of the existential-social dialectic to the exclusion of all or most of the others. As a consequence, all have been found inadequate, even in their own terms. The sections that follow will summarize and analyze major models of explanation. All will be considered to make contributions to understanding, and none to exclude the actual or potential contributions of the others. Implicit in this approach is the assumption that leisure is changing rather than static. It includes both existential and social dimensions that are integrated into the action scheme of individuals and the social forces of the society. Leisure is not a separate domain of human action, dichotomous with any other domain or segregated from other kinds of action. Leisure is very much a part of life as we know it, on the levels of both the actor and the social system. As such, it is multidimensioned, complex, and always in the process of being created and re-created.

MODELS OF EXPLANATION

One approach to models of explanation is by discipline. There is, however, considerable overlap among, and adoption of similar factors by, different disciplines. Therefore, despite the history of leadership of some modes of analysis by sociologists, psychologists, or economists, the approach here will focus on dimensions of explanation and their employment. Also, what follows is not intended as an encyclopedia of references, but as a critical overview.

Social Determination Models

The terminology may be misleading. Are there "determinants" of leisure behavior in a causal sense, or is the analysis stochastic and statistical? It might be more accurate to refer to "correlates" of behavioral aggregates. Correlation coefficients between, for example, age and participation in football are high and negative, but between age and golf relatively low. Age is not itself strictly a "determinant," but indexes a number of factors that decrease participation in physical contact team sports. Further, the second part of the correlation is measured in aggregate terms: percentages of those in specified age categories. The expectation has been that social aggregates would be found to have distinctive leisure patterns.

The model was simple: a series of socio-economic variables was correlated to participation rates in one or more activities. Usually data were obtained from samples of populations in communities, states, or nations. For some employing the model, it was atheoretical, just a matter of using a method. For others there was the implicit theory of structure-functional sociology underlying the study. Differential socialization and access to opportunities were assumed to be indexed by variables such as gender, race, occupation, income, education level, and marital status. Age was considered more a measure of interests and abilities, but was entered into most studies.

The disciplinary source was mainstream sociology. In the 1960s most leisure research was being done by sociologists who were focused on such issues as the determination of leisure by work roles, social status and class in the community context, and the unifying power of integrated social institutions. Leisure was usually defined as residual time. Research approaches measured leisure, however, in terms of participation in listed activities. Surveys often asked for some frequency measure, while time-budget methods measured duration. Results were usually analyzed by correlating mean participation rates with the socio-economic and demographic indices. This method was supported by new computer technologies that facilitated dealing with large samples and multiple variables, and by various economists who included the same variables in their demand equations as proxies for resources and tastes.

How well did it work? At first the method seemed reasonably successful, as statistically significant correlations were found in most studies, especially those with large samples. Other studies compared and contrasted occupational groups (Smigel 1963). Especially when the activities measured were those most differentiated by social status, such as membership in community organizations, the results appeared to validate the assumptions.

The correlations were not large except for a few selected activities, but were almost always significant. Since the likelihood of statistical significance is also correlated to sample size, an N of 1000 or so seemed to ensure probabilities of 0.01. Time-budget studies indicated small but consistent differences in average times spent in various kinds of activities by much the same aggregates. Moreover, some of the correlations were strong: education level to the arts, age and gender to most sports, social status to community organizations, and rural background to hunting and fishing.

In the 1930s, community studies in North America approached leisure in the context of community institutional stratification. In "Middletown," leisure was viewed as a major social space expressing the value systems of the community (Lynd and Lynd 1956). In "Elmtown," leisure was a significant environment for adolescent development as well as for the reinforcement of social stratification (Hollingshead 1949). The study of suburban leisure by Lundberg and associates (1934) analyzed leisure as a derivation of the value scheme of the new upper-middle-class setting. In such community studies, leisure was seen as a product of the social context, but not as strictly determined by a single set of institutional relationships.

In the 1970s and 1980s, however, the model has been subjected to considerable attack. One source was methodological. When multivariate analyses that measured the strength of correlations (the proportion of variance accounted for) were employed, the results were surprisingly unimpressive. One analysis of outdoor recreation surveys found that the variance accounted for averaged less than 5 percent for most activities and approached 10 percent for only a few special-resource activities (Kelly 1980). The previously-found relationships were there, but not with the predictive power presumed.

Altogether almost 20 such surveys were conducted in the 1970s, with numerous analyses of the major national surveys (Snepenger and Crompton 1985). A second crack in the approach was produced by giving attention to social groups as agents and contexts of decision, rather than to aggregate analysis (Field and O'Leary 1973; Cheek and Burch 1976). It was demonstrated that the immediate social contexts of participation, especially family and friendship groups, differentiate participation more than income and occupational indices. An important shift in attention began that has now become commonplace in the study of leisure.

A consensus began to emerge that was in direct conflict with the tacit assumptions of the "determination" or functional model:

1. Although there are demographic and socio-economic variations in leisure and recreation participation, they are only moderately predictive.
2. Much of the variation that is statistically measured can be ascribed to certain constraints (see Goodale and Witt's chapter):
   - the poor are excluded from many kinds of participation, especially any that require travel or other costly investments;
   - other variations are due to past discrimination in access to opportunities, such as for women in physically demanding sports;
   - regional variations are often due to climate and other resource differences in availability and access;
   - excluding the very wealthy and the poor, commonalities of leisure participation appear to be far greater than differences. Such commonalities were more likely to be found in time-budget research and in other designs that included the full range of ordinary activities; and
   - period in the life cycle, and especially child-rearing, has a considerable impact on leisure and recreation patterns.
3. More attention was given to questions of "how?" rather than "what?" That is, style of engagement rather than just frequency would be found to vary according to socialization factors such as education and occupational level.

Ordinarily established premises and methods are abandoned slowly and with some conflict. Although surveys continue to be sponsored and completed, the currently expected results are much more limited than a decade ago. Even the most complete surveys with the largest samples must be interpreted carefully to identify trends and projections (Kelly 1987b). In the case of the overly-simple socio-economic determination model, its retreat was hastened by more sophisticated statistical techniques that undermined its results, as well as by changes in focus. The computer that made the simple survey possible contained the potential for its own dissolution.

Economic and Opportunity Models

At the same time, another determination model was being explored. The assumption was simple: the economic domain of life determines all others. The framework was usually set as a dichotomy — work and leisure. Underlying the agenda-setting volume edited by Erwin Smigel (1963) was the assumption that the diminution of work would make leisure a problem for the social system.

Stanley Parker's influential study, *The Future of Work and Leisure* (1971), was based on a set of models of the relationship. While separation was admitted as one possibility, the bias of the author was that the economic sphere was the major determinant of leisure.

The formulation of the premise was somewhat loose. "Work" was really a tacit way of referring to economic roles, whatever their productive or marginal nature. "Leisure" referred to those activities that occupied time other than that required by the economic roles, self and household maintenance, and domestic tasks. The mixtures of meanings in activity such as child-parent interaction or entertaining at home, for example, were largely ignored, as were gender and life course variations (see Bella's chapter).

Economic models tend to assume that both work and leisure are quantifiable as time. The relationship between the two was usually expressed as a trade-off in which remunerated time on the job is chosen or rejected in favor of non-remunerative time called leisure (Kreps 1968; Linder 1970; see also Vickerman, this volume). Values are indexed by dollars of income or expenditure, or by time as a proxy for economic value.

Parker (1971) proposed that the relationship of work and leisure might be the extension or spillover of identity, the opposition of contrast, or the segmentation of separation. He later suggested that the direction of determination might not all be one-way (1983: 88). Nevertheless, the persistent themes of this and other works are that the economic domain of life is pre-eminent. Nonwork elements of life tend to be shaped by economic roles. This was translated into research that sought to find consistent patterns of leisure differentiated by types of occupation or by occupational status.

The issues, however, tended to be more complex (Zuzanek and Mannell 1983). They include the allocation of time between work and leisure, the impacts of work scheduling variations on leisure, relative values placed on the different domains, the relation of work commitment to leisure valuation, and the carry-over of work attitudes and values to leisure. Fundamental, however, has been the attempt to measure direct effects of economic roles on leisure choices and styles.

Some research has found weak spillover effects or multivariate effects that cannot be captured by a single model (Zuzanek and Mannell 1983). Several studies found little relationship between workplace satisfaction or alienation and leisure (Bacon 1975). Currently, more sophisticated studies are employing complex analysis to identify the carry-over of employment dimensions such as intellectuality and complexity (Miller and Kohn 1982).

A number of factors reinforce this complexity and multidimensionality. On the one hand, individuals with different economic roles have many common histories of socialization, education, and cultural environments. On the other hand, schedules and economic resources are dependent on work roles. Further, there may be reciprocity in learning and expression among such activity elements as skill, sociability, modes of communication, and interaction styles. Negative dimensions of alienation, damage to self-esteem and positive identities, and expression of freedom may have some spillover from work to leisure and family (Torbert 1973). More profoundly, nonwork spheres of life may come to be defined in terms of market participation, possession, and the purchase of commodified experiences (Kelly 1986).

What seems clear is that the multifaceted and multidimensioned relationship between economic and other roles and relationships cannot be reduced to any simple model of occupational determination of leisure activity choice. The same seems to be the case when attention is shifted to economically-derived social position. Social class analysis divides the social system into layers measured by "life chances," or the opportunities derived from economic roles. Rather than a direct occupational determination model, social class analysis presupposes that placement in a stratified socio-economic system determines access to opportunities, as well as the resources the actor brings to those opportunities.

In relation to leisure, there would appear to be some clear ties between social class and leisure. First, the lowest class, the poor and disinherited, are excluded from the opportunities and resources that others take for granted. They have no discretionary income, little likelihood of developing skills and interests in educational settings, and no position that admits them to leisure environments. Their leisure, then, tends to be relatively cost-free and without travel and high equipment costs.

Second, the very wealthy are able — through travel and the purchase of access to special resources — to demonstrate leisure styles in which many of the impediments to leisure for others are avoided. They enter a world of private resources that can be purchased at prices that eliminate crowding by more ordinary classes.

Third, one element of class is that of education. Education not only is an essential credential for economic opportunity, but also is a social space in which tastes and abilities are developed.

Fourth, economic resources to purchase or rent access to leisure opportunities are indexed by social class. With many kinds of leisure offered through the market with prices attached, income is one factor in what can be done and in the style of participation.

Fifth, there is a likelihood that those in the upper investment segments of the economy, as well as many managers and professionals, have more control over their work schedules than those working for hourly wages in the manufacturing or retail sectors of the economy. They are able to integrate work and leisure schedules flexibly, rather than be limited to the time made available by factory or shop schedules.

Perhaps most salient is the fact that those who are marginal economically may be left out by those who supply many leisure markets. Among the costs of stratification in a market economy is that pricing policies offer certain goods and services only to those in the upper strata of the system.

The result is that both resources and opportunities are available, or not, in ways that have economic bases. For this evident reason, it has been assumed that measures of socio-economic class would be powerfully correlated with the activity patterns of leisure participation. In general, however, the results have been disappointing. When the costly travel of the wealthy and the extreme limitations of the poor are excluded, differences in activity choices by upper-middle, middle, and working class people in North America have not been dramatic. When education history is controlled, those differences almost disappear. What seems to be the case is that styles vary more than the activities themselves. Rates of camping, listening to music, watching television, or engaging in sports are little different. What may differ is the place and style of participation. Only costly activities such as downhill skiing and golf have substantial class variations (Kelly 1987b).

This tends to shift attention to what has been called "social status." Class is based on access to and control of economic resources. Status is a matter of style. And it seems to be styles of leisure that vary most. People eat out — some at fast food chains and a few at exclusive clubs. They travel — most by car, staying with friends and at budget motels, and a few by Concorde to pricy resorts. They entertain at home — most with cookouts and potlucks and a few with catered soirées. Even golf may be played on crowded public links or at private clubs so exclusive that even money cannot buy a membership. There are differences in style based on social status, but we have little research on such issues.

SOCIAL FACTORS IN LEISURE

Styles of leisure participation vary with a number of other factors. Economic resources are only the beginning, and not always the most significant. For example, across a wide spectrum of class or status layers, parents of young children orient much of their leisure towards developmental activity and the expression of family bonds. Social variables such as gender, place in the life course, family status, ethnic background and cultural heritage, age-indexed abilities and expectations, and educational histories are all factors in leisure styles.

Again, there have been many attempts to identify and measure the "determinants" of leisure. If economic roles alone did not produce clearly differentiated patterns of leisure participation, then the addition of demographic and social factors might complete the task. Two general sets of assumptions were operative. The first was the Opportunity Model and the second the Socialization Model.

The Opportunity Model was derived from the economic approach. The argument was that access to resources and opportunities was the consequence of a combination of economic and social factors. The economic factors alone, at least for those who were not quite wealthy or not quite poor, did not distinguish different participation patterns. If, however, a fuller set of determinants were to be introduced, then the results would be more persuasive. Gender, age, ethnic identification, education level, marital status, urban-rural residence, and other social variables were added to the economic-occupational ones. Each was presumed to measure some differential access to resources or opportunities that would lead to different kinds of activities being chosen.

The Socialization Model was somewhat more sociological. The premise was that a number of factors produced different life histories. As a consequence, different interests and values were learned in a lifelong process. Gender and educational history, especially, were presumed to index different socialization patterns.

The results were generally significant but not spectacular. Again, differences in both opportunity and socialization produced considerable male predominance in such activities as team sports, hunting, bar visiting, and some individual and pair sports. Females, on the other hand, were disproportionately represented in the fine arts and in some domestic activities. Those with higher education experiences made up almost all the participants in most fine arts engagement, both doing and appreciation. Even when controlling for economic resources, socialization factors were found to be significant.

The results, however, continued to obscure differences due to the focus on frequency of participation in designated activities. Styles of engagement were ignored, as were locales. Swimming was undifferentiated — in public pools versus private and club pools, at exclusive resort beaches versus public urban beaches, or in social versus competitive settings. A trip was a trip, a party a party, and reading anything from the sports page of the newspaper to Thomas Hardy was just reading.

Styles tend to vary more than can be demonstrated by time diaries and activity lists. The styles of behavior learned as appropriate are age-based, gender-differentiated, and culture-varied. Socialization into leisure is a lifelong process in which taking up and discarding activities is only one dimension. Going to concerts, one category in the national recreation surveys, is not much alike for the teen rock crowd and the adult symphony audience. There is a variety of leisure styles within social categories as well as similarities across social strata. The institutional context of participation and socialization incorporates factors of contexts, opportunities, resources, orientations, values, and cohort, as well as personal, histories.

The Life Course Approach

One response to this complexity is to employ the computer to sort out every-thing imaginable that can be put into a research design. Inclusive designs, although they tend to account for somewhat more variance than simpler ones, are plagued by two problems. The first is methodological: the more variables that are included, the more they are likely to overlap. As a consequence, the explanatory power added by the twentieth or even the tenth factor is quite small. A second limitation is that such designs contribute little to explanatory theory. Additions of 0.02 to variance accounted for is of little help in developing models of explanation. This is especially true when single measures are purported to represent complex socialization processes.

When it is admitted that no model seems to include all factors or to order them into a single all-encompassing explanatory model, then the strategies of explanation are somewhat more modest. Perspectives are chosen that do not pretend to do it all. Rather, any metaphor of explanation (Kelly 1987a) focuses on some aspects of the totality, to the exclusion of others. The issue becomes one of choosing metaphors that are most closely aligned with explanatory models that fit what is known of the phenomenon under investigation.

For leisure, a new focus was gaining support. It replaced statistical aggregates with groups, categories with communities. Further, the Socialization Model was given substance in the content of its framework. Moving from family studies (Rapoport and Rapoport 1975), attention to social bonds (Cheek and Burch 1976), and discovery of immediate communities of family and friends as the primary school context of leisure (Burch 1969; Field and O'Leary 1973), the metaphor of the life course was given increased attention.

The dialectic of leisure behavior is demonstrated in this perspective. On the one hand, leisure is viewed as profoundly social, embedded in the roles and relationships that change through the life course. On the other hand, it is seen as purposive action with intentions that include both the immediate experience and longer-term outcomes of personal development. Leisure is one dimension of life in which action is oriented towards "becoming," as well as towards the present.

One aspect of the dual perspective is that of socialization. Leisure is learned behavior, attitudes, and meanings. We are socialized into leisure through our histories of experiences and choices. Leisure socialization is learning how to be leisure actors.

There is, however, also socialization *in* leisure. In leisure events and episodes we are in the process of becoming. We are learning and developing. This learning is both positive and negative, as the self develops strength or fears, competence or inhibitions.

In general, the life course in contemporary societies consists of three bio-social periods: preparation, establishment, and culmination (Kelly 1983a; 1987a). In the preparation period, learning and growing are the central tasks as the young person is getting ready for adult or productive life. The central social institutions are the school and the family of socialization. In establishment, the themes are productive activity and securing a place in the social system. The family of procreation and the economy are salient social institutions. In the final or culmination period, the end point of death is anticipated in ways that make meaning and the passing on of life's outcomes significant. Life is seen as a journey in which the human actor seeks to have some continuity of meaning and identity, rather than just a series of experiences.

From this developmental perspective, leisure is found to be an integral dimension of the entire process, not "time out" from its meaning. Activities are more than time-fillers or discrete forms of action and interaction. Leisure takes place in contexts that change through the life course. These contexts include institutional roles with opportunities and expectations that change through life's journey. For example, all the organized and informal possibilities for sport, the arts, entertainment, and interaction that are associated with the school are left behind in the transition to the establishment period. As a consequence, participation in many kinds of leisure declines suddenly and may be replaced with activity more related to the home and community.

Opportunity structures change through the life course, as do role expectations and self-definitions. In early establishment years, leisure has been found to be altered by the assumption of the roles of spouse and parent as well as full-time worker. Along with the changing social expectation and opportunity contexts, the value systems and world views of individuals may be altered as they move through their life spans. The kinds of travel, parties, sports, and cultural engagements sought by students may be avoided by the same persons five years later as they seek to find accepted places in the adult world. Again, the changes may be more a matter of styles than of activity designations. Locales, attire, companions, and modes of interaction considered appropriate at one age may be seen as damaging to social identity at a later period.

Socialization into leisure is a dialectical process that continues through the life course. As we learn leisure interests and skills, we also learn something about ourselves. We make decisions both in the context of perceived opportunities and expectations and of how we perceive ourselves. We learn in leisure engagement to define and re-define our aims and our selves. We are always in process of becoming, selecting life investments in changing situations.

Csikszentmihalyi (1981) has argued that it is in leisure experiences that we are most likely to develop criteria for the rest of life. Expressive activities may be those in which experiences of the highest quality become the standard by which other experiences — as in work or education — are judged. We may become dissatisfied with events and circumstances that are largely instrumental and devoid of their own meaning. That is, we come to expect some expressive and developmental dimensions in most social spaces.

One aspect of much leisure is that its relative openness allows for more immediate and direct feedback than in many routinized contexts in which the outcomes are predetermined. In the leisure of games, there are discrete and measured outcomes. In social situations, we may choose companions whose feedback is most salient to us. We try new and different initiatives, portrayals, and ventures, knowing that the outcomes are significant for us but not fateful for our major social roles. As a consequence, we may be most likely to learn and develop in such times of relative openness.

There are a number of models of the life course. Each emphasizes one or more dimensions of the life journey. The "family life cycle" stresses the predictable sequences of family roles and contexts. The "life span" model points to age-related changes in the individual and often combines biological with psychological factors in explanation. The "life course" approach defines continuities and transitions in multiple roles that intersect in a variety of ways in each life period. The "crisis" model suggests that there are traumatic upheavals at crucial points in the life journey that realign self-definitions as well as role commitments. The "developmental" perspective proposes certain sequential stages of development that build on previous ones and require some completion in order. Each approach stresses dimensions that have relevance for understanding shifts in leisure activities, social contexts, meanings, and styles through the life course (Kelly 1987a: 66-68).

Identifying just how leisure changes through the life course is too complex a task for this chapter. It is clear that both continuity and change characterize the individual actor as well as social roles and contexts (Kelly 1983a). Leisure is not a separate domain of life, but is woven through all sorts of roles and relationships (Rapoport and Rapoport 1975). As the transitions and traumas of life develop and have their impacts on everything — resources, opportunities, values, self-images, and aims — so leisure takes on different meanings and functions (Kelly 1987c). Further, such changes are different for men and women, those with economic security and the poor, those with intact families and those without, and others with significant differences.

Continuity and change in leisure through the life course can be approached in terms of changes in the individual, in contexts and opportunities, and in expectations and aims. Another approach focuses principally on the kinds of activities pursued. The "core plus balance" model proposes that one element in the failure to find dramatic differences in activities across population categories, or even through the life course, is the persistent core of activities that occupy most adults most of their lives. This core consists of engagements that are relatively accessible and low cost. Watching television, interacting informally with other household members, conversing in a variety of settings, and engaging in sexual activity are common to adults through most of the life span. Other such activity includes reading, walking, residential enhancement such as lawn and garden activity, and meeting with kin and friends. This core occupies the greatest amount of time, especially in those periods between scheduled events. Further, such core activities often express and develop those primary relationships that are highly valued by most adults.

The balance, on the other hand, suggests variety. It also offers one way of answering the old questions about whether leisure is a compensation for work requirements or a spillover from its content (Wilensky 1963). Is leisure escape or intense engagement, relaxation or focus, solitary or social, restful or demanding, physical or mental, and so on? The balance approach suggests that the usual answer for an individual is "both/and" rather than "either/or." In patterns that change through the life course, we usually seek both engagement and separation — in different activities and settings and at different times. Leisure is multidimensional, not monothematic. Further, the balance shifts as we and our lives change. Most people do not seek just one kind of activity to the exclusion of all others, but do a variety of things in a variety of ways.

Social factors, then, reflect both external factors such as resources and opportunities as well as different sets of relationships and roles. They may be indexed by demographic categories that give some measure of differences in socialization as well as of life circumstances. These factors may be analyzed from a number of perspectives, of which that of the life course is one of the most inclusive and useful.

LIFE STYLES: THE ETHNICITY OF LEISURE

When we focus on styles of leisure, how people act and interact rather than which activities they undertake, it becomes apparent that there is little research on the issue. William Burch (1969) offered an analysis of styles of camping that was based on observation rather than surveys. More recently, a wider spectrum of camping styles has been described from a combination of survey and observational analysis (Kelly 1987d). This range of variability in how leisure is done is based only on one activity.

Much more fundamental is the evidence that the entire mix of cultural elements shapes every aspect of leisure. Studies of the social interaction patterns of poor white urban dwellers, urban Italian families, Hispanic families, and others demonstrate how all the learned and transmitted values, modes of communication, interaction expectations, and cultural heritages make a difference in how people gather and form social events (Kelly 1982). Not only are there differences among national, regional, and religious cultures, but also among subcultures within geographical areas. Leisure, like all domains of life, is thoroughly ethnic, *in* and *of* particular cultures.

The concept of style incorporates both what people do and how they do it. The evident diversity in environments, activities, aims, and outcomes is only the beginning. Take as simple an event as a family dinner. How many are invited, the frequency and timing of the event, the foods prepared, how the eating is sequenced, where people gather in sub-groups differentiated by gender, age, marital status, and position in the family, affective behaviors and expressions of emotion and affection, topics of conversation, language conventions, and many other elements differ from one ethnic group to another. And those differences have meaning beyond the single event, as identities are presented, tested, evaluated, and reinforced or rejected.

One danger is that leisure becomes stereotyped. Stereotypes are a form of convenient classification, labels usually based on a single identifying factor. Leisure stereotypes presuppose that individuals are essentially monothematic in their leisure. The stereotype of the passive blue-collar worker or the aesthetic professor, the "jock" or the artist, suggests that they devote most or all of their leisure to one kind of pursuit. It is true that there are those who are quite single-minded in their leisure engagement. They hone the skills of an activity, fashion their social relationships around its groupings, and define themselves in terms of that leisure identification. Such "amateurs," however, are exceptions to the majority core-plus-balance patterns. Their focused commitment is remarkable, partly because it is extraordinary. It is no surprise to find that research on such devotees begins with the special group rather than with population samples (Stebbins 1979).

One particular research methodology for a time threatened to produce an artifactual analysis. Factor analysis that grouped recreation participants according to the sets of activities that differentiated them was employed to delineate varieties of leisure styles. Factors were based on commonalities in participation beyond those that were common to most of a sample. Early results seemed to indicate that "status-based," "sports," "water-based," "backwoods," and even "fast living" might characterize the leisure of identifiable aggregates of people.

A number of assumptions, however, were being overlooked. Different samples produced different factors (Schmitz-Scherzer *et al.* 1974). Heterogeneous lists of activities did not produce the same neat categories as more limited sets (Kelly 1983b). In fact, often the same activities were found in different factors from one sample to another. There were several reasons for these discrepancies. First, individuals have leisure patterns that involve engagement across factors. Stereotyping individuals according to a single factor is misleading. Second, many activities that rank highest on frequency and duration of time do not enter the factors at all. These informal and accessible activities, the "core" already discussed, do not differentiate sets of participants just because they are most common. Yet, to ignore television, reading, and informal socializing when typologies are formulated requires fixing on the occasional at the expense of the ordinary.

This does not mean that there are no single-minded individuals who pursue a "high risk" sport, fine arts production, or some social organization to the exclusion of almost all else. Nor does it mean that there are no significant differences in leisure styles, in how people do what they do. For most of the population, however, stereotypes are blurred by the commonalities in leisure, as well as by the relative diversity in interests and commitments through the life course.

One fundamental flaw of many leisure typologies is that they presume a segregation of leisure. That is, participation in some set of activities is analyzed as a domain of life separated from everything else. Therefore, participation alone is the subject of the analysis. This is a more serious problem even than ignoring the commonalities of the core. It returns to the old survey method of taking lists of activities as representative of the domain of leisure and assuming that all participation in each is the same. All the dimensions of motivation, satisfaction, aims, and styles are brushed aside to focus on the activity label and frequency.

Such an approach neglects both the existential and the social dimensions of leisure. The "becoming" or existential element of leisure that combines experience with decision and developmental aims is forfeited in utter concentration on what occurs in the events and episodes. The social dimension of roles and relationships that are a larger context of engagement is also excluded from the analysis. Leisure is reduced to how often individuals do certain specified activities formed into distinguishing sets. The full range of discretionary activity, tied and connected into our networks of relationships and expressing something of what we believe we are now and what we seek to become, is lost to a method that identifies one factor in differences.

The dialectic proposed at the beginning of this chapter presupposes that leisure is not a part of life separated from all else by some mystical label of "freedom" or "intrinsic motivation." Rather, it is woven into the reality of what we are as individuals and as social and cultural beings who have learned to be what we are. We do not cease to become parents, spouses, kin, lovers, workers, neighbors, friends, colleagues, rivals, or learners the moment we begin a leisure activity. We do not cease to be aggressive or hesitant, rational or emotional, confident or unsure, initiating or responsive, challenge-seeking or security-minded because we are not being paid to do something. The developing and the social self go with us everywhere, including into leisure. To follow the meanings of leisure requires that, at the very least, we come equipped with the questions and the tools of developmental and social psychology and of sociology, inclusively defined.

One summary statement may suffice if we take it in the fullness of its ramifications: leisure is ethnic. That is, it is behavior learned in particular cultures and sub-cultures. It is interpreted in the symbols and language forms of a culture, studied with the methods accepted in salient disciplines, carried out with the forms accepted and provided in a particular social context, and evaluated with the value systems learned in actual social institutions. It is separate from nothing that significantly affects our lives. It is integrated into the full fabric of life, of all that we are and seek to become.

SOURCES OF LEISURE STYLES

One current cliche is that "it's a multivariate world out there." That is surely the case with leisure. Viewed simply from a methodological perspective, narrowing leisure explanation to a few variables that fit neatly into a research method, any method, is deceptive. Truncated designs, no matter how sophisticated the statistical programs employed or how accepted the instrumentation, cannot encompass the variegated reality of leisure.

The limitations in the number of variables that can be included in a single analysis is matched by the sketchiness of most measures. For example, an estimate of household income is used to represent all the complexities of a household budget. Ranked occupational status is said to index the full history of employment and its meanings. Marital status and family life cycle are purported to measure all the variations of family responsibilities and investments. And one or a few scaled items summarize all that makes up satisfaction with the complex dimensions and domains of life. Further, one-time measures are assumed to give an adequate picture of the process of life, with all its transitions and traumas.

It's not just a matter of a somewhat more inclusive methodology or an improved method of analysis. Rather, every research method only touches on the phenomenon, gives a biased picture, and leaves out more than can be included. That is why we always need "triangulation," not only of measures, but also of designs and strategies. Good research design can never forego skepticism and self-criticism.

Research, however, is only the beginning. The more fundamental question is that of leisure as a phenomenon. As already suggested, leisure is multidimensional. It is existential in being developmental, processual, and individual. It is social in being historical, cultural, and contextual. As a consequence, when we attempt to account for leisure behaviors and styles, we select perspectives that focus on some elements to the exclusion of others. Our research-based explanations are always incomplete.

What, then, are the sources of leisure styles and behaviors?

First, we recognize that we are dealing with "how" as well as "what," with "why" as well as "where" and "when."

Second, leisure is a phenomenon of the actor. It is action in the sense of being intentioned as well as responsive, directed as well as determined by opportunities and resources. As each individual is always in the process of becoming, the directions of development, as well as the self-images, self-definitions, and social identities of the present, are part of leisure decisions and meanings. There is always a tension between being and becoming, between what we perceive ourselves to be and what we seek to become. In this sense, leisure is action, not in the simple sense of just doing an activity but in the fuller sense of expressing what we are and aiming towards what we might become. The state of consciousness of the immediate experience is central to the meaning that reaches back into the past of personal history and forward into the future of becoming.

Third, leisure is a social phenomenon. The forms and interpretations of leisure are given in a historical context. They have developed in ways that are specific to a culture and its traditions. They are tied to the ecology and the economy, to the polity and religion, to learning in the school and the home. Not only what is done, but how and why, are thoroughly ethnic, learned in the realities of a cultural time and place. Further, leisure is social not only in involving other people but in having orientations that are connected with the values, traditions, symbol systems, and all that are part of our learned evaluative and conceptualizing processes. Leisure is never separate from the social institutions of the social system and the roles that actors play in them. Therefore, those social ties influence the behaviors and styles of leisure.

Life, then, is both complex and connected, both diverse and integrated. Leisure is not different from other identified domains of life in this way. Rather it is one element of life, distinguished by its relative openness and lack of pre-specification of outcome. It is a life space that offers particular opportunity for existential action. However, it is also a dimension that may be found in the work, family, school, church, and other institutional contexts of life. It is different, but not separate. As a consequence, we cannot list any set of factors that determine leisure styles and behaviors, select indices of those factors, and run them through any program of analysis to give the final and complete word of explanation.

Such a perspective is both sobering and challenging. Although there may be no "magic bullet" in our computers that will do it all, there is the challenge of complexity. There is always the task of bringing together dimensions of leisure in different ways, both complicated and parsimonious, that give a new and useful view of the phenomena. Further, the target is always moving. Leisure is constantly changing in a socio-cultural context that is in flux. No final word is possible, since we are always dealing with what was in the past rather than the truly contemporaneous.

Such a view leads to limitless agendas for research and theory-building. Nothing is settled with finality. Rather, any approach that even begins to be adequate for delimited questions takes something like the following form:

- First, the theory, model, or metaphor (Kelly 1987a) on which the attempt at explanation is based is identified and relevant limitations specified.
- Second, previous research and explanation are critically reviewed, not as a listing of references, but as an analysis of what is known and how that knowledge is limited or contains contradictions.
- Third, a research approach is selected and presented in ways that are as clear about what is not done as about what is done.

- Fourth, the results are offered as a contribution to explanation, rather than as discrete findings with some derivative "implications."
- Fifth, the building, deconstruction, or revision of the theory metaphor adopted is attempted in the light of what has been discovered.

The field, then, is not ruled by methods or by conventions. It is not closed off to innovation by what is taught or accepted at any level. Accounting for leisure behaviors and styles, then, is not just doing more and doing it better. Finality does not wait for that super-measure or supreme statistical package. Rather, real contributions to understanding begin with the complex actions and meanings that are labeled leisure and recreation. Leisure and research are both dialectical, both multidimensional, and both without final resolution. And isn't that what makes the enterprise of leisure research and theory intriguing?

References

Bacon, W. 1975. "Leisure and the alienated worker." *Journal of Leisure Research* 7: 179-190.

Berger, P. and T. Luckman. 1966. *The Social Construction of Reality*. New York: Penguin Books.

Burch, W.R. Jr. 1965. "The play world of camping: Research into the social meaning of outdoor recreation." *American Journal of Sociology* 69: 604-612.

Cheek, N. and W.R. Burch, Jr. 1976. *The Social Organization of Leisure in Human Society*. New York: Harper and Row.

Csikszentmihalyi, M. 1981. "Leisure and socialization." *Social Forces 60:* 332-340.

Field, D.R. and J.T. O'Leary. 1973. "Social groups as a basis for assessing participation in selected water activities." *Journal of Leisure Research 5:* 16-25.

Hollingshead, A. 1949. *Elmtown's Youth*. New York: John Wiley.

Kelly, J.R. 1980. "Outdoor recreation participation: A comparative analysis." *Leisure Sciences 3:* 129-154.

Kelly, J.R. 1983a. *Leisure Identities and Interactions*. London: George Allen and Unwin.

Kelly, J.R. 1983b. "Leisure styles: a hidden core." *Leisure Sciences 5:* 321-338.

Kelly, J.R. 1986. "Commodification of leisure: Trend or tract?" *Loisir et Société 10:* 455-476.

Kelly, J.R. 1987a. *Freedom to Be: A New Sociology of Leisure*. New York: Macmillan.

Kelly, J.R. 1987b. *Recreation Trends Toward the Year 2000*. Champaign, IL: Management Learning Laboratories.

Kelly, J.R. 1987c. *Peoria Winter: Styles and Resources in Later Life*. Boston: Lexington Books, D.C. Heath.

Kelly, J.R. 1987d. "Parks and people: what do we know?" In *Proceedings of the Conference on Science in the National Parks, 1986*. R. Hermann and T. Bostedt-Craig, eds. Ft. Collins, CO: The U.S. National Park Service and the George Wright Society.

Kreps, J. 1968. *Lifetime Allocation of Work and Leisure*. Report No. 22. Washington, DC: U.S. Department of Health, Education, and Welfare.

Linder, S. 1970. *The Harried Leisure Class*. New York: Columbia University Press.

Lundberg, G. *et al.* 1934. *Leisure: A Suburban Study*. New York: Columbia University Press.

Lynd, H. and R. Lynd. 1956. *Middletown*. New York: Harcourt Brace Jovanovich.

Miller, K. and M. Kohn. 1982. "The reciprocal effects of job conditions and leisure-time activities." Paper presented at the 10th World Congress of Sociology, Mexico City.

Parker, S. 1971. *The Future of Work and Leisure*. New York: Praeger.

Parker, S. 1983. *Leisure and Work*. London: George Allen and Unwin.

Rapoport, R. and R.N. Rapoport. 1975. *Leisure and The Family Life Cycle*. Boston: Routledge and Kegan Paul.

Schmitz-Scherzer, R., G. Rudinger, A. Angleitner, and D. Bierhoff-Alfermann. 1974. "Notes on a factor analysis comparative study of the structure of leisure activities in four different samples." *Journal of Leisure Research 6:* 77-83.

Smigel, E. 1963. *Work and Leisure*. New Haven: College and University Books.

Snepenger, D. and J. Crompton. 1985. "A review of leisure participation models based on the level of discourse taxonomy." *Leisure Sciences 7:* 443-466.

Stebbins, R. 1979. *Amateurs: On the Margin Between Work and Leisure*. Beverly Hills: Sage Publications.

Torbert, W. 1973. *Being for the Most Part Puppets*. Cambridge: Schenkman Books.

Wilensky, H. 1963. "The uneven distribution of leisure: The impact of economic growth on free time. In *Work and Leisure*, ed. E. Smigel. New Haven: College and University Press.

Zuzanek, J. and R. Mannell. 1983. "Work-leisure relationships from a sociological and social psychological perspective." *Leisure Studies* 2: 327-344.

CONCEPTS AND MEASURES OF LEISURE PARTICIPATION AND PREFERENCE

Janet E. Stockdale

INTRODUCTION

Aims and Methods of Leisure Research

Leisure is now accepted as an identifiable research area, but its diversity and consequent fragmentary nature raise important questions about the fundamental aims of leisure research and the methods that should be used to achieve them. The understanding of leisure behavior requires an integrated interdisciplinary approach which uses contrasting parent disciplines as a source of strength rather than of weakness (see Burdge's chapter, this volume). This requires open-mindedness and intellectual curiosity from leisure researchers with respect to theoretical perspectives and empirical orientations. If leisure research is to be regarded as a scholarly topic with the capacity for making a major contribution to our understanding of an important area of human behavior, then certain criteria must be fulfilled.

      First, the major research questions which will aid our explanation and prediction of leisure behavior in all its facets and of the role of leisure in people's lives must be identified. It is imperative that leisure researchers, irrespective of the disciplines from which their interest in leisure originates, reach some consensus about the aims and objectives of leisure research, if it is to provide a cohesive and synthetic body of knowledge. This demands not only that researchers consider more carefully their research aims but also that they provide a theoretical basis for their research. A major criticism of leisure research is that the majority of reported empirical studies are atheoretical, lacking any linkage of the central concepts under examination to an explicit theory (cf. Riddick, DeSchriver, and Weissinger 1984). If leisure research is to progress beyond a collection of interesting but dissociated and sometimes trivial findings to a systematic and integrated analysis of leisure, its antecedents and consequences, then research must be firmly grounded in theory.

The emphasis on a sound theoretical basis does not imply that any one discipline is better suited than another to the analysis of leisure. The questions which need to be answered if we are to understand leisure may fruitfully be identified and tackled by researchers originating in a range of different disciplines (see Jackson and Burton's opening chapter). However, the potential benefits of diverse perspectives will only be realized if empirical research is convergent. This does not imply the loss of freedom for leisure researchers, nor does it imply a uniformity of methodological approach or unit of analysis. What convergence *does* imply is explicit and coherent theorizing about the nature and origins of leisure behavior, and empirical studies that will enhance our understanding of leisure and which will reveal how adequately our explanations and predictions fit the real world.

A second and related criterion concerns the methodological adequacy of leisure research. There are several facets of methodology which deserve attention: choice of method and its implementation; the unit of analysis and its measurement; and the technique of data analysis. Some of the methodological issues have been raised by Riddick *et al.* (1984). In their view, not only does leisure research suffer from chronic measurement problems, but a bias toward survey research methods and scarcity of alternative methodologies results in a leisure literature lacking in depth and richness. Furthermore, many researchers fail to report critical methodological information, which hinders comparison across studies and the development of a reliable body of knowledge. Methodological adequacy should not be equated with assigning priority to methodological predilection over theory. Methodology and statistical analyses are integral parts of the research process, but the research questions must come first. The research and analytic techniques are important only insofar as they provide the means of answering these questions.

Objectives

The objectives of this chapter are wide-ranging, but all reflect concerns about the current status and future directions of leisure research. The first is to provide an overview of definitions of leisure and some of the key concepts used in analyzing leisure behavior. A second and related objective is to highlight some of the conceptual and methodological problems by providing an analysis of how certain key concepts have been operationalized in empirical studies of leisure. The analysis focuses on the uncertain relations among theory, methods, and data and, in particular, raises the "quantity-quality" problem which pervades leisure research. A third aim is to outline an integrative framework — the theory of social representations — within which to examine such fundamental questions as: "What is leisure?" and "How do people perceive leisure and what is its meaning?" A recurrent theme throughout the chapter is the argument that complementary and potentially convergent techniques should be used in the analysis of leisure in order to understand the meaning of leisure, participation patterns, and preferences. Finally, there is an attempt to outline a possible research agenda and a menu of methodological approaches which would further our understanding of leisure behavior in the context of economic, technological, and social change and encourage rapprochement across disciplinary divides.

LEISURE AND RECREATION: THEORETICAL APPROACHES AND DEFINITIONAL ISSUES

An Overview

Leisure is an elusive concept. The word is widely used, but is probably more frequent in the vocabularies of researchers, policy makers, planners, and politicians than in the vocabulary of leisure consumers. Leisure has positive connotations of enjoyment, freedom of choice, self-fulfillment, and self-actualization, yet is seen as a problem in the context of the social change demanded by a postindustrial society. Changing patterns of work, and the declining dependence on paid work as a means of organizing one's life and that of one's family, make it inappropriate to consider leisure as time free from work, when one is free to choose what to do. Equally, it is inappropriate to consider work only as a job for which one is paid. Over half the population — dependent children, housewives, the retired, the unemployed, students — are not in paid employment and therefore are not included in the conceptual boundaries of such a definition of leisure. (The importance of examining women's experience of leisure is highlighted elsewhere in this book by Bella, and the role of leisure in the lives of the unemployed is analyzed by Glyptis). Such considerations have forced us to re-examine existing views of leisure, the work-leisure relationship, and the factors affecting leisure choice.

Three essential meanings of leisure are identifiable from an analysis of popular definitions. Leisure is seen as a period of time, as an activity, and as a state of mind. Of these, the most prevalent view of leisure has been as a period of time which is often described synonymously as "free time." Neulinger (1980) draws a critical distinction between subjective (or psychological) conceptualizations of leisure, which view leisure as a state of mind, and objective (or residual or sociological) conceptualizations, which view leisure as something else, be it time or activity.

Objective or "residual" definitions typically focus on the antithesis between work and leisure, but they vary as a function of their conception of work and the extent to which all non-work can be seen as leisure (e.g. Kelly 1972; Parker 1971). Subjective definitions of leisure have their origins in the writings of ancient Greece, and more recently such ideas have emerged in the writings of DeGrazia (1962), Pieper (1963), Neulinger (1974, 1976, and 1981), Iso-Ahola (1980), Mannell (1980), Harper (1981) and Kelly (1983). Current subjective definitions vary in their scope. Whilst some definitions emphasize the quality of an activity or the state of mind of the individual engaging in the activity, others attempt to be holistic and comprehensive. Such definitions characteristically attempt to integrate notions of work, discretionary time, freedom, contemplation, and the achievement of satisfaction by the individual. A frequently quoted example of this form of definition is that offered by Kaplan (1960), who lists seven essential elements of leisure, and argues that leisure is none of these by itself, but all together in one emphasis or another. While definitions such as that given by Kaplan may more than adequately encompass leisure, their complexity reduces their value as a practical vehicle for debate, and they often defy translation into measurable variables within leisure research. Furthermore, a dichotomous concept of work and leisure, combined with an emphasis on freedom from obligation, make the concept of leisure meaningless to women with family responsibilities (see Bella's chapter).

Recreation presents us with similar conceptual ambiguities and definitional problems. Whilst retaining connotations of restoration and renewal for work, and of purpose and social acceptability, the pragmatic and realistic approach of leisure planners and providers has led to recreation being equated with those activities in which people participate during their leisure. Such a view presupposes that what constitutes leisure can be identified. However, as Tork-ildsen (1983) points out, this traditional view of leisure is heavily slanted in pre-conceived directions, such that, for many people, recreation is synonymous with physical recreation and sport. The activity approach does offer a number of practical advantages: ease of identifying who participates in what activity, where, when, for how long and how often. However, the activity approach essentially ignores questions of need, motivation, satisfaction, attitude, experi-ence, and choice. Analysis of recreation in terms of activities frequently assumes that supply determines preferences — and sometimes that supply will generate demand — and causes providers to assume that they are providing for recreation by providing for activities, without any knowledge of whether those activities are the most appropriate and whether they are meeting people's needs. The approach encourages planners to base projections of demand on past types and rates of participation and does not question what latent preferences are not being met.

The contrasting view of recreation as experience has the advantage of recognizing the potential power of the psychological response to an activity as an analytic tool in unravelling the meaning of both leisure and recreation, but has the major disadvantage of making it difficult, if not impossible, for the rec-reation practitioner to define it operationally. Experience does not easily generate tangible criteria on which to base planning and management decisions. The issue of a subjective versus an objective definition, of experience versus activity, underlies discussions of both leisure and recreation. As I shall argue later, the adoption of a broader theoretical framework means that both approaches are equally valid, the choice of approach depending on what the researcher is trying to examine. The issue at this juncture is whether we need the dual concepts of leisure and recreation. On the one hand, it can be argued that the similarities outweigh the differences — both leisure and recreation can be described in terms of either activity or experience — and that equating the two concepts offers both conceptual simplicity and operational convenience. This view implies that preference for one or other of the two terms appears to reflect researcher orientation — upbringing, training, and current affiliation and job demands — rather than a valid distinction. At one level, this does reflect the status of the two terms. On the other hand, if one takes the view that leisure and recreation are different concepts, then failure to distinguish between the two reflects imprecision on the part of the researcher. In my view, leisure and recreation *do* differ in terms of their range of applicability and in the role that they play in our social world. Recreation has certain attributes in common with leisure, but is not identical with it. For example, recreation lacks the time dimension that is clearly evidenced in the definition of leisure as free time. Moreover, the meanings that we attach to leisure and recreation are subtly different, and therefore the activities that have the potential to provide the experience of leisure or that of recreation are not necessarily the same.

One interpretation of recreation is as a social institution, reflecting the provision of facilities and organization of programmes and activities to meet the leisure needs of a community. These facilities and organizations may be funded by the public or private sector, by voluntary agencies, or other social or community bodies, but all share the aim of meeting an expressed need to use leisure time in a responsible and socially acceptable way. These connotations are a less salient feature of leisure, although there is a trend to institutionalize leisure, with increased commercial provision of leisure facilities.

The differences between leisure and recreation are important in some contexts but trivial in others. If one is concerned with finding out the currency that the terms "leisure" and "recreation" have within a society, then their meanings become the object of study. However, for the planner whose task it is to set priorities for the future, it is of less consequence whether the activities are described as constituting leisure or recreation.

Key Concepts

Theoretically, the leisure experience is available to everyone and may be achieved through participation in a wide range of activities. Equally, it is clear that individuals express preferences for certain activities over others, and also that a variety of factors has the potential to constrain — or to facilitate — an individual's choice of leisure activities from those which are ostensibly available to him or her. The list of studies that have examined the relationship between resource availability, cultural and social influences, personal characteristics, and leisure behavior is extensive. Fewer studies have focused on the relationship between these variables and leisure preference or that between leisure preference and choice.

The list of factors which have the potential to affect leisure choice is daunting, especially as it is likely that they interact in a complex fashion. Money, time, and the physical location of facilities are prime examples of resource factors. Cultural and social norms and expectations associated with gender, age, ethnic origin, social status, family structure, and stage of life cycle affect both leisure socialization and current leisure choice. An individual's personality characteristics, motivations, and attitudes further complicate the picture.

Green *et al.* (1980) group the plethora of factors which support or inhibit leisure satisfaction, either directly or indirectly via their effects on leisure-related behavior, into three groups: predisposing, enabling, and reinforcing factors. Predisposing factors are related to the motivation of an individual or group to act, and include such variables as age, gender, knowledge of leisure opportunities, and leisure values. Enabling factors relate to the resources available to an individual, such as money. Reinforcing factors, such as stress, affect the satisfaction that individuals derive from their leisure lifestyle.

The growing interest over the past decade in the antecedents and consequences of non-participation in leisure and recreation is reflected in the growth of research focusing on leisure constraints. As Jackson (1988) points out, although the bulk of the leisure constraints literature is empirical, more recent papers raise conceptual and management issues. This development reflects the growing awareness of the potential offered by examining leisure constraints and non-participation. As well as providing a means of assessing latent demand and the adequacy of recreation delivery systems, they are key concepts in analyses of leisure behavior (Jackson and Dunn 1988). Recognition of the impact of constraints on leisure decision-making processes has led to the emergence of models of their nature and influence (e.g. Crawford and Godbey 1987; Godbey 1985; Iso-Ahola and Mannell 1985; Jackson and Searle 1985; see also Goodale and Witt, this volume). Such conceptualizations can also provide a valuable framework for considering the methodologies used to examine the factors affecting leisure choice (Stockdale 1987).

Such analyses raise questions about the model we assume underlies leisure choice, the relations between concepts such as demand and preference, and the inferences that can be drawn from participation measures and other indices of leisure consumption. A distinction between preference and participation is implicit in our recognition of the wide range of influences which affect leisure choice. The underlying model is one in which a variety of factors act first to delineate a set of leisure preferences for the individual, and then to constrain or facilitate expression of those preferences in observed behavior. Participation cannot be assumed to reflect preference alone, and neither should it be assumed to reflect demand accurately. Typically, however, demand studies simply project past consumption, by combining examination of past participation in a set of given opportunities with an estimate of future growth rate. The failure to recognize that participation is a function of the user's opportunity, time, and money means that demand studies have contributed little information about the actual preferences of the population. Measures of participation are incomplete indices of both preference and demand (cf. Jackson and Dunn 1988). Surveys of preference can provide useful information about latent demand and gaps in current provision, but there will always be a mismatch between expressed preference and actual participation, between the ideal and the real world.

Despite the inadequacy of participation as a measure of demand, the concept of demand plays a key role in economic analyses of leisure-related behavior, on which there is an extensive literature. (An analysis of the contributions of economics to the study of leisure is provided by Vickerman (1983) and elsewhere in this book). In particular, the desire to estimate demand for particular facilities is an important factor underlying the analysis of consumer choice in economic terms. Clearly, individuals choose their leisure activities within the range of opportunities available to them, and leisure expenditure competes with other forms of consumer expenditure for the individual's or family's disposable income.

Vickerman (1983) outlines the development of consumer choice analysis from demand curve estimation, through discrete choice models, to the analysis of subjective elements in demand, and the contribution of cost-benefit evaluation to the understanding of leisure behavior. Such analyses encounter a number of difficulties. For example, the data available consist of the outcome of people's choices about their patterns of leisure activity in the market situation. However, as Vickerman points out, this cannot be taken as representing the demand for an activity or entity at the going price, since it ignores any other factors which affect the attainment of equilibrium between supply and demand in the market. Moreover, economic models are difficult to apply to the more diffuse categories of leisure behavior, such as social activity or entertainment. This has led to a concentration of research on leisure activities with more easily identifiable costs and benefits, specifically outdoor recreation activities. This activity bias, which also characterizes spatial analyses of supply and demand (cf. Coppock 1982; Smith, this volume), encourages a restricted view of the activity domain that should be studied empirically.

RESEARCH ISSUES

The Empirical Analysis of Leisure

What functions do empirical studies of leisure serve? At one level, they provide a body of knowledge about the domain of study, that both describes the phenomena which constitute leisure and informs the construction of theory. Empirical studies are also the means by which theoretical conceptualizations may be refined and models of leisure behavior tested. For those whose job it is to plan leisure provision, the findings of empirical studies provide the rationale for planning decisions. The implications of certain findings also extend outside the domains of leisure and recreation, in that they inform our view of society, its values, and direction of change. At another level, a somewhat cynical view might argue that some empirical studies merely serve the career needs of researchers. Then there are functions that particular types of research may fulfil. For example, some survey and interview research, if properly used, allows leisure consumers to make their views felt and so has the potential to inform and influence decisions about leisure provision.

The different and often conflicting concerns of researchers, providers, policy makers, and consumers have given rise to a substantial body of data about leisure. However, it is less clear that the enthusiasm for data collection has been matched by a predilection for theoretical development. The evolution of leisure research has given rise to a disjunction between theory and data. Theories about the nature of leisure clearly do exist, but those theories which attempt to do justice to the complexities of leisure are difficult, if not impossible, to use as a basis for data collection. The "theories" addressed in other empirical studies are often so specific that they are better described as ideas about certain features of leisure or correlates of leisure behavior rather than as theories in the explanatory sense. Then there are the data gatherers who do not attempt to provide any theoretical rationale for their work.

The separation of theory and data leads to the paradox that leisure research is both atheoretical and theory-laden. On the one hand, a substantial proportion of leisure research is not embedded within a well-developed theory with explicit assumptions. On the other, the wealth of data about leisure testifies to the existence of implicit assumptions about what constitutes leisure and models of human behavior (see Rojek's chapter). Both researchers and consumers inevitably construct a view of leisure which pervades the research process. It is important that the theory-laden nature of leisure research is made explicit, with researchers making clear the assumptions underlying their choice of research question, terminology, data collection method, and methodological and analytical techniques, and consumers having the opportunity to reveal their views of leisure.

The Measurement of Leisure Participation and Choice

Dominant questions in leisure research are: Who does what and how often? What factors affect leisure preference and choice? Is leisure demand predictable? Leisure participation has been described in terms of frequency, duration, and expenditure. Similarly, studies which have focused on leisure resources and facilities have described usage and user characteristics in terms of number of visitors, number and frequency of visits, cost and length (time and distance) of journey. Many of these descriptive studies have also collected data relating to the demographic or psychological profiles of leisure participants or site visitors.

The major research instrument for gathering data remains the survey questionnaire or interview. Examples of such research in the UK include surveys of leisure and recreational participation in general, surveys of specific categories of users, such as occupiers of second homes (Coppock 1977) or visitors to particular areas, such as the coast (e.g. Duffield 1979). Time budget studies represent another important tool in monitoring the "who," "what," "when," and "where" of leisure activity. Time-budget research encompasses a variety of different approaches which together represent a popular method of securing a record of leisure and recreation activities based on people's accounts of their own activities. As Gershuny and Jones (1987) point out, time budget research has a long history. Furthermore, it has been widely used, with at least fifty national studies having been carried out in at least twenty countries, including the twelve-nation study (Szalai 1972). These approaches have been supplemented by observational studies, field inspections, and other methodologies designed to address specific research areas, such as landscape evaluation or the impact of recreation on the countryside.

Both surveys of leisure participation and time budget studies have repeatedly demonstrated a relationship between measures of participation and resource utilization and a variety of demographic, personal, social, and psychological variables. The analysis of correlational patterns between socio-demographic variables (such as social class, occupation, income, car-ownership, education, gender, and marital status) and leisure participation patterns may be traced back to the ORRRC studies of the early 1960s, and the bias toward this kind of analysis has remained a dominant feature of leisure research. The collection of participation data by means of surveys or time use studies and descriptive and simple correlational analyses of such data are clearly important components in the early stages of leisure research, when there is an obvious need to build up a body of "facts." However, there are grounds for questioning whether descriptions of leisure behavior patterns and the socio-demographic characteristics of participants should continue to occupy the dominant position that they have done in the past.

If our ultimate aim is to explain and predict leisure choice, then we cannot afford to rely solely on non-articulated but essentially descriptive models and *ex post facto* analysis. Irrespective of whether our motivation to explain leisure choice arises from our desire to understand this important aspect of human behavior or the more practical need to plan for leisure provision, we must adopt a theory-driven rather than a data-driven approach which reflects our concern with predictive validity. Gershuny and Jones (1987) suggest that the lack of appropriate theories is one of the reasons why the contribution of time budget research has rarely extended beyond a descriptive level. They point out that we have, as yet, no adequate theorizing about the determination of time use patterns and, in their view, perhaps even more importantly, there have been few theoretical applications of time use information.

The extensive use of socio-demographic variables in leisure research offers an example of the way research can be data-driven and leads to a "bottom-up" rather than a "top-down" approach. Socio-demographic variables are not sufficient to predict and explain leisure choice. Even if one accepts the view that socio-demographic variables are relevant to decisions about leisure choice, it is difficult to imagine them acting singly. However, the examination of relationships between socio-demographic variables and leisure participation is often restricted to a series of unidimensional tables detailing participation rates by age, social class, etc. When such factors are examined in combination, there is evidence that socio-demographic characteristics are related in different combinations and in different degrees to participation in different activities. Moreover, socio-demographic variables, although commonly described as "predicting" leisure choice, frequently account for only a small percentage of the variance in leisure participation rates (e.g. Kelly 1980 and this book).

Socio-demographic variables alone offer, at best, a crude description of individual differences, sampling only some of the potential influences on leisure choice at a gross level of analysis. Although it may be possible to describe some differences in leisure participation profiles in terms of socio-demographic differences, any claim that they explain leisure choice is illusory. The ability of socio-demographic variables to act as surrogates for, or operational indicators of, the factors that constrain or facilitate the expression of leisure preference in the selection of activities is doubtful. Furthermore, the lack of equivalence between socio-demographic variables and the factors which enter into decisions about leisure participation is likely to become even more marked with changes in the composition of the workforce, work patterns, and economic priorities within the household and less stereotyped role expectations associated with gender, social class, and educational level. It is important that we recognize and attempt to measure the meaning and significance of leisure in people's lives and the range of resource, social-personal, and social-cultural factors that shape leisure choice.

The Quantity-Quality Problem

A move away from a "bottom-up" approach which is essentially atheoretical toward a "top-down" approach based on explicit theorizing raises a number of questions about the way in which leisure-related behavior, its antecedents, and its outcomes should be operationalized and measured. Questionnaire and interview surveys, the majority of which focus on the more easily measurable aspects of behavior, and frequently use pre-coded response categories and activity checklists, clearly impose certain constraints on respondents. As well as defining the activity boundaries of leisure and its subdivisions, the survey typically reduces the individual to a static entity lacking a personal, social, and cultural context. In contrast, time budget studies, which in theory provide an accurate, detailed, and exhaustive record of how individuals spend the total time resources available to them, should provide the basis for both generation and testing of theory about the nature of leisure and its role in people's lives. However, the methodological problems inherent in such studies are substantial, and these have reduced the impact of this type of research on leisure theory (cf. Gershuny and Jones 1987).

The major problem, which I refer to as the "quantity-quality problem," arises as follows. When the research instrument is designed to provide sound quantitative data, it is easy to lose the essential richness of an individual's leisure experience and the diversity of people's leisure lives. When the research instrument tries to capture these complexities, it can be difficult to analyze responses systematically, because the description of the activities is usually in the hands of the respondents themselves. Thus, there are biases toward quantity as opposed to quality, and vice versa. For example, the time budget method has obvious advantages over the constraints imposed by a pre-coded activity questionnaire, but coding free-response data satisfactorily is a complex and laborious task. It is necessary to classify the activities without losing the great variety of responses, whilst providing a basis for comparison among classes of individuals. However, such coding procedures are based implicitly, if not explicitly, on a model of what constitutes leisure.

The desire both to allow respondents as much freedom as possible in describing their experience and activities, and at the same time to find ways of quantifying concepts and relationships, is a dilemma that pervades leisure research. For example, the quantity-quality problem is relevant to multivariate analyses of the attributes of leisure which typically employ a restricted set of stimuli and response options, and to qualitative studies of the meaning of leisure and related life domains which attempt to exploit the richness inherent in people's own descriptions. Furthermore, the necessity to generate data which will permit the rigorous testing of complex relationships and models of leisure behavior and choice, whilst doing justice to the diversity that constitutes leisure, underlies the methodological debate in leisure research and provides the rationale for the use of complementary methods. The quantity-quality issue has further implications for time budget and other research approaches which attempt to capture the richness of people's leisure lifestyles. For example, the diversity of people's lifestyles and the range of circumstances in which they live mean that large sample sizes are needed to provide sufficient data at an aggregated level for clear patterns to emerge and for meaningful sub-sample comparisons.

One of the ways that time budget research has been used is in analyses of the balance between work and leisure in people's lives. However, the quantity-quality problem also affects this application of time use data. A fundamental aim of these analyses is to determine whether work and leisure are valued equally or whether one is more important than the other. Comparative data concerning the balance between work and leisure have also been used to support the contention that attitudes to work and leisure are changing and that they differ from country to country. These questions have acquired greater salience with the advent of structural unemployment and its attendant consequence of enforced free time, and with the assumption that, for many workers, leisure is increasing as a result of changes in the working week, the amount of paid holiday, and the retirement age, as well as more subtle changes arising from such factors as the availability of household gadgets and the advent of convenience foods. It must be emphasized, however, that for the unemployed, free time cannot necessarily be equated with leisure (Kelvin and Jarrett 1985). Furthermore, the perception of society as leisured may be illusory rather than real (cf. Hunt 1981; Shipley 1980); where an increase in non-work time does exist, it may not be translatable into the positive experience which we label as leisure.

Appraisals of the balance between work and leisure rely primarily on analyses of working hours, the size and composition of the work force, and expenditure patterns. Such analyses typically take as their premise a residual definition of leisure and a narrow definition of work, which is frequently equated with paid employment. As Neulinger (1981) points out, the research questions which would emerge from a subjective conceptualization of leisure would be very different. Analyses of time budget or expenditure data, for example, use time and money as objective indicators of value. These indicators provide the basis for inferences about the role that leisure plays in people's lives and its importance relative to work. However, in failing to take account of constraints, such as availability of resources and possession of skills, such measures cannot be regarded as indicating subjective value and preference.

Questions concerning social change and cultural differences, when considered in the light of Szalai's cross-national study and other studies (e.g BBC 1984; Gershuny *et al.* 1986; Mercer 1985), highlight the fact that comparisons across countries or across time require the use of common research procedures and practices. In particular, inconsistency of activity classifications is a major problem for inter-temporal comparisons of time use patterns. Again, this problem reflects, in part, the quantity-quality conflict. At the micro level, the desire to provide an exhaustive and accurate account of behavior favors the collection of individual accounts, but at the macro level, the need for an aggregate description demands the imposition of a classificatory system to permit quantification. The classification schemes that emerge are frequently data-driven, inevitably reflect the purposes for which the data were collected and the researcher's grouping of leisure activities, and are therefore inconsistent across studies. Gershuny and Jones have overcome the problem by combining analysis of their own data with the secondary analysis or re-analysis of existing historical time budget material, using a common forty-category classification system. Although there have been inter-temporal time use comparisons in the USA and elsewhere (e.g. Robinson 1977), the extended time period of the UK historical time use data series, together with the fact that it is the only example which uses data from surveys originally collected for other purposes, combine to make it a powerful data resource.

Multivariate Analyses of the Attributes of Leisure

Traditionally, one popular approach to understanding the structure of leisure and its definition has relied on multivariate techniques, such as principal components, factor, and cluster analysis, which seek to identify defining features of leisure on the basis of relationships among attributes, activities, or individuals. The majority of studies focus on groupings of attributes or activities, rather than on groupings of individuals. Examples of studies which identify groupings of activities on the basis of their similarity include those by McKechnie (1974), whose factor analysis of participation in 121 activities revealed seven factors, and Bishop (1970), Burton (1971), and Witt (1971), all of whom identified different numbers of factors from sets of activities of different sizes. Cluster analysis was used by Tinsley and Kass (1978) to group ten leisure activities, and by Tinsley and Johnson (1984) to group 34 activities on the basis of their similarity across a number of need-satisfactions and psychological benefits of participation, respectively. Examples of studies which identify groupings of attributes include that by Ragheb and Beard (1982), which focused on attitudes, and that of Tinsley and Kass (1979), which examined leisure need-satisfiers.

The strategy of deriving subject groupings has been less popular, but examples of this approach include work by Duncan (1978), who used a Q-type factor analysis to search for "types" of people who exhibited similar patterns of leisure behavior across 59 activities, and by Tatham and Dornoff (1971), Romsa (1973), and Ditton, Goodale, and Johnson (1974), all of whom used cluster analysis. London, Crandall, and Fitzgibbons (1977) used three-mode factor analysis to identify the factor structure of individuals, activities, and needs and their interrelationship.

These and other studies which have attempted to derive the latent properties of leisure vary in a number of ways: the number and nature of the activities studied; the range of attributes measured; the population of individuals sampled; and the particular multivariate approach adopted. The limitations of a particular approach and the variation across studies raise questions about both the validity and generalizability of the inferences that may be drawn about the nature of leisure from this class of studies (cf. Stockdale 1987).

Procedures differ in the freedom of response they permit respondents, but they typically define either the set of leisure activities, or the attributes of leisure to be examined, or both. In some studies, subjects are asked to respond to an extensive set of activities, such as 71 activities derived from time budget data in Burton's (1971) study. In other studies, respondents are asked to focus on only one "activity." This "activity" may be leisure *per se* (e.g. Beard and Ragheb 1980, 1983; Neulinger and Breit 1969, 1971; Neulinger, Light, and Mobley 1976; Ragheb and Beard 1982); a specific activity, such as television viewing (e.g. Rubin 1981a, 1981b), mountaineering (Ewert 1985), or river recreation (Heywood 1987); a favorite leisure activity (e.g. Pierce 1980a, 1980b, 1980c); an activity about which they know most (e.g. Tinsley *et al.* 1983, 1985); or to which they they are assigned at random (e.g. Tinsley, Barratt, and Kass 1977). Moreover, some studies focus on only one aspect of leisure, such as participation (e.g Bishop 1970; Gudykunst *et al.* 1981; Witt 1971; Yu 1980), whilst others sample in varying degrees of exhaustiveness from a domain such as motivation (Beard and Ragheb 1983; Ewert 1985), need satisfaction (Tinsley and Kass 1979), descriptions and characteristics (Pierce 1980b, 1980c), attitudes (e.g. Neulinger and Breit 1969, 1971; Ragheb and Beard 1982), satisfaction (e.g. Beard and Ragheb 1980; Pierce 1980a) and psychological benefits (e.g. Tinsley and Johnson 1984; Tinsley *et al.* 1983, 1985).

A number of issues arise from the selection of attributes and activities. Although participation measures constitute a major source of data for analyses of similarity among activities, there is no logical requirement that a high correlation between two activities reflects any underlying psychological similarity. An individual may choose to participate in activities that are complementary rather than similar to or even substitutable for one another. Furthermore, low correlations between activities may not be a function of dissimilarity but may arise because participation in one activity precludes participation in another. This will occur, for example, when activities compete for the same resource, such as time, money, space, or other facilities. Hence, participation data alone may provide misleading information about the basic similarity among leisure activities, and therefore about the meaning of those activities to the participants.

A recognition of the limitations of empirical classification methods, and a call for caution in their use, should not be interpreted as meaning that such methods offer no advantages or opportunities for leisure researchers. Their application offers considerable potential benefits in both confirmatory and exploratory analyses. For example, they can provide empirical verification of intuitively derived groupings (e.g. of activities) which can provide the opportunity to draw inferences at a more general, and theoretically useful, level of analysis (e.g. Jackson 1986). Also, systematic comparison of the results derived from participation data with those derived from other attributes, such as activity preferences, perceptions, or satisfactions, can help in determining how far participation measures can be used to represent the psychological reality of leisure pursuits. Although such analyses suggest some stability in the activity groupings derived from participation and preference data (e.g. Chase and Cheek 1979), this type of convergent analysis is underrepresented in the literature.

The choice of activities is also not without its problems. For example, in many studies, the number of activities examined is too small to represent adequately the domain of leisure and is sometimes biased toward a particular type of activity (e.g. Ditton *et al.* 1974). Also, insufficient consideration is given to the comparability of studies of "leisure" *per se* and those which focus on activities.

Further problems arise in terms of the sampling procedures and the choice of multivariate method and algorithm. The dubious validity of using students in leisure research, unless one is specifically interested in the leisure life of students, has been raised elsewhere (Stockdale and Eldred 1982). There is clearly value in looking at the dimensions of leisure as they exist in "special" populations, for example adolescents, the retired, or the unemployed; but it is important that we recognize that the results may be specific to the populations considered and may not generalize to individuals without those special characteristics. The importance of interpreting dimensions of leisure in the context of the subject (and activity and attribute) samples from which they were derived is illustrated by the work of Allen, Donnelly, and Warder (1984); Chase, Kasulis, and Lusch (1980), Schmitz-Scherzer *et al.* (1974), and Yu (1985).

The choice of multivariate method will depend on, amongst other things, whether or not one conceives of the leisure domain in dimensional or typological terms, and whether or not one wants to adopt a particular statistical model. The important point is that the choice of method, or particular algorithm, and the rationale for these choices, should be made explicit.

Comparisons across the wealth of studies which aim to identify the defining attributes of leisure are made difficult by the use of different activity and attribute sets, different measurement scales, different samples, and different grouping methods. Although the results do suggest some stable groupings, they also indicate substantial variations, which are likely to reflect, at least in part, methodological and procedural variations.

Multidimensional scaling (MDS) techniques offer an alternative multivariate approach to the understanding of the dimensions of leisure. MDS refers to a family of data analysis methods (cf. Schiffman, Reynolds, and Young 1981) which enable the researcher to uncover the "hidden structure" underlying the relationships among a set of objects (e.g. leisure activities) and to represent that structure in a form that can usually be understood easily. The major advantage of these methods derives from the nature of the MDS task, which typically involves subjects judging the similarity between all possible pairs of stimuli on the basis of any criteria that they choose. In contrast with the traditional quantitative approaches, this task does not specify the attributes along which the stimuli are to be judged. This minimizes the likelihood that the dimensions that emerge reflect the researcher's choice of attributes, rather than the respondents' perceptual structure. The researcher is still faced with the problem of selecting the stimulus activities to be judged, and of identifying the dimensions that emerge from the analysis, although more objective methods exist for this than for the labelling of components, factors, or clusters.

MDS has been used primarily to examine the perceptual attributes underlying judgements of similarity. Becker (1976) and Bergier (1978) used restricted sets of activities, and so the dimensions identified cannot necessarily be generalized to all leisure activities, while both Ritchie (1975) and Stockdale (1985) used more representative activity sets. Other applications of MDS to the analysis of leisure include studies by Holbrook (1980), who re-analyzed Duncan's (1978) participation data, and Hirschman (1985), who used MDS to analyze media content preferences.

The use of multivariate techniques to identify the defining characteristics of leisure and to establish typologies of leisure activities and consumers clearly lies on the quantitative side of the quantity-quality debate. Studies which take this approach constrain respondents' views about leisure in terms of the activities which are seen to be relevant to the leisure domain, or the attributes from which the defining dimensions or groupings are expected to emerge, or both these aspects. There is variation in how far respondents are constrained — although the activity set remains of critical importance in MDS analyses, they typically offer considerable freedom of response — but all rely on the quantification of some aspect of participation in, or reaction to, a limited range of activities, which are predetermined by the researcher. There is little doubt that these applications of multivariate methods have both advantages and disadvantages. Apart from the systematic data reduction which their use can achieve, they offer the opportunity to establish empirically-based descriptions of a number of facets of leisure. However, there is a real danger that they cannot capture the amazing diversity of pursuits in which people indulge, and that they sacrifice some of the richness of the experience which leisure pursuits and occasions provide.

Qualitative Approaches to the Meaning of Leisure

Qualitative techniques have an important role to play in elucidating consumers' conceptions of leisure and related life domains. Multivariate analyses of the defining features of leisure, of the kind described above, and quasi-experimental studies of selected attributes hypothesized to be associated with leisure (e.g Iso-Ahola 1979a, 1979b; Kelly 1978) focus respondents on attributes defined by the experimenter and do not permit them to use their own conceptual framework. In contrast, the use of direct questioning and depth interviewing of respondents has allowed researchers to infer attributes which people use in defining leisure (cf. Gunter 1987; Neulinger 1981; Roadburg 1977; Shaw 1985; Stockdale 1985; Young and Willmott 1973).

The data obtained in such studies are typically referred to as qualitative, and such data are frequently compared unfavorably with quantitative data. Research which yields quantitative results is seen somehow as more respectable, as more precise, and as closer to the common understanding of science. For example, Faulkner (1982) suggests that the way that qualitative data are often analyzed and presented encourages the view that the results are preliminary or exploratory, rather than empirically-grounded findings, derived from innovative methodologies. Furthermore, they are seen as a means of generating hypotheses rather than as a means of testing them. This is seen as the task of researchers using quantitative, and, in particular, multivariate data. However, qualitative data should not be seen as merely exploratory but as a valid source of information about the meaning of leisure, in terms of both experience and the activities and times that are able to provide that experience. Howe (1985) expresses a similar view, arguing that different methods are appropriate for different situations, and that studying leisure as a meaning or experience may demand the use of a qualitative approach. This is likely to gain in popularity with the increasing emphasis on the need to examine the leisure experience systematically (cf. Gunter 1987; Mannell 1980; Tinsley and Tinsley 1986).

Qualitative data are attractive (cf. Miles and Huberman 1984). They are a source of rich descriptions and explanations of processes which are embedded in the context. Qualitative studies also have a quality of "undeniability." in that words or descriptions have a concrete, vivid, and meaningful flavor that may be more convincing to another researcher, practitioner, or policy-maker than the results of a complex multivariate analysis. However, the value of qualitative enquiry depends on the ways in which the data are collected and the methods of analysis. Qualitative studies should not be seen as immune to the issues of design and analysis that are inherent in multivariate research. The process of inferring valid meaning from qualitative data does not refer to intuitive insights based on responses from a handful of unrepresentative individuals.

Content analysis of written or spoken material is the major qualitative method that has been used to examine the meaning and experience of leisure. However, a number of those who have tried to exploit the richness of qualitative data have done little to protect themselves from methodological criticism. The quantity-quality problem again gives rise to a number of important issues. The richness of detail inherent in text precludes analysis without some form of data reduction, and the key to content analysis lies in choosing a strategy which reduces the amount of information to be analyzed, but which yields substantively interesting and theoretically useful findings. Reliability and validity are two basic quality criteria which any content analysis should seek to fulfill (cf. Krippendorf 1980). Also, Weber (1985) emphasizes that the best content analytic studies utilize both qualitative and quantitative operations on text, and thus combine what are usually thought to be antithetical modes of analysis. Examples of the possibilities provided by Weber range from detailed and quantitative analyses of word or phrase usage, or occurrence of thematic units, to the use of multivariate analyses to identify themes in the text or to relate content themes to external criteria.

Until comparatively recently, there have been relatively few attempts in the leisure field to approach qualitative data in a systematic way, or to use a combination of qualitative and quantitative methods of data collection and analysis. Shaw (1985) used discriminant analysis to determine whether attributes extracted from interviews with respondents (sixty married couples) accurately predicted whether activities were defined as leisure or non-leisure. This combination of methods represents a valuable example of the potential offered by complementary methods. However, it is a source of concern that the coding of attributes — a fundamental part of the qualitative analysis — was done by the researcher alone to avoid inter-observer reliability problems (Shaw 1985: 9). This bypasses the problem of achieving coding reliability for open-ended questions, but it does make it difficult to counter the arguments of those who raise questions of bias or experimenter contamination. Elsewhere, I have emphasized the importance of developing an explicit coding scheme in dealing with open-ended data and of achieving a reliable categorization of subjects' response (Stockdale 1985). In my analysis of responses from 120 subjects to questions about leisure, free time, and work, two coders categorized the total set of responses and a high level of inter-coder reliability was achieved. In an ideal world, one might argue for using three coders who were independent of the project, but the realities of research funding mean an ideal world is rarely achieved.

Gunter's (1987) analysis of 140 self-report essays on the leisure experience highlights another source of concern. He states that the properties of the leisure experience are simply reported in a somewhat rough order of the frequency of their appearance in the essays and the intensity with which each seemed to be held by the participants (Gunter 1987: 118). He makes his position clear. He makes no claim to scientific representativeness, either in the selection of subjects or their experiences, and he does point out that this technique for identifying the common properties of leisure experiences needs to be sharpened and used in combination with others. However, it is questionable whether all researchers who adopt this approach, one which I fully support, will recognize the importance of trying to achieve the highest possible methodological standards within the limits of funding and other aspects of the research process. The important point is that, if qualitative research is not to be seen as the poor relation, we should strive to apply the same methodological criteria that we seek to apply in quantitative research. It is important to recognize that the collection of qualitative data does not preclude quantification. Moreover, something that is perhaps obvious, but often forgotten, is that all data analysis, including the results of quantitative analyses, rests on interpretation. It is dysfunctional to consider qualitative and quantitative methods as dichotomous.

AN INTEGRATIVE FRAMEWORK

The Theory of Social Representations

In order to do justice to the complexity of leisure, it is important that it is not seen as a reified entity, separable from the social and cultural contexts which give it meaning. Rather, leisure should be regarded as an integral component of the experience and behavior of individuals who operate in the increasingly complex and changing matrix of personal and social considerations and societal expectations. This requires some consensual understanding of the world in which we live. Recent theoretical developments within social psychology in Europe illuminate the status of concepts such as leisure, free time, recreation, and work.

Moscovici (1981, 1984) describes a class of phenomena known as "social representations," which are culturally conditioned ways of understanding the everyday or "common-sense" world, and which determine the nature of social reality. The concept of social representations is derived from Durkheim's concept of collective representations, but Moscovici offers a somewhat different formulation. Rather than seeing social representations as explanatory devices, irreducible by any further analysis, they are seen as phenomena, deserving of study in their own right. Furthermore, Moscovici limits the range of applicability of the term "social representation" arguing that: "Social representations should be seen as a specific way of understanding, and communicating, what we know already. They occupy in effect a curious position, somewhere between concepts, which have as their goal abstracting meaning from the world, and introducing order into it, and percepts, which reproduce the world in a meaningful way" (Moscovici 1984: 17).

Moscovici argues that social representations are dynamic. They underlie our understanding of the world around us, and their content and structure changes and is transformed as society changes and individuals are confronted by new objects, events, and concepts. Through processes of anchoring and objectification, the unfamiliar is transformed into the familiar, such that new or ill-defined ideas become meaningful and socially significant. The nature of social representations cannot be dissociated from their purpose and the functions that they serve. They play an essential role in all social processes, by providing the shared or conventional meanings through which communication and coordinated social interaction occurs.

When applied to leisure, the social representations approach emphasizes its social and cultural construction, and its dynamic nature, incorporating societal values, images, beliefs, and myths. Representations of leisure will influence the pursuit of leisure and resource provision. They are fundamental to leisure choices and lifestyles, and to the role of leisure in society. Although expressed in different terms, Kelly presents a similar perspective in the preceding chapter, when he argues that leisure is a social phenomenon, both in terms of its context and orientations. Its forms and interpretations reflect a culture and its traditions, and it is always in the process of being created and re-created.

This new framework for examining people's beliefs and commonsense knowledge raises a number of questions of theoretical interest and practical importance for leisure studies. Do we have distinct social representations of leisure and recreation and, if so, how do they relate to representations of other life domains? How do representations of leisure and related concepts vary from one group to another? How are these representations changing in response to the profound economic, technological, and social changes that have taken place over the past decade? What methods can we use to examine the content and structure of people's representations, and how do those representations relate to behavior? An analysis of leisure and recreation in terms of social representations offers an elegant and productive means of countering some of the criticisms which were highlighted in the introduction to this chapter. Social representations provide a theoretical framework within which to examine leisure and its role in people's social lives, but which allows researchers from different disciplines to emphasize different aspects of the nature and functions of social representations.

Among recent sociological analyses of leisure, for example, Featherstone (1987) argues that leisure tastes, like other lifestyle tastes, can be related to class structure (cf. Bourdieu 1984). Featherstone aims to generate a perspective which goes beyond the familiar debate within the sociology of leisure concerning the freedom/constraint, expressive/instrumental, and autonomy/determinism polarities. Specifically, Featherstone argues that leisure choices cannot be dissociated from the broader set of lifestyle tastes which reflect the cultural expectations of the particular class or class fraction. The "same" activity may have a different significance, be stylized in different ways, and occupy a different position within the lifestyle universe of different class, occupational, gender, and age divisions. In other words, leisure choices can be understood in terms of the social representations that individuals have of leisure, recreation, and work; of individual activities that constitute potential leisure choices; and the group membership that consensual understanding imparts. Indeed, as Kelly (this volume) points out, leisure, like all domains of life, is ethnic. It is woven into the social reality we have constructed from our experience and interpretation of our culture and its sub-cultures.

From the psychologist's viewpoint, social representations offer the opportunity to examine the meaning of leisure, and to relate this to participation patterns and preferences. An emergent trend in both economic and spatial analyses of recreation behavior and leisure participation is the recognition that the analysis of leisure choice in economic terms, and of the relationships between the location and distribution of facilities and supply and demand, cannot be assessed independently of psychological factors, in which social representations play a fundamental role. The framework of social representations also offers a common language, through which disparate disciplines can inform their own theory, and a rich source of collaborative concepts. For example, as Farr (1987) points out, not only is the synthesis provided by the study of social representations a sociological form of social psychology, but it encourages rapprochement between psychology and anthropology. The framework of social representations, by encouraging cooperation and synthesis across disciplines and approaches, is particularly relevant to a topic such as leisure and recreation research, which is inherently interdisciplinary in nature.

Empirical Approaches to the Study of Social Representations

The framework of social representations has generated an increasing body of research, primarily in Europe, which has used a variety of methods in both field and laboratory-based studies (cf. Breakwell and Canter, in press; Farr and Moscovici 1984). The majority of field studies have employed complementary methods, both qualitative and quantitative, in order to observe and describe the content of social representations, their evolution and transformation, their role in behavior and social interactions, and their relationship to social and cultural circumstances. The use of complementary methodologies to examine social representations of leisure serves to highlight those attributes which emerge irrespective of the technique used and those which are made salient by a particular methodology. For example, the results of quantitative and qualitative analyses, whilst they may overlap, may not be entirely convergent, because the methods emphasize different aspects of our commonsense view of leisure.

Exploration of social representations requires research methodologies which allow the richness and complexity of people's representations to emerge, thus mirroring the complexity of the social environment and the social construction of reality. In examining social representations of leisure, it is important to allow subjects maximum freedom, both in terms of how they define the domain of leisure and the meanings they attach both to activities within that domain and the experiences they provide. All too often, leisure researchers focus on formal leisure pursuits, which constitute only a small proportion of many people's leisure time, but which tend to be overrepresented in lists of leisure pursuits because they are more readily labelled than other, less formal, behaviors. Also, their popularity is frequently over-estimated by participation figures, since such activities constitute "good" or socially acceptable leisure according to our "middle class" view of the world. In comparison, the importance of informal activities, such as "doing nothing" or "talking to one's family or friends," tends to be underestimated, either because people are reluctant to admit they indulge in such activities, or because such pursuits are not readily labelled as "activities."

Social representations also provide a framework within which to test the applicability of existing conceptualizations of leisure. For example, an analysis of people's perceptions of leisure activities and the meanings they attach to leisure, using both quantitative and qualitative methods, has indicated the importance of relaxation in social representations of leisure. Relaxation emerged as a potent definer of leisure for many people — both in London and in New York (cf. Stockdale 1985; Stockdale, Wells, and Rall, in preparation). Other important psychological attributes of leisure included freedom of choice, lack of constraint, the contrast with work, and the opportunity for enjoyment and social interaction, although the salience of these attributes varied according to personal circumstances.

Relaxation was also the major reported characteristic of the "pure" leisure experience. Over eighty percent of London subjects nominated a particular holiday, usually a summer holiday abroad in the sun, as an occasion when they felt "completely at leisure," and they described a similar set of feelings: complete relaxation; freedom from worries about work, family, or other obligations; freedom to do what you want; separation from the everyday, mundane, and routine world; and happiness and contentment.

The finding that holidays appear to constitute a major source of "pure" leisure is important in the context of social representations. Communication — the sharing of experience — is of fundamental importance in social representations, in that it serves to embed new or apparently unrelated objects, events, or concepts within a common frame of experience. Leisure activities and occasions, in particular holidays, are a major form of currency in social exchange. In my view, many current analyses of leisure do not put sufficient emphasis on the social nature of leisure, in terms of either the informal contact with others that constitutes a major part of many people's lives, or the role that this social contact serves in generating a common view of the world.

The social representation of leisure, in terms of the experience which it provides and the role that it plays in our society, is shared with other members of our culture. However, certain aspects of the representation may be more or less salient, depending on our personal and social circumstances.

It is helpful to conceive of social representations as a system of overlapping hierarchies of meanings, which move from the general to the particular, from the abstract to the concrete and, in the case of leisure, from experience to those times and activities with the potential to provide that experience. This analysis is useful in that the debate as to whether leisure is experience, time, or activity, or a combination of these, becomes irrelevant. Leisure is all of these: they represent different levels of analysis of the way that we represent leisure.

As one moves down the hierarchy from the abstract representation of leisure to the individual realization of leisure in an individual's leisure lifestyle, the nature and impact of constraints changes. At the macro-level, the way that society is structured, the political climate, the economic and social values, the nature of employment, the work ethic, and assumptions about the "wholesome" use of leisure, will be factors that constrain the way that leisure is represented. At the more micro-level, individual constraints, such as disposable income, family responsibilities, and individual beliefs will be the more potent influences. Within the framework of social representations, they are different ways of talking about the same things: we might term them "sociological" and "psychological" views of leisure. Social representations offers the prospect of integrating the views of these and other disciplines. The framework gives full recognition to the social and cultural context in which leisure is embedded: individual views are moulded by the social context and, in particular, by discussion and communication leading to a shared view of the world. It renders unimportant the stultifying debate about what leisure is and is not — leisure may be conceptualized as experience, or as time, or as activities — and highlights the importance of using complementary methodologies to capture the multidimensional nature of leisure.

AN OVERVIEW: PROBLEMS AND STRATEGIES

The Use of Complementary Techniques

Integration within the leisure field is necessary at the levels of theory, methods, and data. The theory of social representations is, in my view, a powerful catalyst in achieving such integration. It clarifies the conceptual confusion that has been rife within leisure research, and emphasizes the need to examine leisure at different levels of analysis using a range of complementary techniques.

Clearly, the ways in which leisure is conceptualized and the research methods used to examine the nature of leisure, the choice of leisure activities, and the role that leisure plays both in an individual's lifestyle and in society, are not independent of each other. A major implication of the social representations approach to leisure is that one cannot understand leisure if it is studied in a way that is devoid of a social and cultural context. Descriptive studies and head-counting exercises are a necessary first step toward chronicling leisure behavior, but they offer no explanatory power. Similarly, simple statistical analyses that attempt to encapsulate leisure by means of a single indicator (although they may be helpful in testing specific restricted hypotheses) fail to recognize both the multidimensional nature of leisure and its grounding within the social fabric of society.

Leisure phenomena — meanings, functions, attitudes, preferences, and participation choices — are complex and subject to a variety of different influences. No single research technique or method of data analysis offers the "right" approach, but there must be a recognition of the problems that leisure research faces, and an appreciation of which methods are best suited to the challenge inherent in particular research questions. These decisions must not take place in a vacuum but within a sound theoretical framework, which makes explicit the researcher's model of the world and which attempts to cross the disciplinary divides — in language and concepts — that exist within the leisure field.

Multivariate research methods are essential aids to understanding and predicting leisure phenomena for both leisure researchers and providers. Survey data have always been essentially multivariate, but the application of multivariate techniques provides an opportunity to investigate systematically the interrelations among all variables simultaneously, which is a prerequisite to understanding leisure behavior. As well as providing an opportunity to explore the structure of leisure activities and their psychological attributes, they also allow the researcher to study the multiple influences of several aspects of people's worlds on a number of different measures, and therefore mirror the actual complexity of behavioral reality better than simpler methods (cf. Kerlinger 1986: 566).

However, as I have argued in the past (Stockdale 1987), multivariate techniques are not the panacea for all ills in leisure research. The measurement problems which confront much social behavioral research are characteristic of leisure research. Analytic methods, no matter how powerful they may be, are no antidote to poorly operationalized and inadequately measured variables. Multivariate methods are demanding of the researcher and they can never compensate for an inadequate theoretical base or for an ill-conceived research strategy. If judiciously chosen and properly applied, they can provide leisure researchers with useful insights into the nature and role of leisure; they are an important aid to planners and providers in their decision making for the future, and ultimately are the means by which we may test complex structural models of leisure behavior.

The benefits of multivariate methods depend upon the identification, operationalization, and measurement of variables within an explicit theoretical framework. Elegant and complex procedures applied to poor data gathered with little regard to theory and logical analysis can provide little of scientific interest. The combination of multivariate methods with computer implementations is not an invitation to researchers to imbue the results with unchallengeable sanctity and should not encourage researchers to suspend their critical judgment.

However, we should not lose sight of the quality side of the quantity-quality distinction. There is a clear argument for the use of both quantitative and qualitative methods of data collection and analysis. We need to recognize that the distinctions frequently drawn between them are artificial, with quantification playing an important part in the analysis of qualitative data, and the judgment of the experimenter being a key element in quantitative analyses. Quantitative and qualitative research methods should not be seen as polar opposites but as complementary approaches (cf. Fielding and Fielding 1986). The stereotypical view of qualitative data as "soft, subjective, and speculative" and of quantitative data as "hard, objective, and rigorous" is a disservice to both traditions. A combination of both approaches — with sufficient attention to the methodological adequacy of their implementation — offers the opportunity to counter the claims of the two opposing factions: that researchers who use quantitative methods substitute their own reality for that of their respondents, by choosing what are suitable things to quantify; and that qualitative data inevitably fail to yield generalizable findings, or to generate causal explanations.

Moreover, the use of multiple data sources and complementary methods provides the means of validating findings through the process of triangulation (cf. Fielding and Fielding 1986; Hammersley and Atkinson 1983). The rationale underlying triangulation is the fallibility of any single measure or method as a means of representing social phenomena and psychological constructs. We need to recognize this fallibility if we are to understand the experience of leisure and the lifestyle options that can provide that experience. A similar argument has recently been applied to the study of tourism by Hartmann (1988), who proposes that research in this area could benefit from the combination and integration of different field methods.

The Role of Meta-Analysis

Many researchers have recognized the need for strategies which will provide a systematic body of knowledge about the nature and role of leisure, rather than a set of dissociated and fragmented findings. One step toward achieving this goal is the formulation of a sound theoretical base. Another step is the cumulation of results across studies which focus on the same issue, in order to establish facts which will inform theory building. Leisure research is ripe for the application of methods designed for cumulating knowledge across studies, in particular the methods of meta-analysis, developed by Glass and his colleagues (cf. Glass 1976, 1977; Glass, McGaw, and Smith 1981), and extended by Schmidt and Hunter (cf. Hunter, Schmidt, and Jackson 1982). Meta-analysis encompasses a range of techniques for summarizing or synthesizing the results of independent pieces of research, by the use of one (or more) objective procedures (e.g. counting within categories, measuring effect size, summarizing probabilities of results). While meta-analysis is a powerful analytic technique, it is not without limitations, and a number of authors have expressed a need for caution in its use (e.g. Cook and Leviton 1980; Gallo 1978; Leviton and Cook 1981; Rosenthal 1980; Strube and Hartmann 1982, 1983). Clearly, the technique is limited by such factors as: the biased selection of studies; reporting inaccuracies; poor quality data; conceptual, methodological, and statistical invalidity; and lack of independence in the studies reviewed (cf. Strube and Hartmann 1982). Whilst recognizing the limitations of meta-analysis, others have emphasized its considerable potential in contributing to the production of useful cumulative knowledge (e.g. Cooper 1982; Rosenthal 1984).

A number of benefits can accrue from the application of meta-analytic techniques to leisure. Strube and Hartmann (1983) note that a meta-analytic review of a research area can serve a number of functions. These include helping to direct future research more effectively; increasing the effectiveness with which policy decisions are made; and disseminating scientific information to a wider audience. Fiske (1983) points to the demands which meta-analysis places on researchers, such as requiring researchers to exercise greater concern about the operationalization of variables and to conceptualize and theorize more sharply. Leisure research cannot afford to ignore the potential that meta-analysis offers for clarifying confusing sets of results and for aiding research practice, theoretical development, and policy decision making.

THE CONTEMPORARY CONTEXT AND FUTURE SCENARIOS

Conceptualizations of society in the years to come range from the tentatively optimistic to the emphatically pessimistic, but all focus on potential changes in the nature and role of both work and leisure in a "postindustrial" society. Analyses of leisure cannot ignore the profound economic, technological, environmental, and social changes which have occurred in the recent past or those that are predicted to occur in the future. The way in which we represent leisure, the range of leisure options available to us, and our choice of leisure pursuits cannot be divorced from the historical and contemporary context in which they are generated. Forecasts of a decline in paid employment, and the advent of structural unemployment, combined with the increasing proportion of women entering the workforce, require that we consider the impacts of changing work patterns and disposable income on leisure and recreation (see the chapters by Glyptis and Vickerman). In the United Kingdom, the rapid increase in video ownership, and the prospect of an explosion in the number of television channels available, focuses attention on the home-based leisure market and highlights the importance of political decisions in shaping leisure provision. In terms of outdoor recreation, increased pressure on National Parks and Wilderness Areas raises issues of conservation, resource management, and environmental attitudes (see the chapters by Jackson and Swinnerton). Such issues are accentuated by recent growing concern about environmental pollution, acid rain, the "greenhouse effect," and global climatic change (see Wall's chapter). Furthermore, changing expectations with respect to such diverse areas of our lives, as health-promoting lifestyles, increased contact with different cultures through cheap foreign travel, variability in family structure, and increased life expectancy, affect the social context of leisure.

These examples raise a number of questions about the extent and nature of the impact that changes in our values, priorities, and attitudes will have on leisure. How will our representations of leisure change? What range of leisure options will develop? How will leisure choices be constrained? Will particular groups within society, such as women, continue to be "leisure-deprived?" In short, what are our leisure "futures?"

These are not questions that will be answered easily. Nor is it the case that we will like all the answers we get or find it easy to adapt to the changes they demand. Concern about our leisure "futures" also focuses attention on the contribution of leisure to individual well-being within the general population (cf. Allen and Beattie 1984; Andrews and Withey 1976; Campbell, Converse, and Rodgers 1976; London, Crandall, and Seal 1977) and in special populations such as the elderly, who form an increasing proportion of the population (e.g. O'Brien 1981; Riddick 1985). A related issue which is receiving increasing attention, especially in North America, is the presumption that people need to strive for personal growth and self-fulfillment, not only through work as employment, but also through their leisure. The recognition of the fundamental importance of leisure and recreation in individual identity (see the concluding remarks in Godbey's chapter) has led to a rapid growth in the field of leisure counselling and programs designed to ensure that leisure contributes to an individual's value structure and his or her engagement in meaningful activities (cf. Blocher and Siegal 1980; Loesch 1980; McDowell 1980; Tinsley and Tinsley 1980).

Individual researchers, providers, planners, and politicians will decide their own priorities within the wide range of questions that we can ask about the meaning of leisure, its role in people's lives, leisure choice and the role of constraints, and the organization and provision of leisure. In my view, understanding the way leisure is represented is of fundamental importance, if we are to reinstate leisure in its social and cultural context and recognize the influence of social and cultural values, beliefs images, and symbols. Furthermore, we need to appreciate how our representation of leisure affects our leisure choices. For example, we need to appreciate the changing meanings and patterns of both leisure and work, among young people, many of whom lack the contrast between employment and leisure (cf. Chamberlain 1983; Marsland 1982); among unemployed adults who have lost both this contrast and the structure and self-identity usually provided by their work role; and among women, for the majority of whom traditional conceptions of leisure have little overlap with experience. We also need a clearer understanding of the constraints that operate on leisure choice, so that we may be able to extend the range of leisure options which constitute a "real" choice. Identifying the processes involved in leisure socialization and preferences will become increasingly important as pressures to develop "education-for-leisure" become more prominent. Evaluations of changing patterns of leisure provision in the public and private sectors, and the accessibility and value of this provision to different groups within the population, is critical if public policy and commercial decisions are to be well-informed and therefore of benefit to potential consumers (cf. Burton 1982).

Whatever scenario one envisages for the future, leisure will play a fundamental role. Irrespective of whether leisure is viewed as a social problem, or as a positive contributor to perceived quality of life, it is important that our assessments of the role leisure plays in people's lives recognize the richness of the leisure experience and the diversity of activities, occasions, and times that constitute the leisure domain. Equally, irrespective of whether leisure is conceptualized as an agent or a product of social change, it is important that our leisure policies and planning provide people with real leisure opportunities.

An adequate analysis of the nature and role of leisure, both now and in the future, rests on insights from a variety of disciplines whose traditions offer different but complementary approaches to the challenge of developing a sound theoretical base and repertoire of methodological techniques. Connecting theory, method, and data is an integral part of fulfilling whatever particular goals we set ourselves within leisure research. Social representations and complementary methods together offer one way of reducing the frustrations and increasing the fascination of leisure research.

References

Allen, L.R. and R.J. Beattie. 1984. "The role of leisure as an indicator of overall satisfaction with community life." *Journal of Leisure Research 16:* 99-109.

Allen, L.R., M.A. Donnelly, and D.S. Warder. 1984. "The stability of leisure factor structures across time." *Leisure Sciences 6:* 221-237.

Andrews, F.M. and J.B. Withey. 1976. *Social Indicators of Well-being.* New York: Plenum Press.

Beard, J.G. and M.G. Ragheb. 1980. "Measuring leisure satisfaction." *Journal of Leisure Research 12:* 20-33.

Beard, J.G. and M.G. Ragheb. 1983. "Measuring leisure motivation." *Journal of Leisure Research 15:* 219-228.

Becker, B.W. 1976. "Perceived similarities among recreational activities." *Journal of Leisure Research 8:* 112-122.

Bergier, M.J. 1978. "An examination of consumers' leisure time choice behavior: A multi-dimensional scaling approach to the study of spectator sports." Ph.D. thesis, State University of New York at Buffalo.

Bishop, D.W. 1970. "Stability of the factor structure of leisure behavior: Analyses of four communities." *Journal of Leisure Research 2:* 160-170.

Blocher, D.H. and R. Siegal. 1980. "Toward a cognitive developmental theory of leisure and work." *The Counselling Psychologist 9:* 33-44.

Bourdieu, P. 1984. *Distinction: A Social Critique of the Judgement of Taste.* London: Routledge and Kegan Paul.

Breakwell, G.M. and D. Canter. In press. *Empirical Approaches to Social Representations.* Oxford: Oxford University Press.

British Broadcasting Corporation. 1984. *Daily Life in the 1980s.* London: BBC Data Publications.

Burton, T.L. 1971. *Experiments in Recreation Research.* London: George Allen and Unwin.

Burton, T.L. 1982. "A framework for leisure policy research." *Leisure Studies 1:* 323-335.

Campbell, A., P.E. Converse, and W.L. Rodgers. 1976. *The Quality of American Life.* New York: Russell Sage Foundation.

Chamberlain, J. 1983. "Adolescent perceptions of work and leisure." *Leisure Studies 2:* 127-138.

Chase, D.W. and N.H. Cheek. 1979. "Activity preferences and participation: Conclusions from a factor analytic study." *Journal of Leisure Research 11:* 92-101.

Chase, D.W., J.J. Kasulis, and R.F. Lusch. 1980. "Factor invariance of non-work activities." *Journal of Leisure Research 12:* 55-68.

Cook, T.D., and L.C. Leviton. 1980. "Reviewing the literature: A comparison of traditional methods with meta-analysis." *Journal of Personality 48:* 449-472.

Cooper, H.M. 1982. "Scientific guidelines for conducting integrative research reviews." *Review of Educational Research 52:* 291-302.

Coppock, J.T. (ed.). 1977. *Second Homes: Curse or Blessing?* Oxford: Pergamon.

Coppock, J.T. 1982. "Geographical contributions to the study of leisure." *Leisure Studies 1:* 1-27.

Crawford, D.W. and G. Godbey. 1987. "Reconceptualizing barriers to family leisure." *Leisure Sciences 9:* 119-127.

De Grazia, S. 1962. *Of Time, Work and Leisure.* New York: Doubleday.

Ditton, R.B., T.L. Goodale, and P.K. Johnson. 1974. "A cluster analysis of activity frequency and environment variables to identify water-based recreation types." Unpublished paper, Department of Recreation and Parks, Texas A&M University.

Duffield, B.S. 1979. "People and the coast: current demands and future aspirations for coastal recreation." In *Recreation and the Coast,* CCP127, pp. 62-94. Cheltenham: Countryside Commission.

Duncan, D.J. 1978. "Leisure types: factor analyses of leisure profiles." *Journal of Leisure Research 2:* 113-125.

Ewert, A. 1985. "Why people climb: The relationship of participant motives and experience level to mountaineering." *Journal of Leisure Research 17:* 241-250.

Farr, R.M. 1987. "Social representations: A French tradition of research." *Journal for the Theory of Social Behaviour 17:* 343-369.

Farr, R.M. and S. Moscovici (eds.). 1984. *Social Representations.* Cambridge: Cambridge University Press.

Faulkner, R.R. 1982. "Improvising on a triad." In *Varieties of Qualitative Research,* eds. J. van Maanen, J.M. Dabbs, and R.R. Faulkner, pp. 65-101. London: Sage Publications.

Featherstone, M. 1987. "Leisure, symbolic power and the life course." In *Sport, Leisure and Social Relations* (Sociological Review Monograph 33), eds. J. Horne, D. Jary, and A. Tomlinson, pp. 113-138. London: Routledge and Kegan Paul.

Fielding, N.G. and J.L. Fielding. 1986. *Linking Data.* Beverly Hills, CA: Sage Publications.

Fiske, D.W. 1983. "The meta-analytic revolution in outcome research." *Journal of Consulting and Clinical Psychology 51:* 65-70.

Gallo, P.S. 1978. "Meta-analysis - a mixed metaphor?" *American Psychologist 33:* 515-517.

Gershuny, J. and S. Jones. 1987. "The changing work/leisure balance in Britain, 1961-84." In *Sport, Leisure and Social Relations* (Sociological Review Monograph 33), eds. J. Horne, D. Jary, and A. Tomlinson, pp. 9-50. London: Routledge and Kegan Paul.

Gershuny, J., I. Miles, S. Jones, C. Mullings, G. Thomas, and S. Wyatt. 1986. "Time budgets: Preliminary analyses of the national survey." *Quarterly Journal of Social Affairs 2:* 13-39.

Glass, G. 1976. "Primary, secondary and meta-analysis of research." *Education Researcher 5:* 3-8.

Glass, G. 1977. "Integrating findings: The meta-analysis of research." *Review of Research in Education 5:* 351-379.

Glass, G., B. McGaw, and M.L. Smith. 1981. *Meta-analysis in Social Research.* Beverly Hills, CA: Sage Publications.

Godbey, G. 1985. "Non-use of public leisure services: A model." *Journal of Park and Recreation Administration 3:* 1-12.

Green, L., M. Kreuter, S. Deeds, and K. Partridge. 1980. *Health Education Planning: A Diagnostic Approach.* Palo Alto, CA: Mayfield Publishing Co.

Gudykunst, W.B., J.A. Morra, W.I. Kantor, and H.A. Parker. 1981. "Dimensions of leisure activities: A factor analytic study in New England." *Journal of Leisure Research 13:* 28-42.

Gunter, B.G. 1987. "The leisure experience: Selected properties." *Journal of Leisure Research 19:* 115-130.

Hammersley, M. and P. Atkinson. 1983. *Ethnography: Principles in Practice.* London: Tavistock.

Harper, W. 1981. "The experience of leisure." *Leisure Sciences 4:* 113-126.

Hartmann, R. 1988. "Combining field methods in tourism research." *Annals of Tourism Research 15:* 88-105.

Heywood, J.L. 1987. "Experience preferences of participants in different types of river recreation groups." *Journal of Leisure Research 19:* 1-12.

Hirschman, E.C. 1985. "A multidimensional analysis of content preferences for leisure-time media." *Journal of Leisure Research 17:* 14-28.

Holbrook, M.B. 1980. "Representing patterns of associations among leisure activities: A comparison of two techniques." *Journal of Leisure Research 12:* 242-256.

Howe, C.Z. 1985. "Possibilities for using a qualitative research approach in the sociological study of leisure." *Journal of Leisure Research 17:* 212-224.

Hunt, E.H. 1981. *British Labour History, 1815-1914.* London: Wiedenfeld and Nicholson.

Hunter, J.E., F.L. Schmidt, and G. Jackson. 1982. *Meta-analysis: Accumulating Results Across Studies*. Beverly Hills, CA: Sage Publications.

Iso-Ahola, S.E. 1979a. "Basic dimensions of definitions of leisure." *Journal of Leisure Research 11:* 28-39.

Iso-Ahola, S.E. 1979b. "Some social psychological determinants of perceptions of leisure: Preliminary evidence." *Leisure Sciences 2:* 305-314.

Iso-Ahola, S.E. 1980. "Toward a dialectical social psychology of leisure and recreation." In *Social Psychological Perspectives on Leisure and Recreation,* ed. S.E. Iso-Ahola, pp. 19-37. Springfield, IL: Charles C. Thomas.

Iso-Ahola, S.E. and R.C. Mannell. 1985. "Social psychological constraints on leisure." In *Constraints on Leisure,* ed. M.G. Wade, pp. 111-151. Springfield, IL: Charles C. Thomas.

Jackson, E.L. 1986. "Outdoor recreation participation and attitudes to the environment." *Leisure Studies 5:* 1-23.

Jackson, E.L. 1988. "Leisure constraints: A survey of past research." *Leisure Sciences 10:* 203-215.

Jackson, E.L. and E. Dunn. 1988. "Integrating ceasing participation with other aspects of leisure behavior." *Journal of Leisure Research 20:* 31-45.

Jackson, E.L. and M.S. Searle. 1985. "Recreation non-participation and barriers to participation: Concepts and models." *Loisir et Société 8:* 693-707.

Kaplan, M. 1960. *Leisure in America: A Social Inquiry.* New York: Wiley.

Kelly, J.R. 1972. "Work and leisure: A simplified paradigm." *Journal of Leisure Research 4:* 50-62.

Kelly, J.R. 1978. "A revised paradigm of leisure choices." *Leisure Sciences 1:* 345-363.

Kelly, J.R. 1980. "Outdoor recreation participation: A comparative analysis." *Leisure Sciences 3:* 129-154.

Kelly, J.R. 1983. *Leisure Identities and Interactions.* London: George, Allen and Unwin.

Kelvin, P. and J.E. Jarrett. 1985. *Unemployment: Its Social Psychological Effects.* Cambridge: Cambridge University Press.

Kerlinger, F.N. 1986. *Foundations of Behavioral Research.* New York: Holt, Rinehart and Winston.

Krippendorf, K. 1980. *Content Analysis: An Introduction to its Methodology.* London: Sage Publications.

Leviton, L.C. and T.D. Cook. 1981. "What differentiates meta-analysis from other forms of review." *Journal of Personality 49:* 231-236.

Loesch, L.C. 1980. "Leisure counselling with youth." *The Counselling Psychologist 9:* 55-67.

London, M., R. Crandall, and D. Fitzgibbons. 1977. "The psychological structure of leisure: Activities, needs, people." *Journal of Leisure Research 9:* 252-263.

London, M., R. Crandall, and G.W. Seal. 1977. "The contribution of job and leisure satisfaction to quality of life." *Journal of Applied Psychology 2:* 238-244.

Mannell, R.C. 1980. "Social psychological strategies and techniques for studying leisure experiences." In *Social Psychological Perspectives on Leisure and Recreation,* ed. S.E. Iso-Ahola, pp. 62-88. Springfield, IL: Charles C. Thomas.

Marsland, D. 1982. "It's my life: Young people and leisure." *Leisure Studies 1:* 305-322.

McDowell, C.F. 1980. "Leisure: Consciousness, well-being and counselling." *The Counselling Psychologist 9:* 3-31.

McKechnie, G.E. 1974. "The psychological structure of leisure: Past behavior." *Journal of Leisure Research 6:* 27-45.

Mercer, D.C. 1985. "Australians' time use in work, housework and leisure: Changing profiles." *Australian and New Zealand Journal of Sociology 21:* 371-394.

Miles, H.B. and A.M. Huberman. 1984. *Qualitative Data Analysis.* Beverly Hills, CA: Sage Publications.

Moscovici, S. 1981. "On social representations." In *Social Cognition: Perspectives on Everyday Understanding,* ed. J.P. Forgas, pp. 181-209. London: Academic Press.

Moscovici, S. 1984. "The phenomenon of social representations." In *Social Representations,* eds. R.M. Farr and S. Moscovici, pp. 3-69. Cambridge: Cambridge University Press.

Neulinger, J. 1974. *The Psychology of Leisure.* Springfield, IL: Charles C. Thomas.

Neulinger, J. 1976. "The need for and the implications of a psychological conception of leisure." *Ontario Psychologist 8:* 13-20.

Neulinger, J. 1980. "Theory and method of social psychology of leisure and recreation: Introduction." In *Social Psychological Perspectives on Leisure and Recreation,* ed S.E. Iso-Ahola, pp. 5-18. Springfield, IL: Charles C. Thomas.

Neulinger, J. 1981. *To Leisure, An Introduction.* Boston: Alyn and Bacon.

Neulinger, J. and M. Breit. 1969. "Attitude dimensions of leisure." *Journal of Leisure Research 1:* 255-261.

Neulinger, J. and M. Breit. 1971. "Attitude dimensions of leisure: A replication study." *Journal of Leisure Research 3:* 108-115.

Neulinger, J., S. Light, and T. Mobley. 1976. "Attitude dimensions of leisure in a student population." *Journal of Leisure Research 8:* 175-176.

O'Brien, G.E. 1981. "Leisure attributes and retirement satisfaction." *Journal of Applied Psychology 66:* 371-384.

Parker, S.R. 1971. *The Future of Work and Leisure.* New York: Praeger.

Pieper, J. 1963. *Leisure, the Basis of Culture.* New York: New American Library.

Pierce, R. 1980a. "Dimensions of leisure I: Satisfactions." *Journal of Leisure Research 12:* 5-19.

Pierce, R. 1980b. "Dimensions of leisure II: Descriptions." *Journal of Leisure Research 12:* 150-163.

Pierce, R. 1980c. "Dimensions of leisure III: Characteristics." *Journal of Leisure Research 12:* 273-284.

Ragheb, M.G. and J.G. Beard. 1982. "Measuring leisure attitudes." *Journal of Leisure Research 14:* 155-167.

Riddick, C.C. 1985. "Life satisfaction determinants of older males and females." *Leisure Sciences 7:* 47-63.

Riddick, C.C., M. De Schriver, and E. Weissinger. 1984. "A methodological review of research." *Journal of Leisure Research 16:* 311-321.

Ritchie, J. 1975. "On the derivation of leisure activity types: A perceptual mapping approach." *Journal of Leisure Research 7:* 128-140.

Roadburg, A. 1977. "An enquiry into meanings of work and leisure: The case of professional and amateur football players and gardeners." Ph.D. Dissertation, University of Edinburgh.

Robinson, J.P. 1977. *How Americans Use Time: A Social Psychological Analysis of Everyday Behavior.* New York: Praeger.

Romsa, G.H. 1973. "A method of deriving outdoor recreational activity patterns." *Journal of Leisure Research 5:* 34-36.

Rosenthal, R. 1980. *New Directions for Methodology of Social and Behavioral Science: Quantitative Assessment of Research Domains.* San Francisco: Jossey-Bass.

Rosenthal, R. 1984. *Meta-analytic Procedures for Social Research.* Beverly Hills, CA: Sage Publications.

Rubin, A.M. 1981a. "An examination of television viewing motivations." *Communication Research 8:* 141-165.

Rubin, A.M. 1981b. "A multivariate analysis of 60 minutes viewing motivations." *Journalism Quarterly 58:* 529-534.

Schiffman, S., M.L. Reynolds, and F.W. Young. 1981. *Introduction to Multidimensional Scaling.* London: Academic Press.

Schmitz-Scherzer, R., G. Rudinger, A. Angleitner, and D. Bierhoff-Alfermann. 1974. "Structure of leisure activities in four different samples." *Journal of Leisure Research 6:* 77-83.

Shaw, S.M. 1985. "The meaning of leisure in everyday life." *Leisure Sciences* 7: 1-24.

Shipley, P. 1980. "Technological change, working hours and individual well being." In *Changes in the Quality of Working Life. Proceedings of an International Conference on Changes in the Nature and Quality of Working Life*, eds. K.D. Duncan, M.M. Gruneberg, and D. Wallis, pp. 39-53. Chichester: John Wiley and Sons.

Stockdale, J.E. 1985. *What is Leisure? An Empirical Analysis of the Concept of Leisure and the Role of Leisure in People's Lives*. London: The Sports Council and Economic and Social Research Council.

Stockdale, J.E. 1987. *Methodological Techniques in Leisure Research*. London: The Sports Council and Economic and Social Research Council.

Stockdale, J.E. and J.G. Eldred. 1982. "Research methods appropriate to the task." In *Leisure Research: Current Findings and the Future Challenge*, ed. M.F. Collins, pp. 15-29. London: The Social Science Research Council and Sports Council.

Stockdale, J.E., A.J. Wells, and M. Rall. (In preparation.) *The Psychological Meaning of Leisure and Work: A Comparison of London and New York*.

Strube, M.J. and D.P. Hartmann. 1982. "A critical appraisal of meta-analysis." *British Journal of Clinical Psychology 21*: 129-139.

Strube, M.J. and D.P. Hartmann. 1983. "Meta-analysis: Techniques, applications, and functions." *Journal of Consulting and Clinical Psychology 51*: 14-27.

Szalai, A. 1972. *The Use of Time: Daily Activities of Urban and Sub-urban Populations in Twelve Countries*. The Hague: Mouton.

Tatham, R.L. and R.J. Dornoff. 1971. "Market segmentation for outdoor recreation." *Journal of Leisure Research 3*: 5-16.

Tinsley, H.E.A., T.C. Barrett, and R.A. Kass. 1977. "Leisure activities and need satisfaction." *Journal of Leisure Research 9*: 110-120.

Tinsley, H.E.A. and T.L. Johnson. 1984. "A preliminary taxonomy of leisure activities." *Journal of Leisure Research 16*: 234-244.

Tinsley, H.E.A. and R.A. Kass. 1978. "Leisure activities and need satisfaction: A replication and extension." *Journal of Leisure Research 10:* 191-202.

Tinsley, H.E.A. and R.A. Kass. 1979. "The latent structure of the need satisfying properties of leisure activities." *Journal of Leisure Research 11:* 278-291.

Tinsley, H.E.A., J.D. Teaff, S.L. Colbs, and N. Kaufman. 1983. "The psychological benefits of leisure activities for the elderly." A manual and final report of an investigation funded by the AARP Andrus Foundation, Department of Recreation, Southern Illinois University, Carbondale, IL.

Tinsley, H.E.A., J.D. Teaff, S.L. Colbs, and N. Kaufman. 1985. "A system of classifying leisure activities in terms of the psychological benefits of participation reported by older persons." *Journal of Gerontology 40:* 172-178.

Tinsley, H.E.A. and D.J. Tinsley. 1980. "An analysis of leisure counselling models." *The Counselling Psychologist 9:* 45-53.

Tinsley, H.E.A. and D.J. Tinsley. 1986. "A theory of the attributes, benefits and causes of leisure experience." *Leisure Sciences 8:* 1-45.

Torkildsen, G. 1983. *Leisure and Recreation Management.* London: E & F N Spon.

Vickerman, R.W. 1983. "The contribution of economics to the study of leisure: A review." *Leisure Studies 2:* 345-364.

Weber, R.P. 1985. *Basic Content Analysis.* Beverly Hills, CA: Sage Publications.

Witt, P.A. 1971. "Factor structure of leisure behavior for high school age youth in three communities." *Journal of Leisure Research 3:* 213-219.

Young, M. and P. Willmott. 1973. *The Symmetrical Family.* London: Routledge and Kegan Paul.

Yu, J.M. 1980. "The empirical development of typology for describing behavior on the basis of participation patterns." *Journal of Leisure Research 12:* 309-320.

Yu, J.M. 1985. "The congruence of recreation activity dimensions among urban suburban and rural residents." *Journal of Leisure Research 17:* 107-120.

WOMEN AND LEISURE: BEYOND ANDROCENTRISM[1]

Leslie Bella

THE ANDROCENTRISM OF LEISURE

Androcentrism is a pattern of thought that takes male experience as central, and studies and evaluates women's experiences by referring to those of men. For example, to evaluate women's mental health using instruments developed by studying only men is androcentric. So, also, is the application to women of a concept of leisure developed with reference to men's lives. The concept of leisure has been built on bourgeois men's experience of family and employment in an industrial age. The concept incorporates an artificial dichotomy between work and leisure, and is often assumed to require a level of freedom from obligation rarely available to women (or to men with ongoing responsibility for others). Such an androcentric concept cannot reveal meaning in the lives of women, or for those parts of men's lives having to do with relationship and responsibility.

As a result, leisure research reaches sexist conclusions. Sexism is "the socially structured expectation that people perform certain social roles and not others simply on the basis of their sex" (Eichler 1983: 65). Sexist and androcentrist approaches lead to sexist conclusions, and unacknowledged sexist language can conceal the androcentrism in an idea or approach (Eichler and Lapointe 1985; McCalla Vickers 1984). Leisure research using time budget studies, for example, cannot reveal the meaning of people's lives, and has particularly impoverished our understanding of women's lives. Such research ignores expressive rather than instrumental activities, and cannot access the multilayered meaning and interdependencies of human lives. Familist assumptions lead leisure researchers to focus on such phenomena as "family leisure." The possibility that leisure experienced by some family members may entail work for others is also inaccessible.

I propose, instead, an approach to understanding human experience that returns the right to label an experience to those to whom the experience belongs. The multilayered, relationship-bound experience of being human (whether male or female) can then be more fully appreciated and understood. Preliminary results of an exploratory study of the creation of Christmas celebrations in families demonstrate a future research direction that could prove more fruitful than research structured by preoccupation with "freedom from obligation" and with a "work" and "leisure" dichotomy (Bella 1987, 1988).

Dichotomies and Patriarchal Thought

Western thought has been constructed on a number of dichotomies such as man/ woman, instrumental/expressive, rational/emotional, and public/private (Wilson 1980). Daly (1973) describes this tendency to create artificial dichotomies as part of the "dichotomizing-reifying-projecting" syndrome that is characteristic of patriarchal consciousness. The invention of dichotomies is essential to the definitions and categories which are the foundation of positivist social science. However, these dichotomies are then treated by social scientists as naturally occurring, rather than as intellectual constructions (McCalla Vickers 1982).

Several of these dichotomies have been treated as parallel. For example, the dichotomy between male and female is paralleled in other dichotomies, so that one side of each is seen as the domain of the male, and the other of the female. Men, through this line of argument, are involved in rational, instrumental activities in the public world — activities which we call "work." Women, being expressive and emotional, are involved in a private world in something that is not work, and has even been called "leisure" by some social scientists (Dumazedier 1967; Pruette 1924; Veblen 1899). This tendency to dichotomize has, therefore, led to an exaggeration of the differences between men and women, with men portraying themselves as the standard and women as "other" and different (DeBeauvoir 1974: xx). In our society, the characteristics on the male side of these dichotomies are valued more than those on the female side.

> In actuality the relation of the two sexes is not quite like
> that of two electric poles, for man presents both the positive and the
> neutral, as is indicated by the use of "man" to designate human
> beings in general (DeBeauvoir 1974:xx).

Thus, man has the power to name his own pole as the norm, the standard, and the ideal — and woman as the "other." Power (including both economic resources and status) belongs to men working in the public world, rather than women living outside the workforce in the privacy of their families. This construction of multiple and mutually reinforcing dichotomies, with advantage accruing to one side rather than being evenly distributed, is clearly sexist in the sense of the term used by Eichler (1983) — producing an expectation that people perform social roles on the basis of their sex.

The dichotomy between work and leisure is part of this construction. It may appear to have relevance for men with jobs, who work in the "public" world and have "leisure" in the private worlds of their families. However, the work/leisure dichotomy ignores the experience of women (and men) creating and maintaining those families. It cannot comprehend the significance of relationship, caring, or obligation, or the emotional work essential to family life. Also, as Stockdale points out in this book, such a concept has little relevance when half the population is not in employment.

The dominant liberal ideology of the western world has led to the addition of "freedom" to the concept of "leisure." The concept of "freedom from work," even freedom from obligation, became a significant part of the concept as industrial workers obtained shorter work weeks, and eventually paid vacations. The idea of "freedom from obligation" makes the experience of leisure even more inaccessible to those whose lives involve responsibilities for people dependent on them. Obligation to one's children persists, for example, even when they are not present. The idea of leisure as freedom ignores the part of human existence that has dominated most women's lives, and is crucially important today for both men and women. It ignores what Marxist feminists have called "reproductive labor" — the work required to nurture and support existing workers and the children who will be in the future workforce.

Androcentric Leisure Theory

A brief historical review of some of the "great works" in leisure studies will show the androcentric (and sometimes misogynist) bias in this tradition. Veblen was the first of the modern social scientists to take up the study of leisure explicitly. Writing in 1899 he described a class of nonproductive leisured males, the "leisure" class, whose conspicuous leisure and conspicuous consumption served to demonstrate their social status. Wives and servants provided tangible evidence of the status of these men by passing their days in transparently useless activities. Veblen called their activities "second hand" or "vicarious" leisure, pursued to bring honor upon the male household head:

> ... not a simple manifestation of idleness or indolence. It almost invariably occurs disguised under some form of work or household duties or social amenities which prove on analysis to serve little or no ulterior end beyond showing that she does not and need not occupy herself with anything that is gainful or that is of substantial use (Veblen 1899: 82).

Woman's life was naturally ancillary to man's, according to Veblen, either as the dutiful "drudge" of the working class (and he used the word drudge, describing a woman in this position as more happy than her more idle middle class sister), or as the conspicuously unoccupied lady of the house in the middle and upper classes. His ideal world would be one where the housewife, instead of "passing her time in visible idleness, as in the best days of the patriarchal regime," would "apply herself assiduously to household cares" (p. 96). Gone would be that tangible trapping of idleness — the corset! On the other hand, demands for the emancipation of women and for a place in the workforce (demands which might be the logical conclusion for a man who believed that leisure was idle and corrupt) signalled to Veblen a reversion to a subhuman state (p. 361).

Veblen showed almost no understanding of how a large household actually worked. He seemed to have no sympathy for the complexity of the tasks involved in running a household consisting of many servants and children. Children are totally absent from his work. In 1899, they were also absent from his life. In 1888, he had married a classmate, the daughter of a university president, but they had no children. She left him, and they were divorced in 1911. *The Theory of the Leisure Class*, and its biting commentary on the lifestyles of the upper and middle classes, was written in the bitterness of a failed marriage. He was involved in a long series of affairs with women admirers (Dobnansky 1957) and, in 1914, married a divorcée with two daughters. His second wife appeared, at first, to be more content with her housewifely duties than his first, more intellectual, wife had been. She protected and looked after him, taking:

> ... complete care of her eccentric husband, doing his typing,
> washing his laundry, and keeping her children out of his way
> while finding time to make their clothes (Diggins 1978: 162).

She also was unhappy, however. She suffered a mental collapse in 1918, complete with "delusions of persecution," was "incarcerated in a sanatorium," and died in 1920. One of her daughters inherited her responsibility for Veblen, and nursed him until he died, in 1929, at the age of 72. Whatever Veblen's life, its result is a penetrating analysis of a class-based and patriarchal society. The critique, however, reveals no sympathy or affection for women. His many affairs with women were not because he admired them — rather the reverse. Veblen, one would judge from *The Theory of Leisure Class*, was a misogynist.

Veblen's work was influential. In 1924, Lorine Pruette reiterated his views that many of women's household chores were "useless," and that homemaking was a part-time job, leading women to be "dissatisfied," at least until they "grow fat and soft from too much leisure, want something more to do" (Pruette 1924). For Veblen and those he influenced, there was a complete parallel between the dualities of work/leisure, public/private, and man/woman, at least for the upper classes. These women inhabited a private world of "vicarious" leisure.

De Grazia, in his classic of 1962, was less penetrating, but as much a misogynist as Veblen.[2] He rooted his conceptual discussions in the ideas of classical Greece (touched upon by Cooper in this book). De Grazia abandoned the dichotomy between "work" and "leisure." He emphasized leisure as freedom, rather than leisure as the absence of work. "Free time," not "leisure," was the antonym of work, and free time was not leisure. The classical ideal of leisure was a "philosophical state," free from the need to be purposive, so that one could pursue thought, contemplation, and the liberal arts, and excellence in all of these. Happiness was only possible "in leisure." This superior state of being was only obtainable in the classical period by citizens, who relied on slaves to perform the drearier chores of life. According to De Grazia, women could not experience leisure. He only mentions them in order to explain briefly why leisure was inaccessible to them. Wives of the citizens in Sparta had time on their hands, but lacked the education for leisure. As a result, they abandoned themselves to "license and luxury" rather than leisure. De Grazia editorialized on the modern tendency for women to take jobs:

> Aristotle had said, you may recall, that the only slave the poor man has is his wife. The times, it seems, have taken even that away from him. Perhaps his wife is a better wife — I am no judge of that — but for his free time's sake, he could still use a slave.... The hardship (of extra work) is greatest among working men with wives at work too (De Grazia 1962: 74).

There is no mention of hardship for those wives!

The male bias in De Grazia's conceptual work is blatant. Women's experience of work or leisure is of no interest to him at all. This lack of interest is reflected in flaws in his empirical work, which are referred to later in this chapter. His conceptual base, with its concern for "freedom," is reflected in the leisure theory of the subsequent generation of leisure researchers.

French theorist Dumazedier re-embraced the work/leisure dichotomy abandoned by De Grazia. He explicitly described leisure as apart from the "obligations of work, family, and society," as something "to which an individual turns at will, for either relaxation, diversion, or broadening his knowledge and his spontaneous social participation, the free exercise of his creative capacity" (Dumazedier 1967: 16-17).[3] Leisure does not include the job, or supplementary work, or domestic tasks, or personal care, or family rituals and ceremonies, or "necessary" study. Dumazedier acknowledges the problem that women's domestic responsibilities create for understanding their "leisure." He describes women's responsibilities as "semiobligatory, semipleasurable activities," not always done as a result of necessity, and with the time committed to their completion varying in response to the homemaker's level of interest (Dumazedier 1967: 93-95).[4] Like Veblen before him, he invented a new term to cover this activity, and to include the "puttering" that men do with their automobiles and in the garden. He called both of them "semi-leisure." This choice revealed the inability of the concepts of either "work" or "leisure" to reveal fully the meaning of the things people do within the context of the reciprocal obligations of family and other primary relationships.

In his *Contemporary Society and the Growth of Leisure*, Roberts (1978) also used the definition of leisure as "relatively freely undertaken non-work activity." This, he believed, was "broadly consistent with everyday use," incorporating both the work/leisure duality and the idea of freedom. Roberts, though, tried to move beyond the concept of "leisure," to look at lifestyle, commenting that:

> Real life possesses a holistic quality. Individuals do not so much engage in *ad hoc* miscellanies of activities as develop broader systems of leisure behavior consisting of a number of interdependent elements and specific leisure interests that are often only explicable in the contexts of the wider life-styles to which they contribute (Roberts 1978: 37).

But, while Roberts acknowledges the significance of a holistic understanding of people's lives, he is still loath to dispense with the idea of "leisure" as a means for structuring his understanding of those lives. He finds that the major determinants of leisure can be found primarily in sex and in the family life cycle (p. 115). He points out that inequalities in the "distribution of leisure time within families make the contrasts that can be drawn between social classes pale to insignificance" (p. 96). Even in dual-career families, women still did proportionately more housework, and had a smaller number of social contacts and fewer leisure choices beyond the family. He concludes with the comment that this did not necessarily mean that women's lives were less satisfying than men's. And here his argument stops, for the concepts of "work" and of "leisure" do not allow him to penetrate the meaning, significance, or satisfactions inherent in experiences that do not fit his definitions of either work (a job) or leisure (a freely chosen and intrinsically satisfying non-job).

Kelly (1983) defined leisure as "relatively self-determined nonwork activity." Freedom, as reflected in a range of choices, in exercise of discretion in using resources, in a perception of alternatives and a relative lack of coercion, remained essential to the concept. The duality with work remained. He excluded "primarily instrumental activities," focusing only on those producing primarily intrinsic satisfaction (p. 14). This led him to sympathize with the plight of homemakers with small children in low-income families, who "seem to have little of the freedom characteristic of true leisure." Interaction with family and friends was "the main dimension of leisure" for such wives. He acknowledged that both British and American studies revealed a "general picture of leisure constrained by role responsibilities, uncertainties in relationships, limited resources and a generally narrow view of life's possibilities" (p. 39). Although Kelly understood that the concept of leisure is limited in revealing the meaning of people's lives, he did not take the further step of trying to understand those lives from the perspective of role responsibilities and their meaning, rather than imposing the predetermined meaning implied by the terms "work" or "leisure." In his most recent work, Kelly (1987) reviews a wide range of approaches to and understanding of leisure, but shows little interest in gender differences and no appreciation of the androcentric bias in the theories and concepts he outlines.

So, the two problems with the concept of leisure are its dichotomous structure, and its emphasis on freedom from obligation. The dichotomy between work and leisure parallels other dichotomies, leading to sexist conclusions abut the position of women (as in the works of Veblen, De Grazia, and Dumazedier), and special terms to describe women's experience ("vicarious leisure," "semi-leisure"). The idea of leisure as freedom from obligation also does not apply to the lives of women. This can be seen in the dead-ends reached by Kelly and Roberts in their attempts to discuss a homemaker's leisure. The concept cannot be used to understand the lives of those who have obligations for others, or conversely the lives of those who are dependent. Both the restrictions of dependence, and the limitations associated with obligations, render leisure as "freedom from obligation" inaccessible. For women in families in particular, then, the concept of leisure is meaningless.

WOMEN IN LEISURE RESEARCH

The tenets of positivist social science require operational definitions of "work" and "leisure" that are mutually exclusive, and can be identified through some standard procedure. A dichotomous concept of work and leisure meets these requirements. Specific visible activities are labeled "work activities" or "leisure activities." These activities can then be observed or reported, and analyzed to produce a description of "work" and "leisure." Unfortunately, individual respondents have generally not been asked to identify the work and leisure content of their own activities (was it work, leisure, both, or neither?) or to report their experience of doing a number of things (some of them probably invisible) at the same time.[5]

Since positivist social science requires that leisure be visible and measurable, leisure studies have tended to focus on activity — on the instrumental rather than the expressive parts of life. These studies have been blind to those expressive, contemplative, and relational activities that cannot be observed, measured, or reported by traditional methods of social research. As a result, the activities that are stereotypically associated with men have been studied, but those expressive and relational activities associated with women have not been seen. We find out about the activity, but not about the relationship with the person who shares that activity. For instance, is the activity with a person for whom one is responsible (one's child, an older relative or friend who requires special care, or one's student or employee)? Or is the activity with a peer, such as a friend, a spouse, an adult sibling? Or is it with someone on whom one is dependent (such as a supervisor or teacher, or a parent if one is a child, or some other person in a caretaker role)?

As an example, one evening I simultaneously taught my teenage daughter how to iron her cotton shirts while we both watched television. I also ironed a number of my own shirts, and we discussed the costume she might wear for a 1950s dance at school. I would hesitate to call that experience "work" or "leisure." The closest I can come, without stripping too much meaning from the experience, would be "parenting." As Ross (1985) has suggested, women's (and probably men's) lives are multilayered, a seamless web of activities and relationships. Studies of leisure have not gained access to these multiple layers and meanings, and do not reveal the texture and meanings of our lives.

Empirical studies of women's leisure are flawed by the androcentrism of the concept itself. This bias is reflected in the choice of research questions and methodology. The tenets of positivism have resulted in an emphasis on the dichotomy between work and leisure, with less emphasis on leisure as associated with "freedom." The perceived freedom of an activity or lifestyle is difficult to measure using positivist methodology. Hence, an aspect is ignored which might reveal the difficulties of the concept in understanding the place of obligation and dependency in people's lives. Instead, the dichotomous concept of leisure as the antonym of work dominates empirical studies, resulting in an impoverished understanding of the way people lead their lives.

Two particular methodological approaches have been selected to demonstrate these problems.[6] Time budget analysis attempts to measure leisure as activity within time periods, and hence strips the activity from its social context. Second, the familist assumptions in leisure also distort our understanding of women's and men's lives.

Time Budget Studies

De Grazia was among the first to apply time budget methods to an analysis of leisure. In the first part of the book, *Of Time, Work and Leisure*, De Grazia used a definition of leisure as a philosophical state, and therefore as a presumably subjective experience. This definition could not be used, however, in his empirical work, so he returned to a dichotomous concept of leisure as "not work." This allowed him, and others after, to do time budget studies of people's lives, using techniques developed in the Tayloristic study of people's work. Time budget studies could now "establish the duration and the time structure of the activities performed by man within the framework of one 24-hour day" (Stajkov and Petkov 1975: 49).[7] The terminology "time budget" analysis suggests a reference to economics, to saving time, to the costs of time, and ultimately to the logic of the capitalist marketplace. As Andrew (1981) points out, it is no accident that the study of leisure followed on the coattails of the Tayloristic management of work.

In De Grazia's study, activities are divided into those at home and those away. Activities outside the home include a job, traveling, shopping, visiting a restaurant, tavern or barber, visiting a friend or relative's home, and "leisure" (as in games, sports, or church). At-home activities could include "leisure," "leisure other than reading," miscellaneous work at home, eating or preparing food, dressing, bathing, and sleep. Using this set of categories, De Grazia showed that women had slightly more "leisure" than men — an average of 5.1 hours a day compared with 4.5 hours — a conclusion that would not lead De Grazia, or anyone else, to consider that the two sexes might experience leisure, or their lives, differently.

But his categories are a serious problem. First, children do not seem to exist in these households, and responsibility for their care is invisible. Perhaps it is something that people do *while* visiting relatives, or *while* going to church, or *while* one is supposed to be asleep! Second, a number of the categories contain activities that may be leisure-like for some and not for others. For example, collapsing "preparing food" and "eating" into the same categories seems to combine the work-like activity of cooking with the experience of a family meal, which may be leisurely for some family members. Also, to categorize "sports event" together with "family attendance at church" seems ridiculous. De Grazia has designed categories that ignore the different meanings of the activities to the individuals involved.

Dumazedier, writing in 1967, followed De Grazia's methodology, but changed the categories. He listed activities "indisputably contrasted to the notion of leisure":

1. The job.
2. Supplementary work or occasional odd jobs.
3. Domestic tasks (housework, animal care, miscellaneous chores, gardening).
4. Care of the person (meals, bathing, dressing, sleep).
5. Family rituals and ceremonies, social or religious obligations (visits, anniversaries, political meetings, church duties).
6. Necessary study (for study circles, for school or professional examinations) (Dumazedier 1967: 13).

Again, like De Grazia, Dumazedier made no explicit reference to children in this categorization, although he did consider the number of children in his analysis of the results. He concluded that housewives worked a 34-hour week if they had no children, and a 70-hour week with three children. The free time of a married woman, he concluded, "would vary between fourteen and twenty-one hours a week." His conclusions reveal the insensitivity of the time budget method. Anyone — man or woman — responsible for three young children would recognize that the time "free" from responsibility is minimal — certainly not 14 hours a week. This lack of freedom is particularly evident for women who have been socialized to accept this responsibility.

The impression of women as leisured continues in more recent work. Roberts (1978) noted, without reference to research, the reduction in family responsibilities for women:

> Household gadgets, canned and frozen foods and even more
> important, the advent of the small planned family, have released
> the wife/mother from total domesticity, but for paid employ-
> ment rather than a life of leisure, again testifying to the public's
> preference for higher incomes and standards of consumption
> rather than for more free time (Roberts 1978: 17).

Feminists have challenged propositions like this. Armstrong and Armstrong (1978) have defined the work included in making a family or household operate as: 1) housework (now generally recognized); 2) child-care (invisible to De Grazia and Dumazedier); 3) tension management; and 4) sexual relationships.

Tension management includes the generally supportive and stroking behavior to comfort or encourage a spouse, child, or friend — the emotional work of keeping people together and in harmony. Armstrong and Armstrong also include work to develop and maintain the sexual relationship, including making oneself attractive, preparing a seductive environment, as well as responding to a sexual advance. Good sexual relationships, they recognize, require effort.

Time budget studies have been conducted in only one of these four areas — housework. Such studies show that the work week for homemakers actually increased from 52 hours in the 1920s to 55 in the 1960s, with some studies showing 70 to 75 hour weeks for those with young children (Armstrong and Armstrong 1978; Berk and Berk 1981; Gershuny *et al.* 1986; Luxton 1983). This contrasts dramatically with Roberts' assertions — probably because there are fewer servants, fewer helpful live-in relatives, and because older children are in school. Armstrong and Armstrong also suggest that housekeeping standards may have increased and that shopping has become more time-consuming. In addition to these long hours on the job, full-time homemakers are always "on call," and even women without children did 4.2 hours of housework on their "day off" (Armstrong and Armstrong 1978: 64).

Women in the workforce worked even harder, and sacrificed their leisure, though in general their spouses did not. Armstrong and Armstrong showed that:

> Husbands in childless families increased their regular housework time by six minutes a week when their wives joined the labor force; in families with children, the husband's contribution to regular housework increased by an hour a week when their wives obtained paid employment (p. 55).

Using in-depth interviews that revealed the meaning of activities, rather than just describing the activities themselves, Luxton (1983) studied working class households in Flin Flon, Manitoba. She showed women coming home from work "dead tired" and having to "work, cook and be with the kids" while their husbands lay around "drinking beer and watching TV" (Luxton 1983: 34). If men helped, it was to do something that the woman had done while she was doing three other things at once (such as preparing the salad while she made the rest of the meal). Men did not accept roles in management or pre-planning. Men "babysat" their children; the woman still had to find the day care center.

Many women dislike housework, finding it boring and repetitive (Horna 1985; Oakley 1974: 41-60). Although some chores are made less burdensome because they are part of a more significant role of caring for others (DeVault 1985), domestic life does not consist of "vicarious leisure," "semi-leisure," or the "semi-pleasurable" activity identified by some male leisure theorists. "Leisure" activities, Armstrong and Armstrong (1978) found, were often concurrent with those boring household tasks. Some hobbies were related to household maintenance; visiting also involved child-care; entertaining involved serving food; and watching television could include rocking the baby.

Shaw (1982) and Glyptis et al. (1987) have both expanded the time budget method by asking respondents to label their own activities as "work," "leisure," a "mixture," or "neither." Shaw found that men and women experience leisure in different activities. Men were more likely to find leisure in cooking, child-care, and shopping. Women were more likely to find leisure in listening to the radio (Shaw 1982: 136). She also found that only half of people's self-defined leisure occurred in time free from obligation: the social science concept of leisure as freedom from obligation does not appear to correspond with popular conceptions. Shaw confirmed earlier findings about women's comparative lack of leisure, for by their own definitions they had less than men, particularly during that period of supposed leisure, the weekend. She also found that women's employment status had little impact on their perceptions of their own leisure. However, Shaw did not take the next step in understanding her respondents' experiences. Her work remains bound within the limits of the dichotomous concept of work and leisure.

Some researchers have argued for a reintegration of the two halves of the work/leisure dichotomy. Govaerts (1969) and Deem (1982), for example, also show that women have less leisure. Deem points out that much of what women do is an extension of household or paid work, and is "not leisure at all." Colley (1984) and Horna (in press) show, further, that this leisure is home-based and family centered. This leads Gregory (1982) to suggest more qualitative studies of the integration of "work" and "leisure" in women's lives. Henderson and Rannells (1988) pursued this form of study in their oral history project involving farm women. But integration of the two parts of the dichotomy fails on two counts. The two phenomena are defined in reference to one another, and these definitions become meaningless if the division between them is lost. Second, the integration of the two phenomena is still less than the whole as experienced by people in their real lives. An approach is needed that is not structured either by the concept of work, or by the concept of leisure, or by some muddy amalgam of the two.

Time budget studies may help to describe the external forms of people's lives, which may be a useful contribution in itself. However, such studies have stripped activities of their context, analyzing what is done and for how long, rather than looking at the meaning of those activities in the context of an entire life and the relationships it entails. Feminist researchers have applied the time budget method to instrumental activities such as housework, but most child-care activities, tension management, and sexual relationships aspects of people's roles as spouse and parent are not accessible to such studies. The methodology of time budget analysis omits from analysis the expressive aspects of human activity that have been predominantly women's responsibility. Such analysis cannot comprehend the complexity of parenting, the significance of people's emotional work in tension management, or in building and maintaining satisfying sexual relationships.

Familism in Leisure Research

A second problem that has exacerbated the androcentric bias in leisure research is the tendency to treat women's leisure as an extension of the family. Most of the major theorists do this. Veblen saw women solely in relationship to their husbands, or, in the case of female servants, in relationship to their masters. De Grazia attempted a time budget of activities for men and women in families. Dumazedier saw leisure as a challenge for the family, and as a source of new family cohesion. Roberts (1978) asserted that the family is powerful in shaping leisure behavior. Kelly (1978) acknowledged the tension between the intimacy and role responsibilities within the family, and its key position in providing leisure that relies on freedom and autonomy. He studied what he called "family leisure," its limitations and satisfactions (Kelly 1987). Witt and Goodale (1982) and Bernard (1984) described leisure as contributing to family "stability," and reducing the impact of stress. Horna (in press) invented a category of "family leisure," in which "family" and "leisure" coexist. All these approaches fall into the "familist" trap. They all assume *the* family to be monolithic in its internal workings, and to approximate the nuclear two-parent family norm.

Eichler (1983) has challenged both these familist assumptions. She has shown that the participants in a marriage may have very different experiences of that marriage, and that marriage is better for men than for women. Married men are, on the whole, happier in their marriages, and healthier, than married women. The same event can be experienced differently by two participants, even when those two people are married to one another. Much leisure research is "familist" because of an assumption that the family as a whole experiences "leisure" together. For example, Kelly's (1978) study of "family leisure" suggests that "playing with children," "family outings," and "child centered activity" are leisure for all family members. This ignores the work needed to organize such experiences. Roberts (1978) falls into a similar trap, acknowledging that the major function of the family is "providing recreation" (p. 126) without recognizing that someone in the family has to work to make that recreation possible. Horna's idea of "family leisure" also fails to recognize the different experience of that "leisure" for various family members. Who, for example packs the picnic, makes sure people are dressed appropriately, and have extra sweaters and raincoats? Who puts gas in the car and checks the tire pressure? Who selects activities for others' pleasure rather than their own (tobogganing when one would rather be cross-country skiing; going to a "family" movie when there's an adult movie that one would prefer; or rereading a particular bed time story for the zillionth time)? Who manages the tension and ensures that everyone has a good time, that children don't fight in the back seat, or make a scene in the restaurant, or swear when Granny is within hearing?

"Family leisure" may not exist for all members of the family. Camping holidays, for example, can be stressful rather than pleasurable (Rosenblatt and Russell 1975), as the site of household chores is moved to a site without accustomed conveniences (Cerullo and Ewen 1984). Leisure researchers, as people involved in training recreation administrators, should, of all people, be willing to acknowledge that family leisure requires organization by somebody! Interviews with women show that they work extremely hard, for example, in organizing and producing family celebrations such as Christmas (Bella 1987, 1988). By calling the experience of leisure in families "family leisure," studies by Kelly, Roberts, Horna, and others have rendered invisible the work done to make that leisure possible.

These assumptions about "the family" and "its leisure" are combined in the leisure literature with assumptions about "the role" of the husband (as breadwinner) and the wife (as homemaker). Roberts, writing in the United Kingdom in 1978, still believed that "dual-career families" were sufficiently uncommon to attract little notice, even though the majority of married women were already in the labor force (United Kingdom 1980: 16). Iso-Ahola interpreted sex differences in leisure motivation with reference to traditional gender roles. He found that, for men, work-related activity could become leisure if there was a perceived choice in doing the activity. For women, the degree of choice was not a factor in their identifying or experiencing "leisure" — rather it was intrinsic motivation, regardless of perceived choice. He commented on these differences:

> These two findings pertaining to sex differences can best be explained in light of the socialization process. Since men are typically socialized to be breadwinners and women housewives and homemakers, the latter may consequently become more open to, and appreciative of, leisure than the former. Thus, in the socialization process, women may learn to value the intrinsic aspects of leisure because leisure becomes a more important source of satisfying their need to be competent and self determined than does work (Iso-Ahola 1980: 188-189).

This is a typically sexist interpretation of a leisure research finding. It focuses on explaining one difference between men and women (the difference in intrinsic motivation in leisure) with reference to traditional sex roles, without acknowledging the extent to which these roles are changing. Over half the women in Canada over 15 years of age are in the labor force. One third of children under six years of age have both parents in the labor force. Labor force participation reduces women's access to leisure without substantially changing that of men (Shaw 1987), which might suggest that women all lead unbalanced lives. However, women working outside the home were happier and more satisfied with their marriages than those who did not (Eichler 1983). The difference related to perceived choice, identified by Iso-Ahola, could relate to the objective conditions of any person with primary parenting responsibilities, rather than to socialization. Women, living as they do in a network of relationships of mutual obligation, accept obligation as an inevitable part of life, not as a barrier to be overcome. It could be that these relationships, not the intrinsic leisurely character of the activities in which those relationships are built, give women their sense of meaning, competence, and confidence.

The familist bias is also evident in Allen and Donelly's (1985) study of the social unit of participation for favorite leisure activities. They report choices of recreation with "family," "friends," "family and friends," or "alone." They do not differentiate, however, between the different kinds of family experiences that are possible in "family" recreation. Is this a parent describing favorite activities with children? Or with a spouse or adult sibling? What is the dependence context of that relationship? Such a dependence dramatically shifts the meaning and significance of that "favorite" activity.

The leisure literature also tends to rely on assumptions that all families are close to the "two adults and two children" norm. However, while the permanent pair bond, raising two of their own children, may dominate the literature, Eichler (1983) has dismantled this assumption. Such traditional families no longer dominate the real world. Of children born in the mid-seventies, about 45% will likely live in a one-parent family at some point, and most of those will also become part of a new two-parent family (Eichler 1983). The single parent, the non-custodial parent, and the blended family have all become permanent features of our social organization.

The leisure literature has not yet caught up with this new reality. In 1978, Roberts still believed that lifelong monogamy was the rule rather than the exception, that "dual career families" were still "uncommon," and that the housewives of the affluent middle class were satisfied and content (pp. 127-129). His report on "family leisure" included the "married" and the "unmarried," with only the "married" listed as having children (p. 99). This was at a period when, in the United Kingdom, one-fifth of marriages could be expected to end in divorce (United Kingdom 1979: 10). By 1984, over a third of the marriages taking place in that country were remarriages for one or both parties (United Kingdom 1986: 20). But these newly emerging family patterns and diversity did not seem to interest Roberts, even though divorce may have a considerable impact on family leisure, as the noncustodial parent seeks to organize leisure experiences which he (or she) may enjoy with the children who are no longer part of his (or her) own household.

Kelly (1978) also devoted a chapter to "Leisure and the family," describing the "integration of family and leisure" as a "social fact" (p. 129). His findings were not broken down by sex (a regrettable omission, given the different perceptions that men and women have of their families). However, Kelly found that people appear to enjoy the "relatively constrained" leisure within their families more than they enjoy pure unconditional and unconstrained leisure. This he seemed to find somewhat puzzling, but indisputable. Unlike Roberts, Kelly acknowledged contemporary shifts in family structure, but his suggestions reflected his ambivalence over the value of "family leisure" as compared with the abstract ideal of "unconstrained leisure."

Longer life spans, and decisions not to have children, have brought more pure unconditional leisure for some — which Kelly values. However, he also describes the decline of the traditional nuclear family as the loss of a resource for a form of leisure people enjoy. He acknowledges that the transitions between family forms may be painful, and that leisure can perform an ameliorating or bridging role. However, he also acknowledges that for those who might need this bridge most acutely (single parents with custody of their children), leisure is too scarce to be an adequate bridge. Two-worker families will have more income to purchase their leisure needs, but at the cost of time for that leisure. Women in two-worker families, in particular, have "scheduling constraints," and may have to lower their expectations for themselves as parents and homemakers.

Kelly identifies typical "family leisure" as vacations such as camping trips, scheduled events such as school concerts, or informal exchange around the dinner table, in the garden or puttering in the garage. Kelly seems to have ended up in confusion. He wants to retain his original notion of unconstrained leisure as a conceptual ideal type; yet his data seem to show that other things — the restraints of family ties and relationships — are more important to the people he is studying. Also, his analysis of "family leisure" has ignored the reality of the work required to organize that leisure.

Horna (in press) has attempted to solve the problem of leisure in families by introducing two separate domains, "family" and "leisure,"which intersect and overlap. She labels the area in which both occur as "family leisure." This area was larger, she found, for women than for men, whereas men had more leisure outside their families. However, she did not take the next step of analyzing the meanings of "family leisure" to different family members, or to identifying the work that is required by some family members to produce leisure for others.

THE POWER TO NAME THE EXPERIENCE

A new approach is needed, which will give primary importance to people's understanding and perceptions of their own lives, rather than relying on androcentric and dichotomous concepts such as work and leisure. The assignment of a label to a phenomenon is never a politically neutral act. To name, and thereby classify, an experience, an activity, or even a time-span, is an active exercise of power. Foucault (1965) showed that by labeling something "madness," the isolation of those so labeled was legitimized. By labeling something "criminal" (Foucault 1979), or "diseased" (Foucault 1973), other treatments were also legitimized. He also showed how the meanings of these labels have shifted historically, related to the dominant paradigm or "episteme" of a specific period. The paradigm of the Renaissance, concerned with resemblances and accepting the identity of the thing and the language used to describe it, for example, gave way to the Classical age when things were understood within taxonomies, and the language itself disappeared as an object of study. Only in the Post-Positivist era does language re-emerge as distinct from phenomena, as a focus of study in itself, and with a history of its own (Foucault 1970).

The concept of leisure, like the concepts of "madness," "criminal," and "disease," has political implications. To label or name something carries implications of social, psychological, and political importance. To name is an act of power:

> Discursive practices are political and social practices, that to speak within an established mode of speaking is not simply to support some individuals or groups over others, but also to reproduce and affirm the existing system of power in the society (Shapiro 1981: 163).

To label something is an active exercise of power (Foucault 1982). If that which is labeled is part of one's own life, then the act is self-empowering, in the sense used by the women's movement and the peace movement. If that which is labeled is part of someone else's life, then the act of naming is an active exercise of power over that person. The act of naming is then controlling and alienating (Smith 1979). The naming of one person's experience as "leisure" by another is an example of alienation through naming. For example, if an unemployed person's activities were labeled as "leisure," many would conclude that, since this activity is not work, it is not socially productive. Such conclusions have led many to condemn the unemployed and to question the value of unemployment insurance and other social security programs. Since leisure is pleasurable to the individual, the unemployed person is thought to be resented even though we know unemployment has destructive impacts on individual health and family life (Glyptis, this volume). Similarly, if I use the term "leisure" (or "semi-leisure" or "vicarious leisure") to describe homemaking, I am suggesting that this activity also is not work. Homemaking becomes some marginally useful activity, which automatically brings pleasure to the individual. Further benefits for homemakers, such as pensions or disability benefits, shorter hours, days off, and regular holidays, appear illegitimate. Marxist feminists have used the phrase "reproductive labor" in their insistence that this homemaking is not leisure — but they have done so without penetrating the mass consciousness. We still need to reclaim, and rename, this part of women's experience.

Piché (1985: 5) has observed that "family leisure is often experienced as work by women." Daly (1973) describes the evolution of women's liberation as the claiming of this right to name. She identifies particularly the need to rename the phenomena that have been named in the "dichotomizing-reifying-projecting syndrome" characteristic of patriarchal consciousness (p. 33). "Work" and "leisure" have been named as part of this patriarchal syndrome. Daly argues for a new hearing and a new naming of women's experience to replace such names.

Women, I believe, should reclaim their experiences by finding words other than "work" and "leisure" to name the experiences that make up our lives. This, I believe, is where the renaming of that experience called "leisure" should begin. This new hearing and naming would lead us to understand and appreciate some of the characteristics of women's lives that have to this point been inaccessible to our knowledge. I believe that many of these new understandings would be concerned with relationships, and the ways that these are built through activity. In her critique of malestream psychology, Wine (1982) has used the term "relationality" to name the "principle centrally representative of women's experience." She shows a number of ways in which this "relationality" is expressed:

> Women's self-esteem is tied to their perceptions of their own morally good and bad behavior, reflecting concern for the consequences of their behaviors on others, while men's self-esteem is tied only to self-perceived good behaviors (Wine 1982: 84).

This principle is reflected in women's superior skills in listening, in interpreting emotional social messages, and in pro-social rather than anti-social behavior. Correspondingly, our sense of personal identity is based in our relationships to others, and our responsibilities in those relationships, rather than solely in terms of their job (Wine 1982: 86). Women's friendships also have a different quality from those of men. Our friendships seem to stress expressiveness, while men's stress activity. Women have friendships that are more empathetic and altruistic, while male friendships are more companionate, involving doing things together (Mackie 1983: 153). Girls focus their play on intensive relationships with a small group of "best" friends. Boys play in larger groups, where "liking" or "not liking" is less crucial, and where ability to play the game is more important (Mackie 1983: 157).

These differences all reflect the principle which Wine names "relationality." This principle leads to a better understanding of the meanings of people's lives than the dichotomy of work and leisure. The willingness of women to give up, upon marriage, many of the friendships and activities enjoyed while single, can perhaps be understood, for example, in terms of the significance of the new relationships associated with marriage — in terms, in other words, of relationality. The meaning of the activity is in one's relationship to those with whom one is doing the activity. The meaning lies not in the activity itself — whether it is washing dishes, playing squash, or reading aloud — but in the context of relationship and responsibility. Both "work" and "leisure" are irrelevant to our understanding of the meaning of the activity. Similarly, the principle of "relationality" leads women to place a high value on obligation to others. Leisure as "freedom from obligation" has no value to one who values relationships with others as supremely important. Within the new principle, claimed and named "relationality" by Wine, leisure as freedom from obligation has no meaning or value.

This approach to understanding human lives would involve the newer methodologies conjured up by such phrases as "qualitative research" and "grounded theory." The focus of study would be on the various aspects of group life that have been traditionally considered to be part of leisure (family celebrations; vacations; perhaps even the evening meal), to analyze the meaning of these events to the various family members. Kelly (1987: 214) suggests that leisure affords "the opportunity to celebrate," in both secular and religious festivals. However, the production of the rituals associated with celebration is also work.

The work required to produce family leisure (including celebrations) deserves further study. DeVault's (1985) discussion of the ways that the organization of a family meal produces group life is an example of the needed work. We also need to know more about how families produce the rituals that are essential to their stability and security (Wolin and Bennett 1984). We need more understanding of Sunday suppers — the kind when adult children return with their own children; of Christmas and Thanksgiving; of family vacations (Cerullo and Ewen 1984); of eating out; of picnics and other family outings; of the contribution of sports events (e.g. Grey Cup or Super Bowl parties) to group life; of family reunions of various kinds; of the use of telephones and letters to retain ties with distant friends and family; of the contributions of community organizations to various forms of family life (including everything from the events sponsored by recreation and religious organizations to the services of commercial fast food outlets and games parks). In every instance, we will need qualitative studies that seek to understand the context of relationship, as well as a description of activity. In all cases we will need to understand the various meanings to all members of a family, and seek to tease out the contributions that all family members make to the group experience. Only then can we reveal the full significance of those contributions that have typically been made by women — contributions that have been invisible to positivist researchers using androcentric concepts such as "leisure."

FAMILY LEISURE AS WOMEN'S WORK: THE CASE OF CHRISTMAS

An exploratory study of the work women do to create what might be called "family leisure" has focussed on the production of the family Christmas. This seasonal celebration is generally expected to be a happy, family-oriented holiday, but the happiness of the holiday requires work, and even then is not always attainable (Robinson and Coppock Staehili 1982). Christmas can be excruciatingly painful. The production of Christmas brings into focus the invisible emotional work (as well as the more visible physical work) that women do to create happy experiences in their families.

Interviews with a variety of women have demonstrated the depth and significance of the work that women do to create Christmas for their families (Bella 1987). Some women described the physical work done by their mothers and grandmothers, which subsequently became the model for their own expectations of themselves:

NA The very first Christmas I remember, my mother did most of the work. She did most of the cleaning; she did most of the cooking; she did all the organizing, bringing everyone together.... And my Dad basically sat back and watched everything.

NB Based on other families that I have known, and families that I have seen, it is more often than not that the female gets the brunt of all the Christmas responsibilities, and all the chores that go along with it.

BS It was the female, the mother, who would do all that social organization. I felt there was a heavy responsibility on her, although she accepted it as her role.

MW Frankly, it was mostly the three women who lived in the house who did the major preparations.

RM She's the pivotal character in everything, not just celebrations.... Even when she was working she would do everything.

KK Everything would appear magically, and who makes it appear? Mother! It's so ingrained.

PM She did the gift buying, she did the house decorations, she did the cooking, she did the baking, she did the Christmas cards, any of the contact that was established annually.

Their emotional work was also recognized:

RM She would always be pushing things under the carpet and she would want to ignore anything at all costs — and just keep up the front.

RM My mother was responsible for all aspects of it, including keeping the peace most of the time.

Most of the women continued these traditions in their own homes and families. When asked why, in view of all of the physical work involved, they suggested that they wanted to both reproduce the happy memories and experiences of their own childhood Christmases, and to affirm to family members that they were important and valued.

BD I always try to do it the way it was when I was a kid. Keep everything just the same, as much as I can without really thinking why, but just because it feels right.

NA We make everything very special. The table is set beautifully. My grandfather's silverware is used, and we have flowers and stuff. The whole house is decorated in a very special way.

Of course, they would try to reproduce a Christmas-card Christmas, but fall short because of the work involved.

> **KK** Each year he says, "This year you and I are really going to do Christmas properly. We are going to invite friends in, we are going to cook weeks in advance." But Christmas comes and he's overworked, I'm overworked. It hasn't really happened.

The purpose of Christmas celebration was seen in terms of "relationality:"

> **BS** It's the time when people stop and think about who they are, and it's an important time. People start to think about themselves, and gatherings and letting their defences down.
>
> **NB** Communication is important. It's a time of year when you can say, indirectly or directly, "I really care about you" and "you mean a lot to me" and "you've enhanced my life."
>
> **RM** Meaningful is the key word. It isn't the ritual *per se*, but the connection with somebody. You sort of knock down the barriers a bit and people just relax and enjoy one another's company as one human being to another. That's probably what makes Christmas special.

The rituals of Christmas were valued because they symbolized this connectedness and relationship between people, including connectedness with absent parents and grandparents. Food was more than nourishment; it was something to bring people together, to tell people they mattered. Gifts, also, said something special and affirming to those who were to receive them.

All the women worked hard to produce and reproduce Christmas. Some continue to work physically hard, reproducing the specific rituals associated with the celebration. In some instances the symbols have been simplified, to reduce the physical work. In some families the chores have been shared, so that all participate. But still, the woman remains in the center, organizing, planning, distributing chores, encouraging, keeping the peace, trying above all to ensure that through her efforts and those of others the family is celebrated and its members are affirmed. This is an example, I think, of the work need to create any satisfying experience — including those which occur in the intimacy of our families.

BEYOND ANDROCENTRISM? A DIRECTION FOR LEISURE STUDIES

Leisure has been defined in reference to a dichotomy between work and leisure, and has been associated with the idea of freedom from obligation. This chapter has shown that this traditional conception has led students of leisure to neglect or misperceive women's lives, and those parts of men's lives having to do with dependence and relationships. Examinations of time budget studies and of the familist assumptions in the leisure literature have demonstrated the extent to which women's lives have been misunderstood.

Time budget analysis tends to ignore the invisible emotional and relational work that women in their families do while also engaged in physical chores or other more leisure-like activities. Familist assumptions underlie the idea of "family leisure," preventing us from appreciating the work required by some family members in order that the family experience "leisure." Women's comments about their experience in producing Christmas illustrate the work required to produce this family celebration. "Family leisure," they suggest, is women's work.

This discussion has implications for the direction of leisure studies. Can the concept of "leisure" be rescued from its androcentric origins, or would this require so radical a redefinition that we would be studying a new phenomenon for which a new label should be coined?

I believe we might overcome the androcentric bias inherent in the work/leisure dichotomy by shifting from the idea of "dichotomy" to one of "dialectic." If one conceived of leisure as a phenomenon that always, by definition, entailed work, one might be able to reach an understanding that would acknowledge women's contribution to that work. De Grazia recognized the role that slaves played in enabling their owners to experience leisure. We should perhaps reintroduce that question in our present studies, and ask who had to work in order to make a particular experience possible. The answers would not only allow us to illuminate women's work in producing family leisure, but also the work people do as employees to produce experiences for others, and the work we do to produce opportunities for ourselves. The idea of work and leisure as a dialectic rather than a dichotomy might ensure that we always recognize that someone pays the cost (in terms of work) in order that others experience leisure.

However, even this reconceptualization will, I believe, prove insufficient. The idea of leisure has little relevance for those bound by relationships of dependence and interdependence, for obligation is always present. This does not mean that the lives of those so bound are necessarily less satisfying or more impoverished than the lives of those with sufficient freedom to experience "leisure." A person living or working in a setting of reciprocated affection and obligation may be very well satisfied. Women, we learn from psychologist

Wine (1982), consider the building and maintenance of relationships as life's work. Activities, she suggests, are valued because of the relationships they enhance and the people whose value they affirm. The organizing principle of women's lives (and probably also the lives of many men) is "relationality." The significant questions, then, have to do with relationships served through an activity, not whether that activity can be described as "leisure," or even as "work." The meaning of the activity is in the relationships served through that activity, not in the activity itself.

Footnotes

1. The ideas which form the core of this chapter were presented at a conference of the Canadian Research Institute for the Advancement of Women held in Moncton, New Brunswick, in November 1986, under the title, "Androcentrism and the sociology of leisure." Feedback to these ideas was invaluable for formulating this chapter.
2. A male colleague criticized my use of the term "misogynist." A female colleague commented, "the gendered character of the ideological conceptual frame is manifest in the impact of such horrific and misogynist views."
3. Note the androcentric use of the generic "he." Social scientists studying leisure have generally used the generic "he" to include both men and women (De Grazia 1962: 18; Farina 1980: 28; Kaplan 1975: xi; Owen 1969: 3; Pieper 1952: 22; Roberts 1978: 63, 90, 92). However, the use of the generic "he" produces images of men in the minds of readers and writers, even though the intention may be to include women (Schneider and Hacker 1973). Women reading such texts understand their own experience to be invalid or less important (Moulton 1981). Some of the attempted solutions to this problem have created confusion. Iso-Ahola tried to correct his use of the generic "he" with a comment, in the preface, that all references to "he" in his book should be read to include women (1980: ix). Some of his references, however, are to data that do not apply to the same extent for men and women (Spreitzer and Snyder 1976). Parker (1979) wrote about "people" while referring to conclusions that are primarily true for men. Eliminating masculinist language involves more than eliminating sex-specific pronouns. Writers must ensure that their data actually include both men and women, and that their assertions are true for both men and women (Eichler and Lapointe 1985).
4. We now have scientific confirmation that women do not find housework pleasurable, but generally find it overwhelmingly disagreeable (Horna 1985: 32).
5. Shaw's research (1982, 1985) is an exception — she permitted her research subjects to classify their own experiences. Also, a B.B.C. study (British Broadcasting Corporation 1984) reports simultaneous activities. However, a

recent international study which gathered data on simultaneous activities found them difficult to analyze, and returned to the idea of primary activities (Gershuny *et al.* 1986).

6. Other instances of research showing an androcentric bias can be found in this book. For example, Smith's spatial perspective focuses on locations away from home, ignoring those within the home or immediate neighborhood, where most women's "leisure" takes place. Also, women are invisible in Jackson's chapter on environmental attitudes, although his recommendation for "decentralized, small-scale, and individualistic" leisure opportunities could increase access for women.

7. Again, note the use of the generic "man."

References

Allen, L.R. and M.A. Donnelly. 1985. "An analysis of the social unit of participation and the perceived psychological outcomes associated with most enjoyable recreation activities." *Leisure Sciences 7:* 421-446.

Andrew, E. 1981. *Closing the Iron Cage: The Scientific Management of Work and Leisure.* Buffalo, NY: Black Rose.

Armstrong, P. and H. Armstrong. 1978. *The Double Ghetto: Canadian Women and Their Segregated Work.* Toronto: McClelland and Stewart.

Bella, L. 1987. "An exploration of the work women do to produce and reproduce family leisure: The example of Christmas." Paper presented at the CRIAW Conference, Winnipeg, MB.

Bella, L. 1988. "The invisible work of Christmas: The message in women's magazine advertisements." Paper presented at the Feminist Research Conference, University of Saskatoon, Saskatoon, SK.

Bernard, M. 1984. "Leisure-rich and leisure-poor: The leisure patterns of young adults." *Leisure Studies 3:* 343-361.

British Broadcasting Corporation. 1984. *Daily Life in the 1980s.* London: B.B.C. Data.

Cerullo, M. and P. Ewen. 1984. "The American family goes camping: Gender, family and the politics of space." *Antipode 16:* 35-45.

Colley, A. 1984. "Sex roles and explanation of leisure behaviour." *Leisure Studies 3:* 335-341.

Daly, M. 1973. *Beyond God the Father.* Boston, MA: Beacon Press.

De Grazia, S. 1962. *Of Time, Work and Leisure.* New York: Anchor.

DeBeauvoir, S. 1974. *The Second Sex.* New York: Vintage.

Deem, R. 1982. "Women, leisure and inequality." *Leisure Studies 1:* 29-46.

DeVault, M. 1985. "Mothers' household work." Motherhood Workshop, Simone DeBeauvoir Institute, Concordia University.

Diggins, J.P. 1978. *The Bard Savagery: Thorstein Veblen and Modern Social Theory*. New York: Continuum.

Dobnansky, L.E. 1957. *Veblenism: A New Critique*. Washington, DC: Public Affairs Press.

Dumazedier, J. 1967. *Toward a Society of Leisure*. New York: Free Press.

Eichler, M. 1983. *Families in Canada Today: Recent Changes and their Policy Consequences*. Agincourt, ON: Gage.

Eichler, M. and J. Lapointe. 1985. *On the Treatment of the Sexes in Research*. Social Sciences and Humanities Research Council of Canada.

Farina, J. 1980. "Perceptions of time." In *Recreation and Leisure: Issues in an Era of Change*, eds. T.L. Goodale and P.A. Witt, pp. 19-29. State College, PA: Venture Publishing.

Foucault, M. 1965. *Madness and Civilization: A History of Insanity in an Age of Reason*. New York: Random House.

Foucault, M. 1970. *The Order of Things: An Archeology of the Human Sciences*. London: Tavistock.

Foucault, M. 1973. *The Birth of the Clinic: An Archeology of Medical Perception*. New York: Pantheon.

Foucault, M. 1979. *Discipline and Punish: The Birth of the Prison*. New York: Random House.

Foucault, M. 1982. "The subject and power." In *Michel Foucault: Beyond Structuralism and Hermeneutics*, eds. H.L. Drefus and P. Rabinow, pp. 208-226. Chicago: University of Chicago Press.

Gershuny, J., I. Miles, S. Jones, C. Mullings, G. Thomas, and S. Wyatt. 1986. "Time budgets: Preliminary analysis of a national survey." *Quarterly Journal of Social Affairs 2:* 13-29.

Govaerts, F. 1969. *Loisir des Femmes et Temps Libre*. Belgium: Université Libre de Bruxelles.

Gregory, S. 1982. "Women among others: Another view." *Leisure Studies 1:* 47-52.

Henderson, K.A. and J.S. Rannells. 1988. "Farm women and the meaning of work and leisure." *Leisure Sciences 10*:41-50.

Horna, J.L.A. 1985. "Desires and preferences for leisure activities: More of the same." *World Leisure and Recreation* 28-32.

Horna, J.L.A. In press. "Family leisure." In *Family and Marriage: A Cross-Cultural Introduction*, ed. K. Ishwaran. New York: Oxford University Press.

Iso-Ahola, S.E. 1980. *The Social Psychology of Leisure and Recreation.* Dubuque, IA: William C. Brown.

Kaplan, M. 1975. *Leisure: Theory and Policy.* New York: John Wiley and Sons.

Kelly, J.R. 1978. "Family leisure in three communities." *Journal of Leisure Research 10:* 47-60,

Kelly, J.R. 1983. *Leisure Identities and Interactions.* London: George Allen and Unwin.

Kelly, J.R. 1987. *Freedom to Be: A New Sociology of Leisure.* New York: Macmillan.

Luxton, M. 1983. "The hands of the clock: Changing patterns in the gendered division of labour in the home." *Studies in Political Economy 12:* 27-44.

Mackie, M. 1983. *Exploring Gender Relations: A Canadian Perspective.* Scarborough, ON: Butterworth.

McCalla Vickers, J. 1982. "Memoirs of an ontological exile: The methodological rebellions of feminist research." In *Feminism in Canada: From Pressure to Politics*, eds. A. Miles and G. Finn. Buffalo, NY: Black Rose.

McCalla Vickers, J. 1984. *Taking Sex into Account: The Policy Consequences of Sexist Research.* Ottawa: Carleton University Press.

Moulton, J. 1981. "The myth of the neutral 'man'." In *Sexist Language: A Modern Philosophical Analysis*, ed. M. Vetterling-Braggin, pp. 100-115. Totowa, NJ: Littlefield.

Oakley, A. 1974. *The Sociology of Housework*. New York: Pantheon.

Owen, J.D. 1969. *The Price of Leisure*. Buffalo, NY: McGill Queens University Press.

Parker, S. 1979. "Retirement: Leisure or not" *Loisir et Soci été 11:* 329-340.

Piché, D. 1985. "Interacting with the urban environment: Two case studies of women and female adolescents." Paper presented at the Canadian Urban Studies Conference, University of Winnipeg, Winnipeg, MB.

Pieper, J. 1952. *Leisure: The Basis of Culture*. New York: Random House.

Pruette, L. 1924. *Women and Leisure: A Study of Social Waste*. New Hampshire: Ayer Co. (Reprinted 1972).

Roberts, K. 1978. *Contemporary Society and the Growth of Leisure*. White Plains, NY: Longman.

Robinson, J. and J. Coppock Staeheli. 1982. *Unplug the Christmas Machine*. New York: Willam Morrow.

Rosenblatt, P.C. and M.G. Russell. 1975. "The social psychology of potential problems in family vacation travel." *The Family Coordinator* 24: 209-215.

Ross, B. 1985. "The lodging of the time budget method in sexist bedrock: A feminist excavation." Unpublished paper, Ontario Institute for Studies in Education, Toronto, ON.

Schneider, J.W. and S.L. Hacker. 1973. "Sex role imagery and use of the generic 'man' in introduction texts: A case study in the sociology of sociology." *The American Sociologist 8:* 12-18.

Shapiro, M. 1981. *Language and Political Understanding: The Politics of Discursive Practices*. New Haven, CT: Yale University Press.

Shaw, S. 1982. "The sexual division of leisure: Meanings, perceptions, and the distribution of time." Unpublished Ph.D. thesis, Carleton University, Ottawa, ON.

Shaw, S. 1985. "The meanings of leisure in everyday life." *Leisure Sciences* 7: 1-24.

Shaw, S. 1987. "Female employment: Its impact on the distribution of time and leisure experiences of married women and their husbands." Paper presented at the Fifth Canadian Congress on Leisure Research, Dalhousie University, Halifax, NS.

Smith, D.E. 1979. "Using the oppressor's language." In *Resources for Feminist Research*, eds. M.K. Shirley and R.E. Vigler. Toronto, ON: Ontario Institute for Studies in Education.

Spreitzer, E. and E.E. Snyder. 1976. "Socialization into sport: An exploratory path analysis." *Research Quarterly 47:* 238-245.

Stajkov, Z. and P. Petkov. 1975. "A year long investigation of the time budget." In *Time Budgets and Social Activity*, ed. W. Michelson, pp. 48-64. Toronto, ON: University of Toronto, Centre for Urban and Community Studies.

United Kingdom. 1986. *Britain: An Official Handbook.* London: Central Office of Information. Volumes for 1986, 1983, 1980 and 1979.

Veblen, T. 1899. *The Theory of the Leisure Class.* New York: Macmillan.

Wilson, J. 1980. "Leisure and the private sphere." *Loisir et Société 3:* 299-322.

Wine, J.D. 1982. "Gynocentric values and feminist psychology." In *Feminism in Canada: From Pressure to Politics*, eds. A. Miles and G. Finn, pp. 67-88. Buffalo, NY: Black Rose.

Witt, P.A. and T.L. Goodale. 1982. "Stress, leisure and the family." *Recreation Research Review 9:* 28-32.

Wolin, S.J. and L.A. Bennett. 1984. "Family rituals." *Family Process 23:* 401-420.

LEISURE AND UNEMPLOYMENT

Sue Glyptis

Contemporary leisure concepts and rationales for provision are rooted in a climate of abundance. Though leisure has never been shared equally by all members of society, the 1960s and early 1970s brought promise of change. Full employment, rising incomes, shorter working weeks, longer holidays, earlier retirement, greater longevity, and improved mobility combined to create the prospect of greater leisure for all. An age of leisure seemed both inevitable and inviting.

From the mid 1970s, however, it became apparent that, for many people, release from work was to be more a burden than a blessing. Major structural shifts in the economy, the rapid adoption of new labor-saving technologies, and, in some countries, the deflationary economic policies of national governments, conspired to unleash unemployment as a dominant social and economic issue of the late twentieth century throughout the western world. Unemployment is no mere passing phase, but seems set to persist as one of the defining features of post-industrial society. Whereas, in the past, unemployment had been largely frictional in origin, resulting from the movement of people from one job to another, there is now an overall shortage of employment opportunities and a fundamental mismatch between the available labor force and the structure of production. Unemployment is structural, caused by the decline and closure of major sectors of traditional industry, coupled with the adoption of new labor-saving technology. Its effects have been compounded, in the UK, the U.S.A., and elsewhere, by the fact that the proportion of people entering the labor force has increased, particularly among women. Work is in short supply, and shared unequally. By the late 1970s, the age of leisure was being reinterpreted as the collapse of work (Jenkins and Sherman 1979).

The emerging era of unemployment confronts social scientists and leisure providers alike with new challenges. A key issue for practitioners and researchers is whether, and in what ways, leisure might assume a more prominent role in the lives of people without jobs. Unemployment also requires that concepts of leisure be looked at afresh. If leisure were simply non-work, then our non-workers would be the first arrivals in the age of leisure. However, if leisure begins where the obligations of work end, the unemployed have no leisure at all. Both precept and practice are put to the test.

In the academic literature, work and leisure have been treated in the past as a natural couplet, the first often invoked to help define the second. It must be said at the outset, of course, that "work" is widely acknowledged to encompass more than just paid work; in its broadest sense it comprises all that entails effort (see, for example, Parker 1983), though some forms of effort should probably be excluded, e.g. that expended and enjoyed in a game of squash freely undertaken for personal pleasure. However, in everyday parlance the conceptual trimmings tend to be cast aside, and "work" is often used simply to mean paid employment. Work, so used, was the more tangible and central concern, against which leisure, the more inexpressible domain, was located. Work was a touchstone, too, against which to interpret the satisfactions sought and derived in leisure. Kaplan (1975) went as far as to say that leisure has to be earned through work, or work-like commitments, or it is accompanied by feelings of guilt.

Roberts (1978) and Parker (1983), drawing also from the writings of many others (notably Argyle 1972; Bishop and Ikeda 1970; Kando and Summers 1971; Kelly 1976; Meissner 1971; Parker 1971; Rousseau 1978; Salaman 1971; Staines 1980; Wilensky 1960) have discussed three broad work-leisure relationships. First, leisure may be pursued as an "extension" of work (where certain work-based tasks, activities, or social contacts "spill over" substantially into the choice of leisure activity); second, leisure may be in "opposition" to work (where leisure activities and social networks are deliberately different from those of work); and third, leisure may be unrelated to work (where leisure is used neither to consolidate nor compensate for attributes of paid employment).

It is not solely the rise in unemployment which calls these connections into question. Those who *do* enter paid employment tend to start later, after an extended period of education, retire earlier, and live longer; compared with the past, within the typical lifespan, paid work is a shrinking domain, both for the employed and the unemployed. Concepts of leisure must adapt to, and accommodate, these new social contexts.

In the realm of professional practice, leisure providers in the past quarter-century have been geared principally to providing opportunities for public enjoyment outside working hours. The "market" has comprised predominantly employed people (and their families) seeking out-of-home relaxation, entertainment, and enjoyment on weekday evenings, at weekends, and on holidays, and with the mobility, finances, and social networks to create and fulfil their leisure aspirations. The obvious role for the newly institutionalizing leisure profession in the buoyant economic times of the 1960s and early 1970s was to provide (or encourage the provision of) facilities, such as sports centers, swimming pools, playing fields, and country parks. Soon, however, in the UK and elsewhere, there was a growing recognition, within the public sector, of leisure as "part of the general fabric of the social services" (House of Lords Select Committee on Sport and Leisure 1973: para. 67). In this context, it became increasingly clear that in leisure opportunities, as in wealth and welfare generally, there were the "haves" and the "have nots." If leisure opportunities were to be truly accessible to all, then facilities alone were not enough (see also Goodale and Witt, this volume). Certain sectors of the population, notably women, the elderly, the disabled, school leavers, ethnic minorities, and unemployed people, were markedly under-represented in most forms of out-of-home leisure activity. The late 1970s and early 1980s, therefore, witnessed a change of emphasis from a facility orientation to a community orientation, with policies and provisions increasingly aimed at the (assumed) needs of specific "target groups" whom traditional facility provision had manifestly failed to serve (Sports Council 1982, 1984). Goodale and Witt, elsewhere in this book, chart the emergence of similar welfare concerns and interventionist approaches in the United States. In the 1980s, the most widespread development of such provisions in the United Kingdom has been in relation to the unemployed.

In considering these changes, this chapter addresses three main themes. First, the characteristics and circumstances of the unemployed are briefly described. Second, the lifestyles of unemployed people are discussed, drawing mainly from empirical sources on the time use of unemployed people. Third, the response of the leisure profession to high unemployment is addressed, with particular reference to public sector provision in the UK. The chapter concludes by summarizing some key issues to be addressed by leisure providers in attempting to cater for the needs of the unemployed, and by discussing the ability of conventional concepts of work and leisure to adjust to the realities of a postindustrial society.

UNEMPLOYED PEOPLE: THEIR CHARACTERISTICS AND CIRCUMSTANCES

In the UK, the dramatic rise in unemployment came at the end of the 1970s. The fragility of full employment first aroused widespread public consciousness when, in 1975, the number of unemployed topped one million. Then, after further steady growth, it doubled in less than two years, from 1.4 million in 1979 to 2.8 million in 1981. Registered unemployment (which understates the true level of unemployment by excluding certain categories of women ineligible to claim benefits, together with approximately three-quarters of a million people engaged on government training schemes) has exceeded or approximated 3 million since September 1982, and currently (August 1988) stands at 2.3 million, representing just under 9 percent of the labor force. Forty-three percent of the unemployed have been out of work for over a year, and 10 percent for over five years (Department of Employment 1988). Though the details may differ, the same basic pattern is mirrored elsewhere. Taylor (1986), for example, has reported that the unemployment rate in Canada in the 1980s was double that of the 1970s.

While unemployment touches all sectors of society, the brunt of the impact is borne selectively by particular types of people and places. The concentration of unemployment in particular industries has geographical ramifications. In the UK, there is a virtual threefold difference in unemployment rates between the least and worst hit regions. In November 1987, unemployment rates ranged from 6.5 percent in East Anglia and 6.6 percent in the South East, to 17.6 percent in Northern Ireland (*Employment Gazette*, January 1988). Locally, the contrasts are sharper still: the Northern region unemployment rate of 14 percent includes rates of 19.2 percent for the town of Middlesbrough and 21 percent for Hartlepool. In many neighborhoods, the rates are higher again, as the Archbishop of Canterbury's Commission on Urban Priority Areas (1986: xiv) found: "We have been confronted with the human consequences of unemployment, which in some urban areas may be over 50 per cent of the labour force and which occasionally reaches a level as high as 80 per cent." Such variations are echoed elsewhere, albeit in softer relief. In October 1986, unemployment in Alberta varied from 3.8 percent in the Eastern region to 10.8 percent in the North West (Taylor 1986).

Stark as the figures may be, they still present only the most visible face of unemployment. They convey nothing of the duration of unemployment, or of the recurrent, episodic unemployment experienced especially by many young workers and female workers. There are hidden offshoots too. Especially among young people, there is considerable evidence of sub-employment (Norris 1978; Roberts 1982): people with qualifications "trade down" their career aspirations and take any jobs they can get. This reduces — and, perhaps, completely removes — the prospects of those without qualifications, who are already at the bottom rung of the career ladder. There is evidence, too (for example, North Tyneside Community Development Project 1978), that the threat of unemployment makes people stay in jobs they dislike, and even, in extreme cases, turn down the offer of better jobs because they fear that a move to a new firm would leave them, as the newest arrivals, more vulnerable to redundancies.

Any attempt at a detailed social profile of the unemployed will quickly become dated, but a broad description is necessary to set the contemporary scene. Sinfield (1981: 18-19) puts it thus: "those most likely to be unemployed are people in low-paying and insecure jobs, the very young and the oldest in the labor force, people from amongst the disabled and handicapped, and generally those with the least skills living in the most depressed areas." There are ethnic variations too. Over the period 1984-1986, the average UK male unemployment rate was 10 percent for whites, 17 percent for Indians, Pakistanis and Bangladeshis, and 21 percent for West Indians and Guyanese (Central Statistical Office 1988). Other ethnic minorities bear a similar burden. Raymond (1984) refers to concentrations of unemployment among young blacks and Hispanics in Chicago. However, whatever the aggregate social characteristics of the unemployed, they experience unemployment as individuals, and, as Hudson (1983) reminds us, in terms of personal characteristics, values, motivations and satisfactions, "the unemployed are as varied as the rest of us."

The impact of unemployment, and strategies for coping with it, thus vary greatly. In the same way that leisure means different things to different people (see, for example, Glyptis, McInnes, and Patmore 1987; Stockdale 1985), so too does unemployment. With such diversity of personal characteristics, it would be idle to pretend that the unemployed are homogeneous in circumstances or needs, or that leisure can be prescribed as a blanket remedy.

In order to gauge whether leisure might replace some of the fulfillments hitherto derived from work, the effects of joblessness on the individual must first be appraised. Limitations of space necessitate a generalized account, focusing on key issues and typical reactions. Suffice it to stress in passing that what is true of the aggregate will not apply universally to all individuals: there will be many unemployed people whose experience of unemployment contrasts markedly with the patterns and processes depicted by the majority. Inevitably, too, the individual's response to unemployment will change over time. As the Pilgrim Trust (1938: 67) recognized: "the unemployed are not simply units of employability who can, through the medium of the dole ... be put in cold storage and taken out again immediately they are needed. While they are in cold storage, things are likely to happen to them."

Again, generalizations cannot speak for all, but many studies (Bakke 1933; Clarke 1982; Hill 1977; Jahoda, Lazarsfeld, and Zeisel 1972) have identified a cycle of adaptation to unemployment which people typically experience, reacting sequentially with shock, optimism, pessimism, and fatalism. Moynagh (1985: 12) comments on the initial part of the cycle: "the person's emotions may not be ready to take in the possibility of how much has been lost. They need to hang on to the pretence that very little has changed in practice. The idea, shared by many at the beginning of their unemployment, that being out of work is like a holiday, fits this need particularly well. This denial of reality is a form of psychological armor."

After the initial adjustment, most people are optimistic that work will be available, and many use their new found freedom to enjoy their hobbies and catch up on decorating and other jobs — described by Clarke (1982: 53) as "the Handyman-about-the-House Syndrome." Alongside an optimistic search for jobs, some even take up new leisure interests in a conscious attempt to be constructive and purposeful. With time, however, such interests lack conviction as major time-fillers, and phases of pessimism, purposelessness and, finally, fatalism set in.

On employment depends not just our daily bread. Certainly, for most of the unemployed, there is a substantial drop in income upon job loss (Miller 1982; Telford Development Corporation 1982) and, though few unemployed people in the welfare states of the West suffer absolute poverty, their *relative* poverty compared with their own previous material wealth and that which surrounds them in the broader society is real enough. Where economies in personal spending are called for, it is likely that expenditure on recreation and leisure activities will be sacrificed.

However, the non-financial consequences of unemployment can have an impact as great as, or greater than, the financial effects. Jahoda (1979) identifies five such categories of work "reward" which unemployment removes. First, employment structures our time, providing daily, weekly, and yearly routines, objectives to be attained, deadlines to meet, and a framework for daily activity. Evidence shows that few people are able to "believe in," follow, and derive fulfillment from routines they devise for themselves (Friedmann and Havighurst 1954; Hill 1978; Jahoda 1982; Jahoda, Lazarsfeld, and Zeisel 1972; Marsden and Duff 1975). As Kelvin (1981) asserts, any routine or structure must contain a core of necessity or perceived necessity if it is to lend certainty and predictability to people's thoughts, feelings, and actions; for most people, this means it must be devised or validated externally.

A second, related, point is that employment imposes enforced activity. Without a fixed time structure and sense of external obligation and purpose, many unemployed people suffer apathy and depression, because they have nothing "meaningful" to do.

Third, employment provides regularly shared experience beyond the context of the home and family. It brings us into purposeful, and usually pleasurable, contact with fellow-workers, clients, customers, and the community generally; it entails social interaction and imparts a sense of belonging. Unemployment severs these connections.

Fourth, through employment we are linked to goals and purposes that transcend our own. For most people, even those whose jobs are boring, repetitive, and irritating, employment imparts a sense of social importance: the product or service which the individual contributes toward is perceived to be socially or economically valuable. Workers thus perceive themselves to be "playing their part" and contributing to a communal purpose. Unemployment removes that external purpose.

Fifth, from employment derives much of our sense of personal and social identity. Employment arguably exerts the greatest single influence on the way in which others see us, and the way in which we see ourselves. As Brown (1978: 55-56) persuasively argues, occupation can be a measure of much more than merely job content: "'What does he do?' remains the most illuminating question to ask about someone met for the first time. It is illuminating precisely because a man's or a woman's work, or the fact that they do not need to or cannot work, is indicative of so much else about their social situation and their likely life experiences."

Much of the personal and social interpretation placed upon employment derives from the Protestant Work Ethic. In marked contrast to pre-Reformation times, when leisure (though not idleness) and the contemplative life were signs of status, work came to be held in high esteem not simply as a means to an end, but as an end in itself, and as a necessary prerequisite for salvation. As Kelvin (1980) explains, "in essence that ethic transformed work from something which was necessary into something which was virtuous — and then made a necessity of virtue." Whereas in the past a person's work (or the lack of it) was derived from his or her social status, the position was now reversed: status was to be attained through work. In this context, those who do not work may be seen as idle, insignificant, and ineffective, a judgment still made of (and by) the unemployed today, even in the face of massive structural unemployment. Many unemployed people thus feel inadequate and inferior: they lose not only their sense of worth but their sense of personal identity. As one of the unemployed men interviewed by Hill (1978: 118) put it, "I've become a statistic, I'm unemployed."

THE LIFESTYLES OF UNEMPLOYED PEOPLE

There is as yet little evidence of how unemployed people use their time. Certainly, though, the "life of leisure" often attributed to the unemployed by the popular press must be refuted. Very few unemployed people feel a sense of freedom, though Roberts (1982) shows that young unemployed people living in high unemployment areas are less troubled by their situation than most and are accustomed to being on the fringes of the workforce. The boom years of the 1950s and 1960s, he argues, when firms facing labor shortages could only attract school leavers by offering good pay and training, brought unusual rewards and prospects for young workers. At other times, young people have been hired and fired with equal readiness, according to the need for cheap and expendable labor. Roberts (1982: 15) further shows that some youth unemployment, while not relished, is voluntary: "Few ... young people relish unemployment. Nor are they masochists. They are simply retaining certain standards, like expecting to be paid for working." They are also more likely than their elders to alternate between short periods of employment, training schemes, and unemployment. As Roberts (1983: 2) concludes: "It is now normal for 16-20 year olds to be supported by parents and/or state allowances while in education or training. In addition, today's youth have the bricolage of post-war youth culture with which to interpret and respond to their predicaments. Some are coming to terms with the shortage of jobs by adopting sub-employment as the basis for alternative life-styles.... Peer relationships are not undermined but consolidated during spells between jobs. They act as the base for the life-styles and values through which the young people appraise education, training and employment opportunities."

Several factors ease the impact of unemployment for young people. Many have never worked, and none have identities anchored in lifetime attachments to particular jobs or industries. Many are long accustomed to unemployment in their own families and neighborhoods, and few have family responsibilities. Their difficulties should not be berated, however. Youngsters applying for jobs tread a circular path: no experience means no job; and no job means no experience. After school, a job is the natural next step. It signals independence and adulthood, and full participation in society. Unemployment, in effect, impedes the transition from adolescence to adulthood. Even most of the young people who cope reasonably well with it find unemployment unattractive, unrewarding, and unleisurely.

Stockdale (1985) portrays the conceptual mismatch between leisure and unemployment: "enforced free time as experienced by those who are unemployed does not necessarily possess the positive features of leisure. The free time of the unemployed is not perceived as 'earned'; it does not have the structure of free time within the normal working day, and there are social and financial constraints on its full use and enjoyment."

Kelvin, Dewberry, and Morley-Bunker (1984), undertaking fieldwork among the unemployed, encountered the practical difficulties: "We came to use the word 'leisure' very circumspectly in our interviews, because from our earliest piloting it was too likely to be greeted with irony or positive bitterness."

Little is known, indeed, about whether unemployed people perceive of leisure at all, let alone how, if at all, they pursue it. More is known of how the unemployed feel about unemployment than of what they spend their time doing. Bunker (1984: 1), distilling the findings of several empirical enquiries (Bunker and Dewberry 1983; Chappell 1982; Colledge and Bartholomew 1980; Jones 1972; Marsden and Duff 1975; Trew and Kilpatrick 1984), puts it plainly: "there can be few areas of social research where a single broad message emerges with such force and clarity. Unemployment is generally and intensely demoralizing, boring, and depressing."

Those who show the greatest resilience to unemployment are those who can keep themselves occupied. Hepworth (1980: 139), for example, concluded that "the best single predictor of mental health during unemployment was whether or not a man felt his time was occupied." Miles (1983) and Trew and Kilpatrick (1984) echoed that conclusion.

Studies of the effects of unemployment have been preoccupied with effects on men rather than women: "though women do feature in the literature on unemployment, they do so first and foremost as the wives of unemployed men, and as the mothers of such men's children" (Kelvin and Jarrett 1985: 65). Much the same is true of the literature on leisure. Indeed, as Bella (this volume) argues, traditional employment-based concepts of leisure have little relevance to women. As Rapoport (1982) noted, it is often assumed that unemployment is a lesser problem for women than for men, because women will transfer to the relatively invisible but socially acceptable role of housewives. Setting aside for the moment the fact that not all women are housewives, and not all housewives want to *be* full-time housewives, the traditional domestic role of women may mean that they find it easier than men to organize their own routines. Traditional domestic roles have other repercussions, too, such as young unemployed women becoming pregnant and attaining the positive role of motherhood. This is little more than conjecture, however, as empirical evidence to date is slight and inconclusive.

Few leisure participation surveys contain representative samples of unemployed people large enough to permit valid generalization. In the present context, a single illustration must suffice, based on data from the 1980 *General Household Survey* of 20,000 adults (age 16+) in England and Wales (Veal 1986). As Table 1 shows, participation by unemployed people in most out-of-home pursuits was lower than average; the disparities were particularly marked in the case of golf, camping and caravanning (trailer camping), table tennis, indoor bowling, rugby, and motor sports, where the participation rate by unemployed people was less than half that of the population in general. In some cases, though, the unemployed were apparently over-represented, notably in fishing, football (soccer), tennis, cycling, bowls, darts, and billiards and snooker. Proper interpretation of these contrasts, however, is impossible without full details (as yet unpublished) of the sub-sample sizes for specific activities and population sub-groups.

Participation surveys, in any case, provide better profiles of activities than of people; while they usefully examine the probability of particular types of people engaging in particular activities, they convey little of the "packaging" of activities, or lifestyles, of the people concerned. Time-use studies can do this much more effectively, though they are rarely used in this way, nor recorded for long enough to be more than illustrative of daily routines. However, mention must be made of time-use studies which have attempted to compare the activity patterns of employed and unemployed people, and one, in particular, which compares activity patterns before and after job loss.

The reality for most unemployed people tends to be a reduction of activity levels, particularly a withdrawal from out-of-home and social pursuits. Kelvin, Dewberry, and Morley-Bunker (1984) examined the time use patterns of 192 unemployed people, and asked respondents to compare the amount of time spent on various activities in the previous month with that in their last month of employment. While there was little evidence to support the popular assertion that unemployed people spend all day in bed (on average they slept for just under eight and a half hours per day; those aged 16-20 slept for about an hour longer), the dominant theme was of passive, home-based routines. Over two-thirds (68 percent) of the waking day was spent at home, 12 percent of which was allocated to subsistence activities (washing, eating, getting dressed), 18 percent to household duties (mainly cooking, cleaning, and child care),

Table 1
Participation in Selected Activities: England and Wales, 1980

	Unemployed people*	All adults aged 16+*
Outdoor Sports & Physical Activities	**32.8**	**37.8**
Walking	15.8	18.5
Swimming (sea)	4.8	6.1
Golf	1.2	2.1
Fishing	3.7	3.1
Soccer	3.2	2.7
Tennis	3.1	2.8
Camping / trailer camping	0.9	2.7
Bicycling	1.5	1.3
Lawn bowling	1.7	1.5
Cricket	0.9	1.4
Running	1.0	1.1
Indoor Sports & Games	**20.5**	**22.7**
Darts	7.8	7.4
Indoor swimming	5.3	6.0
Billiards / snooker	9.0	6.7
Squash	1.3	2.5
Badminton	1.5	2.2
Table tennis	1.3	2.0
Keep fit / yoga	0.7	1.6
Indoor / ten pin bowling	0.4	1.2
Spectator Sports	**10.5**	**10.2**
Soccer	3.6	4.0
Rugby	0.3	0.7
Motor sports	0.4	0.8
Cricket	1.4	1.5
Countryside Activities	**22.2**	**28.5**
Historic buildings	10.5	17.2
Visiting seaside	12.0	15.5
Visiting countryside	4.6	6.7

Table 1 (Continued)

	Unemployed people*	All adults aged 16+*
Visiting parks	4.6	5.8
Museums	3.1	5.2
Exhibitions	1.4	3.5
Zoos	2.3	3.1
Car outings	2.8	2.5
Boat trips	0.9	1.0
Wildlife parks	0.6	1.0

* Percent taking part in four weeks prior to interview.
Source: Adapted from Veal 1986, Table 5.

and 38 percent to "leisure" (as defined by the researchers). Unemployed women spent more time than unemployed men on household duties, but there were no significant age or gender variations in the time spent on leisure.

Of the average of nearly five and a half hours spent on leisure, five hours were spent watching television, though viewing was not necessarily the main activity throughout this time; there was some evidence that the regularity of programs provided something of a time anchor, and television gave a sense of contact with the real world outside. Away from home, shopping was the dominant activity, occupying over one and a quarter hours per day. Walking took up 20 minutes, and sport 5 minutes. The entire time spent by unemployed people out of the home amounted to less than that spent by employed people at their place of work.

Compared with their time use when employed, respondents reported that they now watched more television, did more housework and reading, and spent more time on hobbies. They spent less time on social activities and going out. Their participation in religious and community activities, creative pursuits, and playing games was unchanged. There was no increase in sports participation since becoming unemployed (involvement in swimming, football (soccer), tennis, bowls, and table tennis actually decreased), nor in live spectating. Watching sport on television, however, did increase.

Miles (1983) corroborates these findings: a time budget survey of 200 unemployed men in Brighton showed that they spent 48 percent of their time alone, and 65 percent at home. Single men and the older unemployed spent even more time alone, though the singles were less tied to home. Neither Miles, nor Trew and Kilpatrick (1984) found evidence of increased time spent sleeping.

Gershuny *et al.* (1986), comparing the time budgets of unemployed men and women, reported that unemployed men engaged in three times as much domestic work as employed men, with the increase concentrated, interestingly, in cooking and cleaning rather than child care.

For most unemployed people, then, leisure activity is curtailed rather than becoming a central source of structure and significance. There is evidence, too, that even among those who do take part regularly in newly adopted leisure pursuits, leisure retains its normal role. It does not become a work substitute. Kay (1987) examined the lifestyles of unemployed people who, after becoming unemployed, took part regularly in sport. They experienced the usual negative effects of job loss, including financial loss, loneliness, and boredom, but most had developed a more positive approach towards coping with it, and had a stronger sense of self-identity and self-confidence than most of the unemployed. Unemployment had affected their activity patterns in two significant ways. First, they were active not only in sport but in other ways, too. As with most unemployed people, they had increased (slightly) their involvement in home-based pursuits and decreased (slightly) their involvement in out-of-home activities. More surprisingly, they had increased their involvement in civic activities, hobbies, study, and education. Overall, for most, unemployment had led to an increase in leisure activities rather than the usual decrease. Furthermore, most had had previous spells of unemployment when they had suffered the more typical, wholly negative experience; in this latest spell they were deliberately constructing active lifestyles as a way of keeping busy.

The second effect of unemployment was evident in the emergence of "purposeful" activities, such as taking educational courses and doing voluntary work. For most, sport was not taken up as a substitute for work; it fulfilled its usual function as a leisure activity, and leisure carried the same meanings as for employed people. The "purposeful" activities, by contrast, were not seen as leisure. People attached greater importance to purposeful activities than to leisure, and there was some evidence of the purposeful activities functioning as a work substitute.

Piecemeal it may be, but the tentative evidence available does produce some common threads. Most unemployed people tend to reduce the time spent on active, out-of-home, and social activities, and increase their passive, solitary, and home-based pursuits. Most dislike being unemployed, and many find it difficult to fill their time. If leisure means anything to the unemployed, for most it finds little expression in enhanced use of facility-based recreations which form the traditional mainstay of public sector provision. How far this is caused by financial hardship and how far it is attributable to the psychological state of the unemployed is unclear. However, several studies (for example Kelvin 1981; Seabrook 1981) have revealed a general tendency toward retreatism among the unemployed.

UNEMPLOYMENT:
THE RESPONSE OF PUBLIC SECTOR
LEISURE PROVIDERS IN THE UNITED KINGDOM

The first manifestations of a strengthened public sector commitment to community recreation provision in the UK unfolded in the late 1970s. The Sports Council, for example, launched a new category of grant-aid to assist projects in "Areas of Special Need," and similar schemes were funded through programs concerned with "Football and the Community" and "Urban Deprivation." Projects established through these programs were aimed at the disadvantaged in general, including school leavers, ethnic minorities, pensioners, the disabled, low income groups, and the unemployed.

The turn of the decade brought a two-fold impetus to develop further programs of this type: first, the dramatic surge in unemployment gave striking visibility to this particular target group; and second, the urban riots of Brixton, Toxteth, and elsewhere brought the instability and social conditions of many inner-city communities starkly into prominence. It is often implied that unemployment *causes* crime, but the evidence is far from conclusive. A Home Office study in 1979 (referred to in Harris 1984), found a significant association between unemployment and crime among whites, but not among blacks and Asians. However, Carr-Hill and Stern (1979) and Tarling (1982) refute these connections, and point out that it is at least as likely that crime leads to unemployment, because having a criminal record makes it harder to get a job. Even more tenuous are arguments that the provision of leisure and community facilities prevents or cures problems of unrest (see, for example, Henry and Bramham 1986), though such claims have been enshrined into conventional wisdom at the highest level (Scarman 1982).

Thus, public sector leisure providers, who have never wielded massive political clout simply by "providing for public enjoyment," could now offer leisure as a means to other ends. Leisure provisions were needed in order to occupy and enhance the quality of life of unemployed people with time on their hands; and, in urban areas, leisure opportunities would be a strong contributor to improving social conditions and a positive community spirit. Such claims are not new, but recall a duality of purpose which has underpinned recreation provision from the mid-nineteenth century. Municipal provision, usually at the instigation of energetic voluntary initiative, has long sought to facilitate freedom of opportunity for the disadvantaged, and yet simultaneously to control its form. This was evident in Britain, for example, in the Rational Recreation Movement and the Civilizing Mission To The Poor, in the Recreation Movement of the U.S.A., and in the Playground Movement in Canada.

The cynical view, however, must be restrained. Well before the major urban riots, the Sports Council had begun preparing for the launch of three national demonstration schemes of sport for the unemployed: these, located in Leicester (The Sports Training and Recreation Scheme, or STARS),

Derwentside, and Hockley Port (Birmingham), were launched in the fall of 1981, initially for a three-year experimental period, with a substantial pump-priming grant from the Sports Council. Shortly afterwards, a similar program, Action Sport, was announced, to work with a broader range of target groups, initially in the urban communities of Greater London and the West Midlands. Both projects were the subject of extensive monitoring and evaluation programs fully reported elsewhere (Glyptis, Kay, and Donkin 1986a, 1986b; Rigg 1986); attention here must be confined to the salient achievements of the three schemes, the characteristics of which are summarized in Table 2, on pages 196 and 197.

The schemes aimed to make sport and recreation opportunities more readily available to the jobless and their families, and each involved a funding partnership between the Sports Council and other public and voluntary agencies which, it was hoped, would continue the schemes beyond the experimental period. All three did, in fact, continue, albeit in reduced or modified form. Each scheme brought together a team of sports leaders, at new or existing facilities, to offer the local unemployed a wide-ranging activity program, free or at nominal cost, and with transport and equipment provided. Several staff posts in all three schemes were funded by the Manpower Services Commission, the government training agency. None of the schemes required users to give proof of their unemployed status, as this might cause stigma and deter potential participants; instead the schemes were, in practice, open to all. Publicity was targeted towards the unemployed.

Impressive levels of participation were achieved. In the initial three-year period the Derwentside scheme, with a potential catchment of nearly 8,000 registered unemployed people in the District, attracted some 4,000 users, who generated over 50,000 attendances; in Leicester, with approximately 20,000 registered unemployed, 6,400 users generated over 30,000 attendances. The Hockley Port scheme experienced wide fluctuations in usage, largely because staff numbers — and therefore the extent of the program offered — varied considerably from year to year.

The participants came overwhelmingly from the intended target group. In Leicester, for example, unemployed people accounted for 98 percent of all attendances. Among these were many long-term unemployed people: half of the users had been out of work for over a year, and a third for over two years.

Men outnumbered women three to one, and the age profile was heavily skewed toward the younger unemployed. However, this should not be surprising. Sport generally appeals more to the young than the old, and more to men than women; the schemes for the unemployed simply mirrored these patterns.

It might be expected that the appeal of the schemes would be limited to those unemployed people who were already keen sports participants. Indeed, 60 percent of users of the Leicester scheme had previously taken part in the activities they did at STARS; however, 40 percent had never participated previously, and even among the 60 percent, half had long since given up sport.

The schemes thus succeeded in generating new recruits for sport, and in resurrecting lapsed interest. What they failed to do, though, by and large, was to retain that interest. For a committed minority (about one in ten users) sport became a central interest: they attended the schemes several times a week, some also took part in sport elsewhere, and several spent time with friends they met initially at the sports schemes; a few groups set up their own self-supporting clubs. For the majority, however, sport was something to taste, and perhaps occasionally dabble in: three-quarters of all users of the STARS scheme attended on five occasions or fewer. This is not necessarily a mark of failure, nor is it greatly at variance with the participation habits of young people generally. The scheme clearly provided an important opportunity for casual "dropping in"; most of the unemployed are not likely to become frequent sports players, but the fact that high levels of usage were sustained throughout (and beyond) the three-year period was a strong sign of demand for something to do on an occasional basis.

For many, the rewards for attending were more social than sporting. Social incentives proved important in motivating people to take part, and social benefits were prominent among the satisfactions gained. Social barriers were sometimes the cause of dropping out.

People heard about the schemes mostly from friends, and all but a few attended with friends. Mixing with other people, being able to relate to the sports leaders, and generally gaining a sense of purpose and confidence, were important benefits, as the comments of users confirm: "Before I went I hated myself, because I wasn't putting anything into society, but now I feel fit and more sure of myself"; "it's enjoyable company. You make friends"; "I have become more confident with people since starting these sports"; "It gives people who are unemployed something to look forward to as well as getting them out of the house."

For some unemployed people, however, the very idea of "special" provision created a form of social stigma in itself: "I feel that the STARS scheme is an insult to a person's identity ... a bit like going on an outing for underprivileged kids and everyone feeling sorry for you because you've never seen the sea before. Being unemployed is bad enough, without new stigmas being created ... for which someone is getting paid to organize them."

The main value of the national demonstration schemes lay in the lessons learned for application elsewhere; as blueprints for others to adopt fully, however, they were too large and too expensive (even though they involved only small numbers of staff) for most local authorities to contemplate. Furthermore, many authorities felt unable to wait for the results of a three-year experiment; more immediate action was called for. Throughout the 1980s, therefore, a great many local authority programs of recreation for the unemployed have been established, with varying styles of provision and varying success.

Table 2

Sport for the Unemployed: Sports Council (England) National Demonstration Schemes

	"Stars" Leicester	Derwentside Recreation Scheme	Hockley Port, Birmingham
Nature of scheme	Up to 40 weekly sports sessions at venues throughout Leicester. Activities included badminton, roller hockey, basketball, horse riding, running, football, 5-a-side, swimming, canoeing, trampolining, archery, table tennis, rock climbing, multi-activity sessions, and outdoor pursuits.	Sports sessions at over 40 venues throughout Derwentside District. Activities included 5-a-side, carpet bowls, swimming squash, badminton, canoeing, table tennis, hill walking, golf, keep fit, and outdoor pursuits.	Based at disused canal port in Handsworth. Some new facilities provided: small sports hall, kick-about area, playing field. Also organized activity program, at Port and other local facilities, including canoeing, jogging, badminton, netball, keep fit, weight training, swimming, and outdoor pursuits.
Sports Council funding	£117,000 over 3 years, towards staff costs, equipment, transport, and residential trips.	£175,000 over 3 years, towards staff costs, equipment, coaching courses, and publicity.	94,000 over 3 years, of which £51,000 towards new facilities and 43,000 towards staff costs, transport, equipment, and residential trips.
Host authority	Leicester City Council, Department of Recreation and Arts.	Derwentside District Council.	A voluntary group, the Cut Boat Folk Ltd.

Target group	Unemployed throughout Leicester. Scheme required no proof of unemployment.	The unemployed, their families and friends. Scheme open to all adults not in employment. No proof of unemployment sought.	Particular emphasis on young unemployed in Handsworth. Scheme required no proof of unemployment.
Unemployment rate	Registered unemployment, City of Leicester, 1984, 15%.	Registered unemployment, Derwentside District, 1984, 25%.	Registered unemployment, 1984 Soho Ward 36%, Handsworth Ward 30%.
Area covered	City-wide, but concentrating on selected priority areas with highest unemployment rates. Made use of spare capacity at existing leisure centers, community colleges, club facilities, etc.	District-wide, operating in the towns of Consett and Stanley, and villages in rural hinterland. made use of facilities owned by District Council, County Council, private clubs, and voluntary groups.	Site-based, concentrating on immediate community. Site is 5 acres, taken over by CBF in mid-1970s for development as adventure center for underprivileged children. Aims now broadended to providing general community resourse base. Comprises canal basin, associated buildings, sports facilities, city farm, riding center, boating activities, craft workshops, cafeteria, and youth and community clubs.

Source: Adapted from Table 1 in S.A. Glyptis and T.A. Kay, 1986

These have twice been reviewed nationally, first for England and Wales only (Glyptis and Riddington 1983) then, in greater depth, for the UK as a whole in 1985-87 (Glyptis and Pack 1988). A comparison between the years under review shows an increase in the number of local authorities making "special" provision for the unemployed, and a shift of emphasis in types of provision (Table 3). In 1982, 53 percent of local authorities in England and Wales had recreation policies and provisions specifically aimed at the unemployed, and a further 7 percent offered more general price concessions available to the unemployed and others. By 1985, both the amount of provision nationally and its scale within particular authorities had increased. By then 64 percent of authorities (61 percent in England) were operating special schemes for the unemployed, and 7 percent offered general price concessions. The basic characteristics of each type of provision, and the response generated, may be summarized as follows.

Table 3
Local Authority Sports Provision for the Unemployed in the UK

| | Percent of Local Authorities | | |
	England 1982	England 1985	UK 1985
No provision	40	30	29
Price concessions for all users	7	8	7
Price concessions for unemployed	42	33	33
Organized sessions	-	4	5
Concession cards	5	16	14
Sports leadership	5	8	9
Other	1	-	3
Base, and % of all local authorities	316 (79%)	334 (90%)	454 (90%)

Sources: Adapted from Glyptis and Pack 1988; Glyptis and Riddington 1983.

Price concessions for all users

These generally offered the use of facilities at reduced prices at specified, mostly off-peak times; some were restricted to school term times. Several authorities running this type of scheme were disappointed at the response of the unemployed. There were some successes, however, such as Knowsley Borough

Council's scheme, which in 1986 attracted over 4,000 attendances per week at six facilities from a total catchment population of 169,000 (including 19,000 registered unemployed).

Price concessions for the unemployed

Over two-thirds of these schemes applied only to the unemployed; in the remainder the concessions extended to other target groups. Many schemes required proof of unemployed status in the form of the Unemployment Benefit Card (UB40) issued to registered unemployed people. The concessions offered varied; nearly one in five schemes gave free use to the unemployed. Again, several authorities reported a low response.

Organized sessions

These schemes offered one or two activity sessions per week, mostly with a choice of activities available and the provision of basic coaching. Attendances were generally low, though schemes which actively promoted a club-like atmosphere, engendering a sense of belonging among users, fared rather better. So, too, did those which offered more unusual activities. The leader of one such project, providing two-day mid-week activity breaks for unemployed people, was under no illusions about how much could be achieved: "We know that these activities will never substitute for work, but they're really to get away from the day-to-day drudgery of the situation they're in ... a way of trying to break through and give them some sort of active interest."

Concessions cards (or "Passports to Leisure")

These schemes comprised a season ticket, whereby users were issued with cards or "passports" valid at specified facilities for a given period. Over a third were aimed specifically at the unemployed, the remainder encompassing additional target groups. As many as one in four of these schemes reported a disappointing response. Others, however, had attracted substantial interest from the unemployed. Birmingham City Council, for example, sold approximately 24,000 Passports to Leisure annually, 49 percent to unemployed people; Gateshead Metropolitan Borough Council sold nearly 12,000 Leisure Cards, 3,000 to the unemployed.

Sports leadership schemes

These offered programs of supervised activities, some free of charge and others at nominal cost, for a range of target groups, especially unemployed youngsters. Some included formal coaching but most were offered on a casual "turn up and play" basis. The scale of projects varied from just two or three staff to over sixty. Outreach work was a key aspect of most leadership schemes, with sports leaders actively promoting participation by contacting members of the target group through other organizations (e.g., Careers Service), through personal house-to-house canvassing, and in streets and shopping centers. Most programs were dominated by swimming, football (soccer), basketball, table tennis, badminton, weight training, and keep fit, and in some cases competitive leagues had been established which helped to retain participants' interest and gave structure to their involvement. A few schemes contained non-sporting activities, such as arts and crafts, music, car maintenance, and discussion groups.

By contrast with the pricing schemes, there was a general feeling of success among authorities providing sports leadership projects. Many consistently attracted large numbers of users, but, in line with the national demonstration projects, most reported that it was difficult to attract regular attendances by the unemployed, and difficult to encourage certain groups, notably young unemployed women, to take part at all.

CONCLUSIONS

Practical Issues

The practicalities of leisure provision for the unemployed may be addressed at both the tactical and strategic levels. The tactical questions concern how best to design, establish, manage, and promote leisure services in order to ensure maximum benefit for unemployed people. The strategic questions relate to policy and priorities, namely to what extent can (and should) leisure providers play a part in enhancing the quality of life of the unemployed; and, within leisure policy, what forms of provision are appropriate. The experience of the UK to date provides a wealth of guidance on tactics, but only pointers, rather than prescriptions, for strategy. The detailed lessons are fully documented in the published reviews; the broader practicalities are as follows.

Staff training for leadership schemes

Sports leaders and motivators need a special mix of skills, beyond that needed for conventional facility management. In the UK, most have a sporting background, but very few have been trained in community contact, outreach work, or social work. Most are expected to cope with running activity sessions, providing coaching, promoting awareness, recruiting and motivating users, and perhaps helping users to establish their own self-running activities. Community sports leadership training is becoming more widely available (notably through an award scheme of the Central Council of Physical Recreation), but the majority of leaders appointed to schemes to date have had to learn their community skills on-the-job.

Community self-help

Many schemes, especially sports leadership projects, set out with the intention of generating leadership from within the community, so that users can in due course take over the running of their own activities. As an officer of Corby District Council put it, the aim is "to innovate and abdicate."

This has not proved easy. In most cases unemployed people are not keen to commit themselves to attending regularly, nor to assume a leadership role. Indeed, if another agency is already providing leadership, users may see little point in taking on the responsibilities for themselves; they become, in that sense, dependent upon the schemes.

Meeting the needs of the unemployed

All but a few schemes of provision in the UK have been founded on the basis of assumed need, and sustained on the basis of assumed benefits (for further discussion, see Schreyer and Driver, this volume). While assumptions may be the only basis for making policy when aiming for "unknown" targets, they are hardly the proper basis for continuity when there is evidence of poor response. At the strategic level, leisure policy for the unemployed must be viewed in two ways. First, in the context of social need and social policy generally, leisure is not a high priority for most unemployed people; they have greater needs — for jobs, income, and comfortable homes. Only a few can adopt sport and recreation as a central source of structure and satisfaction in their daily lives. Second, however, within leisure policy the unemployed are important constituents, and the evidence in the UK to date is that sport and recreation can provide some enjoyment and purpose at some times for some unemployed people. However, there is as yet too little honest introspection about the extent of benefit actually accruing, and too little building upon lessons previously learned. Above all, there is a remarkably narrow focus in the range of provisions offered: the vast majority of schemes are reactive, in the sense that they simply reduce the cost of using existing facilities (almost exclusively sports facilities); or, if proactive, as in leadership projects, they are still virtually all confined to sports activities. There is a need for much greater understanding of what unemployed people actually want to do; a far greater willingness to extend policy initiatives across the whole spectrum of recreation and leisure; and a much fuller blurring of traditional boundaries between leisure provision, education, and social services. Given that traditional facility-based sport within the community as a whole is as yet a minority activity, it is scarcely likely to become a life-line for the majority of the unemployed.

Conceptual Issues

In postindustrial society, the traditional work-leisure relationship can no longer be regarded as an adequate basis for defining the nature and purpose of leisure. This is the case not just for the unemployed but also for the retired, housewives, and people in full-time education; together, these groups already comprise over half the UK population. Stockdale (1985: 117) concluded from her analysis of the concepts of work and leisure that: "it is important to look more closely at particular target groups for whom the role of work may be different from that which they had previously experienced or that which society had led them to expect. The fact that the attributes of leisure and work show minimal overlap suggests that the replacement or partial substitution of work by leisure will not be feasible unless there are fundamental changes in both an individual's and society's views of leisure and work."

Unemployment, for most of the people affected by it, is a wholly negative experience. People expect to work, by and large they want to work, and they derive psychological as well as financial rewards from doing so. The financial difficulties of the unemployed place a significant constraint on their leisure: far from taking on new and more varied leisure interests to absorb the time released from work, most unemployed people cut back their leisure participation. If the unemployed could share equally in the wealth of the community, many of their difficulties would be eased. Political and economic realities prevent the adoption of new, alternative lifestyles. However, we can only speculate on the likely role of leisure if the wealth of the unemployed were enhanced. If they had more money, additional leisure activities and more frequent participation would become possible. Whether it would become any more desirable is not clear, but the evidence to date suggests not.

Leisure can fulfill several of the functions traditionally derived from work. It can fill time. It can provide interest, and a sense of involvement in worthwhile activity. It can foster the development of skills and the attainment of results. It can forge and sustain friendships and a sense of belonging. In a limited way, it can provide structure, for example when activities have to be undertaken at set or prearranged times. Unlike work, however, which is regarded as important in itself, leisure lends structure to these experiences only spasmodically, and for the duration of specific incidents of participation. Above all, what leisure, conventionally defined, *cannot* impart is a sense of compulsion and purpose beyond the pursuit of an activity for its own sake. It cannot provide the central source of structure and purpose on which we have come to depend. As Kelvin (1982: 23) has argued, imposing a sense of structure and purpose on ourselves is not easy: "leisure activities which have become emotionally significant to an individual may become much more demanding and stressful than work; for emotionally significant leisure activities require not only that one meets the demands of the activities as such, but also that one continuously generates for oneself the pressures to meet them. There is no doubt that this may be morally admirable; nevertheless it is also very difficult. Paradoxical as it may sound, a Leisure Ethic is potentially much more puritanical than a Work Ethic." Work and leisure are not just a conceptual couplet; they are experienced as a couplet.

Jenkins and Sherman (1979, 1981) seek the answer in a blurring of the distinction between work and leisure, so that leisure can be recognized and respected as a central life interest in its own right. Stokes (1983: 280) believes that the central focus should shift from "work" to being constructive: "No longer can leisure be considered a residual period of relatively unorganized activity. It must be treated seriously, structured and used so that people may develop their potential and feel they are making a contribution to society."

However, Kelvin (1981) refutes these possibilities, for three main reasons. First, many leisure activities, he argues, even if they involve attending clubs and groups, are essentially individualistic: hardly any demand the continuing social interdependence of work relations. Second, work is perceived as a necessity, whereas leisure is freely chosen. Third, though leisure activities may fill time, they are unable to structure it. His empirical work reaffirms this: "the central finding of our enquiry is clear: the 'leisure' activities of the unemployed do not constitute alternatives to work; they are at best palliatives for boredom, and mostly, for most unemployed, they are inadequate as that" (Kelvin, Dewberry, and Morley-Bunker 1984: 1).

The inadequacy of leisure to form a substitute for work in practice, however, is no reason to discard the concept of leisure in its own right. Hargreaves (1981: 200), though, calls for a radical re-think: "Perhaps the concept of leisure has outlived its usefulness and can be discarded; certainly the concept of work will have to be transformed and disconnected from paid employment. Perhaps it would be easier to speak of 'ways of life' or 'life styles.' At least we might then review the issues unencumbered by concepts which may well restrict our imagination. Should we not now be working out what we mean by a 'life ethic' to displace the 'work ethic'? Is is not important to consider how people can lead a 'full life' rather than worrying about how to return to 'full employment'?"

From the evidence to date, leading a full life depends on having a source of structure. Leisure cannot provide it, though it can retain its conventional role as part of a balanced lifestyle if a source of structure and purpose exists alongside it. If work, in the sense of traditional employment, cannot survive, then work is the concept to be re-examined. Miles (1983) emphasizes the need to think of work in a broader sense than formal employment and to find new forms of work which are both satisfying to undertake and useful to society; various forms of voluntary work, for example in the caring services, could provide such alternatives. Gershuny (1977) advocates the continuing growth of the "self-service economy," whereby people increasingly buy goods and equipment (e.g. washing machines, food processors, do-it-yourself tools) with which to provide their own services, rather than buying the services directly. Perhaps, as Rapoport (1982: 16) argues, the key resource is resourcefulness — the capacity of people to use their own personal and social resources to develop interests and pursue activities which bring personal and social satisfaction. She warns, though, that some highly skilled people — "the one-dimensional men of our specialized society" — are unresourceful. Our education systems, therefore, need to nurture our full range of potentialities, not just the narrowly academic, and our governments need to allow for much greater community initiative and action at the local level in mutual service delivery. Leisure will not become a substitute for work, but new forms of purposeful activity — such as voluntary work, study, and community service — might do so. People need "work" which is satisfying to undertake and which they believe is useful to society. Leisure will survive as a concept and in practice if there are other sources of structure to surround it.

References

Archbishop of Canterbury's Commission on Urban Priority Areas. 1986. *Faith in the City*. London: Church House Publishing.

Argyle, M. 1972. *The Social Psychology of Work*. Harmondsworth: Penguin.

Bakke, E.W. 1933. *The Unemployed Man*. London: Nisbet.

Bishop, D.W. and M. Ikeda. 1970. "Status and role factors in the leisure behaviour of different occupations." *Sociology and Social Research 54:* 190-208.

Brown, R. 1978. "Work." In *Work, Urbanism and Inequality in UK Society Today*, ed. P. Abrams, pp. 55-159. London: Weidenfeld and Nicolson.

Bunker, N. 1984. "Use of time and the effects of unemployment: A brief summary of research." Paper to Unemployed Workers Association, Birmingham, UK.

Bunker, N. and C. Dewberry. 1983. "Unemployment behind closed doors: Staying in and staying invisible." *Journal of Community Education 2:* 37-45.

Carr-Hill, R.A. and N.H. Stern. 1979. *Crime, the Police, and Criminal Statistics*. London: Academic Press.

Central Statistical Office. 1988. *Social Trends 18*. London: HMSO.

Chappell, H. 1982. "The family life of the unemployed." *New Society 62:* 75-79.

Clarke, R. 1982. *Work in Crisis. Dilemma of a Nation*. Edinburgh: Saint Andrew Press.

Colledge, M. and R. Bartholomew. 1980. "The long term unemployed: Some new evidence." *Employment Gazette 88:* 9-12.

Department of Employment. 1988. *Employment Gazette 96:* 28-39.

Friedmann, E.A. and R.J. Havighurst. 1954. *The Meaning of Work and Retirement*. Chicago: University of Chicago Press.

Gershuny, J.I. 1977. "The self-service economy." *New Universities Quarterly 32:* 50-66.

Gershuny, J., I. Miles, S. Jones, C. Mullings, G. Thomas, and S. Wyatt. 1986. "Time budgets: Preliminary analyses of a national survey." *The Quarterly Journal of Social Affairs 2:* 13-39.

Glyptis, S.A., T.A. Kay, and D. Donkin. 1986a. *Sport and the Unemployed. Final Report on the Monitoring of Schemes in Leicester, Derwentside and Hockley Port, 1981-4.* London: Sports Council.

Glyptis, S.A., T.A. Kay, and D. Donkin. 1986b. *Sport and the Unemployed. Lessons from Schemes in Leicester, Derwentside and Hockley Port.* London: Sports Council.

Glyptis, S.A., H.A. McInnes, and J. A.Patmore. 1987. *Leisure and the Home.* London: Sports Council/Economic and Social Research Council Joint Panel on Leisure and Recreation Research.

Glyptis, S.A. and C.M. Pack. 1988. *Local Authority Sports Provision for the Unemployed. An Appraisal of Provision in the UK.* London: Sports Council.

Glyptis, S.A. and A.C. Riddington. 1983. *Sport for the Unemployed. A Review of Local Authority Projects.* Research Working Paper 21. London: Sports Council.

Hargreaves, D.H. 1981. "Unemployment, leisure and education." *Oxford Review of Education 7:*197-210.

Harris, M. 1984. "How unemployment affects people." *New Society 67:* 88-90.

Henry, I. and P. Bramham. 1986. "Leisure, the local state and social order." *Leisure Studies 5:* 189-209.

Hepworth, S.J. 1980. "Moderating factors of the psychological impact of unemployment." *Journal of Occupational Psychology 53:* 139-45.

Hill, J.M. 1977. *The Social and Psychological Impact of Unemployment.* London: Tavistock Institute of Human Relations.

Hill, J.M. 1978. "The psychological impact of unemployment." *New Society 43:* 118-20.

House of Lords Select Committee on Sport and Leisure. 1973. *First Report.* London: HMSO.

Hudson, S. 1983. "Sporting opportunities and the needs of older unemployed women and men." London: Camden Council of Social Services.

Jahoda, M. 1979. "The impact of unemployment in the 1930s and the 1970s." *Bulletin of the British Psychological Society 32:* 309-14.

Jahoda, M. 1982. *Employment and Unemployment: A Social-Psychological Analysis.* Cambridge: Cambridge University Press.

Jahoda, M., P.F. Lazarsfeld, and H. Zeisel. 1972. *Marienthal: The Sociography of an Unemployed Community.* London: Tavistock Institute. (First published 1933.)

Jenkins, C. and B. Sherman. 1979. *The Collapse of Work.* London: Eyre Methuen.

Jenkins, C. and B. Sherman. 1981. *Leisure Shock.* London: Eyre Methuen.

Jones, M. 1972. *Life on the Dole.* London: Davis Poynter.

Kando, T. and W. Summers. 1971. "The impact of work on leisure." *Pacific Sociological Review 14:* 310-27.

Kaplan, M. 1975. *Leisure: Theory and Policy.* New York: Wiley.

Kay, T.A. 1987. "Leisure in the lifestyles of unemployed people: A case study in Leicester." Unpublished Ph.D. thesis, Department of Physical Education and Sports Science, Loughborough University of Technology, UK.

Kelly, J.R. 1976. "Leisure as compensation for work constraint." *Society and Leisure 8:* 73-82.

Kelvin, P. 1980. "Social Psychology 2001: The social psychological bases and implications of structural unemployment." In *The Development of Social Psychology,* eds. R. Gilmour and S. Duck, pp. 293-316. London: Academic Press.

Kelvin, P. 1981. "Work as a source of identity: The implications of unemployment." *British Journal of Guidance and Counselling 9:* 2-11.

Kelvin, P. 1982. "Work, unemployment and leisure: Myths, hopes and realities." In *Work and Leisure: The Implications of Technological Change.* Proceedings of the Leisure Studies Association Seminar 1980, pp. 11-25. Edinburgh: Tourism and Recreation Research Unit.

Kelvin, P., C. Dewberry, and N. Morley-Bunker. 1984. *Unemployment and Leisure.* Report to the Sports Council/Economic and Social Research Council Joint Panel on Leisure and Recreation Research. London.

Kelvin, P. and J. Jarrett. 1985. *Unemployment: Its Social and Psychological Effects.* Cambridge: Cambridge University Press.

Marsden, D. and E. Duff. 1975. *Workless: Some Unemployed Men and Their Families.* Harmondsworth: Penguin.

Meissner, M. 1971. "The long arm of the job: A study of work and leisure." *Industrial Relations 10:* 239-60.

Miles, I. 1983. *Adaptation to Unemployment.* Brighton: Science Policy Research Unit, University of Sussex, UK.

Miller, J. 1982. *Situation Vacant. The Social Consequences of Unemployment in a Welsh Town.* London: Community Projects Foundation.

Moynagh, M. 1985. *Making Unemployment Work.* Tring: Lion Publishing.

Norris, G.M. 1978. "Unemployment, sub-employment and personal characteristics." *Sociological Review 26:* 89-108 and 327-47.

North Tyneside Community Development Council. 1978. *In and Out of Work.* London: Home Office.

Parker, S. 1971. *The Future of Work and Leisure.* New York: Praeger.

Parker, S. 1983. *Leisure and Work.* London: George Allen and Unwin.

Pilgrim Trust. 1938. *Men Without Work.* Cambridge: Cambridge University Press.

Rapoport, R. 1982. *Unemployment and the Family. The Loch Memorial Lecture, 1981.* London: The Family Welfare Association.

Raymond, L. 1984. "The effects of unemployment on the leisure activity participation of unemployed steelworkers." In *Le Temps Libre et le Loisir: Proceedings of Congress of the World Leisure and Recreation Association*, pp. III 5 62-7. Paris: ADRAC.

Rigg, M. 1986. *Action Sport: An Evaluation*. London: Sports Council.

Roberts, K. 1978. *Contemporary Society and the Growth of Leisure*. London: Longman.

Roberts, K. 1982. "Contemporary youth unemployment: a sociological interpretation." Paper presented at the Annual Meeting of the British Association for the Advancement of Science, Liverpool.

Roberts, K. 1983. "Sidelines or forefront: The role of leisure in an age of rising unemployment." In *Urban Leisure Provision and Unemployment: Issues and Solutions*, ed. S. Glyptis, pp. 1-3. London: Leisure Studies Association Newsletter Supplement 1.

Rousseau, D.M. 1978. "Relationship of work to nonwork." *Journal of Applied Psychology 63:* 513-17.

Salaman, G. 1971. "Two occupational communities: Examples of a remarkable convergence of work and non-work." *Sociological Review 19:* 389-407.

Scarman, The Rt. Hon. the Lord. 1982. *The Brixton Disorders, 10-12 April 1981*. Cmnd. 8427. London: HMSO.

Seabrook, J. 1981. "Unemployment now and in the 1930s." In *Unemployment*, ed. B. Crick, pp. 7-15. London: Methuen.

Sinfield, A. 1981. *What Unemployment Means*. Oxford: Martin Robertson.

Sports Council. 1982. *Sport in the Community. The Next Ten Years*. London: Sports Council.

Sports Council. 1984. *Participation: Taking up the Challenge. Proceedings of Sports Council Recreation Management Seminar*. London: Sports Council.

Staines, G.L. 1980. "Spillover versus compensation: A review of the literature on the relationship between work and nonwork." *Human Relations 33:* 111-130.

Stockdale, J.E. 1985. *What is Leisure? An Empirical Analysis of the Concept of Leisure and the Role of Leisure in People's Lives.* London: Sports Council/Economic and Social Research Council Joint Panel on Leisure and Recreation Research.

Stokes, G. 1983. "Work, unemployment and leisure." *Leisure Studies 6:* 269-286.

Tarling, R. 1982. *Unemployment and Crime.* Research Bulletin 14, pp. 28-33. London: Home Office Research and Planning Unit,

Taylor, J. 1986. "Leisure and unemployment." Discussion paper for Alberta Recreation and Parks. Edmonton: Department of Recreation and Leisure Studies, University of Alberta.

Telford Development Corporation. 1982. *Out of Work in Telford.* Telford: TDC.

Trew, K. and R. Kilpatrick. 1984. "The daily life of the unemployed: Social and psychological dimensions." Belfast: Queen's University.

Veal, A. J. 1986. *People in Sport and Recreation 1980. Summary of Data from the General Household Survey for England and Wales.* London: Centre for Leisure and Tourism Studies, Polytechnic of North London.

Wilensky, H. 1960. "Work, careers, and social integration." *International Social Sciences Journal 12:* 543-560.

LEISURE FORECASTING, POLICYMAKING, AND PLANNING

Thomas L. Burton

The Three Solitudes

In principle, forecasting, policymaking, and planning are closely related processes and activities — if only because each is concerned with the future. Forecasting is predictive. It attempts to predict what will happen or, more realistically, what is likely to happen, under a given set of expected circumstances. Policymaking, in contrast, is prescriptive. Policies are designed to give direction, coherence, and continuity to a course of action aimed at achieving a preferred condition or situation. They prescribe what must be done to reach this condition. Finally, planning is a means of implementing policy. Like policymaking, it is prescriptive, but it is also something more. For not only does it prescribe *what* must be done to achieve a desired condition, it also states *how* this may be done and embraces a range of mechanisms and instruments for achieving it. Planning, therefore, is *procedural*, offering an array of methods for securing a desired condition.

Perhaps the most famous example of the interplay between forecasting, policymaking, and planning is to be found in the Bible, in the book of Genesis. It is the story of the years of plenty and famine in Egypt. The story begins with a prophecy, or a forecast: "Behold there come seven years of great plenty throughout all the land of Egypt: And there shall arise after them seven years of famine; and all the plenty shall be forgotten in the land of Egypt; and the famine shall consume the land" (*Holy Bible*, King James Version, Genesis 29-30). This is followed by a proposed course of action, a policy for dealing with the expected consequences of the forecast and for achieving a desired or preferred situation. Pharaoh was advised to "... look out a man discreet and wise, and set him over the land of Egypt ... let him appoint officers over the land ... let them gather all the food of those good years that come.... And that food shall be for store to the land against the seven years of famine" (Genesis 33-36). Finally, a plan was devised for carrying out this policy. Storehouses were set up in the cities for receiving, storing and, later, distributing food. Joseph's agents "... gathered up all the food of the seven years, which were in the land of Egypt, and laid up the food in the cities" (Genesis, 48). Then, during the years of famine, "... Joseph opened all the storehouses and sold unto the Egyptians" (Genesis, 56).

The story of the years of plenty and famine in Ancient Egypt is a powerful and moving tale, but the causal relationship between forecasting, policymaking, and planning which it exhibits is an overly simplistic one that benefits greatly from several assumed conditions not generally found. Most significant, of course, is the fact that the original forecast, the prophecy, dealt not only with a single variable — crop production — but it was also wholly accurate in all respects. Such a circumstance is unlikely to be experienced in any modern situation. Also, the governmental and administrative structure of Pharaoh's kingdom made the formulation of policy simple and effective. All it required was the King's fiat. Such would not normally be the case today. Finally, the story failed to outline and discuss the myriad of administrative details, mechanisms, and instruments that made up the plan for implementing Pharaoh's (or rather Joseph's) policy. It, therefore, ignored the potential for, and the likelihood of, institutional and administrative conflict (whether deliberate or otherwise), inadequate resources, human error, and so on. In a modern world of industrialized nations, planning must take these and other factors into consideration and, in so doing, it becomes a much more complicated exercise.

Notwithstanding these reservations, there is considerable value in reflecting upon the Biblical tale of the years of plenty and famine in Egypt. For, not only does it illustrate, clearly and cogently, the distinctions between a *predictive forecast, a prescriptive policy*, and a *procedural plan*, it also emphasizes the significant processual links among and between them. A predictive forecast (or a series of alternative forecasts) sets the stage for policymaking. A forecast states what will likely happen if events are permitted to unfold without any intervention beyond that which already occurs. Thus, the forecast provides a basis against which the policymaker may judge the need for, or desirability of, intervention in order to regulate the system in a manner that will be more beneficial than self-regulation (Vickers 1965). The more detailed and specific is the forecast (or series of alternative forecasts), the greater will likely be the number of options for intervention available to the policymaker.

Once the policymaker has decided upon one or more prescriptive courses of action designed to provide direction, coherence, and continuity to events, the basis is set for the development of a plan (or plans). The latter is concerned to identify what particular actions must be taken to implement the chosen policy, how these may be implemented, and what specific mechanisms and instruments are readily available to be used. The logical progression is from the statement of general goals or ends, to the production of forecasts indicating whether or not these goals will likely be achieved without intervention, to policies designed to lay out the broad types and forms of intervention to be undertaken (in the event that intervention is deemed necessary), to plans designed to implement policies. The process is not always simple and linear. Sometimes, for example, a forecast precedes the statement of goals. (In the Biblical story cited, the goal was not enunciated until after the forecast of plenty followed by famine was made). Nevertheless, few would disagree with the notion of a general progression from forecasts to policies to plans.

Yet, in reality, such a progression occurs only in a very rudimentary fashion — at least when it comes to the provision of leisure opportunities. Most leisure plans are accompanied by crude policy statements of the kind that advocate increased facilities for particular types of activities or for specified population groups. And these policy statements are usually based upon unsubstantiated predictions of increasing needs or demands for those same facilities or from those same groups. Reading leisure plans, one frequently feels like Alice, who, having stumbled through the looking glass, finds a world of bizarre contradictions in which reality is whatever one wishes and chooses it to be! Observing, analyzing, and participating in the provision of leisure opportunities in modern industrial nations often leads one to conclude that, far from being "closely related processes and activities concerned with the future," leisure forecasting, policymaking, and planning are three solitudes, each existing in its own small world. In short, there appear to be plans in search of policies that take no cognizance of forecasts. One can cite many exemplary (and expensive) efforts at forecasting leisure behavior. One can discover numerous comprehensive (and complex) leisure policies. And one can burrow, knee-deep, in voluminous (and voluble) leisure plans. But rarely can one trace the links among and between them.

LEISURE FORECASTING

It was suggested almost two decades ago that the history of leisure forecasting was one which, to that time, had passed through four principal phases (Burton 1971). It was during the mid-1950s that it became apparent, initially to recreation administrators and urban planners, that it would be necessary to do something about planning for leisure. The evidence of increasing levels of participation in leisure pursuits, firstly in the United States and subsequently elsewhere in the industrialized world, was an indication of the need for some form of planning to accommodate individual demands for access to leisure resources; and planning, of course, implied some kind of forecasting. Thus, there grew up a need for forecasts of future leisure behavior. The first stage in the development of leisure forecasting itself consisted of the initial reaction to this expressed need, and it was one of considerable pessimism. In Taylor's words, "it was the phase when serious scholars said that it was something that could not be done" (Taylor 1969). It was argued that there were too many non-measurable causal factors, so that even if one could forecast the effects of the measurable influences on leisure behavior, the results would be subject to such a degree of error as to make them of little or no practical use.

The first phase lasted for a relatively short period of time and was replaced by a somewhat more optimistic approach, the use of estimates: that is, the development of the informed judgments of administrators, planners, and other experts into predictions of future behavior. These estimates, based upon a great deal of detailed information and experience, were, it was believed, the most credible types of forecast that could be achieved. The difficulty with this approach was that these estimates often became confused with what may be called prospectives. That is, the experts frequently produced estimates of what they wished to happen, or what they believed ought to happen, rather than what they expected would happen. In other words, estimates tended to move away from simple forecasting towards deterministic or goal-oriented planning. (This is not to suggest that such planning is illegitimate or unacceptable, but merely to say that it is not forecasting). The other problem with these estimates, of course, is that they were only as good as the informed judgments of those making them and, in many instances, this meant that they were wildly inaccurate. Indeed, since nobody had previously experienced the explosion in leisure behavior and participation that occurred in the 1960s — and few had the imagination to anticipate it — most estimates were, in fact, gross under-estimates of what actually occurred (see Clawson and Knetsch 1966).

The third stage in the development of leisure forecasting was inherently optimistic. This consisted of the use of extrapolation to predict the numbers of participants in particular leisure pursuits and the numbers of visitor days to particular facilities and areas. Here was the first scientific approach to forecasting: scientific, that is, in the sense that it was based wholly upon an objective mathematical system which excluded value judgment directly — though some would argue that such judgment is always present indirectly (e.g. in the very choice of method). In this sense, the extrapolations of numbers of participants in particular leisure pursuits constituted the first crude mathematical models for leisure forecasting. Of course, many of the early writers cautioned about the weaknesses and limitations of such extrapolations (see Burton 1971). From the present perspective, however, what is important is not the accuracy of these extrapolations, but the approach that they represented. Leisure forecasting had become a respectable academic and scientific field of endeavor.

The scientific approach to leisure forecasting truly blossomed in the fourth stage of development, the construction of predictive models. This is generally agreed to have begun with the work of the Outdoor Recreation Resources Review Commission (ORRRC) in the United States between 1958 and 1962, although there had been some general discussion of the applicability of such models before this. The specific achievement of the ORRRC study, however, was that it produced precise numerical forecasts of participation levels in selected leisure activities by a process which involved the extrapolation of more than one variable (Outdoor Recreation Resources Review Commission 1962). In essence, it used a model which combined (presumed) causal variables in such a way that the interrelationships between them could be identified and incorporated into the resultant forecasts. The importance of the ORRRC study, and subsequent models, lies in the recognition of the fact that there is rarely one single cause of any particular event or trend. Many more sophisticated models have been developed since the ORRRC original, but the latter remains a landmark in the field of leisure forecasting. (It should be noted here that the techniques employed in both extrapolation and predictive modelling were not new in themselves. They had been adopted and adapted from other fields of study where they had been more fully developed, particularly from traffic engineering and economics. What was new at the time was the acceptance of the view that such techniques could be applied, with a fair expectation of success, to the forecasting of leisure behavior).

If one examines the state of leisure forecasting today, one will find that there have been some significant developments since the above "history" was written in 1971. What will be most apparent to the careful observer, however, is the fact that many of the leisure forecasting techniques that exist and are employed today are similar to, or variants upon, the three principal approaches that were identified in the 1971 review. In one of the most comprehensive recent reviews of the subject, Veal (1987) has suggested that there are nine discrete leisure forecasting methods: speculation; trend extrapolation; respondent assessment; the Delphi technique; scenario writing; the comparative method; spatial models; cross-sectional analysis; and composite methods. Each of these has its genesis in one or more of the three approaches identified in the 1971 review. All are, wholly or partially, quantitative in character, implying that leisure forecasting is aimed at producing relatively precise quantitative predictions about leisure behavior, and not simply descriptive statements about the dominant characteristics of leisure activity in some unspecified future. That is, leisure forecasting sets out to determine how many people will likely engage in a specified leisure activity at a specified time, and not simply that a particular type of activity will be popular at that time. A brief commentary will be given here on each of the nine methods, but the reader is directed to Veal's own work for a detailed analysis and critique of each.

Speculation, identical to what were called estimates in the 1971 review, consists of the informed judgments of administrators, planners, and other experts about future developments. Often based upon observations of past trends and current developments, such predictions are generally made in terms of broad orders of magnitude. Burton, for example, predicted in 1970 that there would be both absolute and relative increases in the popularity of individual sports in Britain, while participation in team sports would increase in absolute terms, but would decline relatively to individual sports. He also developed an index of projected changes in leisure-related variables, at quinquennial intervals, for the period 1960-1985. Thus, for example, the number of registered automobiles in Britain was anticipated to rise by 280 per cent, from an index value of 100 in

1960 to 380 in 1985 (Burton 1970) — something which never, in fact, material-ized. For, as Veal pointed out, while speculation can be a source of ideas both for policymaking and research, it is highly subjective and frequently inaccurate. Its strength lies not in its findings, but in the ideas it often generates (Veal 1987: 130). This is especially true with respect to policymaking, since, as noted earlier, such speculations frequently embody elements of what their proponents believe ought to happen and, therefore, can be readily incorporated into prescriptive policies.

Trend extrapolation (or time series analysis) is identical to what was called extrapolation in the 1971 review. Simply put, it involves the examination of past changes in patterns of participation in particular leisure pursuits and the continuation of these patterns into the future. It is, of course, an unsophisticated approach, based on the presumption that the variable under consideration — for example, levels of participation in team sports — will continue to change in exactly the same way in the future as it has done in the past. In consequence, it has a tendency to produce improbable forecasts when employed injudiciously.

Respondent assessment consists in asking respondents to leisure surveys to indicate the kinds of activities — or, indeed, the specific activities — that they plan to take up, or would like to take up, in the future. The responses are then employed as indicators of probable future levels of participation in the particular activities, or types of activities. It is a form of predictive modelling based upon stated intentions or aspirations. Its weakness lies in the fact that, in the absence of specified and real constraints, people will tend to indicate activities that, in reality, for a variety of reasons, they cannot or would not actually take up. The realization that there can be, and often is, a significant difference between "the idea and the reality" limits the potential effectiveness of respondent assessment as a method of leisure forecasting. The technique has been employed extensively in local surveys in both Britain and North America and, even, on occasion, at the regional and national levels (Alberta Recreation and Parks 1988a; British Travel Association/University of Keele 1967; North West Sports Council 1972). The operational problems involved in testing the validity of this type of approach are such that this has never been done.

The *Delphi Technique* is, essentially, a means of distilling expert views about the future. It involves a series of stages whereby various experts in a given field are presented with questions concerning the likelihood of a range of events happening in a given time period. The results of these experts' views are collated, assigned average probabilities based upon results, and a new list of possible developments is created. This second list is then sent back to the experts, with a request that they reconsider and, if they wish, re-state their views. This process can go on for many rounds, or can simply be completed in two rounds. What is critical to the technique is, of course, the choice of the panel of experts, for these must obviously be people who are readily familiar with the topic under consideration, but who are not rigidly aligned with the "status quo."

The technique is similar to that of speculation or estimate, noted earlier, except that the views of many experts are taken into consideration and the resultant range of views is quantified. The technique has become highly popular in leisure forecasting in recent years, whether for the forecasting of general leisure trends (Shafer, Moeller, and Russell 1975) or as a means of identifying and focussing upon particular issues and concerns, such as manpower needs in the leisure industry (Ng, Brown, and Knott 1983) and tourism potential (Kaynak and Macaulay 1984).

Scenario writing is akin to the Delphi Technique — and, indeed, is often confused with the former. It is different, however, in that it involves the construction of alternative possible futures according to designated key variables and the interrelationships between and among them. Typically, one of these variables has to do with economic growth and, equally typically, the scenarios involve high-growth, moderate-growth, and low-growth alternatives. The implications of the different assumed variables are then outlined in the form of a possible future. Unlike the previous methods, scenario writing is not aimed at producing precise predictions so much as presenting a series of alternatives to policymakers. In effect, the various scenarios indicate to decision makers what will happen, or is likely to happen, if a particular set of circumstances occurs, or can be made to occur. Thus, it provides decision makers with an entry point to, and a perspective on, the range of prescriptions which they may choose to pursue. Scenario writing is not prescriptive in and of itself, but it offers a range and variety of alternatives from among which policymakers may choose — and, hence, prescribe — a desired future. One of the earliest and most comprehensive attempts to apply scenario writing to leisure forecasting was carried out in Ontario, Canada, in the mid-1970s, as part of a wider project aimed at the development of a fully integrated provincial transportation network (McCalla 1983) — although there is no evidence to suggest that any of the resultant scenarios was adopted, in whole or in part, as formal government policy.

It has been suggested that the *comparative approach* originated with Dumazedier (1974). In essence, it is based on the notion that future developments in a particular society can frequently be predicted by reference to a more advanced society. Thus, Dumazedier suggested, in 1974, that Western European societies in general could look to the United States as a means of studying their own futures. He recognized, of course, that differences in cultural, political, historical, and environmental situations would make the process of comparison extremely difficult. Nonetheless, he felt that it could be developed in such a way that account could be taken of these particular problem areas. It is an interesting concept and one which builds upon Veblen's theories, developed at the turn of the century, about pecuniary emulation, whereby the lower classes in society sought to emulate the behavior and styles of the social groupings immediately above them (Veblen 1899). Veblen's theory attempted to explain leisure behavior by reference to social emulation. Dumazedier, in contrast, did not suggest that Western European societies should, or would, emulate the United States, either in whole or in part, but only that the various factors likely to affect their futures could be seen in active form in the more advanced society of the United States. Time has proven him right, at least in part, since many of the characteristics of leisure — especially popular culture — that existed in the United States in the late 1960s are clearly evident in many other advanced industrial nations in the 1980s. On the other hand, there are many other characteristics of leisure in the United States in the late 1960s — for example, the fascination with wilderness and the outdoors — which have not appeared, to anything like the same extent, in other countries today.

Spatial models are a specific form of mathematical model which focus upon the effects on leisure behavior of the spatial distribution of opportunities for participation (see Smith, this volume). These models offer mathematical representations of leisure travel. They have been employed with considerable success in several areas, from day travel to urban, regional, and countryside parks to international tourism. One of the earliest examples was Veal's work in Birmingham, England, designed to provide a basis for municipalities to determine the optimum location for a proposed new facility of a given kind (Veal, in Burton 1971). Further studies in this area were undertaken by Duffield (1976) in Britain, but, largely because of data limitations and high cost, the technique has fallen into relative disuse in recent years.

Veal has suggested that *cross-sectional analysis* is probably "the most widely used technique in leisure forecasting today" (Veal 1987: 146). The method consists in examining levels of participation in leisure pursuits among a cross-section of the population. The basis of the forecasting, then, is the proposition that the changing social composition of the population in the future will lead to corresponding predictable changes in levels of participation in the specified leisure pursuits. Thus, for example, if it is found that visits to historic sites in Alberta, Canada, are directly related to levels of education, such that the numbers of visits increase with higher levels of education, then should the proportion of the population attaining higher levels of education increase in the future, one may expect visits to historic sites to increase also. The method is mathematical in that it employs statistical techniques of multiple regression and discriminant analysis to quantify relationships between levels of participation in particular leisure pursuits and the chosen social characteristics of the population. The method, like those of trend extrapolation, the comparative approach, and spatial modelling (as well as, perhaps, others), faces one significant major problem — the assumption that the future is directly and *specifically* reflected in the past. Thus, for example, in the case of the known relationship between per capita disposable income and per capita visits to national parks in the United States, the difficulty for the forecaster is to determine the extent to which the numerical value of the correlation between the two variables will remain constant or will fluctuate in the future. Because the cross-sectional approach focuses upon the effects on levels of participation of selected social and economic variables, and does not focus directly on the leisure pursuit itself, it assumes that the relationship between the given variables and the level of participation in the particular leisure pursuit will remain constant. It is a reasonable and valid assumption that, for example, levels of per capita disposable income will continue to influence per capita visits to national parks in the United States. The critical question, however, is will the scale of this influence increase or decline in intensity, or will it remain at approximately the same level? Thus, it is not the *fact* of the relationship between past and future that is at issue — short of prophecy, little else seems possible — but, rather, the *specificity* of the relationship that is assumed in cross-sectional analysis.

The final leisure forecasting method, which Veal calls the *composite method*, is, in fact, a combination of several of the techniques that have been identified and discussed here. In a way, it is not unlike the original method of speculation, except that it is generally based upon the findings of several of the other techniques. Veal has illustrated the method well: "... while future purchases of video recorders might be predicted by means of simple extrapolation of trends in recent years, this must be set against, and if necessary modified by, knowledge of the 'product life-cycle' of such new consumer durables, 'cross-sectional' information about which groups in society are buying the machines, and the overall trends in disposable income and the share of that income available for leisure products" (Veal 1987: 155). He added further that the monitoring of events in other countries — that is, the use of the comparative method — could also be part of the array of techniques that could be employed in the composite method when addressing such a specific issue as the example cited. The composite method is greatly in vogue at this time, especially in the commercial leisure field (see, for example, Martin and Mason 1984).

It is evident from even this brief review that each of the various leisure forecasting techniques has both strengths and limitations (Table 1). It is a preoccupation with the weaknesses that has led, most recently, to the growing emphasis upon the composite method. This has occurred in the hope that the strengths of one technique will compensate for the weaknesses of another. (Of course, it is quite possible that the limitations of several techniques could compound each other). The demand for leisure forecasts is high. In theory, at least, they are the basis for both policymaking and planning — though, as was argued earlier, this relationship is considerably more nebulous than is generally supposed.

There have been significant developments in methods of leisure forecasting during the past two decades. But, for the most part, these have consisted of improvements to, and adaptations of, methods that already existed — especially estimates and various types of quantitative models. Perhaps the most important advance over the period has been a recognition of the limitations of purely objective, scientific, and quantitative techniques. Cross-sectional

Table 1
A Brief Summary of Leisure Forecasting Techniques

Technique	Description	Principal Strengths	Principal Limitations
Speculation	Informed judgement of administrators, planners, and experts.	Draws upon experience. Source of ideas for both research and policymaking.	Frequent confusion between prediction and prescription.
Trend Extrapolation	Extension of past changes in behavior into the future.	Simple and effective in surprise-free short-term forecasting.	Cannot account for sudden changes. Often, past data do not go far enough back in time to be reliable.
Respondent Assessment	Asks respondents to surveys which pursuits they plan, or would like, to take up.	Indicates preferences and aspirations of leisure participants.	Does not distinguish between "wishful hope" and firm intention. Ignores real world constraints.
Delphi Technique	Seeks judgements of experts. Feeds back findings, seeking any changes to judgements. Can go several rounds.	Distills expert views on the future. Iterative process often brings forth "new" ideas.	Depends heavily on the "vision" of the experts. Frequent confusion between prediction and prescription.
Scenario Writing	Construction of alternative possible futures on basis of key variables and their interrelationships.	Offers a range and variety of alternatives as the basis for policymaking.	Cannot account easily for sudden changes. Requires "global" or holistic capabilities among writers.

Comparative Method	Assumes that future developments in a society can be predicted by reference to current conditions in a more advanced society.	In a "shrinking" world, some trends do, indeed, cross national and cultural boundaries.	Does not really account for cultural, political, historical, and environmental differences between countries.
Spatial Models	Mathematical representations of leisure travel employed to predict spatial need for leisure opportunities.	Produces precise forecasts of behavior relative to specific facilities and areas.	Deals principally with "micro-level" concerns (i.e. particular activities/facilities). Needs large amounts of varied data. Expensive process.
Cross-Sectional Analysis	Examines participation among a cross-section of a population. Forecasts changes in participation on basis of forecasts of changes in composition of population.	Recognizes that leisure participation differs for different segments of a population.	Does not forecast changes in leisure participation directly. Does not account for changes in supply. Expensive process.
Composite Methods	Combinations of two or more of the above techniques.	The strengths of one technique may compensate for the limitations of another.	Limitations of technique could compound each other. Requires extensive knowledge. Frequently, an expensive process.

analysis may be the most widely used approach today, but it has become readily apparent to its proponents that it fares best when combined with other approaches, specifically those that cull the judgments, opinions, and perceptions of experts. In the final analysis, leisure forecasting requires that quantitative findings be mulled over, adjusted and, where appropriate, contested by informed judgments. Perhaps this is the principal message that lies behind the development of the Delphi technique, scenario writing, and composite methods.

LEISURE POLICYMAKING

Unlike forecasting, policymaking is *prescriptive*. Policies are designed to give direction, coherence, and continuity to a course of action aimed at achieving a desired or preferred end or condition. Policies prescribe what must be done in order to reach a desired end. One of the earliest writers on the subject suggested that the central characteristic of policymaking is its concern with values (Vickers 1965). He noted that policymaking is merely part of regulation, or, rather, part of a regulatory process. Any system, left to itself, will be self-regulating. The sole purpose of the regulatory process is to regulate the system at some level more acceptable than that which would be achieved through self-regulation. Thus, Vickers concluded, policymaking implies and, indeed, assumes values. There is no such thing as a value-free policy. Writing in the mid-1960s, Vickers suggested that policymaking was the art of judgment. While one could learn valuation skills and appreciative systems, the exercise of judgment was central to policy formulation.

If policymaking is, indeed, value-laden, it follows that policies will usually reflect the dominant political ideologies of society. In other words, policymaking cannot, and should not, be divorced from politics and political activity. Bella (1986) makes this point well in her analysis of the politics of preservation, the political ideologies, currents and influences that lay behind the creation of National Parks in Canada, the United States, and England and Wales. She shows, for example, how beliefs about private property and about the distribution of political influence, which are central to the dominant ideology of liberal pluralism, have played a significant part in the development of National Parks in the United States. The point here is not to deny the efficacy of policymaking, nor to belittle its significance in action, but, rather, to emphasize that it occurs within different political contexts, which play an important part in shaping its focus and direction.

Several writers, building upon Vickers' notion of policy as judgment, have attempted to develop theories explaining how policymaking actually occurs. Doern and Phidd (1983) have summarized these efforts at theory building by suggesting that there are, in fact, four principal models: the rational model; incrementalism; the public choice approach; and the class analysis model.

According to *rationalist theory,* the policymaker becomes aware of a problem, states a goal, identifies and evaluates alternative means, and chooses a preferred course of action. The norms, standards, and criteria for decision making are known and applied. The rationalist model emanates, in part, from the notion of the ideal behavior of economic man (as both consumer and producer) and, in part, from a belief in science and the scientific method — that is, a preoccupation with the need to identify causality, to establish facts, and to distinguish facts from values. The rationalist model has been strongly criticized on the grounds that values — and, hence, goals — are pluralist rather than singular in nature, that information about alternative means is limited, and that the consequences of alternative means are endless. In short, it is argued that the model is unrealistic and unworkable and that most decisions and policies are simply not made in a rationalist manner. While agreeing with much of this criticism, Doern and Phidd note that, while indeed "the rational model does not explain most government policies," it remains important because "it supplies, for many policy actors and organizations, a general, albeit often vague, normative standard against which many decisions and policies, and the policy process as a whole, are tested in a rough and ready way, particularly in the rhetoric of debate" (Doern and Phidd 1983: 140).

There have been few efforts to develop leisure policies through a rationalist approach. One of the earliest, perhaps, that falls into this category is the outdoor recreation policy for the United States that emanated from the work of the Outdoor Recreation Resources Review Commission (ORRRC) between 1958 and 1962. But, in truth, the ORRRC studies, like many pioneer projects, were focussed principally upon fact-finding and research (Outdoor Recreation Resources Review Commission 1962). An attempt was made to prepare a work program leading to the development of a Canadian Federal Outdoor Recreation Policy in 1976, but this was abandoned before any of the work was begun (Burton 1976). A significant recent example, however, is the policy for the Alberta Ministry of Recreation and Parks. Carried out over a four-year period from 1984 to 1987, and involving a household survey, forty-four specially commissioned Discussion Papers, submissions from more than one hundred organizations and individuals, a survey of visitors to Provincial Parks, nine regional workshops, three specially commissioned research studies, special meetings with related national organizations, a survey of Ministry staff, and two major workshops which examined an early draft of the policy, it culminated in the Summer of 1988 in a document, entitled *Foundations for Action*, which defines the corporate aims of the Ministry (Alberta Recreation and Parks 1988b). It is probably the most formal rational attempt to date to develop a leisure policy. It remains to be seen how it fares in implementation.

The *incremental model* — sometimes called disjointed incrementalism or "the science of muddling through" — is, in many respects, the opposite of the rational model. Incrementalism claims to describe how policy decisions are really made and how, indeed, they should be made. According to incremental-ism, the policymaker focuses only on those policies that differ incrementally from existing ones. Only a limited number of alternatives is considered. Only a restricted number of the important consequences of each alternative is examined. The problem is constantly redefined incrementally. There is no correct decision, only a constant refocussing. Essentially, the model is remedial in character. It, too, has been criticized, on the grounds that it does not distinguish between fundamental decisions and incremental ones, does not provide an explanation of how criteria are set for assessing incremental decisions, and tends to neglect basic societal innovations. In other words, it is a conservative model. It proceeds with existing policies, regardless of their origins, making only incremental or marginal changes as and when problems arise.

There are many examples of leisure policies which are incremental in character, especially, though not exclusively, policies set at the local and regional levels. A national example, developed by a group of non-government organizations in Britain, is the statement on a *Leisure Policy for the Future* (Sports Council 1982a). With a little suggested tinkering here and there, this is principally an endorsement of what presently exists. Another example, suggest-ing more significant incremental change, is the British Sports Council's own proposed policy, *Sport in the Community: The Next Ten Years*, which seeks to expand sports participation among those who presently do not participate (Sports Council 1982b). Examples of local and regional policies of an incre-mental kind include the *Parks and Recreation Policy* for the City of Edmonton covering the years 1979 to 1983 (City of Edmonton 1978), as well as many others.

The rationalist and incremental models occupy opposite extremes along a spectrum, which led Etzioni (1968) to propose a variation upon them which he called mixed scanning. Doern and Phidd perceive this as a variation upon the rationalist and incrementalist models, rather than a distinct model in itself. Etzioni's approach is based upon the assumption that there are two distinct kinds of policy decision processes. On the one hand, there are those of a high order — fundamental policy processes which set basic directions for society. Secondly, there are incremental decision processes which prepare for fundamental deci-sions and work them out after they have been reached. Fundamental decisions are made by exploring the major alternatives seen by the decision maker in light of his or her goals; but unlike rationalism, the details are left out. The aim, in effect, is to obtain an overview of a particular area. Incremental decisions are made within the contexts set by fundamental decisions. It is argued by Etzioni and his supporters that incrementalism reduces the unrealistic aspects of rationalism, while contextuating rationalism helps overcome the conservative slant of incrementalism. As Doern and Phidd have remarked: "In simple terms, this approach suggests that societies do have a capacity to be fairly rational about a very small handful of decisions which they scan and identify, but that they leave the great majority of decisions to the inexorable drift of incremental-ism" (Doern and Phidd 1983: 143). The mixed scanning approach does not qualify as a distinct model, for it is really a combination of rationalism and incrementalism. Essentially, it states that a form of rationalism occurs for only a few decisions, while, for the great majority, incrementalism operates. There have been few examples in the leisure field, though the development of the *Alberta Sport Development Policy* (Alberta Recreation and Parks 1983) and the Canadian national policy for tourism (Tourism Canada 1985) probably qualify as examples.

The *public choice model* reflects the increasing importance attached to the part played by economists in the study of government. The model applies assumptions about the self-interest calculating behavior of individuals that underlies the application of micro-economic theory to the study of public decision making. Individual policymakers are viewed simply as persons whose behavior is best explained not in terms of the pursuit of the public interest but, rather, in relation to the pursuit of their own self-interests. As developed by Hartle (1979), the policy process in the public choice model is seen as a series of interlocking games: the special interest group game; the political game; the bureaucratic game; and the media game. Each group's behavior is best understood in relation to the self-interest maximizing behavior of its leaders. Thus, it is a form of elite theory, which regards public policy as a reflection of the values and preferences of various elites. Public policy reflects the values of these elites and serves their purposes, one of which may, or may not, be the welfare of the general public. In effect, whether or not public policy will concern itself with the welfare of the general population depends principally on whether it is a priority of the elite.

Group or elite theory is a component of the public choice model, dealing specifically with the special interest element within it. The theory is based on the notion that interaction and struggle among groups is central to political life and, thus, to public policymaking. A group of people with common attitudes or interests — usually (though not always) drawn from the same social class or socioeconomic group — coalesces and makes demands upon other groups in society. When the group makes this claim through a government institution, it becomes a political interest group. The more powerful a group is, the more attention its claim will receive. Public policy thus reflects the desires of the dominant, powerful interest groups in society. As groups lose or gain power, as their influence upon politicians, bureaucrats, and the media waxes and wanes, policy is altered to reflect these changes.

There have been some notable examples of the application of the public choice model to the development of leisure policy. Elite individuals have had some demonstrable impacts: Iona Campagnolo's views had an important influence on the development of the Canadian Federal policy on fitness and recreation when she was the Minister holding that portfolio during the period 1978-79 (Fitness and Amateur Sport Canada 1979); and the British report,

New Jobs from Pleasure, strongly reflected the political philosophies of Prime Minister Thatcher and some of her colleagues and, later, influenced policies, indirectly, in several aspects of leisure (Banks 1985; Veal 1987). As for interest groups, they have played a critical part in the development of both Canadian and British national parks policy for more than a century (Bella 1987; Cherry 1985). They were instrumental in the creation of a cultural policy for the City of Edmonton (Molnar 1988). And, certainly, they have played a significant role in the formulation of sports policies at every level, from the local to the international (Redmond 1986).

The *class analysis* model has its origins in the notion of a struggle between social classes, specifically over the means of production (Lipset 1968; McPherson 1953). The model has, as its central concern, inequities of power. Unlike the elite notion within the public choice model, which sees a constant ebb and flow of power-based relationships among and between competing interest groups, the class analysis model sees only a struggle between the "haves" and the "have-nots," between those who control the means of production and those who do not. Thus, economics dictates policy. Maintenance of the status quo, or marginal (incremental) changes to it that do not disrupt patterns of ownership of the means of production, are perceived to be the goals of policy. Recent class analysts have recognized the autonomy of the state, that it is not simply an enforcement agency for those who own the means of production. Yet, this does not appear to have changed their general view of the nature of policymaking: "Thus, despite recent acknowledgments of autonomy, the class analysis approach still overwhelmingly sees the direction of causality in public policy flowing from economy to polity" (Doern and Phidd 1983: 148).

There are no obvious examples of the development of recent leisure policies according to the class analysis model, although it is difficult to make the claim one way or another, since the basis lies in the motives attributed to the policymaker. Thus, for example, when the British Sports Council proposes to expand sports participation among those who do not presently participate (Sports Council 1982b), is this intended to be a means of expanding sports participation generally (incrementalism) or is it intended to be a means of legitimation and coercion (class analysis)? Certainly, there are writers who endorse the class analysis model, either by reference to the past (Bailey 1978; Gruneau 1983; Meller 1976) or to the present (Hargreaves 1985). It seems logical, in fact, that almost any leisure policy could be examined from the class analysis perspective, and a case made for a class-based motivation for the development of that policy.

As was the case with leisure forecasting, it is apparent from this brief review of policymaking models that none alone can explain satisfactorily how leisure policies are actually made. The four models are, essentially, alternative explanations, each of which has particular characteristics, discernible weaknesses, and potential or apparent strengths (Table 2, pages 228-229). Current policies can be analyzed by reference to a particular model, but rarely can one say unequivocally that a particular policy wholly reflects the application of a particular model. The leisure policies that have been attributed to particular models in the text appear to best fit these approaches, but all display aberrations from the models — sometimes of a significant kind. The field of policy science has developed considerably during the past two decades, but it is a long way from espousing an all-encompassing explanation of how policy is actually made.

LEISURE PLANNING

Planning has two differing, but related, meanings (Hall 1970). First, it refers to a set of processes for decision making that include such things as goal formulation, the setting of objectives, forecasting, the development and evaluation of alternative courses of action, and the like. Such processes are to be found in many realms of public and private decision making — in education, budgeting, hydro development, communications, and others. Second, planning also refers specifically to the application of these processes to physical settings, the natural and man-made environments, including cities, towns, regions and, even, countries. This interpretation of planning — called, variously, urban and regional planning, town and country planning, and city planning — incorporates specialized components, such as leisure planning and transportation planning. The term leisure planning, then, refers to the application of a set of decision making processes of the kind noted earlier to the physical development of areas and facilities for leisure activities and pursuits.

   Through an analysis of major writings, Faludi (1973) has identified six distinct models of planning: blueprint planning; process planning; rational comprehensive planning; disjointed incremental planning; functional planning; and normative planning. (There are also other types of planning, such as advocacy planning and transactive planning. It is the author's view, however, that these constitute variations upon the six, or else merely emphasize particular aspects of these). Faludi's six ideal types are not independent of each other, but represent extremes along three continua. Blueprint planning is conceived in opposition to process planning; rational comprehensive planning is contrasted with disjointed incremental planning; and functional planning opposes normative planning (Figure 1).

Blueprint Planning ———————————— Process Planning

Rational
Comprehensive Planning ———————————— Disjointed
Incremental Planning

Functional Planning ———————————— Normative Planning

Figure 1
Faludi's Planning Models

Table 2
A Brief Summary of Major Theories of Policymaking

Model	Description	Principal Strengths	Principal Limitations
Rationalism	A structured process moving *from* recognition of a problem *to* statement of a goal *to* identification and evaluation of all alternative means *to* choice of a preferred course of action.	Attempts to consider all options. Seeks to identify causality. Supplies decision makers with, at least, a general normative standard for decisions.	Fails to recognize plurality and conflict in societal goals. Assumes ready availability of necessary information. Assumes that one can know the full range of consequences of each alternative.
Incrementalism	Focuses only on policies that differ incrementally from existing ones. Considers only a limited number of alternatives, and only a limited number of consequences of each. Constant incremental redefinition of problems.	Recognizes limitations of knowledge and information available to decision makers. Remedial in character, seeking to improve rather than to maximize.	Does not explain how criteria are set for assessing incremental decisions. Conservative. Neglects basic societal changes.
Public Choice	Policy reflects the self-interests of policymakers, the desires and wants of the dominant and powerful groups in society. It emerges from the interplay of these groups.	Recognizes plurality and conflict in societal goals. Recognizes that policy derives from the possession of power. Perceives policymaking as a political exercise.	Fails to account sufficiently for the broad "public interest". Gives undue weight to consumer (group)-based economic considerations in policymaking.

Model	Description	Principal Strengths	Principal Limitations
Class Analysis	Policy is designed to reinforce the class structure of society. Its principal purposes are to foster capital accumulation, social harmony (legitimation), and social order (coercion).	Recognizes that policy derives from the possession of power. Perceives policymaking as a sociopolitical exercise in class relations.	Fails to account adequately for the autonomy of the state. Gives undue weight to class-based economic considerations in policymaking.

Blueprint planning, as its name implies, is concerned with fashioning a blueprint. The image of what is to be planned is firm and static: a long-term ideal desirable state is assumed. The planner presumes that total control of the environment of planning is possible. The principal planning problem becomes one of coordinating the means of implementing plans and manipulating these in order to ensure the attainment of the original objectives. In this model, planning is a mechanistic, technical, and professional exercise, concerned solely with the proper ordering of change. There is a long gestation period for the development of plans. The finished Master Plan becomes almost an end in itself and the principal, if not the sole, measure of the success of planning. Information is perceived simply as an input to planning, while monitoring is a minor and peripheral activity (Figure 2).

In contrast is the *process planning model*, which is an approach that attempts to adjust continuously to change. It has no fixed image of what is to be planned, assuming no wholly desirable end-state. There is no pretension to total control of the environment of planning. Planning becomes response-oriented, concerned primarily with reacting to issues as they arise. It is a flexible and behavioral exercise, concerned not with the ordering of change but with understanding how the nature of order itself changes. The horizon of planning is

BLUEPRINT PLANNING		PROCESS PLANNING
A long-term ideal desirable state is assumed	————	There is no wholly desirable end state
Total control of the environment is assumed	————	There is no pretension to total control
Principal planning problem is coordination and manipulation	————	Planning is response-oriented, concerned with responding to issues
Planning is a mechanistic, technical, and professional exercise	————	Planning is a flexible and behavioral exercise
Planning is concerned solely with the ordering of change	————	Planning is concerned with understanding how the concept of order itself changes
There is a long gestation period for the development of plans	————	The view is short-term and incremental
The MASTER PLAN becomes almost an end in itself, and the sole measure of success	————	The PROCESS of PLANNING is the overriding measure of success
Information is input; monitoring is peripheral	————	An efficient monitoring and information base is central

Figure 2
Blueprint Planning versus Process Planning

short-term and incremental, with the process itself serving as the primary measure of success. An efficient and effective monitoring and information base is essential to this process.

The characteristics of blueprint planning and process planning are diametrically opposed to each other.

Rational comprehensive planning starts from the premise that planning should cover everything that is considered legitimate and relevant. It requires a rational and comprehensive treatment of all variables. Planning is conceived as being total, holistic, comprehensive, optimal, and rational. Centralized planning functions are assumed, as is the possibility of consensus in the formulation and achievement of goals and objectives. Planning is a scientific, diagnostic, and clinical exercise, focussed more on the means of action than upon the identification of ends. In short, rational comprehensive planning is to Planning what the rational model is to Policymaking.

Rational comprehensive planning is antithetical to *disjointed incremental planning*, which perceives planning as covering only a range of limited alternatives (Figure 3). Here the focus is upon incremental change through trade-offs between variables. Planning is conceived as being incremental, remedial,

RATIONAL COMPREHENSIVE PLANNING		DISJOINTED INCREMENTAL PLANNING
Planning should cover everything that is considered legitimate and relevant	————	Alternatives are limited
There is a rational and comprehensive treatment of variables that are rational and comprehensive	————	There is incremental change through trade-offs between variables; rationality is abstract
Planning is total, holistic, comprehensive, optimal, and rational	————	Planning is incremental, remedial, serial, exploratory, and fragmented
Centralized planning functions are assumed	————	Fragmentation of planning functions is assumed
Consensus is possible in the formulation and achievement of social goals	————	Bargaining and compromise are the bases for formulation and achievement of goals
Planning is a scientific, diagnostic, and clinical exercise	————	Planning is a subjective, diffuse, and political exercise in "muddling through"
The concern is with means of action rather than ends	————	The ends justify (moral) means

Figure 3
Rational Comprehensive Planning versus Disjointed Incremental Planning

serial, exploratory, and fragmented. It is assumed that planning functions are dispersed among many different (often competing) agencies and groups, for whom bargaining and compromise are the twin bases for the formulation and achievement of goals and objectives. Planning becomes a subjective, diffuse, and political exercise in "muddling through." In disjointed incremental planning, the ends justify (moral) means. Thus, disjointed incremental planning is to Planning what incrementalism is to Policymaking.

Functional planning begins with the premise that goals and objectives are formulated outside the planning process. They are set externally, the responsibility of planning then being to devise appropriate means for their realization. The principal concern is with the execution of duties. Planning is portrayed as a functional, administrative exercise carried out within a closed, hierarchical structure, the primary purpose of which is to perform duties that have been defined outside the system.

Normative planning, in contrast, begins with the premise that the formulation of goals and objectives is a central concern of planning itself. Planning is not value-free: on the contrary, it is expected to deal with the determination of values and, hence, with goals and objectives. The emphasis is upon the ends of planning, with a primary concern being to develop effective ways of mobilizing and institutionalizing commitment. Planning is a (largely) political exercise, characterized by a high degree of autonomy in the setting and execution of duties and an open administrative structure.

The characteristics of functional planning and normative planning are clearly antithetical to each other (Figure 4).

FUNCTIONAL PLANNING		NORMATIVE PLANNING
Goal setting is EXTERNAL to planning	———————	Goal setting is INTERNAL to planning
Planning emphasizes the coordination and articulation of means	———————	Planning emphasizes the ends or products
Central concern is with the execution of duties	———————	Central concern is with mobilizing and institutionalizing commitment
Planning is a functional, administrative exercise	———————	Planning is a (largely) political exercise
The structure is concerned with the execution of duties that are defined elsewhere	———————	There is a high degree of autonomy in the planning structure
There is a closed, hierarchical administrative structure	———————	There is a tight, but open administrative structure

Figure 4
Functional Planning versus Normative Planning

Although there are sufficient differences between Faludi's models to justify their classification as six distinct types, there is a sense in which they can be grouped more broadly into two general categories. Blueprint planning, rational comprehensive planning and functional planning all emphasize means over ends, closed administrative structures, ordered procedures, and specialized expertise. In so doing, they reflect an *organizational view of planning*. In contrast, process planning, disjointed incremental planning, and normative planning all give primary significance to ends over means and emphasize flexible procedures, relatively open structures, and lay (non-professional) involvement. They reflect an *experiential view of planning* (Table 3).

Table 3
The Organizational and Experiential Views of Planning

	Organizational Planning	Experiential Planning
Features		
	• Emphasizes means over ends	• Emphasizes ends over means
	• Exhibits closed (tight) administrative structures	• Exhibits open (loose) administrative structures
	• Encompasses ordered (fixed) procedures	• Encompasses flexible (varied) procedures
	• Reflects specialized knowledge and expertise	• Encourages lay (non-professional) involvement
	• Seeks control	• Seeks compromise
Types		
	• Functional planning	• Normative planning
	• Blueprint planning	• Process planning
	• Rational comprehensive planning	• Disjointed incremental planning

Faludi's models offer a useful framework for assessing the evolution of leisure planning in Canada and, by extension, in other advanced industrial nations. The earliest form of such planning can be best described as a kind of functional planning. The concerns of planners were with the coordination and articulation of various means of meeting leisure goals that were set externally —

or often were not consciously set at all, but were simply assumed or borrowed from elsewhere. The emphasis was upon the provision of particular kinds of recreation areas and facilities, such as city and neighborhood parks, playgrounds, swimming pools, ice arenas, and tennis courts. The decision to provide an area or facility was taken by reference to arbitrarily-determined standards of provision. The dominant example of this was the urban open space standard, though there were also many leisure facility standards. Most Canadian communities had formal urban open space standards expressed either in acres per thousand population or as a percentage of the developed area. These were usually borrowed from other communities or set according to an ideal national standard. The most famous example is the national standard of 6 acres of municipal parks per 1,000 population, enunciated in Britain in the 1928 by the National Playing Fields Association (National Playing Fields Association 1928). The United States standard of 10 acres per 1,000 population was then declared in the 1950s, and re-stated in the 1960s (American Society of Planning Officials 1965). Others followed, so that, in 1973, the Sports and Recreation Branch of the Ontario (Canada) Ministry of Community and Social Services was able to publish a booklet entitled *Guidelines for Public Recreation Facility Standards*, giving standards for facilities and spaces ranging from indoor ice arenas to community centers to swimming pools to tennis courts (Ontario Ministry of Community and Social Services 1973). Earlier, in 1968, the British Central Council of Physical Recreation had produced a more technical document outlining methodologies for determining local standards for sports grounds, swimming pools, sports halls, and multi-sports centers (Central Council of Physical Recreation 1968). The latter was a more sophisticated document than the former, but it still represented an approach based on provision rather than planning. It said little about location and even less about access. It simply defined a more elaborate standard.

This standards approach to planning was carried out within a closed hierarchical administrative structure by a professional and technical bureaucracy. Leisure planning was a component of general urban planning in that proposals for leisure areas and facilities, identified as necessary through the application of standards, were generally contained in comprehensive municipal plans. There were many examples of such plans, but, perhaps, one of the most notable was the plan for Centre County, Pennsylvania (Centre County Planning Commission 1972).

During the late 1960s, the functional standards approach gave way to a form of blueprint planning. Broad goals were laid down which called for the provision of a wide range of leisure areas and facilities to serve the population of the planning area. Following this, specific objectives were formulated in terms of standards, which again were often culled from a national or provincial guide to standards, or were adopted from another similar community. Once these standards were determined, the planners set out to collect and analyze data about the existing state of affairs in the planning area: the size and structure (for example, age and sex) of the population; the kinds and numbers of existing leisure areas and facilities; potential areas for leisure development and use; and so on. This was then followed by the formulation of a Master Plan, based upon the difference between needs (as determined by the application of the standards to the population data) and existing levels of provision (as measured by the inventory and analysis of current areas and facilities). The Master Plan reflected a long term desirable state. It was the end product of a mechanistic, technical, and professional exercise, concerned principally with the coordination and manipulation of the means of planning — that is, the standards.

This form of blueprint planning began a process which was to lead to an increasing separation of leisure planning from general urban planning. In Canada, communities began to produce distinct *Recreation Master Plans* which were entirely separate from *General Municipal Plans*, the only connection being that "green" spaces were designated in the latter as being for "recreational use" or, even, merely for "public use." The detailed uses to which these spaces would be put — parkland, reserve, athletic ground, swimming pool, and so on — were to be found in the separate *Recreation Master Plan*. Again, there were many examples of such plans, with one of the most notable being the plan for the Grand River in Ontario, Canada (City of Kitchener 1973).

Yet another change occurred in the mid-1970s — from blueprint planning to a form of rational comprehensive planning, although this did not entirely reflect Faludi's ideal model. The focus was still upon the production of a Master Plan. Indeed, in Alberta, Canada, the preparation of such a plan was made a formal requirement for municipalities to be eligible for capital facility grants from the provincial government to assist in the construction of major cultural and leisure facilities. But the emphasis was now upon the rational and comprehensive treatment of all relevant data. This was the period which saw a great upsurge in the use of social surveys to acquire information about the leisure activities of the people living in the planning area: what activities they did, where they did them, how often, and with whom. Public involvement was first tolerated and then encouraged, but only as a means of adding to the store of information that was to be subjected to rational analysis by the planners. The Master Plan, it was assumed, would be total, holistic, comprehensive, optimal, and rational. Where this approach diverged, at least in part, from the ideal model, was in the separation of leisure planning from general urban planning. For, while *Recreation Master Plans* were prepared by centralized planning units within municipal Recreation and Parks Departments (or by planning consultants to these departments), these groups worked in relative isolation from municipal Planning Departments. Although there was often informal (and, sometimes, even formal) liaison and consultation, there was rarely any attempt to work together in joint planning teams. It was sufficient that the *Recreation Master Plan* be consistent with the *General Municipal Plan*. There was no requirement that the two be integrated.

The dominant approach to leisure planning in Canada (and many other advanced industrial nations) today is this form of rational comprehensive planning. Its principal characteristics are a preoccupation with rational and comprehensive analyses, carried out in a scientific and diagnostic manner by leisure planners, with limited community input; a centralized planning system within a Recreation and Parks (or Leisure Services) Department, often isolated in large measure from the general urban planning function; an assumption that consensus is possible in the formulation and achievement of community leisure goals; an emphasis upon the preparation of *Recreation Master Plans* which are concerned with means of action rather than ends or goals; and an underlying belief that leisure planning is a process that can be total, holistic, comprehensive, optimal, and rational. Some excellent examples of this type of leisure planning include the plans for Halifax, Canada (City of Halifax 1976), for Edmonton, Canada (City of Edmonton 1978), and for Strathcona County, Canada (Planning Consultants Consortium 1985).

Leisure planning in Canada and other advanced industrial nations has moved from being a form of functional planning through a phase of blueprint planning to its current form of rational comprehensive planning (Table 4). The time frames have not always been the same in each country. Nor have all of the characteristics been present in every case. (In Britain, for example, there was not the separation of leisure planning from general urban planning that occurred in Canada. Indeed, this was not always the case in every community in Canada). But virtually all countries appear to have adopted an organizational approach to planning, in the sense noted earlier. The principal emphasis has been upon the central characteristics of this perception of planning: means over ends; closed administrative structures; ordered and orderly procedures; and specialized expertise.

Perhaps the greatest problem in leisure planning in Canada and elsewhere springs, paradoxically, from the efforts of planners to be holistic, objective, and logical. The rational comprehensive approach requires that there be a rational and comprehensive treatment of variables that are themselves rational and comprehensive. It assumes that the planner can know everything that needs to be known — that is, that he or she has all the relevant information. In short, it tends to assume away uncertainty. In reality, since this cannot be done, plans emerge characterized by a spurious rationality and a presumed comprehensiveness.

Twenty years ago, Friend and Jessop (1969) identified three kinds of uncertainty in planning. Uncertainty about the relevant environment (UE) refers to "the conventional kind of uncertainty which expresses itself in bad forecasts of behavior within the system that is being planned for" (Hall 1980). Simply put, leisure planners cannot accurately and easily predict mass leisure behavior. Uncertainty about decisions in related decision areas (UR) refers to the fact that there are other groups of decision makers (for example commercial leisure businesses and school authorities) who can, and do, make decisions that will profoundly affect leisure proposals and plans. The critical point is that the leisure planner often cannot easily and accurately predict such decisions and

Table 4
The Evolution of Leisure Planning in Canada

Phase	Period	Type of Planning	Characteristic Features
One	1950s to mid-1960s	Functional Planning	• Implicit rather than stated goals • Arbitrarily-determined standards of provision • Closed, hierarchical administrative structure • Technical and professional bureaucracy • Emphasis upon provision rather than planning • Recreation provision was part of general urban planning
Two	Late 1960s to mid-1970s	Blueprint Planning	• Formulation of objectives in terms of standards • Collection and analysis of sociodemographic data • Preparation of a Master Plan • Mechanistic, technical and professional exercise • Separation of recreation planning from general urban planning
Three	Mid-1970s to the present	Rational Comprehensive Planning	• Recreation participation surveys • Public involvement as a form of input to planning • Locally-based standards • Scientific, diagnostic exercise by professionals • Complete separation of recreation planning from general urban planning

their impact on leisure plans. Uncertainty about value judgments (UV) refers to the fact that planning decisions are made in a value context. The leisure planner may be able to gauge a population's value system (albeit crudely) at the time that a leisure plan is developed, but rarely is it possible to predict how these values will shift over time. There were, for example, few (if any) who predicted the change in values towards health and fitness that has occurred in Canada over the past decade or so. Yet this has had major impacts upon leisure planning: for example, in the escalating demands for bicycle paths, jogging trails, and cross country ski trails.

The existence of the above three types of uncertainty means that a rational comprehensive planning approach can never really be satisfactorily achieved. This, in turn, necessitates a retreat from the Master Plans of the kind that dominated leisure planning through the 1960s and 1970s — and, indeed, still predominate. This is especially true for plans which incorporate large scale, high cost, technologically innovative major capital projects. The history of such plans, both in leisure and more generally, has been one of fatal miscalculation. Overly optimistic forecasts of demand have been combined with overly optimistic forecasts of cost. Invariably, the demand forecasts have been excessively high, while the cost forecasts have been excessively low. Examples from the leisure field include the Sydney Opera House in Australia, Montreal's Olympic Stadium, and Calgary's Olympic Saddledome. Leisure planning in Canada (and, perhaps, elsewhere) has been closely aligned with the development of capital projects, even if, in most instances, these have not been based in wholly new technologies. Indeed, as noted earlier, the existence of an approved *Recreation Master Plan* was a formal requirement for municipalities to be eligible to receive provincial grants to assist in the construction of major cultural and leisure facilities in Alberta, Canada. In light of this, it is not surprising that many Master Plans emphasized major capital projects. But even when they have not done so, *Recreation Master Plans* have usually reflected a rational comprehensive approach, which experience has now shown is not only likely to be highly inaccurate over time, but also often raises unrealistic expectations within the community.

SCIENCE AND JUDGEMENT

The central problem with current attempts at leisure forecasting, policymaking, and planning is a fascination with science and the scientific method. One senses an overwhelming need to identify, demonstrate, and quantify causality, a desire to separate "facts" from "values." This is accompanied by an almost blind trust in the notion of scientific management. Yet, such an attitude and approach flies in the face of *the art of judgment*. It also faces severe practical problems when it attempts to deal with the future. For the one thing about the future of which one can be sure is that it will be continually surprising!

It was noted earlier that any consideration of the future — whether in the form of a predictive forecast, a prescriptive policy, or a procedural plan — must recognize not just the existence of uncertainty, but also the dominant role that uncertainty plays in forecasting, policymaking, and planning. Given this, what one must seek is not science versus values, but science in the service of values. And this, surely, requires a retreat from the rationalist approaches to forecasting, policymaking, and planning that have been so dominant during the past two decades.

It was also suggested earlier that leisure forecasting has already begun to move away from a solely scientific, rational, and quantitative mode to one which combines this with informed judgments derived from values. What is proposed here is that leisure policymaking and planning should follow this same route. To the extent that leisure policymaking may be conceived as being more than just the accommodation of the interests of competing political groups, it should be incrementalist in character. And so should leisure planning. In incrementalist policymaking and planning, bargaining and compromise among competing groups form the basis for the formulation and achievement of goals. Change is incremental and is brought about through trade-offs between groups. Policy and planning are: *incremental,* concerned with marginal change from the status quo; *remedial,* concerned with remedying present inadequacies and inequities; *serial,* carried out through a series of (often minor) changes to the status quo; *exploratory,* exploring ways of adapting the existing system; and *fragmented,* occurring by way of separate (often unrelated) activities and decisions. Most of all, there is no grand policy or Master Plan. There is only a current state in the evolution of an ongoing process. Disjointed incremental policymaking and planning also implies greater cooperation and consultation between leisure policymakers and planners and those in other fields — especially, though not exclusively, those in general urban planning. Incremental policymaking and planning starts from the premise that alternatives are limited and that change is brought about through trade-offs. They also seek, as the name implies, to increase net social benefits, as distinct from optimizing or maximizing them. One way of achieving this is through the integration of resources and activities. This, in turn, is more likely to occur if policies and planning proposals are examined and evaluated in a broad context. A leisure policy and plan, which incorporates and meets one or more of the objectives of health, transportation, and general urban policies and plans, will likely receive greater consideration in a situation where alternatives are limited and trade-offs predominate, than one which meets only leisure objectives. Like education, health, and transportation, leisure requires separate policymaking and planning attention and expertise, but it should not be divorced from these other fields.

Incremental policymaking and planning is a subjective, diffuse, and political exercise in "muddling through." It is not to be confused with an absence of policymaking or planning, nor does it eliminate the need for careful quantitative analysis and evaluation. Incremental policymaking and planning will lead to the commitment of resources, just as any other kinds of policymaking and planning do, and decision makers must know, to the extent possible, what types and quantities of resources will be required. But what incremental policymaking and planning offer, in contrast to rational comprehensive approaches, are greater flexibility in managing uncertainty, greater recognition of plurality and competition among community groups, fewer grand schemes but more attainable ones, and greater adaptability in the use of existing and new facilities. As Hall has remarked, "muddling through is no bad prescription for the ordering of public affairs, if it is done with intelligence and foresight" (Hall 1980). Most importantly, incrementalism employs the products of science to assist in applying the art of judgment.

References

Alberta Recreation and Parks. 1983. *Sport Development Policy*. Edmonton: Alberta Recreation and Parks.

Alberta Recreation and Parks. 1988a. *General Recreation Survey*. Edmonton: Alberta Recreation and Parks.

Alberta Recreation and Parks. 1988b. *Foundations for Action: Corporate Aims For The Ministry of Recreation and Parks*. Edmonton: Alberta Recreation and Parks.

American Society of Planning Officials. 1965. *Standards for Outdoor Recreation Areas*. Chicago: American Society of Planning Officials.

Bailey, P. 1978. *Leisure and Class in Victorian England*. London: Routledge and Kegan Paul.

Banks, R. 1985. *New Jobs from Pleasure: A Strategy for Producing New Jobs in the Tourist Industry*. London: Conservative Central Office.

Bella, L. 1986. "The politics of preservation: Creating national parks in Canada, and in the United States, England and Wales." *Planning Perspectives* *1*:189-206.

Bella, L. 1987. *Parks for Profit*. Montreal: Harvest House.

British Travel Association/University of Keele. 1967. *Pilot National Recreation Survey*. Keele: University of Keele.

Burton, T.L. 1970. (ed.) *Recreation Research and Planning*. London: George Allen and Unwin.

Burton, T.L. 1971. *Experiments in Recreation Research*. London: George Allen and Unwin.

Burton, T.L. 1976. *A Work Program for Determining a Federal Outdoor Recreation Policy*. Ottawa: Environment Canada (Mimeograph).

Central Council of Physical Recreation. 1968. *Planning For Sport*. London: Central Council of Physical Recreation.

Centre County Planning Commission. 1972. *Centre County Recreation and Open Space Plan - Volume I. Recreation Standards.* Centre County, PA: Centre County Planning Commission.

Cherry, G.E. 1985. "Scenic heritage and national parks lobbies and legislation in England and Wales." *Leisure Studies 4:*127-139.

City of Edmonton. 1978. *Parks and Recreation Master Plan 1979-1983.* Edmonton: City of Edmonton.

City of Halifax. 1976. *Recreation Master Plan.* Halifax: City of Halifax.

City of Kitchener. 1973. *Grand River Open Space Study.* Kitchener: City of Kitchener.

Clawson, M. and J.L. Knetsch. 1966. *The Economics of Outdoor Recreation.* Baltimore: Johns Hopkins Press.

Doern, G.B. and R.W. Phidd. 1983. *Canadian Public Policy: Ideas, Structure, Process.* Toronto: Methuen.

Duffield, B.S. 1976. "Forecasting leisure futures: An exercise in understanding and analysis" in Haworth, J.T. and Parker, S.R. (eds.) *Forecasting Leisure Futures.* London: Leisure Studies Association.

Dumazedier, J. 1974. *Sociology of Leisure.* Amsterdam: Elsevier.

Etzioni, A. 1968. *The Active Society.* New York: Free Press.

Faludi, A. 1973. *Planning Theory.* Oxford: Pergamon Press.

Fitness and Amateur Sport Canada. 1979. *Toward A National Policy on Fitness and Recreation.* Ottawa: Supply and Services Canada.

Friend, J.K. and W.N. Jessop. 1969. *Local Government and Strategic Choice.* London: Tavistock Publications.

Gruneau, R. 1983. *Class, Sports and Social Development.* Amherst: University of Massachesetts Press.

Hall, P. 1970. *Theory and Practice of Regional Planning.* London: Pemberton Books.

Hall, P. 1980. *Great Planning Disasters*. Berkeley: University of California Press.

Hargreaves, J. 1985. "From social democracy to authoritarian populism: State intervention in sport and physical recreation in contemporary Britain." *Leisure Studies 4:* 219-226.

Hartle, D. 1979. *Public Policy, Decision Making and Regulation*. Montreal: Institute for Research on Public Policy.

Holy Bible, King James Version, Genesis.

Kaynak, E. and J.A. Macaulay. 1984. "The Delphi Technique in the measurement of tourism market potential." *Tourism Management 4:* 87-101.

Lipset, S.M. 1968. *Agrarian Socialism*. New York: Doubleday (Anchor Books).

Martin, W.H. and S. Mason. 1984. *The U.K. Sports Market*. Sudbury: Leisure Consultants.

McCalla, J. 1983. "Future recreation scenarios for Ontario" in Burton, T.L. and Taylor, J. (eds). *Proceedings of the Third Canadian Congress on Leisure Research*. Edmonton: Canadian Association for Leisure Studies.

MacPherson, C.B. 1953. *Democracy in Alberta*. Toronto: University of Toronto Press.

Meller, H. 1976. *Leisure and the Changing City, 1870-1914*. London: Routledge and Kegan Paul.

Molnar, W. 1988. "A cultural policy for Edmonton." Edmonton: University of Alberta. (Unpublished Paper).

National Playing Fields Association. 1928. *Open Space Standards*. London: National Playing Fields Association.

Ng, D., B. Brown, and W. Knott. 1983. "Qualified leisure services manpower requirements: A future perspective." *Recreation Research Review 10:* 13-19.

North West Sports Council. 1972. *Leisure in the North West*. Salford: North West Sports Council.

Ontario Ministry of Community and Social Services. 1973. *Guidelines for Public Recreation Facility Standards*. Toronto: Ontario Ministry of Community and Social Services.

Outdoor Recreation Resources Review Commission. 1962. *Outdoor Recreation for America*. Washington: U.S. Government Printing Office.

Planning Consultants Consortium. 1985. *Strathcona County Recreation and Parks Development Plan 1985-1989*. Edmonton: Planning Consultants Consortium.

Redmond, G. (ed). 1986. *Sport and Politics*. Champaign, IL: Human Kinetics Publishers.

Shafer, E.L., G.H. Moeller, and E.G. Russell. 1975. "Future leisure environments." *Ekistics 40:* 68-72.

Sports Council. 1982a. *A Leisure Policy for the Future*. London: Sports Council.

Sports Council. 1982b. *Sport in the Community: The Next Ten Years*. London: Sports Council.

Taylor, G.D. 1969. "History and techniques of recreation demand prediction." in *Predicting Recreation Demand*. East Lansing: Michigan State University, 4-13.

Tourism Canada. 1985. *Towards A Canadian Tourism Strategy*. Ottawa: Regional Industrial Expansion.

Veblen, T. 1989. *The Theory of the Leisure Class*. New York: Viking Press.

Veal, A.J. 1971. "A strategy for the provision of recreation facilities." in Burton, T.L. *Experiments in Recreation Research*, pp. 307-344. London: George Allen and Unwin.

Veal, A.J. 1987. *Leisure and the Future*. London: Allen and Unwin.

Vickers, G. 1965. *The Art of Judgment: A Study of Policy Making*. New York: Basic Books.

PART THREE

Building Blocks

One of the most important themes of this book, and one that appears explicitly in several chapters — most notably Kelly's in Part Two and Godbey's in the last part — is that the artificial separation of leisure and recreation from other aspects of people's lives and lifestyles will ultimately preclude a comprehensive understanding of leisure and recreation. It will prevent us from interpreting the meaning and significance of these phenomena with reference to the social and cultural context within which they are embedded. Yet, at the same time, it is almost impossible to conduct scholarly research unless at least some conceptual, operational, and substantive boundaries — albeit arbitrary ones — are imposed on an investigation. The success of leisure studies, as in virtually every other field of scholarly inquiry, depends on achieving a delicate balance between the desire to provide broad contextual understanding and the necessity to conduct careful, systematic, and focused research.

Thus, while broad, holistic approaches are not absent from leisure studies, many leisure scholars have addressed themselves almost exclusively to narrowly defined questions, such as the understanding of why people recreate (motivations), the outcomes of participation (satisfaction and other benefits), leisure constraints, conflict, capacity, special populations, and so on. And it is the exception, rather than the rule, to encounter an empirically-based paper in any of these sub-fields which attempts to review more than the literature in the same area. Unfortunately, this increasing specialization within leisure studies has strongly contributed to the sense of fragmentation and frustration currently being experienced by many leisure scholars, as we have argued elsewhere in this book.

It is true that each of the review chapters in Part Three focuses on a specific topic, theme, or approach in leisure studies — motivations, satisfaction, spatial analysis, economic frameworks, environmental attitudes, benefits, and leisure constraints. What sets the contributions in this section of the book apart from most such efforts, however, is that, by and large, the authors place their subject-matter within a far broader context than is the norm. Each chapter, in its own way, demonstrates the crucial linkages which exist with other branches of leisure studies.

If the chapters in Part Two can be thought of as the essential foundation upon which future leisure studies will rest, then the seven contributions in this part of the book — the building blocks — represent many of the fundamental themes around which the structure of leisure studies will be built in the coming decade or more. They are also an appropriate transition between the theoretical and conceptual concerns of the preceding section and the more concrete, issue-oriented subject-matter of the one that follows.

Part Three encompasses a broad sweep of ideas which cut across many of the specific issues that have concerned leisure scholars and will continue to preoccupy them. Iso-Ahola and Mannell deal with matters that broaden our understanding of why people participate in leisure and recreation, and the satisfaction they gain from participation. Smith and Vickerman summarize two important approaches to leisure studies — the geographic and the economic — without which our understanding will never be complete, despite the apparent neglect of these important frameworks in leisure studies in recent years. Jackson offers a value-based interpretation that goes well beyond much of the current conventional wisdom about why people recreate. Similarly, Schreyer and Driver provide an innovative perspective on the benefits of leisure that challenges the usefulness of the narrow definition of "benefit" that has recently come to dominate the field. Finally, Goodale and Witt address the interconnected issues of recreation non-participation and barriers to leisure, matters which have come to be recognized as important by leisure scholars only in the last decade, but ones which are almost certain to be among the dominant themes in leisure research in the next few years.

As a set, the chapters in Part Three offer compelling models and examples for leisure researchers. While all are written by contributors with clearly-defined disciplinary backgrounds and training, they simultaneously convey a respect for the contributions of other disciplines and acknowledge the necessity of breaking down restrictive boundaries from around the subject-matter of leisure studies.

E. L. J.
T. L. B.

MOTIVATION FOR LEISURE

Seppo E. Iso-Ahola

INTRODUCTION

One of the most basic questions about leisure concerns motivation. Why do people do what they do in their leisure? Are there leisure needs? (Veal 1988) Are leisure choices and behaviors guided by natural instincts, or are they based upon rational and calculated decisions? Are people born with innate senses that tell them when to do something leisurely, or do they learn to do certain leisure behaviors when growing up? In short, what is it that makes people engage in activities they like and do not like during their leisure? In an effort to answer these and related questions, this chapter examines the theoretical and empirical foundations of leisure motivation. One of the themes towards which the ensuing review is directed is the identification of the most fundamental and key motivations for leisure.

Why is it important to study leisure motivation? The answer is two-fold. First, understanding what makes people do their leisure activities is important in and of itself. Such knowledge is fundamental to explanations and predictions of leisure behaviors (Ingham 1986, 1987; Iso-Ahola 1988). There is hardly anything more basic to leisure behaviors than the factors or mechanisms that prompt such behaviors. It is also important to know how much these mechanisms vary under different conditions and for different groups of individuals. Second, there are practical reasons for studying leisure motivation. If we know the basic principles of leisure motivation, we can apply them in practical settings and contexts of leisure services delivery. For example, it is difficult to imagine how recreation programs for the elderly in nursing homes could be planned without considering motivational factors underlying participation in these programs. This is especially true because motives are inextricably linked to expected outcomes of recreation participation (Kleiber 1985; Knopf 1985; Pierce 1980). If social interaction, for instance, is the main motivator among nursing home residents, then it would be foolhardy to plan recreation programs around activities that do not facilitate social contacts.

It is possible to approach the study of motivation from different perspectives and with different premises or assumptions. Perhaps the most important assumption deals with the question of how cognitively active or passive humans are thought to be. While behaviorists view people as passive, mechanistic beings, cognitive social psychologists start from the premise that people are active, construing organisms. The approach taken here is the latter one. Accordingly, the S-O-R model underlies the ensuing discussion, and assumes that the organism (0) variables (i.e. cognitions and emotions) play crucial mediating roles in stimulus-response (S-R) connections. Thus, it is not automatic that a given stimulus (e.g. a sunny day) invariably leads to the same reinforcing response (e.g. playing tennis). Cognitions and emotions mediate the effects of stimuli on responses. This suggests that the study of motivation should be focused primarily on understanding cognitive and emotional aspects of motivation.

WHAT IS MOTIVATION?

While motivation is one of the most basic concepts in psychology, it is also one of the most controversial ones. This is mainly due to two facts: (1) motives cannot be observed, but must be inferred from self-reports or actual behaviors; and (2) there is no single motivational mechanism or theory that can explain all human motivation — motives vary depending on physiological and social bases.

Regardless of their differences, psychologists agree that a motive is an internal factor that arouses and directs human behavior. People do not simply walk, run, or play various games; they strive for some objects and escape from others. Most human actions are directed, and an inner motive (a purpose or a desire) leads to actions that bring people closer to their goals (cf. Gleitman 1986). The question of where this inner motive comes from is generally answered by saying that internal and external stimuli give rise to human motivation. Internal stimuli refer to such things as memory of a good time in playing recreational sports, whereas external stimuli are likened to factors in the physical and social environments (e.g. a sunny day; a good friend calling and asking to play tennis).

Physiological Needs

An important question about motivation deals with its physiological foundations. It is well established that organisms exist in the stable internal equilibrium called homeostasis. Regardless of considerable fluctuations in the external environment, the human body maintains, for example, temperature and water conditions at remarkably constant levels. If, however, certain conditions create homeostatic imbalance, they then lead to motives to restore the internal equilibrium. In this way, some motives grow directly from the organism's regulation of its own internal state. Of these motives, hunger and thirst are most frequently mentioned.

It is important to note, however, that the simple equation of a physiological need or homeostatic imbalance with a psychological motive or drive is not justified (Murray 1964). While the two are correlated, they are not the same. For instance, feeling hungry may result not only from a physiological need but also from external stimuli, such as smelling a sizzling steak. On the other hand, not all nutritional needs result in hunger. What all of this means is that a physiological need is a biological process involving homeostatic imbalance, whereas much more is involved in psychological motives than homeostatic imbalance (Murray 1964). While these non-homeostatic motives can be physiologically influenced, they nevertheless are mainly aroused and shaped by psychological conditions.

Optimum Level of Arousal

Today psychologists generally agree that a search for some optimum level of arousal or general stimulation underlies most psychological motives, but this perspective has not always been accepted. For example, in his famous drive-reduction theory of motivation, Hull (1943) postulated that organisms seek to reduce all stimulation and arousal. The theory, however, was challenged by stimulus or sensory deprivation studies (e.g. Dennis 1960; Dennis and Najarian 1957), some of which showed that stimulus deprivation results in retardation in children's locomotor performance. Other studies demonstrated that, if college students were deprived of all visual, auditory, and touch stimulation, they found such nirvana stressful and could tolerate it only for two or three days (Murray 1964). After that, they experienced periods of confusion, irritability and stress, and began having visual hallucinations. Students' intense desire for external stimulation was indicated by the fact that they wanted to hear a recording of an old stock market report over and over.

Such findings strongly suggest that people seek neither an absence nor an excess of stimulation, but rather an optimal level. Because under- and over-stimulation are physiologically and psychologically detrimental to humans (Hunt 1969), the result is a continuous search for an optimal level of stimulation. Of course, there are variations in this basic tendency, so that what constitutes the optimal level varies from person to person and from time to time.

The search for an optimal level of arousal is quite evident in leisure behaviors. People have not only invented many activities that allow them readily to seek and experience stimulation and excitement (e.g. roller coaster, sky diving), but they have also developed many activities which allow for relaxation and passive enjoyment (e.g. meditation, walking for pleasure, picnicking). Furthermore, people have made living arrangements in which leisure is in opposition to work (free-time after daily work, weekends after work week, and vacation after a year's work); in this way, leisure provides opportunities to balance under- or over-stimulating work.

In their search for optimal arousal, people seek stimulus conditions that are appropriately novel. For example, it is well established that, in their play, children avoid the extremes of total familiarity and total novelty (Fiske and Maddi 1961; McCall 1974). If stimuli are optimally novel, they arouse curiosity and a tendency to approach, but *overly* novel stimuli are likely to lead to fear and avoidance. It is also true that all things lose their novelty with repeated exposure. This process of habituation leads people to look for new experiences or activities, or they do familiar activities in a new way. Of course, the more novel or complex the original stimulus, the longer habituation takes (Murray 1964). It is then reasonable to suggest that leisure activities vary considerably in their ability to resist habituation. Some activities have, by their nature, more elements of novelty and complexity than do others, and therefore provide better opportunities to fulfill one's need for optimal arousal.

Intrinsic Motivation

In their search for optimal arousal, people are motivated by sensory stimulation and novelty and, therefore, are motivated to do and manipulate things. Such activity and manipulatory motivation is especially evident in children. When children discover that they can do something, they repeat it countless times. This interest in an activity for its own sake is also seen among animals. In his classic experiment, Harlow (1950) demonstrated that monkeys learn to disassemble a complex mechanical puzzle without extrinsic rewards. The monkeys worked persistently to learn to open latches that were attached to a wooden board. Because unlocking the latches gave the monkeys no rewards, and yet they continued to do so, the primary motive was presumably to master the manipulatory problem — opening the devices "for the fun of it." Thus, it appears that the intrinsic motives for stimulation and activity are innate, with learning playing only a secondary role (Murray 1964: 81).

The monkeys in Harlow's experiment acted much like human beings often do: they engaged in the activity for its own sake rather than for any extrinsic rewards. Something interesting, however, happened when some animals were given a food reward for solving the mechanical puzzle. These rewarded monkeys used the problem task only to get food, showing little interest in the activity for its own sake. They came to see the puzzle as a means to get extrinsic rewards (pieces of food). In this way, their original intrinsic motivation for the activity was killed by the introduction of extrinsic rewards.

Children's day-to-day activity is, for the most part, intrinsically motivated. Children do activities for curiosity, sheer manipulation, and such intrinsic rewards as feeling competent in dealing with the environment. They can sustain this activity for long periods of time, interrupted by intense homeostatic needs like hunger and thirst. But, as they grow older, especially when they reach school-age, children seem to lose much of their intrinsic motivation and become more extrinsically motivated. In a similar vein, much of adults' day-to-day activity appears to be extrinsically motivated, leaving leisure time the period when most of the daily intrinsic motivation is aroused and put into action (Graef, Csikszentmihalyi, and Gianinno 1983). This is likely to be especially true if working conditions are not stimulating enough. Butler's (1953) research on monkeys suggested that special deprivation conditions like boredom (e.g. boring work) may account for part of the drive behind intrinsic motivation.

Opponent-Process Theory

As noted above, intrinsic motivation serves the human tendency toward optimally stimulating experiences. Because the activities that are done for their own sake are voluntarily chosen, they are expected to bring about an optimum arousal and pleasure. Two things are evident in this formulation: (1) motives and emotions are interwoven; and (2) there is a tendency toward a motivational balance. With his influential theorizing, Solomon (1980) has proposed that the nervous system tends to counteract any deviation from motivational normalcy. If the imagined, expected, or actual experiences take one too far toward either extreme of the pain-pleasure dimension, an "opponent process" takes over and tilts the emotional state to the opposite side. Thus, ecstasy turns into mild pleasure and initial feelings of terror become less intense fear. When the original situation that led to extreme pleasure or fear is withdrawn, the opponent process is unopposed and results in a further movement toward the opposite side of the emotional continuum.

An example of this process can be seen in the experience of sky divers. While these people are intrinsically motivated by the activity in their efforts to find more stimulating and arousing experiences, their emotions and behaviors do not reflect the internal states of people who participate in an activity for the fun of it. The state of panic or terror is evident in most sky divers before their first jump (Epstein 1967). But, when they land safely and after several successful jumps, their emotional reactions change to feelings of elation and happiness. Although they still experience a little anxiety and tension before each jump, they are no longer terrified. After landing safely, the opponent process takes over because the original motivational condition that provoked the opponent process in the first place is withdrawn. The consequence is a shift toward the positive side of the emotional spectrum, and exhilarating feelings result. In short, motivational conditions prompt the opponent process which tends to balance one's emotional state and thereby maintain motivational normalcy.

One of the questions about the applicability of this theory to leisure is whether the opponent process is equally involved in all leisure behaviors or at different levels of regularity of leisure behaviors. It is logical to suggest that the smaller the role the opponent process plays, the more habituated and routine leisure behaviors become. Such routine leisure activities as physical exercise for some, and TV watching for others, apparently do not swing people's emotions too far toward either extreme of pleasure or pain. If so, the opponent process may have little to do with balancing participants' emotional states. On the other hand, non-routine leisure behaviors, such as vacationing and holiday activity, initially provoke exhilarating feelings, and therefore call on the opponent process to take over and swing the emotional state more to the negative side. This may be a reason why many people have severe post-holiday blues and post-vacation blahs.

SELF-DETERMINED BEHAVIOR

It is clear from the above review of research that intrinsic motivation may be at the heart of human behavior. This is not to say, however, that all human behavior is intrinsically motivated because such is not possible, if only for practical reasons. But, whenever possible, people prefer, and opt for, self-determined and autonomous behaviors. There are two basic reasons for this general tendency toward intrinsically motivated behaviors:

1. Intrinsically motivated behaviors facilitate people's attempts to pursue and achieve optimum levels of sensory stimulation and arousal and therefore also their efforts to maintain motivational normalcy; and
2. Intrinsically motivated behaviors are inherently pleasure- and satisfaction-producing.

Constraints on Self-Determined Behaviors

Regardless of the overriding tendency toward intrinsically motivated behaviors, people are often hindered from doing self-determined activities, or their initial intrinsic motivation is significantly undermined by certain factors. One such factor is the use of extrinsic rewards. There is an abundance of empirical evidence in the literature to indicate that, in general, rewards undermine intrinsic motivation (Deci and Ryan 1985). That is, when people are given rewards for doing an activity that they are intrinsically interested in, they subsequently lose much of their interest and willingness to participate in that activity. This "overjustification" phenomenon (Lepper, Green, and Nisbett 1973) is most likely to occur when rewards are expected, salient, and contingent on task engagement. As Deci and Ryan (1985) have suggested, people experience such rewards and feedback as controlling, and therefore perceive them as restricting their self-determination. There are, however, sex differences in these perceptions, in that females are more likely than males to perceive any feedback as controlling (Deci and Ryan 1985). Other factors that undermine intrinsic motivation include the imposition of a deadline for the completion of an interesting activity (Amabile, Dejong, and Lepper 1976; Reader and Dollinger 1982), the mere presence of a surveillant or evaluator (Lepper and Greene 1975), and the provision of information signalling that one's activity is evaluated, even if the subsequent evaluation is positive (Harackiewicz, Manderlink, and Sansone 1984).

Sometimes, a reward is given in the form of positive feedback. Does such feedback or reward undermine intrinsic motivation? The answer appears to be "no." It has been shown that, if positive feedback affirms or elevates one's sense of competence, it then enhances rather than undermines intrinsic motivation (e.g. Koestner, Zuckerman, and Koestner 1987). Further, if doing well at an activity is important to a person, then "positive competence feedback" is likely to increase intrinsic motivation (Harackiewicz and Manderlink 1984). In a similar vein, Sansone (1986) made a distinction between competence and task feedback, and found that feeling competent enhanced intrinsic motivation only if attaining competence was a primary goal of the activity. If, on the other hand, doing well is not thought to be central to activity involvement, the competence feedback can undermine intrinsic interest. In that situation, task feedback would be more appropriate and likely to enhance intrinsic motivation for the activity. Task feedback refers to the information that conveys to people how well they are doing various aspects of the activity, or how well they are improving their activity performance, or how well they are doing by certain accepted activity standards. In this way, the individual's performance is not compared to that of others; rather, the focus is on acquisition of the skills needed to master the activity at individually enjoyable levels.

The opportunity to choose what to do enhances intrinsic motivation, while its opposite, lack of opportunity to choose, undermines intrinsic interest. Swann and Pittman (1977) reported experimental findings indicating a significant decline in intrinsic motivation when an adult rather than the child chose the play activity. Similarly, when college students were given the chance to choose which tasks to work on and to decide how much time to spend in their chosen task, their subsequent intrinsic motivation was significantly higher than that of those who were not given the opportunity to choose the activity (Zuckerman *et al.* 1978).

The importance of choice over rewards was demonstrated in an experiment conducted by Bradley and Mannell (1984). Results indicated that when the subjects were offered the reward prior to the choice to participate in a laboratory game, their intrinsic motivation was significantly less than when the choice was offered first and the reward second. This is consistent with research which has shown that perceived choice or freedom is a critical regulator and determinant of intrinsically motivated leisure experiences (Iso-Ahola 1979a, 1979b). These studies demonstrated that, if subjects did not initially have an opportunity to choose a leisure activity, even the fact that this activity later brought about intrinsic rewards, such as feelings of competence, did not lead to intrinsically motivated leisure experiences. Thus, it appears that freedom of choice is a necessary condition for intrinsic motivation in general and for intrinsically motivated leisure in particular.

A curious, but frequently used, method of controlling children's behavior, and thereby undermining their interest in certain activities, is employed by parents and teachers. "If-then" contingencies such as, "If you do dishes, then you can go out and play with your friends," are common in child-rearing, though not by any means limited to children. In an illuminating experiment, Boggiano and Main (1986) showed that, when preschoolers were presented with this kind of familiar contingency, their interest in the second activity increased but interest in the first activity decreased appreciably. According to the above example, children's interest in washing dishes would have been undermined significantly and their motivation for playing with friends notably enhanced by the use of such a contingency. The problem is that, on subsequent occasions when the children are asked to do dishes, they will not be willing to do it without compensation. In this way, intrinsic motivation for the activity is severely undermined. While "if-then" contingencies may be an effective way of controlling children's behavior, they have definite drawbacks from the standpoint of the development of intrinsic motivation tendencies in children for specific activities.

External rewards, sanctions, and contingencies not only undermine intrinsic motivation but also have negative effects on creativity, cognitive activity, emotional state, and maintenance of behavior change. Experiments have shown (Deci and Ryan 1985) that events that are perceived as controlling (e.g. rewards) tend to lower the creativity of children's artistic and writing products, impair cognitive learning among college students, induce negative feelings in general and create less positive views of others, and undercut the persistence of behavior change following the termination of controlling events (e.g. therapeutic treatment). Deci and Ryan (1985) also reviewed empirical evidence indicating that, if interpersonal contexts and situations are supportive of self-determination and autonomy, they promote perceived competence and self-esteem and curb aggressiveness in children. A series of field experiments (Langer and Rodin 1976; Rodin and Langer 1977; Schulz 1976; Schulz and Hanusa 1978) has demonstrated that such interpersonal contexts promote long-term positive effects on health in the institutionalized aged. As these experiments suggest, it is not only important to raise individuals' perceived control but, above all, to provide opportunities for use of the elevated sense of self-determination and autonomy.

Intrinsic Versus Extrinsic Motivation

It follows that, to foster intrinsic motivation, the occurrence of controlling events should be minimized. Such extrinsic motivators as rewards, surveillance, and if-then contingencies are typically perceived as attempts to control one's behavior, leading to external attributions for behavior. Instead of thinking that I am doing this activity freely on my own, people say to themselves, "I am doing this activity because I have to. I have to play this game to get the trophy, to please someone." When extrinsic rewards and other events lead to such external attributions, they are perceived as controlling. The mere presence of an extrinsic reward does not undermine intrinsic motivation; rather, the perception that the extrinsic reward is controlling (determining) the behavior is what undermines intrinsic interest.

It is important to note, however, that extrinsic rewards and other similar events are not always perceived as controlling. While intrinsically motivated behavior is, by definition, self-determined, extrinsically motivated behaviors can also be self-determined (Deci and Ryan 1987), that is, "chosen extrinsic" behaviors. Many recreational sport activities offer extrinsic rewards like ribbons, trophies, and plaques. People can willingly and freely pursue such rewards and yet be intrinsically motivated by the activity. In that case, rewards would not be perceived as controlling, and behavior could be called "autonomous" (Deci and Ryan 1987). On the other hand, if people are pressured toward achieving such extrinsic goals, then their behavior would be "controlled."

Because, in and of itself, extrinsically motivated behavior is neither self-determined nor controlled, the interpersonal context and events become critical determinants of whether this behavior is autonomous or controlled. It is true, however, that such extrinsic motivators as sanctions, surveillance, and "if-then" contingencies are more likely to be perceived as controlling than as informational. While Deci and Ryan's distinction between autonomous and controlled behavior may be applicable only in the case of extrinsic rewards, it nevertheless seems more appropriate to talk about self-determined versus controlled behaviors than intrinsically versus extrinsically motivated behaviors. Or, if the latter distinction is to be used, it needs to be made clear that intrinsic motivation refers to self-determined behaviors and extrinsic motivation to controlled behaviors, although, again, we have to keep in mind that some behaviors are "chosen extrinsic" behaviors. In fact, this latter point raises a possibility that chosen extrinsic leisure behaviors may be very similar to intrinsic leisure behaviors in terms of satisfaction or contribution to well-being.

THE NATURE OF LEISURE MOTIVATION

The preceding review of the major psychological works on motivation provides a basis for understanding the nature of leisure motivation. Undoubtedly, intrinsically motivated or self-determined behaviors constitute the core of what is called "leisure" (see Cooper's chapter, this volume). In fact, research has shown that freedom of choice at the initiation of a behavior, and such intrinsic rewards as feelings of competence expected to result from the behavior, are the two main determinants of people's defining that behavior as leisure (Iso-Ahola 1979a,

1979b; Shaw 1985). Not only is freedom of choice critical for people's definitions of leisure but also for depth of involvement in the activity (Mannell 1980) and frequency of participation in it (Wankel and Thompson 1978). Those who have had the freedom to choose their leisure activities are more deeply involved in their leisure experiences, and actually participate more frequently in these activities, than those who have not had the freedom to choose their leisure activities.

It is well established that people feel most free when engaged in leisure activities. Such popular leisure activities as socializing with friends, eating meals at home or in restaurants, going to cultural activities, watching television, reading, and playing sports and games are seen as freely chosen more than 85 percent of the time (Csikszentmihalyi and Graef 1979). These activities, in and of themselves, are not leisure activities, however, as reported by the authors. The data from Csikszentmihalyi and Graef indicated that people were most cheerful when they were at such public leisure settings as restaurants, but when they said they had to be there to please a friend or member of the family, they were more irritable than when working. So, once again, we see that freedom of choice is critical for activity involvement to become leisure and enjoyable.

But, does greater freedom mean greater leisure? Mannell and Bradley (1986) addressed this question by conducting a laboratory experiment. The results indicated that the depth of involvement in leisure depended not only on freedom of choice but also on the subject's personality and the structure of the setting in which leisure took place. In this case, "personality" referred to perceived internal versus external locus of control, and "setting structure" to whether or not subjects were given clear guidelines for playing a laboratory game. It appeared that, when setting structure was relatively high, both internals and externals became more absorbed in the game under high choice conditions. On the other hand, when setting structure was relatively low, externals became less involved under high choice conditions, whereas internals became more absorbed with greater choice. This finding suggests that, when recreational games are highly structured, freedom of choice enhances everyone's involvement in leisure experience, but, when these games are less structured, the beneficial effects of freedom of choice depend on one's personality (internal versus external). The results also imply that the quality of leisure experiences cannot linearly and indefinitely be enhanced by providing more and more leisure activities, because leisure is a state of mind. Freedom of choice enhances leisure experiences up to a point, after which individual differences and situational factors mediate such effects of perceived freedom.

While freedom of choice or self-determination is a necessary condition for the occurrence of leisure, it is not sufficient (Iso-Ahola 1980: 189). To have leisure, one must experience enjoyment (Roadburg 1983). Nobody who voluntarily participates in something chooses an activity that is likely to lead to unpleasant and unsatisfying experiences. That is why there is a relatively high positive correlation (in the .40s) between intrinsic motivation and expressed enjoyment (Deci and Ryan 1987). On the other hand, freedom of choice does not necessarily guarantee a high degree of enjoyment: "Choosing to play tennis is one thing; needing to follow after something one finds in playing tennis is something else again" (Harper 1986: 124).

So, in addition to freedom of choice, we look for something else in our leisure experiences, and this something else consists of intrinsic rewards. For one person it may be increased self-understanding, for another feelings of competence, and for yet another simply an opportunity to escape everyday routine and problems. The attainment of these kinds of intrinsic rewards adds significantly to leisure enjoyment or satisfaction. Graef *et al.* (1983) reported that people consistently rate themselves happier and less tense with an increasing level of intrinsic motivation. People with higher percentages of extrinsically motivated (controlled) experiences tend to rate themselves as less happy and more tense, and describe their lives as more boring and their sense of competence lower.

Recent research by Mannell, Larson and Zuzanek (1988), however, suggests that, sometimes, activities *chosen* for extrinsic reasons produce higher levels of intrinsic rewards. A critical aspect seems to be that people perceive the activity as freely chosen in the first place. Under such conditions, people freely and willingly pursue extrinsic rewards, and it should not therefore be surprising that these extrinsically motivated activities can sometimes have great potential for challenging the individual's skills and producing feelings of potency, relaxation, and flow. As noted earlier, Deci and Ryan (1985) have suggested that "chosen extrinsic" behaviors can also be self-determined and autonomous, and therefore similar to intrinsically motivated behaviors in terms of satisfaction and other positive outcomes. There are individual differences, however, in that "given the freedom to choose, some people may also need the feeling of obligation or external compulsion to motivate engagement in activities that require an investment of effort, but as a consequence, produce higher levels of psychological involvement" (Mannell *et al.* 1988).

Optimal Experiences

Intrinsically motivating leisure behaviors are conducive to achieving optimal experiences because people do them from their own free will and pursue rewards that are to be obtained from doing activities for their own sake. It has been suggested that perceived competence is the most important of all intrinsic rewards in leisure (Iso-Ahola 1980: 143). While people strive to balance novelty and familiarity in their leisure, the change from too familiar or too routine experiences to more novel ones occurs within the limits of perceived competence. For example, people who play tennis during their free time and want more change and novelty, replace their tennis partners for new ones of similar caliber.

They do not choose to play with individuals who are much better (cf. Festinger 1954). In this way, the sense of competence and challenge provided by leisure involvement has to be matched in order to have optimal experiences.

The idea of the match between skills and challenges is also central in Csikszentmihalyi's (1982) formulation of optimal or "flow" experiences — what there is to do and what one is capable of doing. If skills exceed challenges, boredom results, and if challenges are greater than skills, anxiety is inevitable. Accordingly, people are motivated to avoid anxiety- and boredom-producing experiences and to approach those that enable them to use their capabilities in challenging ways. The fact that optimal experiences are intrinsically motivating was evidenced by an inverse relationship between "flow" frequency and "wishing to be doing something else." In other words, the more people indicated having flow experiences, the less they wished to be doing something else. In addition, Csikszentmihalyi (1982) reported that the favorite activities of teen-agers were those in which their skills and challenges were matched. He also found that "flow" experiences were the second best predictor of people's affect, that is, how happy, cheerful, and sociable they felt; flow was the best predictor of people's feelings of activation, that is, how active, alert, and strong they felt.

It is evident from Csikszentmihalyi's data that optimal experiences are by no means limited to leisure but can also occur in one's work. When there were "challenging problems at work," the percentage of people mentioning flow experiences in their work was relatively high. Flow experiences are, of course, possible in such jobs because "challenging problems" allow people to apply their skills to problem solving. But, if work does not provide such action opportunities or challenges, flow experiences do not occur in work. Although work is extrinsically motivating for most people, it can be seen as "self-deter-mined" rather than "controlled." If so, money, as the extrinsic motivator, does not prevent one from looking for opportunities to match skills with challenges. Nevertheless, the fact remains that people are more likely to find flow experi-ences in leisure than in work.

This is not to say that all leisure experiences are flow experiences. As Csikszentmihalyi reported, people rated their subjective states more "relaxed" when watching TV than at any other time of the day. Yet, their self-reported levels of concentration, control, alertness, strength, and activation were simulta-neously very low. On the other hand, teenagers rated active leisure pursuits (e.g. sports and games) as much more enjoyable than watching TV — yet they spent two and a half as much time per week watching TV as they did in active leisure (Csikszentmihalyi *et al.* 1977). What this means is that people engage in leisure activities for reasons other than achieving optimal or flow experiences (Shaw 1984). But the existence of these other motivators (e.g. convenience and social obligation) does not deny the fact that the most enjoyable leisure experiences are those that allow people to match their skills with challenges provided by activities and other participants. Therefore, people tend to gravitate toward self-determined, optimal leisure experiences whenever possible. For practical reasons, however, this may not be possible for many people for long periods of time.

Two-Dimensional Theory

Self-determined, competence-elevating experiences constitute the essence of intrinsically motivated leisure. There is, however, another side to intrinsic leisure motivation. This other side has been called "avoidance," "escape," or "leaving everyday routine behind" (Iso-Ahola 1982, 1984). The idea is that people are motivated in their leisure not only to seek such intrinsic rewards as feelings of competence, but also to escape everyday problems, troubles, and routines. This escape in and through leisure becomes an intrinsic reward in and of itself, although it can be combined with the other side of seeking intrinsic rewards. For example, a person wants to get away from the everyday rut, and flies for a few days to the Bahamas. But, because he enjoys tennis, he takes his racquet along and plays every day while there. In this situation, the person manages not only to get away from the routine environment but also succeeds in matching his skills with the challenges of tennis. In fact, these kinds of shorter get-away types of vacations have become increasingly popular in recent years (Mannell and Iso-Ahola 1987).

What is the basis of the escape dimension? First, it has been shown that the desire to escape is an integral part of leisure (Iso-Ahola 1984). As long as we formally and structurally separate leisure from work, be it a 4-40 (4-day, 40-hour week) or 5-40 or whatever work schedule, we automatically build the escape dimension into leisure. Just by doing any leisure activity, one is away from work and is, therefore, able to leave it behind in leisure. Whether a person wants to emphasize this escape dimension at any given time is an empirical question.

Second, working conditions are often such that they promote one's desire to escape work through leisure. One can escape either under- or over-stimulating work. For many people, unfortunately, work is barren, boring, and empty, mainly because they do not have opportunities to use their skills in a challenging way. Confronted with such under-stimulating work, many people turn to what Csikszentmihalyi (1982) called "cheap thrills," that is, nonproductive and often antisocial activities like cock fighting, demolition derby, gambling, drugs, and juvenile delinquency. Compared to the dullness of school or work, these activities provide enjoyment and temporary substitutes in the search for optimal experiences. This supports the earlier notion derived from Butler's (1953) research that sensory or stimulus deprivation conditions (e.g. boring work) in part explain the drive behind intrinsic motivation. Of course, working conditions can also be over-stimulating and stressful, and therefore give rise to the desire to escape from them through leisure. White-collar and managerial positions are often very stressful and demanding. When over-stimulation and stress become psychologically too burdensome, the little free time that is often available is used to escape these taxing conditions (Driver 1972).

Finally, the desire to escape the everyday environment also has its foundations in social learning. Particularly during the winter in colder climates, the idea of escape is heavily promoted by commercial enterprises in the mass media. Airlines and travel agencies advertise on a daily basis in newspapers and on television their warm climate destinations, and they do it cleverly by trumpeting the "need to escape" to such places. It is not surprising that, after repeated exposure to information emphasizing the need to escape, people come to believe that escape through leisure is not only socially acceptable but may also be necessary for their psychological well-being. They have learned to escape. For all the above reasons, the escape dimension is ubiquitous in all leisure behaviors and has to be considered as the second basic force of intrinsic leisure motivation.

Seeking and Escaping

It is important to emphasize that intrinsic leisure motivation consists of seeking *and* avoidance tendencies. It is neither solely seeking nor solely avoiding, however; rather, the stress is on the word "and." These two motivational dimensions or forces are behind all leisure behaviors. In fact, it is impossible to think of any leisure engagement in which both would not be present. Whether seeking is more dominant than avoidance for a certain group of people under certain conditions is, of course, an empirical question. For example, while vacationers may emphasize the escape component, none of them would say that they were not seeking some intrinsic rewards as well (such as social interaction, feelings of competence, and learning about other cultures). Similarly, those who watch TV mainly to escape their everyday environment also get intrinsic rewards as side-products (e.g. relaxation, social interaction, acquiring new information). And often, of course, we watch TV, not so much to escape anything, as to learn something new. On the other hand, those who play tennis after work do so mainly because they enjoy challenging matches and also manage to escape their routine environment in the process. In short, both seeking *and* escaping are two fundamental motivational forces of leisure. Although one motivational force can be more dominant than the other, the two are inseparable in the sense that it is possible to seek by escaping and to escape by seeking.

More specifically, then, what can we seek and escape? It has been theorized (Iso-Ahola 1982, 1984) that the intrinsic rewards that people seek in their leisure can be broken into two components: personal and interpersonal. The former refers to such rewards as feelings of personal competence, expected to be derived from leisure participation. On the other hand, people often want to engage in leisure activities mainly for social contact. They may play tennis, not so much for matching skills and challenges, as for being with good friends. And, of course, some leisure activities are nothing but social interaction (e.g. conversation, parties, picnics). Leisure experiences are a primary vehicle for social interaction and for forming new relationships (Crandall, Nolan, and Morgan 1980).

The importance of social interaction as an intrinsic reward of leisure involvement is well documented (Crandall 1980). In one study, subjects' affective ratings of various aspects of leisure were correlated with their feelings of leisure as a whole (Crandall 1979). It was found that one social item, "the feelings about things you do and the times you have with your friends," correlated more highly to total leisure feelings than other items. Crandall concluded that the best leisure activities seem to be those that involve both friendly interaction *and* an activity. Social interaction, in turn, has been found to be positively related to psychological well-being and mental health (Shaver and Freedman 1975; Schulz 1976). Thus, it seems clear that people seek positive interpersonal contacts in their leisure because social interaction in and of itself is enjoyable and can therefore be the main intrinsic reward of leisure participation. Whether social interaction is the major reward sought after in leisure depends on person, situation, and time.

In a similar vein, people can escape both the personal and the interpersonal world. The former refers to escape from personal problems, troubles, and failures. It can also refer to escape from everyday routine (under-stimulation) and over-stimulating or stressful work conditions. To get away from an interpersonal world means that a person is escaping routine social contacts (e.g. co-workers, the boss, family members). As Figure 1 shows, the two motivational forces pull us in opposite directions: we want to obtain certain intrinsic rewards in leisure but we also want to escape something in it. Again, it is not either/or; motivationally we do both.

This hypothesis was clearly supported in a study of vacationers, which showed that, while people wish to "escape routine" and "be alone and self-discover" during vacations, they also say that they want to "be with family and visit friends and relatives" (Rubinstein 1980). Clearly, they want to escape all interpersonal contacts (to be alone) but simultaneously seek the company of infrequently met friends and relatives. Also, they want to be with their family. Similarly, Copp (1975) found that it was important for hunters to be able to escape family and everyday friends through hunting *and* to be able to hunt with their "buddies."

While all of this seems paradoxical, it is consistent with the ideas of optimum stimulation and arousal. As Rubinstein reported, most people are eager to visit new places, but they want to do so in the company of familiar faces. This does not imply, however, that vacations are always, or even most of the time, done on the 50-50 principle of escaping and seeking. The value of any leisure activity is that it can be used motivationally in different ways at different times.

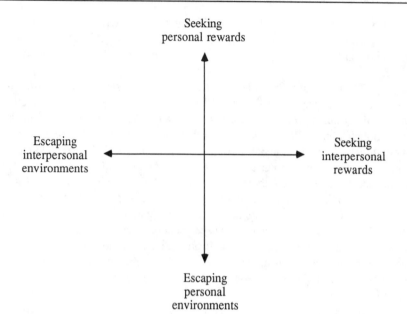

Figure 1
The Seeking and Escaping Dimensions of Leisure Motivation
(Source: Adapted from Iso-Ahola 1984: 111).

That is, at one time a person may go for a short vacation to just visit good friends, but to escape from everyone at another time. Therefore, it becomes important to study the conditions (e.g. sex roles: see Hirschman 1984) that motivate people to engage in leisure activities primarily for seeking purposes and secondarily for escape purposes, and *vice versa*.

The idea of seeking and escaping as components of leisure motivation is not new. It has been supported by numerous empirical studies (Beard and Ragheb 1983; Copp 1975; Crompton 1979; Ewert 1985; Fedler 1984; Hollender 1977; Iso-Ahola and Allen 1982; London *et al.* 1977; Mills 1985; Tinsley and Kass 1978; Tinsley *et al.* 1977). But what *is* new is the suggestion that there are only two fundamental dimensions or forces in leisure motivation: seeking personal and/or interpersonal intrinsic rewards, and escaping personal and/or interpersonal environments. All the individual motives can be incorporated in this 2 x 2 model, so that *no long lists of leisure motives are needed to under-stand leisure motivation*. It is also important to note that these two dimensions are, indeed, motivational forces rather than independent and separate single motives. They are dialectical forces in a sense that they are both, to varying degrees, present in all leisure behaviors and are opposite in their meaning of approach and avoidance. The antecedents and consequences of these motiva-tional forces are largely unknown at the present time.

Lack of Leisure Motivation

To understand leisure motivation better, it is important to consider factors that potentially prevent or undermine the development of intrinsic leisure motivation. The opposite of intrinsic leisure motivation is the lack of it, that is, apathy and boredom. If these constructs are opposite ends of the continuum, it can be assumed that enhancers of boredom perceptions become underminers of leisure motivation. The question, then, is: Why is it that leisure is nothing but boredom for some, while it is the most important thing for others? Or, what factors make people perceive their leisure as boredom?

Recent research (Iso-Ahola and Weissinger 1987) indicates that there are at least six psychological and two sociological factors associated with boredom in leisure. Leisure repertoire, leisure ethic, work ethic, awareness of leisure, constraints on leisure participation, and self-motivation, along with gender and income, were significantly associated with boredom in leisure. Specifically, these findings indicated the following:

- the larger the leisure repertoire, the lower the perception of leisure as boredom;
- the higher the leisure ethic, the lower the perception of leisure as boredom;
- the higher the work ethic, the higher the perception of boredom in leisure;
- the higher the leisure awareness, the lower the perception of boredom;
- the higher the perception of constraints on leisure, the higher the perception of boredom; and
- the higher self-motivation, the lower the perception of boredom in leisure.

It was also found that men more than women and people with high incomes more than those with relatively low incomes, perceived leisure as boredom.

Of the six psychological factors, awareness had much more effect on boredom perceptions than any other factor. In fact, its contribution (30%) to the total variance (60%) explained by all the variables was exactly one half. The second most important contributors to the total variance were leisure ethic, leisure repertoire, and self-motivation, each explaining seven percent of the variance. Importantly, it was not lack of awareness of leisure opportunities, but rather lack of awareness of the psychological value of leisure that contributed greatly to boredom perceptions. As the authors noted, this finding would seem to underline the importance of leisure education and counseling in making people cognitively conscious of the potential of leisure to enrich their lives. Such education is important because by increasing leisure awareness, it enhances intrinsic motivation for leisure.

Besides the awareness factor, the need for leisure education is evident because more positive leisure attitudes and less positive work attitudes were associated with lower boredom perceptions. If leisure education programs can change people's leisure and work attitudes, it is likely that people may become more intrinsically motivated to engage in leisure activities. In a similar vein, intrinsic motivation for leisure may be expected to increase with larger leisure repertoires. In other words, the more and better leisure skills people have, the more they are motivated to do leisure activities for their own sake.

It also makes sense that constraints are associated with boredom in leisure. If a person is inhibited to participate in leisure activities, it is not surprising that he or she would find leisure boring. Of the constraints studied, lack of friends, lack of time, feeling guilty, and lack of money contributed significantly to boredom perceptions. These constraints can, therefore, be seen as significant barriers to intrinsic leisure motivation, especially because "leisure barriers" undermine perceived freedom in leisure (Ellis and Witt 1984). The role of money as a contributor to leisure boredom appears to be somewhat complicated. While lack of money as a constraint increased boredom perceptions, it was also found that people with high incomes were more likely to perceive leisure as boredom than people with low incomes. This apparent contradiction may be explained by the fact that, up to a point, money is necessary for leisure participation (Searle and Jackson 1985), but after that, it does not make much difference. If anything, it becomes troublesome by increasing perceptions of leisure as boredom. Although to a certain degree and under certain conditions, money may help, it cannot buy intrinsic leisure motivation, just as it cannot buy happiness (Shaver and Freedman 1975).

In short, besides a relative lack of predisposition toward self-motivation in general, a person who is likely to have major problems with finding leisure intrinsically motivating and rewarding can be characterized by the following:

- he/she is not aware of the value of leisure in life;
- his/her attitudes toward leisure are poor while his/her work attitudes are very positive;
- he/she has a limited number of leisure skills at his/her disposal; and
- he/she feels that there are several constraints to his/her leisure participation.

In general, to become intrinsically motivated by leisure seems to be more difficult for men than women.

Although there appears to be some evidence (Butler 1953) to suggest that stimulus deprivation conditions, such as boredom, give rise to intrinsic motivation, it is unlikely that this could happen in the absence of the tools needed to become intrinsically motivated. If people do not have awareness, attitudes, and skills for leisure, and feel constrained in leisure participation, it is difficult to see how they could become intrinsically motivated. In this situation, boredom may not be strong enough to stimulate people to look for better conditions, but powerful enough to make them feel more hopeless, worthless, and depressed. On the other hand, this theorizing suggests that having occasional feelings of boredom may be good if people have the aforementioned tools, because, in that situation, boredom may stimulate them to use leisure tools to become intrinsically motivated.

Predisposition Toward Intrinsic Motivation

As the study on leisure and boredom indicated, general self-motivation was negatively (significantly) related to boredom in leisure. In other words, the more self-motivated people are in general, the less likely they are to perceive leisure as boredom. As conceptualized and measured in the study, self-motivation is a personality trait that distinguishes people who are high on the trait from those who are low on it. As one would suspect, this predisposition toward intrinsic motivation protects against boredom and suggests that the tendency to experience leisure as intrinsically motivating is as much a matter of individual capacity as it is a matter of social conditions and structures. Although it is very important for any human community to provide opportunities for intrinsically motivating experiences, it is also important to recognize that intrinsic motivation is an individual capacity (Weissinger 1986). This predisposition appears to be "an inner quality, a psychodynamic dimension that enables the person to discover rewards in mundane events that others find neutral and unrewarding" (Graef *et al.* 1983: 166). In a similar vein, Csikszentmihalyi (1982) concluded that the capacity to experience flow is an important personal skill that cuts across the work/leisure distinction.

The idea that intrinsic motivation is also a rather permanent and stable personality predisposition is supported by extensive research on "hardiness" (Kobasa 1979, 1982; Kobasa, Maddi, and Kahn 1982). Kobasa theorized that individual differences must mediate the relatively weak relationship between stress and illness found in many studies. Specifically, she suggested that people who stay healthy under stressful conditions differ in a "resistance resource" called "hardiness" or a personality disposition toward intrinsic motivation. Those who score high in the three components of intrinsic motivation (challenge, commitment, and control) are less debilitated by stressful life events than others. Over the years, the data have supported this hypothesis, showing that the personality disposition toward intrinsic motivation may decrease one's chance of being ill by 50 percent. Those who score high on stress and low on illness stand out on all the three criteria of the personality disposition toward intrinsic motivation. They are much more actively involved in their work and social lives than those who become ill under stress; they are more oriented toward challenges; and they feel more in control of their life events. Although Kobasa's earlier findings have been replicated (Funk and Houston 1987; Maddi *et al.* 1987), there has been some concern as to whether hardiness is a unitary phenomenon or three separate phenomena (Hull *et al.* 1987).

Regardless of such theoretical concerns, an important question has to do with the acquisition of this predisposition. An answer to this question seems to deal with the socialization process (Weissinger and Iso-Ahola 1984). Exposure to a wide variety of leisure experiences in early years would not only help a person acquire many different leisure skills, but might also contribute to the formation of personality predisposition toward intrinsic motivation — making a person become more oriented toward challenge, commitment, and control. This idea is indirectly supported by the data that have shown a positive relationship between the size of leisure repertoire and indicators of health (Mobily *et al.* 1984). Because personality predispositions are to a great extent a matter of attitude and orientation, they are largely learned from experiences, and can therefore be altered. In theory, then, the predisposition toward intrinsic motivation can be acquired through psychotherapy and counseling, though it may be a difficult task. The best strategy may be to provide opportunities for, and encourage children to pursue different play and leisure activities and skills in their formative years. If early experiences are successful and rewarding, they are likely to instill permanent enthusiasm for leisure and leisure activities.

From Intrinsic Motivation to Addiction

A natural extension of the predisposition toward intrinsic motivation is "serious leisure" (Stebbins 1979). Some people become highly specialized in their chosen activity, like the amateur archaeologists and astronomers studied by Stebbins. Amateurs' leisure is characterized by seriousness and commitment to their activity and is reflected by regimentation (e.g. rehearsals, practice, study) and systematization (e.g. schedules, organization). As Stebbins reported, every respondent in his study listed more rewards than costs, that is, rewards and thrills of their serious leisure outnumbered disappointments, tensions, and dislikes. The rewards that they cited were purely intrinsic, such as self-actualization, self-gratification, self-enrichment, and self-expression.

Consistent with this, it has been reported that those who are classified as "veterans" in given leisure activities stand out on such motives as "to be my own boss," "to develop my skills," "to test my abilities," "to strengthen feelings of self-worth," "to think about personal values," and "to test and use my own (specialized) equipment" (Schreyer *et al.* 1984). These studies suggest that the more specialized and serious we become about our leisure pursuits, the more important are the intrinsic rewards of involvement. As motivators, the psychological value of intrinsic rewards is that they are seen to be durable benefits.

They can be found more readily in serious leisure as opposed to mass or popular leisure. Motivationally, of course, the more serious people become about their leisure, the more they are able to seek intrinsic rewards through their continued and deep involvement.

The potential problem with serious leisure, however, is that it can become addictive. Those who depend exclusively on one activity for a sense of well-being are flirting with addiction (Grant 1988). In particular, this has become a problem with runners in recent years. While most of them started the activity in adulthood as a way of getting in shape or losing weight, many have developed a psychological dependence on it — to the extent that they have to do the exercise daily. If, for one reason or another, they cannot have their daily dose of exercise, they display signs of depression, anxiety, confusion, tension, and irritability. Having to stay away from their exercise regimen for longer periods of time may cause severe psychological problems for those who are addicted: depression, lack of energy, loss of interest in eating, sex, and other activities, decreased self-confidence and self-esteem, insomnia, and weight loss or gain (Grant 1988).

The problem with such leisure addicts is that they put all their "psychological eggs" in one basket. They organize their lives around their single activity, ignoring their spouses, children, and even jobs. For many, workouts are enough to satisfy their desire for social contacts. When carried to such an extreme, leisure becomes psychologically dysfunctional and even dangerous. Of course, these leisure addicts do their activity solely for psychological reasons and rewards — be it a sense of control and competence or self-confidence and self-esteem — and not so much because it is a form of recreation or a path to physical fitness. As Grant noted, exercise is the root of their psychological well-being, the touchstone of their identities. But to become so dependent on one's daily leisure highs as to ignore family and career is psychologically pathological and requires counseling and therapeutic intervention.

These potential problems of "addiction" do not mean that serious leisure will necessarily lead to addiction. Even with a high degree of recreation specialization (Donnelly *et al.* 1986) it is possible to maintain balance among leisure, work, and family. But the fact that leisure can become addictive raises important questions, such as: Do those who become addicted to a leisure activity do so because of their personality tendencies toward compulsive-obsessive behaviors? Or, is leisure addiction a response to a psychologically poor family and work life? Or, are certain activities more addictive than others? These and other relevant questions await empirical answers in our quest to understand the positive and negative sides of intrinsic leisure motivation.

CONCLUSIONS

Summary

Intrinsic motivation is the heart of leisure behavior. There are two basic reasons for the prevalence of intrinsic motivation in leisure: (1) intrinsically motivated behaviors facilitate people's attempts to achieve optimum levels of sensory stimulation and arousal; and (2) intrinsically motivated behaviors are inherently enjoyment- and satisfaction-producing. Intrinsic motivation is largely a matter of self-determination, but it can be undermined by factors that are experienced as controlling. Controlling factors include extrinsic rewards, sanctions, deadlines, surveillance, and external evaluation of one's performance or behavior. In addition, such common techniques as "if-then" contingencies have been found to undermine intrinsic motivation in play and leisure activities. On the other hand, positive feedback affirming or elevating one's sense of competence appears to enhance intrinsic motivation, especially if doing well at an activity is important to a person. It is important to note, however, that extrinsic rewards and similar events are not always and necessarily experienced as controlling.

Intrinsically motivated leisure behaviors are conducive to optimal experiences because they are self-determined and because they imply a match between skills and challenges. An opportunity to use skills in a challenging way produces feelings of personal control and competence, and is therefore a major source of enjoyment. Under- and over-challenging situations are avoided because they lead to anxiety and boredom, respectively. This does not mean that all leisure experiences are optimal experiences, however. People rate active leisure pursuits (e.g. sports and games) much more enjoyable than such passive forms of leisure as TV watching, yet they frequently spend much more time per week watching TV than they do engaged in active leisure. Nevertheless, the fact remains that the most enjoyable leisure experiences are those that are freely chosen and allow one to match skills with the challenges provided by activities and other participants.

People are motivated in their leisure not only to seek such intrinsic rewards as feelings of competence, but also to escape everyday problems, troubles, and routine. Although the desire to escape is an integral part of leisure simply because of the societal structure of leisure in opposition to work, the escape dimension can be made more important by lack of opportunities to use one's skills in challenging ways in work or school. Confronted with such under-stimulating work or school, people turn to "cheap thrills" in their search for optimal experiences. Another factor emphasizing the importance of escape has to do with social advertising of the "need to escape" from hectic, stressful, and over-stimulating work to the Bahamas and similar destinations. In theory, people can escape either personal or interpersonal worlds or both. In and of itself, escape is an intrinsic reward, but it can also be used to help seek other intrinsic rewards (e.g. a person escaping work to the Bahamas takes his golf clubs along).

It is important to emphasize, once more, that there are only two fundamental dimensions to leisure motivation: seeking personal/interpersonal intrinsic rewards, and escaping personal/interpersonal environments through leisure experiences. Leisure motivation is not a matter of either seeking or escaping, but of both. It is also important to note that these two dimensions are indeed motivational *forces* rather than independent and separate single motives. They are dialectical forces in the sense that they both, to a varying degree, undergird all leisure behaviors and are opposite in their meanings of approach and avoidance.

The opposite of intrinsic leisure motivation is the lack of it — a state called boredom. Factors that enhance boredom perceptions, therefore, become underminers of leisure motivation. It has been found that lack of awareness of leisure, relatively poor leisure ethic and high work ethic, absence of many and varied leisure skills, constraints on leisure participation, and not being a self-motivated person are major psychological factors to increase people's experiencing leisure as boredom. In addition, men more than women, and people with high incomes more than those with relatively low incomes, tend to perceive leisure as boredom. Research results also indicate that the personality predisposition toward intrinsic motivation protects against boredom and suggests that the tendency to experience leisure as intrinsically motivating is as much a matter of the individual capacity as it is a matter of social conditions and structures. Exposure to a wide variety of successful leisure experiences in early years might not only help a person to acquire many different leisure skills, but might also contribute to the formation of an intrinsic motivation (personality predisposition).

Sustained intrinsic motivation is likely to lead to what is called "serious leisure." Motivationally, as people become more serious about their leisure, the more intrinsic rewards they are able to extract from their continued deep involvement. Those who have a high degree of specialization in and commitment to a single leisure activity have been found to look for intrinsic rewards from their involvement, such as self-actualization, self-gratification, self-enrichment, and self-expression. Those who depend on one activity for their sense of well-being, however, are flirting with addiction. The problem with such leisure addicts is that they organize their lives around a single activity, often ignoring their family and careers. To become so dependent on one's daily leisure highs as to ignore family and work is psychologically harmful and may require outside help.

Leisure Needs

One of the opening questions of this review was whether there are leisure needs. An answer to this question from the strict physiological standpoint is a categorical "no." Leisure is not necessary for our survival in the same sense as hunger and thirst are. We cannot survive without food and water, but we can without leisure. On the other hand, human life is not a matter of strict physiological exposition. Over the centuries, human beings have evolved well beyond the stage where gratification of the basic needs is the only or main focus of life. This means that the use of human potential and quality of life become central to the discussion of needs.

People (e.g. the socio-economically deprived, prisoners, workaholics) are able to survive the conditions that are not optimally arousing and that are therefore psychologically and even physiologically damaging to them. Such conditions, however, do not facilitate the use of human potential and capabilities. Consequently, quality of life is significantly reduced for individuals who are under-using (the socio-economically deprived) and over-using (workaholics) their potential and skills. Although most people fall somewhere in between these extremes, the issue of human potential and growth is central for both individuals and society. To that extent, leisure plays an important role and helps people balance their lives and achieve a better quality of life. On this basis, it could be argued that there is a social need for leisure.

Another point about the existence of leisure needs has to do with the effect of social environments. While people do not need leisure as such, they can grow highly dependent upon it. Social influences can lead to the point where individuals become "serious" about, and even addicted to, their leisure behaviors. But even if people do not go to the extreme of serious leisure or leisure addiction, they can easily become accustomed to being able to engage in certain leisure behaviors on a regular basis. To that extent, they become dependent on leisure, especially if leisure experiences are enjoyable to them, and begin seeing a need for leisure. This, then, means that leisure needs are social motives that can lead even to addictive behaviors, and therefore appear as "desperate needs." But, they are not physiologically determined or based.

Questions For Further Research

Where do we go from here? For one thing, the theoretical framework put forth in this chapter is open for empirical testing and to questions, such as: What factors and conditions promote the relative dominance of the two motivational dimensions (seeking versus avoidance)? What individual differences are there in these motivational dimensions? Which activities are capable of responding to people's seeking and avoidance tendencies in leisure? How stable are such basic motivations over time and across situations? What implications do the motivations have for physical and mental health?

Another set of empirical questions deals with intrinsic leisure motivation as a personality disposition: How can this personality trait be acquired? How can it be instilled in people? Under what conditions does intrinsic motivation lead to serious leisure and addiction to leisure? Are those who are serious about their leisure, or addicted to it, better off physically and psychologically? Are those youths who are intrinsically motivated for, and serious about, leisure more able to avoid antisocial behaviors (e.g. delinquency and drug use) than those who are not so motivated? Is serious leisure, or addiction to a leisure activity, a form of escape? Is addiction to a leisure activity a way of coping with personal problems and troubles, such as lack of friends, family, and employment?

Finally, there is a question about the effects of a failure to meet certain outcomes or benefits expected to result from leisure motivation and subsequent participation. As noted earlier, leisure motives are inextricably linked to the expected outcomes of recreational involvement, and the benefits sought are personal and/or interpersonal. What happens, for example, when a person decides to play tennis because of expected feelings of competence and mastery and yet the match does not lead to such benefits? Does he feel bad about his leisure experience or does he engage in cognitive compensation? — "Well, I played poorly, but it does not matter because it was a lot of fun to play with him." Do people use such post-decision justifications to balance the inevitable gaps between motives and expected benefits? Can a *primary* motive (e.g. a sense of competence) be compensated by or substituted for a *secondary* benefit (e.g. social interaction)?

Acknowledgments

Thanks are extended to the Department of Leisure Studies, Kuring-gai College of Advanced Education, Australia, for providing me with the opportunity to spend a sabbatical there and for supporting the completion of this chapter. I am also grateful to the following scholars for their thoughtful comments on an earlier draft of this chapter: Charlotte Leedy, Roger Mannell, Tony Veal, and Ellen Weissinger.

References

Amabile, M., W. Dejong, and M.L. Lepper. 1976. "Effects of externally imposed deadlines on subsequent intrinsic motivation." *Journal of Personality and Social Psychology 34:* 92-98.

Beard, J. and M. Ragheb. 1983. "Measuring leisure motivation." *Journal of Leisure Research 15:* 219-228.

Boggiano, A.K. and D.S. Main. 1986. "Enhancing children's interest in activities used as rewards: The bonus effect." *Journal of Personality and Social Psychology 51:* 1116-1126.

Bradley, W. and R.C. Mannell. 1984. "Sensitivity of intrinsic motivation to reward procedure instructions." *Personality and Social Psychology Bulletin 10:* 426-431.

Butler, R.A. 1953. "Discrimination learning by rhesus monkeys to visual-exploration motivation." *Journal of Comparative and Physiological Psychology 46:* 95-98.

Copp, J.D. 1975. "Why hunters like to hunt." *Psychology Today 9* (December): 60-62, 67.

Crandall, R. 1979. "Social interaction, affect and leisure." *Journal of Leisure Research 11:* 165-181.

Crandall, R. 1980. "Motivations for leisure." *Journal of Leisure Research 12:* 45-54.

Crandall, R., M. Nolan, and L. Morgan. 1980. "Leisure and social interaction." In *Social Psychological Perspectives on Leisure and Recreation,* ed. S.E. Iso-Ahola. Springfield, IL: Charles C. Thomas.

Crompton, J. 1979. "Motivations for pleasure vacations." *Annals of Tourism Research 6:* 408-424.

Csikszentmihalyi, M. 1982. "Toward a psychology of optimal experience." *Review of Personality and Social Psychology 3:* 13-36.

Csikszentmihalyi, M. and R. Graef. 1979. "Feeling free." *Psychology Today 13* (December): 84-90, 98-99.

Csikszentmihalyi, M., R. Larson, and S. Prescott. 1977. "The ecology of adolescent activity and experience." *Journal of Youth and Adolescence* 6: 281-294.

Deci, E.L. and R.M. Ryan. 1985. *Intrinsic Motivation and Self-determination in Human Behavior.* New York: Plenum Press.

Deci, E.L. and R.M. Ryan. 1987. "The support of autonomy and the control of behavior." *Journal of Personality and Social Psychology* 53: 1024-1037.

Dennis, W. 1960. "Causes of retardation among institutionalized children: Iran." *Journal of Genetic Psychology 96:* 47-59.

Dennis, W. and P. Najarian. 1957. "Infant development under environmental handicap." *Psychological Monograph 71:* No. 7.

Donnelly, M.P., J.J. Vaske, and A.R. Graefe. 1986. "Degree and range of recreation specialization: Toward a typology of boating related activities." *Journal of Leisure Research 18:* 81-95.

Driver, B.L. 1972. "Potential contributions of psychology to recreation resource management." In *Environment and the Social Sciences: Perspectives and Applications,* eds. J.L. Wohlwill and D.H. Carson, pp. 223-244. Washington, DC: APA.

Ellis, G.D. and P.A. Witt. 1984. "The measurement of perceived freedom in leisure." *Journal of Leisure Research 16:* 110-123.

Epstein, S.M. 1967. "Toward a unified theory of anxiety." In *Progress in Experimental Personality Research,* Vol. 4. ed. B.A. Maher. New York: Academic Press.

Ewert, A. 1985. "Why people climb: The relationship of participant motives and experience level to mountaineering." *Journal of Leisure Research 17:* 241-250.

Fedler, A.J. 1984. "Elements of motivation and satisfaction in the marine recreational fishing experience." In *Marine Recreational Fisheries,* Vol. 9, ed. R.H. Stroud. Savannah, GA: National Coalition for Marine Conservation.

Festinger, L. 1954. "A theory of social comparison processes." *Human Relations 7:* 117-140.

Fiske, D.W. and S.R. Maddi (eds). 1961. *Functions of Varied Experience.* Homewood, IL: Dorsey.

Funk, S.C. and B.K. Houston. 1987. "A critical analysis of the hardiness scale's validity and utility." *Journal of Personality and Social Psychology 53:* 572-578.

Gleitman, H. 1986. *Psychology.* New York: W.W. Norton and Company.

Graef, R., M. Csikszentmihalyi, and S.M. Gianinno. 1983. "Measuring intrinsic motivation in everyday life." *Leisure Studies 2:* 155-168.

Grant, E. 1988. "The exercise fix." *Psychology Today* 22 (February): 24-28.

Harackiewicz, J.M. and G. Manderlink. 1984. "A process analysis of the effects of performance-contingent rewards on intrinsic motivation." *Journal of Experimental Social Psychology 20:* 531-551.

Harackiewicz, J.M., G. Manderlink, and C. Sansone. 1984. "Rewarding pinball wizardry: Effects of evaluation and cue value on intrinsic interest." *Journal of Personality and Social Psychology 47:* 287-300.

Harlow, H.F. 1950. "Learning and satiation of response in intrinsically motivated complex puzzle performance in monkeys." *Journal of Comparative and Physiological Psychology 43:* 289-294.

Harper, W. 1986. "Freedom in the experience of leisure." *Leisure Sciences 8:* 115-130.

Hirschman, E.C. 1984. "Leisure motives and sex roles." *Journal of Leisure Research 16:* 209-223.

Hollender, J.W. 1977. "Motivational dimensions of the camping experience." *Journal of Leisure Research 9:* 133-141.

Hull, C.L. 1943. *Principles of Behavior.* New York: Appleton-Century-Crofts.

Hull, J.G., R.R. Van Treuren, and S. Virnelli. 1987. "Hardiness and health: A critique and alternative approach." *Journal of Personality and Social Psychology 53:* 518-530.

Hunt, J. Mc.V. 1969. *The Challenge of Incompetence and Poverty.* Urbana, IL: University of Illinois Press.

Ingham, R. 1986. "Psychological contributions to the study of leisure - Part one." *Leisure Studies 5:* 255-279.

Ingham, R. 1987. "Psychological contributions to the study of leisure - Part two." *Leisure Studies 6:* 1-14.

Iso-Ahola, S.E. 1979a. "Basic dimensions of definitions of leisure." *Journal of Leisure Research 11:* 28-39.

Iso-Ahola, S.E. 1979b. "Some social psychological determinants of perceptions of leisure: Preliminary evidence." *Leisure Sciences 2:* 305-314.

Iso-Ahola, S.E. 1980. *The Social Psychology of Leisure and Recreation.* Dubuque, IA: Wm. C. Brown Co.

Iso-Ahola, S.E. 1982. "Toward a social psychological theory of tourism motivation: A rejoinder." *Annals of Tourism Research 12:* 256-262.

Iso-Ahola, S.E. 1984. "Social psychological foundations of leisure and resultant implications for leisure counseling." In *Leisure Counseling, Concepts and Applications,* ed. E.T. Dowd, pp. 97-125. Springfield, IL: Charles C. Thomas.

Iso-Ahola, S.E. 1988. "The social psychology of leisure: Past, present, and future research." In *Research about Leisure,* ed. L.A. Barnett, pp. 75-93. Champaign, IL: Sagamore Publishing.

Iso-Ahola, S.E. and J. Allen. 1982. "The dynamics of leisure motivation: The effects of outcome on leisure needs." *Research Quarterly for Exercise and Sport 53:* 141-149.

Iso-Ahola, S.E. and E. Weissinger. 1987. "Leisure and boredom." *Journal of Social and Clinical Psychology 5:* 356-364.

Kleiber, D.A. 1985. "Motivational reorientation in adulthood and the resource of leisure." In *Motivation and Adulthood,* eds. D.A. Kleiber and M. Maehr. Greenwich, CT: JA Press, Inc.

Knopf, R.C. 1983. "Recreational needs and behavior in natural settings." In *Behavior and the Natural Environment,* eds. I. Altman and J.F. Wohlwill. New York: Plenum.

Kobasa, S.C. 1979. "Stressful life events, personality, and health: An inquiry into hardiness." *Journal of Personality and Social Psychology 37:* 1-11.

Kobasa, S.C. 1982. "Commitment and coping in stress resistance among lawyers." *Journal of Personality and Social Psychology 42:* 707-717.

Kobasa, S.C., S.R. Maddi, and S. Kahn. 1982. "Hardiness and health: A prospective study." *Journal of Personality and Social Psychology 42:* 168-177.

Koestner, R., M. Zuckerman, and J. Koestner. 1987. "Praise, involvement, and intrinsic motivation." *Journal of Personality and Social Psychology 53:* 383-390.

Langer, E.J. and J. Rodin. 1976. "The effects of choice and enhanced personal responsibility for the aged: A field experiment in an institutional setting." *Journal of Personality and Social Psychology 34:* 191-198.

Lepper, M.R., and D. Greene. 1975. "Turning play into work: Effects of adult surveillance and extrinsic rewards on children's intrinsic motivation." *Journal of Personality and Social Psychology 31:* 479-486.

Lepper, M.R., D. Greene, and R.E. Nisbett. 1973. "Undermining children's intrinsic interest with extrinsic rewards: A test of the overjustification hypothesis." *Journal of Personality and Social Psychology 28:* 129-137.

London, M., R. Crandall, and D. Fitzgibbons. 1977. "The psychological structure of leisure: Activities, needs, people." *Journal of Leisure Research 9:* 252-263.

Maddi, S.R., P.T. Bartone, and M.C. Puccetti. 1987. "Stressful events are indeed a factor in physical illness: Reply to Schroeder and Costa (1984)." *Journal of Personality and Social Psychology 52:* 833-843.

Mannell, R.C. 1980. "Social psychological techniques and strategies for studying leisure experiences." In *Social Psychological Perspectives on Leisure and Recreation,* ed. S.E. Iso-Ahola, pp. 62-88. Springfield, IL.: Charles C. Thomas.

Mannell, R.C. and W. Bradley. 1986. "Does greater freedom always lead to greater leisure? Testing a person X environment model of freedom and leisure." *Journal of Leisure Research 18:* 215-230.

Mannell, R.C. and S.E. Iso-Ahola. 1987. "Psychological nature of leisure and tourism experience." *Annals of Tourism Research 14:* 314-331.

Mannell, R.C., R. Larson and J. Zuzanek. 1988. "Leisure states and 'flow' experiences: Testing freedom and intrinsic motivation hypotheses." *Journal of Leisure Research 20: 289-304.*

McCall, R.B. 1974. "Exploratory manipulation and play in the human infant." *Monographs of the Society for Research in Child Development 39:* No. 155.

Mills, A.S. 1985. "Participation motivations for outdoor recreation: A test of Maslow's theory." *Journal of Leisure Research 17:* 184-199.

Mobily, K.E., D.K. Leslie, R.B. Wallace, J.H. Lemke, F.J. Kohout, and M.C. Morris. 1984. "Factors associated with the aging leisure repertoire: The Iowa 65+ rural health study." *Journal of Leisure Research 16:* 338-343.

Murray, E.J. 1964. *Motivation and Emotion.* Englewood Cliffs, NJ: Prentice-Hall.

Pierce, R. 1980. Dimensions of leisure I: Satisfactions." *Journal of Leisure Research 12:* 5-19.

Reader, M. and S.J. Dollinger. 1982. "Deadlines, self-perceptions, and intrinsic motivation." *Personality and Social Psychology Bulletin 8:* 742-747.

Roadburg, A. 1983. "Freedom and enjoyment: Disentangling perceived leisure." *Journal of Leisure Research 15:* 15-26.

Rodin, J. and E.J. Langer. 1977. "Long-term effects of a control-relevant intervention with the institutionalized aged." *Journal of Personality and Social Psychology 35:* 897-902.

Rubinstein, C. 1980. "Survey report: How Americans view vacations." *Psychology Today 13 (May):* 62-66, 71-76.

Sansone, C. 1986. "A question of competence: The effects of competence and task feedback on intrinsic interest." *Journal of Personality and Social Psychology 51:* 918-931.

Schreyer, R., D.W. Lime, and D.R. Williams. 1984. "Characterizing the influence of past experience on recreation behavior." *Journal of Leisure Research 16:* 34-50.

Schulz, R. 1976. "Effects of control and predictability on the physical and psychological well-being of the institutionalized aged." *Journal of Personality and Social Psychology 33:* 563-573.

Schulz, R. and B.H. Hanusa. 1978. "Long-term effects of control and predictability-enhancing interventions: Findings and ethical issues." *Journal of Personality and Social Psychology 36:* 1194-1201.

Searle, M.S. and E.L. Jackson. 1985. "Socioeconomic variations in perceived barriers to recreation participation among would-be participants." *Leisure Sciences 7:* 227-249.

Shaver, P. and J. Freedman. 1975. "Your pursuit of happiness." *Psychology Today 10 (August):* 26-32, 75.

Shaw, S.M. 1984. "The measurement of leisure: A quality of life issue." *Loisir et Société 7:* 91-107.

Shaw, S.M. 1985. "The meaning of leisure in everyday life." *Leisure Sciences 7:* 1-24.

Solomon, R. 1980. "The opponent-process theory of acquired motivation: The costs of pleasure and the benefits of pain." *American Psychologist 35:* 691-712.

Stebbins, R.A. 1979. *Amateurs: On the Margin Between Work and Leisure.* Beverly Hills CA: Sage Publications.

Swann, W.B. and T.S. Pittman. 1977. "Imitating play activity of children: The moderating influence of verbal cues on intrinsic motivation." *Child Development 48:* 1128-1132.

Tinsley, H.E.A., T.C. Barrett, and R.A. Kass. 1979. "Leisure activities and need satisfaction." *Journal of Leisure Research 9:* 110-120.

Tinsley, H.E.A. and R.A. Kass. 1978. "Leisure activities and need satisfaction: A replication and extension." *Journal of Leisure Research 10:* 191-202.

Veal, A.J. 1988. "The concept of recreational 'need' reconsidered." Paper presented at the World Leisure and Recreation Association's First World Congress "Free Time, Culture and Society," Lake Louise, AB.

Wankel, L.M. and C.E. Thompson. 1978. "The effects of perceived activity choice upon exercise attendance." Paper presented at the NRPA-SPRE Research Symposium, National Recreation and Park Association, Miami Beach, FL.

Weissinger, E. 1986. "The development and validation of a scale to measure individual differences in intrinsic leisure motivation." Paper presented at the SPRE Leisure Research Symposium, Anaheim, CA.

Weissinger, E. and S.E. Iso-Ahola. 1984. "Intrinsic leisure motivation, personality and physical health." *Loisir et Société 7:* 217-228.

Zuckerman, M., J. Porac, D. Lathin, R. Smith, and E.L. Deci. 1978. "On the importance of self-determination for intrinsically motivated behavior." *Personality and Social Psychology Bulletin 4:* 443-446.

LEISURE SATISFACTION

Roger C. Mannell

If there is a "paradigm" guiding current efforts to study leisure, it is that leisure can be most profitably understood from the *subjective perspective* of the participant. Measuring leisure satisfaction is one conduit into the recreationist's head (Mannell and Iso-Ahola 1987). The following are a few examples of statements that have been used to measure leisure satisfaction:

"Considering all things, how satisfied are you with your leisure?" (Trafton and Tinsley 1980: 37);

"I am frustrated in my free time" (Beard and Ragheb 1980: 27);

"How much would 'experiencing excitement' either add to or detract from the level of satisfaction you would receive as a result of a three-day backpacking trip in a Colorado wilderness or back country area?" (Rosenthal, Waldman, and Driver 1982: 92-93);

"How satisfied were you with each of the following aspects of the raft-race day? — Rest room facilities; the safety of the rafters (etc.)" (Noe 1987: 169).

While apparently similar, these statements are based on different conceptualizations of leisure satisfaction. The present chapter will provide, first, an analysis of the leisure satisfaction construct. As we will see, it is not unidimensional. A typology will be suggested for classifying the various approaches and uses of the construct. Examples of these approaches and uses will be provided, and the state of the theory and research evaluated. Second, what we know about the factors that contribute to leisure satisfaction and about the relationship of leisure satisfaction to other constructs will be reviewed. Finally, issues and directions for future research will be explored.

THE SATISFACTION CONSTRUCT

The term *satisfaction* is typically used as a stimulus to elicit Likert scale ratings of a respondent's state of mind. Also typically, it is left undefined and treated as a "naive" psychological term. However, as technically defined by researchers, the term *satisfaction* has a variety of different meanings and uses. These differences parallel, and in fact have their roots in, the different conceptual and theoretical treatments of satisfaction found in the social science literature.

Conceptualizations of leisure satisfaction will be distinguished along two dimensions — *motivation-based* and *level of specificity*, and roughly classified into the four cells resulting from the cross-classification of these two dimensions (Figure 1).

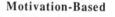

Figure 1
Leisure Satisfaction Construct Typology

The level of specificity of the satisfaction construct being used in any particular study can be distinguished on the basis of the range or scope of the domain of behavior, life experience, or need, with which the satisfaction is associated or derived. The more molar, and therefore the less molecular, the level of specificity of the unit of behavior, life experience, or motivation, the more global is the measure of satisfaction.

A second way in which conceptualizations of satisfaction differ is the extent to which satisfaction is a motivation-based construct anchored to an explicit theory of human needs. Satisfaction can be conceptualized and used in ways that make no assumptions about basic human motivation and needs. This approach views satisfaction as a form of appraisal, assessment, or evaluation of the extent to which an individual's life or daily existence meets with current expectations. At the other end of the continuum, satisfaction is directly anchored or defined by those needs believed to be essential for human survival and well-being.

APPRAISAL-SATISFACTION

General Construct

This non-motivational approach to conceptualizing and measuring satisfaction has emerged from the extensive research that has been done over the past several decades on the subjective well-being of working-aged and elderly adults. The approach consists of asking respondents to rate their satisfaction with life as a whole or some aspect of it. Initially, these types of studies focused on pathology and coping (Gurin, Veroff, and Feld 1957), but later the issue became subjective well-being (Bradburn 1969), or the quality of life as a whole (Campbell, Converse, and Rodgers 1976).

The approach reflects a concerted effort to assess the quality of contemporary life other than with the use of objective measures. For example, economists have equated well-being with the gross national income, public health researchers with decreases in high risk health behaviors, ecologists with the quality of the environment, and sociologists with levels of crime, suicide, public violence, and family disintegration. However, it has been argued that "we cannot understand the psychological quality of a person's life simply from a knowledge of the circumstances in which that person lives" (Campbell 1980: 1), or gain more than a partial explanation of why some people find their lives enjoyable and satisfying and some do not.

Well-being, then, is treated "as a strictly internal construct, independent of the exterior conditions of a person's life" (Larson 1978: 110). It is generally assumed that people "are able to describe the quality of their own lives, not as precisely as one might like, but with a kind of direct validity that more objective measures do not have" (Campbell 1980: 12).

A major task for researchers has been to achieve consensus for the definition and operationalization of well-being (Campbell 1980; Kozma and Stones 1978; Larson 1978; Stock, Okun, and Benin 1986). Based on a review of the literature, Larson (1978) and more recently Stock *et al.* (1986) have identified three constructs — happiness, satisfaction, and morale — that have been used to conceptualize well-being. *Happiness* is considered to reflect the affective feelings of the present moment. *Morale* is considered to reflect a more future-oriented optimism or pessimism. Different from happiness and morale, *satisfaction* "implies an act of judgement, a comparison of what people have to what they think they deserve, expect, or may reasonably aspire to. If the discrepancy is small, the result is satisfaction; if it is large, there is dissatisfaction" (Campbell 1980: 22). The expectations or standards of comparison on which these judgements or appraisals are made are usually left unspecified. Satisfaction has a past orientation — an appraisal of how things have gone up until the present. Whereas happiness and morale reflect the more changeable aspects of well-being, level of satisfaction is considered to be quite stable over time (Campbell 1980; Stock *et al.* 1986).

The level of specificity of the behavior or domain of life experience being appraised has also been considered an important factor. It has generally been assumed that, by examining satisfaction with the major divisions of life, often called "domains," a more detailed picture of well-being can be obtained. Because of the centrality of work to North American life, work or job satisfaction has been the focus of extensive research and theoretical efforts (for recent reviews see Fincham and Rhodes 1988; O'Brien 1986). Interest in satisfaction with leisure has emerged only in the last decade.

Leisure Satisfaction: Facet-Appraisal

In the leisure research that has used the appraisal approach, satisfaction has been conceptualized and measured at various levels of specificity. Researchers with more "molecular" concerns have examined satisfaction with particular facets or subdomains of leisure behavior or experience. Subdomains of leisure behavior examined include satisfaction with provincial park campgrounds (Foster and Jackson 1979), tourist destinations (Pearce 1980), and outdoor recreation activity during a day trip (Vaske *et al.* 1982). These studies used a single satisfaction measure of the leisure subdomains under study.

Research has also been reported that takes the "molecularization" even further. Pizam, Neumann, and Reichel (1978) found that eight subdomains described tourist satisfaction with a well-known seaside destination. Graefe and Fedler (1986) examined satisfaction with a chartered recreation fishing outing. They not only measured overall satisfaction with the trip, but satisfaction with various sub-components or elements of the experience (e.g. enjoyment of the outdoors, types and number of fish caught, challenge). Noe (1987) surveyed spectators at a raft-race event. He measured overall satisfaction with the event, as well as satisfaction with twenty-four specific aspects of the event (e.g. the rafters, food facilities, parking signs, music).

Leisure Satisfaction: Global-Appraisal

At the other end of the specificity continuum, we find a number of studies that are concerned with satisfaction with the whole leisure domain of life. Single-item measures are frequently used, and the domain of behavior to be assessed has been identified in different ways. Subjects have been asked to rate satisfaction with their "present level of leisure participation" (Guin 1980: 200), "amount of spare time" (Lounsbury *et al.* 1982: 290), and "leisure in general" (Iso-Ahola and Weissinger 1987: 360; Trafton and Tinsley 1980: 37).

Studies can be distinguished that also focus on satisfaction with the whole leisure domain, but measure satisfaction by having subjects appraise various facets and summing or averaging across these sub-components to arrive at a global satisfaction score — a "molecular-molar" approach. London, Crandall, and Seals (1977) averaged Likert scale ratings based on their respondents' satisfaction with activities done with friends, family, other social activity, organizational involvements, recreational facilities frequented, and various forms of entertainment. Ragheb (1980) and Francken and van Raaij (1981) had respondents rate their satisfaction with activities representing most types of leisure behavior, and computed an overall leisure satisfaction score from these ratings. Backman and Mannell (1986) had subjects recall the recreational activities they had engaged in during the week preceding an interview. The subjects rated their satisfaction with each recalled activity, and the researchers computed a global leisure satisfaction score based on these molecular ratings.

The research reported using satisfaction as a global appraisal of the whole leisure domain has had several different purposes. One purpose has been to examine the factors that determine satisfaction or dissatisfaction with the leisure domain. To do this, researchers have examined the relationship between leisure satisfaction and other leisure phenomena, such as participation, attitudes, awareness, and boredom. For example, Ragheb (1980) found that leisure participation and attitudes were positively related to leisure satisfaction. Francken and Raaij (1981) found leisure satisfaction to be higher for people who are older, have an optimistic outlook, and perceive themselves as having the personal interests and capacity for leisure activity participation. Iso-Ahola and Weissinger (1987) found that the greater the individual's "boredom in leisure," the less his or her satisfaction with leisure.

A second use of the global leisure appraisal-satisfaction approach has been to examine the contributions of leisure to the overall quality of life. These types of studies often assess the relative contributions of other domains as well. Several studies have found a positive relationship between leisure satisfaction and life satisfaction. However, this relationship appears to have been moderated by job status (Willmott 1971), gender (Hulin 1969), and marital and employment status (Haavio-Mannila 1971). In a widely cited study, London, Crandall, and Seals (1977) found that job satisfaction and leisure satisfaction contributed independently to the quality of life, and that leisure satisfaction was the better predictor. As with earlier research, however, they found the pattern to be more pronounced for some people than others. For example, neither leisure nor work satisfaction were important to the quality of life of relatively disadvantaged groups, and leisure satisfaction was more important for individuals with lifestyles not dominated by work activity. This latter finding was supported by Guin (1980), who reported that, among retired recreational vehicle tourists, leisure satisfaction was strongly associated with life satisfaction. However, leisure satisfaction has not always been found to be significantly associated with life satisfaction, as Trafton and Tinsley (1980) have noted in a study of blue-collar workers.

Issues and Future Directions

Measurement of leisure satisfaction

Can we assume that people know how satisfied they are? Even Campbell (1980), who has used the method extensively, expressed some doubt about this assumption. He found that people change their ratings of satisfaction very little over time, suggesting, perhaps, that they adapt their level of expectation to prevailing circumstances and therefore experience little change in levels of satisfaction.

Few standardized measures have been developed, and the advantages of multiple-item versus single-item scales have not been demonstrated. These scales also seem limited in their ability to penetrate the respondent's feelings, particularly when the meaning of satisfaction is left to the respondent. There is also a lack of "time depth" with this approach (Campbell 1980). A single assessment at one point in time cannot record the fluctuations in a respondent's feelings. Although the respondents are asked to describe their leisure "these days" or "in general," they may be influenced by recent events or swings in mood.

Facets and causes of leisure satisfaction

How is the basis for dividing more molar domains of leisure behavior into facets or subdomains to be determined? For example, global leisure satisfaction may be a function of satisfaction with subdomains based on various types of recreational and cultural activities (e.g. social, sport, hobbies, high culture), which at a more molecular level could be a function of satisfactions derived from the specific activities comprising each type (e.g. sport activity type: squash, hockey, and bowling). On the other hand, another researcher might feel that the relevant underlying dimension is the location of participation (e.g. indoor versus outdoor activities).

There is currently no theory to guide researchers in selecting the most meaningful and appropriate factors that might affect the quality of leisure satisfaction. As a consequence, research using appraisal-satisfaction appears fragmented and lacking in clear direction.

Objective-subjective links

The very strength claimed for the appraisal-satisfaction construct seems to be a limitation as well. If the objective circumstances in which people find themselves cannot be used to predict satisfaction, of what use is a measure of satisfaction in assessing the adequacy of the actual leisure opportunities, choices, and services available to them? The attempt to find relationships between the objective features of leisure settings, activities, and services has been relatively unsuccessful.

One area that has received considerable attention using the appraisal-satisfaction construct is social carrying capacity. However, researchers have had difficulty establishing stable and consistent relationships between measures of the number of participants in a recreation setting and their satisfaction (Manning 1986; see also the chapter by Stankey and McCool in this book).

Iso-Ahola and Weissinger (1987) found that subjectively-based variables were better predictors of leisure satisfaction than more objectively-based variables. Mannell and Bradley (1986) demonstrated that perceptions of choice were more influential in affecting the quality of a leisure experience than the actual number of alternatives for participation. However, in this latter study, personality differences in perceived control appeared to provide some explanation for individual differences in subjective perceptions of the objective setting. Research is needed to identify the factors that mediate the link between the objective circumstances in which people find themselves and their perceptions of these circumstances. After all, managers and practitioners typically have more control over the environment and over opportunities than they do over participant perceptions.

This limitation of the appraisal-satisfaction approach is reflected in the criticism that program evaluators have levelled at the practice of asking the ubiquitous question, "How satisfied were you with ... ?" to evaluate services and programs. While it may have its place, more attention should be concentrated on identifying and measuring other outcome measures that reflect opportunity and service impacts, as well as the impacts of leisure activity choice and participation on the quality of life.

Appraising satisfaction at more than one point in time would also help. Researchers should monitor changes in satisfaction over time, while carefully assessing changes in the factors theorized to affect these shifts in satisfaction. More elaborate experimental and quasi-experimental procedures could also be implemented. For example, Backman and Mannell (1986) examined the leisure satisfaction of a group of institutionalized older adults who participated in one of several counselling and non-counselling programs. Leisure satisfaction was measured before, during, and immediately after the programs, and during a follow-up interview six weeks later. Not only were changes in leisure satisfaction related to differences among the programs in which people participated, but also to changes in recreation behavior and leisure attitudes, which were also monitored.

More leisure appraisal-satisfaction research?

Little research has been reported examining the relationship between satisfaction with the leisure domain and other domains. One exception is a study by Lounsbury *et al.* (1982), which found that if workers were satisfied with their jobs, then the higher was their level of leisure satisfaction, and the less likely was their intention to leave. However, studies of work-leisure relationships have typically focused on the behavioral impact of work on leisure, rather than on how satisfaction with one influences the other (Mannell and Iso-Ahola 1985).

There is also little appraisal-satisfaction research that builds on previous work. Research focusing on the effect of crowding and user density on satisfaction with outdoor recreation is an exception (see Manning 1986). However, even in this well-researched area, clear-cut, consistent patterns and relationships have been difficult to establish — which raises questions about the utility of the construct. Dissatisfaction with the satisfaction construct has emerged in the study of other domains of human behavior, as well. For example, researchers have been frustrated by the problems of finding factors in the work environment that consistently affect satisfaction with work, and by their inability to predict job performance levels and turnover rates from a knowledge of job satisfaction (Orpen 1985).

NEED-SATISFACTION

General Construct

With the need-satisfaction approach, the state of "being satisfied" is commonly conceptualized to be the result of the fulfillment of drives, motives, needs, or expectations. When people are deprived of (or deficient in) something that is important to their well-being, a need is created. The classical approach has been to divide needs into physiologically and socially-based types that are the basis of the mechanisms responsible for arousing, energizing, and directing the diversity of human behavior. Social needs have also been referred to as non-physiological, cognitive, and acquired needs.

Agreement exists about the list of basic physiological needs, since these are founded upon "tissue deficits" or biochemical imbalances in the body. There is considerably less consensus on what constitutes basic social needs, or even if there are social needs common to all people. Classical views of motivation describe all non-physiological needs as learned. Yet, some theories and supporting research have suggested that there are social needs that are not learned. Foremost among these is the need for variety and change, which seems to be based upon the need to maintain an optimal level of arousal in the central nervous system. Cognitively-based research in social psychology has identified social motives, such as the need for cognitive consistency (Festinger 1957) and the need for perceived freedom (Brehm 1966), which are assumed to be present in all people to some degree. Similarly, the need for competency seems to be an essential feature of human nature (Deci 1975). Even the desire to maintain contact with other people, called the need for affiliation (that most social of social needs), has been seen as so nearly universal in human beings that some theorists have considered it inborn (e.g. Skeels 1973).

While recent approaches consider most behavior to be the result, to varying degrees, of biological, learned, and cognitive motivational components, there is little consensus as to what constitutes a complete set of human needs, or to what extent they are learned or inherited (Franken 1982). There are, however, theorists who have attempted to identify the full range of human needs that form the basis of human behavior, regardless of whether they have their roots in tissue deficits, the central nervous system, cognition, learning, or all of these. These approaches postulate a relatively manageable list of basic needs.

Murray's (1938) need theory is a well-known example of this approach. He proposed a list of twenty-eight physiological and social needs. Among these were the needs for achievement, affiliation, dominance, order, understanding, play, autonomy, aggression, and sex. Maslow (1968) proposed another well-known need theory. Like Murray's theory, it holds that there are a few basic needs. Its distinctive feature concerns the proposition that there is a hierarchical arrangement of the needs common to all humans, with basic survival needs at the bottom and the uniquely human ones at the top. Both theories have been used to guide researchers in the selection of leisure needs and satisfactions. Researchers have not suggested or "discovered" needs and satisfactions that are unique to leisure. Leisure is seen as one of a number of domains of behavior that has the potential to provide for the satisfaction of the full range of human needs. Indeed, there seems to be a belief that leisure may be the best domain for this purpose. The individual is freer to choose engagements and so can more easily match current needs with activities known to provide the appropriate satisfactions.

Satisfactions are linked to needs through the *motivational sequence* (Figure 2). This model is most clearly illustrated with reference to physiological needs — for example, food, water, air, rest, and so forth. A *need* arises within the organism when a biochemical imbalance occurs, resulting in a state of arousal known as a *drive* or *motive*, in which the organism is ready to respond to relevant stimuli. These stimuli are called *goal objects*, and they can provide *reward* or *satisfaction* for the behaving organism. The organism's goal is to satisfy its need, and the goal object is an appropriate object, or event, for doing

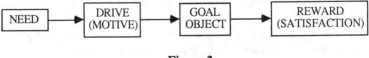

Figure 2
Motivational Sequence

so. In thirst, water is the goal object; consuming it reduces arousal and is the reward. The organism does not remain fully satisfied for long, however. Needs occur in cyclic fashion and, sooner or later, another sequence is required.

Does this motivational sequence describe the relationship between non-physiological needs and satisfactions — including those associated with leisure behavior? Cognitive needs — for example, perceptions of freedom (also an important "leisure" need) — have been conceptualized to operate in an analogous manner. The reactance, negative psychological arousal, produced by threats to freedom, leads to attempts to restore a sense of freedom. The behaviors and cognitions chosen to restore feelings of freedom are the "goal object," and the reduction of the arousal is the "reward" or "satisfaction."

Social needs, many of which may be viewed as leisure needs, have also been conceptualized as fitting this model. For example, McClelland *et al.* (1953) assumed that success is the reward or satisfaction linked to the achievement motive. Murray (1938) saw a need as creating tension somewhere in the brain. When aroused, the person seeks goal objects that reduce the tension. Individuals learn to associate particular goal objects with the satisfaction of particular needs. Maslow (1968) felt that advancement up the need hierarchy could not be achieved if needs at the current level and lower levels were not being regularly satisfied.

There has been little research or discussion concerning the tendency of social and, consequently, leisure needs to reappear in "cyclic fashion." These needs are generally seen to be situationally aroused by cues present in the immediate environment.

Need-satisfaction has been operationalized in several ways. Generally, it is assumed that satisfying a need means that the need is no longer active in arousing, energizing, and directing behavior or experience. As a consequence, cessation or a shift in behavior or cognition can be an indicator of satisfaction (Franken 1982). Many theorists also consider satisfaction to be the cognitions and/or feelings that accompany the meeting of the need. The cognition may be the replacement of the awareness of one need by another (Heckhausen and Kuhl 1985). Satisfaction is also viewed as positive or pleasurable affect. McClelland *et al.* (1953) argued that satisfaction of the need for achievement was accompanied by "felt" positive affect. Deci (1975) has also described intrinsic satisfaction in affective terms.

Leisure Satisfaction: Facet-Need

Researchers studying leisure need-satisfaction have had a conceptual or theoretical basis for "molecularizing" satisfaction — that is, the need structure of the individual. The general assumption underlying most of the theory and research from this perspective is that leisure engagements are goal objects for a number of human needs and provide corresponding leisure satisfactions. The research methods and measurements used have had respondents provide retrospective accounts of the needs that typically motivate their participation, or of the satisfactions they usually receive from this participation. Consequently, leisure satisfactions are treated as personality traits; that is, the links between leisure needs, engagements, and satisfactions are considered consistent and stable over time. The assumption is that people have a history of participation in various recreation engagements, have undergone some sort of socialization process, and have learned that, when certain needs are aroused, specific recreation engagements will lead to the satisfaction of these needs. It is not surprising, then, that the terms "motivations," "satisfactions," "psychological outcomes," "experience expectations," "need-satisfying properties," and "psychological benefits" have been used interchangeably in the literature.

A few researchers have examined single needs. Cheron and Ritchie (1982) and Crandall (1979) analyzed needs such as risk-taking or social interaction, respectively. Iso-Ahola (1980; 1982) has stressed the centrality of intrinsic motivation and the need for variety and change. However, most researchers have attempted to identify the full range of needs satisfied through leisure (for reviews see Crandall 1980; Iso-Ahola 1980; Knopf 1983; Manning 1986; Tinsley 1984). Scales have been developed to identify and measure leisure needs and satisfactions to address specific research questions (e.g. Buchanan, Christensen, and Burdge 1981; Iso-Ahola and Allen 1982; Pierce 1980; Ulrich and Addoms 1981). Several efforts have also been made to refine and assess the psychometric qualities of pencil-and-paper inventories over a series of studies (Beard and Ragheb 1980; Rosenthal, Waldman, and Driver 1982; Tinsley and Kass 1979).

The relatively large number of needs identified is typically reduced through multivariate analysis to a smaller number of need dimensions. Tinsley and Kass (1978) identified eight clusters of needs and satisfactions: self-expression; companionship; power; compensation; security; service; intellectual aestheticism; and solitude. Tinsley (1984) compared the list of needs or need clusters found in his research on general leisure behavior with those found by other researchers. In spite of the varying numbers of need-satisfaction clusters reported, the different names used to label them, and the variety of methodologies used, he concluded that there was substantial agreement. Driver has developed thirty-nine separate satisfaction scales, and has recently examined the psychometric properties of the eight that research has shown are important to recreationists using back country areas (Rosenthal, Waldman, and Driver 1982). These include exploration, escaping role overload, general nature experience, introspection, exercise, being with similar people, seeking exhilaration, and escaping physical stressors. "Travel" needs have also been identified by Crompton (1979) — included were escape, exploration, self-discovery, relaxation, prestige, regression, family bonding, and social interaction.

With the facet-need approach, researchers have asked people what satisfactions they receive from specific recreation activities or from their participation in selected recreation settings. The hope is that activities or settings can be distinguished and grouped on the basis of the different satisfactions they provide. Tinsley and Kass (1979) had respondents indicate the satisfactions they typically received from ten activities; Pierce (1980) used six activities; and Tinsley and Johnson (1984) used thirty-four. In this latter study a taxonomy of nine activity types was suggested. For example, activities such as working crossword puzzles, watching television, going to the movies, and reading fiction were found similar in providing satisfactions labelled "intellectual aestheticism" and "solitude," and contributed very little to the satisfactions of companionship, security, service, or self-expression. In contrast, respondents reported that activities such as picknicking and visiting friends and relatives provided high levels of satisfaction of the needs for companionship, service, and security, and little satisfaction of the needs for solitude or power.

Researchers concerned with outdoor recreation management have developed classification or zoning systems for recreation areas based on the leisure satisfactions they provide (e.g., Driver *et al.* 1987). It is assumed that re-creationists select different settings in which to pursue wilderness recreation because different needs require different environments for their satisfaction. For example, users of three wilderness areas were found to have different prefer-ences for environmental settings (Manfredo, Driver, and Brown 1983). Williams and Schreyer (1981) compared the motives of visitors to alpine areas and to desert/canyon areas. Visitors to the latter environment saw it as providing higher satisfactions for tension release, competence, testing, escape, and family togetherness.

These differences in the need-satisfying properties of activities and settings are seen as useful knowledge for recreation practitioners for the devel-opment and management of physical resources and park areas (Driver *et al.* 1987). Tinsley (1984) has suggested that therapeutic interventions and leisure counselling would also benefit from this knowledge.

Leisure Satisfaction: Global-Need

The facet need-satisfaction approach has focused on identifying and assessing the separate and distinct satisfactions derived from specific activities and settings. Assessment of the extent to which all of an individual's needs are met through leisure has been less frequent. The little research reported on global need-satisfaction is based on a scale developed by Beard and Ragheb (1980). These studies have asked research questions similar to those asked by research-ers using the global appraisal-satisfaction construct discussed earlier.

Ragheb and Griffith (1982) have reported that the higher the level of leisure participation, the higher the level of leisure need-satisfaction, which in turn, is positively related to life satisfaction. Russell (1987) also found support for this relationship between leisure need-satisfaction and life satisfaction. Riddick (1986) found no age differences in leisure satisfaction among eighteen to sixty-five year olds, and knowledge of leisure resources and positive leisure values were strong predispositions for high leisure satisfaction.

Issues and Future Directions

Due to the lack of reported research, little can be said about the use of the global need-satisfaction construct. Beard and Ragheb's scale has six satisfaction subdomains. However, researchers have typically used only the total scale score in assessing leisure need-satisfaction. Further research is required to determine whether the measurement of these sub-dimensions provides useful information beyond that provided by the global score.

It should be noted that as popular as the Beard and Ragheb (1980) scale has become, its adequacy as a measure of leisure need-satisfaction may be in question. The scale purports to measure six types of need-satisfaction, these satisfactions supposedly based on six major needs met through leisure. However, a leisure need scale developed by these same researchers (Beard and Ragheb 1983) identified only four major need dimensions. If their satisfaction scale has an underlying motivational basis, why does it not reflect the four-factor leisure need structure evident in their need scale? Further conceptual and empirical work with the satisfaction scale seems to be in order before it is accepted as a standard measure of the need-satisfaction construct.

Criticism of the facet need-satisfaction construct ranges from a wish to see the research move from its infancy, to doubt about the validity of the approach altogether. In the former instance, Knopf (1983: 227) has suggested that "we have done little more than collect information on reasons why people visit recreation areas." On the other hand, Iso-Ahola (1980: 241) has questioned the validity of itemizing so-called leisure needs and satisfactions. He argues that people do not walk around "with 45 leisure needs in their minds" for careful review before choosing to participate.

Iso-Ahola also reminds us that the need for variety and change seems, under some conditions, to motivate behavioral and cognitive responses aimed at increasing arousal levels and hence satisfaction. As we have seen, much of the need-satisfaction research is based on an arousal-reduction model. His chapter in this book suggests that the need for variety and change, coupled with intrinsic motivation, may be the critical motivation underlying leisure behavior and experience.

Measurement of leisure satisfaction

The measurement of need-satisfaction turns out to be as much a problem as is the measurement of appraisal-satisfaction. The main access to need and satisfaction states is through the questionable avenue of self-reports. The ability of people to assess their cognitive processes has been severely questioned (Nisbett and Wilson 1977). This argument has been applied to recreationists' abilities to report leisure need and satisfaction states accurately. Iso-Ahola (1980: 248) points out that the answers people usually give, when asked what satisfactions they receive from participation, are often stereotypic, and it "remains to be determined when the expressed leisure needs are accurate indicators of underlying leisure motivation and when they simply mirror cultural explanations." Important motivations and satisfactions may also be unconscious (Franken 1982). To complicate matters further, Buchanan (1983) suggests that measures of leisure needs and satisfactions do not distinguish how much of the satisfaction reported is derived from secondary activities. Also, inconsistencies have been found in responses when measurement occurs at different times. For example, Manfredo (1984) found differences in the reported satisfaction of escaping physical stress among fishermen, when measured both on-site and four months later.

Researchers could try to monitor behavior in recreation settings more closely, and infer needs from the direction and intensity of behavior. However, the danger is that we might end up with a different need for every identifiable behavior. There is no completely satisfactory solution to these problems inherent in the classification of need and satisfaction states. Need theorists generally look for convergent evidence from a variety of measurements, observations, and experimental results. The leisure need-satisfaction research to date has shown an over-reliance on the pencil-and-paper survey approach.

Links between leisure satisfactions, activities, and settings

While substantial faith is given to the existence of links between satisfactions, and activities and settings, Manning (1986: 107) concludes that the relationship "between motives, settings, and activities has received little empirical testing." The link is tenuous because it exists in the mind of the participant, and participants differ in attitudes, values, and personalities. Driver and Brown (1984) recognized this basic limitation of leisure activity taxonomies and recreation setting classifications. They pointed out that, in the most fundamental sense, it is visitors who produce recreation and opportunities, not managers.

Researchers need to examine individual differences in the perceptions of the links between leisure satisfactions, and activities and settings. The little research reported to date has been contradictory. Tinsley and Kass (1978) and Pierce (1980) found few sex differences, while Hirschman (1984) found differences not for biological gender, but as a function of psychological sex-role identity. London, Crandall, and Fitzgibbons (1977) also found systematic individual differences in the satisfactions their subjects perceived to be derived from the same recreational activities. Knopf (1983) has noted that there is some evidence that the link between recreation settings and satisfactions is influenced by the social group with which one participates, as well as a person's history of past experiences. Schreyer, Knopf, and Williams (1985) have suggested that motives and satisfactions, as typically measured, are too general to expect that stable links with preferences for specific leisure behaviors and environments would be found. Iso-Ahola (1980: 245) has suggested that we have ignored how the satisfactions we derive from our various leisure involvements change over the life-cycle, and following changes in our current life circumstances. Knopf (1983: 229) has charged that we have not answered the questions, "How do people get to know recreation environments?" and "How do they learn where to gratify their needs?" More research is needed; in particular, studies such as Stebbins's (1981) qualitative analysis of the longitudinal changes in the motivation of amateurs to engage in serious leisure should be emulated.

If the link between leisure satisfactions and activities and settings is to be taken seriously, there is also a need to monitor the immediate conscious experiences accompanying these engagements, and not to rely strictly on retrospective measures of the needs satisfied (Mannell and Iso-Ahola 1987; Schreyer *et al.* 1985). The ability to examine the leisure "motivational sequence," and, consequently, the link between needs, activities, and satisfactions, has been shown by several studies. Iso-Ahola and Allen (1982) measured the needs of participants in an intramural basketball game before and after the engagement. Need-satisfaction was defined by the difference in pre- and post-game need scores. They were able to demonstrate that the satisfaction derived from this activity was systematically related to individual differences among the participants, and to the outcome of the game. Using the experiential sampling method to monitor the flow of experience while engaged in leisure and non-leisure activities, Mannell, Larson, and Zuzanek (1988) found that, under some conditions, activities chosen for extrinsic reasons produce more intrinsic satisfaction than those intrinsically motivated. Certain activities were implicated more than others in this unexpected finding. The links between the activity, the motives for engaging in it, and the resulting satisfaction are often complex and a result of individual differences and situational factors.

A Final Note

The leisure satisfaction construct, whether appraisal- or motivation-based, has attracted the interest of leisure researchers because of its potential as an indicator of important psychological outcomes of leisure behavior, and because of its potential for management and counselling applications. However, significant problems of measurement plague both approaches. Closely associated with these problems of measurement is the difficulty researchers have had in finding links between satisfaction and the objective world of behavior, and social and physical environments. It would seem profitable to concentrate on methods of measurement and data collection other than retrospective, pencil-and-paper inventories — methods that involve on-site monitoring and observation.

References

Backman, S. and R.C. Mannell. 1986. "Removing attitudinal barriers to leisure: a field experiment among the institutionalized elderly." *Therapeutic Recreation Journal 20:* 46-53.

Beard, J.G. and M.G. Ragheb. 1980. "Measuring leisure satisfaction." *Journal of Leisure Research 12:* 20-33.

Beard, J.G. and M.G. Ragheb. (1983). "Measuring leisure motivation." *Journal of Leisure Research 15:* 219-228.

Bradburn, N. 1969. *The Structure of Psychological Well-Being.* Chicago: Aldine.

Brehm, J. 1966. *A Theory of Psychological Reactance.* New York: Academic Press.

Buchanan, T. 1983. "Toward an understanding of variability in satisfactions within activities." *Journal of Leisure Research 15:* 39-51.

Buchanan, T., J.E. Christensen, and R.J. Burdge. 1981. "Social groups and the meanings of outdoor recreation activities." *Journal of Leisure Research 13:* 254-266.

Campbell, A. 1980. *The Sense of Well-Being in America.* New York: McGraw-Hill.

Campbell, A., P. Converse, and W. Rodgers. 1976. *The Quality of American Life.* New York: Russel Sage.

Cheron, E.J. and J.R.B. Ritchie. 1982. "Leisure activities and perceived risk." *Journal of Leisure Research 14:* 139-154.

Crandall, R. 1979. "Social interactions, affect and leisure." *Journal of Leisure Research 11:* 165-181.

Crandall, R. 1980. "Motivations for leisure." *Journal of Leisure Research 12:* 45-54.

Crompton, J. 1979. "Motivations for pleasure vacations." *Annals of Tourism Research 6:* 408-424.

Deci, E.L. 1975. *Intrinsic Motivation*. New York: Plenum Press.

Driver, B.L. and G.H. Brown. 1984. "Contributions of behavioral scientists to recreation resource management." In *Behavior and the National Environment*, eds. I. Altman and J.F. Wohlwill, pp. 307-339. New York: Plenum Press.

Driver, B.L., P.J. Brown, G.H. Stankey, and T.G. Gregoire. 1987. "The ROS planning system: Evolution, basic concepts and research needed." *Leisure Sciences 9:* 201-212.

Festinger, L.A. 1957. *A Theory of Cognitive Dissonance*. Evanston, IL: Row, Peterson.

Fincham, R. and P.S. Rhodes. 1988. *The Individual, Work and Organization*. London: Weidenfeld and Nicolson.

Foster, R.J. and E.L. Jackson. 1979. "Factors associated with camping satisfaction in Alberta provincial park campgrounds." *Journal of Leisure Research 11:* 292-306.

Francken, D.A. and W.R. van Raaij. 1981. "Satisfaction with leisure time activities." *Journal of Leisure Research 13:* 337-352.

Franken, R.E. 1982. *Human Motivation*. Monterey, CA: Brooks-Cole.

Graefe, A.R. and A.J. Fedler. 1986. "Situational and subjective determinants of satisfaction in marine recreational fishing." *Leisure Sciences 8:* 275-295.

Guin, R. 1980. "Early recreational vehicle tourists: Life satisfaction correlates of leisure satisfaction." *Journal of Leisure Research 12:* 198-204.

Gurin, G., J. Veroff, and S. Feld. 1960. *Americans View Their Mental Health*. New York: Basic Books.

Haavio-Mannila, E. 1971. "Satisfaction with family, work, leisure, and life among men and women." *Human Relations 24:* 585-601.

Heckhausen, H. and J. Kuhl. 1985. "From wishes to action: The dead ends and short cuts on the long way to action." In *Goal-Directed Behavior: Psychological Theory and Research on Action*, eds. M. Frese and J. Sabini. Hillsdale, NJ: Erlbaum.

Hirschman, E.C. 1984. "Leisure motives and sex roles." *Journal of Leisure Research 16:* 209-223.

Hulin, C.L. 1969. "Sources of variation in job and life satisfaction: The role of community and job-related variables." *Journal of Applied Psychology 53:* 279-291.

Iso-Ahola, S.E. 1980. *The Social Psychology of Leisure and Recreation.* Dubuque, IA: W.C. Brown.

Iso-Ahola, S.E. 1982. "Toward a social psychological theory of tourism motivation: A rejoinder." *Annals of Tourism Research 12:* 256-262.

Iso-Ahola, S.E. and J.R. Allen. 1982. "The dynamics of leisure motivation: The effects of outcome on leisure needs." *Research Quarterly for Exercise and Sport 53:* 141-149.

Iso-Ahola, S.E. and E. Weissinger. 1987. "Leisure and boredom." *Journal of Social and Clinical Psychology 5:* 356-364.

Knopf, R.C. 1983. "Recreational needs and behavior and natural settings." In *Behavior and The Natural Environment,* eds. I. Altman and J.F. Wohlwill, pp. 205-240. New York: Plenum.

Kozma, A. and M.J. Stones. 1978. "Some research issues and findings in the study of psychological well-being in the aged." *Canadian Psychological Review 19:* 241-249.

Larson, R. 1978. "Thirty years of research on the subjective well-being of older Americans." *Journal of Gerontology 33:* 109-125.

London, M., R. Crandall, and D. Fitzgibbons. 1977. "The psychological structure of leisure: Activities, needs, people." *Journal of Leisure Research 9:* 252-263.

London, M., R. Crandall, and G.W. Seals. 1977. "The contribution of job and leisure satisfaction to quality of life." *Journal of Applied Psychology 62:* 328-334.

Lounsbury, J.W., S.R. Gordon, R.L. Bergermaier, and A.M. Francesco. 1982. "Work and nonwork sources of satisfaction in relation to employee intention to turnover." *Journal of Leisure Research 14:* 285-294.

Manfredo, M.J. 1984." The comparability of onsite and offsite measures of recreation needs." *Journal of Leisure Research 16:* 245-249.

Manfredo, M.J., B.L. Driver, and P.J. Brown. 1983. "A test of concepts inherent in experience based setting management for outdoor recreation areas." *Journal of Leisure Research 15:* 263-283.

Mannell, R.C. and W. Bradley. 1986. "Does greater freedom always lead to greater leisure? Testing a person X environment model of freedom and leisure." *Journal of Leisure Research 18:* 215-230.

Mannell, R.C. and S.E. Iso-Ahola. 1985. "Work constraints on leisure: A social psychological analysis." In *Constraints on Leisure*, ed. M. Wade, pp. 155-187. Springfield, IL: Charles C. Thomas.

Mannell, R.C. and S.E. Iso-Ahola. 1987. "Psychological nature of leisure and tourism experience." *Annals of Tourism Research 14:* 314-331.

Mannell, R.C., R. Larson, and J. Zuzanek. (1988). "Leisure states and 'flow' experiences: Testing perceived freedom and intrinsic motivation hypotheses." *Journal of Leisure Research 20:* 289-304.

Manning, R.E. 1986. *Studies in Outdoor Recreation*. Corvallis, OR: Oregon State University.

Maslow, A. 1968. *Toward a Psychology of Being*. 2nd ed. Toronto: Van Nos Reinhold.

McClelland, D.C., J.W. Atkinson, R.A. Clark, and E.L. Lowell. 1953. *The Achievement Motive*. New York: Appleton-Century-Crofts.

Murray, H.A. 1938. *Explorations and Personality*. New York: Oxford University Press.

Nisbett, R.E. and T.D. Wilson. 1977. "Telling more than we can know: Verbal reports on mental processes." *Psychological Review 84:* 231-259.

Noe, F.P. 1987. "Measurement specification and leisure satisfaction." *Leisure Sciences 9:* 163-172.

O'Brien, G.E. 1986. *Psychology of Work and Unemployment*. Toronto: Wiley and Sons.

Orpen, C. (ed.) 1985. *Job Satisfaction*. Amsterdam: Elsevier.

Pearce, P.L. 1980. "A favorability-satisfaction model of tourists' evaluations." *Journal of Travel Research 19:* 13-17.

Pierce, R.C. 1980. "Dimensions of leisure. I: Satisfactions." *Journal of Leisure Research 12:* 5-19.

Pizam, A., Y. Neumann, and A. Reichel. 1978. "Dimensions of tourism satisfaction with a destination area." *Annals of Tourism Research 5:* 314-322.

Ragheb, M.G. 1980. "Interrelationships among leisure participation, leisure satisfaction, and leisure attitudes." *Journal of Leisure Research 12:* 138-149.

Ragheb, M.G. and C.A. Griffith. 1982. "The contribution of leisure participation and leisure satisfaction to life satisfaction of older persons." *Journal of Leisure Research 14:* 295-306.

Riddick, C.C. 1986. "Leisure satisfaction precursors." *Journal of Leisure Research 18:* 259-265.

Rosenthal, D.H., D.A. Waldman, and B.L. Driver. 1982. "Construct validity of instruments measuring recreationists' preferences." *Leisure Sciences 5:* 89-108.

Russell, R.V. 1987. "The importance of recreation satisfaction and activity participation to life satisfaction of age-segregated retirees." *Journal of Leisure Research 19:* 273-283.

Schreyer, R., R.C. Knopf, and D.R. Williams. 1985. "Reconceptualizing the motive/environment link in recreation choice behavior." In *Proceedings — Symposium on Recreation Choice Behavior*, eds. G.H. Stankey and S.F. McCool, pp. 9-18. USDA Forest Service General Technical Report INT-184. Intermountain Forest and Range Experiment Station, Ogden, UT.

Skeels, H.M. 1973. "Adult status of children with contrasting early life experiences: A follow-up study." *Monograph for Social Research on Child Development*, 31, No. 3, Serial No. 105.

Stebbins, R. 1981. "Science amators: rewards and costs in amateur astronomy and archaeology." *Journal of Leisure Research 13:* 289-304.

Stock, W.A., M.A. Okun, and M. Benin. 1986. "Structure of subjective well-being among the elderly." *Psychology and Aging 1:* 91-102.

Tinsley, H.E.A. 1984. "The psychological benefits of leisure counselling." *Society and Leisure 7:* 125-140.

Tinsley, H.E.A. and T.L. Johnson. 1984. "A preliminary taxonomy of leisure activities." *Journal of Leisure Research 16:* 234-244.

Tinsley, H.E. A. and R.A. Kass. 1978. "Leisure activities and need satisfaction: A replication and extension." *Journal of Leisure Research 10:* 191-202.

Tinsley, H.E.A. and R.A. Kass. 1979. "The latent structure of the need satisfying properties of leisure activities." *Journal of Leisure Research 11:* 278-291.

Trafton, R.S. and H.E.A. Tinsley. 1980. "An investigation of the construct validity of measures of job, leisure, dyadic and general life satisfaction." *Journal of Leisure Research 12:* 34-44.

Ulrich, R.S. and D.L. Addoms. 1981. "Psychological and recreational benefits of a residential park." *Journal of Leisure Research 13:* 43-65.

Vaske, J.J., M.P. Donnelly, T.A. Heberlein, and B. Shelby. 1982. "Differences in reported satisfaction ratings by consumptive and nonconsumptive recreationists." *Journal of Leisure Research 14:* 195-206.

Williams, D.R. and R. Schreyer 1981. "Characterizing the person-environment interaction for recreation resources planning." In *Proceedings of Applied Geography Conference*, Volume IV, eds. J.W. Frazier and B.J. Epstein, pp. 262-271. Tempe, AZ: Association of Applied Geographers.

Willmott, P. 1971. "Family, work and leisure conflicts among male employees." *Human Relations 24:* 575-584.

THE SPATIAL ANALYSIS OF RECREATION AND LEISURE

Stephen L.J. Smith

THE SIGNIFICANCE OF THE SPATIAL PERSPECTIVE TO RECREATION AND LEISURE RESEARCH

In 1963, the editors of *The Geographical Review* invited Roy Wolfe, the "godfather" of recreation geography, to write a review of the recently released 27-volume *Final Report of the Outdoor Recreation Resources Review Commission*. Wolfe's (1964) review turned into a comprehensive overview of the field of outdoor recreation research — which was virtually synonymous with leisure research in the early 1960s. To provide the reader with a coherent picture of outdoor recreation, showing how everything (activities, resources, user conflicts, social trends, public agencies, research, planning, and so on) related to everything else, Wolfe decided to develop a schematic showing the key elements of outdoor recreation and their connections. He began by placing the most important element — the participant — in the middle, with the other elements and connecting lines surrounding the participant. It did not work. After several attempts, Wolfe found the only way to make a coherent and intelligible diagram was to put mobility in the center. As Wolfe was later to comment, the reason was clear in hindsight. The people are here, the resources are there. They must be brought together. And most of the time it is the people who must move through space to the resource.

While people are still the most important element in recreation, of course, Wolfe's serendipitous insight emphasizes that the concept of travel through space is central to an understanding of many forms of recreation behavior, from outdoor recreation to cultural events. If one begins with the facts that resources and people are often spatially separated and that people must move to reach the resources, one is very quickly led to the examination of such issues as:

- Where are the people? How many are there in each location? What are their personal, social, and economic characteristics? How do they differ from people at other locations?
- Where are the resources? What is their quality and capacity? What effect will use of those resources have on the resource base and the local environment? What will the effect be on other people who live in the area and on other users?
- How easy is it for people to travel to the resource or facility? What are their travel costs? Are there other constraints, such as problems of physical accessibility, inconvenient scheduling, excessive admission fees, and racial, linguistic, and social barriers?
- What new facilities or resources need to be supplied? What areas have priority for the new supply? Who should pay to support those who play? How many people are expected to use a new facility at a given location?
- What are the regional differences in recreation preferences? Why do these exist? Do they represent differences in tastes, culture, or historical inequalities?

While not an exhaustive list of questions that must be answered to understand recreation and leisure participation, these questions illustrate that the spatial perspective is essential for a full understanding of recreation and leisure. They should also help to illustrate that the spatial perspective is not limited just to outdoor recreation. It is ironic, nonetheless, that Jackson and Burton's survey results, presented in the first chapter of this book, reveal a widespread ignorance among many contemporary leisure researchers about the nature and contributions of the geographic perspective.

The purpose of this chapter, therefore, is to introduce leisure researchers to the spatial perspective by surveying some of its major contributions to the social scientific study of recreation and leisure. These contributions are grouped into two major themes: locational research and travel research. Although these are presented separately, both are aspects of an underlying phenomenon — space. Recreational space is defined by the dispersion of people, recreation places, and recreation resources across the landscape. These do not exist, however, as discrete "islands," unconnected to each other. Travel of people across the landscape to enjoy different resources and facilities creates a continuous landscape or surface of movement and activity. This surface is defined by concentrations of people, resources, transportation linkages, and other spatial phenomena. Given the current lack of understanding of the role of geography and spatial analysis in recreation and leisure research, it may be useful to begin with a brief overview of some fundamental spatial phenomena and concepts: nodes, trips, travelers, networks, hierarchies, and regions. Examples of how these concepts are used in leisure research will be found later in the chapter.

REVIEW OF BASIC SPATIAL CONCEPTS

Nodes

Nodes are locations of people or resources. The two most common types of nodes are origins (households, neighborhoods, urban areas) and destinations (city, provincial, or national parks, cottage communities, resorts). Interaction or transportation interchange points (airports, railroad stations, highway interchanges) may also be considered nodes.

For the purposes of statistical analysis, nodes are often represented as geometrically dimensionless points. For example, Wood Buffalo National Park or the New York Metropolitan Area — both covering hundreds of square miles — can be represented as points. The reason for such an unrealistic representation is the ease of analysis. The distance between origins and destinations, for example, can be defined only after origin and destination have been abstracted as discrete points. Although both origins and destinations, when abstracted as points, are considered to occupy no space, they may still be assigned important quantities, such as potential demand (perhaps based on total population) or attractiveness (perhaps based on resource inventory). Interaction points may be assigned qualities relating to the volume of traffic or the number of business transactions that occur at them.

Trips

A trip, in its simplest conception, occurs when a recreationist leaves a node, often his home (but sometimes a temporary accommodation such as a hotel room), travels to a destination, and returns. In practice, a trip may include one or more destinations, side trips, or a circuitous tour with no particular destination. Researchers who study trips are often interested in the mode (or modes) of transportation used, the motivations for travel, and the total amount of money spent on various commodities and activities.

Recreation trips may be operationally defined in terms of maximum or minimum lengths of stay or travel distances. As a trivial illustration, most people intuitively define a trip to be a journey longer than a trip to the backyard or a neighbor's house. On the other hand, trips that keep the individual away from home for more than six months or a year are frequently considered to be a change of residence, not a trip.

Individual parts of trips are sometimes separated for special attention. Trip *segments* or *legs* refer to periods of travel between changes of location, modes of transportation, specific carriers, or type of accommodation. As noted previously, trips usually begin at origin nodes and lead to destination nodes, before returning to the origin. Those without identified destination nodes are *touring trips.* The length of stay at a destination node, or the duration of stay in a region or political jurisdiction different from the one of usual residence, is a *visit.* Visits and trips may be measured in terms of *person-nights*, the product of the number of people in the travel party and the number of nights the travel party is away from home. Shorter trips may be measured as *person-days* or *person-hours.*

Certain types of trips may involve very restrictive definitions. For example, the Organization for Economic Cooperation and Development (OECD) defines *vacation-trips* as trips taken primarily for pleasure and lasting for a minimum of four nights and not more than 365 nights (Organization for Economic Cooperation and Development 1973). The Ontario Ministry of Tourism and Recreation defines a "trip" for the purposes of its Travel Survey to be any trip greater than 40 kilometers one-way, irrespective of the duration of stay.

Regardless of the operational definition of a trip, social scientists are interested in many different aspects of travel, including the time of year trips are made, the duration of trips, the distance traveled, the purpose of the trips, and the mode of transportation.

Travelers

While all the concepts reviewed here are closely related, the connection between trips and travelers is especially close. Once an operational definition of a trip has been established — perhaps a trip of more than 100 miles away from home, lasting overnight, for any purpose other than work or school — a traveler is anyone who makes that trip. For some purposes, the interest of the researcher is not necessarily on the individual traveler but on the traveling party, whether one individual or a group of 2, 10, or 100 people. The reason for this is that many travel decisions and travel events are affected by groups of people traveling together. Understanding their behavior requires not the analysis of their individual characteristics, but those of the group. Common socio-economic variables used in the study of travelers include their age, sex, education, occupational status, occupation, annual income, family composition, and party composition.

Networks

The pattern created by nodes and the trips made by individuals and groups between them defines a network. Most travel is confined to relatively narrow and permanent corridors (trails, highways, air routes). The network of these corridors may be conveniently represented as a map, like the familiar highway or topographic maps, showing the precise locations of nodes and transportation linkages, or as a highly stylized graph, simply showing which nodes are directly connected to which other nodes, with no particular regard for direction or distance. Anyone who has traveled on a subway or other rapid transit system has probably seen this type of cartogram. One can abstract the network still further and reduce it to a connectivity matrix, showing the distance or other measures of the ease of travel between every pair of nodes in the network.

The issue of distance between pairs of nodes in a network is one of the most fundamental in spatial analysis. Distance may be measured in many ways. The most familiar is a simple straight line (or great circle if the distance is many thousands of miles on the surface of the earth). Actual highway distance may be more relevant if one is studying patterns of automobile travel, and if the highway is especially sinuous. A special form of highway distance is "Manhattan distance," which is the physical distance between points in urban areas measured along the sides of streets laid out in the familiar rectilinear street network of most North American city cores. Other measures used by researchers have included perceptions of distance (Timmerman 1982), travel time, the number of airline or train stops, and travel costs. Even the number of street crossings can be used, as in a study by Dee and Liebman (1970), of children's trips to playgrounds.

One question that is often raised in the study of any network is the relative degree of interconnectivity of nodes. In other words, how dense is the number of linkages between nodes, especially in comparison to the total number possible? A statistic that is useful for answering this question is the connectivity index:

$$C = \frac{L}{3(P-2)} \tag{1}$$

Where: C = connectivity index
L = number of links
P = number of nodes

Equation 1 is essentially the ratio between the actual number of linkages and the number possible. Its value ranges between 0.00 for a network of unconnected points to 1.00 for a network totally connected. C may be meaningfully calculated for any network with three or more points. In this particular form, C applies to a planar network — a network that exists in only two dimensions, like the surface of the earth — and where every crossover between two linkages defines a node. In three dimensions or where the crossing of linkages does not necessarily define a node, connectivity is calculated by:

$$C = \frac{L}{(0.5)P(P-1)} \tag{2}$$

Where: variables are as defined previously.

Hierarchies

There are bigger nodes and smaller nodes, and there are bigger networks and smaller networks. Behind this apparently trivial observation are some very important spatial principles. Generally, the larger the origin or the more important the destination, the greater its influence and the greater the range of services associated with that node. For example, Toronto, Ontario, is the largest metropolitan area in Canada. Newspapers, television networks, banks, department stores, and many other commodities and services offered by Toronto-based firms extend to all parts of Canada. Individuals and families from a hundred or more miles away regularly travel to Toronto for shopping or an evening's entertainment. Hamilton, Ontario — a medium-sized Canadian city — draws visitors usually from a maximum distance of 50 miles. Its newspapers, television and radio stations also have a more restricted range. The diversity of commodities offered in Hamilton, while large, is not as great as those found in Toronto. Smaller still is Elmira, Ontario, with only about two thousand residents. Elmira serves the immediate farms surrounding the town; its weekly newspaper has a very limited distribution, and there are no locally-based television or radio stations. Elmira residents import these and many other services from nearby, larger communities, including Toronto and Hamilton.

The role of hierarchies in the space economy of a region was originally developed by Christaller (1933) and Lösch (1944). Their analyses are quite complex, but some of their most important principles can be summarized as follows:

1. A minimum population (the population threshold) exists for most goods or services. Nodes with populations below the threshold will normally not offer that particular commodity.
2. The threshold varies with different commodities. The willingness of people to travel to acquire a given commodity also varies with different commodities. These two effects combine to produce market areas, the sizes of which vary with each commodity. A fast food restaurant or a motion picture theater will usually have a much smaller population threshold and a smaller market area than a professional hockey team or ballet company.
3. Nodes (referred to as central places by Christaller and Lösch) form hierarchies based on the sizes of the market areas. Small towns tend to offer only locally consumed goods with small thresholds; large cities offer both locally-consumed goods with small thresholds and commodities that require much larger thresholds and market areas.

The body of research based on these principles is known as central place theory. A major question in central place theory concerns not only the size of nodes or central places and their market areas, but also the number of central places of different sizes and their location on the landscape. Further information on central place theory and its relevance to recreation can be found in Smith (1983a).

Regions

A region is an area on the landscape that is characterized by some set of internal qualities that give it a sense of unity, yet make it distinct from other areas that surround it. Regions are defined by social scientists for three major reasons. First, they are used to name part of the world. Whether one wishes to talk about a neighborhood with specified needs for recreation services, or a part of the natural landscape that should be protected in its natural state as a preserve, one needs to be able to draw a boundary around that area and to assign a name to it. The point is not just the attachment of labels, but the identification of an area that is distinct from other areas on the face of the earth and the provision of a convenient way of referring to it.

Second, regions help to simplify and order knowledge. The Rocky Mountains region actually includes many different locales with significant variations among them — large cities, small towns, rural communities, primitive areas, undisturbed wilderness. While the recognition of these differences is important in some contexts, at other times it is desirable to be able to simplify or to ignore the differences, categorizing all these places as being essentially the same — as part of the Rockies. Without the ability to simplify or stereotype regions, planning and research would become impossibly complex, detailed, and disaggregated.

Third, regions allow researchers to make predictions and to conduct analyses on important social or natural phenomena. For example, Gunn (1979) has noted certain regional characteristics that he believes are important determinants of the potential for that region to support tourism. The concept of a region allows him — and other researchers — to make and test such predictions. The results will eventually help us to better understand tourism and to plan and manage recreation systems more effectively for the regions in which they are located.

Despite the importance of regions for the analysis of recreation, they still represent an inadequately researched topic. Pressing tasks associated with the study of regions include the development of better techniques for defining regions, improved procedures for conducting regional resource inventories, examination of user patterns within and between regions, and improvements in how regions are incorporated into the recreation planning process. Smith (1983b; 1987) provides further information about the use of regions in recreation research and illustrates two different methods for defining regions.

LOCATIONAL RESEARCH

Researchers interested in the locational aspects of recreation and leisure services examine a wide range of topics, from the development of models for the most efficient spacing of recreation facilities to examining the causes of differences in regional participation in sports. Two general topics are especially important in studying the locational aspects of recreation and leisure: (1) the description of locations; and (2) site selection.

The Description of Locations

The description of locations is the study of differences. Regions, by definition, differ from each other. Some locations encourage substantial outdoor recreation activity; others experience no recreational use whatsoever. Canadians who live in the western provinces tend to be more physically active than those who live in Atlantic Canada (McPherson and Curtis 1986). New York City and Las Vegas are both popular urban tourism destinations, but they have greatly different types of attractions. These simple dichotomies illustrate that one of the most basic and important tasks involved in the spatial analysis of recreation and leisure is the description of locations and the differences among them.

The methods and topics of description are numerous, but they may be grouped into three general categories: (1) description of places; (2) description of people or participants; and (3) inventory of resources.

Places and facilities

At the simplest level, the description of places and facilities involves defining the types of places or facilities to be described, followed by a simple inventory of the number or location of these. Slightly more sophisticated measures, such as ratios, are also useful. For example, a ratio that has been used in tourism research is Defert's tourist function, *Tf*, defined as:

$$Tf = \frac{N \times 100}{P} \qquad (3)$$

Where: N = the number of beds in commercial accommodations in a particular origin.
P = population of local residents at that origin.

Tf is a measure of the relative capacity of a tourism destination for accommodating overnight visitors. It has been used in a variety of settings, such as Colorado (Thompson 1971), Provence (Atlas de Provence 1974), and New Zealand (Pearce 1979). It is useful for comparisons among similar destinations, but less useful when the destinations are quite dissimilar in size. For example, cities such as New York or Tokyo have *Tfs* that are relatively small, reflecting the fact that tourism plays only a small role in their total economy. On the other hand, Niagara Falls or Atlantic City have high *Tfs*, reflecting the importance of tourism in their local economies. However, the significance of New York or Tokyo as tourism destinations dwarfs the importance of Niagara Falls or Atlantic City. *Tf* indicates only the *relative* importance of tourism within a destination's economy. It fails to indicate anything about the importance of that particular destination in the larger regional or national economy.

A more complex use of description in the study of recreation facilities may be found in Smith's (1983c; 1985a) work on restaurant location. After specifying a classification system for urban restaurants based predominantly on menus, he mapped the distribution of each category of restaurant in a number of different cities. He then employed a battery of spatial descriptive techniques to identify hidden patterns and relationships in the mapped distributions. These included an examination of surrounding land uses, correlation of locations with traffic volumes, and distances to other restaurants of both the same type and different types. One of the more important spatial statistics that Smith used was the nearest neighbor ratio (Clark and Evans 1955). This statistic is designed to indicate quantitatively whether an observed pattern is clustered, random, or dispersed. It is based on comparing the observed average distance to each point's (in Smith's case, the points were restaurants) nearest neighbor to the average distance expected if the pattern were random:

$$R = \frac{\bar{r}_o}{\bar{r}_e}$$

Where: $\bar{r}_e = \dfrac{1}{2\sqrt{n/A}}$ (4)

$\bar{r}_o$ = observed average to nearest neighbor

n = number of points

A = area of study region

On the basis of the nearest neighbor ratio, Smith was able to obtain evidence that fast food restaurants cluster close to each other, whereas donut shops and pizzarias tend to disperse from each other. More complex patterns were also described concerning the relationships between restaurant locations and other land uses as well as traffic volumes. On the basis of this description, Smith formulated a series of hypotheses regarding successful restaurant locations that can be tested by further research. Another example of the application of nearest neighbor analysis, in a rural setting, is Glyptis's (1981) study of English countryside recreation patterns.

Participants

Describing the location of participants is often more difficult than describing the location of facilities. Participants move. In particular, they move from their home to a facility; thus, a basic question is whether to describe participants and their participation in activities in terms of their residence or the site of participation. Both are used, depending on the purposes of the description.

Descriptions of participants based on some type of survey work on-site often require specialized techniques to obtain information. Mechanical traffic counters at access points can provide basic information on the numbers of people or vehicles entering a facility. Voluntary registration systems, records of ticket sales, aerial photography, random areal sampling, and cordons of field surveyors hidden in strategic locations are some of the methods employed to provide basic descriptive and inventory information about participants.

Some common information often collected about participants was listed above. Other variables include activities participated in, motivations for participation, sources of information used in selecting a particular location, and measures of satisfaction with the recreation experience. Another type of variable that is sometimes employed in describing patterns of participation is the location quotient. This quotient is a type of per capita measure that describes the degree to which participation in each of a set of zones departs from the average participation over an entire region:

$$l_i^a = \frac{a_i}{k} \tag{5}$$

Where: l_i^a = the location quotient for activity a in zone i.

a_i = the number of people participating in activity a in zone i.

k = the average participation in activity a for the entire region (composed of numerous individual zones).

Smale (1984) calculated the location quotients for membership in Family YMCAs/YWCAs for London, Ontario and Kitchener-Waterloo, Ontario in two different years. The location quotients, derived from membership records, provided a quantitative description of the relative concentrations of YMCA/YWCA members in each census tract of the two communities. Smale then compared the patterns of location quotients before and after the construction of new facilities for both organizations in the two cities. After identifying those census tracts with the highest concentrations of members, Smale obtained socio-economic information from Statistics Canada for each of those census tracts. This allowed him to develop rough social and economic profiles of the memberships of each YMCA/YWCA before and after the new facilities were developed.

He was able to deduce, for example, that the London Family YMCA/YWCA had begun to attract a much more affluent and overwhelmingly adult membership in contrast to its previous membership. The Kitchener-Waterloo Y increased its membership, but retained roughly the same socio-economic profile of members after new facility construction.

Shaw (1984) provides another example of social area analysis in her study of recreation participation variations in British neighborhoods, based on the ACORN system (A Classification of Residential Neighbourhoods). ACORN defines eleven different types of neighborhoods with forty classifying variables.

A different and more conceptual approach to describing the patterns of participation is seen in the work of Ryan (1984). Ryan examined the morphology of a large city with reference to the routine recreational activities of citizens in their home community. Borrowing a general urban landscape model first proposed by Murdie (1969), he suggested that the recreation landscape can be abstracted as an oculus or bulls-eye. The concentric rings of his oculus are the central city, the suburbs, and the urban fringe. These are characterized by a gradient from indoor to outdoor, passive to active, and public to personal recreation land use. Cutting through these concentric bands are sectoral concentrations, usually centered on transportation corridors. These sectoral concentrations tend to reflect class and ethnic divisions. After describing his model, Ryan then empirically tested it using data from Cincinnati, Ohio. His particular focus was on whether there are activity clusterings in the various sectors. The available evidence offered support for his model, but as Ryan noted, more thorough analysis, especially analysis over time, would help to yield greater understanding. The validity of Ryan's model is still open to question, but it is sufficiently provocative to warrant examination in other cases.

Resources

As with the description of places or people, the description of resources can be as simple as counting the number of specific resources and measuring their size. An early, typical example of this arithmetic approach to resource description is the U.S. Outdoor Recreation Resources Review Commission's examination of shoreline recreation resources (Campbell *et al.* 1962). Campbell and his team inventoried the total length of shoreline, bluff shore, marsh shore, beach shore, and total areas of public as well as restricted land along the Great Lakes, Atlantic, Gulf of Mexico, and Pacific shores of the United States. The findings were aggregated and mapped by state as a reference for state-level and national-level planning and policy analysis.

A slightly more sophisticated method of inventorying resources is to examine, map, and interpret a wider range of resources that interact to influence the potential for recreation in a region. One example of such a group of interacting variables is weather. Wind chill and the humidex are two derived measures combining ambient temperature and wind speed or humidity. Crowe, McKay, and Baker (1977) collected data related to outdoor recreation in both the summer and winter for Ontario, and produced provincial-level maps on a month-by-month basis showing the relative potential for different forms of recreation across Ontario. The variables the authors examined included:

Summer	*Winter*
Air temperature	Duration of winter daylight
Humidity	Air temperature
Precipitation	Wind speed
Cloud cover	Precipitation
Visibility	Cloud cover
Wind speed	Visibility
Water temperature	Snow and ice cover
Length of season	Length of season

A yet more sophisticated method of describing resources is the use of some form of hierarchical classification. One of the better examples of this approach in recreation planning is Dorney's (1976) inventory system for urban land for recreation planning. Dorney's method is based on a systematic examination of abiotic, biotic, and cultural resources, starting with specific sites and ending with an aggregate map of an urban region.

Variables selected for describing the abiotic resource base include resources related to the air system, subsurface geology, surface geology and soils, hydrology, and noise levels. Each of the variables in these categories was defined and an appropriate scale developed. The distribution and magnitude, intensity, or character of each variable was then plotted on an abiotic landscape map.

Next, aquatic and terrestrial biotic variables were defined, located, and mapped. These included significant stands of vegetation as well as wildlife concentrations. These, too, were combined on a single, biotic landscape map.

Finally, cultural variables related to evidence of pre-Caucasian settlements (if any) as well as existing cultural and recreation resources, such as historic sites, parks, libraries, theaters, churches, and schools, were defined, inventoried, and mapped. Three different cultural maps were produced: one for the dominant culture, one for any specific ethnic or sub-cultural groups, and one for pre-Caucasian settlement patterns, if appropriate.

The last step in Dorney's system was to combine all maps into an aggregate map showing the location of existing recreational features, areas for potential development, and areas that posed barriers for development. Dorney's system has been borrowed by Bastedo, Nelson, and Theberge (1981) for application in national park planning. They have re-labeled Dorney's system as the "ABC Method" (*a*biotic, *b*iotic, *c*ultural). Geographic information systems

(GIS) now allow for even greater flexibility and power in defining regions and conducting complex resource inventories. Their application to recreation analysis, however, has just begun.

Site Selection

Perhaps one of the most obvious answers to the question, "What is the spatial perspective good for in studying leisure?" is that it helps provide guidelines about where to locate recreation facilities. The best location will often be different for public facilities than for private businesses, and it will usually be different for different types of businesses and facilities. The selection is normally not obvious and requires analyses of tradeoffs between advantages and disadvantages.

For public recreation facilities, at least two different criteria may be used to guide the decision about where to locate facilities. The first criterion is the distance that potential users must travel to facilities; the second is the relative need for the services of the recreation facility.

One of the simplest ways of using distance to locate facilities is to select a maximum distance (perhaps on the basis of accepted planning standards or a user survey) that people will normally be willing to travel to reach a facility of a given type. Existing facilities are located as nodes on a map of a city or region, and a service area circumscribed around each facility, the radius of which is equal to the maximum travel distance. Any area falling outside the hinterlands is a candidate for a new facility (Hatry *et al.* 1977). The selection of the specific location in the unserved area which is to receive the next facility then becomes a matter of professional (or political) judgment.

A more sophisticated method is to locate each new facility to minimize the total travel distance that all users accumulate when traveling to the nearest facility (Goodchild and Booth 1980). Although this strategy is easiest to implement as a long-term strategic plan before any facilities are built, such a situation is quite rare for the provision of recreation services. Most communities already have some degree of service, so the task of locating the site that minimizes total distance for a new facility added to an existing system is more complex. The procedure required is known as iterative programming. This involves selecting a tentative location at random or by intuition. Total travel distance is determined by assuming users will go to the nearest facility (a useful, but often incorrect, assumption). The location of the proposed site is shifted slightly and the cumulative distance is again tabulated. This process continues until all possible locations are examined, while the cumulative distances are monitored continuously to identify the minimum. Clearly, such a procedure can tax the resources of even the most powerful computers typically available to planners if the existing facility system is moderately large, with a large user population, and several new facilities are proposed.

This process can be simplified somewhat by aggregating individuals into neighborhoods or census tracts, so that one works with only a score of neighborhoods (or fewer) instead of tens of thousands of individuals. Use of neighborhoods also allows the planner to weigh the presence of different community groups to reflect social or political priorities given to those groups. For example, neighborhoods with a higher proportion of children, seniors, or low income families may be assigned a greater weight so that any new facility may be "pulled" in its direction.

The assessment of relative need also balances the pull of different groups or neighborhoods against each other. Instead of trying to find a compromise location, such as the site that minimizes total travel distance, the assessment of relative need produces a rank ordering of different neighborhoods or regions. The neighborhood with the greatest need will normally be selected as the site for the next facility. The critical issue, of course, is how need is determined. One of the first methods developed, and one that is still used by municipal planners, was described by Staley (1968). Staley suggested comparing need and supply in each of a city's neighborhoods, by combining several variables into a need index and a resource index. His need index included measures of poverty, single-parent families, children, juvenile delinquency rates, and automobile ownership. The resource index reflected public facilities, recreation programs and personnel, and privately-owned recreation facilities, such as swingsets and pools. The need index is then subtracted from the resource index to identify the relative need for each neighborhood.

A variant of relative need assessment is the demand maximization method, proposed by the former U.S. Bureau of Outdoor Recreation as a criterion for awarding recreation grants from the Land and Water Conservation Fund in the 1960s and 1970s. As with Staley's method, demand maximization is still used in some agencies. Its basic premise is that facilities should go where they will generate the greatest increase in per capita use — which is assumed to be an indicator of relative need. With this method the challenge is to be able to predict per capita use.

The usual method for predicting per capita use levels is to correlate observed use levels at existing facilities with various socio-economic variables of the population using the facility. A model is developed that relates certain socio-economic characteristics to per capita use levels for specific activities. Those neighborhoods that have the socio-economic profile associated with the highest use levels are then selected for facility development.

A problem with this approach is that one of the best statistical predictors of the per capita use of recreation facilities is income: the higher the income, the higher the participation rates. This is not always true, but it holds often enough that a decision-maker, relying blindly on the model, will tend to give higher income neighborhoods more facilities while keeping lower income neighborhoods facility-poor. The basic question this model cannot answer with much validity is whether low participation rates in a neighborhood are due to lack of access and past opportunity or to lack of interest. Public surveys and public participation methods have been suggested as ways to help collect this information so that the results of the demand maximization model may be correctly interpreted. But, unfortunately, the most politically-organized and articulate neighborhoods also tend to be those that are the most affluent and well-educated. The political process does not provide any better guarantee for accuracy of information and assessment of true community needs than an economic model. Thus, the issue of setting priorities for public facility development and location continues as a major research need in leisure and recreation (see Godbey's chapter for further discussion of this issue).

The task of locating good sites for recreation businesses involves different criteria than public facilities, but the problem is just as complex. While the fundamental principle guiding the location of public facilities is (or should be) maximizing service to the public, normally the fundamental principle guiding the location of private businesses is maximizing profits. However, just as there are several different ways of defining the level of service, there are also several different ways of defining profitability. A private entrepreneur may be interested in maximizing net profits or return on investment, in minimizing costs, or in maintaining his share of the market. The locational decisions are also likely to be different for the same type of business, depending on whether the decision-maker is the owner-operator of a single independent business, a franchise holder of one outlet, or responsible for the overall locational strategy of multiple franchise outlets (Zeller, Achabal, and Brown 1980).

The process of selecting the best site, or even an adequate site, for a business is a complicated procedure that involves many spatial principles combined with the realities of the real estate market-place and zoning ordinances. The more important spatial principles include:

1. Location is important in determining the ultimate size and success of a firm, but it rarely guarantees success.
2. Site selection involves trade-offs among transportation costs, production costs, the cost of land, access to resources, labor supply, and access to markets, among other concerns.
3. Some businesses benefit by locating close to competitors; others do better if they avoid them; still others are indifferent. Some businesses do well by locating close to complementary businesses, whereas others, such as toxic waste disposal sites, may harm virtually any other business located close to them.
4. Market size and the number and location of competing firms limit the potential for new business growth in relatively predictable ways.
5. Firms that are tied to a specific resource base or that consume heavy or bulky resources tend to locate close to the resource supply. Those that ship relatively heavy, bulky, or perishable items tend to locate close to the market.

TRAVEL RESEARCH

The development of forecasting models for travel represents one of the best examples of cumulative research in recreation and leisure studies. A major reason for this is that an accurate estimate of the numbers of people who are likely to come to a particular facility is one of the most important pieces of information a planner or manager can have. Travel modelling, however, provides other benefits as well. The development of increasingly sophisticated travel models stimulates important research initiatives into understanding human motivations; the importance of spatial variables; how people choose among competing recreation destinations or products; how they perceive distance, travel costs, and recreation opportunities; how the attractiveness of destination, facilities or resources can be measured; and what methods can be employed for assessing the impacts of different numbers of travelers on the destinations they visit. The following sections consider two of the more important models for forecasting travel: gravity models and intervening opportunity models.

It should be emphasized first, however, that travel forecasting issues do not exhaust the scope of travel-related topics. For example, several researchers have examined the impact of travel patterns on the development and use of recreational resources. Campbell (1966), Mariot (1969), and Rajotte (1975) are a few early examples. Each author examined the distinction between "recreational" travel and "tourism" travel. The former is typified by travel originating in urban areas and spreading radially away from cities. The latter also originates in urban areas but tends to form narrowly defined travel circuits. Rajotte has documented the empirical evidence for this common conceptualization using data from the Quebec City region. She has also found distinct land use changes associated with each type of travel — distinctions that became more pronounced over time.

Gravity Models

The gravity model is perhaps the best-known travel forecasting tool of spatial analysts. Although most analysts now consider the basic model rather passé, preferring to use more sophisticated logit or probit stochastic models, an understanding of the basic principles and issues associated with the gravity model is essential to understanding the strengths and weaknesses of other travel models. Further, virtually all extant travel forecasting tools can trace their lineage back to the gravity model. For these reasons it is still appropriate to consider the features of this "old-fashioned" model.

As the name suggests, the gravity model is based on an analogy to the Newtonian law of gravitation, which states that the attraction of two bodies is directly proportional to their mass and inversely proportional to the square of the distance separating their centers of gravity (or the nodes located at the center of each body, assuming the distribution of mass is uniform in each body). When applied to social situations, the gravity model states that the interaction between two bodies, groups, or nodes is proportional to their relative size, wealth, or importance and inversely proportional to the distance separating the two bodies.

Mathematically:

$$T_{ij} = \frac{G\,P_i\,A_j}{D_{ij}^d} \tag{6}$$

Where: T_{ij} = a measure of the interaction between two social entities, i and j, such as the number of travelers from origin i that visit destination j

P_i = a measure of the potential market size of an origin, such as the number of people who own camping equipment

A_j = a measure of the attractiveness or capacity of the destination, such as the number of campsites at a park

D_{ij} = a measure of the distance between i and j
G and d are statistically estimated coefficients

In recreation research, the gravity model is most commonly used to forecast the volume of travel from an origin to a destination. When used this way, Equation 6 no longer operates as a perfect analogy to Newton's model. The "social gravitation" between origin and destination is only one-way: the destination attracts travelers from the origin, but not conversely. In Newton's model the two bodies attract each other equally.

Much of the research that has gone into developing improved gravity models of recreation travel has been concerned with finding better specifications of the three components: P_i, A_j, and D_{ij}. The interpretation of P_i has been variously given as total population, the population of specific types of user groups (such as the number of registered boat owners), disposable income, and so on. The destination component, A_j, has been estimated using various resource inventories and scaling systems, the capacity of campgrounds, perceptual estimates of beauty, levels of public familiarity, and the range of recreational opportunities available. Ewing and Kullea (1979) have developed and tested a measure of attractiveness based on the ability of a destination to attract visitors away from closer destinations. Finally, D_{ij} has been estimated using straight line distance, highway or Manhattan distance, travel time, travel costs (sometimes including estimates of the value of the travel time of the motorists), and estimates of the number of intervening opportunities.

The success of the gravity model in the basic formulation is mixed, but most forecasts have been 40 percent to 60 percent accurate. Greater levels of accuracy have been obtained with more highly aggregated problems, such as modelling travel from every U.S. state to the U.S. National Park system as a whole, with much poorer results obtained for highly disaggregated models, such as forecasts of travel from individual neighborhoods to individual local parks (see Young and Smith 1979, for a discussion on the issue of aggregation in travel forecasting).

In addition to the desire to develop more powerful and accurate forecasting models, travel researchers have worked to overcome some problems in the simple gravity model represented in Equation 6. A basic problem is that the equation is unconstrained. That is, there is no inherent upper limit to the number of trips that it can predict. If the value of P_i were to double, perhaps through a doubling of a city's population, the equation predicts a doubling of visits to park j. So far so good. But if the population triples, and the value of A_j triples, perhaps through a tripling of campground capacity, it predicts that visitation will increase 3 x 3 = 9 times. While some increases are reasonable and expected, there must be some upper limit to the increases possible, due to competition of other facilities, limits of time and budget, and so on. Equation 6 does not accommodate these limits to growth.

The solution is to modify the equation so that it becomes constrained. This is usually accomplished by developing a two-stage model. The first stage is a trip-generation component, often some form of a multiple regression equation relating social and economic characteristics in an origin to the potential number of trips that the origin can produce. The other component statistically distributes the trips among various destinations on the basis of their relative attractivity or capacity. Wennergren and Nielson (1968) and Cesario (1975) provide examples of constrained gravity models.

Another problem observed frequently in connection with the traditional gravity model is its tendency to over-estimate short trips and to under-estimate long trips (Martin, Memmott, and Bone 1961; Whitehead 1965). Drawing again from Newtonian physics for an analogy: there appears to be an inertial element in recreation travel. Additional effort is needed to get a trip started — a threshold that is not easily overcome when the trip goal is very short and the motivation for travel slight. Once that threshold is overcome, it takes much less effort to keep on traveling. The momentum of movement helps to keep pushing the traveler along (this, of course, represents a very different conceptualization of distance and the effort of travel than that assumed by the intervening opportunity model, to be discussed later). Following this analogy, Wolfe (1972) proposed the addition of an inertial term to the gravity model, making the response to distance a function of distance:

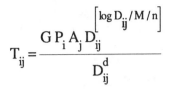

$$T_{ij} = \frac{G\,P_i\,A_j\,D_{ij}^{\left[\log D_{ij}/M/n\right]}}{D_{ij}^d} \qquad (7)$$

Where: M and n are statistically estimated coefficients and other
variables are as defined previously.

The result of this modification is to lower the predicted number of short
distance trips, make virtually no change in the number of intermediate trips, and
raise the predicted number of long-distance trips.

Although dated, Wolfe's inertia model represents, in a sense, the
current trend in travel forecasting. While attention is still paid to the definition
of the various components of the travel forecasting model, researchers now
concentrate on experimenting with the structure of travel models, examining
new ways of estimating the coefficients used to calibrate travel models, and
experimenting with different forms of interactions among the various components. Ewing (1982) in particular, has examined some basic problems associated
with the effects of travel barriers, insufficient variance in observed data sets,
multiple stops on trips, and alternative statistical estimation procedures on the
accuracy of forecasts. His findings have highlighted some recurrent problems in
non-random error in data sets or model mis-specification that will require further
refinement.

Regardless of the actual procedures used for calibrating travel models,
one consistent theme is the importance of distance, space, and other geographic
variables. Many other social science disciplines also have developed predictive
models for recreation participation and travel, but these are usually based
exclusively on traditional socio-economic variables, such as age structure,
income, employment patterns, sex-ratios, and measures of educational attainment. While these variables are important in explaining many forms of recreation participation, they do not tell the full story. In a study designed to test the
relative importance of geographic variables vis-à-vis socio-economic ones,
Smith (1985b) developed three models related to the propensity to take recreation trips. Each model incorporated twenty-two independent variables, including
common socio-demographic variables such as age, education, and income, as
well as geographic variables including supply, population density, proximity to
international borders, and climate. In each case, a model was calibrated that
explained over 90 percent of recreation travel patterns. And in each case, the
most important predictor variables were geographic, not socio-demographic.

While it should be emphasized that the independent variables in this
study were measures of propensity to engage in recreational travel and not
participation in specific activities, it should also be remembered that many forms
of recreation participation require travel. Distance, resource supply, climate, and

other geographic variables are often as important (or more important) in explaining participation patterns as the traditional social science variables used so often in sociology and social psychology.

Intervening Opportunity Models

An observation common to the general public as well as geographers is that attendance at a facility varies inversely with distance. The further people have to travel to reach a particular facility or business, the fewer will patronize it. This observation usually results in forecasting models similar to the gravity model, but there is another possible formulation. To introduce this alternative, consider a common example. A student has been leading a two-hour seminar. At the end of the seminar, he desires to find a drinking fountain. The probability of his selecting any particular drinking fountain is not so much a function of the distance between the seminar room and the drinking fountain in question, but the number of intervening fountains. In other words, the student will go as far as necessary to reach a fountain; the probability of his going to a more distant fountain is inversely proportional to the number of fountains that are closer to his node of origin.

In the context of travel to recreation facilities, a similar logic applies. The reason that people tend to go less frequently to more distant facilities is not that they are further away but that there are intervening facilities available at a lower travel cost that offer the same recreation opportunities. This model does not state that the individual will always select the closest facility, but only that the probability of selecting any facility decreases with increasing numbers of closer opportunities.

Smith (1980) examined the relative importance of distance decay versus intervening opportunities as alternative models for explaining the pattern of travel to urban recreation centers. Using a household survey conducted by the Dallas, Texas, Recreation and Parks Department, he plotted the percentage of users from each of four neighborhoods traveling at least a certain distance against total distance traveled (Figure 1). He also plotted an intervening opportunity curve showing the percentage of visitors traveling a given distance against the number of recreation centers reached or bypassed (Figure 2). The data were also analyzed using a simple regression to permit statistical comparison of the slopes of the lines. The results revealed that there were significant differences in the slopes of the lines for the distance decay curves, reflecting the fact that people in different neighborhoods responded to distance differently. On the other hand, the slopes of the intervening opportunity lines were very similar, suggesting that urban recreationists are guided more by the number of intervening opportunities than by physical distance.

Intervening opportunities, however, do not always act to deter travel. They may, in fact, act as "stepping stones" to encourage travelers to move further afield. Ellis's chapter in this book provides a brief illustration of this phenomenon when he notes that parks located along the Trans-Canada Highway appear to be used as stepping stones for cross-country trips and, thus, are more resistant to the effects of rising fuel prices than parks not located close to the Trans-Canada Highway.

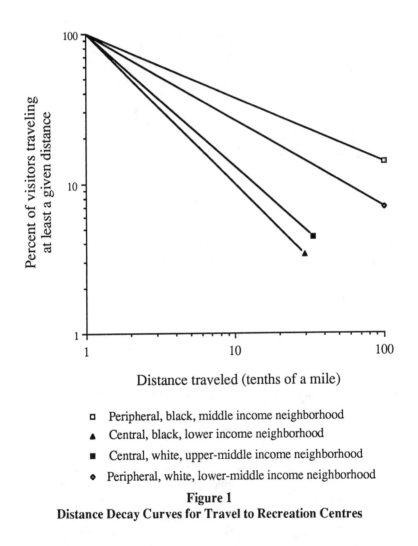

Distance traveled (tenths of a mile)

□   Peripheral, black, middle income neighborhood

▲   Central, black, lower income neighborhood

■   Central, white, upper-middle income neighborhood

◊   Peripheral, white, lower-middle income neighborhood

Figure 1
Distance Decay Curves for Travel to Recreation Centres

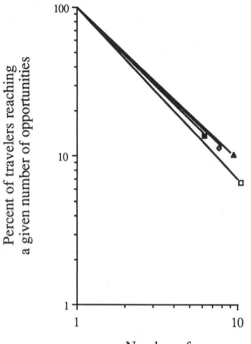

Number of
intervening opportunities

□   Peripheral, black, middle income neighborhood
▲   Central, black, lower income neighborhood
■   Central, white, upper-middle income neighborhood
◆   Peripheral, white, lower-middle income neighborhood

Figure 2
Intervening Opportunity Curves for Recreation Centres

CONCLUSIONS

We have barely scratched the surface of spatial analysis in recreation and leisure studies. Space limitations have prevented us from considering, for example, the growing body of regional analyses, such as Rooney's (1974) and McPherson and Curtis's (1986) work on regional differences in sport participation; Mathieson and Wall's (1982) work on regional variations in impacts of tourism; Murphy's (1986) spatial perspectives on the development and management of community tourism; Butler's (1984) geographic analysis of the history of rock music; and much, much more. A more comprehensive survey of the spatial perspective in recreation and leisure is available in *Recreation Geography* (Smith 1983). Interested readers should also review issues of the *Journal of Leisure Research, Leisure Sciences,* the *Journal of Travel Research, Annals of Tourism Research,* the *Professional Geographer,* the *Canadian Geographer, Transactions of the Institute of British Geographers, Geography, Regional Studies, Urban Studies,* and *Environment and Planning (A)* for examples of current spatial research on recreation and leisure topics.

As a concluding observation, perhaps a useful way of summarizing the spatial perspective in recreation and leisure studies is to visualize the subject as a tree (Figure 3). The tree continues to grow every year, drawing its nourishment by sending its roots deep into other disciplines. The trunk is split into two major branches: locational research and travel research. Each of these is divided into increasingly specialized research initiatives. As the tree image suggests, the trend in spatial research in recreation and leisure (as in most fields) is for established research problems to lead to new, more precise, or more specialized topics.

As researchers explore different and new topics in recreation, there is frequent cross-fertilization, resulting in similar topics emerging on different branches. Such a development is not simple duplication or redundancy, but an opportunity for the research community to examine the same problem from different perspectives. For example, the issue of the impacts of visitors to destination regions has emerged as a joint topic of research by both people interested in locational problems and those interested in travel problems. The locational researchers tend to emphasize social and environmental impacts, while the travel researchers often emphasize the economic impact arising from the transfer of wealth by travelers from origins to destinations. Both perspectives are needed to provide a balanced and comprehensive view of the impacts of travel on destination communities. Other examples can be found in the analysis of recreationists' choice-making processes, evaluation of landscapes, and the definition and description of different types of regions.

The scope of problems in recreation and leisure to which the spatial perspective contributes is literally as broad as the world. From oceans to deserts, from wilderness to big cities, from the most developed regions to the poorest, least developed regions, the spatial perspective has much to say and much to contribute to a better understanding of recreation and leisure in our world.

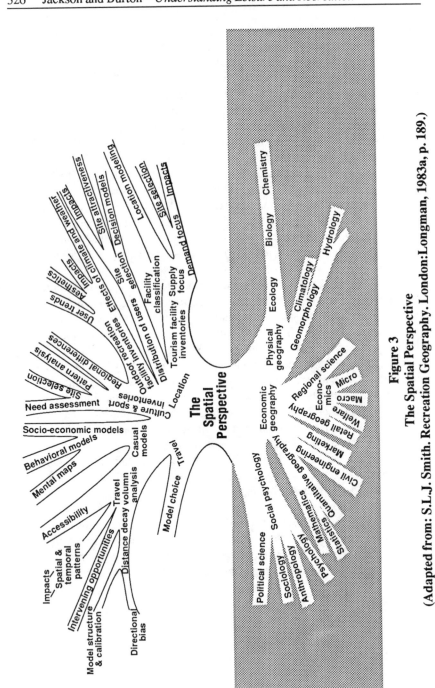

Figure 3
The Spatial Perspective
(Adapted from: S.L.J. Smith. Recreation Geography. London:Longman, 1983a, p. 189.)

References

Atlas de Provence. 1974. *Atlas de Provence: Côte d' Azur.* Le Paradou: ACTES.

Bastedo, J.D., J.G. Nelson, and J.T. Theberge. 1981. "An ecological approach to resource survey and planning for environmentally significant areas: The ABC method." *Environmental Management 8:* 125-134.

Butler, R.W. 1984. "The geography of rock: 1954-1970." *Ontario Geography 24:* 1-33.

Campbell, C.K. 1966. "An approach to research in recreational geography." In *B.C. Geographical Series*, No. 2, pp. 85-90. Vancouver, B.C.: Department of Geography, University of British Columbia.

Campbell, R.D., K.L. LeBlanc, and M.A. Mason. 1962. *Shoreline Recreation Resources of the United States.* Outdoor Recreation Resources Review Commission Study Report 4. Washington, DC: U.S. Government Printing Office.

Cesario, F.J. 1975. "A new method for analyzing outdoor recreation trip data." *Journal of Leisure Research 7:* 200-215.

Christaller, W. 1933. *Die Zentralen Orte in Suddeutschland.* Jena: Gustav Fischer.

Clark, P.J. and F.C. Evans. 1955. "On some aspects of spatial patterns in biological populations." *Science 121:* 397-398.

Crowe, R.B., G.A. McKay, and W.M. Baker. 1977. *The Tourism and Outdoor Recreation Climate of Ontario.* Toronto: Atmospheric Environment Canada.

Dee, N. and J.C. Leibman. 1970. "A statistical study of attendance at urban playgrounds." *Journal of Leisure Research 2:* 145-159.

Dorney, R.S. 1976. "Biophysical and cultural-historic land classification and mapping for Canadian urban and urbanizing land." In *Proceedings of the Workshop on Ecological Classification in Urban Areas.* Toronto.

Ewing, G.O. 1982. "Modelling recreation trip patterns: Evidence and problems." *Ontario Geography 19:* 29-56.

Ewing, G.O. and T. Kulka. 1979. "Revealed and stated preference analysis of ski resort attractiveness." *Leisure Sciences 2:* 249-275.

Glyptis, S. 1981. "Room to relax in the countryside." *The Planner 67:* 120-122.

Goodchild, M.F. and P.J. Booth. 1980. "Location and allocation of recreation facilities: Public swimming pools in London, Ontario." *Ontario Geography 15:* 35-51.

Gunn, C. 1979. *Tourism Planning.* New York: Crane Russak.

Hatry, H.P. et al. 1977. *How Effective Are Your Community Services?* Washington, D.C.: The Urban Institute.

Lösch, A. 1944. *Die Raumliche Ordnung der Wirtschaft.* Jena: Gustav Fischer.

Mariot, P. 1969. "Priestorové aspekty cestovného rucho a otázky gravitacného zázemia náusternych miest." *Geograficky Casopis 21:* 287-312.

Martin, B., F. Memmott, and A. Bone. 1961. *Principles and Techniques of Predicting Future Demand for Urban Area Travel.* Cambridge, MA: MIT Press.

Mathieson, A. and G. Wall. 1982. *Tourism: Economic, Physical, and Social Impacts.* London: Longman.

McPherson, B.D. and J.E. Curtis. 1986. *Regional and Community Type Differences in the Physical Activity Patterns of Canadian Adults.* Ottawa: Fitness Canada.

Murdie, R.A. 1969. *Factorial Ecology of Metropolitan Toronto, 1951-1961.* Research Paper No. 116. Chicago: Department of Geography, University of Chicago.

Murphy, P.E. 1986. *Tourism: A Community Approach.* London: Methuen.

Organization for Economic Cooperation and Development Tourism Committee. 1973. *Tourism Policy and International Tourism in OECD Member Countries.* Paris: Organization for Economic Cooperation and Development.

Pearce, D. 1979. "Towards a geography of tourism." *Annals of Tourism Research 6:*245-272.

Rajotte, F. 1975. "The different travel patterns and spatial framework of recreation and tourism." In *Tourism as a Factor in National and Regional Development*, pp. 43-52. Occasional Paper No. 4. Peterborough, ON: Department of Geography, Trent University.

Rogers, D.S. and H.L. Green. 1978. "Analog modelling: A new perspective in store site selection." *Proceedings of the Applied Geography Conference* 1. Kent, OH: Kent State University.

Rooney, J.F. 1974. *A Geography of American Sport.* Reading, MA: Addison-Wesley.

Ryan, B. 1984. "Activity clustering in urban recreation." *North American Culture 1:* 3-34.

Shaw, M. 1984. *Sport and Leisure Participation and Life-Styles in Different Residential Neighbourhoods: An Exploration of the ACORN Classification System.* London: Sports Council/Economic and Social Research Council Joint Panel on Leisure and Recreation Research.

Smale, B.J.A. 1984. "An examination of membership change under new facility provision." Unpublished report to the Ontario Ministry of Tourism and Recreation.

Smith, S.L.J. 1980. "Intervening opportunities and travel to urban recreation centers." *Journal of Leisure Research 12:* 296-308.

Smith, S.L.J. 1983a. *Recreation Geography.* London: Longman.

Smith, S.L.J. 1983b. "Identification of functional tourism regions in North America." *Journal of Travel Research 22:* 13-21.

Smith, S.L.J. 1983c. "Restaurants and dining out: geography of a tourist business." *Annals of Tourism Research 4:* 515-549.

Smith, S.L.J. 1985a. "Location patterns of urban restaurants." *Annals of Tourism Research 12:* 581-602.

Smith, S.L.J. 1985b. "U.S. vacation travel patterns: Correlates of distance decay and the willingness to travel." *Leisure Sciences 7:* 151-174.

Smith, S.L.J. 1987. "The regional analysis of tourism resources." *Annals of Tourism Research 14:* 254-273.

Smith, S.L.J. and D.C. Thomas. 1983. "Assessment of regional potentials of rural recreation businesses." In S.R. Lieber and D.R. Fesenmaier, D.R. (eds). *Recreation Planning and Management*, pp. 66-83. State College, PA: Venture Publishing.

Thompson, P.T. 1971. *The Use of Mountain Recreational Resources: A Comparison of Recreation and Tourism in the Colorado Rockies and the Swiss Alps*. Boulder, CO: Graduate School of Business Research, University of Colorado.

Timmermans, H. 1982. "Consumer choice of shopping centres: An information integration approach." *Regional Studies 16:* 171-182.

Wennergren, E.B. and D.B. Nielsen. 1968. *A Probabilistic Approach to Estimating Demand for Outdoor Recreation*. Bulletin 470. Logan, UT: Utah Agricultural Experiment Station.

Whitehead, J.I. 1965. "Road traffic growth and capacity in a holiday district (Dorset)." *Proceedings of the Institute of Civil Engineers 30:* 589-608.

Wolfe, R.I. 1964. "Perspective on outdoor recreation: A bibliographic survey." *The Geographical Review 54:* 203-238.

Wolfe, R.I. 1972. "The inertia model." *Journal of Leisure Research 4:* 73-76.

Young, C.W. and R.W. Smith. 1979. "Aggregated and disaggregated outdoor recreation participation models." *Leisure Sciences 2:* 143-154.

Zeller, R.E., D.D. Achabal, and L.A. Brown. 1980. "Market penetration and locational conflict in franchise systems." *Decision Sciences 11:* 58-80.

ECONOMIC MODELS OF LEISURE AND ITS IMPACT

R.W. Vickerman

Much has been made of the importance of leisure in people's lives, and in society as a whole, as a source of fulfillment and as both a complement to and compensation for work. The economist's view of leisure has been largely within this model. For the individual, leisure is time left over after work. For the fortunate few, it can be traded with work, such that the loss of one is always the opportunity cost of the other. Time as a resource may often be a much more binding constraint than money. For society, leisure time is important as a maintenance element in human capital, keeping people fit and productive. But what people do, in aggregate, with their leisure time might be much more important as a source of pressure on other scarce resources, such as transport and the environment. This has sidetracked much of the development of a consistent approach to the economic issues involved in leisure into one of simply providing evaluations of costs and benefits. Hence, the basic model of choice has concentrated on implied valuations of time.

The approach taken in this chapter is an attempt to redress this balance. It concentrates, therefore, on the economic building blocks towards an understanding of leisure decisions and behavior, to the exclusion of a detailed review of the full economic consequences of those decisions. This enables more easily the drawing of parallels with other disciplinary approaches to understanding leisure behavior. It also provides a better basis for an objective critique of more macro analyses. The underlying rationale is that it is wrong to call in the economist just to apply monetary values to observed behavior and add up the results to get an estimate of economic impact. An understanding of economic welfare implies an understanding of the peculiarly economic aspects of decisions governing that observed behavior.

The essence of an economic approach is governed by two basic features. First, the individual or household is making choices under a resource constraint. Any one choice implies foregoing an alternative; this is the opportunity cost of the choice — whether this arises from lack of money, lack of time, an inability to schedule partners' free time together, or that the teenage children have borrowed the family car. Second, individuals' preferred choices, when aggregated, become revealed market demand which interacts with suppliers' decisions to generate a price. This use of the market notion is a very powerful tool for the economist, as it imposes a discipline on what would otherwise be a rather chaotic set of information. The great advantage of the market concept is that it can be used in situations other than the popular concept of an exchange of goods for money. This idea will be used as a unifying theme throughout this chapter.

The chapter starts with a discussion of the development of a basic economic model of consumer choice and leisure activity production. This is then used to examine the impacts which such decisions will have on both the inputs and outputs of such leisure activity. Such an approach enables both the detailed discussion of the economic nature of household leisure activity and consideration of the wider implications for labor markets, leisure goods markets, leisure facilities, and the overall impact of leisure on the economy as a whole. The chapter introduces the language often used by economists, with a brief explanation of terms. The purpose is to show how economic concepts have been, and can be, used as a means of understanding the entire concept of leisure more fully and to provide a link between economic theories and practical problems in leisure.

There are six sections to the chapter. Following an outline of a basic economic approach to leisure, five extensions are considered which define the various impacts on the labor market, on leisure goods, on the environment, on the organization of leisure activity, and on the economy as a whole.

HOUSEHOLD LEISURE CHOICE AND PRODUCTION

Modern analysis of the household activity structure rests on the formal model of time allocation proposed by Becker (1965) and since refined by others (DeSerpa 1971; Evans 1972; Gronau 1977). Becker started with the standard economic model of consumer choice. This allocates a given scarce resource (a money budget) between alternative goods, each of which generates some positive satisfaction or welfare to the individual (usually called utility). Becker's contribution was to examine what happens if a further resource, time, is added to this. This requires each of the consumed goods to have both a money price and a time price. Manipulation of the relationship between the two constraints yields not only an optimal allocation of the two resources, money and time, between activities, but also an implied trade-off between the two. The rate at which time is implicitly traded for money is typically referred to as the value of time, but is more correctly interpreted as a marginal price of time, or value of time savings (i.e. the rate at which an individual will pay money to save time or sacrifice time to save money).

It would be wrong to assume that this was the first attempt either to consider leisure demands or to attempt to model the use of time. Early socialist writers such as Veblen (1899) and Bukharin (1919) had recognized that the basic neoclassical model of consumer choice, as expounded by such writers as Marshall (1920), was essentially applicable only to those groups in society who were freer than most from the binding constraint of working long hours to maintain subsistence. Only these could be argued to have leisure time. However, even for these groups, it would normally be the money constraint which dominated choice and decision. Later, Linder (1970) was to argue that modern society had made the time constraint much more important than hitherto, with the growth of a "time is money" philosophy at a time when modern technology should actually have been creating more time for leisure pursuits.

Concurrently, confronted with the practical problem of evaluation, Clawson (1959) produced what has come to be the central plank in applied leisure economics, a practical means of estimating the time-money trade-off. Clawson's approach was the essentially practical one of observing the way people traded off access time for recreation participation at given sites. By giving this a money value, derived from the costs of access (money and time), one can infer the price, in terms of money, which individuals would be prepared to pay for a given level of activity. Hence, an implied demand curve can be observed, with all the properties which could be expected from the theoretical demand curve derived from the Becker model. There have been many refinements of the basic Clawson method to make it more applicable, in particular to include more than one facility or activity (Cheshire and Stabler 1976; Common 1973; Mansfield 1971; Vickerman 1974), or congestion in facility usage (Anderson and Bonsor 1974: Walsh, Miller, and Gilliam 1983), but the basic idea has stood the test of time. For a useful review of the Clawson method see Baxter (1979), and for a complete exposition of an extended model see Smith, Desvousges, and McGiveney (1983).

The basic Becker-type model is developed in the same way as any conventional economic model of consumer behavior. It is useful to examine this in order to be able to understand its implications. An individual is assumed to derive utility from consumption, but, in this case, the consumption is of activities rather than just goods. These activities are produced by the individual from a range of inputs, principally conventional goods and the individual's own time. The goods are bought, typically for money at market prices, while the individual's time is traded off against its use in alternative activities, one of which is work. In the simplest case, the amount of work time is fixed and generates a fixed income so that two simple constraints operate, a money budget and a time budget. In more complex cases, the income constraint can itself be made endogenous, since individuals may choose to work more or less. Thus, they can vary the values of both the leisure time constraint and the money budget. This model can also apply to those not working in the labor market for a wage, since they will face restrictions on time available and receive at least an implicit income — usually with no trade-off possible (see the evidence presented by Bella and Glyptis in this book).

Thus, formally, we can write the individual's utility function as:

$$U = U(A_1, A_2, \ldots \ldots A_n) \tag{1}$$

where any one activity A_i is defined by:

$$A_i = f_i(x_i, t_i) \tag{2}$$

in which the x_i are the goods used in that activity and t_i is the required time. The individual is then assumed to maximize objective (1) subject to the "production function" constraint of (2) and the overall resource constraints (3) and (4):

$$\sum_i p_i \, x_i = Y \tag{3}$$

$$\sum_i t_i = T - W \tag{4}$$

Equation (3) is a budget constraint in which expenditure cannot exceed income, where the p_i are the money prices of goods and Y is the given money budget. Saving and dissaving are not allowed here, but could easily be incorporated. Equation (4) is a time constraint which clearly is not variable, where T is the total amount of time available (say 24 hours or 168 hours, depending on the appropriate decision period for analysis) and W is the number of hours spent working (i.e. committed to activities other than discretionary leisure).

The solution to the above problem has a familiar form to the economist. Maximizing equation (1) subject to constraints (2), (3), and (4) implies rewriting the problem as:

$$\begin{aligned} V &= U(A_1 \ldots A_n) - \lambda \left(\sum p_i x_i - Y \right) - \mu \left(\sum t_i - T + W \right) \\ &= U'(x_1 \ldots x_m, t_1 \ldots t_m) - \lambda \left(\sum p_i x_i - Y \right) - \mu \left(\sum t_i - T + W \right) \end{aligned} \tag{5}$$

where λ and μ are constants (Lagrangean multipliers). This gives a set of first-order conditions. These imply the optimal allocation of the two resources between activities in terms of their marginal utilities (the increase in "utility" from consuming an extra "unit" of one activity as given in Equation(1)). Expenditure is allocated between activities such that the marginal utility gained by spending an extra unit of each resource in each activity is equated. This gives us for the money constraint:

$$\frac{\delta U_i}{\delta U_j} = \frac{p_i}{p_j} \tag{6}$$

where δU_i is the marginal utility of x_1, i.e. $\delta U / \delta x_i$.

And

$$\frac{\delta U}{\delta t_i} = \frac{\delta U}{\delta t_j} = \mu \tag{7}$$

where μ measures rate of change of U as we relax constraint (4), in effect a marginal utility of increasing available time. An additional condition expresses the relative marginal utility from a relaxation of each resource constraint and hence gives us a money price of time:

$$\frac{\delta U/\delta x_i}{\delta U/\delta t_i} = \frac{\lambda p_i}{\mu} \tag{8}$$

This implies a price of time equal to μ/λ where λ is the marginal utility of money and p_i serves as a numeraire price of goods. These sets of conditions determine the optimal allocation of given resources between goods, and hence we can derive conventional demand curves for goods and for time in terms of prices, the value of time and income:

$$x_i = g(p_i \ldots p_m, \mu/\lambda, Y) \tag{9}$$

For a given price, we thus have an optimal (in terms of an individual's preferences and constraints) level of demand, demand being defined as a willingness and ability to pay for a given level of goods or quantity of activity.

There are certain restrictions with the above model which require some modification. First, it implies both that the value of time is constant over all activities and that it is possible to make a smooth and continuous substitution of time for goods. Both of these seem unlikely and unrealistic. The simplest way of dealing with this is to specify a minimum time input for an activity as a techno-logical constraint:

$$t_i \geq \alpha_i x_i \tag{10}$$

which will limit this substitution and make time specific to each activity. However, this is not a completely satisfactory specification, because it still implies that goods are specific to activities, activity i has one set of goods associated with it x_i and these x_i are only used in the production of A_i. It does, however, allow for activities where the only expenditure on goods is that incurred in reaching the location where it takes place and that consumed during the activity. For example, travel to a theme park and the cost of admission and ice cream are highly activity specific. It does not allow for easy application where more than one activity may be undertaken as part of one journey (unless we redefine the activity accordingly) and particularly does not allow for the use of goods which can be reused. Thus, such a formulation requires different clothes for tennis and squash; or even, to be strictly pedantic, new clothes for every new game played! This is clearly unsatisfactory, and hence we need to respecify equation (2) as:

$$A_i = f_i(x_1, \ldots \ldots x_m, t_i) \tag{2}$$

where $(x_1. \ldots \ldots x_m)$ represents a complete basket of all goods. Further discussion of this is delayed until later in this chapter.

The availability of time is also unsatisfactory in the initial specification, since it implies: (a) that a given fixed time is available for leisure; (b) that the utility derived from leisure activities cannot be compared to that derived from work; and (c) that the individual does not have the option of sacrificing time for more income if that can be used to buy more goods and, hence, of changing the activity-producing technology used in (2') to one which is less time-intensive. The latter process is, however, common. Domestic household appliances are often purchased to free more time from essential domestic pursuits in non-work time, although it has been pointed out that maintenance of such machines can itself absorb time whilst they may also imply the substitution of cheap domestic labor for expensive market labor, thus reducing the leisure time of certain household members (Gershuny 1978). Faster means of transport are used either to reduce the travel time input to the activity or to open up a wider range of possible destinations. This question will be examined more fully in the following section.

Even with a fuller description of time-goods substitution and work-leisure substitution, there remain some further areas for exploration. What happens, for example, when the goods inputs are not efficiently priced by the market? Monopoly influences may lead to a deviation of prices from true resource costs. Further examples of market failure involve the presence of externalities, or public or merit goods aspects, which lead to the deviation of the perceived "private" price for the individual from the true cost to society. The classic problem here is that of congestion, either during access to a leisure facility or during the activity itself. Here, one person's consumption of an activity interferes with that of another. This either changes the time price of the activity, or simply reduces utility through a change in the perceived nature of the output — as in the case of wilderness recreation where solitude is an asset. In other cases, positive utility may be generated by interactions with others: crowded discos and full concert halls change the entire experience.

Thus, the basic economic model appears to be subject to some very severe limitations in terms of its assumptions. It is, nevertheless, like all economic models, extremely powerful in its ability both to yield important implications and to form the basis of an empirical model (Vickerman 1975). The various extensions proposed do not, however, alter the fundamental proposition of an optimal allocation. Before looking at these extensions, it is useful to explore just how far the basic model can be developed. The power of the Becker model lies in its ability, with fairly minimal assumptions about human behavior, to generate a set of observable relationships. The usual way of expressing these is in terms of the demand curve, which highlights the essential economic relationship between a quantity and a price. There may be difficulties in interpreting both of these indicators, as will be discussed in later sections, but both are present in all economic relationships.

Using this underlying notion of consumer behavior, demand relationships have been estimated for a wide range of activities. Some studies have concentrated on the activity, considering frequency of participation as the basic indicator (see the general discussions in Gershuny 1983, Patmore 1983, and Veal 1980). Others have concentrated on the facility where the activity takes place (e.g. Burt and Brewer 1971; Cesario and Knetsch 1976), examining particularly any spatial element involved in the activity; the spatial interaction models discussed in the chapter by Smith can be derived from these fundamental utility maximization hypotheses of behavior. Most of these studies look at single activities, or single facilities, in a partial equilibrium framework. They assume, therefore, that income and all other prices, except for the activity, in question are given such that equation (9) becomes just $x_i = g_i (p_i)$. This does not allow for the ways in which changes affecting one activity may affect others and, through a general equilibrium process, the initial activity (Vickerman 1974; but see Cicchetti, Seneca, and Davidson 1969). This last point is a problem in empirical studies of leisure, since many activities are particularly closely related through either strong substitutability (undertaking one normally precludes another) or strong complementarity (activities are often undertaken either together or attract similar people).

What these studies tell us is that leisure activities tend to display many similarities in terms of their demand characteristics. There are activities that are more income-constrained and those which are more time-constrained. These constraints will vary with income and social status, such that the income elasticities of demand for different activities will be very different. They also give us considerable information about price elasticities, which are useful in determining the effects of transport improvements, in determining optimal locations for facilities, and in assessing the scope for alternative pricing policies for the use of such facilities. As well as the cross-sectional information about different activities and facilities implicit in the above, there are also potential explanations of time series trends in participation in activities and in the use of specific facilities.

Economic studies of consumer behavior do not only have the positive purpose of yielding sets of quantified demand relationships. They also have the normative objective of evaluating these in terms of individual welfare. Since the demand relationships derive from an explicit utility formulation governing consumer behavior, one can also infer the extent to which changes in the arguments (i.e. the causal variables) of any demand relationship (income, price, time price, etc.) will affect not just levels of consumption but also the value of that consumption. This recognizes, for example, that increases in consumption at the margin are not necessarily valued equally with the consumption of existing units. Such an exercise is particularly important where, in the cases of market failure discussed earlier, either the price mechanism is not an efficient allocator of resources (and hence non-pecuniary benefits form a large share of total benefits) or where one is dealing with demands for a public-good type of resource which is available as a free-good to potential users.

Assessment of social benefit, and also by implication social costs where there are negative external effects, has become one of the main uses of economics in leisure studies. To some extent, it could be argued that this has hindered the development of a more satisfactory conceptual and theoretical basis for this appraisal, since the requirement has too often been just for a quantification, however simplistic the underlying basis of that quantification may be. The assessment of social benefit has centered around two key values implicit in individual behavior, those of time and congestion. Much of the early work on recreation concentrated on outdoor, countryside, or wilderness recreation, in which these two values play a key part. The pressure on natural resources which derived from increased mobility and accessibility to the countryside in Britain and many other countries in the 1960s led to greater demands for justifying transport infrastructure on the basis of leisure traffic. Similarly, the recognition that major water resource and hydro-electric schemes also had tremendous recreational potential which could both generate new demands and disturb traditional uses of the countryside led to a further need for quantification and evaluation, as seen in many of the classic studies on both sides of the Atlantic.

At the same time, the limits of the strictly partial approach which the Clawson method provided became apparent. It was no longer clear whether new facilities were creating totally new demands or were, to a large extent, simply diverting a given total level of traffic away from existing facilities. This diversion could also have both positive and negative elements for the existing facilities. Moreover, if as a result of improved access, individuals were perceived to be spending the same (or even longer) times in gaining access to more remote sites, how could benefits be assessed from a model which presumed that time was a scarce resource? The use of such a resource should presumably be minimized whenever possible, especially when used in seemingly wasteful activities such as transport. Some of the explanation naturally lay in the intrinsic characteristics of the facilities, which neither price nor access costs would reflect. Such characteristics could be extremely difficult to measure objectively, although some studies have attempted to do this. For wilderness recreation, for example, it has been suggested that congestion at the facility, as measured by encounters, would give an appropriate indication (Cicchetti and Smith 1976).

This raises the basic definitional problem as to what constitutes an activity. Since part of wilderness recreation as an activity is the enjoyment of a unique wilderness experience, wilderness areas are, in one sense, not close substitutes for one another. On the other hand, swimming pools, badminton or tennis courts are likely to be much closer substitutes. The problem is, therefore, how to specify the choice set of activities in the first place, since this will typically affect the nature of the answer. One solution is to use the slightly different approach to the problem suggested by Lancaster (1966), which formulates the consumer's problem as one of choosing an optimal set of quantities of characteristics of goods and activities. In other words, instead of aggregating goods into activities, as in the Becker model, goods and activities are decomposed into a (smaller) set of characteristics. The "production technology" is then concerned with the ways in which different goods and activities combine these attributes rather than how goods and time enter into activity production.

Such an approach does have limitations, since it is not clear that consumers always have such good and unambiguous knowledge of this technology, especially for normal goods purchases. (Critics of the approach have suggested that oranges are oranges and apples are apples, although avid readers of the labels detailing the contents of chocolate bars may be getting close to being true Lancastrian consumers, and television advertisers clearly differentiate their otherwise identical soap powders and hamburgers by appealing to some particular variation in the ingredients or in the method of preparation). However, for leisure activities, it may offer a useful way forward, since the variations in technology are often greater and the nature of the consumer as producer means that the level of awareness is considerably higher.

What has been developed, therefore, is a fairly powerful way of both describing the structure of consumers' demands for leisure activities and making evaluations of changes in key "price" parameters. However, the limit of the application of such a model is found essentially in the impact on demands for single facilities for single activities, and their evaluation. The purpose of the remainder of this chapter is to extend this impact in various directions, as a prelude to an assessment of total economic impact.

LEISURE AND THE LABOR MARKET

Perhaps the most basic economic interest in leisure stems from leisure as the antithesis of work. The supply of labor effort is often characterized as the demand for leisure. This interest parallels that of other social science disciplines, for which the relationship between work and leisure has often been seen as critical to an understanding of the role of leisure in society. (We shall need, however, to take into account the criticisms that this limits a model of leisure to a minority group in society, possibly the employed adult male: cf. the chapters by Stockdale, Bella, Glyptis and others in this book).

It has already been suggested that the basic Becker model of time allocation can be modified to incorporate work, and hence income, as choice variables. This produces a slightly elaborated version of much earlier attempts to produce a supply of labor relationship using leisure time in the aggregate as one argument of the utility function (Robbins 1930). The critical interest of the labor economist in this was to determine under what circumstances individuals would respond to rising hourly wage rates by increasing work effort and hence generate the expected upward sloping supply curve of labor effort. It is relatively easy to show, however, that if leisure has a strong positive income effect (the higher the income the greater the demand for leisure time) then, even though it becomes more expensive (in the sense that the opportunity cost of foregone income rises as wage rates rise), people consume more leisure as their income rises (see Bosworth and Dawkins 1981, for a general discussion). Which of these outcomes is the more likely depends on the relative strengths of these income and substitution effects (the tendency to substitute cheaper things for dearer ones), and that is an empirical rather than a theoretical result (Brown, Levin, and Ulph 1976; Frost and Jamal 1979; Gronau 1977; McEvoy 1974).

This work-leisure trade-off model depends on the extent to which individuals are free to choose working hours. A common criticism is that many individuals may not be able to vary their hours of work at all (except possibly in the discrete amounts provided for by overtime working). A further group of salaried workers will often receive no variation in remuneration (at least in the short term) for working longer hours. However, if individuals were forced permanently into non-optimal choices by such constraints, they could be expected either to change employment, or even choose unemployment, as alternatives. The model is useful in explaining certain other labor market phenomena.

The pressure for changes in working hours obviously derives from this suppressed demand for additional leisure time, and this has been a recurrent theme in labor negotiations over several decades. The fact that actual hours of work have changed relatively little over this period (as regular time has been replaced by overtime at higher rates of pay) is, of course, a clear demonstration of the balance between income and substitution effects at work (see Bosworth and Dawkins 1981). As society has become richer and the range of leisure opportunities expanded, a higher compensation is required at the margin for foregoing leisure time. This is, of course, different from the frequent finding that people would prefer more leisure. At any given wage rate they would prefer a relaxation of the time constraint, but what they are not prepared to do is buy it at the expense of the income to enjoy consumption in that leisure time.

Second, absenteeism has also a close relationship to wage rates. There is evidence that absenteeism declines towards the end of a pay contract as the demand for income rises. After the start of a new contract with higher wage rates, absenteeism rises as individuals find it easier to achieve their previous target income. Rising expectations and increased consumption needs gradually reduce the absenteeism as individuals adjust to the new relaxed income constraint (Handy 1968).

Perhaps a more serious criticism, however, is the way the demands for leisure time are interpreted. It is not clear that workers can ever appreciate marginal amounts of time. Indeed, it could be argued that the lack of any significant fall in actual weekly hours of work has occurred because negotiated reductions of two or two and a half hours a week (less than half an hour a day, typically) are of little use, especially as commuting times have often increased. This brings us back to the technological constraints on the use of time which require minimum inputs of time. What is significant is the fall in annual hours of work, as increasingly long paid holidays have become the norm, and the major switches from six- to five-day working weeks (or even less). This releases time in useful amounts which can be invested in high time-using activities. By virtue of their time intensity, these were previously seriously constrained, and hence very high marginal utilities are gained.

Discussion of this issue of useful (or useable) time highlights the problem of the non-transferability of time *through time* and, hence, the key question of scheduling activities optimally. This is a question which will be addressed further, below, where problems of queuing and reservation systems are discussed in more detail. Since a very large part of the discretionary time input into the work activity is associated with commuting, there are also strong incentives for economizing on travel time and combining activities. The growth of recreational activities, particularly sports facilities, in central city areas demonstrates this, but, of course, requires that such facilities should have efficient reservation systems.

A further, and more problematic, area of leisure-work relationships arises in what may be termed the maintenance of human capital. Human capital theories (the development of which is also strongly linked with the work of Becker) attempt to show the way in which individuals take a longer time horizon in their consumption decisions, recognizing that they do not simply sell their labor services as consumable items. Skill acquisition and on-the-job training are important elements in determining the lifetime value of those labor services, which will, in turn, affect the potential for lifetime consumption. The major element in the development of human capital is clearly the process of education and skill acquisition, such that individuals can rationally abstain from current consumption and receive lower wage levels whilst training because of the incentives of an enhanced income and consumption stream in the future. This can also influence location decisions and, hence, migration (Sjaastad 1962).

Individuals may also use their future earning potential as security for borrowing to finance this training and, thus, maintain consumption at a higher level than would otherwise be possible.

It is not just a question of investing in human capital, however, but also one of maintaining that capital. Certain activities in non-work time, such as sleeping, eating, and personal hygiene, are clearly ways of maintaining human capital. Time spent on such activities is traditionally excluded from definitions of leisure time, since it is committed rather than available for discretionary allocation. Nevertheless, not all the time spent sleeping, eating, and washing is necessary for maintaining human capital. Indeed, an excess of any of these could actually be injurious to health. There is, therefore, considerable difficulty in determining how much time is essential to the maintenance of a given level of human capital (and, thus, not available for leisure activities) and how much of this time can actually be combined with leisure activities as a jointly produced activity. Many city executives may claim that their daily jogging routine is a purely human capital maintenance activity. The later (and longer) business lunch could be claimed to be a purely leisure activity. In both cases, however, there will usually be some joint production which is difficult to resolve in terms of our basic model (for some evidence see Bassey and Fentem 1981; Department of Health and Social Security 1976).

What has been developed in this section is a number of ideas about the relationship between work and leisure. This is not just the direct choice between one and the other as totally separate entities, but also the interrelationship between them when we investigate further the ideas of committed and discretionary time. Leisure activities may be chosen to enhance the quality of the output of work activities and vice versa. Leisure activities are not just about time, however. There is also a need to look at other inputs; this is the subject of the following section.

LEISURE GOODS MARKETS

One of the fastest growing market sectors in recent years has been that for leisure goods. Some estimates suggest that in the UK this sector accounts for some 25 to 30 percent of all consumer expenditure (Martin and Mason 1984), and has been growing at around 5 percent a year. These figures are only estimates, since it has traditionally been extremely difficult to distinguish the true leisure elements in certain sectors from expenditures essential to the maintenance of human capital (transport, clothing and food being the key examples; see Martin and Mason 1979, for a discussion; also, Henley Centre for Forecasting 1986, for a detailed analysis of expenditure on sport). Forecasting the demand for such goods does, however, require that one take a more detailed look at the structure of leisure activity production. One needs to consider not just the overall demand for the activity, which may be a simple function of income and total prices as for conventional goods, but also the possibilities of techno-logical substitution in production. This substitution may be one of goods for goods, or one of goods for another input, such as time.

It is quite possible for an activity to be normal, in the usual economic sense that it displays a positive income elasticity of demand, whilst the demand for a particular input displays a negative income effect. A simple example of this is the goods-for-time substitution which arises with increasing income as the time constraint becomes more significant. Richer people tend to indulge in more goods-intensive activities. This is particularly true of home leisure activities. Increased demands for domestic appliances, such as washing machines and dishwashers, reflect a desire to economize on time inputs into essential non-work activities used mainly for the maintenance of human capital (though noting that this may for some simply shift time to the maintenance of the appliances). More recent developments have been video recorders and mobile telephones, which assist in the scheduling of leisure activities through time.

Goods for goods substitution can occur in a number of ways. The use of better (i.e. more goods-intensive) equipment can increase the efficiency of many active leisure pursuits, especially sports. A particularly common example of a slightly different sort of purchased input being substituted is the use of more expensive private sports or leisure facilities instead of public ones, again to economize on the increasingly valuable time input, with its logical conclusion in the swimming pool or tennis court at home.

Recent trends in both general leisure, and most particularly sports, suggest a growth in activities which have much larger goods input requirements. These goods are both those provided by the individual, such as clothing and specialist equipment, and facilities provided by either the public or private sectors. Hence, in sports like skiing or sailboarding, the consumer has to equip himself or herself with specialist clothing and either buy or rent equipment. Launching facilities, ski-lifts, and associated capital equipment are also required, plus capital to provide rental of equipment to casual users. This has changed the nature of the way in which leisure and sport are provided, from an essentially casual nature to a much higher level of organization which is generally much more capitalized.

This section has examined the way in which leisure goods relate to the consumer's decision about leisure activities, but stresses the resulting impor-tance of leisure goods markets and the changes in such markets brought about by changes in consumers' preferences. This has an importance for commercial forecasting and for understanding the role of such industries in the economy as a whole. However, there is a further consideration, the extent to which the commercial provision of the services of the leisure goods industries relate to public provision of other inputs. These externality and public goods aspects of leisure are developed in the following section.

LEISURE, EXTERNALITIES, AND THE ENVIRONMENT

Externalities, both positive and negative, have always played a strong role in the economic analysis of leisure. Much of the work on the economic impact of leisure (and especially of recreation) has centered on an evaluation of such externalities, principally environmental ones. The problem here is the interrelationship of individual leisure or recreation decision making with a further set of inputs into the leisure experience, which are typically not capable of being provided by a free market. Hence, one faces either arguments in favor of increasing participation because of public goods or merit goods, or the argument for restricting participation because of congestion or pollution. In both cases, what is being said is that the effective price of the input to the user of the resource differs from the true opportunity cost of that resource to society.

The public/merit good argument suggests that the market price of inputs (e.g. the cost of admission to a swimming pool or sports center) would be too high and, hence, lead to levels of participation in the activity below that which would be socially desirable. Public goods are usually defined as being non-competitive and non-excludable — that is, they are not used up by any one person consuming them and individuals cannot be excluded by, for example, a price mechanism. Pure public goods are difficult to identify, but uncongested open-access recreation facilities and clean air have strong elements of publicness about them. Merit goods, on the other hand, are those for which increased consumption by any one individual benefits society as a whole. Basic education and public health are good examples, as may be increased participation in sport or recreation (see Schreyer and Driver, this volume, for further discussion of benefits).

This notion of social desirability poses problems, since it requires the making of interpersonal comparisons of welfare and the aggregation of society's preferences from those of individuals. It may be possible to obtain some hard evidence relating to this question. For example, a typical argument for increasing participation in active sports is a medical one: greater fitness implies fewer deaths, fewer working days lost and the like, all of which have a directly measurable economic cost (Bassey and Fentem 1981; Sports Council 1982). It is also a distributive argument, however, that high participation fees discriminate against poorer groups in society. Since direct income subsidies to the poor might be spent on other goods, indirect action through prices is often thought preferable. The problem here is that such an approach often fails to identify the way leisure activities are produced, such that there may be difficulties in effecting the sort of substitution implied. This contrasts with the case of subsidizing final goods which feature directly in an individual's utility function.

This notion of the structure of production of leisure activities has been most fully worked out by Knapp and Vickerman (1985) and Vickerman (1985). A careful distinction needs to be made between the final output of the activity and these intermediate outputs. The latter are those in which participation is typically measured, such as the use of a sports center or admission to an outdoor recreational facility, but these strictly speaking are only inputs to the final activity's production. It is the final activity which generates utility to the consumer, produced by combining the intermediate outputs with other factors such as the consumer's own time and skill. The critical issue here is the extent to which the final consumer can substitute between these intermediate outputs without changing the welfare content of the final output.

One specific issue which has rightly received considerable attention is the question of congestion, since this clearly has important repercussions both on the way an activity is chosen to be produced (i.e. production technology) and on the final production of welfare (the consumer's utility). More directly, it raises the difficult issue of the optimal management of a facility which suffers congestion, as well as the appropriate pricing strategy and its distributional implications. The economic significance of congestion is that, while an individual can perceive the direct personal costs of congestion in increased time spent on the activity or simply in reduced enjoyment and, hence, alter production and consumption patterns accordingly, what the individual does not perceive is the increased cost imposed on other consumers of the resource. Any increase in demand for a given resource with a given capacity will lead to an increase in the effective cost not only to the marginal user, but also to all existing intra-marginal users. Hence, the marginal social cost is greater than the marginal private cost. The demand curve perceived by the individual can be thought of as a "constant crowding demand curve," *ccdc* (Anderson and Bonsor 1974; Dorfman 1984), in which the individual evaluates consumption decisions as if congestion remained constant. As can be seen from Figure 1, the observed demand curve will tend to imply a higher level of aggregate benefit (consumers' surplus) than does the constant crowding curve at any level of demand.

This raises difficulties for the management of such facilities, since a given level of prices set according to observed demand and supply conditions may lead to unexpected changes in demand. For example, consider an increase in capacity from S_1 to S_2 in the diagram. The observed demand curve suggests a price of p_2 as an equilibrium price. However, at price p_2, assuming constant crowding, demand actually increases to D_2, leading to excessive attempted use, a shift downward in the ccdc to $ccdc_2$ and, hence, aggregate benefits less than were to be expected.

There is a further issue to be considered here, however. Queuing, which implies an increase in the time devoted to an activity, rather like that involved in congestion, may actually be used as an allocational device because of the distributional implications of direct pricing. This, again, may lead to problems, because of the implicit view that it is the resource being allocated which is the object of final consumption. The use of queues as an allocational device has been analyzed for the general case of merit goods such as health care (Barzel 1974; Bucovetsky 1984; Nicholls, Smolensky, and Tideman 1971). Here, the

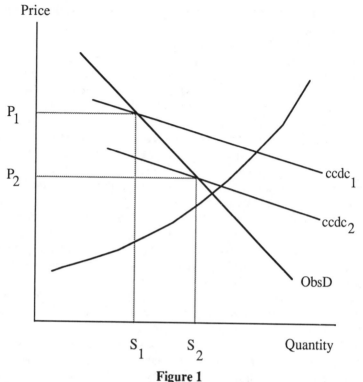

Figure 1
Effects of Congestion on Consumer's Demand for Leisure

allocational principle is that, because the poor have a lower marginal value of time but a severer financial constraint, allocation by waiting is more equitable than by price. Since the rich, with a higher marginal value of time, will be penalized by this, they will seek alternative sources of supply, where price is used as an allocator (i.e. a parallel private market). This has the double advantage of concentrating lower priced facilities on those groups who need them most and of simultaneously reducing the implicit supply price to them by reducing the length of queues. This is an outcome rather like the effects of hard currency shops in Eastern European countries.

Applying this approach to leisure raises a number of further questions, however. Barzel (1974) has pointed out that, where the income elasticity of demand for an activity is (numerically) greater than the price elasticity (which is frequently the case with leisure activities requiring high usage of intermediate goods), the demand will increase more rapidly with income than does the value of time. Hence, the implicit time price of the waiting does not increase rapidly enough to ration demand by those with the fastest growing incomes, who can, thereby, exclude the poor. Second, there is the question of whether queuing time can be resold. Clearly, for most personal services, it is the recipient of the service who has to do the queuing, unlike, for example, the situation in an economy with general rationing, where the "professional queuer" may occur, plus a differential price for gaining access to the parallel market such as with a currency black market. However, there may be an intermediate stage to this, where a booking or reservation system is used to allocate facility time, but where the booking has to be done in person on a first-come first-served basis. Here, there is clearly scope for trading the time in the queue. Third, and of greatest complexity, is the fact that, in many leisure activities, there is no fixed consumption time; hence, waiting time and activity time may be tradeable. Many swimming pools, for example, ration time spent in the water as an alternative to the development of either long queues at the entrance or congestion in the water. Other facilities which have several uses may schedule them at busy times for use only by large groups, regardless of the actual benefits likely to be achieved.

It is in this area of leisure economics and management that much needs to be done to improve the allocational efficiency of the resources which go into the production of leisure activities. A prerequisite to such an improvement is much more research on this aspect.

ORGANIZING LEISURE: THE ROLE OF EFFICIENCY AND INFORMATION

The preceding sections have emphasized the importance of understanding the way in which leisure activities are produced. As in most economics, the assumption has been made that individuals have perfect information, so that they can do this in the most efficient way. The fact that they do not have such perfect information leads to a further important market area, the market for information itself. This has two principal consequences — a need for education and a role for the organizational structure within which these activities take place.

The role of education clearly overlaps in significance the question of external effects discussed in the preceding section, since one of the most important roles of education is in enhancing awareness of the significance of leisure activity itself and its role as a utility generator (Vickerman 1980). In its most general sense, this is the role of "Sport for All" and similar campaigns. However, there is a more subtle way in which education can be used to increase productivity and efficiency in the use of leisure resources. This is a question both of matching specific skills to specific activities and of increasing awareness of alternative means of producing a given activity. The latter of these is often the role of both continuing education (adult education is dominated by classes in essentially leisure-based activities) and the media. The former has some more interesting connotations, since it can be related also to the assessment of the total economic impact of sport through sporting success.

This raises the question as to whether a goal of policy should be to identify potential sporting superstars and invest heavily in them because of the way their success can lead to productivity increases by others for reasons of prestige. This effect has been noted, at least apocryphally, at both local and national levels, and lies behind both the great investment in sport generally in Eastern European countries and the rise of particular sports following local successes: ice skating in the UK and tennis in West Germany are good recent examples of this.

The market for organization in leisure activities is possibly of even greater significance, especially for those activities which require both large intermediate goods inputs of facility resources and large inputs of individual time: that is, resource intensive activities. The former of these will typically be managed by the organization controlling the facility which will have some concept of timetabling use to maximize some objective, whether this is profit for a private sector interest or some notion of weighted participation or usage in the case of a public sector resource. The latter we have already met to some extent in the context of congestion and queuing. But there is a further dimension to this which is caused by the interdependence of different individuals' utility functions in the case of leisure. Here, the utility derived by one individual is not just a function of prices and income but additionally of the utility of another individual or group of individuals. While economists normally like to steer clear of inter-personal factors in consumption, it is obvious that very large numbers of leisure activities are not only *not* undertaken alone, but the degree of satisfaction obtained depends critically on producing the activity jointly with others. The most obvious case which we have met earlier is that of household decision making.

This jointness in production between producers can be thought of as another intermediate good in which the services of another person — time, skill, and so on — are a critical input to the production process. What it also suggests, however, is that, often, considerable energy must be spent on coordinating these inputs, which are neither available on an open market nor under the direct control of the individual. This may be one reason for the growth of voluntary organizations, such as sports clubs, which serve the function of bringing people together and act as a screening device (see Bishop and Hoggett 1986, on the voluntary sector in leisure; and Stiglitz 1975, for a general discussion of screening).

AGGREGATE ECONOMIC IMPACT OF LEISURE

The previous sections have concentrated on explaining the ways in which leisure activities interact with other activities and with resources. The remaining task is to look at the aggregate effect which such interactions have, as a guide to a measure of the total impact of the leisure sector on the economy as a whole, at both local and national levels.

The conventional way of looking at economic impact is the rather narrow one, used in most cost-benefit studies, of simply trying to derive a measure of total user benefits and non-user or external effects. There is usually little examination of the origin of the external effects and hence of the basis for evaluation. This is considered simply in terms of total expenditure, or even just direct employment creation, which then has a multiplier effect in that each additional job or unit of expenditure will create demand and, hence, further jobs or expenditure (for a general introduction to local multiplier studies, see Armstrong and Taylor 1985).

User benefits are assessed by aggregation of consumer's surplus over all users. Consumer's surplus is the benefit that a consumer derives from undertaking an activity at a given price, which is below the price that he or she would be prepared to pay. In diagrammatic terms, it is the area under the demand curve above the market price (ABC in Figure 2). Algebraically, it is found by integrating a demand curve, such as equation (9), over the relevant range.

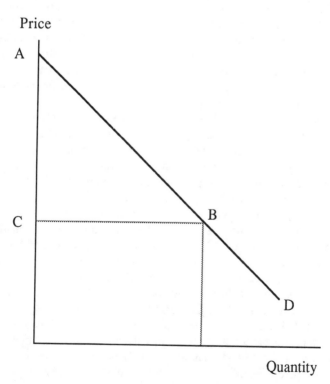

Figure 2
Consumer's Surplus as a Measure of User Benefit

The multiplier is a measure of the way any direct injection of new expenditure or employment into an economy leads to additional rounds of expenditure and/or employment creation, as the recipients of the initial injection spend their increased incomes. Consider, for example, the income generated by a given injection of new expenditure, E. The expenditure starts off an increase in the incomes of those employed in the sector. Some of this initial injection will not be spent on consumption in the region; either it will leak into savings or it will leak out of the immediate region or country as it is spent on imports. At each succeeding round, the effect reduces and the total income and/or employment created is a finite multiple of the initial injection. The size of this multiplier is critical, and depends principally on the size of the leakages. If we write the propensity to consume out of income as c and the propensity to import out of consumption as m then the total increase in income can be written as:

$$Y = \frac{1}{1 - c\,(1 - m)}\;E$$

where the fraction 1/1 - c(1-m) is the multiplier. Hence the propensity to spend of the initial recipients of the increase in income, and where they choose to spend it, are key determinants. Since smaller regions will have greater leakages by definition, local multipliers are usually much smaller than national multipliers. This is only a simple example of the formulation of the multiplier; there is a large literature on the multiplier concept and on good and bad practice in its application which will not be developed further here (cf. Sinclair and Sutcliffe 1982, for a useful discussion in the context of tourism).

As well as assessing the total impact of specific projects or changes in leisure provision, it is also becoming increasingly important to have some measure of the aggregate economic impact of leisure and its main components, such as sport or outdoor recreation. It can be seen from the preceding sections that leisure and recreation have a pervasive influence on a wide range of human activities and, hence, on human economic welfare. Because much of this is not conducted through markets which provide a direct economic valuation, or because even where they do exist, such market evaluations are often inadequate or inappropriate, there is no readily available measure of the size of the leisure sector which can be derived from national accounting procedures. Various attempts have been made to extract the measurable elements to provide such an estimate (see, for example the estimates for the UK by Martin and Mason 1979; and for sport alone in the UK by the Henley Centre for Forecasting 1986). One of the principal difficulties is that large elements of recreation do not appear anywhere in national accounting procedures, the operation of the large voluntary sector in leisure being a good example of this. These studies have suggested that around 20-22 percent of all consumer expenditure is on leisure activities. The detailed study of sport by the Henley Centre (1986) suggests that consumers' expenditure on sport alone (including gambling) could have been as much as £4.4bn in 1985. Adding other expenditure, such as direct government expenditure, investment and exports, would raise this to £5.4bn, or 1.2 percent of total final expenditure. As a "product," therefore, consumers are spending about as much on sport as they do on furniture or bread. As an industry, value-added by sport-related activity (£4.1bn) is larger than that of motor vehicles and parts (£3.6bn) or clothing and footwear (£2.9bn). Similarly, total employment of 376,000 compares with 352,000 in chemicals and 336,000 in agriculture, forestry, and fishing.

Such figures are cautious estimates, but they do give some indication of the potential direct economic importance of one small part of the leisure and recreation sector. One difficulty to be faced is that of defining the leisure components of the expenditures surveyed, since, as we have already seen, it may be difficult to identify the true leisure (discretionary time) expenditures on many activities from that which is thought necessary for human capital maintenance. This returns us to an old question, the extent to which leisure is a substitute for, or a complement to, work.

CONCLUSIONS

Although this has been a fairly wide-ranging examination of the fundamental economic aspects of leisure and their likely aggregate impacts, it has not been possible in the space available to give a full account of all of the possible developments, nor of all the quantitative estimates of these effects and impacts. What has been attempted is a coherent account of the way in which economists view leisure and the implications of this for providing sensible answers to the many questions which a consideration of leisure poses as a problem for social scientists.

Since it lies at the base of any consideration of consumers' choice between leisure activities and consequently of economic evaluation, the starting point for this has been the model of consumers' choice. This is the background to understanding the Clawson model and so much of what has been done on the economic evaluation of recreation. However, it has been shown that an economic approach can, and should, go much further than this, to include questions of the supply of work effort, the role of the leisure goods industries, public or private provision of leisure, and the role of education and information, all as part of an overall assessment of the economic role of leisure.

Because the market and its operations lie at the core of an economic treatment of the problem, markets have been used as a unifying theme throughout this chapter. This is not to claim that a *free*-market solution is always believed to be best in dealing with leisure questions, but rather to provide a convenient basis on which to make comparisons. This framework has been used, in particular, to show the way in which consumers' production of leisure activities needs to be broken down into stages of production. This is necessary both to provide a better basis for the *evaluation* of the economic welfare benefits of leisure activities and to understand more clearly which parts of the process can be left to private sector, *market*, provision and which require *public sector* intervention.

The story is far from complete, however. There is still room for considerably more theorizing about the economics of leisure. This involves both the structure of consumers' production of leisure activities, and the production of welfare from them, as well as the vexed question of relating individual behavior to that of households or families, which may be the more appropriate decision-making unit for leisure activities. Such developments may bring economics much closer to the theorizing of other disciplines; these questions are addressed in the chapters by Bella and Glyptis. In the meantime, however, there is still a strong demand for the production of consistent evidence about the role of leisure in the economy and for the evaluation of particular activities or facilities. It is the responsibility of economists to ensure that such empirical studies are based on rigorous theoretical bases and that the results are properly interpreted, since it is such empirical studies which form the basis of leisure investments, and leisure policy, by both private and public sectors.

References

Anderson, F.J. and N.C. Bonsor. 1974. "Allocation, congestion and the valuation of recreational resources." *Land Economics 50:* 51-57.

Armstrong, H. and J. Taylor. 1985. *Regional Economics and Policy.* Oxford: Philip Allan.

Barzel, Y. 1974. "A theory of rationing by waiting." *Journal of Law and Economics 17:* 73-96.

Bassey, E.J. and P. Fentem. 1981. *Exercise: The Facts.* Oxford: Oxford University Press.

Baxter, M.J. 1979. *Measuring the Benefits of Recreational Site Provision: A Review of Techniques Related to the Clawson Method.* London: Sports Council/Social Science Research Council.

Becker, G.S. 1965. "A theory of the allocation of time." *Economic Journal 75:* 493-517.

Bishop, J. and P. Hoggett. 1986. *Organising around Enthusiasms: Mutual Aid in Leisure.* London: Comedia Publishing.

Bosworth, D.L. and P.J. Dawkins. 1981. *Work Patterns: An Economic Analysis.* Aldershot: Gower Press.

Brown, C.E. Levin, and D. Ulph. 1976. "Estimates of labour hours supplied by married male workers in Great Britain." *Scottish Journal of Political Economy* 23: 261-277.

Bucovetsky, S. 1984. "On the use of distributional waits." *Canadian Journal of Economics 17:* 699-717.

Bukharin, N. 1919. *The Economic Theory of the Leisure Class.* London: Lawrence.

Burt, O.R. and D. Brewer. 1971. "Estimation of net social benefit for outdoor recreation." *Econometrica 39:* 813-821.

Cesario, F. and J.L. Knetsch. 1976. "A recreation site demand and benefit estimation model." *Regional Studies 10:* 97-104.

Cheshire, P. and M.J. Stabler. 1976. "Joint consumption benefits in recreational site 'surplus': An empirical estimate." *Regional Studies 10:* 343-352.

Cicchetti, C.J. , J.J. Seneca, and P. Davidson. 1969. *The Demand and Supply of Outdoor Recreation: An Econometric Analysis.* New Brunswick, NJ: Bureau of Economic Research, Rutgers University.

Cicchetti, C.J. and V.K. Smith. 1976. *The Costs of Congestion.* Cambridge, MA: Ballinger.

Clawson, M. 1959. *Methods of Measuring the Demand for and the Value of Outdoor Recreation.* Washington, DC: Resources for the Future.

Common, M.S. 1973. "A note on the use of the Clawson Method for the evaluation of recreational benefits." *Regional Studies 7:* 401-406.

Department of Health and Social Security. 1976. *Prevention and Health: Everybody's Business.* London: H.M.S.O.

DeSerpa, A.C. 1971. "A theory of the economics of time." *Economic Journal 81:* 828-846.

Dorfman, R. 1984. "On optimal congestion." *Journal of Environmental Economics and Management 11:* 91-106.

Evans, A.W. 1972. "On the theory of the valuation and allocation of time." *Scottish Journal of Political Economy 19:* 1-18.

Frost, P.J. and M. Jamal. 1979. "Shiftwork attitudes and reported behaviour: Some associations between individual characteristics and hours of work and leisure." *Journal of Applied Psychology 64:* 77-81.

Gershuny, J. 1978. *After Industrial Society: The Emerging Self-Service Econ omy.* London: Macmillan.

Gershuny, J. 1983. *Social Innovation and the Division of Labour.* Oxford: Oxford University Press.

Gronau, R. 1977. "Leisure, home production and work: The theory of the allocation of time revisited." *Journal of Political Economy 85:* 1099-1123.

Handy, L.J. 1968. "Absenteeism and attendance in the British coal mining industry: An examination of post-war trends." *British Journal of Industrial Relations 6:* 27-50.

Henley Centre for Forecasting. 1986. *The Economic Impact and Importance of Sport in the U.K.* Study 30. London: Sports Council.

Knapp, M.R.J. and R.W. Vickerman. 1985. "The conceptualization of output and cost-benefit analysis for leisure facilities." *Environment and Planning A 17:* 1217-1229.

Lancaster, K. 1966. "A new approach to consumer theory." *Journal of Political Economy 74:* 132-157.

Linder, S.B. 1970. *The Harried Leisure Class.* New York: Columbia University Press.

Mansfield, N.W. 1971. "The estimation of benefits from recreation sites and the provision of a new facility." *Regional Studies 5:* 55-69.

Marshall, A. 1920. *Principles of Economics.* 8th ed. London: Macmillan.

Martin, W.H. and S. Mason. 1979. *Broad Patterns of Leisure Expenditure.* London: Sports Council/Social Science Research Council.

Martin, W.H. and S. Mason. 1984. *A New View of Leisure.* Maastricht: European Centre for Work and Society.

McEvoy, J. 1974. "Hours of work and the demand for outdoor recreation." *Journal of Leisure Research 6:* 125-139.

Nicholls D., E. Smolensky, and T.N. Tideman. 1971. "Discrimination by waiting time in merit goods." *American Economic Review 61:* 312-323.

Patmore, J. A. 1983. *Recreation and Resources: Leisure Patterns and Leisure Places.* Oxford: Blackwell.

Robbins L. 1930. "On the elasticity of demand for income in terms of effort." *Economica 10:* 123-129.

Sinclair, M.T. and C.M.S. Sutcliffe. 1982. "Keynesian income multipliers and first and second round effects: An application to tourist expenditures." *Oxford Bulletin of Economics and Statistics 44:* 321-338.

Sjaastad L.A. 1962. "The costs and returns of human migration." *Journal of Political Economy 70:* 80-93.

Smith V.K., W.H. Desvousges, and M.P. McGiveney. 1983. "The opportunity cost of travel time in recreation demand models." *Land Economics 59:* 259-278.

Sports Council. 1982. *Sport in the Community: The Next Ten Years.* London: Sports Council.

Stiglitz, J. 1975. "The theory of screening, education and the distribution of income." *American Economic Review 65:* 283- 300.

Veal, A.J. 1980. *Trends in Leisure Participation and Problems of Forecasting.* London: Sports Council/Social Science Research Council.

Veblen T. 1899. *The Theory of the Leisure Class.* New York: Viking Press.

Vickerman, R.W. 1974. "The evaluation of benefits from recreational projects." *Urban Studies 11:* 277-288.

Vickerman, R.W. 1975. *The Economics of Leisure and Recreation.* London: Macmillan.

Vickerman, R.W. 1980. "The new leisure society: An economic analysis." *Futures 12:* 191-200.

Vickerman, R.W. 1985. "On output measurement and benefit evaluation in leisure." *Loisir et Société* 8: 485-492.

Walsh, R.G., N.P. Miller, and L.O. Gilliam. 1983. "Congestion and willingness to pay for expansion of skiing capacity." *Land Economics 59:* 195-210.

ENVIRONMENTAL ATTITUDES, VALUES, AND RECREATION

Edgar L. Jackson

In the survey of active leisure and recreation researchers described in the first chapter of this book, and in reply to the question about required future research, one of the respondents made the following observation: "I feel strongly that a major research effort needs to be mounted concerning the 'psychic' experience of recreation and leisure. Fairly recent changes in national purpose and mood — growing materialism, not to mention hedonism — suggest that we know less about how and why people recreate than we think we do." Clearly, the respondent was concerned about the levels of acquisitiveness and materialism in society and their implications for leisure and recreation preferences; he was suggesting the need to investigate people's values and how they influence recreation and leisure. This chapter addresses that issue.

Few attempts have been made to date, however, to assess the role of values in recreation and leisure. Burton's remark (1981: 40) that "the central problem of virtually all recreation forecasting is that it has failed to take account of, or to come to terms with, the notions of individual and societal values, and changes in these," applies as much to recreation and leisure research in general as it does to forecasting.

Researchers have tackled the issue, at least tangentially, by investigating socio-economic variations in participation. Notwithstanding Kelly's reservations (this volume) about the limited explanatory power of socio-economic variables, such variables have often been used as surrogates for values (Burton 1981). But, given the growing complexity of society and the rapidity of social change, traditional socio-economic configurations of values no longer exist to the extent they once did. Socio-economically-defined segments of society are becoming increasingly characterized by an internal diversity of values and attitudes, and less by a shared view of the world. The assumption of a socio-economic consistency of values — and, therefore, recreational lifestyles — is no longer tenable.

Thus, explicit attention to the values that influence recreation choices is required. A research thrust that offers fruitful prospects for investigating values — at least in *outdoor* recreation — is the small body of literature that has focused on the relationship between outdoor recreation participation and environmental attitudes. This literature is summarized and discussed in the first part of this chapter. Then, the framework of the "consumer society" versus the "conserver society" is used as a device to evaluate the recreational implications of competing values. Finally, the chapter concludes with a discussion of some of the practical (especially forecasting) and theoretical implications of research on environmental attitudes, values, and recreation.

RECREATION, TRENDS, AND VALUES

In the last few decades, per capita participation in leisure and recreation activities has grown enormously in the industrialized world. When multiplied by population growth, this increase in total participation can only be described as explosive. Essentially, five factors have been responsible (Sadler 1978): (1) population growth; (2) an increase in the amount of non-work time on a per capita basis; (3) growth in per capita disposable income; (4) increasing mobility; and (5) a change in attitudes and perceptions, stimulated partly by increasing urbanization. Merely to list factors of this sort, however, adds little to our knowledge of recreation behavior or to its planning applications, largely because of uncertainty about how much each will change in the future and about whether or not they will continue to affect patterns of recreation and leisure in similar ways in the future as they have in the past. Researchers and practitioners need to identify a somewhat different set of trends that can help explain present patterns of recreation and forecast future ones. The obviously vast and complex range of specific factors can be reduced to five main influences.

First, the health of the economy translates into the level of employment and per capita disposable income. It therefore affects the amount of leisure time that people have, how they choose to fill it, and how much money is available for leisure pursuits (see both Glyptis and Vickerman, in this volume).

Second, population size, growth rate, and changing structure (especially by age), and patterns of migration and residence are powerful influences on recreation. Other social factors include family structure and household size and composition, each subject to constant, if not precipitous, change (see the chapters by Kelly and Bella, volume).

Third, technological innovations affect people's recreational choices. They do not do this deterministically, but rather in the sense that innovations often create new leisure opportunities, or ameliorate barriers to participation in activities that already exist (see Goodale and Witt's chapter, this volume).

Educational trends are a fourth influence, partly because education helps people make informed choices. Education also shapes values, and thus people's recreational preferences, as well as the tradeoffs that they are willing to make to achieve them.

The fifth factor is political, both in the narrow sense of which political party is in power, and more broadly in the sense that the political arena is the forum within which society's preferences are expressed. Politicians and bureaucrats make decisions about the relative roles of the private and public sectors in the delivery of recreation services and the allocation of financial and natural resources in the public sector. The development or preservation of wilderness, for instance, is a political question with obvious implications for outdoor recreation (Jackson 1987; see also Swinnerton's discussion, this volume).

Each of the preceding trends is ultimately a reflection of individual and societal values. The economy, disposable income, and unemployment are not necessarily the result of uncontrollable forces; they reflect the emphasis that society as a whole places on material consumption, as well as the tension between private well-being and the public good. Social factors, too, reflect values; interpersonal relationships, the importance attached to children and the family, and where and how people choose to live are all matters of values. Technology, perhaps, is less so; technology *per se* is neutral, but the amount, kind, and scale of technology are not neutral — like the other factors, technology depends on choices. What is emphasized in education, and the level of educational funding, are also matters of values. Clearly, from this perspective, the political process is essentially a concrete expression of society's values, even if these are only implicit in day-to-day political decisions.

The understanding and forecasting of leisure and recreation are enhanced by knowing about relevant values and how they ultimately translate into recreational choices. Key questions include: (1) What are society's present values? (2) How do they affect recreation and leisure choices? (3) How are they changing? (4) What are the implications of these changes for recreation and leisure? Before these questions can be addressed, it is useful to review, in some detail, previous studies of outdoor recreation and environmental attitudes, as it is this body of research that provides us with the empirical evidence upon which interpretation and speculation can be based.

RESEARCH ON THE RELATIONSHIP BETWEEN OUTDOOR RECREATION AND ENVIRONMENTAL ATTITUDES

Rationale and Assumptions

A relationship between values and attitudes towards the environment, on the one hand, and outdoor recreation participation, on the other, has often been assumed by writers on recreation. For example Carls (1980: 157) has observed, "over greater or lesser periods of time the values of people, as reflected in their attitudes, change in ways that are often trivial ... and sometimes profound...

Outdoor recreation has frequently been the recipient and at times the protagonist of these attitudinal oscillations." Referring to wilderness attitudes, Wall suggests that North American perceptions of the land have shifted, historically, from an emphasis on dominance and fear towards an appreciation of wilderness, with the implication that "these changed attitudes stimulated increased interest and participation in outdoor recreation" (Wall 1982: 17). In the British context, too, concern for scenic heritage has been connected with claims for public rights of access to the countryside for various types of recreational activity (see, for example, Cherry 1976, 1985; Council for National Parks 1986).

The preceding sources imply a reciprocal relationship between environmental attitudes and outdoor recreation. On the one hand, participation in outdoor recreation may increase as people become aware of, and concerned about, the environment; on the other hand, participation in recreation can stimulate environmental awareness and concern. Both formulations of the relationship have been used as the basis for the development of hypotheses in past research.

Regarding the effects of recreation on the development of environmental attitudes, Van Liere and Noe (1981) have argued that "a major concern in the sociology of natural resources has been the orientation of Americans toward the natural environment. It is often suggested that attitudes and values which emphasize exploitation of natural resources rather than stewardship or conservation have resulted in damage to local ecosystems as well as threatening the larger biosphere. As a result, a dominant research concern over the past decade has been to identify factors associated with the development of pro-environmental orientations" (p. 505). Among the factors cited by Van Liere and Noe were knowledge about environmental issues, exposure to environmental degradation, commitment to dominant social values, and participation in outdoor recreation. Thus, early investigations of a relationship between outdoor recreation and environmental attitudes may be viewed as an important component of more broadly based efforts to explain a growing concern for the environment (see Buttel 1987 for further discussion).

Van Liere and Noe based their assumption about the effect of outdoor recreation participation on the formation of environmental attitudes both on the general literature alluded to above and, more specifically, on a research paper by Dunlap and Heffernan (1975). Dunlap and Heffernan noted frequent suggestions that increasing participation in outdoor recreation directly stimulated the emergence of the environmental movement and widespread concern for environmental quality in the late 1960s and early 1970s. This occurred, they believed, because outdoor recreation participation "creates an awareness of environmental problems by exposing people to instances of environmental deterioration; creates a commitment to the protection of valued recreation sites; and ... cultivates an esthetic taste for a 'natural' environment which fosters a generalized opposition to environmental degradation" (Dunlap and Heffernan 1975: 18).

Dunlap and Heffernan argued that the existence of a relationship between outdoor recreation participation and environmental concern could have important practical implications. If the relationship were correct, then more widespread and intense concern for environmental quality could be expected to emerge as participation increases, leading to growing support for pro-environmental political candidates and ballot measures, if not necessarily to personal involvement in environmental action or conservation organizations.

Knopp and Tyger (1973) also saw some practical value in investigating the relationship. In their case, however, recreation participation (as measured by the type of activity chosen) was viewed as dependent upon attitudes rather than the reverse. Noting that attitudes towards the environment were changing in the early 1970s, Knopp and Tyger proposed that increasing support for less consumptive forms of recreation could be anticipated. A similar logic was followed by Jackson (1986, 1987), who has suggested that changing environmental attitudes might be symptomatic of evolving social values, with important implications both for outdoor recreation similar to those foreseen by Knopp and Tyger, and for the degree of public support for conservationist land management strategies.

Empirical Studies

The relationship between outdoor recreation and environmental attitudes was first studied empirically in the early 1970s. Knopp and Tyger (1973) investigated attitudinal differences between cross-country skiers and snowmobilers to explain conflicts between them. Two hypotheses were tested:

1. People who engage in motorized forms of recreation are less likely to have environmentalist values than those who prefer self-propelled forms of recreation;
2. People who engage in motorized forms of recreation are less likely to understand or sympathize with the concept of devoting specific recreation areas for distinct purposes than are those who prefer activities with less environmental impact (pp. 7-8).

Knopp and Tyger's study, conducted in Minnesota in 1971, used nine Likert-type items to measure environmental attitudes and six items to assess views on recreation land management issues. As was common in studies of public concern about the environment in the early to mid-1970s, Knopp and Tyger's items were highly specific — that is, they did not tap fundamental beliefs and values in the manner of subsequent studies. For example, the items included statements such as "We need the Alaskan oil pipeline in spite of possible environmental hazards," and "Mass transit systems should be substituted for the automobile in our cities." Further, differences between cross-country skiers and snowmobilers on each item were analyzed on a one-to-one basis — a procedure now recognized as being inadequate and inaccurate (see Van Liere and Noe 1981). Nevertheless, Knopp and Tyger's results supported both hypotheses.

Although Knopp and Tyger were the first to provide empirical evidence of a relationship between outdoor recreation participation and environmental attitudes, and were usually cited in later publications, their study was not the most influential of the early papers. Rather, the "mainstream" of this body of research began with a 1975 paper by Dunlap and Heffernan, whose hypotheses have been re-examined in one way or another by all subsequent researchers. Progress in ensuing research has effectively consisted of incremental modifications (hypotheses, measurement, and analysis) to Dunlap and Heffernan's original study.

Dunlap and Heffernan (1975: 20) tested three hypotheses:

1. There is a positive association between involvement in outdoor recreation and environmental concern;
2. The association is stronger between appreciative activities and environmental concern than between consumptive activities and environmental concern;
3. There is a stronger association between outdoor recreation and concern with protecting aspects of the environment necessary for pursuing such activities than between outdoor recreation and other environmental issues such as air and water pollution.

Three outdoor recreation pursuits were selected as examples of "appreciative" activities (hiking, camping, and visiting state parks and scenic areas), while two examples of "consumptive" activities (fishing and hunting) were chosen.[1] Dunlap and Heffernan argued that preferences for one or the other type of outdoor recreation activity are consistent with underlying values and attitudes to nature. Consumptive activities, they suggested, "involve taking something from the environment and thus reflect a 'utilitarian' orientation toward it. [In] such a stance ... nature is viewed as existing for man's utilization" (p. 19). Appreciative activities, in contrast, "involve attempts to enjoy the natural environment without altering it. Such activities are thus compatible with the 'preservationist' orientation which attempts to maintain the environment in its natural state" (pp. 19-20). Data deficiencies prevented Dunlap and Heffernan from examining a third category of outdoor recreation, namely the use of snowmobiles, trail bikes, and all-terrain vehicles (which were labeled as "abusive," because of the environmental degradation they were deemed to produce).

Dunlap and Heffernan used eight indicators of environmental concern, all reflecting support for funding for environmental quality relative to other societal goals. Two were closely related to recreation issues ("Protect forests and other natural areas for future enjoyment" and "Preserve areas of unspoiled natural beauty for the future"). The rest were defined as more "distant" (e.g. "Prevent serious industrial pollution of water"; "Prevent serious agricultural pollution of water from fertilizers, pesticides and animal wastes"; "Control air pollution from motor vehicles").

Using data from a 1970 survey of Washington State residents, Dunlap and Heffernan found only weak support for their first hypothesis. While most associations were in the expected direction, the majority were of negligible magnitude. On the other hand, the concentration of negative coefficients among fishing and hunting supported the desirability of distinguishing between appreciative and consumptive recreationists, i.e. the basis of the second hypothesis. Generally, associations between participation in appreciative activities and the various measures of environmental concern were higher than those between participation in consumptive activities and environmental concern. As Dunlap and Heffernan observed, "while 14 of the 24 associations between environmental concern and appreciative activities reached a non-negligible level, this was true for only 2 of the 16 associations between environmental concern and consumptive activities. Furthermore, the only negative associations were between hunting and environmental concern" (p. 23).

The third hypothesis was also supported. Involvement in outdoor recreation was more likely to be associated with a concern for protecting nature for recreational purposes than for controlling pollution.

Because certain socio-economic variables were known to be related to both the dependent and the independent variables, Dunlap and Heffernan checked for spuriousness by re-examining the original bivariate relationships while controlling for age, sex, residence, education, and income. The initial findings were supported. In summary, Dunlap and Heffernan's results, although weak, were sufficiently encouraging to warrant their call for further investigation of the relationship between outdoor recreation participation and environmental concern.

Dunlap and Heffernan's first and second hypotheses were re-examined using data from a 1974 rural-based survey in Wisconsin by Geisler, Martinson, and Wilkening (1977), in which both the independent and dependent variables were measured more broadly than in the earlier study. Geisler *et al.* added what they called an "abusive" category, exemplified by snowmobiling, to the measure of outdoor recreational activity. They also complemented the indicators of environmental concern (defined as support for public action) with several items dealing with the awareness of various environmental issues (e.g. stream, lake, noise and air pollution; wildlife reduction; soil erosion). They argued that "this broader conceptualization of environmental concern permits us to compare cognitive states with actual support for public action to protect the environment and, by inference, to enhance recreation" (p. 242).

The results of this study, however, were at odds with those reported by Dunlap and Heffernan. There was support for the first hypothesis at the zero-order level of analysis, namely that environmental concern is associated with outdoor recreation participation. Evidence for the second hypothesis was also present, albeit weaker than for the first. However, socio-economic variables (especially age, but also income and education) were more strongly related than outdoor recreation behavior to environmental concern. Furthermore, the associations were greatly attenuated when the socio-economic variables were controlled. Thus, "the ... analysis suggests that environmental concern is affected more by respondent characteristics than by recreational habit" (p. 246). Geisler *et al.* concluded that "this study leads us to question the generalization that specific types of recreation produce varying degrees of environmental concern or commitment to public policies regarding natural resources. At most it can only be said that particular forms of outdoor recreation are related to particular environmental concerns at particular times and places" (p. 248).

A study conducted in Louisiana in 1974 by Pinhey and Grimes (1979) appears, on face value, to question further the validity of Dunlap and Heffernan's hypotheses: Pinhey and Grimes found only weak and inconsistent relationships between outdoor recreation and environmental concern. They did find that active participants in outdoor recreation activities were more likely (42%) than non-active respondents (28%) to cite ecological or recreational reasons for evaluating Louisiana's natural marsh regions as valuable, whereas the latter group more frequently cited other reasons or did not perceive such resources to be valuable. Pinhey and Grimes assessed this association to be "weak to moderate" (p. 5). However, there was no difference between "actives" and "inactives" with regard to preferences for preservation versus other uses of these areas, nor did consumptive and appreciative recreationists differ on either measure of environmental concern. Further analysis indicated that socio-economic variables were better (although still weak) predictors of environmental concern than were measures of recreational activity. Pinhey and Grimes concluded that their results were more consistent with those reported by Geisler *et al.* than with those found by Dunlap and Heffernan.

It is not unduly critical, however, to point out that the two highly specific and localized measures of environmental concern used by Pinhey and Grimes were extremely poor, even in view of the modest advances in measurement that had been achieved by the mid-1970s (and especially so in the light of more recent developments). Thus, as Van Liere and Noe (1981: 507) subsequently commented, Pinhey and Grimes's findings "may not be too surprising given [their] operationalization of environmental concern as valuing natural marsh areas. Duck hunters, for example, may value marshland highly while being less concerned about other environmental issues. This points to a major weakness in the Pinhey and Grimes study — their restricted measures of environmental concern." Thus, it comes as no surprise that Pinhey and Grimes failed to replicate Dunlap and Heffernan's original findings, and it would not be reasonable to accept their results either as a refutation of Dunlap and Heffernan's, or of the original premises upon which this body of research was founded.

For several reasons, a more recent study reported by Van Liere and Noe (1981), conducted among visitors to Cape Hatteras National Seashore, represented an important stage in the evolution of research on outdoor recreation and environmental attitudes . To begin with, it was the first true replication of Dunlap and Heffernan's original study in that it was, to that date, the only project to have been designed and conducted after the appearance of Dunlap and Heffernan's paper. (The papers by Geisler *et al.* and Pinhey and Grimes were published after Dunlap and Heffernan's, but the research on which they were based was conducted earlier).

Second, the way in which Van Liere and Noe measured environmental attitudes represented a marked improvement over the methods of previous studies. They used a general measure, namely the 12-item "New Environmental Paradigm" (NEP) scale developed by Dunlap and Van Liere (1978). The measurement of this broader "worldview" was deemed to be important because "it is exactly these beliefs (such as 'the balance of nature is delicate and easily upset') which participation in outdoor recreation is purported to arouse and cause to be internalized (and ultimately generalized to concern about specific problems)" (Van Liere and Noe 1981: 509). Also, as a multiple-item instrument, the NEP scale was viewed as more reliable than the single-item measures used in previous studies.

Third, the terminology used by Van Liere and Noe — "environmental attitudes" as opposed to "concern" — represents an important conceptual shift. As the authors observed, their scale "asks respondents to express their general orientation toward the environment rather than awareness or concern about specific environmental problems" (p. 509). Thus it was the first real effort in this body of research to conceive of environmental attitudes as values, and to tap deep-seated influences that might explain recreational choices, as opposed to more superficial perceptions (concern) which grow out of it. Alternatively stated, Van Liere and Noe recognized that outdoor recreation participation can be viewed as a dependent variable which is influenced by environmental attitudes (a conceptualization that has important implications for recreation forecasting).

Despite their conceptual and methodological improvements, however, Van Liere and Noe found only mixed support for the hypothesis of an association between outdoor recreation participation and environmental attitudes — coefficients for some activities were close to zero or even negative. There was support for a second hypothesis, namely of a stronger association between appreciative activities and environmental attitudes than between the other forms of recreation and environmental attitudes. Even so, the coefficients were no larger than in previous studies.

Van Liere and Noe suggested three possible reasons for their findings:

1. The hypotheses are true but were inadequately tested. Further improvements in measurement and study design might lead to stronger associations.
2. There is indeed no relationship between outdoor recreation participation and environmental concern. (Van Liere and Noe rejected this reason because their results, although weak, were not spurious, i.e. controlling for socio-economic variables did not attenuate the zero-order relationships, as was the case in the Geisler *et al.* study).
3. The hypotheses may be true but the linkages among variables are more complex than previously assumed.

Rather than abandon research on environmental attitudes and outdoor recreation, Van Liere and Noe urged that "research focus on specifying more complex models linking these two variables. What needs to be identified are those influences which might cause individuals to interpret their outdoor experiences in a manner that creates awareness and concern about the environment and causes them to manifest that concern in their actual behavior" (pp. 511-512). Van Liere and Noe suggested several such variables, including recreational socialization during childhood, membership in recreational groups with a particular environmental orientation, and the environmental attitudes of social groups in which the activity is shared (p. 512).

Another such variable, recreational specialization, exemplified by Bryan's (1977) study of trout fishermen, received some attention from Van Liere and Noe. They inferred from Bryan's research that participants within the same activity should not necessarily be assigned to one or the other of two distinct groups, "appreciative" or "consumptive." Rather, they might vary from consumptive to appreciative, depending on their past experiences and, in turn, on the meaning they attach to the activity and on their attitudes and values about it. This hypothesis, which Van Liere and Noe suggested might apply widely in outdoor recreation, is consistent with the observations of Kelly and Godbey on leisure styles, elsewhere in this volume. Furthermore, a recent study by Doberstein (1988) provides some support for Van Liere and Noe's suggestion. An investigation of environmental attitudes among three types of campers in Kananaskis Country, Alberta, showed that backcountry campers expressed the strongest environmental attitudes, followed by those in limited amenity campgrounds. Campers in full amenity campgrounds consistently expressed weaker environmental attitudes than their counterparts in other camping settings.

The sixth and final study summarized here (Jackson 1986) was conducted in Edmonton and Calgary, Canada, in 1984, and addressed some of the measurement problems discussed by Van Liere and Noe. The objective of the

Canadian study was consistent with, but more broadly defined than, the research described above — namely to interpret the relationship between attitudes towards the environment and preferences for different types of outdoor recreational activity in the context of the diverging values of the "consumer" and "conserver" societies. Two hypotheses were formulated, based upon those originally developed by Dunlap and Heffernan (1975):

1. Participants in appreciative (self-propelled) activities will exhibit stronger pro-environmental attitudes than participants in extractive and mechanized activities;
2. There will be a stronger association between outdoor recreation participation and attitudes towards specific aspects of the environment necessary for pursuing such activities than between outdoor recreation participation and attitudes to more "distant" and general aspects of environmental issues.

The Canadian study departed from previous research in three main ways. First, a more appropriate comparison was made of the attitudes of participants in different activities. With the exception of the Pinhey and Grimes study, all previous analyses of attitudinal differences between activities were conducted indirectly, by examining the relative strength of differences between more intense and less intense participants in a particular activity, or between participants and non-participants in the activity. As explained below, a more direct set of comparisons between types of recreational activity was made in the Canadian study.

Second, the 21-item scale designed to measure environmental attitudes was more comprehensive than in previous studies. Although it was based upon the rationale and content of the NEP scale used by Van Liere and Noe (1981), several items from Dunlap and Van Liere's (1984) "Dominant Social Paradigm" (DSP) scale were also included, together with several new items. To test the second hypothesis, a six-item recreational attitudes scale was developed, using items from Knopp and Tyger (1973) and Wong (1979; see also Jackson and Wong 1982).

Third, respondents' scores on the environmental attitudes scale were factor analyzed to identify the dimensions of environmental attitudes and values that best distinguished among recreationist categories. Four factors emerged, labeled as "Negative consequences of growth and technology," "Relationship between mankind and nature," "Quality of life," and "Limits to the biosphere."

The analysis of relationships between outdoor recreation participation and environmental attitudes was confined to eight outdoor activities, classified into three groups: self-propelled activities[2] (cross-country skiing, hiking, and canoeing), mechanized activities (snowmobiling, motor boating, and dirt biking), and extractive activities (hunting and fishing). The validity of this classification was verified in a factor analysis of participation rates (Jackson, in press).

Tests of differences in attitudes were conducted on the basis of 26 "exclusive pairs" of activities, i.e. by comparing people who had participated exclusively in one or the other of each pair of activities. Participants in both activities in a given pair were excluded to avoid the problem of double-counting, as were participants in neither, because these people were irrelevant to a given analysis (but not necessarily to any other "exclusive pairs" analysis). For example, in the case of cross-country skiing and snowmobiling, comparisons were made between respondents who had participated in cross-country skiing but not snowmobiling and those who had participated in snowmobiling but not cross-country skiing. People who had participated in both or neither of these activities were excluded from this particular analysis.

The results supported the first hypothesis. With one exception, there were no differences in environmental or recreational attitudes either within or between the mechanized and extractive pairs of activities. The main differences were between participants in self-propelled activities on the one hand, and participants in mechanized and extractive activities on the other. Equally important was the finding that the dimensions of attitudes which best distinguished between these groups of recreationists were those having to do with the quality of life and the relationship between mankind and nature; these are the key differences between the core values of the consumer and conserver societies (see below).

The data also supported the second hypothesis: coefficients for relationships between outdoor recreation participation and the recreation scale were almost universally larger than those for the environmental scale. The comparable magnitudes and significance levels of the zero-order and partial coefficients indicated that the relationships could not be accounted for by socio-economic variables alone, and therefore were not spurious.

In summary, the most recent evidence supports the original premise that participation in different forms of outdoor recreational activities is related to environmental attitudes. People who prefer self-propelled activities, such as cross-country skiing, canoeing, and hiking, more frequently hold environmental attitudes consistent with the "New Environmental Paradigm" than participants in "consumptive" activities such as fishing and hunting, and "mechanized" activities such as snowmobiling, motor boating, and dirt biking. These latter types of outdoor recreationists tend to express weaker pro-environmental attitudes, and even, in some instances, anti-environmental attitudes. Moreover, the dimensions of attitudes which best distinguish among these types of recreationists — views on the quality of life and the man-nature relationship — are precisely those which simultaneously differentiate between the values of the consumer and conserver societies.

SOCIETY, LEISURE, AND RECREATION: A FRAMEWORK FOR INTERPRETATION

In and of itself, the small body of literature on the relationship between outdoor recreation and environmental attitudes represents a useful contribution to knowledge, especially regarding the understanding and interpretation of factors that influence outdoor recreation participation. Yet the potential also exists to use this knowledge in a broader social context, and to seek answers to the questions raised earlier about the roles of values in recreational and leisure choices. For this purpose, the concepts of the "consumer society" and "conserver society" provide a useful organizational and interpretive device. These notions have begun to receive increasing attention in the literature, especially in Canada (Orfald and Gibson 1985; Science Council of Canada 1977; Thompson 1982).

Leisure and Recreation in the Consumer Society

Many commentators have suggested that modern western industrial society is dominated by a "consumer ethic." The fundamental values of such a society are characterized by an internally consistent set of perceptions: (1) the biosphere is viewed as unlimited with regard to its supply of materials and its capacity to absorb wastes and other impacts; (2) faith is placed in the unbounded ability of science and technology to exploit nature, while unbridled optimism about the prospects for sustained economic growth is expressed; and (3) the quality of life is assessed primarily in material and quantitative terms, equating satisfaction and success with material yardsticks, such as growth in individuals' income and in the Gross National Product (Boulding 1966; O'Riordan 1976; Russell 1979).

Several other important values associated with the consumer society may be identified by drawing upon the work of Dunlap and Van Liere (1984). These authors have attempted to identify and measure the core values associated with the consumer lifestyle, which they label the "Dominant Social Paradigm." Dunlap and Van Liere describe the DSP as "a useful shorthand term for the constellation of common values, beliefs, and shared wisdom about the physical and social environments which constitute a society's basic 'worldview'" (p. 1013). They suggest that the DSP is "transmitted from generation to generation via institutional socialization ... and forms the core of a society's cultural heritage. And while it may not receive universal endorsement, the DSP nonetheless provides general guidance for both individual and societal behavior" (pp. 1013-1014). One of Dunlap and Van Liere's most important points is that "environmental problems arise ... because [the] DSP was formed during a bygone era of extraordinary abundance, and thus much of it ... is no longer adaptive in an era of ecological limits." Thus, "individual commitment to the DSP results in support for practices and policies that lead to environmental degradation and to opposition to policies needed to create a more ecologically sustainable society" (Dunlap and Van Liere 1984: 1014).

Among the values of the DSP identified by Dunlap and Van Liere, and which have direct implications for recreation and leisure, are the following: faith in science and technology; support for individual rights; support for economic growth; faith in material abundance; and faith in future prosperity. In sum, these values assert the possibility and the desirability of personal consumption, unconstrained by environmental, social, economic, political, or technological limits.

What, then, are the implications for leisure and recreation? The most complete discussion of leisure and recreation in the consumer society has been provided by Spry (1980). A consumer society is "a world in which the emphasis is constantly on the apparatus of living, not on the quality of life itself" (Spry 1980: 147). The goal is having, not being. Consequently, in a consumer society, leisure is associated with "lavish spending." Thus:

> Of all [the] varied ways of putting in leisure time, some entail
> very heavy demands on material and environmental resources.
> Travel means jet planes, the fuel they use, and the cloud cover they
> create. Automobiles mean using up metals and gasoline and creating
> smog. Television means cameras and lights, congested air waves,
> production studios, elaborate transmitting and receiving equipment,
> including satellites and other apparatus of space technology. Movies
> mean cameras, sound recording equipment, filmstock, sets and
> costumes, cutting rooms, theaters and projection apparatus, to say
> nothing of the extravagances of the glamor industry. The record
> industry has similar requirements as does sport, both professional
> and amateur, organized as entertainment. International competitive
> sport has escalated jet set glamor and the kind of emulation that
> gives rise to Olympic extravaganzas. Even unassuming, personal
> participation in sport has become the raison d'être for promoting
> sales of elaborate equipment and clothing....
>
> Underlying the expansion of the mass media — TV, radio,
> records, computers, the press and periodicals — and their role in
> leisure time, is the proliferation of sales promotion and advertising.
> Shopping as a pastime simply adds to the perpetual pressure to buy
> more, have more, and consume more. Increasing leisure time has
> become a market to be exploited through the ruthless promotion of
> the idea that more and ever more elaborate possessions and
> expenditure will add immensely to the satisfaction that can be won
> from leisure time. Power boats and snowmobiles, ten-speed bicycles
> and fancy skis, stereophonic record players and computers are
> becoming widespread items of household equipment, besides TV
> sets, radios, telephones, and cars. Emphasis is given increasingly
> to the apparatus used in leisure time activities. This is generally true
> of affluent societies (Spry 1980: 143-144).

Some additional characteristics of leisure in a consumer society might include the following: severe impacts on the natural environment (Wall and Wright 1977); heavy demands on natural resources, especially energy, reflected in types of equipment , the scale of facilities, and patterns of recreational travel (Foster and Kuhn 1983; Ritchie and Claxton 1983); and centralization, facility-orientation, and standardization. Consumer society leisure provides instant or short-term gratification ("quick thrills") and involves competition with others, even if only in subtle ways (e.g. status seeking).

Leisure and Recreation in the Conserver Society

Like the consumer society, the conserver society (or "New Environmental Paradigm," to use Dunlap and Van Liere's terminology), exhibits an internally consistent yet directly opposite complex of beliefs and preferences. A limited biosphere is viewed as imposing constraints on technology and the possibility for economic growth. In turn, the latter is seen as undesirable, given the inevitable negative environmental and social consequences that could result if the "growth ethic" is not rejected. A re-direction of material aspirations is therefore required and the quality of life is assessed using primarily qualitative criteria (Boulding 1966; O'Riordan 1976; Russell 1979). Thus, the conserver society rests upon acceptance of the tenets of the NEP, which represents an alternative "worldview" based on a reaction against the values and beliefs of the DSP. Founded on ecological principles, it is more conducive than the DSP to pro-environmental behavior and support for environmental protection and preservation (Dunlap and Van Liere 1978).

Describing leisure in a conserver society, Spry makes the following observations:

> The popularity of jogging, of [cross country] skiing, and of cycling suggests that simple activities, without a great elaboration of apparatus, are coming into their own. [These and many other activities] make very little demand on material support systems. Gardening, crafts, carpentry, and all sorts of do-it-yourself activities, ranging from home dress-making to household repairs, may actually conserve material and environmental resources, since they combine recycling of materials with satisfaction of the instinct of workmanship. Leisure time pursuits should be undertaken, not in the hope of winning Oscars or Olympic gold medals, but for their own sake, because they are fun or interesting, or because they contribute to a cause that is considered to be useful or worthwhile (Spry 1980: 145-146).

To this, it can be added that recreation and leisure in a conserver society would likely be decentralized, small-scale, individualistic, and oriented towards the non-consumptive enjoyment of the natural environment. They would demand lower levels of equipment and would rarely be mechanized. They would, therefore, tend to be low in energy use per capita or per recreational engagement. The goal of leisure activity would be personal, long-term, physical and mental development. In short, the conserver society places "increasing emphasis on leisure time as an opportunity for the enhancement of human quality and the enrichment of creative experience, rather than as an opportunity for the elaboration of entertainment, escalation of self-indulgence, and multiplication of apparatus" (Spry 1980: 151). If Spry is correct, then the emergence of new forms of leisure and recreation may be interpreted as evidence of the restructuring of societal values and behaviors, at least partially as a result of changing perceptions of ecological limits and resource constraints.

Voluntary Versus Enforced Change

How likely is a shift from the consumer society to the conserver society? Too few people, it might be argued, share the values and lifestyles of the conserver society to make a difference, and the number is unlikely to grow in the foreseeable future; too many constraints prevent the conserver society from materializing. Yet a growing body of opinion has emerged over the past couple of decades which *does* accept that there are limits to growth (e.g. Brooks 1981; Lovins 1977; Miles 1976; Ophuls 1977). Some writers argue that a new era of limits will enforce changes in resource use, and therefore ultimately in leisure and recreation. Dunn (1980: 116), for instance, having accepted the notions of resource scarcity and the escalating environmental impact of human activity, suggests that "a fundamental challenge confronting all nations in coming decades will be which leisure activities can or should be continued or encouraged, which discontinued or discouraged, which modified, and which new experiences need to be devised or invented." Similarly, in discussing the implications of a Canadian study of relationships between recreation and energy, Ritchie and Claxton (1983: 880) remark that there are "certain activities of high energy intensity for which there appear to be no obvious substitutes. If energy conservation became a primary social objective, there may be no alternative but to consciously discourage such activities."[3]

Is there any evidence, though, of voluntary, as opposed to enforced, change in values and behavior? There always has been and probably always will be a small but significant number of people whose values and lifestyles echo, by choice, those of the conserver society. But there are also signs that new and more widespread perceptions, attitudes, and behaviors towards resources and the environment are emerging (Dunlap and Van Liere 1978, 1984; Farhar *et al.* 1980; Jackson 1988; Jackson and Foster 1982; Kelly 1982; Kuhn 1987, 1988).

There is, too, an increasing tendency to question personal values related to work, material consumption, the family, leisure, and so on, and more generally the type of society and economy in which we live (Cotgrove 1982). People are asking whether the supposed benefits of the consumer society are worth the sacrifices, when all the advantages and disadvantages are weighed. Spry (1980: 150) contends that, just as concern is growing "for the quality of life that cannot be measured in Gross National Product figures, so may concern be growing for human quality that is not demonstrated by lavish expenditures and an elaborate apparatus of spare time enjoyment." Similarly, Sewell and Mitchell (1981: 262) suggest that "significant segments of the public at large are concerned about such matters as to what constitutes the good life.... They wonder about the relative emphasis that should be placed upon the pursuit of high levels of economic growth, the attainment of a more egalitarian society, and the preservation of environmental quality. The traditional consumer society is now being challenged by a small but vociferous group which believes that a conserver society is superior."

It has also been argued that conserver society values will not remain those of a minority for long, but will eventually gain ascendancy. Balmer (1979: 546), writing about Canada, has suggested that, by the end of the twentieth century, "there will be a decline in values associated with materialism, private ownership, capitalism, and unqualified economic growth. Increasing emphasis will be placed on concepts such as quality of life ... [and] a new focus on the ecological ethic." Moreover, the notion of a conserver society implies neither the wholesale rejection of consumer values on the part of an individual, nor universal endorsement across society. What is does imply, though, is a more widespread acceptance of conserver values than at present.

Synthesis

Most of the preceding discussion can be expressed in five propositions:

1. Variations in leisure preferences are consistent with societal differences in values.
2. As societal values change, so do lifestyles, leisure, and recreation.
3. Our present society may be described as a "consumer society"; its values can be identified, and leisure and recreation preferences are consistent with these values.
4. A small but significant minority of people has adopted values and attitudes that are at least partly consistent with those of a conserver society. Much of their recreation and leisure is spent in activities consistent with these values.
5. Growing acceptance of conserver-society values would result in measurable changes in recreational and leisure preferences.

To elaborate, the first proposition suggests that people's recreation and leisure preferences are consistent with their values. Sub-groups of society exist which share a common core of values, lifestyles, and leisure. People who enjoy a particular form of recreation are likely to resemble, in their values and life-styles, those who participate in the same types of activity; people who prefer other kinds of recreation probably share a different lifestyle and values. Conversely, if we can recognize sub-divisions of society based on the values that they hold, and which distinguish them from other groups, then we should expect to find simultaneous and consistent variations in leisure and recreation.

The second proposition assumes that values are not fixed, but are subject to constant change, even if this change is very slow and, sometimes, rather difficult to detect. The third and fourth propositions are more speculative. The third states that we currently live in what can be called a consumer society. The consumer society has certain identifiable values and lifestyles to which the majority of people subscribe, and the dominant recreation and leisure pursuits are consistent with these values. These statements can be summarized in a model (Figure 1).

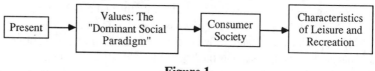

Figure 1
The Consumer Society

This, then, takes us to the fourth and fifth propositions. As was the case for the third, a model will suffice to establish the linkages (Figure 2). The propositions suggest that new values will be associated with growing acceptance of a conserver society and that, in turn, new forms of recreation and leisure will develop alongside these social and value-based changes.

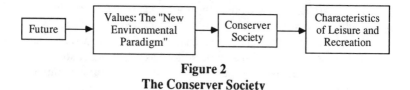

Figure 2
The Conserver Society

The preceding remarks can now be synthesized, by combining the two models with the characteristics of recreation and leisure described previously (Figure 3). As we move from the present to the future, values and attitudes might evolve from those of the current "Dominant Social Paradigm" to the "New Environmental Paradigm"; the growth ethic is replaced by a steady-state economy; the current exploitative attitude to nature is replaced by a perception of the importance of ecological balance; and we seek solutions other than the large-scale application of technology. The consumer lifestyle evolves into the conserver lifestyle, and recreation and leisure undergo the changes outlined above.

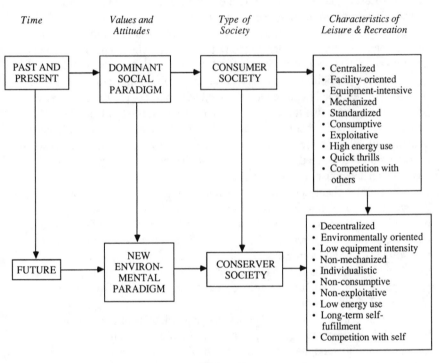

Time	Values and Attitudes	Type of Society	Characteristics of Leisure & Recreation

Figure 3
Values, Types of Society, and Characteristics of
Leisure and Recreation

IMPLICATIONS

Practical Implications

Social and attitudinal changes of the kind described in this chapter are likely to be reflected in new and emerging patterns of leisure activity. In turn, they will influence personal spending on recreation, as well as preferences about the quantity, quality, location, and management of public recreation resources. Hence, they must be recognized by practitioners. Thus, knowledge of the relationship between outdoor recreation participation and environmental attitudes should assist recreation policy makers and planners in anticipating (if not precisely predicting) future trends in outdoor recreation participation (see Burton, this volume).

Furthermore, the time horizon over which such research would have practical relevance is quite different from that which is consistent with traditional forecast methods. Socio-economic variables can be used to produce reasonably reliable immediate predictions of specific activity changes; focusing instead on the values and attitudes related to recreation should allow practitioners to come to grips with emerging long-term trends, which tend to be "easily overlooked in the bustle of day-to-day and fiscal operations" (Carls 1980: 159).

What predictions about recreation, then, can we make on the basis of the research described in this chapter? Changes in outdoor recreation activity preferences will occur if those who foresee even a modest shift from the consumer to the conserver society are correct. Under conditions of a voluntary evolution of values, preferences for appreciative, self-propelled activities should become more widespread, while a decline should occur in preferences for mechanized and consumptive activities.

Similar changes should occur even if social evolution is enforced because of resource and financial constraints: mechanized activities require relatively high levels of energy consumption, directly in the use of mechanized equipment, but also indirectly in its manufacture and transportation (see Ellis, this volume). The economic costs of such activities should, therefore, become significantly greater than those for appreciative activities. Consequently, some participants in the former may begin to seek other, less expensive, pursuits (Jackson 1986, pp. 19-20).

One criticism that could be leveled at predictions of this kind is that they are highly speculative, and rest on some tenuous assumptions about the direction, rapidity, and magnitude of attitudinal and social change. The current predominance of consumer-society values may well continue, in turn supporting preferences for mechanized and extractive activities. Another valid criticism is that such speculations refer most appropriately to outdoor recreation. Yet, the findings of research are consistent with Spry's broad-brush pictures of leisure in the consumer and conserver societies. Thus, it is not an over-generalization to project them beyond the narrow confines of outdoor forms of recreation.

Theoretical Implications

Equally as important as the practical implications, the investigation of the relationship between outdoor recreation participation and environmental attitudes is theoretically significant. Typically, social scientists have tended to recognize only the "horizontal" (descriptive) linkages among various facets of human behavior ("a" in Figure 4). Studies of the relationship between recreation and energy use, for example, have generally focused on two reciprocal issues:

the effects of changes in energy availability and price on recreation behavior; and the pressures that various forms of recreation place on the consumption of energy resources (Converse and Machlis 1986; Foster and Kuhn 1983; Kuhn 1983; McCool 1981; Ritchie and Claxton 1983).

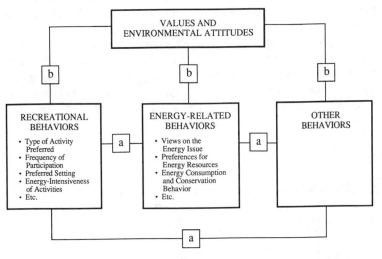

Figure 4
Horizontal and Vertical Linkages Among Behaviors

The implications are much deeper, however. Because environmental attitudes are also known to influence perceptions, preferences, and behaviors towards energy (Farbrother 1985; Jackson 1985, 1988; Kuhn 1987, 1988; Rodgers 1987), the recreationist who prefers low-impact, low-energy-use, self-propelled and appreciative activities consistent with pro-environmental attitudes is also more likely to prefer "soft energy paths" for the future (Lovins 1977) and to emphasize the importance of individual efforts to conserve energy. The more technocentrically-oriented recreationist is likely to favor "hard energy paths" based on the expansion of energy resource supplies, and to down-grade the need for conservation and the use of renewable resources.

What this means is that each individual's choices, both about recreation and energy use, are not only consistent with each other but are also traceable back to his or her attitudes and values towards resources and the environment. From the perspective of these ideas, any given behavior may be viewed as one specific outcome of fundamental values and attitudes. If recreation, energy use, and other behaviors stem from these basic factors, then "vertical" (explanatory) linkages between apparently quite different forms of behavior become apparent ("b" in Figure 4). Such linkages provide a much more powerful theoretical construct than the more superficial horizontal or functional linkages. This implies two things: first, that recreation and leisure are best viewed as closely linked with other aspects of human behavior rather than as something separate and apart, as seems to be the perspective in much contemporary leisure research (see Godbey, this volume, for further discussion); and, second, that the frameworks and hypotheses developed for research on recreation, environmental attitudes, and values can be applied to other topics traditionally of interest to social scientists.

Finally, this formulation offers a common conceptual framework for leisure scientists in several disciplines. Thus, the recognition of the fundamental effects of environmental attitudes and values may help to break down some artificial disciplinary barriers, since these variables are clearly of equal significance to sociology, social psychology, behavioral geography, and many other branches of the social sciences.

Acknowledgments

I wish to thank the following people for their helpful comments on earlier versions of this chapter: Linda Jackson, Richard Kuhn, David Whitson, Riley Dunlap, Brent Doberstein, and Sylvia Harron.

Footnotes

1. A value-bias on the part of these and subsequent researchers may be detected in their use of the terms "appreciative," "consumptive," and, especially, "abusive."
2. The term "appreciative" was used in the original paper; the label has been changed here, in the spirit of the point made in footnote 1.
3. Energy conservation would, indeed, be a primary social objective in a conserver society.

References

Balmer, K.R. 1979. "Canadian societal futures: implications for the leisure research community." In *Contemporary Leisure Research: Proceedings of the Second Canadian Congress on Leisure Research*, pp. 545-558. Toronto: Ontario Research Council on Leisure.

Boulding, K. 1966. "The economics of the coming spaceship earth." In *Environmental Quality in a Growing Economy*, ed. H. Jarrett, pp. 1-14. Baltimore: Johns Hopkins.

Brooks, D.B. 1981. *Zero Energy Growth for Canada*. Toronto: McClelland and Stewart.

Bryan, H. 1977. "Leisure value systems and recreational specialization: The case of trout fishermen." *Journal of Leisure Research 9:* 174-187.

Burton, T.L. 1981. "You can't get there from here: A personal perspective on recreation forecasting in Canada." *Recreation Research Review 9:* 38-43.

Buttel, F.H. 1987. New directions in environmental sociology. *Annual Review of Sociology 13:* 465-488.

Carls, E.G. 1980. "So long Frank Buck: Some changes in the ecology of outdoor recreation." In *Recreation and Leisure: Issues in an Era of Change*, eds. T.L. Goodale and P.A. Witt, pp. 154-164. State College, PA: Venture Publishing.

Cherry, G.E. 1985. "Scenic heritage and national parks lobbies and legislation in England and Wales." *Leisure Studies 4:* 127-139.

Converse, R.S. and G.E. Machlis. 1986. "Energy and outdoor recreation: A review and assessment of the literature." *Leisure Sciences 8:* 391-416.

Cotgrove, S. 1982. *Catastrophe or Cornucopia: The Environment, Politics and the Future*. Chichester: John Wiley.

Council for National Parks. 1986. *National Parks: The Celebration and the Challenge*. London: Council for National Parks.

Doberstein, B. 1988. "Inter-activity differences in environmental attitudes: a comparison of three types of campers." Unpublished B.Sc. Honors thesis, Department of Geography, University of Alberta.

Dunlap, R.E. and R.B. Heffernan. 1975. "Outdoor recreation and environmental concern: An empirical examination." *Rural Sociology 40:* 18-30.

Dunlap, R.E. and K.D. Van Liere. 1978. "The 'new environmental paradigm': A proposed measuring instrument and preliminary results." *Journal of Environmental Education 9:* 10-19.

Dunlap, R.E. and K.D. Van Liere. 1984. "Commitment to the dominant social paradigm and concern for environmental quality." *Social Science Quarterly 65:* 1013-1028.

Dunn, D.R. 1980. "Future leisure resources." In *Recreation and Leisure: Issues in an Era of Change,* eds. T.L. Goodale and P.A. Witt, pp. 115-124. State College, PA: Venture Publishing.

Farbrother, S.C. 1985. "The influence of environmental attitudes on energy preferences and behaviours." Unpublished M.A. thesis, Department of Geography, University of Alberta.

Farhar, B.C., C.T. Unseld, R. Vories, and R. Crews. 1980. "Public opinion about energy." *Annual Review of Energy 5:* 141-172.

Foster, L.T. and R.G. Kuhn. 1983. "The energy/leisure interface: A review and empirical exploration." *Recreation Research Review 10:* 49-61.

Geisler, G.C., O.B. Martinson, and E.A. Wilkening. 1977. "Outdoor recreation and environmental concern: A restudy." *Rural Sociology 42:* 241-249.

Jackson, E.L. 1985. "Environmental attitudes and preferences for energy resource options." *Journal of Environmental Education 17:* 23-30.

Jackson, E.L. 1986. "Outdoor recreation participation and attitudes to the environment." *Leisure Studies 5:* 1-23.

Jackson, E.L. 1987. "Outdoor recreation participation and views on resource development and preservation." *Leisure Sciences 9:* 235-250.

Jackson, E.L. 1988. "Public preferences for energy resource options: Long run v. short run." *The Canadian Geographer 32:* 162-165.

Jackson, E.L. In press. "Recreation in Edmonton and Calgary." In *Essays in Honor of William C. Wonders,* ed. P.J. Smith. Edmonton, Alberta: Department of geography, University of Alberta.

Jackson, E.L. and L.T. Foster, L.T. 1982. "North American research on public attitudes to energy resources and conservation: a bibliographic essay." *Environmental Perception Research.* Working Paper, EPR-10. Toronto: Institute for Environmental Studies, University of Toronto.

Jackson, E.L. and Wong, R.A.G. 1982. "Perceived conflict between urban cross-country skiers and snowmobilers in Alberta." *Journal of Leisure Research 14:* 47-62.

Kelly, M.L. 1982. "Attitudes towards the environment: A comparison of six surveys spanning six years." Report No. ECA82-ST/2. Edmonton: Environment Council of Alberta.

Knopp, T.B. and J.D. Tyger. 1973. "A study of conflict in recreational land use: Snowmobiling versus ski-touring." *Journal of Leisure Research 5:* 6-17

Kuhn, R.G. 1983. "An examination of the interrelationships between energy consumption and leisure activities: A case study of Victoria, British Columbia." Unpublished M.A. thesis, Department of Geography, University of Victoria.

Kuhn, R.G. 1987. "Geography, energy, and environmental attitudes: An investigation of policy scenarios and public preferences." Unpublished Ph.D. thesis, Department of Geography, University of Alberta.

Kuhn, R.G. 1988. "Factors affecting energy preferences: Environmental attitudes and reasons for choice." *The Canadian Geographer 32:* 165-167.

Lovins, A.B. 1977. *Soft Energy Paths: Toward a Durable Peace.* Cambridge, MA: Ballinger.

McCool, S.F. 1981. "Energy and wildland recreation: Policy issues, research questions." *Recreation Research Review 9:* 23-30.

Miles, R.E. 1976. *Awakening from the American Dream: The Social and Political Limits to Growth.* New York: Universe Books.

Ophuls, W. 1977. *Ecology and the Politics of Scarcity.* San Francisco: W.H. Freeman.

Orfald, D. and R.Gibson. 1985. "The conserver society idea: A history with questions." *Alternatives 12:* 37-45.

O'Riordan, T. 1976. *Environmentalism*. London: Pion.

Pinhey, T.K. and M.D. Grimes. 1979. "Outdoor recreation and environmental concern: A re-examination of the Dunlap-Heffernan thesis." *Leisure Sciences 2:* 1-11.

Ritchie, J.R.B. and J.D. Claxton. 1983. "Leisure lifestyles and energy use." In *Proceedings of the Third Canadian Congress on Leisure Research*, pp. 871-896. Edmonton, AB: Canadian Association for Leisure Studies.

Rodgers, J.R. 1987. "A comparison of environmental attitudes, energy preferences, and energy conservation behaviour among environmentalists, business executives, and the public." Unpublished M.A. thesis, Department of Geography, University of Alberta.

Russell, M. 1979. "Conflicting perceptions of energy's future role." In *Energy in America's Future: The Choices Before Us*, eds. S.H. Schurr, J. Darmstadter, W. Ramsay, H. Perry, and M. Russell, pp. 401-408. Baltimore: Johns Hopkins.

Sadler, B. 1978. *Forest Recreation in Alberta*. Information Bulletin No. 11, Public Hearings on the Effect of Forestry Operations in Alberta. Edmonton: Environment Council of Alberta.

Science Council of Canada. 1977. *Canada as a Conserver Society: Resource Uncertainties and the Need for New Technologies*. Report No. 27. Ottawa: Science Council of Canada.

Sewell, W.R.D. and B. Mitchell. 1981. "The way ahead." In *Canadian Resource Policies: Problems and Prospects*, eds. B. Mitchell and W.R.D. Sewell, pp. 262-284. Toronto: Methuen.

Spry, I.M. 1980. "The prospects for leisure in a conserver society." In *Recreation and Leisure: Issues in an Era of Change*, eds. T.L. Goodale and P.A. Witt, pp. 141-153. State College, PA: Venture Publishing.

Thompson, D. 1982. "A conserver society: Grounds for optimism." *Alternatives 11:* 3-9.

Van Liere, K.D. and F.P. Noe. 1981. "Outdoor recreation and environmental attitudes: Further examination of the Dunlap-Heffernan thesis." *Rural Sociology 46:* 501-513.

Wall, G. 1982. "Changing views of the land as a recreational resource." In *Recreational Land Use: Perspectives on its Evolution in Canada*, eds. G. Wall and J.S. Marsh: 15-25. Ottawa: Carleton University Press.

Wall, G. and C. Wright. 1977. *The Environmental Impact of Outdoor Recreation*. Waterloo, ON: Department of Geography, University of Waterloo.

Wong, R.A.G. 1979. "Recreational resource use conflict: Perceived conflict between cross-country skiers and snowmobilers." Unpublished M.A. thesis, Department of Geography, University of Alberta.

THE BENEFITS OF LEISURE

Richard Schreyer and B.L. Driver

INTRODUCTION

One of the most trite things it would appear that one could say about leisure participation is that it is beneficial. People would not voluntarily engage in such activities if they did not perceive them to be beneficial. However, once one moves past that basic observation, the question arises, what is really known about the benefits of leisure?

It may be possible to recognize that leisure is beneficial, but in fact there is little precise knowledge about the nature or extent of those benefits. There is often the tendency to perceive them as a luxury, the window-dressing on life, something nice but not necessary. This has had tangible consequences, as the public providers of recreation services and resources continually give these benefits short shrift in terms of the allocation of public dollars and resources. For instance, the Land and Water Conservation Fund, a major source of funding for recreation at the state and federal levels in the U.S., is authorized for expenditures of up to $900 million annually. However, in recent years, Congress has only appropriated about $35 million (National Recreation and Park Association 1987). During the period 1961-1971, Congress gave the USDA Forest Service 96 percent of its budget request for timber management, but only 45 percent for its requests for recreation (Downing 1988). This imbalance still existed in the fiscal year 1989 budget (Coffin 1988). From a professional perspective, there is currently no career entry level position for a professional in recreation for the USDA Forest Service. Entry-level recreation professionals are still hired under the forester, forestry technician, and landscape architecture professional position standards.

It is apparent that leisure is extremely valuable to people. This is evidenced in the growing participation rates at public recreation facilities. Recreational visitation to federal lands in the U.S. rose from about 300 million visitor days in 1965 to about 550 million in 1988 (Task Force on Outdoor Recreation Resources 1988). Further, the 1977 Nationwide Outdoor Recreation Survey indicated that the percentage of Americans engaged in selected activities rose in almost every case between 1960 and 1977. The percentage of persons engaging in picnicking increased from 53 to 72 percent; sightseeing from 42 to 62 percent; walking and jogging from 33 to 68 percent; and bicycling from 9 to 47 percent (Heritage, Conservation and Recreation Service 1977).

Such valuing is also seen in the expenditures people make for recreation. Using constant 1982 dollars, per capita expenditures for recreation in the U.S. rose from $480 in 1970 to $549 in 1986 (Task Force on Outdoor Recreation Resources 1988). From a more disturbing perspective, such valuing is also seen in the growing conflict among persons competing for recreational access to outdoor recreation resources. The 1977 outdoor recreation survey identified "areas too crowded" as the second greatest deterrent to participation among Americans (Heritage, Conservation and Recreation Service 1977).

However, there is still not firm evidence that such behavior means leisure is *vital* to people's well-being. This lack of evidence has important implications for the public support of leisure services. Public health and education receive substantial amounts of public support each year, because their necessity for human well-being is taken for granted. This is not the case with leisure and its benefits. Thus, decision-makers tend to perceive leisure pursuits as the frivolous things people do to fill up their idle time before getting on to the more serious matters of life.

Of course, it is possible to assert that such types of human indulgences should, in fact, be in the domain of the private sector. The provision of leisure services crosses a wide array of non-governmental arrangements, from private industry to public service organizations. The full picture of leisure and the benefits provided by it cannot be understood without a knowledge of the different suppliers and the roles they play. However, governmental involvement is a crucial part of the whole. Open space in cities, greenbelts in urban regions, and the vast acreage of wildlands are inevitably in the domain of public policy and provision.

This, then, points to the dilemma. Leisure is beneficial. But, when the question is directed at how well researchers have scientifically documented the nature of those benefits, at least to the extent of effectively influencing public policy, the answer is, not very well.

OBJECTIVES

Over 2000 years ago, Hippocrates called for cause-effect inquiry in the field of medicine. The history of that science shows that some individuals followed that advice and attributed sources of wide-spread diseases, such as diphtheria and cholera, to food or sanitation. Nevertheless, strongly predictive cause-effect relationships were not established in medicine until 100 years ago, following the work of Robert Koch, Louis Pasteur and others. Since that time, medical knowledge has been advanced greatly by systematic inquiry, including advantageous serendipitous spinoffs such as anesthesia, x-ray technology, and penicillin. Certainly, more needs to be learned, especially in the area of "preventative medicine." Perhaps one of the most significant aspects of this area of inquiry focuses on the contributions of recreation activity to mental and physical health.

The intent of this paper is not to try to play Hippocrates, though a primary purpose is to urge more cause-effect research on relationships between leisure activities and benefits to individuals and society. However, it is important to emphasize that such research is needed as much within the leisure professions as it was in the medical professions.

This chapter draws on the content of several other papers written recently on the subject of recreation benefits, in order to build a perspective on the significance of understanding the benefits of leisure, and particularly in pointing directions for needed research. The scope of consideration of benefits in this chapter will be somewhat limited. While monetary measures of value used by economists for "benefit-cost" analyses are important and necessary, the concern in this paper is not with the monetary worth of the recreation goods and services — or the benefits of recreation as defined by economists. Instead, the focus is upon the *actual* benefits (or utility) on which those economic "benefits" are based.

The primary objectives of the chapter are twofold. The first is to establish the idea that much of the current knowledge about the beneficial consequences of recreational engagements is "soft" scientifically; it is largely intuitive or inferential, having little strong predictability based in empirical evidence. This situation exists because there has been little research that has focused explicitly on benefits as defined here. It is not so much an issue that leisure research has been soft as it is that a void exists for empirically supported knowledge about benefits. The second objective is to encourage more systematic inquiry about benefits in order to fill that void.

DEFINITIONS

As the purpose of this chapter is not to develop a philosophy or theory of leisure, the words "leisure" and "recreation" will be used interchangeably. Any distinctions that the reader might wish to make between these terms are largely irrelevant in this context. More research on benefits is needed, whether of leisure as a mental state, a particular type of recreational engagement, a playful behavior, or of participation in a sport for fun. One need not draw definitive boundaries around these concepts in order to study their basic properties. While recreation and leisure pursuits encompass an extremely wide array of activities and behaviors, this paper generally emphasizes, but is certainly not limited to, outdoor pursuits.

Several definitions of the word "benefit" are in common usage. One focuses on benefaction, meaning "to do well, an act of charity" (The World

Publishing Co. 1968). Another definition is "something that guards, aids, or promotes well being" (G. and C. Merriam Co. 1965), or "anything contributing to an enhancement in condition" (The World Publishing Co. 1968). A third is how economists studying economic efficiency normatively use that word to mean a "potential Pareto improvement" and then use "willingness to pay" as a benefit (Randall 1984a). The fourth — and the definition we will use — is, "a benefit denotes a desirable change of state; it is a specified improvement in condition or state of an individual or a group of individuals, of a society, or even of nonhuman organisms" (Driver, Nash, and Haas 1987). Used in this way, a benefit means a gain of some type (Schreyer and Driver, in press (a)). Thus, the words "benefits," "gains," "improved conditions," and "desirable consequences" or "impacts" will be used interchangeably. As elaborated subsequently, it is much easier to define benefits than it is to specify and measure their magnitudes.

What are the benefits of recreation participation? It is likely that no definitive list will ever be compiled. There are many different types of benefits that could be and have been identified. Any given benefit may be argued concerning the extent to which it actually is a benefit of recreation, unless empirical evidence exists. Further, any listing will involve some organization and classification of different types of benefits that may be associated with one another.

Driver (1986) has identified the major categories as personal benefits, social benefits, economic benefits, and environmental benefits. Personal benefits are benefits to the individual, and are the ones that likely come to mind most immediately. Many of these have been inferred from studies of people's recreation experience preferences. Table 1 shows scales that have been refined over the years through many studies to represent these experience preferences (Driver and Brown 1987). Driver and Brown also list a summary categorization of probable personal benefits, which is shown here as Table 2. Table 3 shows an elaborated version of Table 2, developed from open-ended interviews with river recreationists (Schreyer and Driver, in press (b)).

Broader taxonomies of benefits going beyond the personal have also been developed. Table 4 shows a listing of the potential benefits of wilderness from the paper by Driver, Nash, and Haas (1987). Tables 5 through 7 show the results of a Delphi exercise from a workshop on recreation benefits in which three groups of experts on recreation and leisure attempted to create lists of benefits (Schreyer 1984). Finally, Table 8 presents an indirect listing of benefits. It is the set of topical presentations from a national conference on the benefits of recreation/leisure held in May, 1989 (Driver 1988).

These tables represent a tremendous range of potential benefits. The extent of overlap across the various tables gives some idea of the degree of shared agreement concerning any particular benefit. Space does not allow for an individual discussion of the various benefits, but the tables do give a good picture of what is meant by benefit in this chapter.

Table 1
Recreation Experience Preference Scales Making Up the Recreation Experience Preference Domains (shown in bold)[a]

1. ENJOY NATURE
   A. Scenery
   B. General Nature Experience
   C. Undeveloped Natural Area

2. PHYSICAL FITNESS[b]

3. REDUCE TENSION
   A. Tension Release
   B. Slow Down Mentally
   C. Escape Role Overloads
   D. Escape Daily Routine

4. ESCAPE NOISE AND CROWDS
   A. Tranquility/Solitude
   B. Privacy
   C. Escape Crowds
   D. Escape Noise
   E. Isolation

5. OUTDOOR LEARNING
   A. General Learning
   B. Exploration
   C. Learn Geography of Area
   D. Learn About Nature

6. SHARE SIMILAR VALUES
   A. Be With Friends
   B. Be With People Having
      Similar Values

7. INDEPENDENCE
   A. Independence
   B. Autonomy
   C. Being in Control

8. FAMILY KINSHIP[b]

9. INTROSPECTION
   A. Spiritual
   B. Personal Values

10. BE WITH CONSIDERATE PEOPLE[b]

11. ACHIEVEMENT/ STIMULATION
   A. Reinforcing Self
      Confidence/Self-Image
   B. Social Recognition
   C. Skill Development
   D. Competence Testing
   E. Seeking Excitement/
      Stimulation
   F. Self-Reliance

12. PHYSICAL REST[b]

13. TEACH/LEAD OTHERS
   A. Teaching-Sharing
      Skills
   B. Leading Others

14. RISK TAKING[b]

15. RISK REDUCTION
   A. Risk Moderation
   B. Risk Prevention

16. MEET NEW PEOPLE
   A. Meet New People
   B. Observe New People

17. NOSTALGIA[b]

Source: Driver and Brown 1987

[a] The items that make up these scales have been tested for many types of validity and reliability, with reasonably good results.

[b] These domains have only one scale, with the same title as the domain.

Table 2
A Taxonomy of Some Probable Personal Benefits Gained from Use of Outdoor Recreation Opportunities

A. Personal Development
  1. Self-concept
  2. Self-actualization
  3. Self-reliance
  4. Value clarification/introspection
  5. Humility
  6. Leadership
  7. Spiritual growth
  8. Aesthetic enhancement
  9. Learning

B. Social Bonding
  1. Family kinship
  2. Kinship with significant others
  3. Meeting new people

C. Therapeutic/Healing
  1. Clinical problems (drug abuse, etc.)
  2. Stress/tension mediation
  3. Physical rest

D. Physical Fitness/Health

E. Stimulation

F. Independence/Freedom

G. Nostalgia

H. Commodity-related

Source: Driver and Brown 1987

Table 3
Benefits from Recreation Participation Deriving from Interviews with Respondents at the Delaware Water Gap National Recreation Area and Upper Delaware Scenic and Recreational Rivers

Benefit Categories	No. of Times Mentioned	Percent of Total Sample[3]
A. Personal Development[1]	**48[4]**	**25.4**
1. Self-concept	4	2.1
2. Self-actualization	0	0.0
3. Self-reliance	1	0.5
4. Value clarification/introspection	4	2.1
5. Humility	0	0.0
6. Leadership	3	1.6
7. Spiritual growth	3	1.6
8. Aesthetic enhancement	7	3.7
9. Learning	5	2.6
10. Achievement/skill development[2]	13	6.9
11. Challenge[2]	8	4.2
B. Social Bonding	**108**	**57.1**
1. Family kinship	28	14.8
2. Kinship with significant others	39	20.6
3. Meeting new people	10	5.3
4. Group solidarity[2]	2	1.1
5. To tell others about the experience[2]	2	1.1
6. Nurturance[2]	3	1.6
7. Cultural awareness[2]	1	0.5
8. Solitude[2]	19	10.1
9. Escape family[2]	4	2.1
C. Therapeutic/Healing	**99**	**52.4**
1. Clinical problems	0	0.0
2. Stress/Tension mediation	31	16.4
a. Quiet/peace[2]	25	13.2
b. Stress release[2]	1	0.5
c. To recharge batteries[2]	5	2.6
3. Physical rest/Relaxation	68	36.0

Table 3 (Continued)

D. Physical Fitness/Health	**34**	**18.0**
1. Exercise[2]	11	5.8
2. Getting tan/sun[2]	23	12.2
E. Stimulation	**83**	**43.9**
1. Fun[2]	35	18.5
2. Excitement[2]	17	9.0
3. Recreation[2]	4	2.1
4. Adventure[2]	2	1.0
5. Exploration[2]	3	1.6
6. General stimulation[2]	22	11.6
F. Independence/Freedom	**8**	**4.2**
G. Nostalgia	**7**	**3.7**
H. Commodity-related (catch fish)	**9**	**4.2**
I. Experiential[2]	**73**	**38.6**
1. Good time[2]	16	8.5
2. Passing time/leisure[2]	11	5.8
3. New experience[2]	17	9.0
4. Seeing sights[2]	3	1.6
5. Pleasure/enjoyment[2]	20	10.6
6. Spontaneity[2]	4	2.1
7. Fantasy[2]	2	1.0
J. Relations with nature[2]	**116**	**61.4**
1. Enjoyment of nature[2]	66	34.9
2. To be outdoors/fresh air/water[2]	24	12.7
3. Temperature/good weather[2]	8	4.2
4. Scenery[2]	14	7.4
5. Relationships with place[2]	4	2.1

Source: Schreyer and Driver, in press (b)

[1] Categories patterned after those developed by Driver and Brown (1987).
[2] Categories not identified by Driver and Brown in their more general list.
[3] N = 189.
[4] Category totals represent summations of all subcategories.

Table 4
Taxonomy of Wilderness Benefits

I. **Personal benefits (accruing primarily to individuals and which might or might not benefit society at large)**

    A. Developmental (desired changes in self-concepts and skills)
       1. Self-concept
       2. Self-actualization
       3. Skill development

    B. Therapeutic/healing
       1. Clinical
       2. Nonclinical (stress mediation/coping)

    C. Physical health

    D. Self-sufficiency

    E. Social identity (development/maintenance of desired social relations with family and others)

    F. Educational

    G. Spiritual

    H. Esthetic/creativity

    I. Symbolic (benefits from options to realize that actions are being taken in support of preservation-related beliefs)
       1. Resource stewardship
       2. Anti-anthropocentricism/moralistic
       3. Option demands
       4. Other

    J. Other personal wilderness recreation-related benefits

    K. Commodity-related (benefits to individuals from goods produced from wilderness such as those related to water and to grazing by domestic animals)

    L. Nurturance

Table 4 (Continued)

II. Social benefits (accruing across individuals to society collectively or to large segments of society)

A. Aggregate personal benefits

B. Spin-off benefits

C. Historical cultural benefits

D. Preservation-related benefits
  1. Representative ecosystems
  2. Species diversity
  3. Air visibility
  4. Unique landforms, including areas of outstanding scenic beauty
  5. Historic sites
  6. Educational values
  7. Scientific laboratory
  8. Stewardship (options for future generations)

E. Quality of life

F. Commodity uses (water, minerals, grazing, etc.)

G. Economic benefits
  1. National economic development
  2. Local/regional economic development

III. Inherent/intrinsic (benefits to nonhuman organisms)

Source: Driver, Nash, and Haas 1987

Table 5
Delphi Listing from the Benefits Specification Workshop

I. SOCIAL/PERSONAL

Health - Activity
Group Cohesiveness - Making Friends
   Meeting People
Status
Skills
Learning
Increased Productivity
Conflict Resolution
Courtship

Community Stability and Harmony
Cultural Pride and Nationalism
Historical Understanding

II. MATERIAL

Income
Trophies
Play

Meat
Hides
Community Development

III. ENVIRONMENTAL

Preservation
Conservation
Husbandry
Stewardship

Joint Products (Management)
Baseline Indicators
Ecosystem Appreciation
Understanding Human Dependency

IV. PSYCHOLOGICAL

Independence/Self-Sufficiency
Mastery
"Split Rail"
Atavism
Historical Recall
Group Solidarity
Kinship
Family
Sharing
Leadership
Creativity
Escape
Contrast Value/Compensation
Aesthetics
Diversity
Spiritual/Religious
Nurturance
Simplicity

Prowess
Privacy
Isolation
Bonding
Competence
Virility
Personal Attractiveness
Exploration
Achievement
Risk Taking
Aggression
Danger
Nature Kinship and Empathy
Savagery
Humility
Abasement
Value Clarification

Source: Schreyer 1984

Table 6
Delphi Listing from the Benefits Specification Workshop

INDIVIDUAL

Psychological
Stress Reduction
Stimulation
Happiness

Self
Creativity
Self-actualization, Esteem, etc.

Physical
Learning About Wildlife (Knowledge Gained)
Learning About Physical Environment

Social/Cultural/Historic
Knowledge and Understanding of Cultures

SOCIAL

Social Harmony
Better Relations With Family, Friends

Economic
Increased Productivity
Jobs
Income

Physical
Environmental Protection (many costs too)
Animal Population Control = Ecological Stability

Source: Schreyer 1984

Table 7
Delphi Listing from the Benefits Specification Workshop

Family Solidarity
Cultural Continuity/Adoption
Mental Health - Capacity to Cope
Self-Identity/Frame of Reference
Physical Health
   Well-Being
   Cure/Prevention
Relaxation and Enhanced Concentration
Stress Mediation
Social Bonding/Intimacy/Dyad Formation
Sexual Potency
Group Identification
Enhanced World View -Cognitive
   Maturity
Catharsis/Self-Disclosure
Self-Confidence
Cognitive Efficiency/Integrative
   Complexity
Capacity for Fantasy/Imagery/Creativity/
   Reminiscence/Anticipation
Social Validation/Communication Skills
Socialization/Learning Social Rules
Financial Return/Utility Function
Productivity in Workplace/Everyday
   Environment
Vehicle for Competition
Stability
Point of Transition (Moving from one
   life situation to another)
Jobs

Enhanced Problem-Solving
Spiritual Communication
Humility
Skill Development
   Recreational
   General
      Organizational Skills
      Decision-Making
Sensation of Experience Arousal/
   Entertainment/Play
Thrill/Vertigo
Peak Experience
Sense of Aesthetics
Quality of Life Feeling
Pride/Patriotism
Political Action
Environmental Awareness
Products of Creativity -
   "Works of Art"
Establish Leadership Function
Status/Trophies
Validating Understanding
Locus of Control/Autonomy
Storage Function (Children)
Survival Capacity
Privacy/Withdrawal
Eating/Commensalism
Regional Well-Being

Source: Schreyer 1984

Table 8
Subject Areas for the Recreation/Leisure Benefits Workshop

Community Stability & Satisfaction Benefits of Leisure & Leisure
    Environments
Developmental Benefits of Leisure to Children
Beneficial Economic Consequences of Leisure and Recreation
Social Cohesion Benefits of Leisure & Leisure Environments
Managerial Needs for Information on Benefits
Organizational Wellness
Promotion of Flow Experiences & Self-Actualization
Programmed, Non-Clinical Skill Development Benefits of Wildland Settings
The Cardiovascular Benefits of Physical Exercise
Philosophical Perspectives About Leisure: A Cross-Cultural Inquiry
Philosophical Perspectives About Leisure: The English-Speaking Countries
Self-Identity Benefits of Leisure Activities
Beneficial Changes in Mood and Emotion
Beneficial Economic Consequences of Leisure & Recreation
Enhancement of Good Citizenship from Leisure Activities
Benefits of Leisure & Leisure Environments to Clinically Diagnosed People
Relationships Between Leisure & Leisure Environments and Quality of Life/
    Life Satisfaction
The Benefits of Leisure to Family Bonding
The Learning Benefits of Leisure Activities
Benefits of Leisure to Environmental Protection and Vice Versa
Spiritual Benefits of Leisure Activities & Settings
Needs for Information on Benefits in the Legislative Process
The Cardiovascular Benefits of Physical Activity
Developmental & Well-Being Benefits from Non-Programmed Engagements
Psycho-Physiological Indicators of Leisure-Related Causes of Well-Being
Beneficence of Sports Activities

Source: Driver 1988

THE NEED FOR INFORMATION ON BENEFITS

Several types of need exist for better knowledge about the beneficial consequences of leisure activity. They can be grouped as follows:

1. Advance and promote the leisure professions.
2. Improve resource allocation decisions.
3. Enhance consumer choices.

Each will be described briefly.

Advance the Leisure Profession

The most telling characteristic of a profession is its empirically supported body of knowledge. Of course, there may be some question as to just how professional the various sectors involved in recreation and leisure really are. There is, in fact, no such thing as "the profession" of leisure, and the range of competency of persons in various roles varies dramatically. There are practitioners in areas of leisure services with little formal training. There is no common body of knowledge in recreation and leisure which would be considered the fundamental foundation of a professional position. However, there are many who would seek to develop a level of professional respect for persons in the field of recreation and leisure that would be recognized by the public at large. Certainly, among persons purporting to pursue research to contribute to the existing body of knowledge and theory concerning leisure, the appellation of "professional" is a *sine qua non*.

Since the ultimate product of all service delivery systems is the benefits provided to the users of those services, knowledge about those benefits and about which service opportunities create particular benefits is the "bottom line" for determining whether the professionals delivering those services know what they are doing. This is the reason why medical doctors do not prescribe antibiotics for a nose bleed, and communication experts do not eliminate dialing tones and busy signals on telephones.

The pertinent question is: What benefits are produced from opportunities to camp, play softball, take a continuing education class in fly tying, or attend a symphony? If those benefits are known, the second question is: What are their magnitudes? Answers to these questions are necessary before anyone can compare the social advantages of parks and open spaces with alternative, non-recreational, uses of those lands. Yet, beyond good judgment and intuition, there are really few good answers. Systematically obtained information on the benefits of recreation will also help advance professional bodies of knowledge by leading to firmer theories of leisure. That knowledge would nurture additional research, support existing theories, and spawn new ones.

Knowing better what to do and how to do it will also promote and enhance images and credibility outside the leisure professions — just as medicine had to reduce quackery to gain respect. The implication is not that leisure professionals are quacks, but that limited empirical support for much of the existing knowledge base does lead to a lot of interesting pronouncements and overly assured assertions at professional meetings and in the leisure literature.

One final professional advantage of more systematic knowledge about the benefits of recreation needs to be mentioned. It is a subtle but extremely important one that relates to professional pride. Until quite recently, the field of leisure in academia, research, and practice was commonly perceived by others as having little intellectual content (see the chapter by Cooper). In the extreme, beliefs existed that people entering various careers within leisure could not succeed in other jobs. The question is whether or not this situation has changed considerably as sounder principles have been developed. Indicators of such change would be less defensiveness and better "minds" entering the leisure professions. This may also lead to stronger standards for academic curriculum accreditation. Increased knowledge about the benefits of leisure will promote that pride even more as understanding grows, and practitioners can articulate more clearly why and how leisure services contribute to the betterment of individuals and society.

Improve Resource Allocation Decisions

Research on benefits would facilitate better recreation policy and management decisions in several ways, as identified in other recent papers (Driver 1986; Driver, Brown, and Burch 1987; Schreyer and Driver, in press (a)). Policy makers need to compare the benefits and costs of alternative uses of public resources. These comparisons, which include but go beyond economic measures of benefits, have grown in importance as demands on public resources have increased and broadened. Among other things, information on recreation benefits would help to prevent making allocations for short-term gains that cause undesired long-term effects. Much of what is currently passed as knowledge about the benefits of recreation in public policy discussion is largely intuitive. More systematically documented information is needed.

Once basic public resources have been allocated for a particular type of recreational use, information on benefits would improve the ability of recreation planners and managers to define clear objectives and prescriptions and, then, to establish more explicit standards and guidelines for meeting those objectives. Provision of exercise trails, opportunities for self-testing, quiet places, sites for socialization of many types (such as enhancing family kinships), and options to be free from specific everyday pressure are examples of discrete management actions that can help assure options to realize specific types of benefits.

The extent to which an individual is expected to bear the cost of the public provision of beneficial services varies. Some benefits, such as national defense, are shared by all. Payment for such services is generally embedded in the taxes that citizens bear. Some benefits could be specifically charged for, such as public education, but again these are shared by the general public because of the presumed broader societal benefits that accrue. Within the area of recreation, the provision of specific opportunities by the public sector is often charged for, such as entrance to a state park. However, these fees are often below what the willingness to pay of the individual would be, and the actual cost of provision of such opportunities. This differential is also justified through assumptions concerning broader societal benefits.

On a larger scale, there are few fees charged to individuals who may gain substantial benefits from entering onto and recreating in large areas of public wildlands. Part of this could be attributed to the impracticality of collecting such fees. However, many of the rationales surrounding these policies have more to do with a general philosophy of free access to public lands (with the obvious exception of National Parks). This philosophy is beginning to change, as costs to public agencies for engaging in recreation planning and management grow, and as decisions have to be made concerning the competitive allocation of such lands for recreation as opposed to alternative resource uses which might produce commodities of known economic value. Thus, there is a growing feeling that the beneficiaries of recreation should pay their fair share of the costs of providing those services, although what constitutes a "fair share" is still a thorny issue.

Information on recreation benefits would make it possible to identify better what types and proportions of the benefits from a recreation opportunity accrue primarily to individuals (and to which types of individuals), to society at large, and to future generations. Thus, a better "multiple-part" pricing system could be designed under which particular types of beneficiaries pay user fees while others are subsidized by public taxation to meet clearly defined social objectives.

Better information about benefits could also give a clearer picture about the relationship between certain types of opportunities for participation (e.g. opportunities for activities such as fishing or skiing, or different types of activities, such as developed or primitive camping) and the benefits provided by those opportunities. This could help identify more clearly those benefits unique to particular recreation opportunities, those that are not unique but highly preferred from these opportunities, and those that can be obtained from alternative opportunities with no preference about which particular opportunities actually provide the benefit. The key is to identify how strong the relationship is between a given recreational opportunity and a particular benefit. Such information is needed to identify substitutes for various recreation opportunities, which is important in a world of limited resources. This would also help identify which sectors of society are willing to make such substitutions, and which are not, in order to better accommodate concerns for equity in allocation decisions. In addition to better allocation decisions, these advantages would also help promote the credibility of the leisure professions and increase pride and motivation among practitioners, as mentioned earlier.

Enhance Consumer Choice

Not only will information on patterns of individual gains and losses be useful to public decision makers, it will also likely enhance the rationality of the choices of sovereign consumers and voters. For example, if consumers knew more about the positive effects of different recreation activities, they might value them more highly, engage in them more often, and be more willing to pay for those opportunities through taxes or user fees. Thus, the information on gains and losses to individuals would be useful both to consumers, as well as to public decision makers, by helping each in their respective roles make more informed valuations and, therefore, better choices.

Obviously, a more informed public does not ensure that people will act in beneficial ways. Not all outcomes of recreation are beneficial, either to the individual (e.g. injuries from participation) or to society (e.g. anti-social behavior). Many people still smoke and make other choices that apparently are not good for them. Many of these decisions are based on short-term benefits as opposed to long-term consequences. Nevertheless, it is likely that most consumers and voters do use available information in their choices, especially over time. There appears to be growing support for the general concept of "wellness." For example, consumer behaviors have certainly been influenced by the advantages of using seat belts, reducing cholesterol in the diet, exercising, avoiding substance abuse (including alcohol and tobacco), and stress management. Knowledge of the cardiovascular benefits of habitual, aerobic exercise, of the role of leisure activities in stress management, and user support of therapeutic and adventure recreation programs indicate some reasonableness in human choices about leisure. One of the most important values to be derived is the capacity to give people information about *potential* benefits. Beyond current actual benefits, this may serve as an incentive for people to explore new potentials and, subsequently, to grow and develop.

Particularly relevant to the theme of this chapter is the fact that most of the research on these examples has been done quite recently. The relevancy is threefold: the proposed research can be done; it can influence consumer and resource decisions; and it can disclose both expected and unexpected benefits.

WHY THERE ISN'T MORE SYSTEMATIC DOCUMENTATION

Other papers (Driver 1986; Schreyer and Driver, in press (b)) have identified the major factors that have resulted in the paucity of empirical research on the benefits of leisure. They will be reviewed briefly.

1. Many leisure services are provided by public agencies, which do not promote research on benefits. For instance, Forest Service Research, the research arm of the U.S. Forest Service, is the largest natural resource research organization in the world. However, beyond economists, very few social scientists are employed by the organization, and they are spread across a range of topics, of which benefits is only one. The National Park Service employs researchers who work within individual units of the system, or in cooperative park studies units. The former are almost universally biological or physical scientists, with the rest in archaeology. The cooperative units tend to support projects requested by individual park units, which tend to be disproportionately non-social research. The Bureau of Land Management, the other major land managing agency in the U.S., does not have a formal research program. Social research is not seen as a particularly high priority in these agencies, and the cost of such research is generally perceived as not being justified.

2. For a variety of reasons, the concept of benefit has been increasingly perceived as being in the domain of economics. The economic view of benefit is strongly guided by the assumption that the utility to the individual need not be known, as long as the external behavior is expressed in a pricing situation. In this sense, economists measure the monetary value of benefits by measuring the goods and services that *provide* the benefits, and these are assumed to be the benefits themselves (Driver 1986). For example, Vickerman, in his chapter on economics in this volume, states that "user benefits are assessed by aggregation of consumer's surplus over all users. Consumer's surplus is the benefit that a consumer derives from undertaking an activity at a given price, which is below the price that he or she would be prepared to pay."

A common means of expressing this concept in terms of aggregate benefit in situations in which fees for public recreation opportunities are either not charged or exist at a nominal value are aggregate measures of consumers' "willingness to pay" for a given experience. Thus, as Driver (1986:46) has observed, "'benefits' are equated with the monetary worth of the goods and services to the consumers. The logic is that the willingness to pay reflects the utility (an unmeasurable abstraction used by economists) and improved conditions that users expect to realize from the good or service; that willingness indexes the worth of those benefits by pricing the worth of the goods and services that provided the benefits. But those underlying benefits remain unspecified and unmeasured."

There is obviously no quarrel with the fact that willingness-to-pay studies are an important part of our understanding of the *overall* nature of the benefits of recreation (Randall 1984b). However, there are deeper implications in terms of how agencies respond to the notion of recreation benefit in decision making: "many people, and agency evaluation handbooks, now use the word benefit to refer only to the results of willingness to pay studies" (Driver 1986: 46). Other potential positive outcomes are accounted for, but they are treated in generic terms dealing with qualitative values that do not often have the capacity to compete with the "hard" information provided by such studies.

Vickerman recognizes this issue as well: "To some extent, it could be argued that this has hindered the development of a more satisfactory conceptual and theoretical basis for this appraisal, since the requirement has too often been just for a quantification, however simplistic the underlying basis of the quantification may be." There needs to be greater semantic clarity about the referent of the notion of benefit, which is traditionally referred to as "economic benefit," to provide a better technical accuracy concerning what is being considered. This essentially would not compromise the validity of economic inquiries (Driver 1986), so much as it would expand the range of relevancy concerning what is referred to as benefit and its impact on decision making.

This notion is particularly relevant in the arena of public policy analysis. One of the major means of resource allocation decision making in the public sector has been the use of benefit-cost (B/C) analysis in evaluating potential options. In a situation of increasingly scarce resources, there is a tendency to focus on economic efficiency in budgetary commitments, which is a reason why such seemingly "rational" means of analysis have been favored. A market-driven economy would be particularly prone to support such analyses.

Other types of generic considerations, such as social welfare, could not compete well with such "hard" evidence (Driver 1986). However, this restricts the focus to viewing the benefit of a proposed action strictly in terms of the monetary worth of a good or service to potential and actual users (Peterson, Driver, and Brown, in press). This is tied to the assumption that aggregate expressions of willingness to pay over the costs of providing the goods and/or service will represent benefits in terms of the net increase in material wealth (Randall 1984a).

Of course, broader values are recognized in economic and political analyses. For instance, the Forest Service's Resource Planning Act program assessment (USDA 1980) recognizes four general categories of benefit: promotion of environmental quality; promotion of national economic development; promotion of regional and local economic development; and promotion of national well-being (Driver, Brown, and Burch 1987). The U.S. Water Resources Council (1979) has also adopted a similar range of assessments.

The question remains as to the extent to which the non-economic indicators are actually incorporated into decisions. This depends upon the analytic structures being used to put these elements into perspective. Within the domain of economic analysis, there are two major approaches to the attainment of governmental objectives — efficiency and equity. Economic efficiency deals with how recreational use and expenditure results in a change in the net aggregate economic wealth of the nation. Equity deals with the question of whether such gains are fairly distributed throughout society (Driver and Peterson 1987). The latter requires greater value judgment, and cannot be reduced to aggregate values involving willingness to pay, as there are deeper questions concerning the implications of potential inequities in distribution.

Such considerations may be abetted by the broader conceptual approach being used in this chapter. The basic definition of a benefit being used here is an "improved condition," which covers the full range of consideration addressed above. There is a more fundamental structure through which the concept of benefit may be addressed. First, it is necessary to specify the benefit itself. What are the specific benefits provided by a given recreational opportunity? Health? Stress reduction? Family solidarity? Second, what is the magnitude of benefit for any given participation? What increment of the benefit of stress reduction is, in fact, derived from a particular event? Third, what is the value of that benefit to the individual? It is this latter domain that is best represented by economics.

However, the other two have significant implications concerning the understanding of the provision of services for public well being: "there might be a direct correspondence between the magnitude of benefit and its relative value and there may not be; a small gain can have great importance and vice versa. Failure to distinguish benefits from measures of the value of the benefits has impeded progress in creating knowledge about the benefits of amenity goods and services" (Driver 1986: 47).

Driver, Brown, and Burch (1987) provide a model of the use of two contrasting approaches, one using solely economic indicators and the other using the broader paradigm employed above. Both share two similar steps in the initial process: 1) Management actions that cause changes in outputs of goods and services; 2) Changes in the use of goods and services. Then the two models split. The "utility-based" approach, which is the economic model, proceeds; 3) Consumer utility (not measured); 4) Monetary measures of assigned values. The other model is termed the "condition-based" approach, and it proceeds; 3) Measure the changed conditions of individual and other social units (gains and losses); 4) Monetary and non-monetary measures of assigned values.

Of course, this begs the question, why not just use the economic indicators. Why are they not sufficient to represent the inclusion of these values? Even though economists recognize the presence of non-quantifiable values, they usually do not carry much weight in the overall assessment of resource allocation. This is especially true when economists refer to their information as benefits in general, as opposed to economic benefits. This leaves the impression that all of the benefits can, in fact, be expressed in economic terms.

This is a subtle semantic argument, but it can have significant effects in viewing and assessing the allocation of public resources (Driver and Harris 1981). "While that paradigm has proven to be quite powerful for evaluating resource allocations, its application is seriously complicated for non-rival or non-exclusive goods or where the personal and social consequences of resource use are not well understood" (Driver, Brown, and Burch 1987).

Non-economic measures are intended to address a broader range of concerns than those that can be expressed purely through economic value (Peterson, Driver, and Brown, in press). Resource managers need to understand the consequences of their actions. While economic indicators are one way of expressing those consequences, it is also important to account for the meaning and the importance of those actions (Driver, Brown, and Burch 1987). This is in recognition of the multiple goals that agencies pursue in the provision of various goods and services. "No valuation methods exist now, nor will likely exist in the near future, that provide sufficiently commensurate and comprehensive measures to replace the subjective element of resource allocation decisions. The decision maker must have his or her own weighting system, as well as make many judgments about impact that are suspected but not well defined or measured" (Driver, Brown, and Burch 1987). The more systematically these non-economic values can be documented, the better decision makers will be able to evaluate the potential consequences of any actions.

Further, such evaluations often exist at the aggregate level, summing across all individuals. This is necessary in a broader scale, but there may be considerable value in examining individual gains and losses, such as characterizing what are the specific health gains to individuals from participation in a particular type of recreation. This would not only help decision makers; it could also help individuals make more informed choices concerning their own behavior. This could subsequently be translated to a greater willingness to pay, which would then give decision makers greater impetus to provide such opportunities (Driver, Brown, and Burch 1987). In this sense, such non-economic measures could help improve economic measures by enhancing individual consumers' utility appraisals (Driver 1986).

Economists recognize that intangibles, amenity values, merit goods, and incommensurables exist. However, that recognition does little to advance the capacity to make decisions about them. Unless researchers can systematically document what the gains and losses are, as well as their magnitudes, the provision of leisure services will continue to be forced into the arena of "black box" decision making.

3. The Puritan Work Ethic has deferred systematic inquiry of leisure in general and leisure benefits in particular.

4. In the public sector those services that generate more revenues (cash flows to the treasury) than do leisure services have tended to be emphasized (e.g., the sale of coal from public lands).

5. Until recently, the leisure professions and professionals were not given "fair" recognition in academic, research, and public management institutions. This attitude served to limit budgets, especially for research. This is a somewhat circular logic, in that a previous lack of systematic inquiry and the failure to develop a credible body of knowledge and lack of support serves as a major deterrent to the development of that knowledge base.

6. Related to the preceding point, the advancement of leisure theory has been a quite recent phenomenon. This has served to limit empirical investigations of the benefits of leisure, as the number and depth of integrative frameworks which could guide research are limited.

7. The research on benefits is extremely complex, lacks much precedence, and requires longitudinal studies that result in postponed publications. This has deferred needed research.

Fortunately, these constraints are weakening. There is now a considerable and rapidly growing interest in these benefits. Also, a sizable cadre of highly competent scientists has expressed interest in the topic, as well as a willingness to become involved as additional funds become available.

STUDYING BENEFITS

A central theme to this chapter is that there is little question that recreation provides benefits to people. However, that observation is based primarily on "common sense" or inferential knowledge. While this inferential knowledge may be helpful in articulating the importance of recreation, the nature and, especially, the magnitude of specific benefits have not been confirmed well enough by systematic research. Ironically, when it comes down to documenting benefits in a manner that would be recognized generally as providing evidence for specific benefits, there is little in the way of direct information. Much research has focused on related topics, and this is where most of our knowledge comes from. This research, much of which resulted in the creation of the tables shown earlier, has tended to focus on the initial reasons why people choose to engage in recreation in the first place, rather than focusing on what they actually obtain from the experience in the end. Thus, much of this information is inferred from research on motivations for participation (see the chapter by Iso-Ahola), desired psychological outcomes (Driver 1976), and recreation experience preferences (Driver and Brown 1987).

Other sources of information have been studies on types of satisfaction with recreation (Hendee 1974; Williams, in press). As a more direct source of information, descriptions in the popular literature have been used. Articles by

Driver, Nash, and Haas (1987) and Stankey and Schreyer (1987) used such descriptions to characterize benefits accruing from wilderness.

This chapter is not intended to be a review of the literature on benefits. The state of the knowledge of benefits that does exist has been documented by various recent publications. They include the series of papers on outdoor recreation benefits compiled by Kelly (1981), the 11 papers on monetary and non-monetary measures of benefits that were coordinated by Driver and Peterson for the Literature Review published by the President's Commission on Americans Outdoors (1987, section entitled "Values"), and other papers (Driver 1986; Driver, Nash, and Haas 1987; Schreyer and Driver, in press (a) and (b)). Those papers discussed a particular type of benefit in some detail, or comprehensively developed either lists of probable and known benefits or taxonomies of such, with brief descriptions of the state of knowledge about each.

There have been two broad approaches to the measurement of benefits, as described in this chapter. The first is through introspective measures, that is, by asking people how they think or feel about the benefits they receive. Such studies show a wide range of probable benefits. We say "probable," because most studies relying on introspective measures imply benefits, but do not define them explicitly.

Introspective studies may be further broken down into *direct* or *indirect* measures of benefit. As discussed previously, research has generally used constructs such as motivations, needs, satisfactions, or experience preferences that *indirectly* connote benefits. Examples are family kinship, being with friends, and being away from everyday strains and stresses. Although many introspective studies have been done that enhance our ability to make firmer inferences about benefits, a question remains as to how much evidence these studies provide to document benefits as improved conditions (see the chapter by Iso-Ahola).

Certainly, one can argue that, in a "chain of benefit causality", perceived increase in family kinship logically should lead to greater family solidarity and happiness, which has been identified as a significant contributor to life satisfaction (Campbell 1981). Or, alternatively, perceived respite from a demanding job could contribute to increased work productivity and, thus, to greater economic security and, then, greater life satisfaction — or to increased net national product and better comparative economic advantage to the nation in international trade and thus to a more favorable balance of payments. The fact still remains, however, that the indirect introspective measures only provide information either about rather loosely defined benefits realized at the beginning of the chain of causality, or inferences about specific benefits.

Some introspective studies were identified in the papers cited above that adopted *direct* measures of benefits — with the dependent variables defined explicitly as specified improved conditions. These include studies of improvement in specific abilities (e.g. leadership, skill proficiency), self-concept (Schreyer and Williams 1987; Williams, Haggard, and Schreyer, in press), learning, value clarification (Kaplan 1984), physical and mental relaxation (Ulrich 1981, 1984), and self-reliance (Burton 1981).

Both the direct and indirect introspective measures have generally used self-reports and have relied on ordinal scaling procedures to estimate the importance of the constructs. In most of these studies the rating of a particular "benefit" has been generally done within the context of the relative importance of other "benefits" included in the survey as part of a rather lengthy list. Further, very few of these studies have been predictive, because descriptive statistics were usually employed to test mean differences between specific "motivations," "needs," or "experience preferences," or differences across such items by age, sex, or some other classifying variable.

In a nutshell, direct and indirect introspective studies — while not "soft research" — provide rather soft results with respect to facilitating firm conclusions about the tangible nature, and especially the magnitude, of a specific benefit. Further, such measures lack behavioral correlates to the benefits identified, such as between perceived and physiological measures of improved physical fitness or mental relaxation.

The second approach involves measuring benefits represented by actual changes in behavior. Very few studies have used "behavioral change" measures, where the gains are defined as some type of observed improved performance, such as increased quantity or quality of work output, less absenteeism from work, improved behavior with respect to a spouse, children, or associates, or physiological measures designed to index changes in physical or mental health. Except for research on the cardiovascular benefits of physical activity (Buccola and Stone 1975), a couple of studies of increased academic performance from participation in adventure/challenge types of recreation (Ewert 1987), a few studies of physiological relaxation (Ulrich 1981, 1984), and some (usually not adequately designed) studies of reduction of clinical problems (substance abuse, delinquency, disciplinary problems in youth, etc.; Gibson 1979), the literature discloses very few behavioral change measures of benefits — the type that most convincingly establishes cause-effect relationships. The result is that we know very little about the benefits of leisure.

WHAT NEEDS TO BE DONE

Several needed courses of action have been implied in the foregoing discussion. They include:

1. Additional research.
2. Changes in perspectives about valuations of publicly-provided recreation goods and services.
3. Changes in perspectives by leisure professionals.
4. Changes in orientations within public agencies.

Additional Research

Obviously, more systematic research is needed to increase knowledge about benefits. The emphasis in that research should be on both prediction and causal explanation: What types of recreation opportunities (and characteristics of particular opportunities) cause or facilitate particular types of benefits, to which types of users, and why? Much greater use of behavioral-change (especially physiological) measures are needed. This means that "outside" disciplines, such as medicine, psychiatry, psychophysiology, and even bio-engineering, will need to be encouraged to collaborate on innovative research designs more than they have in the past.

Introspective measures will also be needed, because not all benefits are reflected by readily observable changes in behavior (e.g. increased self-concept, some types of learning, enjoyment, spiritual development, value-clarification). Considerable advancement of knowledge about the benefits would result if future studies focused *directly* on beneficial changes rather than *indirectly* on constructs from which inferences must be made about benefits. This does not mean that the indirect introspective measures are not useful for other purposes, such as to identify user motivations and environmental dispositions. It does mean that if benefits are the dependent variables, then knowledge is advanced better by research that defines specific types of improved conditions than by other constructs from which inferences must be drawn about benefits.

Whether behavior change or introspective measures are used, greater emphasis must be placed on quantifying the magnitudes of the benefits. This will require considerable innovation. While comparisons of relative magnitude are helpful, other measures would be more useful. Beyond relative measures, there is a need to define magnitude on some common metric or standardized scales of measurement that would allow for comparisons of magnitudes across benefits. This is one reason why the behavior-change measures are effective, as they are more prone to quantification.

Future research efforts should also try to avoid the common confusion that exists in the impact assessment literature between measurement of the magnitude of an impact (gain, for our purposes) and the value of that gain. Specifically, there are five analytical exercises involved (Driver and Burch, in press; Peterson, Driver, and Brown, in press):

1. Specify the impact (gain or benefit).
2. Select variables (and parameters of those variables) that will be used to quantify the magnitude of the impact.
3. Measure the magnitude of the impact.
4. Select variables (and parameters) to measure the value of the impact.
5. Estimate the value of the impact.

An example will be used to clarify these differences. Consider the case of a person interested in the value of listening to Mozart's clarinet concerto (K-622) for mental relaxation after a cognitively taxing day at work. First, it is necessary to specify the benefit, which is here called mental relaxation. Second, one must select the variables to be used to measure changes in mental relaxation. This could be some type of introspective measure of mental disengagement, relaxation, or change, using self-reports on a psychometric instrument. But, in line with the theme of this chapter, assume the measure to be alpha amplitude (brain wave) on an electroencephalogram (EEG), which is a widely accepted measure of wakeful relaxation. Third, the magnitude of mental relaxation (the benefit) needs to be measured. This could be done using measures of alpha amplitude before and while listening to the Mozart selection. Fourth, it is necessary to select variables to measure the worth or relative importance of any beneficial changes observed in alpha amplitude. For simplicity here, willingness to pay for a scarce compact disc of the best performance ever of K-622 will be used to represent that worth. Of course, other variables could be used. Finally, and fifth, the amount of willingness to pay a monetary price needs to be estimated. The point is: the magnitude of the benefit might or might not be perfectly correlated with the value of that magnitude; some small beneficial changes have great value and vice versa.

However, even before dealing with issues of magnitude, the first analytical task is one of specifying, or clearly defining, a benefit. This in itself can be difficult and deserves some elaboration. A recent discussion (Driver, Nash, and Haas 1987) addresses this point:

> To answer the question "What are the gains (benefits) ... ?" we need to know who gains and who loses and how. Qualitative analyses (Peterson *et al.*, in press) are needed to help answer these questions, because saying that an impact is a gain or a loss involves a valuation by the gainers and losers or by those who represent them. Those judgments reflect the gainers' and losers' held values (or preferential judgments), and they vary from one context to another (Brown 1984). Various impacts of adding a new area to the Wilderness Preservation System would be considered as gains by members of the Wilderness Society, but that allocation might be perceived as mostly causing losses to a party interested in commodity uses of the same area. Of course, either party might understand the perspectives of the other, but still differ in its preferential judgments about wilderness. Also, what is considered a gain at one point in time may be considered a loss at another by the same party. An avid jogger might later suffer knee injury caused by the jogging. The *ex ante* and *ex post* values assigned opportunities for jogging might differ.

At some stage, gainers and losers should be involved in defining the gains and losses to protect the sovereignty of those whom the proposed allocation will impact. Those impacted must definitely be involved directly in defining any gains and losses that are not yet well specified. Such involvement might, for example, include members of an Indian tribe claiming sacred significance of a land area, recreationists desiring use of the same area, or a mining company seeking profit from mineral extraction. On the other hand, less involvement is now needed where good definitions exist for certain impacts, such as the cardiovascular benefits of using an area for exercise (Buccola and Stone 1975) or the losses associated with wildfire caused by recreationists. Past research along with new studies must be used to achieve comprehensive definitions of the gains ... associated with use of particular amenity goods and services.

There would probably not be a great deal of controversy about the most generally defined benefits of recreation. However, it is the context in which they are defined, and the ways in which they are used in empirical research, that ultimately has become an issue. In any case, the systematic documentation of these benefits will require tapping the perceptions of the public. In this regard, much more qualitative research needs to be done. This type of research is particularly important in specifying these benefits.

Changes in Valuation Perspectives

A recent paper (Driver and Burch, in press), has tried to establish three perspectives regarding measurement and valuation of public amenity goods and services, such as recreational opportunities. First, all public resource agencies pursue multiple goals that frequently conflict, such as the promotion of national, regional, and local economic development or growth and the provision of amenities. Second, no one paradigm for estimating the impacts and values of alternative allocations of public resources for commodity uses (such as timber) and non-commodity uses (such as wilderness) can measure, comprehensively and accurately, all impacts or their values. This means that public decision makers — in the face of severely limited information about all impacts and values — must somehow miraculously and simultaneously weigh and ultimately balance a lot of incommensurate measures to come up with (hopefully) the best allocation. They must reach deeply into their "black boxes" to perform this "magic." Third, better information on the beneficial (as well as the unwanted) impacts of a proposed allocation on individuals and society would open the "black boxes" to much light, and thus enhance the rationality of public resource allocation decisions. The problems are that public decision makers have little empirically supported information about these benefits, and there is an overemphasis on the monetary values of the goods and services that provide these benefits, without comprehensive knowledge about what the actual benefits are. This is particularly important because the decision makers in general have a mandate to advance the well-being of society.

The research proposed in this chapter should help pursue the nature, scope, and magnitude of such benefits. However, not all values can be translated to a common denominator. Even if all the benefits to people were known, monetary measures could not index the worth of some of the benefits (e.g. value clarification, spiritual growth, etc.). Such measures also say nothing about benefits beyond the individuals who reveal their willingness to pay, such as general societal benefits (e.g. greater national pride) that have consequences beyond those individuals. In the final analysis, both the monetary and non-monetary measures of benefits are needed in the decision process, but for different purposes.

The specific need is for the technical analysts, representing different disciplinary perspectives, as well as decision makers, to recognize the need for information on the beneficial impacts to individuals in the resource valuation process. Perspectives are changing, but more progress is needed. In a sense, this may well represent the beginning of a new journey in making decisions about how public resources are used to meet people's needs.

Changes in Perspectives in Leisure Professionals

As mentioned earlier, there is no single leisure "profession," and there is considerable variation in the knowledge, values, and capacities of individuals who work in the provision of leisure services. Frequently, such practitioners tend to focus on the more immediate concerns of management. As such, the whole domain of recreation and leisure becomes one of attention to equipment handling and budget management. One only need skim through the pages of *Parks and Recreation* to gain a clear picture of the extent of this perspective.

When major issues are addressed, they generally have to do with concerns for law enforcement, liability, trash collection, and vandalism. These are, of course, not irrelevant issues for management; but when there is a fixation on such concerns, it blocks consideration of the broader intent of leisure services. There may be philosophical tracts that address the benefits of leisure, but often they are couched in idealistic faith and romanticized elevation that invokes Dorothy and Toto skipping down the Yellow Brick Road, rather than a recognition of the need for systematic inquiry and documentation.

While faith and inspiration are admirable, they carry remarkably little weight in front of Congressional Subcommittees intent on slashing budgets. The tunnel vision that keeps practitioners focused on the day-to-day aspects of coping with management situations and the naive romanticism about the wonderful good things leisure does for the folks — from stopping crime to curing mental illness to reducing the national debt — both serve to prevent the serious articulation of the cause-effect nature of leisure activities in providing specific benefits.

This contributes to the perception that leisure is a "trivial pursuit," that practitioners do not particularly need professional education, and that systematic research is not necessary or, even, particularly desirable. In a circular sense, this prevents the systematic documentation of the benefits of leisure, which then continues to maintain it in the domain of the folklore of nice things to do. While there are many persons external to leisure services who have mind-sets against the importance of leisure and recreation, unless leisure practitioners themselves treat the concept with more respect and recognize the need for more rigor, this situation will not change.

Changing Perspectives Within Public Agencies

Too often, public recreation agency personnel are caught up in the "here and now," while practicing crisis management, frequently of a defensive nature. Recreation tends to get defined as a "problem" to be dealt with. This makes it difficult for people to plan actively to provide opportunities to meet people's needs.

As an added difficulty, few public agencies provide "career ladders" for recreation professionals. It is therefore difficult to cultivate a competent and dedicated cadre of people to advance this type of resource use. In these institutional atmospheres, there will be little support for the research proposed in this paper. Somehow, perspectives need to be changed to focus more on social services and fundamental contributions than on getting the everyday job done. The world is changing in terms of the values people place on recreation. There is a growing need to be able to translate these into terms that can be used in contemporary resource management and planning.

CONCLUSION

People benefit from access to satisfying leisure opportunities. The value of those benefits, from all the indirect indicators it is possible to identify, is substantial. Further, the importance of the benefits derived from leisure appears to be growing through time. This culture is investing increasing importance in the life meanings derived from freely chosen pursuits. People are giving themselves ever greater permission to define themselves through leisure, as a complement to the more structured and pre-determined elements of life (see the chapter by Godbey).

The basis of the criticism in this chapter centers around the belief that these values are not being adequately incorporated into public policy decisions about providing opportunities to assist people in such quests. Research can serve, as it has with medicine, to advance this cause, by providing good, systematic evidence that such values are tangible, substantial, and worthy of pursuit. Perhaps the best service to be rendered in this regard is to be as persuasive as possible in encouraging the documentation of these benefits. Everyone benefits from leisure. What is needed is a better articulation of those benefits from professionals who bear the responsibility for advancing this cause in the public sector.

References

Brown, T.C. 1984. "The concept of value in resource allocation." *Land Economics 60:* 231-246.

Buccola, V.A. and W.J. Stone. 1975. "Effects of jogging and cycling programs on physiological and personality variables in aged men." *Research Quarterly 46:* 134-139.

Burton, L.M. 1981. "A critical analysis and review of the research on Outward Bound and related programs." Ph.D. dissertation, Rutgers University, New Brunswick, NJ.

Campbell, A. 1982. *The Sense of Well-Being in America: Recent Patterns and Trends.* New York: McGraw Hill.

Coffin, J.B. 1988. "FS: Recreation budget lags far behind targets in plans." *Federal Parks and Recreation 6(5):* 3-4.

Downing, K.B. 1988. Personal communication.

Driver, B.L. 1976. "Toward a better understanding of the social benefits of outdoor recreation participation." In *Proceedings of the Southern States Recreation Research Applications Workshop.* General Technical Report SE-9, pp. 163-189. Asheville, NC: USDA Forest Service, Southeastern Forest Experiment Station.

Driver, B. L. 1986. "Benefits of river and trail recreation: The limited state of knowledge and why it is limited." In *Proceedings of the First International Congress on Trail and River Recreation,* ed. S. Seguire, pp. 44-58. Vancouver, BC: Outdoor Recreation Council of British Columbia.

Driver, B.L. 1988. Authors and papers for the recreation/leisure benefits workshop. Fort Collins, CO: USDA Forest Service, Rocky Mountain Forest and Range Experiment Station.

Driver, B.L. and P.J. Brown. 1987. "Probable personal benefits of outdoor recreation." In *President's Commission on Americans Outdoors: A Literature Review.* Washington, D.C.: US Government Printing Office. "Values" section: 63-70.

Driver, B.L. and C.C. Harris. 1981. "Improving measurement of the benefits of public outdoor recreation programs." *Proceedings, Division 4, XVII IUFRO World Congress:* 525-537.

Driver, B.L. and G. Peterson. 1987. "Benefits of outdoor recreation: An integrating overview." In *President's Commission on Americans Outdoors: A Literature Review.* Washington, DC: U.S. Government Printing Office. "Values" section: 1-10.

Driver, B.L., T.C. Brown, and W.R. Burch, Jr. 1987. "A call for more comprehensive and integrated evaluations of public amenity goods and services." In *Proceedings of the 18th IUFRO World Congress: Economic Value Analysis of Multiple-Use Forestry*, eds. F. Kaiser and P.J. Brown, pp. 204-216. Corvallis, OR: Oregon State University, Department of Resource Recreation Management.

Driver, B.L., R. Nash, and G.E. Haas. 1987. "Wilderness benefits: A state-of-knowledge review." In *Proceedings of the National Wilderness Research Conference,* General Technical Report INT-220, ed. R.C. Lucas, pp. 294-319. Ogden, UT: USDA Forest Service, Intermountain Forest and Range Experiment Station.

Driver, B.L. and W.R. Burch, Jr. 1988 "A framework for more comprehensive valuations of public amenity goods and services." In *Amenity Resource Valuation: Integrating Economics With Other Disciplines,* eds. G.L. Peterson, B.L. Driver, and R. Gregory, pp. 31-45. State College, PA: Venture Publishing, Inc.

Ewert, A. 1987. "Values, benefits and consequences in outdoor adventure recreation." In *President's Commission on Americans Outdoors: A Literature Review.* Washington, DC: U.S. Government Printing Office. "Values" section: 71-80.

G. and C. Merriam Co. 1965. *Webster's Third New International Dictionary of the English Language, Unabridged.* Springfield, MA.

Gibson, P.M. 1979. "Therapeutic aspects of wilderness programs: A comprehensive literature review." *Therapeutic Recreation Journal 13:* 21-33.

Hendee, J.C. 1974. "A multiple-satisfaction approach to game management." *Wildlife Society Bulletin 2:* 104-113.

Heritage, Conservation and Recreation Service. 1977. *1977 Nationwide Outdoor Recreation Survey*. Washington, DC: U.S. Government Printing Office.

Kaplan, R. 1984. "Wilderness perception and psychological benefits: An analysis of a continuing program." *Leisure Sciences 6:* 271-290.

Kelly, J.R. ed. 1981. *Social Benefits of Outdoor Recreation*. Urbana-Champaign, IL: University of Illinois, Department of Leisure Studies.

National Recreation and Park Association. 1987. "Commission calls for 'absolute minimum' of $1 billion." *Dateline: NRPA 10:* 1.

Peterson, G.L., B.L. Driver, and P.J. Brown. In press. "The benefits of recreation: dollars and sense." In *Economic Valuation of Natural Resources: Issues, Theory and Applications*, eds. R.L. Johnson and G.V. Johnson. Boulder, CO: Westview Press.

President's Commission on Americans Outdoors. 1987. Section entitled "Values." In *President's Commission on Americans Outdoors: A Literature Review*. Washington, DC: U.S. Government Printing Office.

Randall, A. 1984a. "The conceptual basis of benefit cost analysis." In *Valuation of Wildland Resource Benefits*, eds. G.L. Peterson and A. Randall, pp. 53-63. Boulder, CO: Westview Press.

Randall, A. 1984b. "Benefit cost analysis as an information system." In *Valuation of Wildland Resource Benefits*, eds. G.L. Peterson and A. Randall, pp. 65-75. Boulder, CO: Westview Press.

Schreyer, R. 1984. "The recreation benefit specification workshop." Logan, UT: Institute of Outdoor Recreation and Tourism, Utah State University, 43 pp.

Schreyer, R. and B.L. Driver. In press(a). "The benefits of outdoor recreation participation." In *Proceedings Benchmark 88: A National Outdoor Recreation and Wilderness Forum*, ed. A. Watson. Asheville, NC: USDA Forest Service, Southeastern Forest Experiment Station.

Schreyer, R. and B.L. Driver. In press(b). "The benefits of wildland recreation participation: What do we know and where do we go?" In *Contributions of Social Scientists to Multiple-Use Management: An Update*, ed. B.L. Driver. Fort Collins, CO: USDA Forest Service, Rocky Mountain Forest and Range Experiment Station.

Schreyer, R. and D.R. Williams. 1987. "Episodic vs. continued participation —
implications for self-concept enhancement." Paper presented at the
Fourth World Wilderness Congress, Estes Park, CO.

Stankey, G.H. and R. Schreyer. 1987. "Attitudes toward wilderness and factors
affecting visitor behavior: A state-of-knowledge review." In *Proceed-
ings of the National Wilderness Research Conference*, General
Technical Report INT-220, ed. R.C. Lucas, pp. 246-293. Ogden, UT:
USDA Forest Service, Intermountain Forest and Range Experiment
Station.

Task Force on Outdoor Recreation Resources and Opportunities. 1988. *Outdoor
Recreation in a Nation of Communitie*s. Washington, DC: U.S.
Government Printing Office, 169 pp.

The World Publishing Co. 1968. *Webster's New World Dictionary of The
American Language: College Edition*. New York, NY.

Ulrich, R.S. 1981. "Natural versus urban scenes: Some psychophysiological
effects." *Environment and Behavior 13*: 523-556.

Ulrich, R.S. 1984. "View through a window may influence recovery from
surgery." *Science 224*: 420-421.

USDA. 1980. *The RPA Program — 1980 Update*. Washington, DC: USDA
Forest Service.

U.S. Water Resources Council. 1979. "Procedures for evaluation of national
economic development NED benefits and costs in water resources
planning." *Federal Register 44*: 72950-72965.

Williams, D.R. Haggard, and Schreyer R. In press. "Satisfaction and outdoor
recreation participation." In *Proceedings Benchmark 88: A National
Outdoor Recreation and Wilderness Forum*, ed. A. Watson. Asheville,
NC: USDA Forest Service, Southeastern Forest Experiment Station.

RECREATION NON-PARTICIPATION AND BARRIERS TO LEISURE

Thomas L. Goodale and Peter A. Witt

Besides satisfying basic curiosity about the dynamics of an important area of human behavior, understanding why people recreate has important implications for those who plan leisure services, provide facilities for leisure activities, and develop leisure-related policies. While much of the research in this area is focused on why people recreate, there is growing interest in the other side of the coin — why people do *not* recreate and what are the antecedents and consequences of recreation non-participation. Indeed, the origins of recreation service provision are founded in attempts to overcome the deleterious conditions which precluded or limited recreation participation for one group or another.

EVOLUTION OF RECREATION SERVICES

During the 19th Century, a number of reform movements emerged throughout North America and Europe. These movements sought to redress problems that accompanied the growth and spread of industrialism and organization, particularly those confronting the urban poor and, more particularly, urban children and youth. The recreation movement, the community centers movement, the playground movement, and the city beautiful movement in the United States and elsewhere emerged at this time, as did Britain's "Civilizing Mission to the Poor." The kindergarten movement in Germany and movements to reform education for children in Italy, Germany, the United States, and elsewhere were rooted in similar concerns.

Many of the leaders of these movements were activists seeking reform of social and physical environments (Duncan 1985) which created obstacles to "healthy" physical, social, intellectual, psychological, and moral growth and development. In short, urban parks and playgrounds, community centers and summer camps, and clubs, voluntary associations, and professional organizations all sought to overcome obstacles to "the worthy use of leisure time."

This brief overview of the origins of recreation and leisure services provides the context for the current interest in non-participation and barriers to participation. Clearly, that interest originated in practical concerns about human, social welfare. Academic and theoretical interest, although of comparatively recent origin, is infused with practical concerns and applications.

It must be recognized that concern about barriers, non-participation in recreation activities, and lack of leisure opportunities has always been an important progenitor of park, recreation, and leisure services. From the origin of public and voluntary agency services up to the past two decades or so, the principal strategy for overcoming barriers was the direct provision of facilities and services. That, too, remains a principal strategy. Even the provision of services based on the principle of satisfying demand, or the wish to convert latent demand into manifest or expressed demand, can be seen as addressing the barrier of "lack of opportunity" as a reason for non-participation.

We have come to recognize, however, that although the direct provision of services and facilities may help overcome some barriers for some people, the simple provision of more opportunity is usually not enough. The dynamics of participation or non-participation are complex, encompassing psychological, health-related, and other personal factors. Too, there are both philosophical and practical — social, political, and economic — limits to multiplying facilities and programs. In addition, practical interest in non-participation and barriers can be furthered by direct and disciplined inquiry into the reasons why people do or do not participate, what barriers they encounter, why barriers are indeed barriers, and what, if anything, can and should be done about them.

EVOLUTION OF THE STUDY OF NON-PARTICIPATION AND BARRIERS

The study of non-participation and barriers to participation has moved through at least four stages. These stages can be described as: (1) philosophic and social welfare-based concerns about the causes and consequences of recreation non-participation; (2) the identification of demographic and socio-economic correlates of participation and non-participation and the growth of survey research and quantitative methods; (3) pursuit of social-psychological correlates of barriers to participation, along with a broadening of the operationalization of barriers to include such concepts as barriers to leisure fulfillment or enjoyment; and (4) beginning attempts to develop comprehensive models that take into account the multitudinous factors that affect participation/non-participation, enjoyment/non-enjoyment, and the like. These stages are described briefly in the following pages.

Social Welfare: Philosophy and Practice

For about a century, the park and recreation movement represented an effort to overcome barriers to participation through the direct provision of facilities and services. The rapid transition from rural, agrarian communities to an urban, industrial society resulted in decrements of opportunity to make recreational use of free time and cope with the growing segmentation of time and space. Research consisted, in the main, of gathering information to support causes and initiatives and to provide political education. The struggle between the Social Darwinism of Herbert Spencer and the Instrumentalism of John Dewey came increasingly to be resolved in favor of the latter. Reason, evidence, collective action, and social policy became instruments for social development and improvement. Interventions of reformers and collective responsibility came to supplant fatalistic biology and the natural laws of survival.

Recreation and leisure, as academic and research interests, are included particularly in the rich sociological tradition of community studies, of which there are many well known examples from the first several decades of the twentieth century (e.g. Lundberg *et al.* 1934). Recreation participation and non-participation were studied in a comprehensive way as an important element of community and social life. Quantitative methods were seldom used until, in the 1950s, quantification and descriptive statistics on participants and participation became more characteristic of work on this subject. In the main, practical concern with the provision of opportunity characterized the first stage, from the origin of the park and recreation movement to about 1950.

Demographic and Socioeconomic Correlates

In the 1950s and 1960s, several studies were undertaken to identify the correlates of recreation participation. Thus, basic demographic and socio-economic variables such as age, gender, income, and education were included in community "attitude and interest" surveys and in most studies that sought information about recreation demand. In an early attempt to look at what is now referred to as market segments, preferences for and participation in particular forms of activities were differentiated by age groups, gender, or categories of socio-economic status. Barriers to participation were implied in correlational or other statistical relationships between these variables and measures of participation or desired participation. These efforts were mainly sociological in nature, with the emphasis on an understanding of collective as opposed to individual behavior.

The multi-volume report of the Outdoor Recreation Resources Review Commission (1962) is the best example of this approach and thus is a useful starting point for more a detailed review of non-participation and barriers research. While the Commission was particularly interested in the demand for outdoor recreation and the role of government in the management of resources to meet this demand, some volumes were of particular interest to social scientists and provided further impetus to the study of recreation behavior. Study Report Number 19, *National Recreation Survey* (Ferriss *et al.* 1962) and Number 20, *Participation in Outdoor Recreation: Factors Affecting Demand Among American Adults* (Mueller, Gurin, and Wood 1962) were read widely and referred to frequently by those in academic and research communities. While the ORRRC studies focused primarily on demand, some effort was made to address the questions of non-participation and barriers directly. There was, in addition, some attempt to address the questions of attitude and motivation, although "the scope of (the) study permitted only a very modest beginning" (Mueller *et al.* 1962: 1).

The survey and report of factors affecting demand focused mainly upon the influence of social, economic, and demographic variables (age, gender, health status, race, place of residence, income, occupation, education, and so on). In addition, an opportunity rating, based on availability of resources, was included, along with questions which began to probe the phenomenon of non-participation and the reasons for it. Questions were asked about activities in which respondents would like to begin participating or to participate more often and the reasons respondents did not do so.

For example, Proctor (1962), in Appendix A of Volume 19 of the ORRRC Reports, factor analyzed participation in 15 different outdoor recreation activities, calculated factor scores for each subject for the four derived factors, and then conducted regression analyses for eight subgroups (four regions by gender) to determine the best predictors of each of the four activity scores. Variables such as education, occupation, health status, and income emerged as major predictors of participation, along with age and region.

Proctor's discussion of the results indicated an interest in determining not only what variables predicted increased participation in a given set of activities, but also what variables predicted decreased or no participation. Thus, noting that age is negatively correlated with participation in some set of recreation activities is also to say that age is associated with circumstances that create barriers. A similar case can be made for most variables that are said to predict demand or participation.

The relationship of barriers to demand was also explicitly discussed in the introductory section of the National Recreation Survey results, a major part of the ORRRC Reports (Ferriss *et al.* 1962). Having determined the characteristics (time required to engage, monetary costs of engaging, level of physical activity involved, etc.) of each of the recreation activities included in the survey, the report stated that:

> Characteristics of the activity may predetermine or condition participation in the activity. These characteristics are considered in terms of the limits they specify. In each case weassume that the commitment of a person to an activity is related to the ratio between the input necessary to participate and rewards he perceives receiving as a result of participation....
>
> Consider a young person of excellent health, no physical impairments, and high vitality; an input of physical activity would

be of little cost to him and might, in fact, contribute to his reward system; but, since he is young and dependent financially, an input of money might make the activity prohibitive to him (Ferriss *et al.* 1962: 5).

The report also attempted to deal directly with the issue of barriers to participation. The central interest was in determining why people do not participate in outdoor activities to the full extent of their desires. Thus, the sixty percent of the respondents from the overall National Recreation Survey who indicated that they would have liked to engage in more outdoor activity than they did the preceding year were asked: "What was it, mainly, that prevented you from doing them last year?" (Mueller *et al.* 1962: 5-6). The results are included in Table 1. They indicate time, cost, health status, family ties, and availability of facilities as the major factors preventing desired outdoor recreation participation.

Table 1
Factors Preventing Desired Outdoor Activity

Reason Given	%[1]
Lack of time	52
Financial cost, too expensive	17
Ill-health, old age	11
Family ties	11
Lack of available facilities	9
Lack of car	5
Lack of equipment	4
Miscellaneous	9
Don't know or not ascertained	4
(Number of cases)	(1,737)

[1] Adds to more than 100% because respondents could mention more than one reason.

Source: Mueller *et al.* 1962.

In summarizing the results of the demand and barriers portions of the survey, the authors concluded that:

> Most popular are the activities in which barriers to participation
> are minimal — driving for sightseeing and relaxation, and
> picnicking. Activities which require more physical effort and skill
> and more specialized facilities are engaged in by fewer people
> (Mueller *et al.* 1962: 8-9).

Thus, the ORRRC studies provided significant base-line data, an important benchmark, and in some respects a beginning of academic interest and social science research into non-participation and barriers to participation. The National Recreation Survey, however, was typical of studies of the period — and, indeed, many approaches still currently in vogue. Data concerning recreation participation was limited to only 15 outdoor recreation activities; the list of barriers was limited as well. However, while the scope and conceptualization were restricted, the ORRRC studies did bring important attention to the relationship between demand and certain factors that inhibited it.

Broadening the Conceptualization: A More Social-Psychological Approach

Between the publication of the ORRRC reports and the early 1970s, the approach to non-participation research remained for the most part unchanged. In the 1970s, the study of leisure began to take on a social-psychological perspective. Interest in barriers followed a similar path. Part of the stimulus for this emphasis was a product of the self-help, personal growth movement which emerged in the late 1960s. Growing interest in leisure counseling and leisure education dictated a greater interest in information that would be useful in helping individuals reach more optimal levels of leisure functioning. The vocabulary of service delivery expanded to include enabling and facilitating participation as an extension of the traditional commitment to provision of opportunities. This expansion was particularly evident in work with special populations, when the National Therapeutic Recreation Society in the United States adopted a service model that included components specifically aimed at improving leisure functioning by helping individuals identify and remove barriers to participation (National Therapeutic Recreation Society 1982). However, while not as clearly operationalized, facilitating or enabling participation was certainly added to the mandate of park and recreation services.

In addition, there was increased interest in exploring barriers to participation in the context of the state-of-mind approach to operationalizing leisure. With this approach, there is more interest in how people *feel* about what they are doing, as opposed to simply examining what a person is doing or if the individual is participating in a particular activity. Thus, dependent variables were broadened to include variables such as enjoyment (Witt and Goodale 1981), leisure satisfaction (Beard and Ragheb 1980) and perceived freedom in leisure (Ellis and Witt 1984; Witt and Ellis 1985). Focusing on barriers to a particular state-of-mind also influenced the type of barriers that were examined, such as impediments to individuals' perceiving freedom in leisure. Based on attribution theory (Iso-Ahola 1980), factors such as perceived competence and perceived control were seen as influencing perceived freedom in leisure. While Ellis and Witt (1984) included a barriers inventory in their overall "Leisure Diagnostic Battery," the main focus of their efforts was upon identifying personal attributions that hindered "optimal leisure functioning."

Several other research studies broadened the definition of barriers to include the reasons why people cease participation once they start, as opposed to simply why people do not participate in the first place (e.g. Boothby, Tungatt, and Townsend 1981; Jackson and Dunn 1988).

Based on their review of the barriers literature through the early 1980s, Jackson and Searle (1985) sought to identify some commonalities that were represented in research dealing with some aspect of non-participation, barriers to participation, and barriers to enjoyment. They attempted to categorize the *types of barriers* that have been included in the studies reviewed. Thus, research has focused on one of the following:

1. Non-participation because of lack of interest (e.g. Romsa and Hoffman 1980);
2. Non-participation because of the influence of internal or person-specific barriers, such as lack of knowledge of opportunities, motivation, or skills (e.g. Ellis and Witt 1984; Romsa and Hoffman 1980);
3. Non-participation because of the influence of external or situation-specific barriers such as lack of facilities or programs (e.g. Jackson 1983; Jackson and Searle 1983).

The three other categories identified by Jackson and Searle (1985) dealt with the *types of participants* that were studied. Thus, studies have dealt with:

1. Participants who wish but are unable to increase the frequency or intensity of their participation (e.g. Wall 1981);
2. People who were formerly participants in an activity but who have ceased participating (e.g. Boothby *et al.* 1981);
3. People who participate but are unable to achieve the desired level of satisfaction or enjoyment (e.g. Witt and Goodale 1981; Francken and van Raiij 1981).

While systematic classification of existing research brings a degree of clarity to the barriers literature, it also reveals weaknesses in conceptualization and methodological sophistication characterizing much of the research undertaken to date. That, in the main, reflects the highly varied nature of the studies undertaken, as illustrated in Table 2:

1. Studies have varied widely in the actual barriers that have been included in any given study;
2. Studies have focused on widely different groups of activities (e.g. outdoor pursuits, sports);
3. Studies have focused on many different populations (e.g. families, the elderly, outdoor recreation participants);
4. Studies have utilized widely different predictors of non-participation (e.g. socio-economic or demographic variables, social-psychological variables);
5. Studies have utilized different criterion variables (e.g. barriers to enjoyment, satisfaction, or participation; reasons for ceasing participation, for not starting participation, or not participating more).

Thus, conceptual problems in barriers research arise from several sources. The topic is inclusive and complex. The problem of non-participation cannot be isolated from "the more general context of an individual's recreation choices and behavior, together with all the factors, both positive and negative, that influence recreational decisions" (Jackson and Searle 1985: 697; see also Kelly, this volume, for a broader discussion). In other words, barriers can probably be best understood in the context of models that specify why people do what they do and what they derive from their involvements. Noting the absence of such models, and after reviewing much of the barriers literature, Ellis and Rademacher (1986: 1) concluded that:

1. Theory is needed to define the parameters of the barriers topic and to provide guidance to researchers and practitioners who must deal with barriers;
2. Additional interdisciplinary work seems to be essential to developing an understanding of barriers to recreation participation and the effects of those barriers;
3. Research is needed to validate existing findings and assumptions related to both personal and environmental barriers to leisure. The need is for both the replication and the extension of findings;
4. Further research is needed to continue the development and validation of measures of major variables that are affected by barriers to participation (e.g. perceived freedom, user satisfaction, perceived crowding, reactions to knowledge of resources, etc.)

Table 2

Examples of Barriers, Populations, and Activities Included in Typical Research Studies

Author(s)	Barriers	Population Studied	Activities Covered
Boothby *et al.* (1981)	Forty-three specific reasons for ceasing participation in sports, classified into six main groups: loss of interest, lack of facilities, physical disability or inadequate fitness, leaving a youth organization, moving away from the area, and no time to spare.	Sample of youth	Sports activities
Francken & van Raiij (1981)	Two sets of barriers: external circumstances (lack of time and money, geographical distance, and lack of facilities) and internal (personal capacities, abilities, knowledge, and interest)	176 households in three neighborhoods in Breda, Netherlands	11 groups of activities covering the full range of pursuits

Table 2 (Continued)

Author(s)	Barriers	Population Studied	Activities Covered
Godbey (1985)	Twenty-one reasons for non-participation, based on respondents' replies to open-ended questions about the use of public leisure services	1490 households in an eastern U.S. city and 1658 in an eastern U.S. urban county	Leisure services in general as offered by departments in the respondents' community
Bialeschki & Henderson (1987)	Twelve barriers to trail use based on response to a telephone survey	Stratified sample of 423 Wisconsin households	Use of recreational trails in Wisconsin
Howard & Crompton (1984)	Twelve obstacles to participation in park and recreation services	Consumer surveys in Florida, Oregon, and Texas	Extent to which adults used park and recreation facilities and the obstacles that prevented use
Jackson (1983); Jackson & Searle (1983); Searle & Jackson (1985)	Fifteen barriers, including time and money commitments (family and work), lack of opportunities, lack of awareness, lack of ability, shyness, lack of transportation, lack of partners, and overcrowding of facilities	2425 households in Alberta, Canada	Four specific activities (tennis, racquetball/handball, downhill skiing, and golf), plus six groups of other activities including team sports, outdoor activities, and cultural pursuits

Author(s)	Barriers	Population Studied	Activities Covered
McGuire (1980)	Thirty potential constraints responsible for the discrepancy between actual and desired leisure involvements of older adults	125 adults (aged 45-93) in a large U.S. mid-western city	Leisure involvements in general
Romsa & Hoffman (1980)	Four sets of reasons for non-participation: lack of interest, time, facilities, and funds	2968 individuals across Canada	19 outdoor recreation activities
Witt & Goodale (1981)	Eighteen barriers to leisure enjoyment (no classification used). Barriers included time, skills, money, and opportunities	Adults in two Ontario, Canada communities	Barriers to leisure enjoyment in general

See also studies by: Barnett and Kane 1985; Christensen and Yoesting 1973; Dottavio, O'Leary, and Koth 1980; Goodrow 1975; Gramann and Burdge 1984; Mannell and Iso-Ahola 1985; Manning and Ciali 1980; McAvoy 1979; McGuire 1985; Mobily *et al.* 1984.

From these comments it is clear that there is a need to bring further conceptual clarity to the study of barriers and non-participation. While efforts in the late 1970s and early 1980s have helped to move in this direction, explication of theory with a coherent set of definitions is still needed.

Refinement and Consolidation: Concepts, Models and Theories

As was alluded to earlier, nearly all studies of recreation participation are also, *ipso facto*, studies of non-participation and barriers to participation. As Ellis and Rademacher (1986: 2) have remarked, "virtually any study in which a leisure phenomenon serves as a dependent variable ... is related to the topic of barriers to leisure". With so much and so varied research, even if limited to that focused specifically on barriers, the need to refine and consolidate has become increasingly evident (Jackson 1988). This is true for recreation and leisure research as a whole. Recent efforts of several authors have been aimed at developing conceptual clarity, useful models and frameworks, and theoretical bases for barriers and non-participation research. This is the fourth stage of the evolution of social science approaches to the topic, a stage which has only recently begun.

These efforts at refinement and consolidation take many forms and vary as to comprehensiveness, of which there appear to be at least three levels. For convenience, these levels are referred to as meta, meso, and micro conceptualizations, recognizing, however, that even the micro conceptualizations are still broad and comprehensive because human behavior is so complex. In the following paragraphs, these approaches are illustrated by citing examples from the recent scholarly and research literature.

Meta level conceptualizations

Two recent books, *Freedom to Be: A New Sociology of Leisure* (Kelly 1987) and *Why People Recreate: An Overview of Research* (Smith and Theberge 1987) illustrate the meta concept level of analysis. The approaches, however, are quite different and, comprehensive as they are, necessarily limited.

Of the two, Kelly's is the more abstract and inclusive. Sociology and social philosophy are combined in an effort to produce a theoretical understanding of leisure. Kelly discusses eight theories, beginning with the experiential (leisure as immediate experience), and proceeds through a series of spirals to humanistic theory. He views all of these theories as neither valid nor invalid nor mutually exclusive. Rather, he notes the presence of a dialectic of thesis-antithesis characterizing each theory — thus, an evolving spiral of increasingly inclusive theory, each addressing the limits of the previous theory in what he calls "a dialectical hierarchy."

Smith and Theberge, like Kelly, address the often voiced weaknesses of social science research (disciplinary boundaries, weak links between theory and research, piecemeal rather than comprehensive explorations, etc.; see also the first chapter of this volume), and attempt to provide a comprehensive framework for the analysis of recreation behavior. While they build a model and a derivative model based on research into participation in outdoor recreation, the models are not limited to outdoor recreation activities but apply to all forms of recreation.

The authors propose what they refer to as the "ISSTAL" Model and a derivative, a "General Activities Model." ISSTAL is an acronym, the letters standing for Interdisciplinary Sequential Specificity Time Allocation Lifespan (model). The models are intended to further understanding of discretionary time participation. "The ISSTAL Model," the authors note, "is essentially an accounting scheme for keeping track of the many variables that are relevant to explaining participation" (Smith and Theberge 1987: 119). The General Activity Model posits a pattern of covariation among and between activities, and between activities and social, psychological, and contextual influences.

Because of their comprehensiveness, these meta level conceptualizations do not, and were not intended to, point out specific areas of inquiry. Rather, they provide a superordinate framework within which particular areas of inquiry can be viewed in relation to the whole. These meta level conceptualizations, like organization charts, help us understand how interests and activities, such as research on non-participation and barriers to participation, relate to other varied and complex, theoretical and practical interests in leisure-related phenomena.

Meso level conceptualizations

At this level, the refinement and consolidation process provides clearer direction for research. Of the three examples noted here, two (Tinsley and Tinsley 1986; Iso-Ahola 1986) provide logical analyses, using postulates, propositions, derivations, and corollaries that sharpen the theoretical perspective on the phenomena at issue. The third (Ellis and Witt 1984) draws together and empirically tests, via a series of instruments, some of the major determinants of leisure participation and effective leisure functioning.

Tinsley and Tinsley (1986), based on an analysis of theoretical statements about the nature of leisure experience, formulated a series of 21 propositions, many with one or more corollaries. The propositions cover three aspects of the leisure experience: the attributes which clarify the nature of the experience; the conditions necessary to experience leisure; and the effects of the leisure experience on the individual. The authors' format is particularly useful, not only in reflecting previous theoretical statements and relevant supporting empirical evidence, but also in directing research and identifying relationships among the many postulates and corollaries, each of which is testable assuming adequate operationalization of terms.

Citing literature which holds that leisure is a state or condition, the authors are careful to distinguish leisure as a state from leisure as an experience, the distinguishing element being the intensity or strength of feeling experienced. In a sense, the leisure state is reached with "peak" experience. In addition, particularly with reference to barriers and non-participation (or, more precisely, the absence of leisure experience), the authors provide a useful summary of factors which, theoretically, are necessary for an individual to experience leisure (Tinsley and Tinsley 1986: 4). There is much agreement, theoretically and increasingly empirically, that intrinsic motivation and perceived freedom are essential conditions.

Iso-Ahola (1986), using the same format as the Tinsleys, formulated two postulates and, for each, a number of derivations and corollaries. Again, all of these statements are testable and help direct research as well as locate it in a broader framework. This article, "A theory of substitutability of leisure behavior," is particularly related to the matter of barriers and non-participation, for, as Iso-Ahola notes, "for the leisure participant, substitution means that the originally intended or desired behavior is no longer possible" (p. 369). That is, the participant has encountered a barrier or obstacle to continued participation.

Perceived freedom of choice and perceived comparability of alternatives from which to choose are the central elements of the two propositions the author formulated, pointing out again the centrality of perceived freedom. The author was also careful to note that the theory formulated is limited to substituting one activity for another, rather than substituting times or sites for the same activity. He also noted the difference between leisure behavior, activity, and participation, in stating that the terms were used interchangeably only as a matter of convenience and simplicity. Iso-Ahola and others recognize that one of the problems of research, including that regarding barriers to participation, is that terms are sometimes used loosely, as if equitable, and confusion sometimes results.

The third example of meso level analysis is the theoretical and empirical work engaged in by Ellis and Witt (1984) in developing the Leisure Diagnostic Battery (LDB). This work integrated several components of attributes of, and conditions for, leisure experience identified in the literature.

In developing the LDB, the authors postulated that, while a leisure state or condition may be transitory, there may also be traits that endure over time and which predispose individuals to experience leisure states. The traits include an individual's perceptions of control and competence, need satisfaction, capacity to become deeply involved in activity, and playfulness. Correlations among measures of these traits point to a unitary dimension, best characterized as "perceived freedom," with individuals sharing these traits capable of high levels of leisure functioning. Lack of these traits clearly constitutes a barrier to leisure, a barrier which is primarily intrapersonal in nature, and related to self-concept in particular.

Other meso level analyses that combine empirical as well as conceptual work include that of Csikszentmihalyi (1975) on the attributes of peak leisure experience, now widely referred to as flow experience or the flow state, and the paradigm suggested by Neulinger (1981), in which leisure and non-leisure states are distinguished by perceptions of freedom or constraint and by motivation, either internal, external, or some combination of both. Non-leisure appears to be the result, in the main, of interpersonal barriers. Also Ragheb and his collaborators (cf. Beard and Ragheb 1980) have been persistent in examining the concept of leisure satisfaction and the conditions which do or do not give rise to it.

These, and other meso-level analyses, reflect the current preoccupation with consolidation and refinement of theoretical and empirical analyses of leisure. They also reflect the shift toward psychological bases for the study of leisure. And, though not always direct, barriers to participation (or to leisure experience, enjoyment, satisfaction, flow, condition, or state) and non-participation phenomena are clearly implicated in these analyses.

Micro level conceptualizations

The examples of refinement noted below are referred to as micro only because they specifically focus on barriers. Each example includes models or paradigms which provide a conceptual framework for barriers theory and research.

Iso-Ahola and Mannell (1985), drawing particularly on earlier work of the first author, suggest a model of social and psychological "constraints" on leisure. The model addresses three questions about constraints: What are the causes? What are the types? How permanent or temporary are they? Answers are organized in Figure 1.

TYPE / LOCUS

		Social-Personal	Social-Cultural	Physical
STABILITY/ PERMANENCE	Stable/ Permanent	• Abilities • Competencies • Control	• Social norms • Roles • Obligations	• Resources • Finances • Facilities
	Variable/ Temporary	• Attitudes • Motives • Needs	• Social interaction	• Time

Figure 1
Conceptualization of Sources of Constraints on Leisure
(Source: From Iso-Ahola and Mannell. Social and Psychological Constraints on Leisure. Courtesy of Charles C. Thomas, Publisher. 1985.)

As Figure 1 illustrates, six causes or sources of constraints are postulated. The categories "social-personal," "social-cultural," and "physical" correspond to categories used by other barriers analysts. Of particular note in this model is the division of barriers according to the degree to which the barriers are stable and enduring over time or are temporary and transient. Just as notions of state and trait have been noted regarding leisure experience and individuals' predispositions which do or do not lead to such experience, barriers that individuals encounter can be similarly categorized.

In addition, the authors are careful to point out that the model applies particularly to constraints which are felt during or following engagement. This distinguishes, then, between participation and other concepts, such as the enjoyment or satisfaction which result from participation.

Jackson and Searle (1985), using decision making theories and models, propose a model in which barriers are conceptualized as the reduction of alternatives. Theoretically, a broad range of choices is available. Not all of them are practical and, of the practical, not all are possible. In each case, the range of available choices is reduced. Elements of this model appear to be of interest to those focusing on perceived freedom (to choose among alternatives) and the problem of substitutability. Figure 2 (from Jackson and Searle 1985: 703) is largely self-explanatory.

Theoretical Range of Activities	Blocking Barriers			Practical Range of Activities	Inhibiting Barriers						Actual Range of Activities
	Interest	*Awareness*	*Other*		*EB1*	*EB2*	*EB3*	*IB1*	*IB2*	*IB3*	
T1	O	O	O	P1	+	+	+	+	+	+	P
T2	O	O	O	P2	+	+	+	+	+	+	P
T3	O	O	O	P3	+	+	+	-	-	-	NP1
T4	O	O	O	P4	-	-	-	+	+	+	NP2
T5	X	O	O								NP3
T6	X	X	O								NP4
T7	O	O	X								NP5
Tn	O	O	X								NPn

X Blocked choice	+ Favorable to choice	EB External barrier	P Participation
O Open choice	- Unfavorable to choice	IB Internal barrier	NP Non-participation

Figure 2
A Decision-Making Model of Recreation Behavior
(Source: From Jackson and Searle. *Recreation
***Research Review 10*(2):5-12, 1983)**

Of particular note in this conceptualization is the distinction between two types of barriers — those which block participation and thus preclude it, and those which inhibit and thus limit, but do not preclude, participation. In much of the research on this topic, terms such as barriers, obstacles, or constraints are used interchangeably, without distinguishing between blocks and limits. In this model, lack of interest and lack of knowledge are posited as blocking barriers. Other analysts have recently elaborated upon the lack of interest barrier by focusing on the relationship between preferences and participation.

Godbey (1985) developed a model detailing factors associated with the non-use of public leisure services (Figure 3). Godbey's model focuses on the information level of potential users concerning what leisure services exist. "An argument is made that combating lack of awareness is a more cost-effective method of increasing participation than attempting to alter services to enable participation by those who know about such services but are prevented from participating" (Godbey 1985: 1).

Finally, Crawford and Godbey (1987) offer a critique of some of the barriers literature and research and, in particular, the almost exclusive conceptualization that barriers intervene between preferences and participation, i.e. "I would participate (in X activity) but do not because [some barrier intervenes]." Noting the weak relationship between preferences and participation, and noting a number of contributing explanations, including the transient nature of preferences, the authors suggest that there are three types of relationships between preferences, barriers, and participation. These are illustrated in Figure 4 (Crawford and Godbey 1987: 123-24).

Diagram C (Figure 4), for structural barriers, needs no explanation, as it illustrates the presumed relationship between preference and participation, with barriers intervening. Diagram A posits that intrapersonal barriers are determinants of preferences. For example, a person afraid of heights and water will probably have little interest in, or preference for, diving from a ten-meter platform. Lack of interest, the authors suggest, determines preference rather than intervening between preference and participation. Diagram B, representing interpersonal barriers, illustrates that these barriers both condition preferences and intervene between preference and participation. This reflects, in a sense, elements of deference to or accommodation of others, particularly the "significant others" with whom one relates. Although Crawford and Godbey's formulations were addressed particularly to barriers to leisure for families, general applicability to the study of non-participation and barriers to participation seems clear.

Though not exhaustive, and though the stages of development as well as categories of meta, meso, and micro level conceptualizations characterizing the current stage are somewhat arbitrary, the above review does generally represent the current state of social science approaches to non-participation and barriers to participation in recreation and leisure. As we proceed through the present stage of refinement and consolidation, a number of questions and issues will continue to occupy those interested in participation, non-participation, and barriers phenomena.

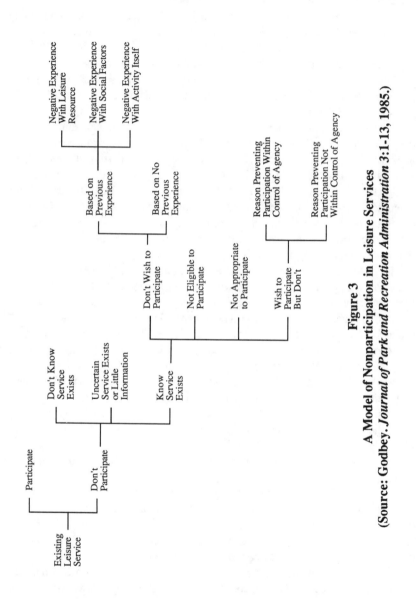

Figure 3

A Model of Nonparticipation in Leisure Services

(Source: Godbey. *Journal of Park and Recreation Administration 3*:1-13, 1985.)

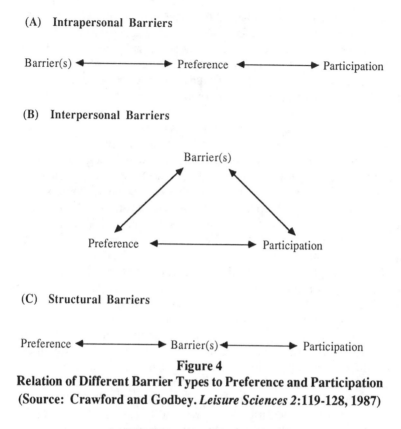

Figure 4
Relation of Different Barrier Types to Preference and Participation
(Source: Crawford and Godbey. *Leisure Sciences* 2:119-128, 1987)

QUESTIONS AND ISSUES

Some of the problems in barriers research and some suggestions for researchers were briefly noted earlier in the chapter. Those considerations, plus the review of efforts to refine and consolidate theories and concepts used in barriers research, highlight two types of questions and issues currently occupying researchers: clarifying concepts and the nature of research.

Clarifying Concepts

Cast in terms of independent and dependent variables or antecedents and consequences, clarity and refinement is being pursued on both sides of our propositions and conjectural statements. The dependent variables used in research include participation, satisfaction, enjoyment, experience, fulfillment, and other terms. While some barriers, such as time, may influence whatever dependent variable we specify, it cannot be assumed that all barriers influence all dependent variables or that they exert the same influence. These dependent variables differ in ways that are not merely semantic; barriers to participation may differ from barriers to enjoyment or satisfaction, since enjoyment and satisfaction presume participation. Also, satisfaction and enjoyment may be quite different, one being experienced but not necessarily the other. And there is the additional complication of when such feelings are felt — during the engagement? Immediately thereafter? Many hours, days or weeks thereafter? In addition, participation does not equal experience, and experience may not equal the leisure state or condition, or what is referred to as peak experience or flow. There appear to be minimal and optimal levels for whatever dependent variable is used, perhaps with identifiable thresholds for those levels.

Even if the dependent variable were limited to participation, which many regard as a step toward (or antecedent to) such dependent variables as enjoyment and satisfaction, further distinctions must be made. Barriers to participation differ from barriers to continuing participation, and both differ from barriers to ceasing from, or increasing the rate of, participation.

This points to efforts to clarify the concept of barriers, and its presumed antecedents in conjectures about non-participation and barriers. One point of clarification sought has to do with the definition of the term barrier itself. Noting the absence of formal definitions of barriers in the literature, Ellis and Rademacher (1986: 2) propose that "a barrier to recreation participation is any factor which precludes or limits an individual's frequency, intensity, duration, or quality of participation in recreation activities." Several terms in such a definition require operationalization, including such dependent variables as intensity or quality of participation. More important is the mixing of terms such as "preclude" and "limit" participation. While the term "barriers" is often used, and used generically, a barrier, presumably, is insurmountable. The term "obstacles" is sometimes used, particularly with reference to special populations (the disabled or handicapped), and the only book which focuses on barriers is entitled *Constraints on Leisure* (Wade 1985). Barriers, obstacles and constraints, then, are different concepts (Jackson 1988). The title, *Constraints on Leisure*, also raises the long-standing question as to whether recreation or leisure should be the focus, and whether or not the research domain should be limited to preconceived notions of what activities are considered recreational.

The additional problem with the barriers concept is determining what constitutes a barrier. As Jackson and Searle argue (1985: 697), barriers are but a sub-set of the myriad of reasons why someone may not at some time participate in some activity. In particular, questions are raised as to whether or not lack of interest is a barrier. Either way, lack of interest is seen not as an antecedent but a consequence for which researchers seek antecedents to that lack.

It may be that lack of time, and, perhaps, even money beyond some level, are not so much barriers but reasons, and perhaps only excuses, for non-participation, increased participation, or continued participation (Jackson 1988). Thus, literature on how the physical, social, political, and economic environments shape preferences and priorities, as well as literature on motivation and motivational strength becomes of interest. For example, do barriers increase or decrease motivational strength, and for whom?

While there is some consistency in categorizing types of barriers, there are various types of categories. The distinction between those that are permanent and those that are temporary (Iso-Ahola and Mannell 1985) is one example, and that example appears in other forms as well — in the growing consensus that the leisure state is transitory, that there may be rather stable personality traits which determine the probability of achieving leisure states, and the recognition that dispositional attributes mix with situational ones in determining participation or non-participation decisions and actions.

These appear to be the major questions and issues involving concepts central to research on non-participation and barriers to participation. That conceptual clarity is a continuing problem and issue reflects, in part, weaknesses in the research. But the nature of research is such that resolutions and refinements lead to new issues and questions, including concepts that need further clarification and refinement.

The Nature of Barriers Research

Critiques of barriers research, leisure research, and social science research in general, abound. That, too, is an essential part of the research process and does not negate observable progress nor decry the fact that there is always more to do. Only a few decades separate attempts to gather data to support preconceived contentions and causes and those that indicate an increasingly theoretical approach to non-participation and barriers phenomena. Studies culminating in descriptions of participants and participation have given way to correlational studies which are now giving way to experimentation and hypothesis-testing.

As noted earlier, analysts such as Tinsley and Tinsley (1986) and Iso-Ahola (1986) have contributed to theory building and have formulated numerous testable propositions. In addition to formulations regarding the attributes of leisure experience (flow), antecedent conditions (awareness, salary increase), effects of experience (pleasant or not), and substitutability (time schedule, location, or activity), much other theoretical work has been drawn into barriers research. By way of illustration, one can find links to internal and external locus of control, attribution theory, communication theory, decision making theory, field dependence and independence, arousal, motivation and motivational strength, and more. It should be noted that, here and throughout this review, the mainly psychological and social-psychological orientations are clear. But that is also clear in the work of researchers who deal with resources which constitute opportunities for recreation and leisure. Thus, theories and concepts such as social carrying capacity, crowding, preference for others and the like, are clearly implicated in barriers research, along with theories of attractiveness and distance decay of attractiveness and use (cf. Graefe *et al.* 1984; Smith 1983).

In short, the gap between theory and empirical research appears to be shrinking. Too, the lack of persistence in pursuing research subjects — to which, incidentally, there are a number of barriers (i.e. barriers to barriers research) — does not characterize a number of researchers, many of whom (Jackson, Ragheb, Mannell, Neulinger, and others) have already been noted. Issues of extension and replication may be addressed as researchers persist in pursuit of focused lines of inquiry. Further shrinking of the gap between theory and empirical research will result as researchers formulate testable propositions suggested by the descriptive and correlation data that have accumulated over the past twenty-five years.

Other issues and questions remain. Self-reported, cross-sectional survey data make up much of the information base of barriers research. There have been many calls in the literature for the use of other methodologies. In particular, there have been calls for qualitative research and for longitudinal studies. Barriers to these types of research are well known, though perhaps surmountable (see Godbey, this volume). Maintenance of support and conducive, long-term situations are needed for research of this type. Too, imperatives to quantify must be overcome, and qualitative research must be strengthened so as to provide increasingly reliable, valid, and generalizable information.

Another extension of methodology would be additional experimentation. That may require, according to the nature of the study, shifting from the field to the laboratory. That has been done successfully, though there are but few examples to date. Mannell (1980) has provided some leadership in this area.

Interest in qualitative, longitudinal, and laboratory research is probably another reflection of the shift toward psychology-based inquiry noted previously. That is evident in the increased attention placed on intrapersonal and interpersonal barriers, with comparatively less on obstacles and opportunities in the physical, political, and economic environments. There are, then, questions and issues about the levels and types of aggregation appropriate to the study of non-participation and barriers. More intensive study of smaller numbers of cases or respondents seems to be indicated by the increased interest in psychological and social-psychological determinants of behavior. This also reflects the shift in practice from the direct provision of opportunity to enabling and facilitating individuals to capitalize on opportunities available.

EVOLVING AGREEMENT

Again, the nature of research (and thus also researchers) is such that agreement is not easily attained, and what there is has been hard won over time. Barriers research is relatively new and appears to be evolving rapidly. Still, there seems to be a growing consensus around a number of matters.

There is general agreement that there are three types of barriers: those which are external (environmental, often physical but sometimes also social, economic, political, etc.); those internal to the individual (psychological, intrapersonal); and those which are social and relational (social-psychological, interpersonal). Elaboration and refinement of categories can be expected, along with refined rationales and criteria for assigning barriers to categories. In addition, Jackson and Searle (1985: 698) suggest a core of five barriers which appear in the literature: interest; time; money; facilities; skills or abilities. Further, Howard and Crompton (1984: 44) identified 12 specific barrier questions used in common by different researchers in three different communities.

There appears to be a growing consensus about the nature of leisure, particularly insofar as that it is regarded as a state or condition, rather than as an activity or participation. That implies, necessarily, that leisure is something other than free time and that all activities, not limited to those thought to be free time or recreational, are potential sources of leisure. In other areas of leisure research, leisure is conceptualized differently, but psychological and social-psychological approaches generally tend toward state or condition conceptualizations.

On these matters, there are still a number of questions and issues, although broad areas of agreement are evident in the literature. There seems also to be strong, perhaps even uniform, agreement that there are at least two antecedents to, or conditions for, leisure. They are: (1) intrinsic motivation, with no objectives or rewards other than those accruing from the activity itself; and (2) perceived freedom, with little or no felt constraint over choices and actions. Antecedents to those conditions have increasingly become the focus of barriers theory and research. There is, of course, agreement that much more needs to be done both as to concepts and theories and to research strategies. Extension and replication of studies is called for, along with "triangulation" involving both a variety of methods and a variety of discipline and sub-discipline bases.

THE BROADER CONTEXT

On the topic of leisure, recreation and the social sciences, the focus is necessarily theory and research. That has been the focus of this chapter, but perhaps some comments about the broader context would be germane before concluding.

Interest in and studies of non-participation and barriers to participation are a clear example of the social sciences as instruments of social welfare and development. Applied and practical knowledge is, finally, the presumed objective, however general and distant that may be. But the desire to understand non-participation and barriers to participation is grounded in the desire to do something about them. Underlying that are predispositions, assumptions, biases, and philosophies which shape research in the social sciences.

There is, for example, an activist, instrumentalist, interventionist character in this body of research. Avoiding, for the moment, the value-laden assumption that something *should* be done, there is the conviction that something *can* be done. Perhaps that reflects the ebb and flow of tides along the nature-nurture continuum. There is a continuing push against fatalistic philosophy and deterministic science, necessarily based on the assumption that human nature, at least, is infinitely malleable. That assumption is necessary in order to discover the limits.

Implicit in the notion that something *can* be done is that it *should* be, though there may be endless debate over whatever it is that should be done. The evidence of time famine and time deepening in our culture appears to reflect an ill-defined belief that everyone should do everything, or at least try. Non-participation and barriers to participation interests assume that, individually and collectively, some participation is better than none, and more is better than less. But there is also a clear notion that participation in some things is better than in others. Perhaps that should be made explicit. That "in life there are no non-participants" is not only a philosophical statement, but one which raises important questions about non-participation. Further, when time-use studies suggest that married couples converse only about four minutes per day, and that parents who work outside the home spend about thirty seconds per day conversing with their children, should "conversing with family members" be included in the list of activities used in barriers research? Increased participation in various activities may not be a panacea, or even an improvement, in a culture where pace, stress, and overload seem already to have exceeded the limits of well-being for many. Withdrawal and avoidance may be indicated for the well-being and happiness of some.

There is, in addition, some distrust with the idea that well-being is promoted, or even mediated, by market-place transactions in goods and services. Many are concerned, then, with the increasing commercialization and privatization of recreation and leisure services. On the other hand, there is also some distrust with the idea that well-being is assured or mediated by the well-intended interventions of a socio-political welfare system, and thus some distrust of social science and scientists. For precisely these reasons, being explicit about assumptions, values, philosophies, and perhaps biases might shed some light on research into non-participation and barriers to participation.

Another aspect of the broader context is people's expectations, of particular outcomes of activities but also of all activities, i.e. of life. The emphasis on rights and entitlements, experience and happiness which characterizes recent decades may mean that, with all our affluence and opportunity, there may be more perceived barriers and less perceived freedom now than ever before. It is clear, then, that everyone encounters barriers at some point, and various obstacles and constraints along the way. Barriers are inevitable. They are also necessary. In a broad context, erecting barriers is as much an interest as dismantling them. Among the tasks of education and other socialization processes is teaching each generation how to find contentment and happiness in a world of constraints and barriers. The absence of perceived freedom and the presence of perceived barriers may reflect, among other things, the ascendance of greed or the decline of socialization processes. While there seems to be no sense of obligation to accommodate greed, research on barriers attends more to desires and demands than to needs, perhaps due to the difficulty of defining and measuring "need."

A further question arises with the notion, primarily of a psychological nature, of perception. Political, economic, social, and philosophical approaches to barriers would likely raise questions not of perceptions but of realities. The practical side of such questions would involve decisions about increasing freedom, in some objective sense, and eliminating barriers. Or it may involve changing perceptions. The counterpart of Skinner's "happy slave" (which may be a fiction) is the liberated wretch. So the social sciences must be concerned with realities as well as perceptions, for while it is true that the same opportunities (time, income, facilities, etc.) may be perceived differently by different people, it is also true that not all people have the same opportunities, or would necessarily want them.

From the standpoint of application and practice among those in the park, recreation, leisure service, and various allied fields, these broader context issues are particularly salient. Practitioners must not only know what can be done but also must decide what should be done. That is not the task of science but the task of all who participate in community and society, including scientists. The allocation of resources to direct provision of facilities and programs, to facilitation processes, to leisure education or to counseling, is something in which everyone has a stake.

The mixing and separating of knowledge and belief, science and philosophy, perception and reality, theory and practice continue to engage, fascinate, and sometimes frustrate those interested in leisure, recreation and the social sciences. Not least among them are those particularly interested in the phenomena of non-participation and barriers to participation, researchers and practitioners alike.

446   Jackson and Burton—*Understanding Leisure and Recreation*

References

Barnett, L.A. and M.J. Kane. 1985. "Individual constraints on children's play." In *Constraints on Leisure*, ed. M.G. Wade, pp. 189-226. Springfield, IL: Charles C. Thomas.

Beard, J. and M. Ragheb. 1980. "Measuring leisure satisfaction." *Journal of Leisure Research 12:* 20-33.

Boothby, J., M.F. Tungatt, and A.R. Townsend. 1981. "Ceasing participation in sports activity: Reported reasons and their implications." *Journal of Leisure Research 13:* 1-14.

Christensen, J. and D. Yoesting. 1973. "Social and attitudinal variants in high and low use of outdoor recreation facilities." *Journal of Leisure Research 5:* 6-15.

Crawford, D.W. and G. Godbey. 1987. "Reconceptualizing barriers to family leisure." *Leisure Sciences 9:* 119-128.

Csikszentmihalyi, M. 1975. *Beyond Boredom and Anxiety.* San Francisco: Jossey-Bass.

Dottavio, F.D., J.T. O'Leary, and B. Koth. 1980. "The social group variable in recreation participation studies." *Journal of Leisure Research 12:* 357-367.

Duncan, M. 1985. "Back to our radical roots." In *Recreation and Leisure: Issues in an Era of Change,* eds. T.L. Goodale and P.A. Witt, pp. 407-415. State College, PA: Venture Publishing.

Ellis, G. and C. Rademacher. 1986. "Barriers to recreation participation." Unpublished paper submitted to the President's Commission on Americans Outdoors. 18 pp.

Ellis, G. and P.A. Witt. 1984. "The measurement of perceived freedom in leisure." *Journal of Leisure Research 16:* 110-123.

Ferriss, A.L. 1962. *National Recreation Survey.* Outdoor Recreation Resources Review Commission Study Report No. 19. Washington, DC: U.S. Government Printing Office.

Francken, D.A. and W.F. van Raiij. 1981. "Satisfaction with leisure time activities." *Journal of Leisure Research 13:* 337-352.

Godbey, G. 1985. "Non-participation in public leisure services: A model." *Journal of Park and Recreation Administration 3:* 1-13.

Goodrow, B.A. 1975. "Limiting factors in reducing participation in older adult learning opportunities." *The Gerontologist 15:* 418-422.

Graefe, A.R., J.J. Vaske, and F.R. Kuss. 1984. "Social carrying capacity: An integration and synthesis of twenty years of research." *Leisure Sciences 6:* 395-431.

Gramann, J.H. and R.J. Burdge. 1984. "Crowding perception determinants at intensively developed outdoor recreation sites." *Leisure Sciences 6:* 167-186.

Howard, D.R. and J.L. Crompton. 1984. "Who are the consumers of public park and recreation services?" *Journal of Park and Recreation Administration 2:* 33-48.

Iso-Ahola, S.E. 1980. *The Social Psychology of Leisure and Recreation.* Dubuque, IA: William C. Brown.

Iso-Ahola, S.E. 1986. "A theory of substitutability of leisure behavior." *Leisure Sciences 8:* 367-389.

Iso-Ahola, S.E. and R.C. Mannell. 1985. "Social and psychological constraints on leisure." In *Constraints on Leisure,* ed. M.G. Wade, pp. 111-154. Springfield, IL: Charles C. Thomas.

Jackson, E.L. 1983. "Activity specific barriers to recreation participation." *Leisure Sciences 6:* 47-60.

Jackson, E.L. 1988. "Leisure constraints: A survey of past research." *Leisure Sciences 10:* 203-215..

Jackson, E.L. and E. Dunn. 1988. "Integrating ceasing participation with other aspects of leisure behavior." *Journal of Leisure Research 20:* 31-45.

Jackson, E.L. and M.S. Searle. 1983. "Recreation non-participation: Variables related to the desire for new recreational activities." *Recreation Research Review 10(2):* 5-12.

Jackson, E.L. and M.S. Searle. 1985. "Recreation non-participation and barriers to participation: Concepts and models." *Loisir et Société 8:* 693-707.

Kelly, J.R. 1987. *Freedom to Be: A New Sociology of Leisure.* New York: Macmillan.

Lundberg, G., M. Komarovksy, and M.A. McInerny. 1934. *Leisure: A Suburban Study.* New York: Columbia University Press.

Mannell, R. 1980. "Social psychological techniques and strategies for studying leisure experiences." In *Social Psychological Perspectives on Leisure and Recreation*, ed. S.E. Iso-Ahola, pp. 62-88. Springfield, IL: Charles C. Thomas.

Mannell, R.C. and S.E. Iso-Ahola. 1985. "Work constraints on leisure: A social psychological analysis." In *Constraints on Leisure*, ed. M.G. Wade, pp. 155-188. Springfield, IL: Charles C. Thomas.

Manning, R.E. and C.P. Ciali. 1980. "Recreation density and user satisfaction: A further exploration of the satisfaction model." *Journal of Leisure Research 12:* 329-345.

McAvoy, L.A. 1979. "The leisure preferences, problems, and needs of the elderly." *Journal of Leisure Research 11:* 40-47.

McGuire, F.A. 1985. "Constraints in later life." In *Constraints on Leisure*, ed. M.G. Wade. Springfield, IL: Charles C. Thomas.

Mobily, K.E., K.D. Leslie, R.B. Wallace, J.H. Lemke, F.J. Kohout, and M.C. Morris. 1984. "Factors associated with the aging leisure repertoire: The Iowa 65+ and rural health study." *Journal of Leisure Research 16:* 334-343.

Mueller, E., G. Gurin, and M. Wood. 1962. *Participation in Outdoor Recreation: Factors Affecting Demand among American Adults.* Outdoor Recreation Resources Review Commission Study Report No. 20. Washington, DC: U.S. Government Printing Office.

National Therapeutic Recreation Society. 1982. *Philosophic Position Statement of the National Therapeutic Recreation Society.* Alexandria, VA: National Recreation and Park Association.

Neulinger, J. 1981. *The Psychology of Leisure*, 2nd ed. Springfield, IL: Charles C. Thomas.

Outdoor Recreation Resources Review Commision. 1962. *Outdoor Recreation for America*. Washington, DC: U.S. Government Printing Office.

Proctor, C. 1962. "Dependence of recreation participation on background characteristics of sample persons in the September 1960 National Recreation Survey." In Ferriss, A.L., *National Recreational Survey*. Outdoor Recreation Resources Review Commission Study Report No. 19. Washington, DC: U.S. Government Printing Company.

Romsa, G. and W. Hoffman. 1980. "An application of non-participation data in recreation research: Testing the opportunity theory." *Journal of Leisure Research 12:* 321-328.

Searle, M.L. and E.L. Jackson. 1985. "Recreation non-participation and barriers to participation: Considerations for the management of recreation delivery systems." *Journal of Park and Recreation Administration 3:* 23-36.

Smith, D. and N. Theberge. 1987. *Why People Recreate*. Champaign, IL: Life Enhancement Publications.

Smith, S.L.J. 1983. *Recreation Geography*. London: Longman.

Tinsley, H. and D. Tinsley. 1986. "A theory of the attributes, benefits and causes of leisure experience." *Leisure Sciences 8:* 1-45.

Wade, M.G. (ed.). 1985. *Constraints on Leisure*. Springfield, IL: Charles C. Thomas.

Wall, G. 1981. "Research in Canadian recreation planning and management." In *Canadian Resource Policies: Problems and Prospects,* eds. B. Mitchell and W.R.D. Sewell, pp. 233-261. Toronto: Methuen.

Witt, P.A. and G.D. Ellis. 1985. "Conceptualizing leisure: Making the abstract concrete." In *Recreation and Leisure: Issues in an Era of Change,* eds. T.L. Goodale and P.A. Witt, pp. 105-117. State College, PA: Venture Publishing.

Witt, P.A. and T.L. Goodale. 1981. "The relationship between barriers to leisure enjoyment and family stages." *Leisure Sciences 4:* 29-49.

PART FOUR

Issues and Applications

As the results of the international survey of active leisure scholars noted earlier tended to suggest, there has been a relative decline, in recent years, in the dominance of outdoor recreation-related research in leisure studies. While a broadening of the scope of the field to encompass much more than outdoor recreation is surely to be welcomed, it is a pity, nonetheless, that many leisure scientists appear to have lost sight of the importance of the environment and natural resources, not only to outdoor recreation, but to virtually all other forms of leisure as well. It is also a paradox that the increasing recognition of the social and cultural embeddedness of leisure and recreation has been accompanied by a neglect of what we might call, in parallel, their environmental embeddedness.

Perhaps this has occurred as leisure studies has shifted away from overtly "applied" and policy-driven forms of research and into the academic, scholarly, and theoretical arena. Is it possible that this reflects a distaste (even a disdain), in some quarters, for practical and practitioner-oriented research? If so, it would be well to heed the message of Driver's chapter, which concludes Part Four. Although the applications touched upon by Driver might seem, at first glance, to be most closely associated with outdoor recreation research, his assessment of the benefits of interaction and cooperation between researchers and practitioners applies to the broad spectrum of leisure studies, and not just to one branch of it.

The importance of the environment — physical and natural, but also cultural and social — is amply demonstrated in the two opening chapters of Part Four. Wall shows how crucial the environment is to all leisure activities, even ones like reading or listening to music. Ellis, similarly, demonstrates that every leisure and recreation activity depends upon, and consumes, energy, not only in the most obvious ways, such as switching on a snowmobile or plugging in a videocassette recorder, but in complex and indirect ways as well.

In addition, each of the chapters in Part Four demonstrates, from one perspective or another, that the interaction between the environment and leisure/ recreation is reciprocal. Not only is the environment the setting for leisure, recreation, and tourism, but these activities can also lead to substantial, frequently detrimental, and sometimes irreversible impacts upon the quality of the natural environment and the processes that are crucial to its maintenance and functioning. This was the essential idea that originally led to the development of the social capacity concept, as Stankey and McCool point out in the third chapter of Part Four, and has been a fundamental theme in the close, century-long, symbiotic relationship between recreation and conservation, as Swinnerton describes in his careful and detailed assessment. The idea is repeated, once more, in Butler's account of the historical development of tourism and the contemporary debate about its impacts, both positive and negative.

The critical reader might argue that, in selecting the contributions for Part Four, we have leaned too heavily in the direction of issues and applications related to the natural environment, natural resources, and outdoor forms of recreation. Four of the chapters — those on environment, energy, social capacity, and conservation — are, seemingly, addressed exclusively to these matters. But the careful reader will discern that a central theme in all of these chapters, individually and in combination, goes far beyond such narrow confines. As this entire set of contributions demonstrates — particularly those by Wall, Stankey and McCool, Swinnerton, and Butler — environments do not impact upon leisure and recreation in deterministic ways. Rather, the key issue is how human *perceptions* of the environment, and our *values and attitudes* towards it, influence the uses we choose to make of it, and how, in turn, those uses affect its quality.

Without question, this is a message that has broad applications in leisure studies: that no serious leisure scholar can afford to neglect the settings in which leisure takes place, the interpretations and meanings which people attach to these settings, and, finally, how these settings are altered by leisure, recreation, and tourism, and indeed all other forms of human activity.

E. L. J.

T. L. B.

PERSPECTIVES ON RECREATION AND THE ENVIRONMENT

Geoffrey Wall

INTRODUCTION

At first sight, a contribution on the physical environment and recreation may appear to be out of place in a volume written predominantly by social scientists. However, it is my contention that a full understanding of recreation is unlikely to be achieved in the absence of an appreciation of the attributes of the places in which people recreate, and of the ways in which environmental factors contribute to and detract from the qualities of recreational experiences.

It is a paradox that participants in recreation are drawn to attractive environments, whether natural or built, but that their mere presence is likely to result in the modification of those environments. There is a real possibility that the environment can be loved to death! On the other hand, the provision of recreation opportunities provides a persuasive rationale for the preservation and creation of attractive environments.

The environment may be both the object of, and the setting for, recreational experiences. Particular elements of the landscape, such as viewpoints, mountain peaks, fish, or historic sites, may be the specific objects of recreational attention, and their attainment and appreciation the major goal of the recreational activity. In other cases, the environment may constitute the backdrop, or context, in which the activity takes place. Thus, the presence of a lake or an ocean vista may make an area particularly attractive to picnickers or campers, even though they may have no wish to engage in water-contact activities.

In some cases, the availability of specific environmental attributes may be essential for an activity to take place: swimming, boating, and fishing are impossible in the absence of water, skiing and snowmobiling require snow, and many sports, if they are to be played properly, require areas of specific dimensions. In other cases, elements of the environment, such as the presence of a rainbow, the song of a skylark, or the fleeting glimpse of a deer, may not be *required* for participation to take place, but their presence *enhances* the quality of the recreational experience. The environment influences the availability of recreational opportunities, and the quantity and quality of recreational experiences which may be obtained, and has a pervasive influence upon all aspects of recreation.

THE NATURE OF ENVIRONMENT

The word "environment" encompasses all aspects of the world around us. According to Nelson and Butler (1974), it is a comprehensive term which overlaps in meaning with "ecosystem." The latter is a biological concept which can be defined as the elements and processes interacting with an organism or organisms. Ecosystem dynamics, which is concerned with the processes of energy flow and the cycling of phosphorous, nitrogen, carbon dioxide, and other nutrients necessary to maintain organic life, implies that an organism is an integral part of its own ecosystem, and that the distinction between organism and ecosystem is a false dichotomy. However, from an anthropocentric perspective and for present purposes, it is convenient to define the environment of a person as the sum total of conditions which surround that human being. Evidently, "environment" is an all-embracing term which defies analysis in its full complexity.

Sonnenfeld (1968) has illustrated this complexity as a nested hierarchy (Figure 1). The entire universe external to the individual is the *geographical* environment. A sub-set of this is the *operational* environment, which consists of those portions of the world that impinge on man, whether he is aware of it or not. That portion of which he is aware is termed the *perceptual* environment.

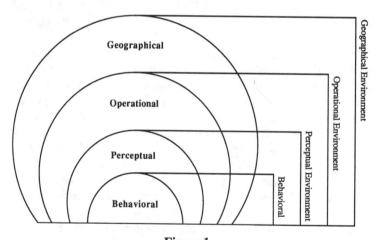

Figure 1
Nested Set of Environments
(Source: Sonnenfeld, "Geography, Perception, and the Behavorial Environment", 1968.)

Awareness may be a result of present sensations or past experiences, and may be derived from direct or indirect (second-hand) stimuli. The innermost level, or *behavioral* environment, is that part of the perceptual environment which elicits a behavioral response. One can conclude from this not only that the environment is extremely complex, but that individuals are aware of, and respond to, only a portion of all environmental stimuli, and that the process is mediated by selective perception. Furthermore, we respond to and manipulate environments both as individuals and as groups or societies. We may, as individuals, decide to visit a national park, but we decide, as a society, to allocate resources to the provision and maintenance of such parks.

The interaction between human beings and environment is a two-way process: the environment provides opportunities and constraints as human beings attempt to satisfy their needs and desires and, at the same time, human beings have the ability to modify the environment. The latter situation has become more prevalent with burgeoning population and modern technology. Thus, a balanced perspective should consider both the implications of environment for human activity and the impact of human beings upon the environment.

The word "environment" is often employed with associated adjectives. The *natural* environment usually refers to nature, more specifically aspects of nature which are natural in that they have not been modified by human beings. In fact, the impact of human activity is so pervasive that there are no longer any truly natural environments. Natural environments are contrasted with *man-modified* environments, such as *urban* environments, which are often called *built* environments. Natural and built environments may both be termed *physical* environments, although some use the terms "natural" and "physical" interchangeably. Others use the term "physical environment" to contrast with the *socio-cultural* environment, which refers to the attributes of individuals and societies which impinge upon us. This chapter will be concerned primarily with physical environments, whether natural, modified, or predominantly man-made, although occasional reference will be made to the socio-cultural setting, particularly in cases of conflict over the use of the same scarce resources of land and water. In addition, for the sake of convenience, attention will focus primarily upon outdoor recreation and, to a lesser extent, tourism, to the relative neglect of recreation in urban and home settings.

A RECREATIONAL TRIAD

Recreational experiences are derived from the interaction of three phenomena: individuals and their attributes; other people, or the social setting; and the environment in which recreation takes place (Phillips 1978).

Recreational experiences are obtained by individuals. Of course, individuals differ in personality, motivations, expectations, skills, backgrounds, financial resources, health, mobility, family commitments, and in many other ways which influence their recreational behavior and experiences. Thus, two individuals fishing at the same time from the same boat may have contrasting experiences, and not merely because they may catch a different number of fish. One may be bored by the seeming dullness of the lack of activity, whereas the other may relish the opportunity to commune with nature. Similarly, one person may be attracted by the excitement of white-water rafting, whereas another may be horrified at the risks involved. Someone else may wish to climb a mountain, and yet another be quite content to view it from a distance. This does not mean that recreation experiences are idiosyncratic and that there are no similarities between individuals — in fact, the grouping of like individuals is essential for many types of recreation research. Rather, it means that people participate in recreation for many different reasons, and that individuals participating in the same activities in similar environments are not necessarily enjoying the same experiences, nor need they be similar in other ways (see the chapters by Kelly, Iso-Ahola, and Mannell, this volume).

Many types of recreation, and most outdoor recreational activities, are group activities — they are undertaken with other people. Many have a social component; the experience is enhanced by participating with family or friends, or by the prospect of meeting new friends. Cheek, Field, and Burdge (1976) have suggested that the composition of the group is one of the most important influences on recreation behavior; thus, families with small children behave similarly whether they are in an urban, state, or national park. The appropriate number of participants varies considerably with the activity, from very few in a wilderness setting to large numbers at a party or a concert. However, there is usually some interaction with others. Very few wilderness users hike or camp alone and, paradoxically, the wilderness experience usually includes a strong social component — most wilderness users like to be "alone together." Even solitary activities, such as reading or listening to records through a head-set, involve interaction with others who have created the work that is the object of attention. Thus, a social component is a part of most recreation activities.

It has already been indicated that the environment, whether natural or modified by human agencies, contributes to most recreation experiences. The interaction of the individual with others and the environment is part of most forms of recreation. Thus, to use mountain climbing as an example, the environment, or mountain, presents a personal challenge which is taken up in association with others, who may even be joined by the same rope. To provide an example in which the environment plays a more passive role, a quiet room with a comfortable chair may constitute a setting that is conducive to the completion of a crossword puzzle.

On the basis of a detailed study of a student sample, employing psychological tests and an inventory of leisure participation, Phillips (1978) identified seventeen groups of recreational activities and environmental settings. Her results can be summarized schematically in a triangular diagram, with each axis representing one of the three components identified above (Figure 2). Nightlife, for example, is portrayed as a set of activities in which the social environment is of more importance than the natural environment. On the other hand, "man in nature," which includes nature study, camping, canoeing, hiking, and membership of conservation organizations, is shown at the high end of the physical environment scale. "Macho" recreation, which includes fishing, hunting, shuffleboard, target shooting, boxing, judo, karate, and kung fu, is located in the center of the diagram, embracing elements of all three dimensions. The diagram demonstrates clearly that the significance of the environment varies from activity to activity.

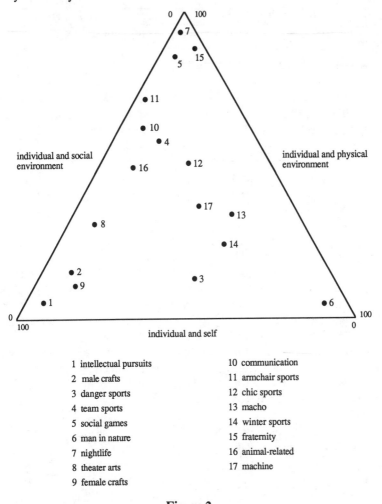

1 intellectual pursuits	10 communication
2 male crafts	11 armchair sports
3 danger sports	12 chic sports
4 team sports	13 macho
5 social games	14 winter sports
6 man in nature	15 fraternity
7 nightlife	16 animal-related
8 theater arts	17 machine
9 female crafts	

Figure 2
Triad of Interactions Inherent in Various Recreation Groups
(Source: Phillips 1978)

INFLUENCES OF THE ENVIRONMENT ON RECREATION

The nature of the physical environment strongly influences the availability of recreation opportunities. The characteristics of the climate, land, water, flora, and fauna in an area are major determinants of the types of outdoor recreation that can be undertaken in that area and of the quality of the recreational experiences that are likely to be obtained. Of course, they are not the only factors: accessibility to recreation sites, capital investment, and management strategies are among the many other factors that influence the supply of recreation opportunities. Nevertheless, the evaluation of the physical environment of an area according to its ability to provide for and sustain recreational uses is essential for the wise provision of recreation opportunities.

Inventorying Recreation Resources

The task of evaluating recreation resources is essentially one of inventory, i.e. the identification of those areas which, because of their characteristics, are able to support particular forms of outdoor recreation. Unfortunately, the diversity of recreational activities, each with its own specific requirements, makes conducting inventories of recreation resources a daunting task. Given the very large number and variety of activities which together constitute outdoor recreation, it is difficult to think of a situation which is not conducive to some form of recreational activity.

In order that recreation opportunities can be inventoried, it is often necessary to develop a classification so that particular types of opportunity can be counted and/or mapped. Many classifications are possible, and the appropriateness of a classification will vary with the purpose for which the inventory is being undertaken. Examples of classifications include the following: urban and rural; resource-based, intermediate, and user-oriented (Clawson and Knetsch 1968); man-modified and natural; public and private; federal, provincial/state, and local; active and passive; formal and informal; intensive and extensive; and fragile and resistant. Some of these categories refer to attributes of the environment, some to the characteristics of recreational activities, and others to jurisdiction over resources. It is not usually a difficult task to inventory existing opportunities for many types of recreation at an elemental level: it is usually straightforward to locate and count libraries, cinemas, arenas, beaches, and parks. However, it is much more difficult to determine the quality of the experiences which they provide. For other types of recreation, such as walking, picnicking, sightseeing, and driving for pleasure, it is extremely difficult to measure the existing resource base, let alone the potential of areas to provide satisfactory experiences given appropriate designation and management.

Although not confined to recreation, The Canada Land Inventory is an interesting example of an inventory of recreation resources (Canada, Department of Regional Economic Expansion 1970). The objectives of the inventory are: to provide a reliable overview of the quality, quantity, and distribution of natural recreation resources within the settled parts of Canada; to indicate comparative levels of recreation capability for non-urban lands based upon present popular preferences; to indicate the types of recreation to which the land is best suited; to identify lands or features possessing outstanding or unique recreational value; and to provide basic information for planning. Numerous assumptions had to be introduced before progress on the inventory could be made. Examples of such assumptions include the following: that management and development practices are sound; that demand and accessibility are uniform; and that the potential of water bodies accrues to the adjacent land. Data were gathered using aerial photographs and field reconnaissance (current inventories may be facilitated by the use of remote sensing), and the result was a series of maps at a scale of 1:250,000, covering the settled portions of Canada, excluding urban areas. Areas are designated in one of seven capability classes, ranging from very high to very low, according to the quantity of recreation which can be sustained per unit area of land per year under perfect market conditions. Further information is provided through the use of numerical and letter symbols. The data are also available for computer manipulation. Although sometimes criticized because of its assumptions and because the level of resolution of the data is not at a scale to suit the needs of all potential users (Hamill 1978), the Canada Land Inventory is a valuable source of information on the potential of Canadian lands to sustain outdoor recreation.

Measurement of Quality

The ability to support recreational use on a long-term basis is a desirable characteristic, but it is not necessarily the same as the provision of a high-quality experience. The measurement of quality is a much more difficult task than the measurement of quantity. However, there has been considerable interest in measuring the quality of landscape in quantitative terms. In part, this has been a reaction to the apparent difficulty which the advocates of greater provision of high-quality, low-intensity recreation opportunities, such as those found in wilderness parks, have experienced in winning battles over the allocation of resources. Proponents of extractive uses, such as forestry and mining, are usually able to provide estimates of the monetary value of production and the number of jobs likely to be created. In contrast, recreation researchers have found great difficulty in evaluating the intangible values of wilderness in similar terms (see Schreyer and Driver, this volume). While usually stopping short of attributing precise monetary values to scenery, students of landscape have developed a large literature on quantitative landscape evaluation.

There are almost as many methods as there are contributors to this literature, and a thorough review is outside the scope of this essay. Fortunately, competent reviews are readily available (e.g. Mitchell 1979). It will suffice to say that landscape evaluation currently lacks a strong theoretical base — although Appleton (1975) has taken some interesting steps to rectify this situation — and is often seen as an intractable technical problem whose solution would resolve many of the difficulties of designating areas for recreation and preservation. This is not the case, for beyond the technical problem is the issue of values. If it were possible to determine the most beautiful area in the world and all could agree on it, the problem of what to do with it would still remain. Some might wish to fence it off and prohibit visitors in order to prevent its desecration, while others might argue that it would be wrong to prevent people from enjoying such a significant part of our heritage.

Although the precise evaluation of scenery remains a daunting task, considerable success has been achieved in providing quantitative estimates of the potential of the resource base to support particular activities. In many cases, it is possible to specify the minimum environmental attributes which must be met for an activity to be possible. If this can be done, then locations can be identified which exceed the criteria and provide conditions which are suitable for the activity. Crowe, McKay, and Baker (1977, 1978), for example, have suggested climatic criteria which must be met if particular recreation activities are to be possible. In the case of downhill skiing, they have suggested that, for successful downhill skiing to take place, a minimum of one inch of snow should be present, winds should be less than fifteen miles per hour, the temperature should be between -5°F and +45°F, visibility should be greater than one-half mile, and there should be no liquid precipitation. Climatic data can be used to determine where and when these conditions are met, and they can even be combined with information on relative relief to identify places which have the potential, based on environmental characteristics, to provide downhill skiing opportunities. The length of the normal operating season and its variability from year to year can be calculated and, when combined with information on rates of visitation and expenditure patterns, the likely viability and profitability of recreation enterprises can be calculated (Lynch, McBoyle, and Wall 1981). Wall and his associates have employed extensions of this technique to assess the implications of possible future climates associated with the greenhouse effect for downhill skiing and camping in Ontario (McBoyle, Wall, Harrison, Kinnaird, and Quinlan 1986; Wall, Harrison, Kinnaird, McBoyle, and Quinlan 1986) and downhill skiing in Quebec (McBoyle and Wall 1987). Micro-climatic information has been employed in the planning of national parks (see, for example, Findlay 1973). At a different scale, Mieczkowski (1985) has examined world climates as they pertain to human comfort and the needs of tourists. Thus, the climatic studies illustrate that the environment has implications for recreation at a wide variety of spatial and temporal scales.

IMPACTS OF RECREATION ON THE ENVIRONMENT

The word "impact" often has a negative connotation; it is frequently associated with undesired changes. But not all changes are "bad," and the environment is often modified so that the requirements of recreationists may be met more satisfactorily. Impacts of recreation on the environment are both purposive and accidental. Areas are set aside and managed for recreational use, structures are erected to entertain and accommodate recreationists, and new environments are created, such as theme parks, which cater to the whims of the recreating public. Many of these areas, such as national parks, are relatively natural, whereas others, such as resorts, are built environments. It is common practice to modify environments and to create new ones to make them more suitable for particular types of visitors. There is a substantial literature on purpose-built recreational environments, particularly upon the morphology of spas (Lawrence 1983; Patmore 1968; Roark 1974; Wightman and Wall 1985), seaside resorts (Gilbert 1939, 1954; Lavery 1971; Meyer-Arendt 1985; Stansfield 1970, 1972) and ski areas (Barker 1982), but this literature is beyond the scope of this chapter. Instead, greater attention will be paid here to relatively natural environments.

Not all environmental modifications are purposive: many are accidental or are the inevitable consequences of recreational use. Whether recreating in natural or built environments, in small or in large numbers, recreationists have side-effects upon the environment, and it is these side-effects that have received the most attention in the literature. This literature is large and growing rapidly but, fortunately, a number of fairly comprehensive reviews are available (Hammitt and Cole 1987; Satchell and Marren 1976; Speight 1973; Wall and Wright 1977), as well as review papers on specific topics. For example, Liddle (1975) and Graefe et al. (1985) have assessed the impacts of trampling upon vegetation; Seabrooke (1981) has drawn together the literature on water-based recreation; Howard and Stanley-Saunders (1979) have compiled an annotated bibliography on impacts on streams; Manning (1979) has examined riparian soils and vegetation; and Liddle and Scorgie (1980) have reviewed the effects of recreation on freshwater plants and animals.

Assessors of changes induced in the environment by recreation are faced with similar challenges to those common to all types of impact research (Wall and Wright 1977). These include the problems of defining a base level against which change can be measured, of distinguishing between human-induced and natural change, of spatial and temporal discontinuities of cause and effect, and of incorporating the full complexities of direct and indirect effects. It is extremely difficult to determine what a place would be like in the absence of recreation, particularly if it has been used for recreation for a considerable period of time, but in the absence of such information it is impossible to be certain of the role which recreation has played in modifying the environment.

Furthermore, environments are not static but evolve naturally: vegetation succession takes place, lakes silt up, and animal populations respond to changes in their habitats.

Activities of human beings may modify energy balances and speed up processes that occur naturally, but at a slower rate. Thus, weathering (the breaking up of rock into small particles) and erosion (the transportation of those particles downslope under the influence of gravity), which are natural processes, may increase in recreation areas and may become management problems. In many cases, the limits of a recreation site do not contain the full causes or effects of change. Thus, many recreational areas may feel the consequence of acid rain or global climate change derived from activities beyond their borders and, conversely, impacts of recreation may extend beyond the recreation site. For example, inadequate waste disposal and leaking septic tanks may pollute river water and cause fish-kills downstream, and destruction of the habitats of migratory species will influence the population elsewhere in the range. Further-more, impacts are both direct and indirect, and it is seldom possible to trace the full impacts of recreation as they reverberate through the complex linkages of an ecological system.

To these common difficulties of impact research may be added a number of others that are more specific to recreation. Just as the diversity of recreational activities poses problems for resource assessment, it also presents a challenge for students of environmental impact, making generalization about the environmental impacts of recreation difficult. Clearly, the consequences of downhill skiing are likely to differ greatly from the changes caused by boating or the environmental perturbations caused by the recreational use of all-terrain vehicles. To compound the problem, recreation takes place in many different environments, each with its own characteristics and susceptibility to change. Obviously, a grassy sward is different from a beach, ski hill, or coral reef, and possesses different potentials for change.

Impact Assessment Methods

Faced with the above problems, investigators have adopted a diversity of research methodologies, each with its own strengths and weaknesses. Three major types of study can be identified: after-the-fact analysis; monitoring; and simulation. Most studies are of the first type (see, for example, Willard and Marr 1970). Impacts are measured after they have occurred, and impacted sites may be compared with sites experiencing no recreational use or impact, the differences between the two being attributed to recreation. Such studies are relatively cheap and easy to undertake, and results are achieved quickly. The methodology is excellent for identifying locations where remedial measures are required, but the investigations are undertaken after the changes have occurred, so that they are akin to "shutting the barn door after the horse has bolted." A further deficiency of such studies is that, while they often provide very detailed information

on environmental changes, it is only the occasional study that provides comparable information on levels and types of recreational use. The manager of
recreation sites needs both types of information if wise decisions are to be made,
for both the environment and visitors are open to manipulation.

Monitoring studies have the potential to overcome the latter limitation.
It may be possible to measure and relate levels of use and associated environmental changes over considerable periods of time, and this may be particularly
informative if sites can be monitored from the moment that they become used by
visitors (see, for example, LaPage 1967). While such studies are intellectually
appealing and are often among the most informative, they are also time-
consuming and expensive to undertake. Thus, they constitute only a small
proportion of all investigations of recreational impacts.

Simulation studies exhibit an experimental approach (see, for example,
Weaver and Dale 1978). Experimental and control plots are exposed to known
volumes and frequencies of recreational use and the consequences are measured
and compared. This approach has the great advantage of examining use and
impact at the same time. The studies are relatively cheap to undertake and they
are becoming relatively more common. They also lend themselves to the examination of recovery rates, since environmental changes can be monitored after the
impacting forces have ceased (Bayfield 1979; Willard and Marr 1971), something which may be difficult to arrange in areas actively used for recreation.

Results of Environmental Impact Research

There are a number of ways of organizing the results of the numerous studies on
the environmental impact of outdoor recreation: by activity, considering the
impacts of different types of recreation; by ecosystem, reporting upon studies
undertaken in different environmental contexts; and by environmental element,
discussing the implications for particular components of the environment, such
as rocks, soil, vegetation, air, water, and wildlife. The last structure will be
adopted here, and a brief synopsis will be provided of a more detailed discussion
available elsewhere (Wall and Wright 1977).

Geology

In most environments, recreation has few implications for geology. However,
the implications can be severe in certain special environments. For example,
rock hounding and collecting fossils can lead to the destruction of interesting
geological sites, and the removal of stalagmites and stalactites can diminish the
appeal of caves. Mountaineers cut holds and leave pitons on rock faces, and
others carve names and paint messages on rock surfaces. These are not major
ecological problems, but they often diminish the quality of the recreation

experience for those who follow. Rock inscriptions may be valued if they are sufficiently old, but it is not clear at what point undesirable graffiti become a valuable archaeological resource.

Soils and vegetation

Most work on recreational impacts has concentrated upon soils and vegetation, particularly in campsites and along trails. The studies indicate that users compact soils, increase the proportion of water running off the surface rather than percolating down through the soil, modify soil moisture and temperature regimes, reduce organic matter and nutrients in the soil (although these may also increase locally due to the deposition of waste materials), increase erosion, and reduce the number and diversity of soil organisms. Vegetation is modified directly through mechanical damage caused by recreationists and their vehicles coming into contact with plants, and indirectly through changes in the soil. The results are that vegetation is destroyed and bare patches may be created; growth rates and reproduction rates may be reduced; the age structure of the vegetation may be modified; species composition is changed as more resilient and often weedy species obtain a competitive advantage; and species diversity is reduced. Although these changes are usually considered to be negative, in some cases habitat diversity may increase as areas are opened up for recreation, and light is allowed to penetrate along trail and campsite edges in areas that were formerly entirely forested. Unfortunately, different researchers measure different variables (e.g. biomass, species diversity, percentage cover) so that comparisons between studies are not easy to make, and it is not clear which measures are of most significance to managers. The situation is extremely complex because the amount of impact is influenced not only by the numbers and types of users, but also by factors such as the season of the year, the amount of soil moisture, soil type, species morphology, and the successional stage of the vegetation.

Air quality

There have been few studies of the influence of recreation upon air quality. The impact of recreation upon the atmosphere is not considered to be a problem in most situations. However, in deep valleys, such as Yosemite, where large numbers of automobile exhausts combine with the smoke from camp fires, air quality can become uncomfortable. Studies have been undertaken of the ability of air masses to disperse pollutants in ski areas such as Aspen, Colorado (Kirkpatrick and Reeser 1976). Few would deny that automobile exhausts are a substantial contributor of pollutants, and, if it is acknowledged that a large proportion of automobile use is for pleasure, then it follows that recreation is a substantial cause of air pollution. However, there is little documentation to substantiate this assertion.

Water quality

Lakes "age" naturally, and the impacts of recreation are likely to differ on oligotrophic ("young") and eutrophic ("old") lakes. Most of the evidence of the adverse effects of recreation on aquatic ecosystems is circumstantial. Water is mobile, and it disperses and dilutes pollutants, often making it difficult to link cause and effect with absolute certainty. Few would deny that recreation can contribute to lower water quality and increased concentrations of pathogens through inappropriate waste disposal and leaking septic tanks. Many cottagers are concerned about water quality in lakes as increased use of lakeshores contributes to nutrient enrichment, especially of nitrogen and phosphorous compounds, leading to greater plant growth and diminished oxygen supply. Although there are simulation studies which indicate that as much as four out of every ten gallons of gasoline may be discharged directly into the water from outboard motors (Barton 1969), there are surprisingly few quantitative studies of cause and effect relationships between recreation and water quality.

Wildlife

Wildlife constitutes the quarry for some types of outdoor recreation — hunters and anglers aim to have an impact upon wildlife as the objective of their activity. Nevertheless, many among their number claim that, because they are concerned about the maintenance of populations of desirable species, their overall impact is benign. Many species adjust quite well to the presence of humans, and most readers will have experienced how tame (and dependent upon human food) many animals and birds can become. There is a substantial literature on bears and bear management which has been developed in response to concerns about human-bear encounters in recreation areas. It does seem unfair, though, that it is usually the bear which is considered the rogue and which is relocated, while the invading visitor remains unchastized.

Impacts of recreation on wildlife take three forms: direct influences on numbers by killing or stocking; alteration of habitat; and disturbance. In all three cases, this may lead to changes in population numbers and species composition. However, animals are mobile, so it is often difficult to distinguish between death and out-migration. Although there are a very limited number of exceptions (see, for example, Busack and Bury 1974), most studies lack population counts taken prior to the incidence of recreation, and there are very few longitudinal studies. This would seem to be essential where much impact is likely to be indirect through habitat modification.

Recent Perspectives

The preceding review is a synopsis of an assessment undertaken by Wall and Wright in 1977, whose work is summarized in Figure 3. Research has continued to flourish since that time, and many additional studies can be added to their bibliography. Many of these papers are to be found in recent issues of *Biological Conservation*, the *Journal of Applied Ecology*, and *Environmental Management*. There have not been major methodological innovations. Rather, the trend has been to apply existing methods to new environments and new activities. Many of the early studies undertaken in temperate grassland and sand dune settings, but the range of environments which have been investigated now encompasses temperate and tropical forests, deserts, wetlands, coastal and riverine areas, and coral reefs, as well as high latitude and high altitude locations.

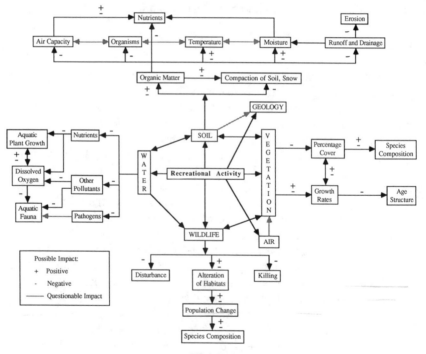

Figure 3
Recreation Impact Relationships
(Source: Wall and Wright 1977)

Most of the early studies concentrated upon the implications of trampling on trails and campsites. These studies are still very valuable, for the impacts of most activities are derived from the cumulative pressures applied by a succession of feet and vehicles. Impacts of canoeing, for example, are few while the craft is on the water, but are concentrated at the shoreline where camping takes place and where the canoe is introduced to and withdrawn from the water.

The trampling studies were soon joined by investigations of skiing and snowmobiling and they, in turn, have been complemented by examinations of off-road vehicles, river rafting, boating, and reef walking. Most studies still concentrate upon soils and vegetation; none attempts to trace the full range of direct and indirect impacts as they reverberate through the ecosystem. Nevertheless, the growth in the number of studies and their extension to new environments and locations represent a substantial degree of progress in the acquisition of information about the impacts of recreation on the environment.

The large number of studies of the impacts of recreation on different environments, and the use of varied methodologies, all point to important generalizations. At a conceptual level, interactions between human beings are now being viewed in a more sophisticated manner. Thus, for example, Liddle and Tothill (1984) have suggested that such interactions can be seen as a three-stage process, termed *alpha* (communication), *beta* (contact), and *gamma* (response). The *alpha* process includes all of the signals that are received before physical contact takes place. The *beta* process begins with first contact and ends when contact ceases. The *gamma* process commences when a response to the *beta* process takes place.

Also, terminology is beginning to be used in a more precise manner. Thus, a distinction can be made between resistance, or the ability to resist mechanical damage (in the case of plants); tolerance, or the ability of a species to survive over a given period; and resilience, or the re-growth and proliferation of individuals and/or parts of plants. Perhaps the most significant practical implication of the studies is the recognition that impacts on the environment occur at relatively low intensities of use, and successive increments of environmental change diminish in magnitude with additional increments of use. In other words, much change takes place at low-use intensities. Furthermore, rates of recovery are relatively slow and take considerably longer than the time required for the impacts to occur. These findings have considerable implications for managers. They suggest, for example, that, unless managers have a very large area at their disposal, it will be difficult to rotate areas of use, designating some as off-limits to visitors while they recover.

THE SIGNIFICANCE OF ENVIRONMENTAL IMPACTS

The purpose of this section is to examine the significance and implications of the impacts which have already been discussed. Although requirements vary considerably from place to place, many countries (as well as states, provinces, and even local jurisdictions) now require environmental impact statements to be prepared in situations where projects or policies appear as if they might put the quality of the environment at risk. Many of the impacts of recreation are individually small, although, cumulatively, they may result in substantial changes in the environment. They have not usually been of great concern in most assessments of environmental impact. Major tourist developments, without question, can have adverse impacts upon the environment, and specific recreation projects, such as the development of ski areas in the national parks of western Canada (Bella 1987: 121-127), have been the object of much controversy. However, while it has been common for concern to be expressed about the adverse effects of other developments on recreational environments, the impacts of recreation have often been viewed, sometimes erroneously, as relatively benign, particularly when recreation takes place at low densities.

Most recreationists are gregarious. While a minority stray far from the beaten track, even in wilderness settings the majority are concentrated in a relatively small area. This means that the most impacts are also highly concentrated spatially. However, there is a tendency for visitors to congregate in highly valued areas such as shorelines and viewpoints, so that, while most impacts of recreation are relatively localized, they often occur in highly-valued places. Nonetheless, most visitors appear not to be adversely affected by many of the changes which have been described above, for they continue to return to the same locations. Conversely, the quality of the experience of a minority of users may be destroyed by quite small modifications to the environment, which they deem to be unacceptable.

Both accidental and purposeful environmental modifications which are acceptable to most users of an urban park may be deemed by the same individuals to be inappropriate if found in a wilderness setting. Also, there may be little relationship between the magnitude of impacts as measured quantitatively by scientists, and their salience to users with very different goals and objectives. In fact, the recreating public may even employ measures which are quite different to those used by the scientist. For example, in the case of water quality, the scientist may be measuring turbidity, pH value, coliform counts, and biochemical oxygen demand, whereas the recreating public may take their cues from color, smell, temperature, and the quantity of debris in the water. The interpretation of the significance of results may also vary dramatically, as is shown when people continue to swim at placarded beaches (Barker 1971); users may be prepared to accept the risk, and the probability of being harmed by the degraded environment may be less than the probability of being involved in an automobile accident on the way to the beach. Thus, relationships between human behavior and environmental modifications are not straightforward, and management of the interactions between the environment and people at leisure continues to pose challenging questions for researchers and for the managers of recreation sites.

The degree to which environmental modification is acceptable to potential users is a function of the experiences which they hope to gain from use of the resource. It is common for goals to vary to such a degree that real conflicts occur between potential users whose objectives are so antagonistic that compromise may not be possible. Recreation may be viewed as competing with other potential uses of the scarce resources of land and water. Conflicts between preservation and use, between forestry, mining, and recreation, between commercial and sport fishing, between agriculture and the development of second homes, and between hunting for sport and subsistence, are just some among numerous possible examples of competition between recreation and other types of resource use. Careful management may permit the coexistence of different activities and a sharing of resources. However, tensions between users are seldom completely eliminated. Multiple use of resources usually involves the segregation of users spatially, as in the case of buffer zones to separate active logging from recreation, or temporally, when snowmobiling takes place on agricultural land during the winter season. Where true multiple use takes place, such as the simultaneous use of lakes for recreation and flood control, there is usually some loss in utility for each function, although total net benefits to society may be greater than from allocation of the resource to a single use.

Conflicts over the allocation of resources between recreation and other uses are usually resolved through the political process. Recreation researchers have devoted greater attention to conflicts within recreation than to investigating conflicts between recreation and other resource uses (Owens 1985). Lucas's (1964) study of users and managers of the Boundary Waters Canoe Area in Minnesota was one of the earliest studies in this genre and it still merits attention. He divided the users into categories based upon the mode of transportation employed, and determined that paddling canoeists penetrated further into the area than motorboaters but regarded a much smaller part of the area as being true wilderness. Neither the canoeists' nor the motorboaters' perceptions of wilderness coincided with the "official" wilderness, which was under the jurisdiction of the managers. Furthermore, relationships between users were asymmetrical, in that the presence of motorboaters usually detracted from the experiences of canoeists, but the converse was usually not the case: motorboaters were generally more tolerant of the presence of other users than were canoeists.

Since the publication of Lucas's study, a growing literature has developed concerning the environmental perceptions of recreationists. Much of this literature has considered individuals participating in different types of recreation, often making a distinction between mechanized and non-mechanized activities. Attention has been drawn to differences in the experiences sought and resulting conflicts between such groups as snowmobilers and cross-country skiers (e.g. Jackson and Wong 1982), sailors, power-boaters, water skiers, and fishermen (Gramman and Burdge 1981; Owens 1977), hikers and riders of trail bikes, and campers using different types of equipment (Clark, Hendee, and Campbell 1971).

The research has generally confirmed the broad findings of Lucas. However, there is a danger that injudicious reporting of survey results may lead to the development and perpetuation of myths. For example, it is usually concluded that mechanized forms of recreation are more demanding than non-mechanized activities. This is a half-truth. While mechanized recreational activities usually require larger areas and may make greater environmental impacts than non-mechanized forms, their devotees are less likely to require a pristine environment and are more likely to be tolerant of the presence of large numbers of other users. But to conclude that they do not appreciate the environment is to perpetuate a falsehood. Rather, they prefer a different relationship with the environment, and their preferred experience may be derived from a different mix of personal, environmental, and social components. Similarly, wilderness camping with fly-in access, space blankets, and freeze-dried food may be just as dependent on modern technology as other forms of camping. Nor is it clear to this author why those who appreciate a comfortable bed should, automatically, fail to appreciate a natural environment. A well-designed lodge may be much less taxing on the environment than many of the eyesores which currently masquerade as campgrounds. The moral is that wilderness devotees, who have been responsible for much of this research, should be more careful to separate their own values from those of their respondents than has sometimes been the case in the past.

Some researchers, such as Dunlap and Heffernan (1975) and Jackson (1986, 1987, and this volume), have examined more broadly based values held by participants in different forms of outdoor recreation and their attitudes towards the environment and environmental issues; McKechnie (1977) has developed and tested an instrument for measuring environmental dispositions. Jackson discusses environmental attitudes in some detail in this volume, so that, other than to draw attention to the imprecise use of terminology, which continues to plague the whole area of so-called "perception" research (Schiff 1971), the reader is referred to his contribution for a thorough discussion of this topic.

Careful analyses reveal that participants in the same activity may have very different expectations and experiences. Bryan (1979) developed the concept of specialization to provide some order to this topic. He proposed that levels of specialization can be distinguished within any activity. He defined recreation specialization as "a continuum of behavior from the general to the particular, reflected by equipment and skills used in the sport and activity setting preferences" (Bryan 1979: 29). Roggenbuck, Smith, and Wellman (1980) used

How can standards of recreation be established?

recreational specialization as the conceptual basis for their study of Virginia canoeists; Graefe (1980) employed it in an investigation of fishermen; Kauffman and Graefe (1984) applied it to canoeists; Donnelly, Vaske, and Graefe (1986) to boaters; and Williams and Huffman (1985), with mixed success, to hikers. Grimm (1987) has provided a useful review of this literature, and has linked it to the concepts of depreciative behavior (Christensen and Clark, 1983; Roggenbuck, Smith, and Wellman 1980), displacement, and succession (Anderson and Brown 1984; Becker 1981; Schreyer 1979).

Managers have a number of options open to them in manipulating the recreation-environment interface in an attempt to provide recreational experiences compatible with their mandates. They can modify the environment, for example by planting vegetation, seeding and watering campsites, stocking fish, or improving habitat for desired species. They might attempt to modify the behavior of visitors. Such an approach can be divided into two main strategies: manipulative and regulatory. Regulatory controls define where, when, and how people may recreate. Manipulative strategies are more subtle and, in many ways, more attractive. They are "less obtrusive practices that control the intensity of use without directly interfering with the user's perceived freedom of choice" (Gilbert, Peterson, and Lime 1972: 136). A bewildering variety of management strategies has been suggested as appropriate to wilderness areas; many of these have been reviewed by Hendee, Stankey, and Lucas (1978). However, this author is not aware of any systematic attempt to assess the extent to which various strategies have been adopted, their relative success, and the circumstances which influence their usefulness.

Much of the literature on the environmental impacts of recreation has developed with the notion of carrying capacity in mind (see Stankey and McCool, this volume). Carrying capacity has been variously defined, but can be considered to be the maximum number of people which an area can support without an unacceptable decline in the quality of the environment or the quality of the recreational experience. The carrying capacity concept is particularly interesting in that it is an attempt to combine human and environmental components within one measure. Shelby and Heberlein (1986) have provided one of the most comprehensive discussions of the topic from a behavioral perspective, including consideration of the tenuous relationship between crowding and satisfaction. Unfortunately, while interest in carrying capacity has generated a large literature on environmental impacts and has drawn attention to the need for managers to specify the goals for their sites with clarity, the failure to develop satisfactory methods for measuring capacity and, more basically, the growing belief that areas do not have an inherent capacity, have led to the notion of carrying capacity falling into increasing disfavor (Wall 1982).

Limits of Acceptable Change (Stankey and McCool 1984) and, particularly, the Recreation Opportunity Spectrum (Driver, Brown, Stankey, and Gregoire 1987) are concepts which incorporate a continuum of recreation-environment interactions and which are attracting an increasing number of devotees. However, they are not the only contenders in the quest to develop an integrated and widely applicable conceptual base for the planning and management of recreation-environment interactions. Others include the Visitor Impact Management framework (Graefe, Kuss, and Loomis 1985) and the Visitor Activity Management Process (Graham, Nilsen, and Payne 1987).

To conclude, research on outdoor recreation and the environment is currently in a transitional stage. However, both from the perspective of the development of conceptual bases to further the understanding of interrelationships between recreation and the environment, and from the viewpoint of providing planners and managers with tools which will assist them in their decision-making, there is strong evidence that considerable progress has been made.

References

Appleton, J. 1975. *The Experience of Landscape*. Chichester: Wiley.

Anderson, D.H. and P.J. Brown. 1984. "The displacement process in recreation." *Journal of Leisure Research 16:* 61-73.

Barker, M.L. 1971. "Beach pollution in the Toronto region." In *Perceptions and Attitudes in Resources Management*, eds. W.R.D. Sewell and I. Burton, pp. 37-47. Ottawa: Department of Energy, Mines and Resources.

Barker, M.L. 1982. "Traditional landscape and mass tourism in the Alps." *Geographical Review 72:* 395-415.

Barton, M.M. 1969. "Water pollution in remote recreational areas." *Journal of Soil and Water Conservation 24:* 132-134.

Bayfield, N.G. 1979. "Recovery of four montane heath communities on Cairngorm, Scotland, from disturbance by trampling." *Biological Conservation 15:* 165-179.

Becker, R.H. 1981. "Displacement of recreational users between the Lower St. Croix and the Upper Mississippi." *Journal of Environmental Management 13:* 259-267.

Bella, L. 1987. *Parks for Profit*. Montreal: Harvest House.

Bryan, H. 1979. *Conflict in the Great Outdoors: Toward Understanding and Managing for Diverse Sportsmen Preferences*. Birmingham: University of Alabama, Bureau of Public Administration.

Busack, S.D. and R.B. Bury. 1974. "Some effects of off-road vehicles and sheep grazing on lizard populations in the Mojave Desert." *Biological Conservation 6:* 179-183.

Canada. Department of Regional Economic Expansion. 1970. *The Canada Land Inventory Classification for Outdoor Recreation*. Ottawa.

Cheek, N.H., Jr., D.R. Field, and R.J. Burdge. 1976. *Leisure and Recreation Places*. Ann Arbor, MI: Ann Arbor Science.

Christensen, H.H. and R.R. Clark. 1983. "Increasing public involvement to reduce depreciative behavior in recreation settings." *Leisure Sciences* 5: 359-379.   GV   1 L 53   Educ PR

Clark, R.N., J.C. Hendee, and F.L. Campbell. 1971. "Values, behavior and conflict in modern camping culture." *Journal of Leisure Research* 3: 143-159.

Clawson, M. and J.L. Knetsch. 1968. *Economics of Outdoor Recreation.* Baltimore, MD: Johns Hopkins.

Crowe, R.B., G.A. McKay, and W.M. Baker. 1977 and 1978. *The Tourist and Recreation Climate of Ontario.* Toronto: Atmospheric Environment Service. 3 vols.

Donnelly, M.P., J.J. Vaske, and A.R. Graefe. 1986. "Degree and range of recreation specialization: Toward a typology of boating related activities." *Journal of Leisure Research 18:* 81-95.

Driver, B.L., P.J. Brown, G.H. Stankey, and T.G. Gregoire. 1987. "The ROS planning system: Evolution, basic concepts, and research needs." *Leisure Sciences 9:* 201-212.

Dunlap, R.E. and R.B. Heffernan. 1975. "Outdoor recreation and environmental concern: An empirical examination." *Rural Sociology 40:* 18-30.

Findlay, B.F. 1973. *Climatography of Pukaskwa National Park, Ontario.* Toronto: Atmospheric Environment Service.

Gilbert, C., G. Peterson, and D. Lime. 1972. "Toward a model of travel behavior on the Boundary Waters Canoe Area." *Environment and Behavior 4:* 131-157.

Gilbert, E.W. 1939. "The growth of inland and seaside health resorts in England." *Scottish Geographical Magazine 55:* 16-35.

Gilbert, E.W. 1954. *Brighton: Old Ocean's Bauble.* London: Methuen.

Graefe, A.R. 1980. "The relationship between level of participation and selected aspects of specialization in recreational fishing." Ph.D. thesis, Texas A & M University.

Graefe, A.R., F.R. Kuss, and L. Loomis. 1985. "Visitor impact management in wildland settings." In *Proceedings, National Wilderness Research Conference: Current Research*, pp. 424-431. Ogden, UT: USDA Forest Service, Intermountain Research Station.

Graham, R., P.W. Nilsen, and R.J. Payne. 1987. "Visitor activity planning and management in Canadian national parks: Marketing within a context of integration." In *Social Science in Natural Resource Management Systems*, eds. M.L. Miller, R.P. Gale, and P.J. Brown, pp. 149-146. Boulder: Westview.

Gramann, J.H. and R.J. Burdge. 1981. "The effect of recreational goals on conflict perception: The case of water skiers and fishermen." *Journal of Leisure Research 13:* 15-27.

Grimm, S. 1987. "Recreational specialization among river users: The case of Nahanni National Park Reserve." M.A. thesis, University of Waterloo, Department of Geography.

Hamill, L. 1978. "Canadian approaches to the description and evaluation of the recreation resources and scenery of near-natural areas, 1961-1976." Paper presented to the Annual Meeting of the Canadian Association of Geographers, London, ON.

Hammitt, W.E. and D.N. Cole. 1987. *Wildland Recreation: Ecology and Management*. New York: Wiley.

Hendee, J.C., G.H. Stankey, and R.C. Lucas. 1978. *Wilderness Management*. Washington, DC: USDA Forest Service.

Howard, G.E. and B.A. Stanley-Saunders. 1979. *Impacts of Recreation Activities Associated with Streams: A Problem Analysis*. Clemson: Clemson University, Department of Recreation and Park Administration.

Jackson, E.L. 1986. "Outdoor recreation participation and attitudes to the environment." *Leisure Studies 5:* 1-23.

Jackson, E.L. 1987. "Outdoor recreation participation and views on resource development and preservation." *Leisure Sciences 9:* 235-250.

Educ.   GV   1 L53

Jackson, E.L. and R.A.G. Wong. 1982. "Perceived conflict between urban cross-country skiers and snowmobilers in Alberta." *Journal of Leisure Research 14:* 47-62.

Kauffman, R.B. and A.R. Graefe. 1984. "Canoeing specialization, expected rewards and resource related attitudes." In *National River Recreation Symposium Proceedings*, eds. J.S. Popadic, D.I. Butterfield, D.H. Anderson, and M.R. Popadic, pp. 629-641. Baton Rouge, LA: Louisiana State University.

Kirkpatrick, L.W. and W.K. Reeser, Jr. 1976. "The air pollution carrying capacities of selected Colorado mountain valley ski communities." *Journal of the Air Pollution Control Association 26:* 992-994.

LaPage, W.F. 1967. *Some Observations on Campground Trampling and Ground Cover Response.* Upper Darby, PA: USDA Forest Service, Northeastern Forest Experiment Station.

Lavery, P. 1971. "Resorts and recreation." In *Recreation Geography*, ed. P. Lavery, pp. 167-196. Newton Abbot: David and Charles.

Lawrence, H.W. 1983. "Southern spas: Source of the American resort tradition." *Landscape 27:* 1-12.

Liddle, M.J. 1975. "A selective review of the ecological effects of human trampling on natural ecosystems." *Biological Conservation 7:* 17-36.

Liddle, M.J. and H.R.A. Scorgie. 1980. "The effects of recreation on freshwater plants and animals: A review." *Biological Conservation 17:* 183-206.

Liddle, M.J. and J.C. Tothill. 1984. *The Ecological Basis of the Interactions between Organisms.* Brisbane: Griffith University, School of Australian Environmental Studies.

Lucas, R.C. 1964. "Wilderness perception and use: The example of the Boundary Waters Canoe Area." *Natural Resources Journal 3:* 394-411.

Lynch, P., G.R. McBoyle, and G. Wall. 1981. "A ski season without snow." In *Canadian Climate in Review - 1980*, eds. D.W. Phillips and G.A. McKay, pp. 42-50. Toronto: Atmospheric Environment Service.

Manning, R.E. 1979. "Impacts of recreation on riparian soils and vegetation." *Water Resources Bulletin 15:* 30-43.

McBoyle, G. and G. Wall. 1987. "The impact of CO_2-induced warming on downhill skiing in the Laurentians." *Cahiers de Geographie du Québec 31:* 39-50.

McBoyle, G., G. Wall, R. Harrison, V. Kinnaird, and C. Quinlan. 1986. "Recreation and climatic change: A Canadian case study." *Ontario Geography 28:* 51-68.

McKechnie, G.E. 1977. "The Environmental Response Inventory in application." *Environment and Behavior 9:* 255-276.

Meyer-Arendt, K.A. 1985. "The Grand Isle, Louisiana resort cycle." *Annals of Tourism Research 12:* 449-465.

Mieczkowski, Z. 1985. "The tourism climate index: A method of evaluating world climates for tourism." *Canadian Geographer 29:* 220-233.

Mitchell, B. 1979. *Geography and Resource Analysis.* London: Longman.

Nelson, J.G. and R.W. Butler. 1974. "Recreation and the environment." In *Perspectives on Environment*, eds. I.R. Manners and M.W. Mikesell, pp. 290-310. Washington, DC: Association of American Geographers.
SC(QI+ 54/ A 84 19 74

Owens, P.L. 1977. "Recreational conflict: The interaction of Norfolk Broads coarse anglers and boat users." In *Recreational Freshwater Fisheries: Their Conservation, Management and Development*, ed. J. Alabaster, pp. 136-152. Stevenage: Water Research Centre.

Owens, P.L. 1985. "Conflict as a social interaction process in environment and behaviour research: The example of leisure and recreation research." *Journal of Environmental Psychology 5:* 243-259.

Patmore, J.A. 1968. "Spa towns in Britain." In *Urbanization and its Problems*, eds. R.P. Beckinsale and J.M. Houston, pp. 47-69. Oxford: Blackwell.

Phillips, S.D. 1978. "Recreation and personality: A systems approach." M.A. thesis, University of Waterloo, Department of Geography.

Roark, C.S. 1974. "Historic Yellow Springs: The restoration of an American spa." *Pennsylvania Folklife 24:* 28-38.

Roggenbuck, J.W., A.C. Smith, and J.D. Wellman. 1980. *Specialization, Displacement and Definition of Depreciative Behavior Among Virginia Canoeists.* St. Paul, MN: USDA Forest Service, North Central Forest Experiment Station.

Satchell, J.E. and P.R. Marren. *1976.The Effects of Recreation on the Ecology of Natural Landscapes.* Strasbourg: Council of Europe.

Schiff, M.R. 1971. "The definition of perceptions and attitudes." In *Perceptions and Attitudes in Resources Management*, eds. W.R.D. Sewell and I. Burton, pp. 7-12. Ottawa: Department of Energy, Mines and Resources.

Schreyer, R. 1979. *Succession and Displacement in River Recreation: Problem Definition and Analysis.* St. Paul, MN: USDA Forest Service, North Central Forest Experiment Station.

Seabrooke, A.K. 1981. "The environmental impacts of water-based recreation." *East Lakes Geographer 16:* 11-19.

Shelby, B. and T.A. Heberlein. 1986. *Carrying Capacity in Recreation Settings.* Corvallis: Oregon State University Press.

Sonnenfeld, J. 1968. "Geography, perception and the behavioral environment." Paper presented to the American Association for the Advancement of Science, Dallas, TX.

Speight, M.C.D. 1973. *Outdoor Recreation and Its Ecological Effects: A Bibliography and Review.* London: University College.

Stankey, G.H. and S.F. McCool. 1984. "Carrying capacity in recreational settings: Evolution, appraisal, and application." *Leisure Sciences 6:* 453-474.

Stansfield, C.A. 1970. "The recreation business district." *Journal of Leisure Research 2:* 213-225.

Stansfield, C.A. 1972. "The development of modern seaside resorts." *Parks and Recreation 5:* 43-46.

Wall, G. 1982. "Cycles and capacity: Incipient theory or conceptual contradiction?" *Tourism Management 3:* 188-192.

Wall, G., R. Harrison, V. Kinnaird, G. McBoyle, and C. Quinlan. 1986. "The implications of climatic change for camping in Ontario." *Recreation Research Review 13:* 50-60.

Wall, G. and C. Wright. 1977. *The Environmental Impact of Outdoor Recreation.* Waterloo: University of Waterloo, Department of Geography.

Weaver, T. and D. Dale. 1978. "Trampling effects of hikers, motorcycles and horses in meadows and forests." *Journal of Applied Ecology 15:* 451-457.

Wightman, D. and G. Wall. 1985. "The spa experience at Radium Hot Springs." *Annals of Tourism Research 12:* 393-416.

Willard, D.E. and J.W. Marr. 1970. "Effects of human activities on alpine tundra ecosystems in Rocky Mountain National Park, Colorado." *Biological Conservation 2:* 257-265.

Willard, D.E. and J.W. Marr. 1971. "Recovery of alpine tundra under protection after damage by human activities in the Rocky Mountains of Colorado." *Biological Conservation 3:* 181-190.

Williams, D.R. and M.G. Huffman. 1985. "Research specialization as a factor in backcountry trail choice." In *Proceedings, National Wilderness Research Conference: Current Research,* pp. 339-344. Ogden, UT: USDA Forest Service, Intermountain Research Station.

RECREATION AND ENERGY

Jack B. Ellis

OVERVIEW OF THE CONNECTIONS BETWEEN RECREATION AND ENERGY

Recreation, like any other human activity, consumes energy. Energy in many forms, injected at various points in the cycle of preparing for and conducting it, is required to actually engage in any occasion of recreational activity. Paradoxically, however, little is known about either the magnitude or importance of reciprocal relationships between energy and recreation — for example, how much energy is consumed in recreational engagements, or, conversely, how energy considerations have affected recreational activity participation.

In considering energy, three forms can be distinguished. In some aspects of recreation ("re-creation"), it truly may be said that human energy is produced by the activity rather than being consumed. This human mental or psychic energy is crucial to an understanding of what recreation is and why we do it, but none of the social and medical sciences to date has been able to measure the "human energy" thus created. Since we do not understand enough about this form of energy in recreation, it is not dealt with in this chapter.

The human physical energy involved in recreation activities is the research domain of the physiologist, the specialist in sports medicine, and related disciplines. The often-used terms "active" and "passive" as descriptors of recreational activities obviously can refer usefully to this form of energy. This topic could belong here, but it is excluded more or less arbitrarily.

The components of recreational energy that are supplied externally, from what are commonly seen as the primary convertible forms of energy — petroleum fuels and electricity — are the subject of this chapter, and only such energy will be considered.

Recreational energy can be seen as having several components: an activity component, which must include both direct and indirect energy content; a locational component, which involves travel modes and distance factors; a qualitative activity modifier, dependent on the level of engagement of the participant — for example, a casual versus elite athlete; and a lifestyle component, in which the number of activities and frequency of participation influence the total recreational energy budget. Perhaps the clearest way to illustrate the concepts that link recreation and energy is in diagrammatic form. Figure 1 shows the basic factors relating energy and recreation that are addressed in this chapter.

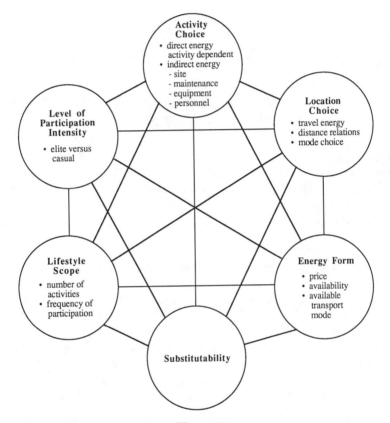

Figure 1
Conceptual Relationships Between Energy and Recreation

One of the major factors affecting the energy content of recreation is activity choice versus locational choice. Since energy content must be assessed for the whole cycle of a recreation occasion, the choice of a distant destination or an inefficient mode of transportation can have a much greater effect on overall energy consumed in a given outing than the choice of an inherently low-energy activity versus an energy-intensive one. The locational choice is so strongly related to travel patterns to and from the site of recreational activity that the two factors can be considered as a single influencing variable. Smith's chapter (this volume) on the spatial analysis of recreation and leisure explores the travel component in some depth.

The main aspects of energy affecting recreation are the price and availability of different forms of energy. Petroleum energy is the primary form involved in outdoor recreation, while electrical energy is dominant for indoor recreation. The latter may, of course, be generated from many primary sources, including petroleum.

The concept of substitutability, which has intrigued and challenged so many generations of leisure researchers, can be seen to affect both the recreation and the energy side of the recreation/energy picture. If a recreationist substitutes a near-home activity for a distant, outdoor, one, for example, there most likely will be a substitution of travel mode — perhaps from the automobile to walking or cycling — as an additional consequence.

ENERGY COMPONENTS OF RECREATION ACTIVITIES

In classifying recreation activities as being more or less energy-intensive, many researchers have used the concept of a "typical" occasion of participation in the activity. This yields a one-dimensional typology or conceptual spectrum of activities from energy-intensive to low-energy. For example, Osborn and Peine (1979), Ritchie (1979), Graef, Gianinno, and Csikszentmihalyi (1980), and Foster and Kuhn (1983) present rankings of activities based on their energy-intensiveness.

It is important to note that a second dimension is also needed for such a typology, since the level of engagement of the participant with the activity also influences the energy requirements significantly. For example, sailing may be a low-energy activity for the average person with a dinghy, but it is a completely different and far more energy-intensive pursuit when sailing in an America's Cup race. In general, the more elite the scale of participation in the activity or the higher the competitive level at which participation takes place, the higher will be the energy content of the activity occasion.

Figure 2 attempts to show this phenomenon in its two-dimensional form, where the inherent energy content of activities and the level of engagement of the participant are both shown as affecting energy intensiveness. The axes have no particular scale, since there are many factors involved in assessing the indirect as well as the direct components of an activity's energy requirements.

The "direct" and "indirect" components of energy use can transform the energy content of a given recreation occasion. The direct use is just that; it comprises the energy it takes to do the activity, including getting to and from the site of doing it. The indirect component includes the energy required to support the activity, such as to build and maintain the facility, to manufacture and distribute equipment, the energy consumed in the lifestyles of any employees, and so forth. Clearly, this indirect component can be rather difficult to measure, or even to identify in some cases.

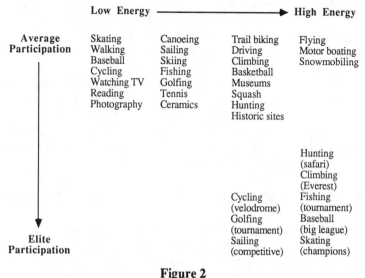

Figure 2
A Typology of Recreation Activities by Energy Intensity
and Participant Engagement

As an example, consider a game of golf. The direct energy component is the average energy consumed by a typical participant going to and from the golf course, and in playing 18 holes. The indirect energy component is comprised of a share of the energy required to maintain the golf course, the nonsocial portion of the club house, and the household energy budgets of club employees. Purists also might insist on charging a portion of the energy costs of infrastructure beyond the golf course itself, such as a portion of the energy to maintain the streets used by golfers to access the club; portions of the personal energy budgets of those employed in making and retailing golf equipment; and so forth, seemingly *ad infinitum*. The concept is simple, but the practicalities of definition and measurement are not.

As noted above, this secondary component of energy becomes important in distinguishing the different levels of participation in a given activity. It is fairly obvious that a typical participant in skating, for example, might use little direct energy and no indirect energy at all, if the skating were done on a frozen pond. A championship-level figure skater, on the other hand, might live as near to an arena as an average skater does to his or her frozen pond, thus using the same direct component of energy use per skating occasion; but the indirect energy component involved in using hours of arena time for practice, extensive travel to competitions, engagement of expert coaches, and so forth, is enormous. This factor of level of participation completely transforms the energy used per occasion of participation. In general, of course, the shift is toward much greater energy inputs as the level of participation becomes more elite. The low-energy activity of sandlot baseball played by children becomes a tremendously high energy activity when it is major league baseball played in an air-conditioned domed stadium.

It would be attractive to conclude this discussion with some definitive data on how trends in recreation activities are affecting energy content, and whether energy considerations are affecting trends in activity participation. Alas, the data are inconclusive as to whether energy is really a prime consideration at all in most recreation settings.

Boating, for example, is an activity where the energy components are fairly visible, and are quite varied depending on the type of boating considered. Often, a superficial argument is made that energy has had the greatest effect on trends in this activity. In most parts of North America, boating has increased significantly in popularity in the years since the early 1970s. In particular, participation in sail boating increased very rapidly as energy costs escalated in the mid to late 1970s, while participation in power boating increased at a much slower rate. More recently, as energy costs have eased, the growth rate of participation in motor boating has picked up while the growth in participation in sail boating has slowed (Hough, Stansbury, and Ellis, 1985). These observations may lead some observers to assume that energy is the prime — or only — cause behind these shifts.

But shifts in tastes and technology have had powerful effects also, and it is too simplistic to attribute major changes solely to energy factors. For example, in addition to rapid energy price increases, the 1970s saw revolutionary changes in the technology of sailboat construction, including the fiberglass hull and the dacron sail. Both innovations radically reduced the costs and maintenance time and effort required of sailors, especially for large sailboats. Two different but powerful "ethos" factors were also at work: to slake their desire to emulate the super-rich, middle class participants now found they could afford some sort of sailing yacht; to "go with the flow" in an eco-environmental sense, many others were attracted to sailing as a clean, silent sport. No-one can say how much of the shift to sailing in the 1970s resulted from energy considerations and how much from other factors. Similarly, the more recent shift to higher growth in large power boating is at least partly a generation or age-cohort related phenomenon: many of the 35-40 year old sailboat purchasers of earlier years find that they wish to switch to a less demanding power boat as they approach their sixties. They can also more readily afford the greater operating costs, of which energy is only one component.

ENERGY RELATIONSHIPS IN RECREATIONAL TRAVEL

Possibly the area in which energy has had the greatest effect on recreation is not in the selection of the activity itself, but in the travel patterns associated with recreation. There are several aspects of recreational travel which different researchers contend were or were not affected by energy considerations. Shifts and trends in the use of different modes of travel and different lengths of trip are noted. Destination substitution through the shifting of destinations or substitution of places for the activity-experience is also explored, but to a limited extent, since so few data are available. Some analysis of shifts in recreational travel patterns is given, and there is some speculation on the future.

The problem is that most of the research noted earlier deals with survey data on intentions, and in some cases with reported behavior, but is rarely substantiated by actual measurements of real-world recreational traffic or use patterns. The findings of Foster and Kuhn (1983) are fascinating — and typical — in this respect. Foster and Kuhn found that respondents to surveys in British Columbia reported changes in leisure behavior to be among the least frequent of 26 energy conserving measures they had adopted. Only 40 percent reported an inten-tion to change leisure behavior if energy prices were to double. But no data were offered on actual attendances or total recreational trip volumes in the field.

The "energy crisis" or "energy crunch," depending on one's view of the situation, has been a factor in most people's thinking and travel decision-making since late 1973. During that time, significant changes have taken place in travel associated with recreation and tourism:

- International air travel has increased markedly, as has domestic air travel in most countries;
- Automobile travel declined somewhat in the late 1970s and early 1980s, although this trend has been reversed more recently. Until the last three years, total fuel demand was less than it had been in earlier peak years, in most countries;
- Rail and bus modes are competing for a shrinking market in North America, although rail travel continues to grow in Europe;
- Standard-route travel by ship is virtually extinct, but pleasure cruise travel is increasing dramatically;
- Few studies have shown any large or sustained declines in levels of participation in energy-intensive recreation activities, such as motor boating or snowmobiling. Rather, they have undergone temporary setbacks or experienced much lower growth rates than counterpart activities that are less energy-intensive, such as sailboating or skiing;
- Pleasure trips taken have tended to be shorter in length, and the automobile mode has a smaller share now than formerly.

Many of the above trends have been commonly attributed to the influence of energy considerations, but it is far from clear that energy has been the only influence, or even the most important one. Important influences on recreation patterns are such factors as changing demographic structures, higher participation rates of women in the workforce, more widespread and attractive forms of electronic entertainment, higher average levels of education and income, and changes in tastes and fashion. No definitive research exists showing just how much of each of these (and other) factors has caused the recreational shifts that have been observed, and to what degree they have done so.

Modal Shifts and Trip Length Patterns

There are some interesting data which can illuminate the question of how much effect energy changes have had on changing recreation patterns even if they do not conclusively explain the shifts. Such data are quite readily available for Canada and the U.S.A., where fairly extensive travel surveys have been conducted in recent years. To place travel pattern and mode data in the context of energy efficiency, Table 1 shows the relative efficiency in passenger-miles per U.S. gallon of petroleum (or equivalent for electric propulsion).

Table 1
Energy Efficiency of Common Transportation Modes

	Passenger-Miles per U.S. Gallon
Commuter Train	100
Intercity Train	95
8-car Subway Train	95
Intercity Bus	120
Urban bus	60 - 100
Early Jet (707)	30
Jumbo Jet (747)	35
Newer Jet (767)	45
STOL Aircraft	28
Automobile	15 - 80
Large Ship (QE II)	8

Sources: Rice (1972); U.S. Department of Transportation (1986)
Reprinted with permission from *Technology Review*, c. 1972

Table 1 makes it clear that the most energy-efficient travel modes are the inter-city bus and the commuter train. But both of these have low shares of the recreational travel market; moreover, these shares are declining. Aircraft efficiency is fairly good, and is rising in the case of newer aircraft types. The automobile has also fairly good potential fuel efficiency if it is not occupied by the driver alone. In the case of most recreational automobile trips, as opposed to trips to work, this is the case. Finally, the relatively low fuel efficiency of large ships has not deterred major increases in cruise trips. The high fuel input per passenger-mile of ship travel must, of course, be seen in the context that the ship provides a whole living environment, not just a place to be seated for a few hours while a destination is reached.

Still, Table 1 and the preceding brief discussion show that there is no evidence at all that recreational patterns are moving uniformly towards the energy-efficient modes of travel. Indeed, the contrary is clearly the case in some instances.

Those interested in specific data on trip-making behavior over the period since the mid-1970s have a number of sources to consult, depending on the area of interest. For Canada, there has been a large-scale Canadian Travel Survey conducted since 1978 (Canadian Government Office of Tourism, quarterly; Statistics Canada, biennial), which is oriented to trips over 50 miles (80 km). Several Canadian provinces have similar surveys of residents, covering various years, as do many U.S. states.

The above-noted surveys have one drawback for this discussion, however, since they do not include all trips, particularly the short ones. These are sometimes measured in urban transportation surveys, but then the geographical coverage is quite specific. The best source of general data is perhaps the U.S. Nationwide Personal Transportation Survey (NPTS), which was conducted in 1969, 1977, and 1983. This survey covers all trips, regardless of length and mode, providing a complete overall picture of travel, including recreational travel.

Space limitations preclude any extensive discussion of the findings of the NPTS, but a few results from the most recent survey are of interest to set the transport and energy component of recreation into some perspective. First, the survey reveals that trips for recreational purposes are fewer in number than trips to work, but their average length is longer. Thus, the average American family travels about as much for recreation as for work, and indeed more than for any other purpose. Table 2 shows this clearly. This is doubly true if some of the family and personal trips are considered recreational, which many probably are. The overwhelming proportion of trips for all purposes is taken by automobile, as might be expected, and the proportion of automobile use for recreation trips does not differ significantly from that for other purposes. Other NPTS data show that this picture also held fairly constant over the 1977-1983 period.

Table 2
Selected Data on Vehicle Trips per Household:
1983 Nationwide Personal Transportation Survey

Purpose	veh-trips/hh /year	/day	veh-miles/hh /year	/day	avg trip length (miles)
Home to Work	414	1.1	3538	9.7	8.5
Social/Recreational	335	0.9	3534	9.7	10.6
Visit Friends/Relatives	147	0.4	1590	4.4	10.8
Pleasure Driving	5	-	132	0.3	22.7
Vacation	2	-	250	0.7	113.9
other	181	0.5	1562	4.3	8.7
Overall total	1486	4.1	11739	32.2	7.9

Source: U.S. Department of Transportation 1986: 173-180.

Destination Substitution and Travel Pattern Shifts

When the effects of increased energy costs on recreational travel are considered, the intuitive or common sense hypotheses are that: fewer trips will be taken; they will tend to be shorter in length; fewer weekend trips will be made; and longer stays at destinations will occur. Research relating to such hypotheses was popular in the 1970s and early 1980s: see, for example: Booz, Allen, and Hamilton, Inc. (1974); Goodale (1975); Kouris (1978); Kemp, Crompton, and Hensarling (1979); Williams, Burke, and Dalton (1979); Canadian Government Office of Tourism (1980); Bryan (1981); Crompton and Gitelson (1981); Smith (1981); Van Doren (1981).

It must be noted, however, that energy costs are just one item in the consumer's budget, and that the overall personal financial situation is the paramount economic influence on travel behavior. The price of gasoline is the energy cost component most immediately felt by the average consumer, and it has undergone some interesting gyrations over the past fifteen years.

The real cost of gasoline escalated dramatically in the years from 1973 to 1981 in both Canada and the U.S.A. In the time period from 1982 to the present, the trends have diverged in the two countries. In the U.S.A., deregulation of oil prices led to reductions in the real price, and recession also reduced demand in 1981-1982. Later, as world oil prices fell, further price reductions occurred. In Canada, the rate of price increase was abated by regulation during the 1970s, but the rise continued in the 1980s as the world price was reached in the domestic market and governments increased gasoline taxation when the world price subsequently fell.

Thus, the gasoline price index in the U.S.A. peaked about November 1981, whereas in Canada it continued to rise until mid-1985. Perhaps the most relevant indicator is the price index for gasoline in relation to the overall consumer price index. This indicator rose rapidly in the U.S.A. to over 150 percent of overall inflation in 1981, then fell drastically to about 85-90 percent in 1985-1987. In Canada, there was a slower but prolonged, and eventually greater, rise in the relative gasoline price, with only slight moderation in 1986-1987 to 135 percent of inflation.

The question of whether changes in energy costs give rise to any significant degree of change in recreational travel patterns was addressed in behavioral surveys, such as those by Bryan (1981), Foster and Kuhn (1983), and Kemp, Crompton, and Hensarling (1979). These deal with survey respondents' intended or reported behaviors, as noted earlier. Evidence from large-scale sources of traffic volumes (Ontario Ministry of Transportation, annual; traffic data processed for the recreational component by the method of Wolfe, 1967, 1969) and recreational use data (Ontario Ministry of Natural Resources, annual) was studied by Ellis (1982). That paper looked at shifts in patterns of recreational travel in the vicinity of 10 varied Provincial Parks in the Ontario system, and confirmed most of the hypotheses noted above. For this chapter, the results of the earlier work were updated by a further four-year interval of data. Some doubt was shed on the validity of the hypotheses by the additional data, since extension of the analysis to 1985 shows that only some of the pattern shifts found to 1981 continued, while others appear to have shifted back to patterns more typical of the "good old days" of the 1970s.

While the results are presented and discussed briefly below, it should be noted that, no matter how fascinating the pattern shifts seem or how much they may confirm some intuitive feelings about leisure in the 1980s, the findings do not — and cannot — separate the energy factors from a much wider range of factors, including changes in the destinations themselves, changes in family composition and lifestyles, or shifts of taste for whole areas of activity, of which Provincial Park camping is only one small item on an ever larger menu of choices available to the recreational consumer.

The analysis compared patterns of highway traffic for recreational purposes and Provincial Park campground use over the period 1973-1985. Mutual interaction between the use patterns was found, and was seen to have shifted over the time period. The parks chosen include two having the largest attendances in the system, and a representative range of smaller parks. The sample included Algonquin Park, long the attendance leader in the Ontario system and arguably among the best-known parks in eastern North America. All parks chosen are located such that one sector of a nearby highway is representative of the recreational traffic to which each park is exposed.

The concept underlying the analysis was to compare the relationship of camper-nights use of the parks with recreation-purpose trip volumes on the nearby highway segments, over the same seasons. For convenience, four-year intervals were chosen to represent the time period of interest: 1973, 1977, 1981, and 1985. These years include the last recreation season prior to the onset of the energy crisis in late 1973, and the interim year of 1977 when Canadians were still enjoying relatively low gasoline prices. The oil price peak and the recession in 1981 are covered, as is the subsequent recovery to 1985.

Another factor examined was the weekend peaking ratio of highway traffic, defined as the ratio of average weekend daily traffic to average weekday daily traffic (summer only). Analysis of this factor and its changes over time gives clues as to whether certain areas are shifting their weekend/weekday patterns or not.

The main findings can be summarized as follows:

- Recreational traffic on a control segment of freeway — Highway 400 just north of Toronto, selected to assess patterns of overall recreational trip volumes near a major urban area — increased progressively and significantly over the period, with a dip only in the recession year of 1981;
- Pinery Park, on Lake Huron, and attracting significant use by U.S. residents, outstripped Algonquin to become the most-used camping location in the system;
- At the five park sites chosen on the basis of progressively increasing distance from Toronto, park use and recreational traffic both declined — in proportion to distance — in four of the five cases;
- The highest overall recreational traffic rises were experienced near Pinery and Sibbald Point Parks. The latter is the closest major campsite to Metropolitan Toronto. The Pinery data show that most of its large increase occurred between 1981 and 1985, reflecting both its location near large U.S. population centers, and the more recent return of U.S. tourists to that part of Ontario;
- The biggest loser in the sample was Algonquin Park, Ontario's largest park and considered by most observers to be its most attractive. In the Algonquin Park corridor, recreational traffic volumes fell by about half;
- The weekend traffic peak in the Algonquin corridor actually disappeared by 1981, although it had been the highest in the sample in 1973 and 1977;
- Weekend peaking, relative to weekday volumes of all traffic, dropped in all corridors between 1977 and 1981, though it recovered in some of them in the period 1981-85;
- By 1985, weekend peaking was most pronounced in the case of the Sibbald Point and Pinery corridors, where peaks now exceed anything in earlier years. The Highway 400 control segment also showed high peaking in 1985.

While it would be unwise to make sweeping generalizations about recreational travel patterns as a whole from the foregoing data and analysis, some indications may be taken as to what has been occurring, and some speculation can be made about the future.

While overall recreational trip-making seemed to be unaffected by changing energy prices, since it increased at a rate faster than the growth rate of household populations, parks more than about three hours' drive from major population centers lost heavily in weekend use, as is illustrated most clearly by the case of Algonquin. This apparent three-hour barrier will likely persist in the future, but perhaps less for energy reasons than because of the time factor.

Energy concerns, to the extent that they were the real cause underlying some of the pattern changes noted, seem to have diminished in areas nearest to population centers. There is now heavier park use, higher volumes of recreational trips, and greater weekend peaking of traffic in such areas. The evidence suggests that more recreational and weekend trips per household are occurring, though trip lengths have fallen off perceptibly. Tastes and personal lifestyle shifts are perhaps as great an influence as energy considerations on recreation trends, including recreational travel.

ENERGY AND RECREATIONAL LIFESTYLES

The question of recreational energy consumed on a given occasion is one matter; the question of how much energy people consume in their entire lifestyles may be quite another. The number of activities will increase in an engaged leisure lifestyle; the level of engagement will affect energy inputs; and the frequency of participation will exact its energy toll.

For these reasons, some gradual beginnings have been made in assessing some sort of energy index for leisure lifestyles. The work of Foster and Kuhn (1983) has shown the way. They defined a value for the energy intensiveness of a given activity (similar to the one-dimensional scales noted earlier) and a factor for the frequency of participation in that activity by a given individual. The "Energy Leisure Lifestyle Index" (ELLI) for an individual was then defined as the product of the energy intensiveness value and the frequency of participation, summed over all activities in which the individual participated. While no major correlations were found between the ELLI and energy conserving practices or values, the concept is a valuable one to add to the repertoire of recreation/energy research concepts.

In future, it may be appropriate to devise more refined measures of energy indices for leisure lifestyles — ones which will weight intensity and location of participation, and explore the two thorny research matters of substitutability and leisure satisfaction. Ritchie and Claxton (1981) are among the few — and brave — researchers who have explored leisure satisfaction in relation to energy factors.

CONCLUSIONS

The principal question for the future is: will there be another energy crunch or rapid price rise? The outlook on this is mixed. Most observers note that oil is a finite resource and its price must rise substantially at some time. Others point to the supply side, in which the exploration and production situations have been transformed by previous enormous price hikes which, in turn, also lowered the rate of increase in demand. Aside from the question of price, chronic political instability in the Middle East leaves open the possibility of actual supply disruptions or shortages, reminiscent of 1973 or 1979.

Even if this happens, what will be the effect on recreational behavior? Wolfe (1979) cited conflicting evidence from European sources as to whether people would make greater use of "car pools" for the journey to work to save gasoline for the weekend recreational trip, or cut down their recreational trips in order to get to work. It all may depend on the relative severity of any shortage, and the locational availability of alternative public transport modes.

In the papers edited by Jackson (1988) there is support for the contention that we still do not know enough about how energy and spatial behavior are related. Usher, Ellis, and Michalski (1987) point out the qualitative and environmental factors involved in recreational spatial behavior.

How, then, will energy affect our leisure and recreation in future? No crystal ball holds the answer, but it is certain that recreation and leisure patterns will continue to shift and evolve. Social, economic, and technological forces will combine to cause the shifts, and changes in energy supply and price will be one of the economic and technical factors. But it is only one, and likely not the most influential.

References

Booz, Allen, and Hamilton Inc. 1974. "Sensitivity of the leisure-recreational industry to the energy crisis." In *Hearings of the House of Representatives Sub-Committee on Environmental Problems of Small Business, August 21-23, 1974*. Washington, DC: Congressional Publications Office.

Bryan, W. 1981. "Improved mileage, discretionary income and travel for pleasure." *Journal of Travel Research 21:* 28-29.

Canadian Government Office of Tourism. 1980. *Energy and Tourism: The Evolving Situation and Some Implications*. Ottawa.

Canadian Government Office of Tourism. Quarterly. *Travel Trends*. Ottawa.

Crompton, J. and R. Gitelson. 1981. "Consumer reactions to the standby motor fuel rationing plan." *Journal of Travel Research 19:* 27-36.

Ellis, J. B. 1982. "Energy costs and the travelling public: Future effects on Canada's park systems." In *Proceedings, Federal-Provincial Parks Conference, October 1982*. Ottawa: Parks Canada.

Foster, L.T. and R. Kuhn. 1983. "The energy/leisure interface: A review and empirical exploration." *Recreation Research Review 10:* 49-61.

Goodale, T. 1975. "Impacts of the energy crisis on parks and recreation." *Recreation Canada 33:* 11-15.

Graef, R., S.M. Gianinno, and M. Csikszentmihalyi. 1980. "Energy consumption in leisure and the quality of life." In *Proceedings of the International Conference on Consumer Behaviour and Energy Use*, pp. 1-14. Banff, AB.

Hough, Stansbury and Associates, and J. Ellis and Associates. 1985. *Recreational Boating in Ontario: An Update to 1985*. Burlington, ON: Canada Department of Fisheries and Oceans, Small Craft Harbours Branch.

Jackson, E.L., ed. 1988. "Focus: Behavioural energy research in geography." *The Canadian Geographer 32:* 162-172.

Kemp, D., J. Crompton, and D. Hensarling. 1979. "The reactions of travelers to gasoline rationing and to increases in gasoline prices." *Journal of Travel Research 17:* 137-141.

Kouris, G. 1978. "Price sensitivity of petrol consumption and some policy implications." *Energy Policy Sept. 1978:* 209-216.

Ontario Ministry of Natural Resources. Annual. *Provincial Park Statistics.* Toronto.

Ontario Ministry of Transportation and Communications. Annual. *Highway Traffic Volumes.* Toronto.

Osborn, P.N. and J.D. Peine. 1979. "Recreation and energy use: a comparative analysis." In *Recreation Planning and Development.* Washington, DC: American Society of Civil Engineers.

Rice, R. 1972. "System energy and future transportation." *Technology Review Jan. 1972:* 31-37.

Ritchie, J.R.B. 1979. *Leisure Activities and Energy Consumption: A Review.* Ottawa: Consumer and Corporate Affairs Canada.

Ritchie, J.R.B. and J.D. Claxton. 1981. "Leisure lifestyles and energy use." In *Proceedings of the Third Canadian Congress on Leisure Research,* eds. T.L. Burton and J. Taylor, pp. 873-896. Edmonton: Canadian Association for Leisure Studies.

Smith, D.C. 1981. "Energy and recreational travel: An overview." In *Proceedings of the Third Canadian Congress on Leisure Research,* eds. T.L. Burton and J. Taylor, pp. 915-924. Edmonton: Canadian Association for Leisure Studies.

Statistics Canada. Biennial. *Tourism and Recreation: A Statistical Digest.* Cat. #87-401. Ottawa.

United States Department of Transportation. 1986. *National Transportation Statistics: Annual Report.* Publication DOT-TSC-RSPA-86-3. Washington DC: Department of Transportation, Research and Special Programs Administration.

Usher, A., J. Ellis, and M. Michalski. 1987. *Beach Use and Environmental Quality in Ontario*. Toronto: Ontario Ministry of the Environment, Policy and Planning Branch.

Van Doren, C. 1981. "Outdoor recreation trends in the 1980s: Implications for society." *Journal of Travel Research 19:* 27-36.

Williams, P., J. Burke, and M. Dalton. 1979. "The potential impact of gasoline futures on 1979 vacation travel strategies." *Journal of Travel Research 17:* 3-7.

Wolfe, R. 1967. *A Theory of Recreational Highway Traffic*. DHO Report # RR128. Toronto: Ontario Ministry of Transportation.

Wolfe, R. 1969. "A tentative procedure for estimating recreational highway traffic." *Traffic Quarterly January 1969:* 105-121.

Wolfe, R. 1979. "Patterns of recreation highway traffic in time of energy scarcity: A progress report." In *Proceedings of the Second Canadian Congress on Leisure Research*, pp. 502-507. Toronto. Ontario Research Council on Leisure.

BEYOND SOCIAL CARRYING CAPACITY

George H. Stankey and Stephen F. McCool

INTRODUCTION

Few topics in the field of outdoor recreation research have commanded as much attention as the issue of carrying capacity. Indeed, as Jackson and Burton report in the opening chapter of this book, 65 percent of the respondents to a recent international survey of leisure scientists viewed carrying capacity as a dominant theme of the last twenty years. Capacity is one of those ideas that seems founded upon the most elementary kinds of common sense. If the use of an area is allowed to continue to increase without limit, at some point the amount of use will lead to a level of impact, either upon the experience of the user, the environment, or both, that is unacceptable. The key to resolving the problem, then, is answering the question "how much use is too much?"

Or so it would seem. To understand the notion of carrying capacity as conventionally used today, it is necessary to understand the historical origins and foundations of the concept as it is applied to outdoor recreation. The roots of carrying capacity are found in such fields as wildlife and range management. Here, the term refers to the numbers of animals of a particular species that can populate a given habitat on a sustained basis, given available food, shelter, and water (Dasmann 1964). Given such a definition and the early influence of biologically trained recreation managers, it is not difficult to see how the concept came to be applied in outdoor recreation. With use levels rising rapidly, particularly during the period of post-war recovery in the 1950s, and facilities deteriorating just as fast, there was general recognition that a framework to address these problems was desperately needed. The framework would help managers make the difficult decisions about how much use an area could receive before controls and limitations on use would need to be introduced. If the framework determined how many people could use an area before unacceptable impacts occurred, there would be an unequivocal foundation for establishing limits on use, with a biologically objective basis as a rationale.

The carrying capacity concept was quickly broadened to include a social or perceptual component in addition to an ecological one. J. Alan Wagar, a pioneering observer of the carrying capacity issue, noted in the preface to his seminal paper, *The Carrying Capacity of Wildlands for Recreation*, that "the study ... was initiated with the view that the carrying capacity of recreation lands could be determined primarily in terms of ecology and the deterioration of areas. However, it soon became obvious that the resource-oriented point of view must be augmented by consideration of human values" (Wagar 1964).

In the 25 years that have passed since Wagar's monograph was published, a vast literature on the carrying capacity question has emerged. Between 1975 and 1986 alone, over 1300 articles and reports on carrying capacity were published, about two-thirds of the nearly 2100 such articles published since the turn of the century (Drogin, Graefe, and Vaske 1986). Both the ecological and social dimensions of the issue have been examined. With this burgeoning literature have come efforts to summarize the state of knowledge; recent examples include Stankey (1982), Graefe, Vaske, and Kuss (1984), Manning (1986), Shelby and Heberlein (1986), and the set of papers in a special edition of Leisure Sciences (Vol. 6, No. 4, 1984). Yet, despite the large level of research attention given to the carrying capacity concept, substantial concerns and doubts remain about its utility and validity for recreation management. Burch (1984) scathingly observes that "there is a growing insistence that never has so much been said by so many on a topic of such inconsequential irrelevance." Other writers (e.g. Bury 1976; Wagar 1974) have questioned whether the profession would be better off to abandon the concept and focus its attention on alternative approaches to recreation management problems.

Despite such reservations about the carrying capacity concept itself, concerns among recreation managers and visitors about the adverse affects of use on resources and experiences continue to plague the field. Similarly, concerns for the development of a framework within which difficult decisions about the management of recreation use can be made and implemented have not been resolved successfully. The concept of carrying capacity continues to be commonly perceived as the most likely source of such a framework.

The purpose of this chapter is to explore the major criticisms of the carrying capacity model and to clarify the essential premises and assumptions which make the concept a useful basis for the formulation of recreation management strategy. Following that, we will review and illustrate some of the major findings of the literature. From this background, we will outline an alternative formulation of the carrying capacity model, in which principal attention is given to the identification of specific desired resource and social conditions, as opposed to the traditional focus on the amount of use. Finally, we will offer some suggestions with regard to issues and topics requiring further research.

COMPONENTS OF THE CARRYING CAPACITY MODEL

It has been generally accepted that determining carrying capacity involves three separate, yet interrelated, components: management objectives, visitor attitudes, and recreational impact on resources (Lime and Stankey 1971). It must be stressed that these components are related in an interactive, iterative manner, each influenced by the others, rather than in a linear fashion.

Management objectives provide the framework within which the type of desired recreational opportunity is defined. In a sense, management objectives constitute the "operating rules" that define what is acceptable and what is not. Probably the greatest difficulty encountered by recreation managers is the lack of clear, well-defined objectives. Typically, good management objectives are defined as being measurable, objective, and attainable (Brown 1985). Without such specificity, objectives are subject to varying interpretation by both managers and the public. For example, an objective calling for the "maintenance of natural conditions" leaves unanswered fundamental questions such as, "how does one define natural?" Depending on how one defined "natural," the implications for recreation management could vary enormously.

Another component of the carrying capacity model is visitor attitudes. Among the various reasons for establishing a measure of recreational carrying capacity is the protection of the recreational experience. The question is, "whose recreational experience are we talking about?" Not all recreationists perceive the environment in the same way; not all want the same kinds of developments, the same types and levels of use around them, or the same levels of environmental quality. Confounding the situation further is the fact that visitors' views about such matters also differ from those held by recreation managers. For example, in a study of National Forest campgrounds in the United States, Lucas (1970) found that ratings of site quality differed significantly between managers and visitors, with the visitors almost always ranking conditions better than managers.

The judgment of acceptable levels of resource impact or numbers of other visitors varies in response to the different values held by the observer. The carrying capacity issue clearly reflects this; a given level of use will be defined by some as acceptable while others may describe it as too low (e.g. people visiting a singles beach don't want to be by themselves), while still others will describe it as "crowded."

The interpretation of visitor attitudes must be made within the context of management objectives. However, there is a kind of "chicken and egg" complexity here. Which comes first — the objectives, with all other inputs considered within that context? Or should objectives be founded in visitor attitudes? As suggested earlier, the process here must be iterative and interactive. Objectives founded without any knowledge of visitor attitudes probably stand little chance of being met, and, as Brown (1985) has suggested, attainability is one criterion of a good objective. Management cannot rely solely on public opinion to make its decisions, but such input is essential in formulating them. A knowledge of public attitudes can help define the spectrum and mix of opportunities needed and can also shed light on how visitors might respond to different management actions.

The third component of the carrying capacity model is the impact on the resource resulting from recreational use. Because any use of an ecosystem results in some level of impact, managers must make a decision, at some point, that any additional impact is "too much." The obvious question is, at what point is the level of impact serious enough to warrant such a judgment?

The relationship between recreational use and resource impact is complex and not well understood. The type of recreation involved, the time of year when it occurs, its duration, and the specific behavior of the participants are all part of the equation (for further detail, see Wall's chapter, this volume). One well-documented finding, however, is that the amount of recreational use has only a limited effect on the level of impact; more use does not *necessarily* lead to more impact, and, from a management point of view, perhaps most importantly, reductions in use do not *necessarily* lead to reductions in impact. As we shall discuss in more detail shortly, it is the relatively minor role that use level plays in defining impact that is the source of much of the criticism of the carrying capacity model, which (at least implicitly) focuses primary attention on the question of "how much use is too much?"

Nevertheless, the resource impact resulting from recreational use is a major concern. Again, management objectives help identify whether a given level of impact is judged as acceptable or unacceptable. A given level of impact judged unacceptable in a wilderness might be entirely acceptable in a regional park; the question of acceptability is a matter of judgment more than science. A knowledge of visitor perceptions and attitudes about the types and levels of impact considered acceptable is also essential in making such judgments.

A knowledge of resource conditions and how they are affected by recreational use is, like visitor attitudes, useful input into the formulation of management objectives. Objectives established in the absence of an understanding of resource values, constraints, and sensitivity may be unattainable and/or lead to the irreversible loss of important resources. But, judgments about acceptable impact must take place within the framework provided by area management objectives.

Although not considered as a distinct component of the carrying capacity model, it is also important to consider that capacity is not a fixed, inherent quality of the site. The capacity of a site to withstand resource impact, for example, can be enhanced through inputs by management. This could include such things as watering and fertilization, planting more impact-tolerant species, or hardening the site through design and engineering measures (e.g. paving trails). The question as to the appropriateness of such steps, however, can only be answered within the context of the objectives established for the area. In a wilderness setting, engineering-type actions would typically be inappropriate, given an objective of creating or maintaining a setting where evidence of human presence is absent or minimal. Here, controlling impacts may be more dependent on control of visitor use. However, in an urban park, extensive modification of the site, including the use of artificial materials, might be considered appropriate as a means of controlling visitor impacts.

In summary, first, the basic carrying capacity model involves three components — management objectives, visitor attitudes, and recreational impacts on resources. Second, area capacity is a function of the interrelationship among these three components. Third, because capacity is not an absolute quality, judgments about capacity will always be space- and time-dependent. An area's carrying capacity is also a dynamic quality, subject to manipulation through various management controls.

This framework of carrying capacity has provided the basic structure within which decisions about use and impact have been made. It contains the primary components that must be considered in establishing capacities and, as presented, defines the various caveats of which one must be aware to apply the model successfully. Nevertheless, many criticisms and concerns about the carrying capacity model have been voiced, and we will now proceed to summarize and evaluate them.

CRITICISMS OF THE CARRYING CAPACITY MODEL

As noted earlier, the carrying capacity model was derived from the biological sciences. Underlying the adoption of the model was an implicit assumption that biological capacity is a discrete and intrinsic quality of the environmental setting, i.e. that a given environmental setting has a fixed and definable limit to the level of use that it can withstand and a fixed population that it can support. However, this fundamental assumption had no basis in fact. Biological scientists have long recognized that the carrying capacity of rangeland is a function of a variety of factors, including the species involved, season of use, the inherent durability of the soils and vegetation, what constitutes proper utilization of the vegetation, and, perhaps most importantly, the level of management invested in the site. Thus, rather than having a *single* biological capacity, most areas have a *variety* of capacities, depending upon exactly how the concept of capacity is defined (Shelby and Heberlein 1986).

The notion of a singular recreational carrying capacity was eventually replaced by more sophisticated concepts, and a number of authors proposed that a recreation area may have several different types of capacities — social or perceptual, biological or ecological, physical, even a facilities capacity (Bury 1976; Lime and Stankey 1971). Common to these extensions of the earlier definitions of carrying capacity, however, was the increasing recognition that site management objectives were a significant influence in determining capacity

— regardless of the type of capacity. For example, Lime and Stankey (1971: 182) noted that "there are many possible carrying capacities for a given recreation area. These capacities can be defined only in light of the objectives for the area in question."

The concept of recreational carrying capacity has also been criticized on the grounds that it focuses undue attention on the physical-biological qualities of a site, to the exclusion of social and psychological issues. This criticism stems from the deficiency discussed above, in which capacity was seen as an intrinsic and fixed quality of the biological regime. (As an aside, there is increasing recognition that decisions about the biology of a site are based on social and cultural values and reflect the judgment of managers.) Additionally, the biologically-based perception of carrying capacity obscures considerations of how an individual area fits into a broader range of areas, what trade-offs and relationships exist among these areas, and what steps might be undertaken to contend with the problems brought on by use.

The substance of this concern is that the fixation on physical site characteristics hinders recognition that recreation is primarily a social-psychological experience. Biological factors, as well as the intrusiveness of management, comprise the "land, labor, and capital" that visitors put together to construct a recreational product or experience. The level of environmental deterioration may have little or nothing to do with the quality of the experience. Because much of the biological impact that inevitably accompanies recreation use typically occurs under fairly low use levels (Cole 1987), the biologically oriented manager can be easily convinced that restriction of use is necessary (Hendee and Pyle 1971). This restrictive mentality, manifested in use regulations, rationing, and the like, is often noted as a product of the carrying capacity approach to management (Burch 1981). Indeed, the very term "capacity" implies that only this limited range of actions is appropriate for management of recreational settings.

There is also a concern that the carrying capacity model obscures the distinction between issues of a technical/scientific nature and those of a value or normative nature. For example, recreation use clearly can produce significant impacts on soils, vegetation, and water quality. Many empirical investigations of these effects have been conducted and their results are of importance to recreation managers in making decisions regarding the use of resources under their administration (Cole and Schreiner 1981). However, such data are not deterministic; they do not, by themselves, prescribe how much use is too much or how much impact is too much. This is a normative question — a value judgment — and, while managers play a key role in resolving it, their technical expertise is no greater credential for settling what is fundamentally a value judgment than are the values, preferences, and expectations of their clients, the recreationists (Socolow 1976). By employing a biologically-founded framework to resolve what is fundamentally a question of competing social values, the inherently difficult nature of the political choices to be made is obscured (Burch 1984).

The essence of concern here is that the traditional carrying capacity model promotes the notion that the establishment of capacities is a deterministic, even mechanistic, process, when, in fact, it involves a resolution of conflicting values over what is appropriate and acceptable. Such resolution is further compounded when, as noted earlier, decisions about capacity are made for one area at a time rather than within a regional or systems context (Stankey 1974).

The conception that areas have a definable recreational capacity also fosters the notion that the key issue in management is the number of persons involved, i.e. that the maintenance of conditions within an area's carrying capacity is largely a matter of managing numbers of people. However, a growing body of research clearly indicates that such is not the case. To the extent that managerial attention is directed at limiting use when the problem is something else, then inappropriate (or even wrong) and ineffective actions will be taken.

Criticism of the capacity model with regard to this issue points to the fact that the amount of use might be, and often is, of only minor importance in determining the magnitude of human-induced impacts. This is true whether one conceives of capacity in physical-biological or social terms. Shortly, we will return to examine this issue further. However, it is clear that the question of whether an area is "crowded" or not is often rooted more in the nature of the *character* and *behavior* of other users, and the value systems of users and managers, than in the *number* of visitors.

Finally, there has been, and continues to be, concern that carrying capacity research too often has lacked sound theoretical formulation, resulting in a series of *ad hoc*, non-additive, and generally atheoretic case studies. As a result, data from many of the studies conducted lack a coherent framework within which they might be interpreted and applied. The plethora of empirical studies has yielded a great deal of data about contact levels, visitor satisfaction, and so forth; but whether they have provided much in the way of a clear understanding of the process of how people cope, react, and adapt to changing use and site conditions, and how managers can deal with these factors, are other questions.

Clearly, the traditional model of carrying capacity is subject to criticism. Some questions are directed at inherent flaws within it, others at the manner in which it has been applied. Still, interest in its utility remains high. And, it does address an issue of major concern: how can the quality of recreational experiences be protected in the face of changing use conditions? Thus, we turn next to a review of some of the major findings of the research literature in order that we may consider what a reformulated model of carrying capacity should take into account.

RESEARCH ON SOCIAL CARRYING CAPACITY

The concept of a social carrying capacity has become intimately linked with the notion of crowding, which, in turn, is defined primarily in terms of levels of use and visitor satisfaction. Increasingly, however, it has become understood that physical measures of use intensity, or density, do not, in themselves, constitute crowding. Density represents an objective measure, such as persons per unit space. Crowding, on the other hand, is an evaluative concept in which a given density is perceived as undesirable, or crowded (Stokols 1972). The extent to which a given density is perceived as crowded is dependent upon a variety of factors, including personal characteristics, experience, expectations, individual norms, and context. Altman (1975) also states that crowding occurs when the desired level of privacy or contact with others is violated. This occurs when the various mechanisms that individuals use to regulate access to themselves (such as personal space or territoriality) do not, for some reason, function effectively.

Thus crowding is clearly a situationally specific state. It varies across settings; what is crowding in wilderness may be its opposite construct — social isolation — on a singles beach. Heberlein (1977) has graphically demonstrated this principle through the use of a series of "return potential" curves for hypothetical wilderness, cocktail party, and city sidewalk recreation experiences. These curves demonstrate that optimal levels of encounters, and the definition of "crowded," vary significantly depending on the experience expected. What is crowded also varies for any individual in terms of time and social context. Desired levels of contact with others will vary according to the social group with whom one participates — family, friends, or by one's self; and it may very well change for an individual over time, and in different settings. Individuals in the same setting may have very different perceptions of crowding, simply because of differing normative standards.

It is also clear that factors other than use levels contribute to a sense of crowding. Gramann (1982), for instance, suggests that a model of goal interference would include not only the impacts stemming from the actual presence of others but from evidence of their previous presence (e.g. litter, physical impacts on vegetation) as well. Also, the behavior of others can have a significant impact on the experiences of visitors. Behaviors that violate generally-ascribed-to norms of appropriateness can lead to the sensation of crowding, irrespective of the numbers of persons involved. In particular, behaviors that interfere with the functioning of the basic social unit found in most recreation settings — the group — likely contribute greatly to the feeling of being crowded. Manning (1986) comments that "solitude in outdoor recreation may have more to do with interaction among group members free from disruption than with actual isolation ... (from others).... As long as contacts with other groups are not considered disturbing, they do not engender feelings of crowding or dissatisfaction."

The normative nature of crowding perceptions lies at the root of much of the conflict between recreation groups. Feelings of being crowded stem as much (or more) from the perception of a sense of "being different" as they do from a sense of there being too many people. For example, Lucas (1964) reported that canoeists in the Boundary Waters Canoe Area complained of crowding more than twice as often as any other group. But much of their concern with crowding stemmed not from the feeling that they had encountered too many people, but from contacts with persons traveling in motor boats. Canoeists indicated they could accept up to five encounters daily with other canoeists, but that any contact with motor boaters was too much. On the other hand, motor boaters said there was no limit to the number of canoeists they could meet without adverse effect. Research by others on conflict (for example, Adelman, Heberlein, and Bonnicksen 1982; Driver and Bassett 1975; Jackson and Wong 1982) shows that "tolerances" for similar types of recreationists are usually higher than for different types.

This variable sensitivity to the presence of other types of groups has been labeled "asymmetric antipathy" by Adelman, Heberlein, and Bonnicksen (1982). It is linked to the idea of "likeness" suggested by Lee (1977); participants seek to find a "scheme of order with others similar enough to themselves to be able to take for granted many everyday normative constraints." The perception of other groups as being similar to one's own contributes to predictability and certainty. Others are accepted, or rejected, on the basis of their demonstrated ability to operate within "the rules" rather than by their numbers. This conclusion is certainly not limited to recreational settings, but most likely typifies the course of human behavior.

Such a perspective of the carrying capacity issue is fundamentally normative in nature. Shared norms of what constitutes acceptable or appropriate behavior result in an avoidance of and reaction to those behaviors that interfere with others. Much of what is defined as crowding stems not from excessive contact with others, but from contact with others in a manner defined as inappropriate. A clear example is in wilderness, where there is a strongly held norm that one should camp "out of sight and sound" from others (Lucas 1980; Stankey 1980).

There has been a tendency to focus upon use level as the key factor in establishing carrying capacities. As we have noted earlier, this stems, in part, from traditional ways of defining problems, as well as from the term itself. However, research has consistently reported that use level, defined either as total numbers of users or more specifically as the number of users encountered, has only a limited relationship to the perception of crowding. Absher and Lee (1981) report that the density of use in the backcountry of Yosemite National Park accounted for only 7 percent of the variance in the perception of crowding.

Use level has little to do with levels of satisfaction. Shelby and Nielsen (1976) found that satisfaction was not related to either density or perceived crowding; even among the 30 percent of respondents who thought there was crowding on their trip on the Colorado River, there was little relationship to the number of people they actually saw. Absher and Lee (1981) conclude that "it seems that the common-sense notion of crowding in recreation settings as a phenomenon dependent upon sheer numbers of other people must be reassessed in favor of more complex formulations that incorporate motivation and individual characteristics." Similarly, Shelby (1981) observes, "the two-variable satisfaction model is obviously oversimplified."

In a major review of the carrying capacity literature, Graefe, Vaske, and Kuss (1984) analyzed the results of over 50 studies. Most studies found no relationship between actual density and satisfaction; and, among the three studies that did report a statistical effect, two showed a positive rather than a negative association. They also examined the relationship between actual contacts among recreationists and their reported satisfaction and again failed to discover any significant association. They did, however, find positive, significant relationships between the number of contacts reported by visitors and perceived crowding; that is, as use levels increased, recreationists were more likely to report the situation as being crowded. They conclude by noting that it seems reasonable to assume that crowding perceptions are influenced by use densities, but that this relationship is mediated by a variety of situational and subjective variables. This would include such things as the preferences and expectations held by visitors.

The reader should note, however, that we are troubled by much of the satisfaction research. There are many different ways to conceptualize and measure satisfaction (Lawler 1973; Williams 1988), and different researchers have used varying approaches, used different measures, or simply did not completely specify the model of satisfaction in use (see Mannell, this volume). Satisfaction is linked to factors other than encounters, particularly in more developed settings, so one should expect low correlations. Nevertheless, the literature supports the notion that crowding is different from use level or encounters.

Preferences and expectations have also received much attention by researchers (Schreyer and Roggenbuck 1978; Shelby *et al.* 1983). In general, the research suggests that expectations are most useful as predictors of how actual use conditions will be evaluated. When actual use is higher than or equal to that expected, crowding usually is reported; when the opposite is the case, reports of crowding are rare. Expectations appear to play the role of normative standards of acceptability.

Also, where expectations are founded upon limited experience, they are less likely to predict the visitor's reaction to other users. Shelby and Nielsen (1976) found that 90 percent of the river runners they sampled on the Colorado River of the Grand Canyon were first-time users and their evaluation of use conditions on the river typically was positive, even though actual use exceeded their expectations. Chambers and Price (1986) similarly report that a variety of intervening variables affect the relationship between crowding and satisfaction and that, in particular, visitors without expectations about use levels are most likely to be insensitive to crowding.

Preferences are also important, primarily as a source of information about desired states of contact with others. They are, therefore, of value in establishing the kinds of evaluative standards called for in carrying capacity models that are founded upon a management-by-objectives basis (Shelby and Heberlein 1986; Stankey et al. 1985).

The lack of association between changing use levels and satisfaction seems, at first, unusual. People do hold strong preferences for contact with others, yet the results of much of the research, as noted earlier, indicate that satisfaction levels among visitors are high, often irrespective of the actual use levels encountered. However, there are several plausible explanations. People obviously employ a range of adaptive strategies to cope with the conditions they encounter. Because recreation is a self-selected, voluntary behavior, strong forces operate to maintain a sense of congruity between an individual's state of mind and reality. Heberlein and Shelby (1977) argue that, because recreation is a freely chosen behavior, we should not be surprised to find high satisfaction levels. In a later book (Shelby and Heberlein 1986), they suggest several other explanations to account for the lack of association between contact and satisfaction, including the idea of *product shift*, in which users change their definitions of desired recreational experiences to cope with excessive use levels, and *displacement*, in which those users dissatisfied with the use levels they encounter leave an area, to be replaced by those who find those levels tolerable or even desirable.

The lack of a clear association between use levels and satisfaction is also a function of the multidimensional nature of satisfaction (Hendee 1974; Manning 1986). In attempting to use it as an evaluative criterion, one is faced with resolving the issue of "satisfaction with regard to what aspect of the experience?" Experiences are composed of a variety of dimensions, which, in turn, vary in their salience to the user (Stankey and McCool 1984). Lucas (1985) reports that, among wilderness visitors who rated solitude as an important dimension of their experience, both their evaluation of the number of others met per day and the resultant satisfaction with that encounter level differed significantly in the predicted direction from those who rated solitude of low importance. Similarly, in a comparison of persons ranking in the upper and lower quartiles on a scale measuring the importance of solitude/stress release, McCool (1983) found that those scoring high tended to react negatively more frequently to the same level of encounters than those who scored low. "Overall measures (of satisfaction)," he concluded, "are most strongly related to evaluations of individual attributes, particularly when the saliency of the attribute can be identified."

We can conclude several things from this brief review. First, social carrying capacity is a complex phenomenon; the view that it is simply a matter of determining "how much is too much" is not useful, nor is it a valid way of conceptualizing problems. The perception of a setting as crowded is shaped by situationally specific norms, mediated by a variety of influences. A diversity of use densities is both appropriate and desired in order to satisfy the range of experiences sought by recreationists (Manning 1985).

Second, although there is a great diversity among recreationists in the kinds of use conditions defined as appropriate, nonetheless, there are patterns in what is sought. The research does reveal the presence of norms about appropriate use levels and behavior.

Third, although it is apparent that people are extremely versatile in their ability to cope with a wide range of use conditions and still report satisfactory experiences, it is also apparent that they do hold strong preferences for the kinds of experiences they would like to find. Such preferences represent an important input into the process of managing recreation settings and implementing management strategies with regard to the types of use conditions which management should strive to provide.

Finally, it is essential to repeat that the process of prescribing carrying capacities remains a judgmental matter. Embodied within the decision to establish a given capacity in a given setting is an inherent value judgment that reflects an emphasis on one type of recreation opportunity at the expense of another. Such a judgment is unavoidable, but, because the issue of carrying capacity is ultimately a matter of satisfying different value systems, it is imperative that the judgments the process must make are done so in an explicit and visible fashion. In most planning systems, this is done through the identification of management objectives.

THE ROLE OF MANAGEMENT OBJECTIVES

Increasingly, research on carrying capacity has acquired a more conceptually sophisticated and theoretically sound base. The preeminent area of agreement in this literature is that carrying capacity is a management concept directed toward the maintenance or restoration of ecological and social conditions deemed to be appropriate and acceptable. These statements of desired condition are embodied in the management objectives established for an area (Stankey and McCool 1984).

Objectives provide the basic framework within which decisions about appropriate conditions will be made. Shelby and Heberlein (1986) argue that, in establishing objectives, particularly as a basis for an area's carrying capacity, there is a need to establish clear "rules," two of which are of especial importance here. First, there must be agreement among relevant groups about the type of recreation experience to be provided — e.g. is the area to be managed for wilderness experiences or for more intensive kinds of recreation? Second, there must be agreement among the relevant groups about the appropriate levels of parameters or variables that define the experience — i.e. there must be agreement about the appropriate resource and social conditions defining the experience to be provided in the area so that measurable standards can be established. Without these kinds of agreements the manager is left in the dilemma of trying to provide for all types of experiences — experiences which may clash in terms of desired social and resource conditions.

A final area of consensus about a framework for social carrying capacity is that managers need to focus on the environmental and social conditions desired in an area and on how changes in those conditions are caused. The absolute number of users, as the brief literature review illustrated, is only one influence on these conditions and is, in many cases, a fairly minor influence. Thus, management attention must consider how a wide range of user characteristics could potentially alter an area's conditions and how those changes relate to those defined as desired in area management objectives.

Thus, the focus of the carrying capacity literature has begun to shift from a question of "how much use is too much?" to the more appropriate question of "what are the desired resource and social conditions within the area?" Such a reformulation of the carrying capacity question has been long in the making and grows out of a variety of sources, including the Recreation Opportunity Spectrum and the concept of management-by-objectives. Recent developments offer alternative approaches to the traditional carrying capacity approach. New systems, such as the Limits of Acceptable Change (LAC) concept (Stankey et al. 1985) and the Visitor Impact Management (VIM) system (Graefe, Kuss, and Vaske 1987) are examples of this. Both give primary attention to the explicit identification of desired conditions, embodied as measurable standards, to which management is directed. An area's carrying capacity, in these systems, is defined as the level of use consistent with the conditions defined as desired by these standards.

A LOOK TO THE FUTURE

What are the issues and challenges facing future work in the field of social carrying capacity? Our brief review suggests that a broader, more realistic, and conceptually rigorous definition of the issues implied by the term social carrying capacity is certainly needed. The complexity of managing human behavior in recreational settings indicates that researchers need to think in terms of recreational setting attributes, saliency, expectations, normative standards, and human responses rather than continuing to rely upon social carrying capacity as a paradigm for inquiry.

This view suggests that it will be appropriate and important to examine a variety of topics. As suggested earlier, a major criticism of past research has been its atheoretic nature. Continuing efforts to increase the theoretical, conceptual, and substantive content of research on human responses to encounters is essential to further progress in both research and management concerning desired and appropriate conditions in wilderness. For example, there is a need to view recreational carrying capacity as a sub-component of a broader effort in the social sciences to understand how people regulate and/or cope with interaction with others. Understanding these processes in a variety of settings and social situations will help managers deal more effectively with encounters and crowding in wilderness.

Much work has been done on this issue in other fields of social inquiry, and both the theoretical frameworks used there, as well as the empirical results, need to be examined. The problems of determining appropriate social conditions in recreational settings can be viewed as special cases of more general social issues of crowding, privacy, solitude, and normative influences on these. Altman (1975), for example, has presented an extremely useful model of privacy regulation that encompasses many of the issues and concerns pursued in attempting to determine appropriate levels of intergroup encounters. Westin (1967) has examined the issue of both the various dimensions of privacy as well as the functions it serves, and these concepts have been tentatively explored by researchers concerned with social conditions (e.g. Hammitt 1982; Hammitt and Brown 1984; Twight, Smith, and Wissinger 1981), but it seems to be an extremely fruitful area for further work. Also, Burch (1981) has argued for increased attention to the use of more rigorously founded approaches to the study of spacing behavior in humans (and other higher primates). Specifically, he calls for greater attention to the role of situational norms, permeability of group and taste territories, and familiarity as an adaptive strategy to strangers.

More attention is needed on the various behavioral and psychological mechanisms employed by people to cope with conditions defined as crowded. It is difficult at the moment to assess exactly what does happen when crowding occurs; do people adapt, do they leave, do they put up with it? In large part, our inability to assess the consequences and implications of crowding is constrained by methodological shortcomings. Much of our data base is derived from one-time, cross-sectional surveys, and we lack long-term, longitudinally-based data. Also, much of the data is focused on attitudes, expectations, and preferences. Data reporting behavioral responses is limited; more is needed to provide a clearer understanding of the behavioral consequences of crowding.

We need to reconsider the utility of user satisfaction as a criterion for the measurement of capacity. As the literature review revealed, there seems to be a limited relationship between use level and satisfaction; yet satisfaction remains a major focus of concern. Alternative models of satisfaction might need further attention, such as Herzberg's two-factor theory of satisfaction (Dorfman

1979; McCool and Petersen 1982). Such a reformulated view suggests that, while low encounter levels might be associated with high satisfaction, there is not necessarily a corresponding decline in satisfaction with increased use levels, because satisfaction and dissatisfaction are conceptually distinct and independent.

It should be clear to the reader that the term "social carrying capacity" no longer does justice to this field of research, nor does it adequately describe the task of managers of wildland recreation settings. Managers develop, maintain, or restore where necessary the desired social (and resource) conditions needed for specific types of recreational opportunities. Only in limited situations does the frequency, alone, of encounters with others bear directly upon the nature of these opportunities or is positively and significantly related to visitor satisfaction. The term "capacity" continues to imply that a "one number" limit on use is an appropriate solution to recreation management problems that are, in fact, complex, multifaceted, and may have little to do with numbers of visitors.

The term capacity implies that limiting numbers of visitors can solve problems of impact and satisfaction. Our review here demonstrates that such an implication may seduce one into feeling that a problem may have been resolved (through limiting use) when in fact it remains or emerges in some other form. Clearly, what managers should be asking is, "what conditions are acceptable or appropriate?" and researchers should be searching for the social and psychological processes that lead humans to prefer these conditions. Unfortunately, the social carrying capacity term itself does not provide an adequate conceptual foundation for either. The question, "how many is too many?" may neither be appropriate nor heuristic. We suggest that the term is no longer useful in guiding research or management.

References

Absher, J.D. & R.G. Lee. 1981. "Density as an incomplete cause of crowding in backcountry settings." *Leisure Sciences 4:* 231-247.

Adelman, B.J., T.A. Heberlein, and T.M. Bonnicksen. 1982. "Social psychological explanations for the persistence of a conflict between paddling canoeists and motorcraft users in the Boundary Waters Canoe Area." *Leisure Sciences 5:* 45-61.

Altman, D. 1975. *The Environment and Social Behavior*. Monterey, CA: Brooks/Cole.

Brown, P.J. 1985. "Management objectives, recreation, and recreation management planning." In *The Management of Human Behavior in Outdoor Recreation Settings*, ed. D.L. Dustin, pp. 1-10. San Diego, CA: Institute for Leisure Behavior, San Diego State University.

Burch, W.R., Jr. 1981. "The ecology of metaphor: Spacing regularities for humans and other primates in urban and wildland habitats." *Leisure Sciences 4:* 213-230.

Burch, W.R., Jr. 1984. "Much ado about nothing: Some reflections on the wider and wilder implications of social carrying capacity." *Leisure Sciences 6:* 487-496.

Bury, R.L. 1976. "Recreational carrying capacity." *Parks and Recreation 11:* 22-25, 56-57.

Chambers, T.W.M. and C. Price. 1986. "Recreational congestion: Some hypotheses tested in the Forest of Dean." *Journal of Rural Studies 2:* 41-52.

Cole, D.W. 1987. "Research on soil and vegetation in wilderness: A state-of-knowledge review." In *Proceedings, National Wilderness Research Conference: Issues, State-of-Knowledge, Future Directions*, R.C. Lucas, compiler, pp. 135-177. General Technical Report INT- 220. Ogden, UT: USDA Forest Service, Intermountain Research Station.

Cole, D.W. and G.S. Schreiner. Compilers. 1981. *Impacts of Backcountry Recreation: Site Management and Rehabilitation: An Annotated Bibliography*. General Technical Report INT-121. Ogden, UT: USDA Forest Service, Intermountain Forest and Range Experiment Station.

Dasmann, R.F. 1964. *Wildlife Biology*. New York: John Wiley and Sons.

Dorfman, P.W. 1979. "Measurement and meaning of recreation satisfaction: A case study in camping." *Environment and Behavior 11:* 483-510.

Driver, B.L. and J.R. Bassett. 1975. "Defining conflicts among river users: A case study of Michigan's Au Sable River." *Naturalist 26:* 19-23.

Drogin, E.B., A.R. Graefe, and J.J. Vaske. 1986. "A citation index for the recreation impact/carrying capacity literature: A descriptive analysis and demonstration." Paper presented at the First National Symposium on Social Science in Resource Management, Oregon State University.

Graefe, A.R., F.R. Kuss, and J.J. Vaske. 1987. *Recreation Impacts and Carrying Capacity: A Visitor Impact Management Framework*. Washington, DC: National Parks and Conservation Association.

Graefe, A.R., J.J. Vaske, and F.R. Kuss. 1984. "Social carrying capacity: An integration and synthesis of twenty years of research." *Leisure Sciences 6:* 395-432.

Gramann, J.H. 1982. "Toward a behavioral theory of crowding in outdoor recreation: An evaluation and synthesis of research." *Leisure Sciences 5:* 109-126.

Hammitt, W.E. 1982. "Cognitive dimensions of wilderness solitude." *Environment and Behavior 14:* 478-493.

Hammitt, W.E. and G.F. Brown, Jr. 1984. "Functions of privacy in wilderness environments." *Leisure Sciences 6:* 151-166.

Heberlein, T.A. 1977. "Density, crowding and satisfaction: Sociological studies for determining carrying capacities." In *Proceedings: River Recreation Management and Research Symposium*, pp. 67-76. General Technical Report NC-28. St. Paul, MN: USDA Forest Service, North Central Forest Experiment Station.

Heberlein, T.A. and B. Shelby. 1977. "Carrying capacity, values and the satisfaction model: A reply to Greist." *Journal of Leisure Research 9:* 142-148.

Hendee, J.C. 1974. "A multiple-satisfaction approach to game management." *Wildlife Society Bulletin 1:* 104-113.

Hendee, J.C. and R.M. Pyle. 1971. "Wilderness managers, wilderness users: A problem of perception." *Naturalist 22:* 22-26.

Jackson, E.L. and R.A.G. Wong. 1982. "Perceived conflict between urban cross-country skiers and snowmobilers in Alberta." *Journal of Leisure Research 14:* 47-62.

Lawler, E.E. 1973. *Motivation in Work Organizations.* Monterey, CA: Brooks/Cole.

Lee, R.G. 1977. "Alone with others: The paradox of privacy in wilderness." *Leisure Sciences 1:* 3-19.

Lime, D.W. and G.H. Stankey. 1971. "Carrying capacity: Maintaining outdoor recreation quality." In *Recreation Symposium Proceedings,* pp. 174-184. Upper Darby, PA: USDA Forest Service, Northeastern Forest Experiment Station.

Lucas, R.C. 1964. "Wilderness perception and use: The example of the Boundary Waters Canoe Area." *Natural Resources Journal 3:* 394-411.

Lucas, R.C. 1970. *User Evaluation of Campgrounds in Two Michigan National Forests.* Research Paper NC-44. St. Paul, MN: USDA Forest Service, North Central Forest Experiment Station.

Lucas, R.C. 1980. *Use patterns and visitor characteristics, attitudes and preferences in nine wilderness and roadless areas.* Research Paper INT-253. Ogden, UT: USDA Forest Service, Intermountain Forest and Range Experiment Station.

Lucas, R.C. 1985. *Visitor Characteristics, Attitudes and Use Patterns in the Bob Marshall Wilderness Complex.* Research Paper INT-345. Ogden, UT: USDA Forest Service, Intermountain Research Station.

Manning, R.E. 1985. "Crowding norms in backcountry settings: A review and synthesis." *Journal of Leisure Research 17:* 75-89.

Manning, R.E. 1986. *Studies in Outdoor Recreation.* Corvallis, OR: Oregon State University Press.

McCool, S.F. 1983. "Wilderness quality and wilderness solitude: Are they related?" In *The Bob Marshall Wilderness Visitor Study,* ed. S.F. McCool, pp. 40-61. Missoula, MT: University of Montana.

McCool, S.F. and M. Petersen. 1982. "An application of the two factor theory of satisfaction to recreational settings." Report submitted to Forestry Sciences Laboratory, Intermountain Forest and Range Experiment Station, Missoula, MT.

Schreyer, R. and J.W. Roggenbuck. 1978. "The influence of experience expectation on crowding perceptions and social-psychological carrying capacities." *Leisure Sciences 1:* 373-394.

Shelby, B. 1981. "Encounter norms in backcountry settings: Studies of three rivers." *Journal of Leisure Research 13:* 433-451.

Shelby, B. and T.A. Heberlein. 1986. *Carrying Capacity in Recreation Settings.* Corvallis, OR: Oregon State University Press.

Shelby, B. and J.M. Nielsen. 1976. "River contact final study report," parts II and III. Grand Canyon National Park (mimeo).

Shelby, B., T.A. Heberlein, J.J. Vaske, and F. Alfano. 1983. "Expectations, preferences, and feeling crowded in recreation activities." *Leisure Sciences 6:* 1-14.

Socolow, R.H. 1976. "Failures of discourse: obstacles to the integration of environmental values into natural resource policy." In *When Values Conflict: Essays on Environmental Analysis, Discourse, and Decision,* eds. L.H. Tribe, C.S. Schelling, and J. Voss, pp. 1-33. Cambridge, MA: Ballinger.

Stankey, G.H. 1974. "Criteria for the determination of recreational carrying capacity in the Colorado River Basin." In *Environmental Management in the Colorado River Basin,* eds. A.B. Crawford and D.F. Peterson, pp. 82-101. Logan, UT: Utah State University Press.

Stankey, G.H. 1980. "Wilderness carrying capacity research: Management and research progress in the United States." *Landscape Research 5:* 6-11.

Stankey, G.H. 1982. "Recreational carrying capacity research review." *Ontario Geography 19:* 57-72.

Stankey, G.H. and S.F. McCool. 1984. "Carrying capacity in recreational settings: Evolution, appraisal, and application." *Leisure Sciences 6:* 453-473.

Stankey, G.H., D.W. Cole, R.C. Lucas, M.E. Petersen, and S.S. Frissell. 1985. *The Limits of Acceptable Change LAC System for Wilderness Planning.* General Technical Report INT-176. Ogden, UT: USDA Forest Service, Intermountain Research Station.

Stokols, D. 1972. "On the distinction between density and crowding: Some implications for future research." *Psychological Review 79:* 275-277.

Twight, B.W., K.L. Smith, and G.H. Wissinger. 1981. "Privacy and camping: Closeness to self vs. closeness to others." *Leisure Sciences 4:* 427-441.

Wagar, J.A. 1964. *The Carrying Capacity of Wildlands for Recreation.* Forest Science Monograph 7. Washington, DC: Society of American Foresters.

Wagar, J.A. 1974. "Recreational carrying capacity reconsidered." *Journal of Forestry 72:* 274-278.

Westin, A.F. 1967. *Privacy and Freedom.* New York: Atheneum.

Williams, D.R. 1988. "Great expectations and the limits to satisfaction: A review of recreation and consumer satisfaction research." In *Proceedings, Benchmark 1988: A National Outdoor and Wilderness Forum.* Asheville, NC: USDA Forest Service, Southeastern Forest Experiment Station.

RECREATION AND CONSERVATION

Guy S. Swinnerton

INTRODUCTION

One of the most urgent and controversial issues in recreation resource management is the relationship between resource protection and recreational use. Although the dilemma of providing opportunities for recreation while protecting the resources on which many of these experiences depend is particularly well illustrated in the context of national and provincial or state parks, the issue is ubiquitous to decision-making in recreation resource planning and management. The purpose of this chapter, therefore, is to provide an overview of the relationship between recreation and conservation, relying primarily on contributions from the social sciences. Permeating the discussion is the recognition that the recreation-conservation interface needs to be addressed at the conceptual, policy, and management levels, both in terms of identifying problems and in finding solutions.

Outdoor Recreation and the Resource Base

Extensive reference is made in the literature to the importance of the resource base for outdoor recreation and tourism (Farrell and McLellan 1987; Wall 1981). Irland and Rumpf (1980: 77) have observed that "outdoor recreation is by definition a land-using activity," and Ferrario (1979: 18) has remarked that tourism should be considered as a landscape industry which "requires the transformation of raw material (the available natural/cultural resources) into a finished tourist product." Several reviews of recreation land capability classification systems (Coppock and Duffield 1975; Smith 1983; Swinnerton 1974) attest to the critical role that the resource base is considered to play in the provision of recreation opportunities. More recently, the application of the recreation opportunity spectrum (ROS) concept has demonstrated the importance of the resource base (physical setting), in conjunction with characteristics of the social and managerial settings, in providing recreational diversity (Driver *et al.* 1987).

Inherent in these and other studies that have examined the resource base for outdoor recreation and tourism is the concern expressed over the ensuing tension between recreation resource use and the level and type of protection required to prevent deterioration or degradation of the attributes of the resource base itself (Pearce 1985; Pigram 1976; Romeril 1985). In addition, the high priority that some tourists place on their destination's cultural and natural heritage has prompted Romeril (1985: 215) to observe that "the message is clear: ruin the natural attractions (resources) of popular destinations and a major reason for their popularity is eliminated."

Several factors have been responsible in accounting for the urgency of the issue associated with the relationship between recreation resource use and protection. First, during the last twenty-five years increased participation in many forms of outdoor recreation and the occurrence of new activities has placed expanding and different pressures on the resource base (Cordell and Hendee 1982). Second is the recognition that all human use, including relatively passive and non-consumptive forms of outdoor recreation, impairs natural resources to some extent (Wilkes 1979). Finally, protection of pristine and unique environments, as represented by national parks and other designated areas, has been given increased visibility as part of the broader concern of environmentalism which evolved during the late 1960s and early 1970s (Boden and Baines 1981). The three components of this environmentalism — institutional, public, and organized (Buttel and Larson 1980) — became evident in the increased attention given to the conservation role of many park systems during the 1970s and 1980s (Swinnerton 1984).

The Nature of the Recreation-Conservation Relationship

The relationship between recreation and conservation is a component of the broader field of study associated with man-environment interrelationships and the planning and management of natural resources. Contributions from the social sciences to these areas of research have been extensive (Miller, Gale, and Brown 1987; Wall 1981).

Although considerable concern has been expressed about the negative repercussions resulting from tourism and the recreational use of natural and cultural resources, Farrell and McLellan (1987: 2) have warned against the danger of attributing "an unreasonable amount of responsibility for landscape change and environmental degradation to tourism." However, the fact that many forms of tourism and outdoor recreation do result in substantial impacts on the resource base (Hammitt and Cole 1987; Wall and Wright 1977; see also Wall's chapter, this volume) has resulted in a growing appreciation of the need for careful environmental planning, particularly in ecologically sensitive areas (Inskeep 1987).

Any exclusively polemic approach to the study of the recreation-conservation relationship fails to take account of the "wide spectrum of generally complex interrelationships and impacts" (Pearce 1985: 248) that do occur. Budowski (1976), for example, has suggested that there are three different forms of relationship that can exist between tourism and conservation. The close similarity between many aspects of tourism and outdoor recreation generally (Gunn 1986; Mathieson and Wall 1982; Murphy 1985) makes his observations equally relevant to the recreation-conservation relationship.

The three possible relationships identified by Budowski (1976) are: (1) coexistence as a result of minimal interaction between tourism and conservation; (2) a mutually supportive or symbiotic relationship; and (3) a conflict situation, where tourism introduces detrimental effects to the environment. The reality is that a state of coexistence rarely remains static and, as a result, the relationship invariably progresses towards one of symbiosis or conflict. Budowski concluded that a relationship of conflict was likely to become increasingly common because of the overall growth of tourism. However, Romeril (1985: 217) has stated that, despite the difficulty of ensuring that environmental awareness permeates throughout the various sectors of the tourist industry, Budowski's symbiotic relationship "is much more a reality now than it was in 1976."

Mathieson and Wall (1982) have examined the latter two relationships suggested by Budowski in considerable detail. With reference to the symbiotic relationship, they refer to Waters' (1966) contention that tourism may provide both the incentive and economic means for conservation. Tourism may act as a stimulant to conservation in a variety of ways including: (1) the rehabilitation of existing historic sites, buildings, monuments, and activities; (2) the transformation of old buildings and sites into new tourist facilities; (3) the conservation of natural resources in parks and outside designated protected areas; and (4) the introduction of administrative and planning controls directed towards protecting and maintaining the quality of the environment.

Numerous examples may also be cited where the provision of selected outdoor recreation opportunities has been an important motivating factor in the conservation of both natural and cultural resources. Such actions are most frequently discernible where the attributes of the setting are an essential component of the recreational experience and where specific interest groups or organizations are involved. The role played by Ducks Unlimited in the protection and enhancement of wetlands as an outcome of the need to improve duck habitat for hunting interests is one example (Swinnerton 1984). Similarly, there are many examples from various parts of the world where the conservation of natural and cultural landscapes associated with linear recreation activities, such as hiking and canoe tripping, has led to the protection of land and water corridors (Seguire 1986).

In contrast to the synergistic relationship between tourism or recreation and the environment, there are a corresponding number of examples which point to the impacts of tourism or recreation on specific environmental components such as vegetation, water quality, air quality, wildlife, and a variety of ecosystems (Mathieson and Wall 1982; Wall and Wright 1977). Not surprisingly, a considerable amount of the research which has examined these issues has focused on recreational experiences and settings which are extremely sensitive to environmental change and modification. Wilderness research is symptomatic of this interest (Lucas 1986). A corresponding level of attention has been directed to the relationship between recreation or tourism and conservation in national parks and other park systems. Marsh (1983) has referred to this relationship as a problematic one because of the evolving priorities over time concerning the balancing of use and protection.

Recreation and Conservation:
The Origin and Evolution of the Dilemma

Runte (1987: xix) has prefaced his examination of the national parks experience in the United States by stating that "no institution is more symbolic of the conservation movement in the United States than the national parks." It is therefore not surprising that the problem of finding an acceptable compromise between recreation use and conservation has been most evident in the case of national parks and other formally protected areas, where this duality of purpose has been enshrined in legislation and policy. Conservation in terms of parks received its initial impetus from a Bill in 1864 granting Yosemite Valley and the Mariposa Big Tree Grove to the State of California for public use, resort, and recreation (Sax 1976). The establishment of this state park not only facilitated the subsequent acceptance of the first national park, Yellowstone, in 1872, but more importantly, raised the issue of the principles of policy and management that should be adopted in connection with such protected areas. Although Frederick Law Olmsted's report entitled "The Yosemite Valley and the Mariposa Big Trees," published in 1865, was largely ignored at that time, the recommendations that the goals for the park should be the preservation and maintenance of the natural scenery and the restriction of artificial intrusions, have remained an important legacy of the park and conservation debate (Nash 1982; Sax 1980).

The establishment of Yellowstone as the world's first national park in 1872 was soon followed by the designation of other national parks in the United States and in other countries, including Royal National Park near Sydney, Australia in 1879, Banff National Park in the Canadian Rockies in 1885, and Tongariro in New Zealand in 1887. To varying degrees, all these designated parks encompassed the mandates of recreation and conservation.

Formal and legislated responsibility for the perpetuation/use dilemma that now characterizes many of the world's national parks is usually accredited to the National Park Act of the United States, which was passed in 1916

(Forster 1973). Section 16-1 of the National Park Service Organic Act states that the fundamental purpose of national parks is:

> To conserve the scenery and the natural and historic objects and wildlife therein and to provide for the enjoyment of the same in such manner and by such means as will leave them unimpaired for the enjoyment of future generations (Lemons 1986: 128).

The relevance of Section 16-1 extends beyond the United States, because other national and even provincial or state park agencies in other countries have frequently adopted this statement of purpose, with minor modification, to provide the basis for their respective park legislation. However, the dual mandate contained within the 1916 National Park Act was largely workable at that time because of the low level of visitor use experienced by the early parks in the years immediately following their establishment (Sax 1980).

The intended coexistence of conservation and the provision of outdoor recreation opportunities, provided for in the legislation and policies of many park systems, conceals a fluctuating but generally apprehensive and tenuous relationship. Studies which have addressed the historical evolution of national parks in the United States point to scenic preservation, fuelled by the forces of romantic idealism, religious naturalism, and nostalgia for a disappearing wilderness, as being particularly prominent during the initial period (Everhart 1983; Sax 1980). Runte (1987) has noted that monumentalism or natural symbolism, together with the economic worthlessness of the designated areas, were important factors in the political decisions that led to park establishment. However, both the Yosemite Grant Act of 1864 and the Yellowstone Park Act of 1872 made specific reference to the use of these areas for recreation and public enjoyment (McCool 1983; Runte 1987).

Scenic protection and the pleasure ground role of national parks was promoted by the railroads in recognition of the revenues that could be gained from tourism. During the early years, support was also forthcoming from specific recreation interest groups, such as the Appalachian Mountain Club and the Boone and Crockett Club (Runte 1987). In addition, preservationists tolerated the promotion of tourism and park visitors, not only on the basis of patronage and necessary public support, but also in the belief that these uses were preferable to utilitarian conservation interests involving dams, reservoirs, and timber development (Runte 1987). Nevertheless, even during the early decades of the twentieth century, preservationists were expressing concern about which forms of public enjoyment were appropriate in national parks and about the meaning of the phrase "leave them unimpaired for the enjoyment of future generations."

The reciprocal relationship between conservation and recreation was also evident in the early park movement in other countries. In the case of Canada's initial national parks, established during the last two decades of the nineteenth century, the role of tourism, economic benefits, and national symbolism was even more evident (Bella 1987; Turner and Rees 1973). As was the case in the United States, recreation constituencies intent on retaining the integrity of national parks for selected forms of outdoor recreation, as well as protecting them from more utilitarian uses, were active conservationists. For example, the Alpine Club established the Canadian National Parks Association in 1923 to protect national parks (Bella 1987). Marsh (1983: 273) has remarked with reference to parks in Canada that "historically, parks, be they city, provincial or national, have always been connected with recreation and tourism."

Although legislative provision for the establishment of national parks in England and Wales did not take place until the passing of the National Parks and Access to the Countryside Act in 1949, the early forces at work may be traced back to the later part of the nineteenth century and include both conservation and recreation interests (MacEwen and MacEwen 1982, 1987). Dower (1978: 3), for example, observed that the national park movement was "rooted in two distinct ideas — the protection of natural beauty, and the provision of access to the countryside." The subsequent evolution of national parks in England and Wales illustrates the attempt to find an appropriate balance between conservation and recreation.

Henwood (1982, 1983), in his examination of the evolution of national parks in New Zealand, has emphasized that, in contrast to the situation in Canada and the United States, where support for national parks came from central government, the advocates for park establishment and effective management in New Zealand were drawn from preservation groups and recreation interests, including skiing and tramping clubs. Likewise Turner (1981), in a study of the development of national parks in New South Wales, Australia, paid particular attention to the involvement of both conservation and recreation lobby groups.

McCool (1983) has observed that the role of national parks in the United States has evolved as the nation's values have moved from those of an industrial to those of a post-industrial society. Similarly, studies that have examined conservation (Devall and Sessions 1985; Jarrett 1958; Nash 1968) and outdoor recreation (Wall and Marsh 1982) reveal significant changes in both the perception and practices of these two interest groups. The current situation is in marked contrast to the conditions prevailing during the first half of the twentieth century. Increased visitor levels and changing patterns of participation in outdoor recreation have not only created conflicts between participants (Schreyer and Knopf 1984) but have also resulted in an increased diversity of activities and a decline in the quality of recreation and park environments (Downie 1986; Dustin and McAvoy 1982). Internal threats to park environments are compounded by external threats, including water pollution, pesticide use, and encroachment by exotic species (Machlis and Tichnell 1985; United States Department of the Interior 1980). Thus Dunn (1980: 119) has commented that "achieving a balance between preservation and utilization is one of the most difficult challenges confronting leisure resource managers.... [The] problems and issues are fundamental, profound, interrelated and international."

Even a cursory review of the academic literature and case examples of outdoor recreation and park planning practice reveals that achieving a compromise between recreation use and conservation is a complex problem. Several factors would seem to account for this difficulty. In the first instance, considerable confusion continues to exist as to both the concept and practice of conservation and specifically its relationship to preservation. This issue will be discussed in more detail later in this chapter. However, it is acknowledged that the confusion reflects, in part, the diversity of backgrounds of researchers and practitioners that have addressed conservation issues in what O'Riordan (1971) has referred to as a fusion of approaches. A second consideration is the realization that the relationship between recreation and conservation is dynamic and may take a variety of forms. Reference has already been made to the insights provided by Budowski (1976) into the different relationships which may exist.

A third major factor is that reaching an acceptable compromise between recreation use and conservation is initially and fundamentally a matter of policy. Policy guidelines and subsequent management decisions provide the framework within which technical tasks are carried out. The latter are well documented and relatively straightforward (Jubenville, Twight, and Becker 1987). Policy making, on the other hand, is much more complex. For example, it is widely recognized that policy making involves decisions which can never be entirely separated from values, matters of judgment, and ethics (Brown 1984; Devall and Sessions 1984; Klosterman 1983; Walther 1986). Both Burton and Godbey have made similar assertions in their chapters in this book. Nelson (1979), for example, has noted that environmental questions and environmental decisions are essentially about values. Lemons (1987), with reference to national park management issues in the United States, has suggested that, because of ambiguous legislation and inadequate scientific research, decisions relating to the protection of park resources have largely revolved around three variables: parks' values; social benefits; and financial considerations. In addition, Stankey (1982a) has recommended that a logical and defensible philosophical framework is required as a basis for conservation and preservation. The following section addresses some of the more important concepts and underlying themes associated with the recreation-conservation issue.

RECREATION AND CONSERVATION: CONCEPTS AND UNDERLYING THEMES

Although most people have an intuitive feeling about what is implied by the terms "leisure" or "recreation," debate continues to exist as to what constitutes an adequate interpretation of these terms (see the chapters by Cooper, Rojek, and others in this volume). For the purposes of this chapter, "outdoor recreation" includes any activity which is undertaken on a voluntary basis during leisure time for personal enjoyment and satisfaction, and where the resource base (natural or cultural) is an important factor in the experience.

The concept of conservation has become an integral part of the field of resource management. However, one of the distinguishing characteristics of conservation studies is the recognition, if not the acceptance, of the diversity of definitions. This acknowledgment is readily made, irrespective of whether the studies have a specifically economic focus (Ciriacy-Wantrup 1968; Howe 1979; Randall 1981), are concerned with environmental quality and resource management (Green 1981; Jarrett 1958; Nash 1968; Warren and Goldsmith 1983), or involve cultural and historic resources (Artibise and Stelter 1981; Denhez 1978; Ward 1986; Weiler 1984).

Resources and Conservation

Reduced to its basic meaning, conservation is synonymous with a philosophical and conceptual framework involving the optimum use of resources over time. Such a definition presupposes an understanding of the term "resource." Traditionally, the concept of resources was associated with land or natural resources and included those "tangible elements of the biophysical environment necessary for the production of certain basic commodities ..." (O'Riordan 1971: 4). O'Riordan (1971: 5) contended that equating resources with materials excluded the important components of technology and appraisal and as a result, resources were considered to be "tangible, single-purpose, and static in their value over time." Because of this perspective, early classifications of resources were based on the concept of renewability or natural substitutability of the resource in relation to society's perceived needs over time. The distinction was therefore made between stock or non-renewable resources and flow or renewable resources (Rees 1985), in the context of society's needs for minerals, agricultural produce, timber, wildlife, and energy. Such a perspective fails to recognize the dynamics of the man-environment interrelationship and society's proactive role in appraising the potential of its environment.

Ciriacy-Wantrup (1968: 28) has suggested that "the concept 'resource' presupposes that a 'planning agent' is appraising the usefulness of his environment for the purposes of obtaining a certain end." This perspective is complementary to the bio-cultural process of resource appraisal discussed by O'Riordan (1971) and based on the earlier work of Zimmerman (1951). O'Riordan (1971: 3) has defined the bio-cultural concept thus: "a culturally defined abstract concept, which hinges upon man's perception of the means of attaining certain socially-valued goals by manipulating selected elements of the biophysical environment."

The concept of resources suggested by Ciriacy-Wantrup, and the bio-cultural process of resource appraisal, have important implications for the recreation-conservation relationship. Recreation clearly becomes a legitimate resource use, with satisfaction and benefits being expected outcomes for both the individual and society (Peterson, Driver, and Gregory 1988; see also Schreyer and Driver, this volume). Conservation, therefore, becomes an appropriate management strategy for attempting to ensure the availability of such benefits over time. The bio-cultural concept of resource appraisal helps to explain why different potential user groups and resource agencies perceive the same component of the biophysical environment in different ways and assign to the component different values and levels of utility. The outcome is competition — and not infrequently conflict — between major resource interest sectors, such as agriculture, forestry, and recreation, as well as between preservationists and pro-development recreation interests. In addition, the dynamics of the bio-cultural perspective imply that society's concept of a recreation resource changes through space and over time. Consequently, at any one point in time, society is unable to identify the attributes of the biophysical environment to which it may assign recreation value at some future date or the amount of the resource base it will require to meet future demand. This element of uncertainty has important implications for conservation policies and practices (Swinnerton 1984).

Another dimension of resources involves the concept of amenity resources (Perloff 1969). Although difficult to define, amenity resources are generally considered to be those resources which contribute to the quality of life and the environment, and which go beyond life's basic necessities (Coppack 1985). Amenity resources therefore include landscape aesthetics, the character of open space, the integrity of irreplaceable natural and cultural environments, and non-consumptive wildlife values (INNTREC Group Ltd. and EDA Collaborative Inc. 1980; Shaw and Zube 1980).

In discussing the full-range of resources, reference should also be made to human-induced changes or additions to the environment which represent a special class of resources in that they are not strictly natural (Barlowe 1972). Buildings, archaeological artifacts, and cultural landscapes, which illustrate the way in which people have purposefully manipulated the natural environment, can be important resources for recreation and tourism. However, these resources can be equally adversely affected by neglect and abuse or destructive action resulting from excessive visitor pressure. Consequently, the concept of conservation is equally applicable to historic and cultural resources as it is to the more traditional natural resource area.

The amenity value of the countryside is strongly entrenched in the provision of outdoor recreation opportunities in Britain, and the humanized landscape of the national parks, which has been largely created and maintained by agriculture, is one of the basic reasons for their appeal (Johnson 1971;

Phillips and Roberts 1973). In both Canada and the United States, concern for environmental quality as manifested in landscape has been focused primarily on wilderness areas and landscapes largely devoid of human intervention. Schauman (1979) and Getz (1975) have commented on these international differences, and Swinnerton (1982) and Tuttle (1980) have noted the recent development in Canada and the United States of moves towards the conservation of the rural integrity of the countryside. Melnick (1983) has also discussed the positive aspects of the integration of conservation efforts involving both natural and cultural resources as represented in rural landscapes. Proposed landscape conservation areas in Nova Scotia (Boggs 1976), greenline parks in the United States (Corbett 1983), and consideration of rural recreation space as an alternative to national parks in Australia (Pigram 1983) illustrate the potential coexistence of recreation and conservation outside the traditional designations of national and provincial or state parks.

This amalgamation of natural and cultural resources is being increasingly referred to under the collective term "heritage resources." The Countryside Review Committee (1979: 5) in Britain, in considering the conservation of countryside heritage, included "landscape, nature, and archaeological sites and historic buildings, things which we value for aesthetic, scientific, cultural reasons." At the Heritage for Tomorrow Assembly to celebrate the centennial of Canada's National Parks, heritage was defined as "the existing context of the past, including all natural, historic and cultural resources" (Nelson, Scace, Sadler, Lemieux, and Washington 1986: 28). Application of the heritage concept at a provincial level has been referred to by the Department of Recreation and Parks of Alberta (1988), in the context of heritage resource protection, as including the protection and preservation of both natural landscapes and features as well as historic and cultural resources.

Recognition of the various dimensions of resources is important to obtaining a holistic perspective on the relationship between recreation and conservation. Particularly relevant is the realization that the recreation-conservation interface is not restricted to achieving an appropriate balance between recreation use and the protection of natural resources within park settings.

Alternative Concepts of Conservation

The preceding discussion on resources emanated from the statement that conservation is synonymous with the optimum use of resources over time. However, the resource utilization aspect of conservation, according to Green (1981), is only one of three kinds of conservation. The other two are maintenance of environmental quality and preservation.

Conservation in terms of the maintenance of environmental quality is associated with the application of quality standards to components of the environment, including water, air, and noise, and, at a broader level, the preparation of environmental impact assessment statements.

For many people, conservation is most clearly demonstrated through the preservation of those features of the environment considered to be of amenity value, including wildlife and natural areas of biological and geological significance, cultural landscapes, and individual buildings and artifacts of heritage value.

Although the three kinds of conservation are not entirely mutually exclusive, and traditional resource agencies frequently argue that the planned use of resources to ensure their continuing supply automatically subsumes the other two, there is considerable evidence to demonstrate that the latter is not necessarily the case. Resource use invariably involves conflicts of interest, even though the different constituencies involved argue their respective cases on the basis of good conservation practices. The debate is a long-standing one and is illustrated by the resource utilization interpretation of conservation expressed by the professional forester Gifford Pinchot, compared to the preservation perspective advocated by the naturalists George Perkins Marsh and John Muir (Nash 1982).

Conservation: Underlying Themes

Any attempt to understand the concept of conservation involves a multidisciplinary approach and the coalescence of a number of interacting themes. Numerous researchers from both the social and natural sciences have examined these themes (Barnett and Morse 1963; Ehrenfeld 1976; Gilg 1981; Green 1981; Rowe 1982). Other researchers have interpreted these themes to emphasize the benefits to be derived from protected natural areas, and in so doing argue the case for the conservation and preservation role of parks, wilderness areas, and other forms of protected reserves (Fuller 1970; Fuller 1987; Lausche 1980; Lemons 1987; Lucas 1984; Pearsall 1984; Rolston 1985, 1986; Rowe 1982; Stankey 1982a).

The underlying themes to conservation, and the justification for the protection of natural areas and the benefits subsequently realized, are broadly twofold: a biocentric perspective and an anthropocentric perspective.

The biocentric perspective and benefits associated with natural areas are based on an ethical orientation that recognizes the inherent and intrinsic value of nature. Aldo Leopold's (1949) "land ethic" enlarged the membership of the moral community beyond human society to include all the constituents of nature. A further dimension of this perspective is the claim that wildlife possesses moral rights and standing and that all living organisms and even natural phenomena should be accorded legal status and rights (Tallmadge 1981). This latter position questions society's right to exploit and exterminate any form of life or natural phenomenon. Stankey (1982a) has suggested that the preservation of natural areas is a symbolic gesture involving society's moral responsibility to protect environmental diversity.

Despite the fact that "many people feel that conservation is somehow a matter of conscience" (Green 1981: 8), ethical arguments are difficult to comprehend, to assign economic value to, and to translate into public policy. As a result, greater recognition tends to be given to the anthropocentric perspective and associated benefits in advocating the need for parks and protected natural areas. O'Riordan (1981: 11) has suggested that, in contrast to the "ecocentric mode," the "technocentric mode" is attractive to governments and their bureaucracies because of its emphasis on rationality, managerial efficiency, and a "sense of optimism and faith in the ability of man to understand and control physical, biological and social processes for the benefit of present and future generations."

The anthropocentric justification for parks and protected natural areas is based on the contention that an appreciation of nature, and therefore support for conservation and preservation, can only be expressed in terms of a human scale of values. As a result, protection of natural areas is ultimately assessed in terms of society's self interest, utility, and proprietorship (Livingston 1981). Stankey (1982a) has described this perspective as an "instrumental" conception of conservation and preservation, in that the protection of natural areas is a means to an end rather than an end in itself.

The benefits associated with an anthropocentric perspective to the conservation and preservation of parks and related natural areas are many but may be categorized as follows.

Although difficult to measure, spiritual benefits are considered by many to be the most significant benefits derived from the preservation of natural areas. These benefits relate to the spiritual renewal, moral regeneration, and the ethical and symbolic values of the natural environment. Godfrey-Smith (1980) has referred to these benefits as pertaining to the "cathedral" view of conservation.

Acceptance of the concept of the recreation opportunity spectrum requires the provision of a range of recreation settings, from primitive to highly developed. Areas such as natural parks and wilderness are essential components of this continuum in that they provide the preferred type of setting for many outdoor recreation activities. The personal, societal, and economic benefits which may be derived from involvement in these activities has been noted by many researchers (Driver, Nash, and Haas 1987; Peterson, Driver, and Gregory 1988; Schreyer and Driver, this volume).

An integral part of many recreation experiences is the aesthetic benefits derived from pleasant scenery, together with the solitude and quiet provided by natural landscapes. All of these are considered to have positive effects on physical and mental well-being (Daniel, Zube, and Driver 1979). The aesthetic value of landscape is not confined to an appreciation of visual grandeur, but can also be attributed to a sense of identity and to the meaning and emotional significance that landscapes can have for the observer.

Proponents of the ecological benefits to be derived from parks and protected natural areas point to the need to retain undisturbed ecological systems for maintaining natural processes upon which human life is dependent. Associated with the ecological perspective is the questioning of the effects of society's activities on the world ecosystem, the availability of resources, and the quality of life for future generations. In its optimistic form there is the belief that new technology will be able to counteract resource and environmental problems. The pessimistic perspective recognizes the ecological limits of the biosphere and the dangers of exceeding the "critical zone" of certain components of the resource base. These contrasting views are part of the broader resource debate discussed by Boulding (1966), O'Riordan (1981), and Russell (1979). Jackson (this volume) uses the labels "conserver" and "consumer" society to outline the key beliefs, assumptions, and values associated with the two opposing perspectives. Further attention is given to this issue in a subsequent section of this chapter.

A second important dimension of ecological benefits is the contribution that protected areas make as *in situ* gene banks. This protective role relates not only to endangered species but also to the need to preserve genetic diversity in terms of many different species and variation within species (Ford-Lloyd and Jackson 1986; Prescott-Allen and Prescott-Allen 1984). Protecting this genetic diversity has implications for both species adaptation and natural selection and the more materialistic application through the use of the world's genetic resources, both realized and potential, for food, fiber, and pharmaceuticals and the genetic stock they may provide for improving existing crops and domestic animals (Webb 1987).

Another major category of anthropocentric benefits associated with parks and protected areas is the need for research areas in undisturbed and natural settings. A specific function of such sites is their use as benchmarks against which to measure natural or man-induced changes and to provide guidance for the rehabilitation of disturbed ecosystems. Educators are also becoming increasingly aware of the value of parks and related reserves as *in situ* classrooms and laboratories for a wide variety of disciplines and educational levels.

Pearsall (1984: 3) has stressed the need to recognize the "*in absentia* benefits of nature preserves, which are those benefits which do not accrue to the user at the preserve." The longer term benefits experienced by recreationists who may use parks or protected areas as settings for compatible recreation activities has already been noted in this section. Option, existence, and bequest benefits are also closely associated with *in absentia* benefits. A further example of *in absentia* benefits is the contribution that natural areas have made as the basis for inspiration in the arts including painting, music, and literature.

Conservation and Preservation

Recognition of the distinction between the concepts of conservation and preservation is not simply a philosophical issue or a matter of semantics. Inskeep (1987: 128), in his discussion of environmental planning for tourism and specifically the relationship between tourism and protected areas, recommends the following:

> The distinction must be made between the concepts of *conservation* which implies "planned management" and controlled use of the area and *preservation* which means virtually no change and restricted use.

National park authorities throughout the world are charged with the responsibility for protecting natural resources; many state and provincial park agencies are charged with the same mandate. Reference to the relevant legislation and policy manuals reveals a pattern of inconsistency and substitutability in the use of the terms "conservation" and "preservation." For example, Section 16-1 of the U.S. National Parks Act states that the fundamental purpose of national parks is "to conserve," whereas the *Management Policies* manual of the National Park Service (United States Department of the Interior 1978: I-II) states that "the areas of the National Park System are managed to place primary emphasis upon preservation and appropriate recreational use of significant natural and cultural resources." An inconsistency is also evident in legislation relating to national parks and the protection of the countryside in England and Wales. Whereas the National Parks and Access to the Countryside Act, 1949 refers to the "preservation and enhancement of natural beauty in England and Wales," the corresponding section of the Countryside Act, 1968 specifies "the conservation and enhancement of the natural beauty and amenity of the countryside." The more recent Wildlife and Countryside Act, 1981 also uses the term "conservation." In New Zealand (Henwood 1983) and Australia (Boden and Baines 1981), the term "preservation" is used with reference to their respective national parks.

The mandate of Canada's National Parks as defined in Section 4 of the National Parks Act, 1930 states that "Parks shall be maintained and made use of so as to leave them unimpaired for the enjoyment of future generations." In 1964, a statement on parks policy referred specifically to preservation (Downie 1986), as does the most recent comprehensive Parks Canada Policy (Parks Canada 1979). Parks Canada, (1982: 102) in its *National Parks Management Planning Process Manual* defines preservation as "the act of maintaining physical and biological integrity. This is usually accomplished in national parks through strict control of human activity." By way of comparison, provincial park legislation in many provinces across Canada makes explicit reference to both the conservation and preservation role of parks as well as facilitating their use and enjoyment for outdoor recreation (Swinnerton 1984; Ward and Killham 1987). Perhaps not surprisingly, few agencies have attempted to distinguish between conservation and preservation (Swinnerton 1984).

Devall and Sessions (1984), in their discussion of natural resource development, contrast Gifford Pinchot's resource utilization and anthropocentric version of conservation with the "righteous management" or the biocentric and preservation perspective of John Muir. Stone (1965), for example, has contrasted the preservation orientation of the U.S. National Park Service with the conservation orientation of the U.S. Forest Service. White and Bratton (1980: 242), in their consideration of preservation both from a philosophical and practical perspective, note that "historically, conservation and preservation in the U.S.A. were distinct and partially antagonistic. Conservationists were motivated by economics.... Preservationists, on the other hand, sought to protect wild lands from any economic use or development." In Canada, these divergent philosophies on conservation did not exist (Turner and Rees 1973). The emphasis was almost exclusively upon resource utilization for economic benefits.

A crucial factor from White and Bratton's perspective is that the early preservationists advocated no human intervention other than to protect areas from human influence. This approach was adopted largely in the belief that natural ecosystems were self-maintaining. From this perspective, there generally evolved the connotation that preservation signified no human use and no human intervention in the form of resource management of a natural area, whereas conservation was characterized by specific management goals with economic and social benefits in mind. However, White and Bratton (1980) correctly point out that, even when reserves are established for preservation purposes, changes take place because of natural processes as well as any human influence. Consequently, they point to the need for management goals and the setting of priorities in preserving protected areas. For example, they distinguish between management to preserve natural ecological processes from management to preserve specific species. In a similar context, Reid (1979) has made the comparison between the preservation of ecological processes, which he has termed the wilderness concept of preservation, and the preservation of an ecosystem or a particular seral stage because of its social desirability, which he regards as the natural features concept of nature preservation. This latter type of preservation, he suggests, is closely allied with educational and recreational interests. Clearly, in those instances where a recreation function is to be accommodated within a protected area, such as national or provincial and state parks, priorities should be established in terms of the preservation of natural systems or processes and the provision of recreational opportunities. Another dimension of the preservation issue with regard to national parks in both the United States and Canada is that both of their respective national parks acts refer to maintaining park resources in an unimpaired state. Lemons (1987) has noted that the usual interpretation of this mandate is maintaining parks' resources in their natural condition. This in turn has given rise to a considerable debate as what constitutes "natural" (Bonnicksen and Stone 1985; Bratton 1985; Devall and Sessions 1984; Dolan, Hayden and Soucie 1978). The specific position taken in such a debate has important implications for strategies that are adopted towards the management of natural resources in parks and other protected areas (Swinnerton 1988).

A recent attempt to distinguish between conservation and preservation has been made by the Department of Recreation and Parks of Alberta (1988: 3) in its *Foundations for Action* report:

> Although "preservation" and "conservation" are both forms of heritage resource protection, they have different meanings and distinct aims. Preservation is the retention of the integrity, authenticity and intrinsic value of a resource in perpetuity. Conservation is the management of a resource in a manner that sustains its capability to meet the needs and aspirations of current and future generations. As it relates to the ministry's programs and services, conservation focuses on retaining or enhancing the capability of an area to offer an experience to visitors or to fulfill a necessary park function.

Further reference to the report suggests that, whereas preservation is concerned with protecting the natural and intrinsic values of natural landscapes and features in perpetuity, conservation involves the protection of an area's capability to support its park or outdoor recreation function through the retention of those elements and attributes of the resource base which are essential for providing a quality experience both now and in the future.

The relationship between conservation and preservation may also be elaborated through an examination of the distinguishing characteristics of these two concepts within the broader framework of resource protection and resource development (Swinnerton 1984). In addition, the distinguishing characteristics used in the framework in Figure 1 provide some insight into the various disciplines and fields of study that consider conservation and preservation issues to be legitimate areas of research and practice. For example, the ethical, social, and economic perspectives that are referred to in relation to the "frame of values" used to distinguish between preservation, conservation, and exploitation illustrate the diversity of disciplines involved. Reference to relevant journals such as *Environmental Ethics, Society and Natural Resources,* and the *Journal of Environmental Economics* provides further evidence of O'Riordan's (1971) contention that conservation involves a fusion of approaches. Despite this reality, Heberlein (1988) has recently commented on the need to improve interdisciplinary research involving resource policy issues and, specifically, the need to better integrate the social and natural sciences in such endeavors.

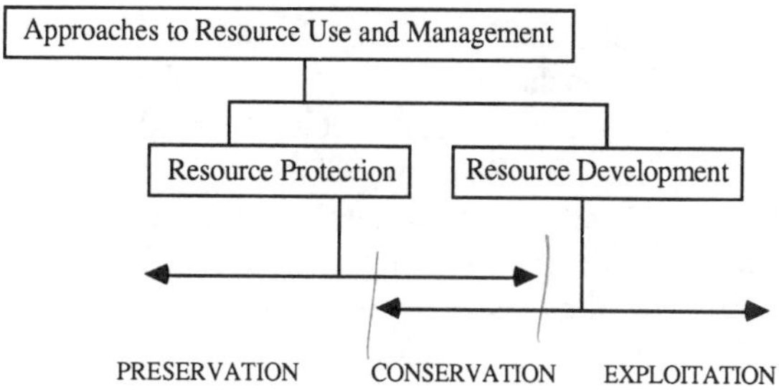

DISTINGUISHING CHARACTERISTICS			
FRAME OF VALUES	Ethical	Social/Economic	Economic
PERSPECTIVE TO RESOURCE	Biocentric/ Anthropocentric	Anthropocentric	Anthropocentric
CONSTRAINTS ON LEVELS OF USE	Conscience/ Ecology	Conscience/ Ecology/ Science/ Technology	Science/ Technology/ Economics
TYPE OF USE	Non-use/Vicarious/ Appreciative/ Non-consumptive	Appreciative/ Consumptive	Consumptive
LEVEL OF USE	Retention of integrity and authenticity	Sustained yield	Depletion/ Exhaustion
OUTPUT/ OUTCOME FROM USE	Human experience/ Satisfaction/ Intrinsic benefits/ Future options	Human experience/ Market product/ Intrinsic & extrinsic benefits/ Future options	Market product/ Extrinsic benefits
ABILITY TO ACCOMMODATE OTHER USES	Difficult	Possible/ Probable	Possible
TIMING OF RESOURCE USE	In perpetuity	Long term	Short term

Figure 1
Distinguishing Characteristics of Resource Protection and Resource Development. (Source: Swinnerton 1984)

RECREATION AND CONSERVATION: POLICY AND PRACTICE

The purpose of the preceding examination of conservation and related themes at a conceptual level was twofold. First, the discussion was in response to the recognized need for greater precision in the application of planning and management terminology in the context of protected areas and outdoor recreation

(Inskeep 1987; Nelson and Day 1985; Swinnerton 1984, 1988). Second, the review acknowledges that a logical and philosophical framework is a necessary underpinning to resource management policies and practices (Hendee and Stankey 1973; Sax 1980; Stankey 1982a, 1982b; White and Bratton 1980). Despite the fact that these issues have been the focus of considerable attention in the literature, many agencies continue to have difficulty in contending with the dilemma of reconciling recreation use with the protection of heritage resources.

Social scientists have examined this issue at two, though not mutually exclusive, levels. The first level encompasses those studies which have primarily been concerned with decision making at a policy level. The second level, which is in part an outcome of the first, puts greater emphasis on planning and management practices that address the need to find a symbiotic relationship between recreation and resource protection.

Principles and Practice at the Policy Level

An appropriate point at which to begin examining the relationship between recreation and conservation is in terms of policy-making and decision-making. O'Riordan (1971: 119) has suggested that "studies of decision making in resource management are significant in that they attempt to relate and assess the *totality* of forces in operation and aid the understanding of the processes involved in the spatial variation of phenomena on the landscape." Another reason for focusing on policy making initially is that it provides the context and framework within which planning and management practices are carried out.

Policy-making and decision-making involving the relationship between recreation and conservation is a complex and frequently controversial undertaking. This situation arises from the fact that policy-making incorporates making choices which can never be entirely separated from the pervading philosophies, values, perceptions, and attitudes of the various constituencies involved. Simeon (1976: 570), for example, has suggested that "fundamentally, these factors may be seen as providing the basic assumptions and framework within which policy is considered." A corresponding viewpoint has been noted by Sproule-Jones (1982), in his discussion of public choice theory and natural resources.

Using Christensen's (1985) classification of planning problems, the recreation-conservation issue is one where the technology is available to deal with most of the problems; the difficulty is primarily associated with the different goals of the constituencies involved. As a result, the distinguishing characteristics of the policy-making and decision-making process are usually those of compromise and the accommodation of multiple preferences.

Park Policies: A Selected Overview

Because of the totality of the picture that studies of policy provide, it is not surprising that a considerable amount of research has been focused on tracing and explaining the vagaries of the recreation-conservation relationship, particularly in the context of the evolution of national parks and other protected areas. Most of these studies point to the complexity and dynamics of the relationship over time. Furthermore, although government-directed policies have recognized that both conservation and the provision of recreation opportunities are worthwhile endeavors, the relative priority given to these two objectives and their level of compatibility have frequently been brought into question.

The recreation and conservation balance within national parks in England and Wales has been the focus of considerable attention (Cherry 1985; MacEwen and MacEwen 1982, 1987; Sheail 1975, 1984). Cherry (1985: 127) has summarized the development of national parks in England and Wales as "a good example of a public sector response to vigorous advocacy, revised preferences and changing circumstances." In his analysis, he identifies three interactive value systems pertaining to the political element, the professions and the bureaucracy, and the community. He also suggests (1985: 127) that these three elements are "internally heterogeneous, rather than homogeneous; they may change direction over time; and none has consistent primacy over the others." The importance of the political element has also been noted by Sheail (1975, 1984). For example, he suggests that the prerequisite for government involvement in the promotion of national parks and nature preservation was that it had to be "perceived as part of a larger movement to preserve rural amenity and opportunities for outdoor recreation" within the context of post-war reconstruction (Sheail 1984: 29). Sheail (1984) has also commented on the fact that the more recent Wildlife and Countryside Act of 1981 is a further illustration of the political dimension in environmental decision-making.

Other studies have been more provocative in their assessment of the national parks in England and Wales. Ann and Malcolm MacEwen (1982), having considered provisions for conservation and recreation, and the diversity of pressures on these areas from agriculture, forestry, and other natural resource interests, suggest that existing policies are largely cosmetic in nature and that a substantial revision of national park policy and practice is required. More recently, they have contended that, despite the British government's token support for the principles of sustainability contained within the World Conservation Strategy, "conservation is an attitude of mind that runs counter to the prevailing ideology of consumerism" (MacEwen and MacEwen 1987: 65). As an indication of this consumerism, they point to the involvement by central government and tourism interests in the promotion within national parks of "particular areas less for their real qualities than for commercial gimmicks" (MacEwen and MacEwen 1987: 86).

In contrast to those authors who have expressed concern about the negative impact of increased recreation pressure on parks and sensitive environments, other researchers have either been more sanguine about the relationship between recreation and conservation or have advocated policies and strategies which are more accommodating of recreation interests (Curry 1985; Donnelly 1986; Fitton 1979). Fitton (1979), for example, has warned that some of the reactions to the growth of outdoor recreation were mildly hysterical and that, as a result, there has been a tendency to introduce policies to contain recreation rather than to explore the possibilities of providing opportunities for recreation in the countryside. Another recurrent theme which Fitton (1979) has discussed is the apparent distinction that some conservation constituencies make between those visitors who are acceptable in the countryside and those who are not. The contentious issue of what types of recreation activity are appropriate in national parks and other protected areas will be addressed in a subsequent part of this chapter.

Curry (1985) has suggested that there is considerable disparity between public policy and public opinion with regard to conservation and recreation priorities in Britain's rural landscape. He attributes this distinction in part to the fact that "conservation is seen as an objective of policy and recreation as a land use problem" (Curry 1985: 4). He pursues this argument by observing that, whereas policies and plans have emphasized conservation, "public attitudes towards conservation and recreation in the countryside clearly favour recreation" (Curry 1985: 4). Curry's (1985: 19) evident support for recreation interests is further illustrated by his conclusion that "all too often, conservation has been the master of recreation and not its servant."

Notwithstanding the contentious nature of this issue, Poore (1982) has suggested that a symbiotic relationship between conservation and recreation, together with the promotion of a vigorous rural economy, could result in Britain's national parks providing a model for the application of the principles of the World Conservation Strategy. Supportive of Poore's (1982) expectations are the results of research carried out by the Countryside Commission, which Phillips and Ashcroft (1987: 327) suggest reveal "that the public's enjoyment of an attractive countryside will grow in importance and [are] a reminder that conservation policies should play a part in future recreation strategies."

A comparison between national parks in Canada, the United States, and England and Wales by Bella (1986) suggests that "in each instance the national parks reflect the dominant political ideology, and have come into being through political processes typical of that country" (Bella 1986: 189). In a detailed study of the development of the national parks of Canada, Bella (1987) shows that many were initially created for economic and political reasons and that, although selected parks within the system were subsequently established for preservation purposes, "certain forms of resource exploration have been limited, but only so that another form of resource exploitation, tourism, can continue" (Bella 1987: 158).

The evolution of provincial parks in Canada reflects a similar variety of motives for park establishment. These motives include commercial profit through tourism, the granting of mineral and timber leases, the provision of intensive recreation opportunities for local populations, and political expediency, as well as the protection of natural environments (Mason 1988; Passmore 1966; Swinnerton 1984, 1987, 1988). Provincial parks accommodate to varying degrees a combination of conservation and outdoor recreation functions. The relative priority given to these two broad functions would seem to be contingent upon a number of factors including: (1) the existence or otherwise of other designated areas to accommodate these functions; (2) the land tenure balance between crown and private land; and (3) the primary focus of the agency which has ultimate responsibility for parks (Swinnerton 1988). Mason (1988: v), in his study of provincial parks in Alberta, has argued that "the nature and pattern of provincial park development in Alberta are the result of an interactive process which has been affected by social, economic, and political factors."

Studies which have addressed the evolution of park and wilderness policies in the United States have also commented on the changing function of these areas and the importance of the wider societal dynamics of change to account for adjustment in policy and practice. These changing functions have invariably had a profound effect on the relationship between recreation and conservation in parks and/or protected areas (Allin 1982; Bratton 1985; Everhart 1983; Ise 1961; Lemons 1987; McCool 1983; Nash 1982; Runte 1987; Sax 1976, 1980, 1985b).

McCool (1983), in his examination of national parks in post-industrial America, discusses the evolution of policy and practice in the context of Alvin Toffler's paradigm of cultural development. Within this framework, McCool (1983: 16) observes that:

Parks are very much products of the culture which creates them; they are social institutions in the truest sense of the term. Their purpose and management policy and direction reflect the dominant values and needs of the society in which they are emplaced.

McCool illustrates this proposition by contrasting the provision of entertainment by park authorities in the industrial era (Toffler's second wave) with the more recent emphasis on experiential planning for the park visitor and greater awareness of the preservation of ecological processes. This conflict between the values of the industrial era and those of the post-industrial (Toffler's third wave) is, according to McCool (1983), largely responsible for the confusion over the role of parks.

These changes discussed by McCool (1983) are also symptomatic of the suggested transition from a consumer to a conserver society and the implications for leisure and recreation and environmental attitudes which are discussed by Jackson elsewhere in this book. The reciprocal relationship between environmental attitudes and outdoor recreation (Dunlap and Heffernan 1975; Jackson 1986; Van Liere and Noe 1981) is characterized in the park context by changes in recreation activity patterns and concern for environmental quality and heritage protection. Indicative of this relationship, for example, is the increased popularity of adventure or risk activities, in which the preference for unmodified natural environments is an important component of the overall recreation experience. According to Jackson (1987: 249), "if the prospect of a conserver society indeed becomes a reality, then an even more widespread and stronger support for the preservation of natural resources than is evident at present may be anticipated." Such dimensions of social and attitudinal change have implications for two other aspects of park policy and practice, namely the priority issue between recreation and conservation and the debate over what recreation activities are appropriate within parks.

Recreation and Conservation: The Priority Issue

One of the primary issues associated with the preservation-versus-use dilemma in national parks is not only how these tensions may be reconciled but ultimately which interest has priority. Most legislation is generally considered to be ambiguous on this issue. However, recent interest has been focused on more careful legal scrutiny of the legislation. Lemons and Stout (1984: 41), for example, have suggested that "a resolution of the preservation versus use dilemma must be based upon the intent of congressional legislation." They point out that few studies have addressed the issue from a judicial perspective. Following a review of U.S. National Park legislation, they contend that "although the actual balance between preservation and use of park resources depends on the individual park, the most basic fiduciary duties of the NPS are to reduce development and promote preservation of resources" (Lemons and Stout 1984: 65; see also Lemons 1987; Lemons and Stout 1982).

  Dustin and McAvoy (1980) have drawn attention to this issue in terms of their application of Garrett Hardin's concept of the "tragedy of the commons" to the increasing use of national parks in the United States, and in so doing implicitly demonstrate the importance of policy to the recreation-conservation debate. For example, they note that, whereas "the National Park Service has a history of attempting to alleviate such problems of overuse with technical solutions" (Dustin and McAvoy 1980: 41), what is required is a more difficult decision but one which involves a change in policy limiting access to a common resource.

  It is also appropriate to mention that policy statements relative to the preservation-use issue in Canada's National Parks (Parks Canada 1979), Alberta's conservation-outdoor recreation system (Alberta Recreation and Parks 1988), and National Parks in England and Wales (MacEwan and MacEwan

1982; Sandford 1974) have implied that, where preservation and use and recreation development are in conflict, the former has to take priority. All of these shifts in policy which are more supportive of resource protection may be explained, in part, by the increased involvement of conservation groups in public policy making and the greater concern expressed by society as a whole in the quality of the environment in recent years.

Recreation and Conservation: Compatibility and Conflict

Reference has already been made to the fact that the emergence of conservation associated with the designation of national parks and protected areas was due in no small part to the latter's tourism and recreation value and the public support that these uses engendered. It has also been acknowledged that an adjunct to the growth of outdoor recreation and resource-oriented tourism during the last quarter century has been an increase in environmental awareness and an enhanced concern for the protection of heritage resources. This reciprocal relationship between recreation and conservation is referred to in several other chapters in this book. Other authors (Clarke 1987; D'Amore 1987; Ritchie 1986; White 1988) have commented upon the positive alliance between tourism and conservation. Clarke (1987: 27), for example, has contrasted tourism with the more traditional forms of resource exploitation by noting that "tourism represents the opportunity for growth based upon natural resource conservation." However, the volatile nature of this apparent symbiotic relationship is equally apparent (Dearden 1983; Downie and Peart 1982).

Broad generalizations about the nature of the recreation-conservation relationship do little to assist in the formulation of meaningful policies and strategies. For one thing, recreation and tourism are collective terms which incorporate a wide spectrum of activities that have an equally diverse range of interactions with the environment. Moreover, the participants themselves demonstrate varying degrees of sensitivity to environmental issues (Dunlap and Heffernan 1975; Jackson 1986, 1987). Marsh (1983: 272) has cogently summarized the situation in the following manner:

> Conflict is serious where tourism of a particular type occurs in a park least suited to that type of tourism or where the demands, of even an appropriate type of tourism, are excessive for the park environment.

However, deciding what is "appropriate" or what is "excessive" is an inherent problem for those policy makers who have to contend with such issues. For, as Butler (1986: 81) has observed, "to a large extent the importance of the impacts of tourism is a matter of perception and attitude, especially with respect to what is acceptable and reasonable."

Perhaps not surprisingly, therefore, an important contribution of the social sciences to the recreation-conservation debate has emanated from studies that have focused on park values, the public's perception of park environments, and environmental attitudes. Researchers have not only addressed the differing perceptions of the overall role of parks but also the appropriateness of specific activities and levels of facility development within parks.

An appropriate introduction to these issues is to reiterate Olmsted's ideas regarding park values. Sax (1980: 22) states that:

> His (Olmsted's) principal goal in seeking preservation of the scenery was to assure that there would be no destruction to impede an independent and personal response to experience.... His concern was with the installation of facilities or entertainments ... where prepared activities would occupy the visitor without engaging him.

Sax's (1980) book *Mountains Without Handrails* provides one of the most comprehensive and reasoned assessments of the intended role of national parks and related reserves and the position that the national park service should take in the conservation-recreation issue. The distinction is made between conventional forms of recreation, which require concession facilities and support services, and reflective recreation, which focuses on experiencing natural resources. Lemons (1987) has suggested that, whereas conventional recreation is consumptive of resources, reflective recreation is not. An alternative way of distinguishing between these forms of recreation and development is to recognize the distinction between intrinsic forms of recreation, which are compatible with and supportive of the park ethic, and those activities and developments which are extrinsic in nature, and which ultimately detract the park visitor from understanding and appreciating the natural environment and the significance of parks' designations as special places (Swinnerton 1985).

The proliferation of activities and facilities of an extrinsic nature invariably precipitates a gradual succession in conditions that result in the compromising of park values, and is reflected in a shift from primitive to urban conditions (see Dustin and McAvoy 1982). Schreyer and Knopf (1984: 10) have described the succession in the following way:

> The prototypical scenario involves swelling numbers of visitors to a recreation environment, the construction of new facilities and other support services to accommodate them, and the subsequent arrival of a new clientele who are attracted to the support services rather than the original character of the setting.

The long-term implications of this trend have prompted Dustin and McAvoy (1982) to comment on the adaptability of visitors to adjust to extrinsic recreation environments and to caution recreation planners and managers against responding to the needs of these recreationists to the exclusion of those who continue to seek intrinsic settings and activities.

An important dimension of this issue from the visitor perspective is the question of displacement and the perception of recreation substitutes (Anderson and Brown 1984; Manfredo and Anderson 1987; Wyman 1982). Manfredo and Anderson (1987: 85), for example, have suggested that "even if sites appear similar, they may not be perceived to be good substitutes." Site characteristics associated with the resource base have also been identified by Jacob and Schreyer (1981) as a factor in recreation conflict. One of these areas of conflict is centered on resource specificity — the significance attached to using a specific recreation resource for a given experience. Another category of conflict, mode of experience, focuses on the varying expectations of how the natural environment will be perceived (Jacob and Schreyer 1981). An important aspect of conflict is the differing perceptions of the impact of recreational use on the resource base expressed by different recreational and preservation interest groups.

Despite the concern expressed by Sax (1980) and other researchers, different interest groups and constituencies have varying perceptions of park environments and the purpose of protected areas. These differences reveal themselves in a variety of forms.

One area of potential conflict is between park agencies and local communities. Bonnicksen (1983), for example, has alluded to the antagonism that exists in some areas in the United States between park officials pursuing a policy that emphasizes the wilderness value of national parks, and local communities that are more disposed towards development and the ensuing economic benefits. Zube (1986) has also commented on the conflicts between park management goals and local interests. Often underlying these conflicts is the issue of resource protection versus development, not only for recreation or tourism purposes but for a broader range of resource industries. Zube (1986) suggests that different permutations of this tension occur in both developed and less developed countries.

This latter observation draws attention to those studies that have made cross-national and cross-cultural comparisons with regard to the recreation-conservation debate and park policies (Armstrong 1977; Nelson, Needham, and Mann 1978) as well as the differing perceptions of the environmental impact of tourism (Liu, Sheldon, and Var 1987). Of particular significance is the growing interest in the repercussions of park and other protected area policies in developing countries and/or where indigenous peoples and subsistence economies are prevalent (Gardner and Nelson 1980; Hunt 1987; Marsh 1987). Harmon (1987: 149), for example, has focused on the cultural ramifications of introducing national parks, which he contends are "a phenomenon of affluent culture," into developing countries. The problems inherent in addressing the recreation-conservation debate, particularly in the context of developing countries, was a major focus of attention at the World Congress on National Parks in Bali, Indonesia, in 1982 (McNeely and Miller 1984). This important facet of park policy and practice cannot in turn be detached from the intent of the broader principle of sustainable development, which is the central message of the World Conservation Strategy (Allen 1980; Nelson 1987).

Despite the growing interest being focused on recreation and conservation issues in developing countries, considerable research continues to be directed towards the primary role of parks and what may be considered to be appropriate activities in western industrialized countries. White and Schreyer's (1981) study of non-traditional uses of national parks revealed that park visitors had only a generalized conception of national parks and regarded them primarily as places to see and enjoy. Smith and Alderdice (1979), in their study of Point Pelee National Park in Ontario, noted variations in the level of environmental concern expressed by respondents, but that, overall, there was a relatively high level of support for the preservation of the park's natural environment. Dunn (1983) examined the perception of park visitors to Dinosaur and Writing-on-Stone Provincial Parks in Alberta. Her study revealed that the majority of visitors to both of these parks expressed a preservation orientation. On the basis of her findings, Dunn (1983) recommended that, although a planning strategy for such parks should recognize the recreation needs expressed by various visitor groups, the emphasis should be on preservation programs relative to recreation programs. Booth's (1987: 60) study of national parks in New Zealand led her to suggest that "public awareness of national parks strongly influences public perception." Her examination of a sample of Christchurch residents revealed that "43 per cent thought that New Zealand should have national parks for their preservation function and did not recognize a recreation function, while 26 per cent acknowledged recreation but not a preservation role. In comparison, one-fifth noted both preservation and recreation functions" (Booth 1987: 61-62).

The fact that Booth's (1987) results were based on a household survey raises another issue, namely the difference between attitudes held by the public in general and park visitors in particular. A comparison between park visitors in Alberta and Albertans in general with regard to the resource protection and recreation role of provincial parks has shown that, although both groups demonstrated strong support for preservation and conservation, this priority was more evident in the responses from park users (Swinnerton 1987). In addition, the same study showed that park users expressed a higher priority to preservation relative to recreation in comparison to the position taken by the Alberta Department of Recreation and Parks, and that the former group was also more restrictive in the types of activities which it thought were appropriate in provincial parks (Swinnerton 1987).

Recreation and Conservation: Economic Values and Benefits

Another dimension of the recreation-conservation dilemma which is applicable both within and outside park boundaries is an assessment of the economic benefits of outdoor recreation and the preservation value of wilderness and park areas to the public. More particularly, the pressure has been put on those pursuing preservation policies to demonstrate the benefit/cost relationship of non-development and specifically the opportunity cost involved in not developing parks and related reserves for recreation and tourism (Ritchie 1986). Many researchers have responded to this and similar challenges (Adamowicz and Phillips 1983; Entwistle 1987; Peterson and Brown 1986; Peterson, Driver, and Gregory 1988; Peterson and Randall 1984; Peterson and Sorg 1987; Roome 1981; Walsh, Gillman, and Loomis 1982; Walsh, Loomis, and Gillman 1986). Such studies not only provide an additional input into decisions concerning resource preservation and recreation development but they also have an important role to play in those circumstances where natural areas are threatened by various forms of resource development.

Many recreation experiences involve the use of scarce or unique resources such as wildlife and wilderness areas. There is, therefore, increasing recognition of the need to take into consideration the willingness to pay for the preservation value in addition to the consumer surplus from current recreation use. Preservation and recreation values include option values, existence values, and bequest values. Option value is the willingness to pay for the opportunity to use environmental resources for recreation use in the future. Existence value is the willingness to pay for the knowledge that certain resources are protected whether or not they are used. Bequest value is defined as the willingness to pay for the satisfaction of endowing environmental resources to future generations. A study carried out in Colorado by Walsh, Gillman, and Loomis (1982) clearly demonstrated the general population's willingness to pay for the preservation of wilderness resources when option, existence and bequest values are taken into account. With the increasing attention being given to economics in resource planning decisions (Cottrell 1985; Johnston and Emerson 1984), it becomes increasingly important that the measurement of non-market values associated with the preservation of unique or representative natural resources can withstand scrutiny and become accepted indicators of value in the decision making process.

Planning and Management Practices

Research by social scientists reveals that park and recreation agencies have responded in various ways in an attempt to reconcile the tension between recreation and conservation. The dilemma conforms to the multiple objectives in outdoor recreation planning which Hill and Shecter (1978) have suggested incorporate efficiency benefits, distributional equity, preservation of natural areas, and choice.

Forster (1973) has reviewed several of the approaches to reconciling resource protection and use in national parks. He has noted that a master plan (management plan) provides the primary control document for reconciling perpetuation and use and serves to "establish the philosophical basis whereby use is reconciled with the conservation of the physical resources upon which the park is based" (Forster 1973: 76). More recently, Elkin and Smith (1988) have reviewed the application of environmental impact statements for screening potential development, both of a recreation and non-recreation nature within Canada's national parks. Indicative of a more proactive approach in dealing with visitors and park resources in Canada's national parks is the recent introduction of the Visitor Activity Management Process (VAMP). This approach, which systematically complements the traditional resource approach to parks planning and management with consideration of visitor appreciation and enjoyment of the resource, has been critically reviewed by Graham, Nilsen, and Payne (1987).

Within park systems, park classification has traditionally been used as a mechanism for ensuring the sustainability of the system and its components, both in terms of the protection of natural and cultural resources and the provision of recreation opportunities for park visitors, to achieve satisfying experiences commensurate with the limitations of the resource base. Yapp and Barrow (1979) have examined the close relationship between park classification, zoning, and carrying capacity, whereas Cattell's (1977) study of zoning within the Canadian national park system was critical of the environmental considerations upon which zoning decisions were based. Walther (1986) has also been critical of zoning as a technique for resource management, not least because of the ultimate subjectivity and value judgements involved in assessing thresholds for environmental degradation, compatibility, and conflict. However, the underlying premise of zoning involving spatial segregation as a means of ensuring sustainability of the resource base and appropriate levels of use is widely accepted and practised (Swinnerton 1984). The issue of subjectivity and value judgements is also relevant to the concept of carrying capacity. Contributions of the social sciences to this aspect of resource management, and specifically the recreation-conservation dilemma, are discussed in this volume by Stankey and McCool, and Wall. Shelby and Heberlein (1986) have also provided a rigorous assessment of the contribution of social science research to the behavioral aspects of carrying capacity.

Other planning and management approaches to reconciling conservation and recreation use include the recreation opportunity spectrum (ROS) (Driver *et al.* 1987; Manning 1986; United States Department of Agriculture 1982). The Limits of Acceptable Change (LAC) System (Stankey *et al.* 1985) also provides an approach for identifying acceptable conditions and prescribing actions for protecting both social and resource conditions in recreation settings. These and other techniques have been extensively reviewed by Brown, McCool, and Manfredo (1987). Although their focus was on wilderness areas, their findings are appropriate to park environments in general as well as to different settings along the recreation opportunity spectrum.

Other studies by Dustin (1985) and McAvoy and Dustin (1983) have focused on visitor management involving both indirect and direct methods. The latter have argued for the direct management approach on both practical and theoretical grounds. Cole, Peterson, and Lucas (1987) have also provided an overview of problems and solutions relating to the recreation use of wilderness areas. They summarize the strategies and tactics for wilderness management under the following headings: (1) reduce use of the entire wilderness; (2) reduce use of problem areas; (3) modify the location of use within problem areas; (4) modify the timing of use; (5) modify the type of use and visitor behavior; (6) modify visitor expectations; (7) increase the resistance of the resource; and (8) maintain or rehabilitate the resource. Particularly relevant to the focus of this chapter, which has considered recreation and conservation, is the observation made by Brown, McCool, and Manfredo (1987) that wilderness research and management have been evolving to integrate both resource protection and recreation experience strategies.

Not surprisingly, a great deal of the research relating to recreational impact in wilderness and backcountry areas and resultant management practices focuses on the North American situation (see Cole and Schreiner 1981; Hammitt and Cole 1987). Studies from Australia (Birrell and Silverwood 1981) and Britain (Goldsmith 1983; Speight 1973) point to the problem being an increasingly difficult one where the demand for recreation in the countryside continues to increase. MacEwen and MacEwen (1987: 82), in their discussion of providing for recreation in national parks, have noted that "other active pursuits require a greater degree of management, however, if the needs of the different users are to be met and the environment and quiet enjoyment of others are to be safeguarded." The Countryside Commission in Britain has been particularly cognizant of the need for active management in reconciling conservation and recreation interests, as well as accommodating the rights of the private landowner (see also Foster 1987). The Snowdonia land management experiment and management strategies for heritage coastlines illustrate the attention given to this issue (Edwards 1987; MacEwen and MacEwen 1982). The Countryside Commission (1987) in its recent publication *Policies for Enjoying the Countryside* has reiterated once again the importance of countryside management. Many of the techniques being advocated are based on the findings from surveys and management experiments involving social scientists (Phillips and Ashcroft 1987).

CONCLUSION

This review of recreation and conservation has illustrated the wide spectrum of interrelationships which occur between these two constituencies, ranging from mutual support and collaboration to situations of conflict. Although the emphasis throughout, for reasons of expediency, has been on recreation and conservation in park settings, the findings are broadly applicable to the environment in general. Some justification for this emphasis is to be found in Sax (1985a: 207), when he states that "parks are not only, and not even most importantly, resources in their own right, but indicators of the general well-being of the society in its management of natural resources."

There is little doubt that the reconciliation of recreation-conservation interests will continue to be a major dilemma for recreation and park agencies as the demands for recreation opportunities increase and as concern for environmental protection expands. Social scientists have made major contributions in seeking a more realistic understanding of the issues involved and the translation of research into policy and practice. The role of the social sciences in the future is likely to be no less significant, for as Zube (1986: 13) has noted with regard to the growing importance of integrating development and conservation:

> Successful linkages will not be realized without understanding the values, perceptions, attitudes and behaviors of local populations and park resources, and the transactions between these populations and park resources and other groups such as managers and tourists.

References

Adamowicz, W.L. and W.E. Phillips. 1983. "A comparison of extra market benefit evaluation techniques." *Canadian Journal of Agricultural Economics 31:* 401-412.

Alberta Recreation and Parks. 1988. *Foundations for Action: Corporate Aims for the Ministry of Recreation and Parks*. Edmonton: Alberta Recreation and Parks.

Allen, R. 1980. "The World Conservation Strategy: What it is and what it means for parks." *Parks 5(2):* 1-5.

Allin, C.W. 1982. *The Politics of Wilderness Preservation*. Westport: Greenwood Press.

Anderson, D.H. and P.J. Brown. 1984. "The displacement process in recreation." *Journal of Leisure Research 16:* 61-73.

Armstrong, G. 1977. "A comparison of Australian and Canadian approaches to national park planning." In *Leisure and Recreation in Australia*, ed. D. Mercer, pp. 200-208. Malvern: Sorrett.

Artibise, A.F.J. and G.A. Stelter. 1981. "Conservation planning and urban planning: The Canadian Commission of Conservation in historical perspective." In *Planning for Conservation*, ed. R. Kain, pp. 17-36. New York: St. Martin's Press.

Barlowe, R. 1972. *Land Resource Economics: The Economics of Real Property*. 2nd edn. Englewood Cliffs, NJ: Prentice Hall.

Barnett, H.J. and C. Morse. 1963. *Scarcity and Growth: The Economics of Natural Resource Availability*. Baltimore: Johns Hopkins Press.

Bella, L. 1986. "The politics of preservation: Creating national parks in Canada, and in the United States, England and Wales." *Planning Perspectives 1:* 189-206.

Bella, L. 1987. *Parks for Profit*. Montreal: Harvest House.

Birrell, R. and R. Silverwood. 1981. "The social costs of environmental deterioration: The case of the Victorian coastline." In *Outdoor Recreation: Australian Perspectives*, ed. D. Mercer, pp. 118-124. Malvern: Sorrett.

Boden, R. and G. Baines. 1981. "National parks in Australia: Origins and future trends." In *Outdoor Recreation: Australian Perspectives*, ed. D. Mercer, pp. 148-155. Malvern: Sorrett.

Boggs, G.D. Associates Ltd. 1976. *Nova Scotia Parks and Recreation System Plan*. Prepared for Parks and Recreation Division, Department of Lands and Forests, NS. Oakville: G.D. Boggs Associates Ltd.

Bonnicksen, T.M. 1983. "The national park service and local communities: A problem analysis." *Western Wildlands 9(2):* 11-13.

Bonnicksen, T.M. and E.C. Stone. 1985. "Restoring naturalness to national parks." *Environmental Management 9:* 479-486.

Booth, K.L. 1987. "The public's view of national parks." *New Zealand Geographer 43:* 60-65.

Boulding, K.E. 1966. "The economics of the coming spaceship earth." In *Environmental Quality in a Growing Economy*, ed. H. Jarrett, pp. 3-14. Baltimore: Johns Hopkins Press.

Bratton, S.P. 1985. "National park management and values." *Environmental Ethics 7:* 117-133.

Brown, P.J., S.F. McCool, and M.J. Manfredo. 1987. "Evolving concepts and tools for recreation user management in wilderness: A state-of-knowledge review." In *Proceedings: National Wilderness Research Conference: Issues, State-of-Knowledge, Future Directions*, compiler R.C. Lucas, pp. 320-346. General Technical Report INT-220. Ogden: Intermountain Research Station, Forest Service, United States Department of Agriculture.

Brown, T.C. 1984. "The concept of value in resource allocation." *Land Economics 60:* 231-246.

Budowski, G. 1976. "Tourism and environmental conservation: Conflict, coexistence, or symbiosis?" *Environmental Conservation 3:* 27-31.

Butler, R.W. 1986. "Impacts of tourism: divots, depression, and dollars." In *Tourism and the Environment: Conflict or Harmony?* Proceedings of a Symposium, pp. 75-83. Edmonton: Canadian Society of Environmental Biologists, Alberta Chapter.

Buttel, F.H. and O.W. Larson III. 1980. "Whither environmentalism? The future political path of the environmental movement." *Natural Resources Journal 20:* 323-344.

Cattell, K.M. 1977. *An Evaluation of the Canadian National Parks Zoning System.* Ottawa: Parks Canada.

Cherry, G.E. 1985. "Scenic heritage and national parks lobbies and legislation in England and Wales." *Leisure Studies 4:* 127-139.

Christensen, K.S. 1985. "Coping with uncertainty in planning." *Journal of the American Planning Association 51:* 63-73.

Ciriacy-Wantrup, S.V. 1968. *Resource Conservation Economics and Policies.* 3rd edn. Berkeley: University of California, Division of Agricultural Sciences.

Clarke, G.B. 1987. "Tourism and the parks, a global perspective on tourism." In *Heritage for Tomorrow: Canadian Assembly on National Parks and Protected Areas,* eds. R.C. Scace and J.G. Nelson, Volume 5, pp. 26-34. Ottawa: Environment Canada, Parks.

Cole, D.N., M.E. Petersen, and R.C. Lucas. 1987. *Managing Wilderness Recreation Use: Common Problems and Potential Solutions.* General Technical Report INT-230. Ogden: Intermountain Research Station, Forest Service, United States Department of Agriculture.

Cole, D.N. and E.G.S. Schreiner, Compilers. 1981. *Impacts of Backcountry Recreation: Site Management and Rehabilitation: An Annotated Bibliography.* General Technical Report INT-121. Ogden: Intermountain Forest and Range Experiment Station, Forest Service, United States Department of Agriculture.

Coppack, P.M. 1985. "The nature of amenity." *Recreation Research Review 12:* 80-87.

Coppock, J.T. and B.S. Duffield. 1975. *Recreation in the Countryside: A Spatial Analysis.* London: Macmillan.

Corbett, M.R., ed. 1983. *Greenline Parks: Land Conservation Trends for the Eighties and Beyond.* Washington, DC: National Parks and Conservation Association.

Cordell, H.K. and J.C. Hendee. 1982. *Renewable Resources in the United States: Supply, Demand, and Critical Policy Issues.* Washington, DC: American Forestry Association.

Cottrell, T.J., ed. 1985. *Role of Economics in Integrated Resource Management.* Edmonton: Alberta Forestry Lands and Wildlife.

Countryside Commission. 1987. *Policies for Enjoying the Countryside.* CCP234. Cheltenham: Countryside Commission.

Countryside Review Committee. 1979. *Conservation and the Countryside Heritage: A Discussion Paper.* Topic Paper No. 4. London: Her Majesty's Stationery Office.

Curry, N.R. 1985. "Conservation and recreation priorities in the rural landscape." *Landscape Issues 2:* 4-21.

D'Amore, L.J. 1987. "Parks and tourism, a global perspective." In *Heritage for Tomorrow: Canadian Assembly on National Parks and Protected Areas*, eds. R.C. Scace and J.G. Nelson, Volume 5, pp. 14-25. Ottawa: Environment Canada, Parks.

Daniel, T.C., E.H. Zube, and B.L. Driver. 1979. *Assessing Amenity Resource Values.* General Technical Report RM-68. Fort Collins, CO: Rocky Mountain Forest and Range Experiment Station, Forest Service, United States Department of Agriculture.

Dearden, P. 1983. "Tourism and the resource base." In *Tourism in Canada: Selected Issues and Options*, ed. P.E. Murphy, Western Geographical Series, Volume 21, pp. 75-93. Victoria: University of Victoria, Department of Geography.

Denhez, M. 1978. *Heritage Fights Back.* Toronto: Heritage Canada and Fitzhenry and Whiteside.

Devall, B. and G. Sessions. 1984. "The development of natural resources and the integrity of nature." *Environmental Ethics 6:* 293-322.

Devall, B. and G. Sessions. 1985. *Deep Ecology: Living as if Nature Mattered.* Layton: Gibbs M. Smith.

Dolan, R., B.P. Hayden, and G. Soucie. 1978. "Environmental dynamics and resource management in the U.S. national parks." *Environmental Management 2:* 249-258.

Donnelly, P. 1986. "The paradox of parks: Politics of recreational land use before and after the mass trespasses." *Leisure Studies 5:* 211-231.

Dower, M. 1978. "The promise: For whom have we aimed to provide, and how was it to be achieved?" In *Countryside for All? A Review of the Use People Make of the Countryside for Recreation: The Countryside Recreation Research Advisory Group Conference,* pp. 3-19. Cheltenham: Countryside Commission.

Downie, B.K. 1986. "A tourism policy for national parks: A growing need." In *Current Research by Western Canadian Geographers: The University of Victoria Papers, 1985,* ed. E.L. Jackson, pp. 159-175. Vancouver: Tantalus Research.

Downie, B.K. and B. Peart, eds. 1982. *Parks and Tourism Progress or Prostitution.* Victoria: National and Provincial Parks Association of Canada. *H 55 FC 215 P 25 1982*

Driver, B.L., P.J. Brown, G.H. Stankey, and T.G. Gregoire. 1987. "The ROS planning system: evolution, basic concepts, and research needed." *Leisure Sciences 9:* 201-212.

Driver, B.L., R. Nash, and G. Haas, 1987. "Wilderness benefits: A state-of-knowledge review." In *Proceedings: National Wilderness Research Conference: Issues, State-of-knowledge, Future Directions,* compiler R.C. Lucas, pp. 294-319. General Technical Report INT-220. Ogden: Intermountain Research Station, Forest Service, United States Department of Agriculture.

Dunlap, R.E. and R.B. Heffernan. 1975. "Outdoor recreation and environmental concern: An empirical examination." *Rural Sociology 40:* 18-30. *HT 401 R94 PMC*

Dunn, D.R. 1980. "Future leisure resources." In *Recreation and Leisure: Issues in an Era of Change,* eds. T.L. Goodale and P.A. Witt, pp. 115-124. State College, PA: Venture Publishing.

Dunn, E. 1983. "Preservation and recreation orientations of visitors to Dinosaur and Writing-on-Stone Parks, Alberta." M.A. thesis, University of Alberta, Department of Physical Education and Sport Studies.

Dustin, D.L., ed. 1985. *The Management of Human Behavior in Outdoor Recreation Settings.* San Diego: San Diego State University, Institute for Leisure Behavior.

Dustin, D.L. and L.H. McAvoy. 1980. "Hardening national parks." *Environmental Ethics 2:* 39-44.

Dustin, D.L. and L.H. McAvoy. 1982. "The decline and fall of quality recreation opportunities and environments?" *Environmental Ethics 4:* 49-57.

Edwards, J.R. 1987. "The UK heritage coasts: An assessment of the ecological impacts of tourism." *Annals of Tourism Research 14:* 71-87.

Ehrenfeld, D.W. 1976. "The conservation of non-resources." *American Scientist 64:* 648-656.

Elkin, T.L. and P.G.R. Smith. 1988. "What is a good environmental impact statement? Reviewing screening reports from Canada's national parks." *Journal of Environmental Management 26:* 71-89.

Entwistle, E.R. 1987. "Methods of economic evaluation of national parks with reference to New Zealand." *New Zealand Geographer 43:* 79-83, 94.

Everhart, W.C. 1983. *The National Park Service.* Boulder: Westview Press.

Farrell, B.H. and R.W. McLellan. 1987. "Tourism and physical environment research." *Annals of Tourism Research 14:* 1-16.

Ferrario, F.F. 1979. "The evaluation of tourist resources: An applied methodology." *Journal of Travel Research 17(3):* 18-22.

Fitton, M. 1979. "Countryside recreation: The problems of opportunity." *Local Government Studies 5:* 57-89.

Ford-Lloyd, B. and M.T. Jackson. 1986. *Plant Genetic Resources: An Introduction to their Conservation and Use.* London: Edward Arnold.

Forster, R.R. 1973. *Planning for Man and Nature in National Parks: Reconciling Perpetuation and Use.* Morges: International Union for Conservation of Nature and Natural Resources.

Foster, J., ed. 1988. *Protected Landscapes: Summary Proceedings of an International Symposium.* International Union for Conservation of Nature and Natural Resources and the Countryside Commission.

Fuller, S. 1987. "Wilderness: a heritage resource." In *Heritage for Tomorrow: Canadian Assembly on National Parks and Protected Areas*, eds. R.C. Scace and J.G. Nelson, Volume 3, pp. 79-121. Ottawa: Environment Canada, Parks.

Fuller, W.A. 1970. "National parks and nature preservation." In *Canadian Parks in Perspective*, ed. J.G. Nelson, pp. 99-110. Montreal: Harvest House.

Gardner, J.E. and J.G. Nelson. 1980. "Comparing national park and related reserve policy in hinterland areas: Alaska, northern Canada, and northern Australia." *Environmental Conservation 7:* 43-50.

Getz, D.P. 1975. "Integration of the outdoor recreation component in urban centered regional planning." M.A. thesis, Carleton University, Department of Geography.

Gilg, A.W. 1981. "Planning for nature conservation: a struggle for survival and political respectability." In *Planning for Conservation*, ed. R. Kain, pp. 97-116. New York: St. Martin's Press.

Godfrey-Smith, W. 1980. "The value of wilderness: a philosophical approach." In *Wilderness Management in Australia*, eds. R.W. Robertson, P. Helman, and A. Davey, pp. 56-72. Occasional Papers in Recreational Planning, Canberra: Canberra College of Advanced Education, School of Applied Science.

Goldsmith, F.B. 1983. "Ecological effects of visitors and the restoration of damaged areas." In *Conservation in Perspective*, eds. A. Warren and F.B. Goldsmith, pp. 201-214, Chichester: John Wiley and Sons.

SCI   QH   75 C 748   1983

Graham, R., P.W. Nilsen, and R.J. Payne. 1987. "Visitor activity planning and management in Canadian national parks: Marketing within a context of integration." In *Social Science in Natural Resource Management Systems*, eds. M.L. Miller, R.P. Gale, and P.J. Brown, pp. 149-166. Boulder: Westview Press.

Green, B.H. 1981. *Countryside Conservation: The Protection and Management of Amenity Ecosystems*. London: George Allen and Unwin.

Gunn, C.A. 1986. "Philosophical relationships: Conservation, leisure, recreation and tourism." In *A Literature Review, The President's Commission on American Outdoors*, pp. Tourism 1-7. Washington, DC.

Hammitt, W.E. and D.N. Cole. 1987. *Wildland Recreation: Ecology and Management*. New York: John Wiley and Sons.

Harman, D. 1987. "Cultural diversity, human subsistence, and the national park ideal." *Environmental Ethics 9:* 147-158.

Heberlein, T.A. 1988. "Improving interdisciplinary research: Integrating the social and natural sciences." *Society and Natural Resources 1:* 5-16.

Hendee, J.C. and G.H. Stankey. 1973. "Biocentricity in wilderness management." *BioScience 23:* 535-538.

Henwood, W.D. 1982. "The national parks system of New Zealand: Its evolution and prospects." *Park News 18(1):* 3-11.

Henwood, W.D. 1983. "The national parks system of New Zealand: Part II - Its evolution and prospects." *Park News 19(3):* 3-9.

Hill, M. and M. Shecter. 1978. "Multiple objectives in outdoor recreation planning." *Journal of Leisure Research 10:* 126-140.

GV 1 J 86   Educ RR

Howe, C.W. 1979. *Natural Resource Economics: Issues, Analysis and Policy*. New York: John Wiley and Sons.

Hunt, C.D. 1987. "A critique of land use and conservation in the Arctic." In *Arctic Heritage: Proceedings of a Symposium*, eds. J.G. Nelson, R. Needham, and L. Norton, pp. 329-334. Ottawa: Association of Canadian Universities for Northern Studies.

INNTREC Group Ltd. and E.D.A. Collaborative Inc. 1980. *Improving Amenities in Downtown Edmonton*. Edmonton: INNTREC Group Ltd. and E.D.A. Collaborative Inc.

Inskeep, E. 1987. "Environmental planning for tourism." *Annals of Tourism Research 14:* 118-135.

Irland, L.C. and T. Rumpf. 1980. "Trends in land and water available for outdoor recreation." In *Proceedings 1980 National Outdoor Recreation Trends Symposium*. Volume 1, pp. 77-87. General Technical Report NE-57. Broomall: Northeastern Forest Experiment Station, Forest Service, United States Department of Agriculture.

Ise, J. 1961. *Our National Park Policy: A Critical History*. Baltimore: Johns Hopkins Press.

Ittner, R., D.R. Potter, J.K. Agee, and S. Anschell, eds. 1979. *Recreational Impact on Wildlands: Conference Proceedings.* Seattle: Forest Service, United States Department of Agriculture, National Park Service, United States Department of the Interior.

Jackson, E.L. 1986. "Outdoor recreation participation and attitude in the environment." *Leisure Studies 5:* 1-23.

Jackson, E.L. 1987. "Outdoor recreation participation and views on resource development and preservation." *Leisure Sciences 9:* 235-250.

Jacob, G.R. and R. Schreyer. 1980. "Conflict in outdoor recreation: A theoretical perspective." *Journal of Leisure Research 12:* 368-380.

Jarrett, M., ed. 1958. *Perspectives on Conservation: Essays on America's Natural Resources.* Baltimore: Johns Hopkins Press.

Johnson, W.A. 1971. *Public Parks on Private Land in England and Wales.* Baltimore: Johns Hopkins Press.

Johnston, G.M. and P.M. Emerson, eds. 1984. *Public Lands and the U.S. Economy: Balancing Conservation and Development.* Boulder: Westview Press.

Jubenville, A., B.W. Twight, and R.H. Becker. 1987. *Outdoor Recreation Management: Theory and Application.* State College, PA: Venture Publishing.

Klosterman, R.E. 1983. "Fact and value in planning." *Journal of the American Planning Association 49:* 216-225.

Lausche, B. 1980. *Guidelines for Protected Areas Legislation.* IUCN Environmental Policy and Law Paper No. 16. Gland: International Union for Conservation of Nature and Natural Resources.

Lemons, J. 1986. "Research in national parks." *The Environmental Professional 8:* 127-137.

Lemons, J. 1987. "United States' national park management: Values, policy and possible hints for others." *Environmental Conservation 14:* 328-340.

Lemons, J. and D. Stout. 1982. "National parks legislative mandate in the United States of America." *Environmental Management 6:* 199-207.

Lemons, J. and D. Stout. 1984. "A reinterpretation of national park legislation." *Environmental Law 15:* 41-65.

Leopold, A. 1949. *A Sand County Almanac: With Essays on Conservation from Round River.* New York: Oxford University Press.

Liu, J.C., P.J. Sheldon, and T. Var. 1987. "Resident perception of the environmental impacts of tourism." *Annals of Tourism Research 14:* 17-37.

Livingston, J.A. 1981. *The Fallacy of Wildlife Conservation.* Toronto: McLelland and Stewart.

Lucas, P.H.C. 1984. "How protected areas can help meet society's evolving needs." In *National Parks, Conservation and Development: The Role of Protected Areas in Sustaining Society,* eds. J.A. McNeely and K.R. Miller, pp. 72-77. Washington, DC: Smithsonian Institution Press.

Lucas, R.C. (Compiler). 1986. *Proceedings: National Wilderness Research Conference: Current Research.* General Technical Report INT-212. Ogden: Intermountain Research Station, Forest Service, United States Department of Agriculture.

MacEwen, A. and M. MacEwen. 1982. *National Parks: Conservation or Cosmetics?* London: George Allen and Unwin.

MacEwen, A. and M. MacEwen. 1987. *Greenprints for the Countryside? The Story of Britain's National Parks.* London: George Allen and Unwin.

Machlis, G.E. and D.L. Tichnell. 1985. *The State of the World's Parks: An International Assessment for Resource Management, Policy, and Research.* Boulder, CO: Westview Press.

Manfredo, M.J. and D. Anderson. 1987. "The influence of activity importance and similarity on perception of recreation substitutes." *Leisure Sciences 9:* 77-86.

Manning, R.E. 1986. *Studies in Outdoor Recreation: A Review and Synthesis of the Social Science Literature in Outdoor Recreation.* Corvallis: Oregon State University Press.

Marsh, J.S. 1983. "Canada's parks and tourism: a problematic relationship." In *Tourism in Canada: Selected Issues and Options*, ed. P.E. Murphy. Western Geographical Series, Volume 21, pp. 271-307. Victoria: University of Victoria, Department of Geography.

Marsh, J.S. 1987. "Tourism and conservation: Case studies in the Canadian north." In *Arctic Heritage: Proceedings of a Symposium*, eds. J.G. Nelson, R. Needham, and L. Norton, pp. 298-322. Ottawa: Association of Canadian Universities for Northern Studies.

Mason, A.G. 1988. "The development of Alberta's provincial parks." M.A. thesis, University of Alberta, Department of Recreation and Leisure Studies.

Mathieson, A. and G. Wall. 1982. *Tourism: Economic, Physical and Social Impacts.* London: Longman.

McAvoy, L.H. and D.L. Dustin. 1983. "Indirect versus direct regulation of recreation behavior." *Journal of Park and Recreation Administration* 1: 12-17.

McCool, S.F. 1983. "The national parks in post-industrial America." *Western Wildlands 9(2):* 14-19.

McNeely, J.A. and K.R. Miller, eds. 1984. *National Parks, Conservation and Development: The Role of Protected Areas in Sustaining Society.* Washington,DC: Smithsonian Institution Press.

Melnick, R.S. 1983. "Protecting rural cultural landscapes: Finding value in the countryside." *Landscape Journal 2:* 85-97.

Miller, M.L., R.P. Gale, and P.J. Brown, eds. 1987. *Social Science in Natural Resource Management Systems.* Boulder, CO: Westview Press.

Murphy, P.E. 1985. *Tourism: A Community Approach.* New York: Methuen.

Nash, R., ed. 1968. *The American Environment: Readings in the History of Conservation.* Reading: Addison-Wesley.

Nash, R. 1982. *Wilderness and the American Mind.* 3rd edn. New Haven, CT: Yale University Press.

Nelson, J.G. 1987. "National parks and protected areas, national conservation strategies and sustainable development." *Geoforum 18:* 291-319.

Nelson, J.G. and J.C. Day. 1985. "Wildlands management of Point Pelee, Rondeau, and Long Point peninsulas." *Environments 17(3):* 65-79.

Nelson, J.G., R.D. Needham, and D.L. Mann, eds. 1978. *International Experience with National Parks and Related Reserves.* Department of Geography Publication Series No. 12. Waterloo: University of Waterloo.

Nelson, J.G., R.C. Scace, B. Sadler, G.H. Lemieux, and S. Washington. 1986. "Heritage issues in Canada: the second threshold, 1985-2085: the national issues paper." In *Heritage for Tomorrow: Canadian Assembly on National Parks and Protected Areas,* eds. R.C. Scace and J.G. Nelson, Volume 1, pp. 13-53. Ottawa: Environment Canada, Parks.

Nelson, R.J. 1979. "Ethics and environmental decision making." *Environmental Ethics 1:* 263-278.

O'Riordan, T. 1971. *Perspectives on Resource Management.* London: Pion.

O'Riordan, T. 1981. *Environmentalism.* 2nd edn. London: Pion.

Parks Canada. 1979. *Parks Canada Policy.* Ottawa: Parks Canada.

Parks Canada 1982. *National Park Management Planning Process Manual.* Ottawa: Parks Canada.

Passmore, R.C. 1966. "Provincial parks in Canada." *Canadian Audubon 28:* 150-156.

Pearce, D.G. 1985. "Tourism and environmental research: A review." *International Journal of Environmental Studies 25:* 247-255.

Pearsall, S.H. 1984. "*In absentia* benefits of nature preserves: A review." *Environmental Conservation 11:* 3-10.

QH 540 E62   SCf

Perloff, H.S. 1969. "A framework for dealing with the urban environment: introductory statement." In *The Quality of the Urban Environment, Essays on "New Resources" in an Urban Age,* ed. H.S. Perloff, pp. 3-31. Baltimore: Johns Hopkins Press.

Peterson, G.L. and T.C. Brown. 1986. "The economic benefits of outdoor recreation." In *A Literature Review, The President's Commission on Americans Outdoors,* pp. Values 11-18. Washington, DC.

Peterson, G.L., B.L. Driver, and R. Gregory, eds. 1988. *Amenity Resource Valuation: Integrating Economics with Other Disciplines.* State College, PA: Venture Publishing.

Peterson, G.L. and A. Randall. 1984. *Valuation of Wildland Resource Benefits.* Boulder: Westview Press.

Peterson, G.L. and C.F. Sorg, eds. 1987. *Toward the Measurement of Total Economic Value.* General Technical Report RM-148 Fort Collins: Rocky Mountain Forest and Range Experiment Station, Forest Service, United States Department of Agriculture.

Phillips, A. and P. Ashcroft. 1987. "The impact of research in countryside recreation policy development." *Leisure Studies 6:* 315-328.

Phillips, A. and M. Roberts. 1973. "The recreation and amenity value of the countryside." *Journal of Agricultural Economics 24:* 85-97.

Pigram, J.J.J. 1976. "The resource base for outdoor recreation." *Journal of Environmental Management 4:* 71-80.

Pigram, J.J.J. 1983. "Rural recreation space: alternatives to national parks." *Leisure Studies 2:* 19-30.

Poore, D. 1982. "The national parks' role in the World Conservation Strategy." In *1982 National Parks Conference: Report of Proceedings*, pp. 25-27. Buxton: Peak Park Joint Planning Board.

Prescott-Allen, R. and C. Prescott-Allen. 1984. "Park your genes: protected areas as in situ genebanks for the maintenance of wild genetic resources." In *National Parks, Conservation and Development: The Role of Protected Areas in Sustaining Society*, eds. J.A. McNeely and K.R. Miller, pp. 634-638. Washington, DC: Smithsonian Institution Press.

Rees, J. 1985. *Natural Resources: Allocation, Economics and Policy.* London: Methuen.

Reid, R.A. 1979. "The role of national parks in nature preservation." In *The Canadian National Parks: Today and Tomorrow Conference II*, eds. J.G. Nelson, R.D. Needham, S.H. Nelson, and R.C. Scace, Volume 1, pp. 105-113. Waterloo: University of Waterloo, Faculty of Environmental Studies.

Ritchie, J.R.B. 1986. "The tourist as an environmentalist: Managerial and financial implications." In *Tourism and the Environment: Conflict or Harmony? Proceedings of a Symposium*, pp. 103-110. Edmonton: Canadian Society of Environmental Biologists, Alberta Chapter.

SCI G155 A1 7718 1986

Rolston, H. 1985. "Valuing wildlands." *Environmental Ethics 7:* 23-48.

Rolston, H. 1986. "Beyond recreational value: The greater outdoors preservation-related and environmental benefits." In *A Literature Review, The President's Commission on Americans Outdoors*, pp. Values 103-113. Washington, DC.

Romeril, M. 1985. "Tourism and the environment: Towards a symbiotic relationship." *International Journal of Environmental Studies* 25: 215-218.

SCI S 900 I62

Roome, N. 1981. *The Evaluation of Nature Conservation Benefits.* Gloucestershire Papers in Local and Rural Planning, No. 10. Gloucester: Gloucestershire College of Arts and Technology, Department of Town and Country Planning.

Rowe, S. 1982. "Why preserve wild areas and species." *Park News 18(3):* 12-15.

Runte, A. 1987. *National Parks: The American Experience.* 2nd edn. Lincoln, NE: University of Nebraska Press.

Russell, M. 1979. "Conflicting perceptions of energy's future role." In *Energy in America's Future: The Choice Before Us*, eds. S.H. Schurr, J. Darmstadter, W. Ramsay, H. Perry, and M. Russell, pp. 401-408. Baltimore: Johns Hopkins Press.

Sandford, Lord (Chairman). 1974. *Report of the National Park Policy Review Committee.* London: Her Majesty's Stationery Office.

Sax, J.L. 1976. "America's national parks: Their principles, purposes, and prospects." *Natural History 85(8):* 57-88.

Sax, J.L. 1980. *Mountains Without Handrails: Reflections on the National Parks.* Ann Arbor: University of Michigan Press.

Sax, J.L. 1985a. "A rain of troubles: The need for a new perspective on park protection." In *Parks in British Columbia: Emerging Realities*, ed. P.J. Dooling, pp. 205-214. Vancouver: University of British Columbia, Department of Forest Resources Management.

Sax, J.L. 1985b. "An American perspective." In *Views of the Green*, ed. P.L. Pritchard, pp. 4-12. Washington, DC: National Parks and Conservation Association.

Schauman, S. 1979. "The countryside visual resource." In *Proceedings of Our National Landscape: A Conference on Applied Techniques for Analysis and Management of the Visual Resource*, eds. G.H. Elsner and R.C. Smardon, pp. 48-54. General Technical Report PSW-35. Berkeley: Forest Service, United States Department of Agriculture.

Schreyer, R. and R.C. Knopf. 1984. "The dynamics of change in outdoor recreation environments: Some equity issues." *Journal of Park and Recreation Administration 2:* 9-19.

Seguire, S., ed. 1986. *Proceedings International Congress on Trail and River Recreation.* Vancouver: Outdoor Recreation Council of British Columbia.

Shaw, W.W. and E.H. Zube, eds. 1980. *Wildlife Values.* Tuscon, AZ: University of Arizona, Centre for Assessment of Noncommodity Natural Resource Values.

Sheail, J. 1975. "The concept of national parks in Great Britain 1900-1950." *Transactions of the Institute of British Geographers 66:* 41-56.

Sheail, J. 1984. "Nature reserves, national parks, and post-war reconstruction in Britain." *Environmental Conservation 11:* 29-34.

Shelby, B. and T.A. Heberlein. 1986. *Carrying Capacity in Recreation Settings.* Corvallis, OR: Oregon State University Press.

Simeon, R. 1976. "Studying public policy." *Canadian Journal of Political Science 9:* 548-580.

Smith, G.C. and A. Alderdice. 1979. "Public responses to national park environmental policy." *Environment and Behavior 11:* 329-350.

Smith, S.L.J. 1983. *Recreation Geography.* London: Longman.

Speight, M.C.D. 1973. *Outdoor Recreation and its Ecological Effects: A Bibliography and Review.* Discussion Papers in Conservation No. 4. London: University College.

Sproule-Jones. M. 1982. "Public choice theory and natural resources: Methodological explication and critique." *American Political Science Review 76:* 790-804.

Stankey, G.H. 1982a. "Philosophy, science and management: The fundamentals of natural area conservation." Paper presented at the Natural Area Management National Workshop Tasmania, Royal Australian Institute of Parks and Recreation, National Parks and Wildlife Service, Tasmania.

Stankey, G.H. 1982b. "The role of management in wilderness and natural-area preservation." *Environmental Conservation 9:* 149-155.

Stankey, G.H., D.N. Cole, R.C. Lucas, M.E. Petersen, and S.S. Frissell. 1985. *The Limits of Acceptable Change (LAC) System for Wilderness Planning.* General Technical Report INT-176. Ogden: Intermountain Research Station, Forest Service, United States Department of Agriculture.

Stone, E.C. 1965. "Preserving vegetation in park and wilderness." *Science 150:* 1261-1267.

Swinnerton, G.S. 1974. "Land classification and environmental planning." In *Land Capability Classification.* Technical Bulletin 30, pp. 109-124. Ministry of Agriculture, Fisheries and Food. London: Her Majesty's Stationery Office.

Swinnerton, G.S. 1982. *Recreation on Agricultural Land in Alberta.* Edmonton: Environment Council of Alberta.

Swinnerton, G.S. 1984. *Conservation in Practice in Alberta: An Examination of the Role of Alberta Recreation and Parks.* Prepared for Alberta Recreation and Parks. Edmonton: University of Alberta, Department of Recreation and Leisure Studies.

Swinnerton, G.S. 1985. "Some reflections on Heritage for Tomorrow: Canadian Assembly on National Parks and Protected Areas." *Park News 21(3):* 31-32.

Swinnerton, G.S. 1987. "The role of Alberta's provincial parks: A government and park visitor perspective." Paper presented at the Fifth Canadian Congress on Leisure Research, Dalhousie University, Halifax, NS.

Swinnerton, G.S. 1988. "Managing natural resources in parks for recreation and conservation: Issues and prospects." Paper presented at the 27th Annual Conference of the Federal-Provincial Parks Council, Québec City, Québec.

Tallmadge, J. 1981. "Saying YOU to the land." *Environmental Ethics 3:* 351-363.

Turner, A. 1981. "National parks and pressure groups in New South Wales." In *Outdoor Recreation: Australian Perspectives*, ed. D. Mercer, pp. 156-169. Malvern: Sorrett.

Turner, R.D. and W.E. Rees. 1973. "A comparative study of parks policy in Canada and the United States." *Nature Canada 2:* 31-36.

Tuttle, R.W. 1980. "The American countryside: A visual resource to value." *Agricultural Engineering 61(9):* 14-16.

United States Department of Agriculture. 1982. *ROS Users Guide.* Washington, DC: United States Department of Agriculture, Forest Service.

United States Department of the Interior. 1978. *Management Policies.* Washington, DC: United States Department of the Interior, National Park Service.

United States Department of the Interior. 1980. *State of the Parks - 1980: A Report to the Congress.* Washington, DC: United States Department of the Interior, National Park Service.

Van Liere, K.D. and F.P. Noe. 1981. "Outdoor recreation and environmental attitudes: Further examination of the Dunlap-Heffernan thesis." *Rural Sociology 46:* 503-513.

Wall, G. 1981. "Research in Canadian recreational planning and management." In *Canadian Resource Policies: Problems and Prospects*, eds. B. Mitchell and W.R.D. Sewell, pp. 233-261. Toronto: Methuen.

Wall, G. and J.S. Marsh, eds. 1982. *Recreational Land Use: Perspectives on its Evolution in Canada.* Ottawa: Carleton University Press.

Wall, G. and C. Wright. 1977. *The Environmental Impact of Outdoor Recreation.* Waterloo: University of Waterloo, Department of Geography.

Walsh, R.G., R.A. Gillman, and J.B. Loomis. 1982. *Wilderness Resource Economics: Recreation Use and Preservation Values.* Denver, CO: American Wilderness Alliance.

Walsh, R.G., J.B. Loomis, and R.A. Gillman. 1986. "How much wilderness to protect?" In *Proceedings - National Wilderness Research Conference: Current Research*, compiler R.C. Lucas, pp. 370-376. General Technical Report INT-212. Ogden: Intermountain Research Station, Forest Service, United States Department of Agriculture.

Walther, P. 1986. "The meaning of zoning in the management of natural resource lands." *Journal of Environmental Management 22:* 331-343.

Ward, E.N. 1986. *Heritage Conservation - the Built Environment.* Working Paper No. 44. Ottawa: Environment Canada, Lands Directorate.

Ward, E.N. and B. Killham, 1987. *Heritage Conservation - the Natural Environment.* Waterloo: University of Waterloo, Heritage Resources Centre.

Warren, A. and F.B. Goldsmith, eds. 1983. *Conservation in Perspective.* Chichester: John Wiley and Sons.

Waters, S.R. 1966. "The American tourist." *Annals of the American Academy of Political and Social Sciences 368:* 109-118.

Webb, C. 1987. *Reserves for Nature.* Edmonton: Environment Council of Alberta.

Weiler, J. 1984. "Reusing our working past for recreation and tourism." *Recreation Canada 42(2):* 36-40.

White, P.S. and S.P. Bratton, 1980. "After preservation: Philosophical and practical problems of change." *Biological Conservation 4:* 241-255.

White, R.G. and R. Schreyer. 1981. "Nontraditional uses of the national parks." *Leisure Sciences 4:* 325-341.

Wight, P. 1988. *Tourism in Alberta.* Edmonton: Environment Council of Alberta.

Wilkes, B. 1979. "The myth of the non-consumptive user." *Park News 15(1):* 16-21.

Wyman, M. 1982. "Substitutability of recreation experience." *Leisure Studies* *1:* 277-293.

Yapp, G.A. and G.C. Barrow. 1979. "Zonation and carrying capacity estimates in Canadian park planning." *Biological Conservation 15:* 191-206.

Zimmerman, E.W. 1951. *World Resources and Industries.* Revised edn. New York: Harper.

Zube, E.H. 1986. "Local and extra-local perceptions of national parks and protected areas." *Landscape and Urban Planning 13:* 11-17.

TOURISM AND TOURISM RESEARCH

Richard W. Butler

INTRODUCTION

It is, perhaps, at first surprising that tourism should be treated as a separate aspect of leisure and recreation, comparable to environmental impact or carrying capacity, because tourism is really a phenomenon as individual as leisure or recreation in its own right. However, the leisure and recreation literature makes scant reference to tourism, despite the fact that many of the elements found in and influencing leisure and recreation apply equally to tourism. Although many of the phenomena studied are essentially the same for both tourism and leisure and recreation — e.g. motivations, facilities, capacity, forecasts, and impacts — the methodologies used, the examples cited, and the individuals involved in the research are often quite different. The same set of disciplines is involved, however, and the relative lack of cross-fertilization between researchers is a major disappointment and, more seriously, a disadvantage to the development of research in both areas.

This chapter reviews the development of, and major issues in, tourism and tourism research in the context of the social sciences. It begins with a discussion of definitions and the context in which tourism falls. It then discusses the origins and development of tourism and its major patterns. This is followed by an examination of the place of tourism in society, the nature of tourism as a business, and the positive and negative impacts that result from its development. A short review of the social, cultural, and environmental aspects of tourism leads to a discussion of the problems involved in planning and controlling this activity. The chapter concludes with a commentary on future research needs and implications.

DEFINITION AND CONTEXT

Tourism, like leisure and recreation, suffers from problems of definition. Implicit in most definitions of tourism is the assumption, if not the requirement, that tourism is something which can only take place during leisure time, or when a person is "at leisure." As tourism also implies travel, and therefore some activity on behalf of the tourist, then it is logically a part of both leisure and recreation, if the latter can be defined as an activity engaged in during leisure time on a voluntary basis for the purpose of enjoyment. The interrelationships among leisure, recreation, and tourism are strong and interdependent ones. The need to consider these interrelationships was recognized with the publication, in 1987, of a special issue of the *Annals of Tourism Research*, and, as the editor of that issue noted, the papers raised "more questions than they answered" (Fedler 1987: 311). The reader is referred, in particular, to papers by Mannell and Iso-Ahola (1987) and Colton (1987) for a more detailed discussion of specific issues.

Mieczkowski (1981), in a deceptively simple diagram, has illustrated the relative place and relationship of each of these elements to the others (Figure 1). The relationship implied is that tourism is an aspect of recreation, which in turn is a component of leisure. While this says something about tourism, it does not give the whole picture; nor does it explain the multitude of definitions of tourism which exist in the literature. Leiper (1979), for example, discusses the definitional aspects of tourism, grouping them into economic, technical, and holistic, but finds major drawbacks to all of these approaches, and suggests that it could be argued that "a definition suitable for general tourism scholarship has not yet emerged." Although his article was written almost a decade ago, there is considerable temptation to agree with his statement today. Indeed, the definition he quotes from the *Oxford English Dictionary* — that tourism is "the theory and practice of touring, travelling for pleasure" (Leiper 1979: 391) — is attractive because of its simplicity, despite its academic inadequacies.

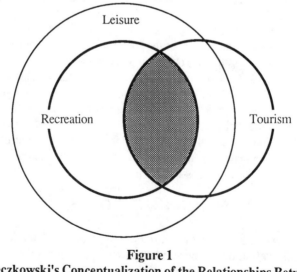

Figure 1
Mieczkowski's Conceptualization of the Relationships Between
Leisure, Recreation, and Tourism
(Source: Mieczkowski 1981: 189)

There are primarily two factors that cause the definitional problems in tourism studies, although other elements are also involved. First and foremost is the multidisciplinary nature of the topic. Any subject which attracts researchers in as many fields as tourism does is bound to face this problem. Anthropologists, biologists, business-managers, economists, geographers, political scientists, psychologists, and sociologists take widely differing approaches to research, using very different methodologies and concepts. To derive a definition which is generally acceptable to all researchers in a single discipline is difficult; to find one acceptable to all disciplines, as well as multidisciplinary and interdisciplinary fields, is virtually impossible. Cohen (1979: 31) has recognized this problem; his conclusion, although specifically focused on the sociology of tourism, has relevance to the field as a whole:

> The complexity and heterogeneity of the field of tourism suggests that there is no point in searching for THE theoretical approach to the study of tourism, just as there is no point in searching for THE conceptualization of the tourist. Rather, a pluralistic and even eclectic research strategy is advocated. The many different empirical problems can only be tackled by utilizing a wide range of concepts and research instruments.... The most fruitful work ... will be accomplished by a skillful blending of different approaches for the elucidation of specific problems.

Second, tourism is still a relatively recent field of study in most disciplines, and has yet to be accepted as a discipline or field of study in its own right. The recency of the academic study of tourism has been noted by several authors, along with the disdain which an apparently "frivolous" subject generates among less enlightened colleagues (e.g. Mathews 1983; Mitchell 1979; Wolfe 1964; and Cooper's chapter, this volume). Research on leisure and recreation predates that on tourism, and yet there is not universal agreement on definitions of leisure and recreation across all disciplines and fields studying those topics. Fedler concludes his introduction to the special issue of the *Annals of Tourism Research* on the interrelationship of leisure, recreation, and tourism by noting:

> the definitional problems of leisure, recreation, and tourism have undoubtedly hindered many attempts at clarifying and specifying any theoretical relationships between the three concepts. It may well be that these definitional problems have been grounded by an inadequate understanding of the forms, functions and processes involved with the Leisure Recreation Tourism experiences (Fedler 1987: 313).

Despite the relatively short period during which tourism has been regarded as an appropriate subject for serious study, considerable progress has been made. The appearance of two major interdisciplinary journals in the decade from 1974, plus a large and increasing number of papers, research reports and books on the subject have done much to further the quality of the study. Both the *Annals of Tourism Research* and *Tourism Management*, along with the earlier established *Tourist Review*, are firmly multidisciplinary in orientation. Perhaps more than any single publication, the *Annals* has furthered the dialogue among researchers in different disciplines by its editorial policy of having associate editors for different disciplines, and by publishing special issues on both thematic topics, e.g. "Evolution of Tourism" (1985) and disciplinary ones, e.g. "Political Science and Tourism" (1983).

Books on tourism have appeared in much greater numbers in the last decade than ever before. Apart from a few noticeable exceptions, such as Ogilvie's *The Tourist Movement*, which was published in 1933, little of real significance appeared before the 1970s. In that decade, however, the first books to challenge the previously positive image of tourism were published. Bryden (1973), MacCannell (1973), Turner and Ash (1975), and Young (1973), to note only a few, challenged the assumptions of the universal benefits of tourism. Later publications, such as those by Gunn (1979), Mathieson and Wall (1982), Pearce (1982), Murphy (1985), and Pearce (1981, 1987), have focused attention on such topics as planning, impacts, perceptions, and development issues. The trend has been from a simple criticism of tourism, to one which includes identification, examination, and proposed amelioration and mitigation of negative effects. The topics studied have been broadened, and have become more focused, moving from global discussions to the identification of particular problems and remedial actions in specific areas, while recognizing, in the process, the commonality of many of the issues. Thus, the lack of general agreement on methodologies, concepts and definitions notwithstanding, research on tourism has advanced a considerable way in what may be regarded as the first quarter century or so of its existence as a topic for serious academic inquiry.

THE ORIGINS AND DEVELOPMENT OF TOURISM

There is little disagreement that tourism as a term owes its origin to the participants in the Grand Tour of the 17th and 18th Centuries. Although the direct influences of this phenomenon are few in number today, epitomized perhaps by "Grand Hotels" and the initials G.T. on automobiles, the indirect influences are quite profound, and evidence of them can be found in much present-day tourist behavior. Considering its importance in influencing 20th-Century tourism, studies of the Grand Tour, its origins, its participants, and its effects have been few and often superficial. One exception is the work of Towner (1985), a researcher who has identified and analyzed original data from participants on the Tour and drawn some interesting conclusions.

While the first tourists were drawn from a very limited and privileged segment of English society, during the two centuries that it remained in its classic form the Tour showed clearly the fact that "mass followed class"; the Tour did not escape the democratization process that leisure in general has followed from time immemorial. Travel away from home clearly predates the Grand Tour. The ancient Mesopotamians had summer palaces, Kublai Khan his pleasure dome, and the Roman elite their villas on the hills surrounding Rome. The idea of seasonal migration for comfort (then to cooler areas from hotter ones), for pursuit of sport, and for pursuit of social activities, predates written records, although for most of human history such migration has been confined to the privileged groups in society.

The significance of the Grand Tour as the origin of tourism as we know it today lies in three important respects. The first is in the places made popular by the Tour, which several centuries later are still popular tourist destinations. This is, in part, because of the second factor, the creation of services and facilities to serve the increasing numbers of tourists travelling — in particular accommodations, transportation facilities, and guide services. The third, and perhaps most revealing, element is in the continuation of the pattern of behavior established by the first tourists. Hibbert (1969: 20) quotes the instructions given to a potential tourist in the 18th Century:

> When settling down to stay in any place the Tourist must remember that he has come abroad to gain knowledge and not to enjoy himself in idleness. He must make an effort not only to perfect his mastery of the language, but to learn all he can about the history, geography, trade, climate, crops, minerals, food, clothes, customs, fauna, flora, politics, laws, art and military fortifications of the district. On entering a strange town he should at once ascend the highest steeple to gain a good view of it and pick out the buildings worthy of further inspection.... Having inspected these buildings he must make drawings of them, take the necessary measurements, endeavour to learn how any curious details were executed, list their valuable contents and striking furnishings, constantly bearing in mind his future as inheritor and patron.... He must also form a collection of prints and drawings of the places and buildings and works of art he has seen, and of specimens of unusual plants, stones or whatever other natural phenomena struck his fancy.... He must avoid his own countrymen, so far as possible, choosing to pass his time with the polite society of the country he is visiting.

The comparisons of such behavior with present day tourist activities are obvious. While contemporary tourists rarely sketch and are unlikely to be able to commission their own works of art, they take photographs, and buy postcards, cheap art, and models of significant features on a scale inconceivable even fifty years ago. A walk around world-famous features, such as the Tower of London, the Leaning Tower of Pisa, the Grand Canyon, or Banff National Park allows one the opportunity to acquire more instant art, plaster of Paris, plastic, rock fragments, and miniature Mounties than one could use in several lifetimes. While the majority of current tourists may not want to learn all the languages and customs of the local population of the place they are visiting, many are at least willing to eat local food (or internationalized versions of it), and certainly to scale the highest buildings, whether they be the Eiffel Tower, the C.N. Tower in Toronto, or the Pyramids of Egypt.

The principal appeal and purpose of tourism, therefore, appears to have changed relatively little in basic terms: it is to experience something different from the normal pattern of existence. What has changed enormously is how this experience is obtained, where it is obtained, and by whom. While nowhere near as universal as leisure and recreation, tourism is now engaged in by vast numbers of people, most of whom do so on a regular basis.

The major growth in numbers participating began in the 19th Century as a result of improved access to mass transportation, especially in the form of the railway and steamships, increased affluence, the introduction of formal holidays with pay, and entrepreneurship. While tourism could not have grown without facilities and services, such as accommodations and entertainments, the role of entrepreneurs in demonstrating and developing the potential market was crucial; yet it has received little attention. Of major significance is the effort of Thomas Cook, who succeeded in revolutionizing tourism with the introduction of package tours (Swinglehurst 1982). Working with an idealistic and welfare focus, Cook invented mass tourism as distinct from individual tourism (albeit involving large numbers of people), which had characterized tourism until the middle of the 19th Century. The story of Cook, his tour innovations, the creation of the first travel agencies, of travellers cheques and international rental agencies, warrants much more attention than it has been given.

Cook was a major force in the democratization of tourism (Graburn 1983: 3), revealing as he did that the attractions of travel and tourism appear to be common to almost all people. The pattern of tourism since the 1850s has witnessed a tremendous expansion in volume and vast technological change, particularly with the appearance of, first, the automobile and, later, the aircraft, but relatively little change in basic purpose and behavior. Perhaps the only true change in tourism in the last century has been the large increase in travel to warmer climes in the winter, although even that is not entirely new and was well established at Nice and other Mediterranean resorts in the mid-19th Century (Pearce 1979).

PATTERNS OF TOURISM

To say that tourism is dynamic is to state a truism of outstanding dimensions. There is no element of tourism which does not change over time — although, paradoxically, there is considerable inertia and stability within the patterns displayed. One of the earliest patterns of tourism to emerge was the movement of people to large bodies of water, most frequently the ocean. Beginning with the stagecoach, followed by the steamship (Wall 1977), this vacation activity increased dramatically with the advent of the railway. The links between railway companies and resort development are common and well documented in both Britain and North America (Hart 1983; Stansfield 1972). The patterns of tourism which were established by the mid-19th Century are still in evidence in Britain today, although the automobile and the jet aircraft have given many tourists wider horizons, as well as the means to reach them.

Of the patterns that have emerged in the last century, that of sun-seeking tourism is the predominant one. The desire to obtain sunshine on a vacation has dominated travel in post-war Europe and has seen Spain replace France as the dominant summer destination of northern Europeans. The Mediterranean pleasure periphery has expanded from France to Spain, and to Italy, to Greece and Malta, and most recently to North Africa. Expansion into Libya and the Middle East would almost certainly have occurred on a large scale by now had not political instability deterred it.

On a global scale the winter search for the sun has resulted in a spectacular growth in tourism in the Western hemisphere, initially in Florida, and then in the Caribbean (Weaver 1983), both by air travel and by cruise ship. In fact, this area has now overtaken the Mediterranean in popularity for cruising (Lawton and Butler 1987). Heliotropic tourism has resulted in the increasing popularity of the South Pacific and the Indian Ocean islands also. While tourists still travel in increasing numbers to temperate destinations, such as Northern Europe and North America, to visit heritage areas and friends and relatives, to experience new cultures, and for a host of other reasons, "sunlust" travel has remained a dominant feature of the patterns of tourism in the last quarter century.

Research on the patterns of tourism, particularly those of a spatial nature, has traditionally been the realm of geographers. Examples include early work on the reciprocity of tourism (Williams and Zelinsky 1970); on patterns of resort development and morphology (Stansfield 1972); on global patterns (Matley 1976); and on regional patterns (Christaller 1963). Geographical research has also been a major component in studies of the process of tourism development, as well as the spatial pattern of that development — for example, in the writings of Pearce (1981, 1987), Murphy (1985), and Wall and Butler (1985). Other researchers have also contributed significantly in these areas in recent years. "The pleasure periphery" as defined by Turner and Ash (1975) has become an established term in the literature, and others, e.g. Ghali (1976), have focused their attention upon regional development and growth.

Of particular concern to researchers studying the development of destination areas has been the nature and process of such development. In 1963 Christaller wrote of the changes which Mediterranean communities went through once they had become popular with tourists, and, since then, several authors have speculated on and researched the process which tourist destinations appear to pass through. One of the most frequently quoted references on this topic has been one by this author on the cycle of evolution of tourism destinations (Butler 1980). Several authors, e.g. Hovinen (1981) and Meyer-Arendt (1985), have used that model to describe and compare the development of, and changes in, the areas studied. Stansfield (1978) has applied a similar cycle to Atlantic City, while Wolfe (1982) has suggested a variation on the same theme. The model proposes that tourism destinations are essentially organic, with a definite life cycle, and that their development can be modeled using an S-shaped curve (Figure 2). While Cohen (1979) has criticized unidirectional models of development, the consensus to date suggests that there are more examples which approximate the model than not. It remains, however, as Heywood (1987) has argued, to determine through formal empirical study if the model is correct.

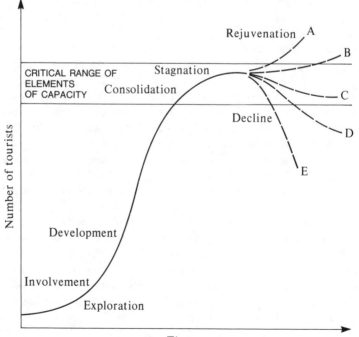

Figure 2
Hypothetical Evolution of a Tourist Area
(Source: Butler 1980: 7)

In a similar vein, an early article by Plog (1977) has gained considerable attention in the literature. Plog suggests that not only is it possible to segment tourists into types by psychographics, but that the types of visitors to destinations change over time, from the trend-setting "allocentrics" to the more sedentary "psychocentrics." He concludes with the question as to whether tourist destinations carry with them the inevitable seeds of their own decline. Intuitively this model, again unidirectional, has great appeal, but it, too, has not yet been tested empirically. To do so for a specific destination would require considerable longitudinal data, which are unlikely to exist.

Whatever the specific merits of the general models discussed above, there is little doubt that both destinations and tourists change over time. Resorts rise and fall in popularity and in real and perceived attractivity. Typologies of tourists are quoted in the literature (e.g. Cohen 1972). Much research remains to be done in this area, which in many respects is at the core of tourism studies, since it deals with the implications facing communities and their populations if they become a part of the global tourist industry. Whether the planning and modification of tourism development is possible and how this could be achieved remains to be seen, but, undoubtedly, if left to its own devices, tourism, in many cases, seems destined to continually reenact the "tragedy of the commons" (Hardin 1969).

TOURISM AND SOCIETY

The place of tourism in society today is clearly very different from that of earlier times. Tourism is now a commonly accepted form of behavior, but has assumed, as with many other commonly held goods such as automobiles, a role as an indicator of status. Smith (1979), for example, noted such behavior in her research sample. How the desire and need for tourism fits into the broader hierarchy of needs, such as those defined by Maslow (1954), remains to be clarified. Dann (1977), along with others, has adopted a more social-psychological view, based upon the examination of the individual needs of tourists in the context of the group of which they are members.

There are, of course, varying views of the roles and purposes of tourism and vacation travel. Krippendorf (1986: 523) argues that society creates the need to travel and that:

> people leave because they no longer feel at ease where they are, where they work and where they live. They feel an urgent need to rid themselves temporarily of the burdens imposed by the everyday work, home, and leisure scenes, in order to be in a fit state to pick up the burden again.

In other words, tourist travel is a form of re-creation. MacCannell (1973), on the other hand, has argued that tourists are not concerned with amusement, but seek authenticity in a manner and with a purpose which makes the tourist essentially a pilgrim, motivated as though on a religious quest. Cohen (1979) has challenged the latter view of tourism as somewhat limited, but shares similar concerns over the authenticity of the phenomena visited by tourists and their effects upon continued authenticity. Between these somewhat extreme views of tourism is the realization that there are, in fact, infinite numbers of reasons for participating in tourism, ranging from combatting boredom, through relaxation, to the search for spiritual replenishment. Each type may have a different set of requirements from the host population and environment, impose different impacts upon them, and consist of widely differing individuals. For example, Iso-Ahola (1984) has proposed an alternative theoretical framework to explain leisure and tourism motivation, which argues that two forces simultaneously influence leisure behavior — change (or novelty) and escape.

A significant emerging trend is the transformation of news events, such as the Seven Country Economic Summit Conference held in Toronto in June 1988, into full-scale media events and, hence, into tourism events. Such is the power of the media to influence public taste and fashion, both directly and indirectly, that it seems impossible now to envisage an America's Cup Competition which would not be a major tourist attraction, primarily because of media attention. Prior to the successful Australian challenge in 1984, the event had been limited to one location; its attraction was restricted principally to yacht enthusiasts, and it received limited media coverage. The hosting of the 1986 challenge in Freemantle, Australia, saw massive investment in tourist-related infrastructure unrelated in any direct way to the racing of several twelve-meter yachts. Given the fact that Freemantle/Perth (and Western Australia generally) was a pleasant but virtually unknown international tourist destination, and that the races themselves were all but invisible to the majority of "spectators," the principal explanation for the attendance of several thousand visitors from overseas has to be the attention generated by the news media, together with some latent "nautical nationalism" among the visitors.

There are some intriguing research possibilities on related items, such as the general boredom of affluent sections of the population, the apparent increasing desire of people to be at the scene of happenings, whether they be conventionally leisure related or not, and the unclear (but likely) relationships among tourism, snobbery, and uniqueness. Surrogate and vicarious participation in international events can be claimed by the collection of photographs, souvenirs, and, particularly in recent years, items of clothing emblazoned with information, often false, implying that the wearer was at, or a participant in, some recent event, or a visitor to a remote or exotic location.[1]

As Lew (1987) has commented, research on tourist attractions is limited, despite the importance of such features to the industry. He argues that tourist attractions "consist of all those elements of a 'non-home' place that draw discretionary travelers away from their homes" (p. 554), but notes that it can be difficult to differentiate between attractions and non-attractions. Perhaps at this point in time more than ever before, this distinction is even harder to make as the range of attractions varies from authentic native rites available for observation to only the confirmed and practised amateur anthropologist, to the Disney Worlds and totally artificial facilities at places such as Las Vegas, and from the deserted spaces of Antarctica to the stores and facilities of West Edmonton Mall in Canada.

While the role and place of tourism in society has changed greatly, so, too, has the society in which tourism occurs. For many centuries, tourism was limited either to areas similar to those from which tourists came (i.e. urban centers), or else to private rural estates, the exceptions being limited to places such as spas, whose special natural attributes eventually gave way to the importance of entrepreneurs, fashion, and specific facilities (Patmore 1968). Over the last century or so, however, communities have appeared whose role or primary function is to cater for tourists and their needs. The earliest resorts were those associated with the railway and with the Mediterranean (Gilbert 1939; Pearce 1979; Stansfield 1972), but they have since taken on a wide variety of functions and characteristics (Lavery 1975).

The study of these special tourist places, destinations of many of the world's tourists, and their unique social and physical composition has remained to a large extent the domain of geographers. Stansfield (1972, 1978), Barrett (1958), and Brown (1985) have all examined the unique and common morphology of traditional resorts and their responses over time to changes in accessibility and markets. While the interest in the communities themselves has not attracted much attention from other disciplines, the study of the perceptions and attitudes of the residents of these communities has attracted much more attention from anthropologists, sociologists, and political scientists as well as geographers.

The often negative attitude toward tourists displayed by locals and by other tourists is one of the other aspects of tourism which appears to have originated with the Grand Tour (Hibbert 1969), a feature which was heightened by the innovations of Cook (Swinglehurst 1982), as the increased numbers of mass tourists were not appreciated by the more affluent and class-conscious individual tourists of the time. Few people today describe themselves as tourists while on holiday — preferring terms such as visitor, sightseer, or even stranger to being characterized as a tourist, with all which that might imply. While the impact of the "Golden Hordes" of Turner and Ash (1975) may be as great as that of earlier waves of barbarians, many individuals feel less sure of themselves abroad than the apocryphal El Syd (Coren 1978), the unworthy but perhaps inevitable descendant of Sir Phillip Sydney, the originator of the Grand Tour.

TOURISM AS A BUSINESS

While the first "tourist" was on a political mission, and earlier seasonal migrants temporarily relocated more for reasons of comfort than anything else, today's tourist is an economic feature. Tourism has assumed such significant economic dimensions in so many parts of the world that it can no longer be allowed to depend upon the whims and preferences of those engaged in pleasure travel. Such, at any rate, is the impression one gathers from the actions of public and private agencies alike over the last quarter-century. Economies of nation states are now dependent on tourism, with many of these states having little or no control over the industry which is shaping their development, or lack of development, as discussed by Britton (1982) and de Kadt (1979). The economic importance of tourism varies widely from region to region across the world. While the dominant countries in absolute figures are the developed countries of Western Europe and North America, in relative terms tourism is more important in other parts of the world, particularly in the "pleasure periphery" described by Turner and Ash (1975). Of 33 nations in which tourism is classified as a leading industry, 25 are developing nations (Richter 1983: 315).

In several parts of the world, the Caribbean probably being the best example, the lives of much, if not most, of the population would be considerably worse without tourism-generated employment and income. This is recognized by politicians, business people, and ordinary citizens alike. What has also become clear, however, is that tourism is increasingly being controlled and manipulated from the center, the regions from which most tourists originate, in which the multinational corporations, which own most of the large scale tourism infrastructure, are located. Thus, many of the profits eventually return to the center from whence they originated. Nash (1977) and others have speculated on "Tourism as a form of imperialism," and Wu (1982), for example, writes of the links between tourism and the political economy of under-development.

The identification and the magnitude of economic benefits from tourism depend to a great degree upon who is conducting the research, together with the definition of who is a tourist and what constitutes tourism. Many agencies involved in tourism development tend to include almost any visitor from out of the country, the area, or the town under discussion. As a result, economic benefits from expenditures by businessmen, students, and even politicians are frequently included in total amounts credited as tourist spending. The media representatives covering events such as the Winter Olympics in Calgary and the Summer Olympics in Seoul, 1988 were certainly not tourists in any generally accepted meaning of the word. There is little doubt, however, that their purchases of accommodation, meals, and services will be included in tourist revenues when the final balance sheets for these events are drawn up.

Even within tourism destinations, it is clear that benefits and costs do not accrue evenly, nor are they perceived to do so (Brougham and Butler 1981). While the private hotel operator and the staff may benefit through revenue generation and salaries, another business may suffer because of increased labor costs caused by labor shortages arising from increased employment in tourism-related developments (Mathieson and Wall 1982). Demand for second homes for tourists may cause inflation in property prices, resulting in increased costs of local houses and land (Coppock 1977). Rapid expansion in tourism-related services and facilities can unbalance the economies of traditional communities — as happened, for example, in the case of Kissimmee, Florida, with the construction of Disney World and associated development. Rapid and sizeable increases in local taxes, in land prices, and in labor costs caused severe problems for long-time residents on fixed incomes, who had no way of benefitting from the unanticipated rate of growth of tourism and economic activity going on around them (personal observation 1973).

A common pattern in such cases is that the benefits accrue to those involved in the industry and to some others in a position to sell goods or services required, but that the costs are borne by others, principally through opportunity costs and inflation. The problem is generally compounded by the fact that the stimulus for, and control of, the development is external to the area experiencing it, particularly as the rate and scale of growth accelerates (Keller 1983). Such a situation seems common to areas as different as the Canadian Arctic and the Caribbean, or Central Florida and the South Pacific. Even where international corporations are not involved, central or national governments may promote the development and growth of tourism at the expense of regional and local populations, which may have to absorb additional costs, such as local road or harbor improvements or the provision of municipal services on a much larger scale than previously.

As more research has been conducted, it has become increasingly clear that the early economic forecasts of the effects of tourism were generally too simplistic, too narrow, and too optimistic. While few reached the level of inaccuracy of the Zinder Report (1969), most displayed the single focus which generally typified the early work of economists, the return on investment. Few economists (Bryden 1973, and Archer 1973a and 1973b being particularly respected exceptions) looked beyond the economic implications of the effects of tourism development. The economic and business domination of tourism is clearly illustrated by Richter (1983: 327), who quotes a convention theme of the Pacific Area Travel Association: "The Consumer: The Only One Who Matters."

In recent years, however, the need to take a wider view of the economic benefits and costs of tourism has been widely accepted. Studies have assessed, for example, the difficulties of using multipliers, and have explored alternative ways of maximizing benefits, depending upon the type of economic development and change desired. Publications such as Finney and Watson's *A New Kind of Sugar: Tourism in the South Pacific* (1977), de Kadt's *Tourism - Passport to Development?* (1979) and Young's *Tourism - Blessing or Blight?* (1973) have not only queried the true nature of the benefits, but have also inquired into the costs of tourism and tourism-associated development. Other researchers, such as Hovik and Heilberg (1980), have reviewed tourism in the context of center-periphery theory, and few studies of the effects of projected or proposed tourism development now assess only the economic effects of that development.

In this respect and in many others, tourism is little different from any other form of economic activity. Where it is different, or perhaps more difficult to control, is in the social and cultural effects which it can bring about.

THE SOCIO-CULTURAL AND ENVIRONMENTAL ASPECTS OF TOURISM

One of the major and most innovative contributions of social science research to tourism has almost certainly been in the wide range of studies into the human effects and interrelationships involved in tourism. This research began in depth in the early 1970s and has become a major research thrust since. Students of tourism were well aware of the effects of tourism upon both tourists and the host population of destination areas well before this period. Thus, as noted above, criticism of tourists is not a new phenomenon, but there had been little systematic study of this problem. What research there was had tended to focus on the more positive economic impacts of tourism rather than the rarely documented problems in the social and cultural fields resulting from development (Butler 1974).

There are several factors influencing such a state of affairs. In the first place tourism, except as a part of development generally, was not seriously studied by academics. Second, research funding bodies, particularly government agencies, were not (and some are still not) sympathetic to research exposing problems resulting from development. Third, as Wall and Wright (1977) have pointed out in the context of environmental impacts of leisure activities, without longitudinal data and established benchmarks and control sites, it is difficult, if not impossible, to ascribe changes and impacts to one single agent, in this case tourism. Especially with impacts in areas such as language, cultural adaptation, crime, attitudes, indigenous skills, and traditional behavior patterns, it is difficult to measure change, let alone identify beyond doubt the agent of change. In the area of language, for example, Cohen and Cooper (1986) identify only two studies dealing expressly with the relationship between tourism and the languages of host populations.

There has, however, been considerable research in anthropology, geography, political science, psychology, and sociology on the effects of tourism on host populations, and on the tourists themselves, including their motivations and desires, their behavior, and their expectations. Two major reports on the effects of tourism (Noronha 1976; Thurot 1975) appeared in the mid-1970s, and were followed by a number of the monographs discussed above. The most comprehensive review of the literature on the impacts of tourism is

contained in the book by Mathieson and Wall (1982), which omits little if
anything of significance published in English before that date. This book is of
particular value, not only because of the extent of the material included, but also
because of the analysis and context in which it is placed, which allow for a
rational assessment of the effects of tourism development in a variety of
settings.

More material has appeared since 1982, although it is fair to say that no
really significant new findings or thrusts have manifested themselves. Rather,
the more recent work has tended to reinforce and complement the findings from
the empirical studies discussed in Mathieson and Wall's book. Some interesting
research has appeared in social psychology (e.g. Furnham 1984; Van Raaij and
Francken 1984); in anthropology (e.g. MacCannell 1984; Wood 1984); in
recreation (e.g. Perdue, Long, and Allen 1987); and in sociology (e.g. Van Den
Berghe and Keyes 1984). The basic issues raised by early writers, such as
Greenwood (1976), Butler (1973), and Jafari (1974), still remain as major items
of interest, specifically, how tourism affects local populations in such areas as
language, traditional patterns of behavior, traditional values, and attitudes
towards the visitors. Several authors have focused upon the latter point, suggesting that changes in the attitudes of locals towards tourists is indicative of
changes in attitude towards tourism in general. Others, such as Lui, Sheldon, and
Var (1987) have examined residents' perceptions of the impacts of tourism,
concluding that perception of "the impact of tourism on the environment is
shared by all the residents regardless of their geographic locations and maturity
levels of tourism" (p. 17).

As may be expected, much of the research by social scientists has
focused on the human aspects of tourism. However, some attention has also
been paid to the environmental effects of tourism on destination areas, particularly by geographers and planners. The environmental effects of recreation are
discussed elsewhere in this volume (see Wall, in particular, but also Swinnerton,
and Stankey and McCool), and are not very different in nature from the impacts
of tourism. Farrell and McLellan (1987:2) in their paper on "Tourism and
physical environment research," note one of the principal problems with
environmental impact research:

> A high proportion of well-educated individuals, through possibly
> ignorance or emotion, attribute an unreasonable amount of resp-
> onsibility for landscape change and environmental degradation to
> tourism. For those concerned with tourism, enormous questions
> are thus raised, and although a number of assertions may seem
> plausible, they are seldom backed with adequate argument. It is
> not unusual to hear an otherwise scientifically sound and thought-
> ful colleague make sweeping allegations concerning the
> destructiveness of tourism.

It can be argued that much the same comments could be made about the effect of tourism on the human environment; Farrell and McLellan's conclusions to that discussion bear repeating in the context of research on any impacts of tourism:

> It is obvious that research is inadequate; that the area is one of supersensitivity and should be treated as such; and management should, in the interests of all concerned, reflect values that society places on environment (p. 2)

Elsewhere, I have argued for the necessity of considering all impacts of tourism together, especially in matters of policy and management formulation, for it is unrealistic to examine human impacts in isolation from physical ones, or physical ones apart from economic ones, since all clearly interrelate in reality (Butler 1974). This argument is particularly true when one considers whether tourism can achieve any sort of symbiotic relationship with, for example, cultural preservation or environmental protection. Hughes (1987) has discussed the links between culture and tourism, while Wall and Sinnott (1980) have demonstrated clearly the appeal of, and strong links between, art and tourism. There is no doubt that tourists find heritage, both environmental and human, of great attraction, and are willing to pay to visit heritage sites. Attendance figures for popular historic sites and national parks throughout the world bear out this point. Many national park systems in the world owe their establishment and protection to the potential tourist market envisaged by governments (Nelson 1973; see also Swinnerton's chapter, this volume), and Innskeep has argued that tourism "can actually be a positive force in achieving conservation objectives and maintaining or even improving environmental quality" (1987: 131). D'Amore (1987) has also expressed these sentiments in calling specifically for closer liaison between, for example, National Park agencies and tourism planners and developers to establish such a symbiotic relationship, echoing the thoughts of Gunn (1976) several years earlier. It must be noted, however, that such developments are more easily called for than obtained. The tourism industry, in most places, is highly fragmented, often does not have agreement among its members, is highly competitive, and appears relatively resistant to government direction and intervention (Butler 1987). Wolfe (1982) has suggested that it is difficult to envisage a situation in which tourism is both successful and not a threat to the human and physical environments, because of its inherent characteristics and the way in which it develops.

TOURISM PLANNING AND CONTROL

The points raised in the previous discussion highlight a major difficulty with tourism, that of planning and controlling development. The principal efforts of governments and public agencies in many parts of the world have traditionally been aimed at attracting and increasing tourism rather than controlling it. Most tourism-related legislation concerns the establishment of tourism boards (agencies, departments, or ministries), the provision of incentives for development, and the marketing and promotion of the host nation. Other regulations may deal with hotel and other accommodation registers and grading, employee training, and operator licensing. Rarely does the legislation deal with limiting or controlling development. Where tourism plans have been developed, in few places are they regarded as more than expressions of preference, easily changed to accommodate those willing to develop, but who wish to develop at locations other than those suggested in a plan.

The reason for this situation is most likely that authorities prefer tourism development of almost any kind to no development at all, to a large extent because, in general, most governments regard tourism as a clean, non-polluting, harmless form of development. "Tourists take nothing but photographs and leave nothing but footprints" was the text of an advertisement promoting the tourism industry in Ontario in the 1970s. Apart from basic inaccuracies in that text, the reactions of much photographed residents suffering from a lack of privacy and the effects of large numbers of footprints in some fragile environments obviously were not considered to be important by the authors of the text.

A related aspect of the problem of numbers is that while vast efforts are made to attract tourists to a destination, commensurate efforts are not always feasible or contemplated to retain that share of the market. While for a period a destination may succeed in attracting visitors because of its growth and reputation, ultimately it is likely to be eclipsed by newer and more trendy competitors, or to outgrow its potential. This state of affairs has been described by Wolfe (1952) as "the divorce from the geographic environment," the reliance upon man-made and social attractions after the natural attractions are degraded or lost. The ongoing appeal of Niagara Falls, for example, probably owes as much or more to the continued addition of artificial creations (wax works, museums, new fantasy or theme worlds) as it does to the natural features which attracted tourists initially.

Very few places have managed to retain much or all of their initial attractiveness and their popularity. Some are capital cities — such as London, Paris, and Rome — where the major attractions remain, and the appeal of the large urban center is still high, based on its being a center of fashion, taste, and power. Other places, however (e.g. St. Moritz, Davos, and, more recently, Aspen), remain attractive for different reasons. They have managed to retain their appeal, charm, and attractiveness, their ambience and atmosphere, by exclusiveness and consistency. In so doing, they have eschewed rapid and large-scale expansion, and have maximized revenues by increasing costs to visitors, rather than by increasing the numbers of visitors. A higher return per head from each visitor, obtained through high quality experiences and high prices, has helped to ensure exclusivity and to reduce the demand for change so as to cater to large numbers of less affluent visitors.

To be able to achieve such a position, however, requires an affluent, up-market clientele at the beginning of development, and a recognition and determination to maintain that clientele. In turn, this requires specific policies and local control over development, and the ability to limit or prevent development, even where this may be encouraged by other levels of government. Such arrangements are not common, nor is local willingness to set limits to tourism growth. In planning as in politics, the long-term benefit is frequently sacrificed for the short-term gain. Coordination and agreement between different levels of government in the public sector, and between the public and private sectors, are also requirements for such sustained success. It is perhaps too soon to say if the other extreme, the Disney operations in California and Florida, may also survive successfully for many decades. These operations are private concerns which operate as municipalities and, thus, have this coordination and agreement, because the private and public sectors are, in effect, combined. As well, the corporation has total power and almost total freedom to institute whatever changes and innovations it desires in order to maintain attractivity to visitors and offer an atmosphere of continual novelty and freshness. Together, the two extremes indicate the importance of power and control residing with the planning agency, whether this be public or private.

All too often, the real power is not vested in the agency responsible for planning, especially at the local level, but resides, rather, in boardrooms and legislative corridors far distant from the destination communities — more likely in the countries of origin of the tourists (Britton 1982). In such cases, the local communities, or even small nation-states, can do little but accept the future and the pattern of development as laid down by the elements shaping the market. They may plan, but must develop and change to stay competitive in a market over which they have no control (Keller 1983).

Despite some consideration of the problem in the 1960s (Bord Failte 1966), the issue of the carrying capacity of destinations, in both human and environmental terms, has received little attention in the tourism field. It is, perhaps, ironic that so much excellent research has been conducted on carrying capacity in wilderness areas in which few or no people live (Lucas 1964; Stankey 1982; Wagar 1964; and the chapter by Stankey and McCool in this volume), but that relatively little has been done in popular tourist destinations where large numbers of permanent residents live and mix with large numbers of tourists. A few studies have looked at manifestations of the problem of too many visitors — e.g. Cheng (1980), Pigram (1980), and more recently Getz (1983) and Graefe and Vaske (1987) — but little attempt has been made to explore the conceptual and theoretical problems inherent in the topic. A major problem is to satisfy competing and often contradictory demands — by visitors for a quality experience, by local residents for privacy and normalcy, and by business operators and governments for maximum revenue (Kienholz 1987).

CONCLUSIONS AND IMPLICATIONS

While researchers in many disciplines, primarily within the social sciences, have conducted studies in tourism, their findings and conclusions have not always been in agreement. Much of the research on tourism has been undertaken by economists and those in the business of tourism. From their perspective, tourism is labor-intensive, requires little skill in many areas, and can use local labor, often young people and women, two groups otherwise generally disadvantaged in the search for employment, especially in developing countries. As well, tourism normally results in an input of foreign currency, or at least a re-allocation of internal funds, from generally high-income urban areas to low-income rural areas. The conclusions of economists in particular, therefore, have understandably tended to focus upon material benefits resulting from development and have been positive about tourism. Researchers in other disciplines, particularly anthropology, sociology, and geography, and more recently political science, have focused much of their attention on the effects of tourism-related development and have generally been more critical (and in some cases even negative) in their conclusions about the overall effects of tourism upon the destinations and host populations.

One of the major difficulties for researchers in a field such as tourism studies is that of being cognizant of relevant research conducted in disciplines other than their own. As most academics are well aware, staying abreast of developments in one's own discipline is increasingly difficult given the growth in the number of publications and in the speed of the flow of information. It is a hard, if not almost impossible, task for a researcher in, for example, geography, to know all of the journals in anthropology, economics, political science, psychology, and sociology, in which articles on tourism might appear, let alone keep up-to-date with them. While keyword searches and the electronic storage and retrieval of data make such a task more feasible than heretofore, there is no doubt that some (perhaps many) studies are missed by most researchers. Examples abound, but one will suffice to illustrate the point.

In an article on "Consumer research on tourism," van Raaij refers to a "vacation sequence" (Van Raaij 1986: 3), introduced by van Raaij and Francken in 1984 "as a framework for describing the main stages of consumers' tourist behavior and experience." This sequence has five stages: generic decision; information and acquisition; decision-making; vacation activities; and satisfaction and complaints. Recreation researchers, especially those with backgrounds in economics and geography, could hardly miss the similarities of this sequence to one of the most well-known models in recreation research, the "recreation experience" proposed by Marion Clawson in the mid 1960s, and fully discussed in the now classic *Economics of Outdoor Recreation* (Clawson and Knetsch 1966). This model proposed five stages in the recreation experience: anticipation; journey to site; on-site experience; journey back; and recollection, with an implied feedback as the next "experience" was anticipated. The purpose of this example is not to denigrate a good article, nor to criticize the breadth of reading by van Raaij. It is easy to imagine how someone who is a professor of economic psychology, writing on vacation behavior, might not find a model on the recreation experience contained in a book on the economics of recreation.

There is no easy solution to this problem, which is compounded by the generally unilingual attributes of most researchers, especially those in North America, which potentially can result in ignorance of research which may have been published in languages other than their own. Tourism, perhaps more than many academic subjects, is international in scope because of its very nature, and knowledge of the global literature is difficult to acquire. Nevertheless, there is clearly a need for more cross-disciplinary and interdisciplinary research in the field of tourism, if the subject is to be fully understood. The fact that the major journals in the field, as also in leisure and recreation, are multidisciplinary, is a great advantage. While articles on tourism (and leisure and recreation) still appear in disciplinary journals, as is entirely appropriate in some cases, many researchers now turn automatically to the specialist subject (as opposed to the discipline) journals to publish their own work and to learn from the results of others.

In the areas in which further research is most needed, these comments are particularly true. Research on the motivations of tourists, for example, has been marked by a variety of approaches and conclusions. In his review article, Gann (1981) notes seven different uses of the expression by 1981. He explains the lack of agreement and the divergent views of motivation as being the result of the multidisciplinary nature of the research, as well as a number of differing theoretical perspectives within given disciplines. Similarly, in the research on impacts, as noted earlier in this chapter (and in detail by Wall in his chapter in this volume), much of the research has been fragmentary, of short duration, and from a multitude of viewpoints, with little coordination or replication of results. Even in the area of forecasting, while there has been more consistency in approach, there has been little by way of hindsight evaluation or assessment of potential impacts of predictions by those making the forecasts.

The dynamic and responsive nature of tourism makes it difficult to predict and to plan. Wolfe (1966) raised the question, many years ago, of what would happen to travel if the world became homogeneous and the distinction between places disappeared. Krippendorf (1986) raises a similar question when he discusses what might happen to tourism if we made our working and living environments and lifestyles more attractive, and thus reduced the need or desire for change. People may still travel because they believe the places they are going to will offer what they desire but cannot obtain at home, and image may become even more important than it is now. Hunt (1975) noted that images may have as much to do with an area's success as its tangible attributes, a point that Colton (1987) discusses in the context of a symbolic interactionism view of leisure, recreation, and tourism. Because we are still so unsure about so many aspects of tourism, we face great difficulties in defining it and managing it. It is but one aspect of life, but one which, like leisure and recreation, appears to be assuming an ever-increasing importance in many people's lives. Graburn (1983:2) has noted:

> Tourism is also a barometer of the dynamics of culture change within a society, for it may portend future cultural patterns for the individual ... and for the society. Furthermore, in patterns of historical trajectory, patterns of tourism may reflect the unfolding of consciousness and interests, e.g. in history, in the environment, and conservation, in health and cures, or in personal awareness.

If that is true, one may ponder the societal implications of a recent advertisement announcing the establishment of a new travel club called "Holidays for Maniacs," which will arrange accommodation and travel for members to war zones in areas such as the Persian Gulf, Iraq and Beirut. One feels that this is not quite what was intended when the United Nations hailed tourism as a "passport to peace."

Notes

1. This section of the chapter was written shortly before President Reagan visited Moscow in May, 1988. On the second day of his visit, the *London Free Press* published a photograph of a seven-year-old Russian girl carrying a canvas shopping bag on which the word "Summit" appeared four times as the pattern. This is perhaps even more commercial than the "Mom and Dad went to X and all they brought me was this T-shirt" slogan seen on small non-tourists at home.

References

Archer, B. 1973a. *The Impact of Domestic Tourism*. Bangor Occasional Papers in Economics No. 2. Cardiff: University of Wales.

Archer, B. 1973b. *The Uses and Abuses of Multipliers*. Tourist Research Paper TUR 1. Bangor: University College of North Wales.

Barrett, J.A. 1958. "The Seaside Resort Towns of England and Wales." Unpublished Ph.D. thesis, University of London.

Bord Failte, 1966. *Planning for Amenity and Tourism*. Dublin: An Foras Forbatha.

Britton, S.G. 1982. "The political economy of tourism in the third world." *Annals of Tourism Research 9:* 331-358.

Brougham, J.E. and R.W. Butler. 1981. "A segmentation analysis of resident attitudes to the social impact of tourism." *Annals of Tourism Research 13:* 569-590.

Brown, B.J.H. 1985. "Personal perception and community speculation: A British resort in the 19th Century." *Annals of Tourism Research 12:* 355-370.

Bryden, J. 1973. *Tourism and Development: A Case Study of the Commonwealth Caribbean*. Cambridge: Cambridge University Press.

Butler, R.W. 1973. "The social impact of tourism." *Proceedings of the 6th International Congress of Speleology*, VII, Fc, 139-146.

Butler, R.W. 1974. "The social implications of tourist developments." *Annals of Tourism Research 2:* 100-111.

Butler, R.W. 1980. "The concept of a tourist area cycle of evolution: Implications for management of resources." *The Canadian Geographer 24:* 5-12.

Butler, R.W. 1987. "Tourism and heritage use and conservation." In *Heritage for Tomorrow*, eds. R.C. Scace and J.G. Nelson, Vol. 5. Ottawa: Ministry of Supply and Services.

Cheng, J.R. 1980. "Tourism: How much is too much? Lessons for Canmore from Banff." *The Canadian Geographer 24:* 72-80.

Christaller, W. 1963. "Some considerations of tourism location in Europe: The peripheral regions - underdeveloped countries - recreation areas." *Papers of the Regional Science Association 12:* 95-105.

Clawson, M. and J. Knetsch. 1966. *Economics of Outdoor Recreation.* Baltimore: Johns Hopkins.

Cohen, E. 1972. "Toward a sociology of international tourism." *Social Research 39:* 164-182.

Cohen, E. 1979. "Rethinking the sociology of tourism." *Annals of Tourism Research 6:* 18-35.

Cohen, E. and R.L. Cooper. 1986. "Language and tourism." *Annals of Tourism Research 13:* 533-563.

Colton, C.W. 1987. "Leisure, recreation, tourism: A symbolic interactionism view." *Annals of Tourism Research 14:* 345-360.

Coppock, J.T. 1977. *Second Homes: Curse or Blessing?* Oxford: Pergamon Press.

Coren, A. 1978. *Tissues for Men.* Harmondsworth: Penguin.

D'Amore, L. 1987. "Parks and tourism: a global perspective" In *Heritage for Tomorrow,* eds. R.C. Scace and J.G. Nelson, Vol. 5. Ottawa: Ministry of Supply and Services.

Dann, M.S. 1977. "Anomie, ego-enhancement and tourism." *Annals of Tourism Research 4:* 184-194.

de Kadt, E. 1979. *Tourism: Passport to Development?* New York: Oxford University Press.

Farrell, B. and R.W. McLellan. 1987. "Tourism and physical environment research." *Annals of Tourism Research 14:* 1-16.

Fedler, A. J. 1987. "Are leisure, recreation and tourism interrelated?" *Annals of Tourism Research 14:* 311-313.

Finney, B.R. and A. Watson (eds.) 1977. *A New Kind of Sugar: Tourism in the Pacific.* Honolulu: East-West Technology and Development Institute, East-West Center.

Furnham, A. 1984. "Tourism and culture shock." *Annals of Tourism Research 11:* 41-58.

Gann, G.M.S. 1981. "Tourist motivation: An appraisal." *Annals of Tourism Research 8:* 187-219.

Getz, D. 1983. "Capacity to absorb tourism: Concepts and implications for strategic planning." *Annals of Tourism Research 10:* 239-263.

Ghali, M.A. 1976. "Tourism and economic growth: An empirical study." *Economic Development and Cultural Change 24:* 527-538.

Gilbert, E.W. 1939. "The growth of inland and seaside health resorts in England." *Scottish Geographical Magazine 55:* 16-35.

Graburn, N.H.H. 1983. "The anthropology of tourism." *Annals of Tourism Research 10:* 9-33.

Graefe, A.R. and J.J. Vaske. 1987. "A framework for managing quality in the tourist experience." *Annals of Tourism Research 14:* 390-404.

Greenwood, D. 1976. "Tourism as an agent of change." *Annals of Tourism Research 3:* 128-142.

Gunn, C.A. 1976. "Tourism-recreation-conservation synergism." *Contact 8:* 128-138.

Gunn, C.A. 1979. *Tourism Planning.* New York: Crane Russak.

Hardin, G. 1969. "The tragedy of the commons." *Science 162:* 1243-1248.

Hart, E.J. 1983. *The Selling of Canada.* Banff, AB: Altitude Press.

Heywood, K.M. 1987. "Can the tourist-area life cycle be made operational?" *Tourism Management 7:* 154-167.

Hibbert, C. 1969. *The Grand Tour.* London: Putnam.

Hovik, T. and T. Heiberg. 1980. "Centre-periphery tourism and self-reliance." *International Social Science Journal 32:* 68-98.

Hovinen, G. 1981. "A tourist cycle in Lancaster County, Pennsylvania." *The Canadian Geographer 25:* 283-285.

Hughes, H.L. 1987. "Culture as a tourist resource: A theoretical consideration." *Tourism Management 8:* 205-216.

Hunt, J.D. 1975. "Image as a factor in tourism development." *Journal of Travel Research 13:* 1-7.

Innskeep, E. 1986. "Environmental planning for tourism." *Annals of Tourism Research 14:* 118-135.

Iso-Ahola, S.E. 1984. "Social psychological foundations of leisure and resultant implications for leisure counseling." In *Leisure Counseling: Concepts and Applications*, ed. E.T. Dowd. Springfield, IL.: Charles C. Thomas.

Jafari, J. 1974. "The socio-economic costs of tourism to developing countries." *Annals of Tourism Research 1:* 227-259.

Keller, C.P. 1983. "Centre-periphery tourism development and control." In *Leisure, Tourism and Social Change*. Edinburgh: T.R.R.U., University of Edinburgh.

Kienholz, E. 1987. *Tourism and the Environment*. Calgary, AB: Canadian Society of Environmental Biologists.

Krippendorf, J. 1986. "Tourism in the system of industrial society." *Annals of Tourism Research 13:* 517-532.

Lavery, P. 1975. *Recreational Geography*. Newton Abbot: David and Charles.

Lawton, L.J. and R.W. Butler. 1987. "Cruise ship industry patterns in the Caribbean, 1880-1986." *Tourism Management 7:* 329-343.

Leiper, N. 1979. "The framework of tourism: Towards a definition of tourism, tourist and the tourist industry." *Annals of Tourism Research 6:* 390-407.

Lew, A.A. 1987. "A framework of tourist attraction research." *Annals of Tourism Research 14:* 553-575.

Lucas, R.C. 1964. *The Recreational Capacity of the Quetico-Superior Area*. Research Paper LS-15. St. Paul, MN: USDA Forest Service.

Lui, J.C., P.J. Sheldon, and T. Var. 1987. "Resident perception of the environmental impacts of tourism." *Annals of Tourism Research 14:* 17-37.

MacCannell, D. 1973. "Staged authenticity: Arrangement of social space in tourist settings." *American Journal of Sociology 79:* 586-603.

MacCannell, D. 1984. "Reconstructed ethnicity: Tourism and cultural identity in third world communities." *Annals of Tourism Research 11:* 375-392.

Mannell, R.C. and S.E. Iso-Ahola. 1987. "Psychological nature of the leisure and tourism experience." *Annals of Tourism Research 14:* 314-329.

Maslow, A. 1954. *Motivation and Personality.* New York: Harper.

Mathews, H.G. 1983. "Editor's page." *Annals of Tourism Research 10:* 303-305.

Mathieson, A. and G. Wall. 1982. *Tourism: Economic, Physical and Social Impacts.* London: Longman.

Matley, I.M. 1976. *The Geography of International Tourism.* Commission on College Geography. Washington, DC: Association of American Geographers.

Meyer-Arendt, K.J. 1985. "The Grand Isle, Louisiana resort cycle." *Annals of Tourism Research 12:* 449-466.

Mieczkowski, Z.T. 1981. "Some notes on the geography of tourism: A comment." *The Canadian Geographer 25:* 186-191.

Mitchell, L.S. 1979. "The geography of tourism: An introduction." *Annals of Tourism Research 6:* 235-243.

Murphy, P.E. 1985. *Tourism: A Community Approach.* London: Methuen.

Nash, D. 1977. "Tourism as a form of imperialism." In *Hosts and Guests: The Anthropology of Tourism,* ed. V. Smith. Philadelphia, PA: University of Pennsylvania Press.

Nelson, J.G. 1973. *Canadian Parks in Perspective.* Montreal: Harvest House.

Noronha, R. 1976. *Review of the Sociological Literature on Tourism.* New York: World Bank.

Ogilvie, F.W. 1933. *The Tourist Movement.* London: P.S. King.

Patmore, J. 1968. "The spa towns of Britain." In *Urbanization and its Problems,* eds. R.P. Beckinsale and H.M. Houston. Oxford: Blackwell.

Pearce, D. 1979. "Form and function in French resorts." *Annals of Tourism Research 5:* 142-156.

Pearce, D. 1981. *A Geography of Tourism.* New York: Longman.

Pearce, D. 1987. *Tourism Today: A Geographic Analysis.* London: Longman.

Pearce, P. 1982. *The Social Psychology of Tourist Behavior.* Oxford: Pergamon Press.

Perdue, R.R., P.T. Long, and L. Allen. 1987. "Rural resident tourism perceptions and attitudes." *Annals of Tourism Research 14.*

Pigram, J. 1980. "Environmental implications of tourist development." *Annals of Tourism Research 7:* 554-583.

Plog, S.C. 1977. "Why destination areas rise and fall in popularity." In *Domestic and International Tourism,* ed. E.M. Kelly. Wellesley, MA: Institute of Certified Travel Agents.

Richter, L.K. 1983. "Tourism and political science: A case of not so benign neglect." *Annals of Tourism Research 10:* 313-335.

Smith, V. 1979. "Women: The taste-makers in tourism." *Annals of Tourism Research 6:* 49-60.

Stankey, G.H. 1982. "Recreational carrying capacity research review." *Ontario Geography 19:* 57-72.

Stansfield, C. 1972. "The development of modern seaside resorts." *Parks and Recreation 5:* 14-17 and 43-46.

Stansfield, C. 1978. "Atlantic City and the resort cycle: Background to the legislation of gambling." *Annals of Tourism Research 5:* 238- 251.

Swinglehurst, E. 1982. *Cooks Tours: The Story of Popular Travel.* Poole: Blandford Press.

Thurot, J.M. 1975. *Impact of Tourism on Socio-Cultural Values.* Aix-en-Provence: Centre d'études du Tourisme.

Towner, J. 1985. "The Grand Tour: A key phase in the history of tourism." *Annals of Tourism Research 12:* 297-335.

Turner, L. and J. Ash. 1975. *The Golden Hordes: International Tourism and the Pleasure Periphery.* London: Constable.

Van den Berghe, P.L. and C.F. Keyes. 1984. "Introduction: Tourism and re-created ethnicity." *Annals of Tourism Research 11:* 343-352.

Van Raaij, W.F. 1986. "Consumer research on tourism: Mental and behavioral constructs." *Annals of Tourism Research 13:* 1-9.

Van Raaij, W.F. and D.A. Francken. 1984. "Vacation decisions, activities, and satisfaction." *Annals of Tourism Research 11:* 101-112.

Wagar, J.A. 1964. *The Carrying Capacity of Wildlands for Recreation.* Forest Science Monograph No. 7. Washington, DC: Society of American Foresters.

Wall, G. 1977. "Recreational land use in Muskoka." *Ontario Geography 11:* 11-28.

Wall, G. and R.W. Butler. 1985. "Themes in research on the evolution of tourism." *Annals of Tourism Research 12:* 287-296.

Wall, G. and J. Sinnott. 1980. "Urban recreational and cultural facilities as tourist attractions." *The Canadian Geographer 24:* 43-50.

Wall, G. and C. Wright. 1977. *The Environmental Impact of Outdoor Recreation.* Publication Series, No. 11. Waterloo, ON: University of Waterloo, Department of Geography.

Weaver, D.A. 1983. "Tourism as a factor in third world development with special reference to the Caribbean." *Ontario Geography 22:* 47-70.

Williams, A.V. and W. Zelinsky. 1970. "On some patterns in international flows." *Economic Geography 46:* 549-567.

Wolfe, R.I. 1952. "Wasaga Beach: The divorce from the geographic environment." *The Canadian Geographer 2:* 57-66.

Wolfe, R.I. 1964. "Perspective on outdoor recreation: A bibliographical survey." *Geographical Review 54:* 203-238.

Wolfe, R.I. 1966. "Recreational travel: The new migration." *The Canadian Geographer 10:* 1-14.

Wolfe, R.I. 1982. "Recreational travel: The new migration revisited." *Ontario Geography 19:* 103-124.

Wood, R.E. 1984. "Ethnic tourism, the state, and cultural change in Southeast Asia." *Annals of Tourism Research 11:* 363-374.

Wu, C.-T. 1982. "Issues of tourism and socio-economic development." *Annals of Tourism Research 9:* 317-330.

Young, G. 1973. *Tourism: Blessing or Blight?* Harmondsworth: Penguin.

Zinder, H. 1969. *The Future of Tourism in the Caribbean.* Washington, DC: Zinder and Associates.

APPLIED LEISURE RESEARCH: BENEFITS TO SCIENTISTS AND PRACTITIONERS AND THEIR RESPECTIVE ROLES

B.L. Driver

INTRODUCTION

When agreeing to write this chapter, I assumed my major charge was to show that leisure scientists are a worthy lot by documenting the tremendous contributions they have made to practice. Toward that end, a form was mailed to more than one hundred leisure scientists to solicit information on the nature and scope of the new technologies they had helped to generate. The "we-are-good" tack was abandoned for several reasons.

- It would be impossible to do justice to all the contributions made by leisure scientists, if for no other reason than space does not exist to describe them properly. Also, there would be a tendency to promote those applications that are national (and international) in scope or generic to a widespread need, which would not do justice to the many studies addressed to particular, local issues.
- Such a paper would be boring and read like an annual report of a research foundation.
- Most importantly, it is difficult to imagine any other established profession attempting to "justify" its research. Would scientists in electrical engineering or medicine feel a need to show their research has been used? Within the past decade, members of the leisure professions have grown in their self-confidence and are regarded more highly by other professions than they were 20 to 30 years ago. Defensive postures reflecting the attitude "Yes, our research really is useful" would not help that evolution.

Despite the decision not to attempt to document the magnitude and significance of the "technology transfer" work of leisure scientists, I emphasize that I disagree strongly with those who argue that leisure research has had little influence on the managerial and policy decisions of those responsible for providing leisure services. Important applications *have* been made at all levels of government and by private organizations. Still, many of these applications occur with a time lag; the "practitioners" frequently need to modify the results somewhat to make them useful; the scientist often is not aware that the results have been used; and many of the research results and most of the applications are never documented in established publications.

Rather than document specific applications of new technology, this chapter considers four aspects of the applications of leisure research: types of applications; benefits of technology-transfer efforts to scientists and to practitioners; conditions that nurture effective applied research efforts; and roles of scientists in public policy analyses. The basic objective is to offer a broad perspective on the application of the results of leisure research and to suggest how wider application might be achieved.

Although some authors distinguish among research results, technology, and applied knowledge, the assumption remains pervasive within the research community that scientists generate new knowledge and technology, and then some "practitioner" uses it. This chapter departs from the conventional wisdom in three ways. First, the view is taken that both the scientist and the practitioner generate new knowledge. Knowledge is derived from many sources, including everyday observation of patterns and of cause and effect, experiential reflection, and valid and reliable results of systematic research. Those trained in the scientific method believe that objective criteria — including statistical testing for error, replicability, reliability, validity, and generalizability — should be applied. Nevertheless, people not trained in the scientific method *do* generate new knowledge and methods and techniques through heuristic problem solving and other means. Although the emphasis in this chapter is on the application of knowledge derived from scientific inquiry, the broader perspective is maintained to emphasize that the scientist and practitioner can learn from each other: the flow of information is not one-way.

The second departure from conventional wisdom is that the word "practical" will be used to refer not just to the use of scientific information by practitioners; instead, a broader definition will denote "the application of knowledge to useful ends" (The World Publishing Company 1968). This definition permits consideration of how the research applications process can be useful to the scientist, too. The main focus, however, will be on the transmission of scientific information to practitioners and their use of that information.

The word "practitioner" will be used to refer to those who directly apply professional knowledge in policy and managerial decisions, including the delivery of social services, whether within clinical or other settings. It is not a good word because scientists are practitioners of science, but it will have to suffice as defined.

The last departure from conventional wisdom is my view that traditional attempts to dichotomize research into basic and applied types generally set up false dichotomies. Both basic and applied research can generate new theories and techniques (including new research methods), and both types frequently are applied by practitioners. Furthermore, many largely applied studies, such as program evaluations, frequently require some basic, developmental efforts.

TYPES OF APPLICATION

Scientific knowledge can be applied in several general ways. The different types of applications include: intrinsic use of knowledge for its own sake; promotion of additional scientific inquiry; advancement of professional bodies of knowledge; and resolution of real-world problems, including evaluation of programs.

The pursuit of new knowledge from any source is often an end in itself. In this Aristotelian sense, knowledge has intrinsic reward. This end requires no other justification, such as the advancement of a professional body of knowledge or the resolution of a real-world problem. Certainly, the intrinsic rewards of discovery, problem-solving, and just knowing motivate most scientists and many nonscientists.

Despite the occasional emergence of a new theory that has little resemblance to other previous thought, most bodies of knowledge build incrementally on previous theories and methods. Thus, an important application of the results of leisure research is to promote additional scientific inquiry.

Most scientists claim an academic discipline and allegiance to one or more professions. The most distinctive characteristic of a profession — as contrasted with a trade or craft — is an empirically supported body of knowledge. Most scientists are committed to advancement of the bodies of knowledge of their professions through the applications of their research results.

Most people think of the application of new knowledge as the solving of real-world problems or in doing things better or in a different way. Practitioners may apply such knowledge in many different ways. A problem-solving application might be using new knowledge acquired on how to quickly resurface an ice-skating rink. An application that demonstrates improvement of an existing technique might be the development of a better system for measuring the use of an area, or for inventorying the recreation potential of wildlands. Program evaluations, too, can be applied to evaluate the degree to which stated objectives are being met and/or how the program can be improved. For example, systematic evaluations of the Youth Conservation Corps program showed which types of enrollees were most likely to drop out, how specific dimensions of program operations could be improved, and what benefits were perceived by the participants (Ross and Driver 1986; Scott, Driver, and Marans 1973). Results of systematic inquiry have also been used to evaluate alternative policy options, as is commonly done in benefit-cost, social impact, and environmental impact analyses. Yet another application of new knowledge might be an improved method of informing and educating the public, such as advocating the need for increased user fees or teaching the public how to reduce user-caused forest fires or other damage. Finally, the most obvious application is the development of a new product to expand the public's choice options, as exemplified by the hula hoop or the hang glider — a type of application common in the commercial sector of the economy.

BENEFITS OF TECHNOLOGY TRANSFER

Benefits to Scientists

Scientists commonly think that the benefits of research application efforts accrue mostly to practitioners. The fact is that scientists also benefit in many ways.

- Without any contact with practitioners, the process of advancing scientific knowledge generates new research ideas that are frequently applied by scientists involved in that process. The scientists benefit by being recognized for their contributions, and they regard their chosen professions more highly as those knowledge bases expand.
- Because practitioners approach problems differently than do scientists, their critiques and insights can do more than help keep scientists relevant; they stimulate new perspectives and insights that would not be obtained otherwise. This often leads to new hypotheses and new methods.
- By working with practitioners, scientists frequently gain access to data otherwise not readily available. The same can be said about access to particular physical areas, equipment, and recreationists, as well as to sources of lodging for research assistants. In addition, internships and future job options for students can be nurtured.
- The scientists gain real-world perspectives; doing applied research and being active in technology transfer provides opportunities for reality testing that helps keep the scientists' feet on the ground. This not only provides a rewarding sense of relevance, but it can offer real-world examples for use in classroom teaching and in research publications.
- The scientists appreciate more fully the tendency of academic disciplines to carve up real-world problems to fit the bag of tools and skills unique to each profession. Work with practitioners reminds the scientist that most problems require multidisciplinary skills, that many problems are either unsolvable or are only partially solvable,

that problems can be difficult to fit into tight research designs, and that most problems are changing and long-term, so only temporary answers can be found. Through these interactions during application, scientists come to understand better the critical dimensions of the practitioners' problems and to which aspects they can most usefully devote their energies and skills.

- Surprising as it may seem, working with practitioners can sharpen the analytical abilities of the scientist. Many managers tend not to set clear and specific objectives, which the scientist needs. Anyone who does much applied research with practitioners soon recognizes the need to establish objectives early on. The process of doing that has spill-over benefits to other scientific inquiry.

- Both the scientist and practitioner learn that each has different values, speaks a different language, operates in different institutional settings, and is rewarded in different ways and for different efforts. This understanding helps promote more productive and meaningful relationships, as elaborated below.

- Writing reports understandable to managers can enhance the researcher's ability to communicate clearly and simply in other contexts. By having to cast off the cloak of disciplinary jargon, the scientist frequently nurtures improved skills in communication and in clarity of thinking.

- Practitioners are frequently providers of funding for future research that would not be funded in other ways.

- There are many "perks" for the scientist, including opportunities to travel, work in interesting environments, rewards and recognition by applied agencies, a sense of being appreciated, and the friendships built.

- Most scientists are not independently wealthy. Those who are supported by institutions that in part have the mission of improving the real-world application of knowledge have a moral responsibility (to those who finance their research) that their work be relevant. Doing applied research can help meet this obligation.

Benefits to Practitioners

On the other side of the ledger is a list of benefits of technology transfer to the applied users of research results.

- Most practitioners derive their academic training from the professional bodies of knowledge that have, at least in part, been developed from empirical research. Thus, without any concerted technology-transfer efforts between scientist and manager, the manager benefits by better professional training. Twenty years ago, for example, few managers viewed leisure in behavioral terms. Most do so today. This type of application is apparently not recognized by the many leisure scientists who argue that there is little application in managerial and policy decisions.

- Specific studies help resolve particular real-world problems, offer more efficient ways of meeting an objective, evaluate the effectiveness of particular programs, provide new options that might promote greater public acceptance, evaluate the consequences of alternative policies, and expand choice options for the users of particular goods and services. This helps the practitioner get the job done.

- Through interaction with scientists, practitioners are provided better opportunities to stay abreast of professional advancements, including improving their options for formal training. This facilitates the acquisition of a different vocabulary and frames of reference, which then enhance the ability of the practitioners not only to communicate with scientists but with the publics they serve. For example, practitioners can learn how to better nurture more effective public involvement in the decision process and how to use that information. This updating of skills also facilitates an enhanced ability to read and follow technical articles.

- Related to the preceding point, the mindset of the practitioner can be expanded. This can lead to a breakdown in tunnel vision, paternalism, and inefficient competition with other entities. For example, biases against economic valuations can be tempered by better understanding of the purposes and limitations of economic efficiency analyses. As a consequence, barriers are removed that once limited broader analytical and conceptual thought processes, possibly leading to the adoption of new methods, better definition of particular problems, clearer articulation of the practitioners' goals and objectives, and greater specificity in delineation of management prescriptions and standards. For example, managers played an active role in developing the Recreation Opportunity Spectrum system (Driver *et al.* 1987). That participation helped managers understand better the meaning of a recreation experience, which in turn has helped them write more specific management objectives for particular areas.

- Probably one of the greatest benefits is a subtle increase in professional pride that accompanies the successful use of new technology. This can lead to higher commitment and motivation. For example, research on recreation needs, experiences, and benefits has helped managers understand better their contribution to social welfare. Many of them enjoy the feeling of being on the "cutting edge."

- Lastly, as for the scientists, the practitioner often gets many "perks," including travel and awards/recognition for their work with scientists and/or applications of new knowledge.

CONDITIONS THAT NURTURE EFFECTIVE APPLIED RESEARCH EFFORTS

Now that the mutual benefits of technology-transfer efforts have been examined, it is appropriate to consider how those efforts can most successfully be pursued. Toward that end, some conditions that nurture successful applied research will be considered. Several such conditions described in other recent papers (Driver and Knopf 1980; Driver and Koch 1981) are modified only slightly here. The central theme is that the scientist must move out of the "ivory tower" and work closely with the practitioner on all aspects of the research, from definition and selection of the problem to implementation of the results — a theme common in other articles on research application (e.g. Beaman 1978).

1. *The problem must be researchable and relevant to the practitioner.* There must be an identifiable problem, which is researchable and relevant to the needs of the practitioner. If neither of these conditions is met, the meaningful application of research results is not likely. Instead, the researcher may be working on an insoluble problem or the practitioner may not be interested in the results. However, the researcher and practitioner often honestly disagree about the relevance of the research results to a particular applied problem. For example, researchers sometimes think that they are doing applied research when they are not. Alternatively, they might be, but practitioners think they are not. Frequently, too, the researcher will want to do more basic research than is needed in a particular context. These situations lead to Condition 2.

2. *The researcher and the practitioner must have a common understanding of the problem and its significance.* If the practitioner and the researcher disagree on the definition of the problem or its significance, there is less chance that the research results will be applied. Either party can identify the problem. However, the early application of results is more likely if, once identified, the problem is defined jointly, with agreement reached as to how research might help.

3. *The researcher and the practitioner must have a personal and a mutual interest in the problem.* The personal interests might differ for reasons explained in Condition 6 below, but the mutual interests must be based on shared goals. For example, the interests of the researcher must go beyond obtaining another publication, while those of the practitioner must go beyond just meeting a set production target. Normally, these shared goals reflect personal values related to mutual professional interests.

4. *The research effort must be a cooperative one between the researcher and the practitioner.* Conditions 1-3 require a commonly understood problem, mutuality of interest in that problem, and a willingness of the researcher and the practitioner to work together. Early transfer of research results is also facilitated if the practitioner is actively involved in all phases of the research effort, if only in order to offer a critique. At a minimum, the practitioner should be kept aware of progress being made. Preferably, the practitioner will help define hypotheses, review study plans and questionnaires, be briefed on general types of data analyses to be performed and how the results will be displayed, review draft reports, and co-author manuscripts submitted for publication. Too frequently, the researcher "takes" the problem and makes no contact with the practitioner until the final report is delivered. The researcher must reserve the option to make final decisions concerning the research design, but input by the practitioner should be given serious consideration. On the other hand, the practitioner must reserve the option to make final decisions regarding applications, but input by the researcher should be considered. The major responsibilities of each in the applied research effort should be specified clearly, preferably in writing. Since the research is applied, the target audience for some of the research reports should be practitioners. It is particularly useful if the practitioner can review drafts of those reports to see if they are understandable, and organized and written in a useful manner.

5. *The researcher and the practitioner must understand each other's job-related needs and responsibilities.* The knowledge transfer process is helped if the researcher understands the budget, time, and knowledge constraints under which the practitioner works and realizes that the practitioner is under intense pressure to meet a set of production targets on time. For example, the practitioner frequently does not need highly sophisticated information. It also helps if the practitioner understands the researcher's needs to follow the rules of scientific inquiry — to define variables and describe methods of investigation in precise language; to have clearly stated purposes (or objectives) that define the problem and state whether it is researchable; to do developmental work; and to test the reliability and validity of the measuring instruments used. Put simply, each participant in the joint research effort must appreciate the professional atmosphere and job-related demands of the other if there is to be mutual respect, tolerance, understanding, and progress.

6. *The researcher and the practitioner must understand each other's basic differences.* People who choose research for a profession probably differ from those who choose careers in application. Researchers tend to prefer to work on abstract problems that may take considerable time to solve, are generally more tolerant of ambiguity or uncertainty, may be less down to earth, and tend to enjoy reading technical papers. Practitioners tend to prefer immediate and

useful solutions that do not equivocate or exceed operating budgets or other constraints. Thus, the researcher and the practitioner tend to be different types of people with respect to their personal interests and how they define and approach problems. Each must understand these differences if they are to work together as an effective team.

7. *Mutual respect and trust must be established and maintained*. This is perhaps the most difficult condition to meet, because it diverts much time away from other tasks. It requires considerable face-to-face interaction between the researcher and the practitioner, and it demands much compromise by both parties. Such trust and respect can be achieved best under informal conditions where formal role barriers to frank and open communication are lowered. As trust is established, stereotypes are broken down and misconceptions can be clarified. Also, defensive postures, reflected by the use of jargon and by some researchers' highly counter-productive propensity to preach or lecture, are lessened. As mutual trust and respect are gained, most of the constraints to the expeditious utilization of research results are overcome. If either party is unwilling to commit the necessary time and patience because of other demands or because they do not view technology transfer as largely a one-on-one process, the likelihood of successful application is greatly reduced.

8. *The mechanism of operation must be coordinated and made as similar as possible for both the researcher and the practitioner*. The deadlines faced by practitioners and researchers have different time structures; these must be made compatible through dialogue and compromise. Through such compromise, research results can be brought "on-line" as soon as possible. Also, because practitioners tend to be transferred from one location to another more frequently than researchers, mutual efforts can be disrupted. For this reason, it is advisable to put in writing how continuity of the project will be maintained if either party is transferred.

9. *The scientific credibility of the research must be maintained*. Researchers cannot help solve applied problems if they do low-quality research; they will give inaccurate results and/or lose the trust and respect of the practitioner. The researcher must be extremely careful not to imply that the data or results are any better than they actually are, or to identify those results as final. When working closely with practitioners, researchers are frequently asked to share results that might not have the statistical precision desired by the researcher but are better than other available information. Alternatively, in doting on a probability level of < 0.05, the researcher frequently forgets the practitioner is often flipping a coin, or using a 50-50 probability. Specifically, the researcher tends to forget about Type II error (i.e. rejecting true findings). Scientists who release preliminary results or do applied research with less demanding

significance levels are often criticized by other researchers. The practitioner who gets such negative feedback may be reluctant to use the results, or possibly any results, of that researcher. Thus, there are risks to the researcher who works closely with practitioners to help assure the early and effective transfer of research results. For example, research results that get passed around informally before systematic review by the researcher's peers and formal publication can be distorted and misinterpreted. Those results, then, may not at all represent the researcher's original position or remain appropriately qualified.

10. *The researcher must be involved in the early stages of application of the research results.* Frequently, practitioners have questions about specific aspects of particular studies or a series of related studies. In other instances, applications of results might need to be made on a trial basis, training sessions on the new technology might be necessary, or draft guidelines for implementation might need to be written. In these situations, the researcher might be the best qualified person to answer questions, clarify instructions, or otherwise help assure that the technology is applied appropriately. In addition, the involvement of the researcher in these early stages of research application leaves the impression that the researcher cares about the practitioners' problems. The goodwill established will carry forward into future joint efforts.

11. *Both the researcher and the practitioner must appreciate that each has different performance evaluation and reward systems.* Rewards given to researchers by most institutions are based primarily on publications, not on efforts to apply research results. Similarly, practitioners can be punished professionally for spending too much time with researchers. Therefore, researchers and practitioners desiring to work together must frequently do so for rewards other than those reflected by higher salaries or advancement in their organizations. Each should be aware of the performance evaluation requirements of the other.

In summary, these conditions require that researchers work on relevant problems defined by researchers and practitioners working together; that practitioners be involved with the researchers throughout the research investigation to such an extent that mutual trust, respect, and understanding are attained; that researchers and practitioners work to help each other and not just themselves; that researchers help in the early stages of research application; and that both members of the team work together to help each other overcome any organizational constraints that serve to encourage separate rather than mutual efforts on a common problem.

These conditions, especially numbers 4, 7 and 10, are not easy to meet, nor would it be appropriate to try to meet each of them in all applied leisure research efforts because of the extra time involved. But, meeting them can help assure that more applied research will be done, that the results of that research will be applied more readily, and that researchers and practitioners will attain a better appreciation of, respect for, and support of each other.

It should be apparent that the approach proposed by these eleven conditions is a "one-on-one" model rather than the more conventional "if-the-results-are-useful-then-they-will-be-used" model. Because the one-on-one model takes more time, it usually reduces the number of publications for any one scientist, but it increases applications of that scientist's work.

ROLES OF SCIENTISTS IN PUBLIC POLICY ANALYSES

This final section considers the special case where scientists either conduct special studies or draw on an existing body of knowledge as input to public resource allocation decisions. Three perspectives are offered with respect to this role of the scientist as public policy advisor.

First, it is appropriate that scientists, as experts, share their specialized knowledge to help increase the efficiency, effectiveness, equity, and responsiveness of public resource allocation decisions. This helps not only the public decision maker; there are also rewards to the scientists, their institutions, and their professions.

Second, the scientists must be ever mindful that they represent a particular disciplinary perspective and usually speak in the vernacular of their professions. As Boulding (1956) said, "One wonders sometimes if science will not grind to a stop in an assemblage of walled-in hermits, each mumbling to himself/herself in a private language that only he can understand." All scientists are guilty of using too much professional jargon when communicating with practitioners including policymakers.

Third, although it is "good" that most scientists represent a particular disciplinary viewpoint — and there are many within most academic disciplines — it is not so "good" if any particular perspective is proffered as the one and only truth. Real-world problems tend not to carve themselves up into disciplines, but are multidisciplinary. The scientist as policy analyst must be extremely careful not to drastically redefine the problem to fit his or her bag of professional tools. This might comfort the scientist, but the problem remains with its real-world complexity.

Freeman and Frey (1986) offer a useful perspective regarding the role of the scientist in assisting public decision makers who must attempt to achieve reasonable compromise among competing interests with different values. They recognize two distinct "levels" of involvement, only one of which is assigned to the scientist. They are "a technical level ... where the analyst (scientist) specifies and justifies value criteria, and a political/ administrative level ... where decision makers make tradeoffs among conflicting value criteria."

Freeman and Frey recognize that public decision makers almost always must consider a multitude of competing values, and they must rely on some personal (usually highly subjective) system for defining and weighing the best — and always limited — information available about those values. For example, public decision makers responsible for making decisions about how the National Forests in the United States are to be used are required by various laws to consider multiple values related to national economic efficiency, local and regional economic development, local community stability, environmental protection, management of Congressionally designated areas (such as Wilderness Areas and areas that qualify for protection of air visibility under amendments to the Clear Air Act), and other values described in Driver and Burch (1988). Many of these values conflict, so the scientist as technical advisor, with expertise in the theories and methods of a particular valuation paradigm (that represents his/her disciplinary perspective), can "specify" and "justify" only one "value criterion" (whether economic efficiency or a particular mode of environmental protection). Many paradigms from many disciplines are needed.

Too frequently, scientists lose sight of the fact that they are strongly conditioned by their disciplinary training. Thus, they tend to be intolerant of a countervailing point of view. Scientists can serve the public decision maker best if they can synthesize and integrate as well as analyze. Not only will this broader perspective best serve the public decision maker, but it will also promote and nurture multidisciplinary efforts through the mutual respect it engenders across disciplines and between scientists having different persuasions within disciplines.

The managers or policymakers not only need technical information but must also be sensitive to the values and needs of the publics they serve as well as the interest groups that support their agencies. And to reiterate, they must somehow consider those agency goals for which the technical states of the art are not sufficiently advanced to provide accurate and reliable information. In addition, the practitioner frequently operates under constraints that make it difficult to incorporate all useful technical information into a decision.

Although circumstances frequently limit the role of the technical advisor, they certainly do not eliminate it, as evidenced by the significant influence of leisure scientists on many policy decisions. Within outdoor recreation, for example, scientists have had a major impact on many types of policy decisions. The list is long, and includes: policies related to user fee schedules; values used in benefit-cost, social impact, and environmental impact analyses; types of inventory systems adopted; visual resource management; and development of management handbooks that guide a large number of field-level decisions such as determination of area carrying capacity, types of interpretive programs to use, and measurement of basic use.

The question is not whether leisure scientists have influenced policy decisions, but, instead, how they can do so more effectively.

References

Beaman, J. 1978. "Leisure research and its lack of relevance to planning, management and policy formulation: A problem of major proportions." *Recreation Research Review 6 (3):* 18-25.

Boulding, K.E. 1956. "General systems theory: The skeleton of science." *Management Science 2:* 197-200.

Driver, B.L. and R.C. Knopf. 1980. "Some thoughts on the quality of outdoor recreation research and other constraints on its application." In *Proceedings, Social Research in National Parks and Wildland Areas,* ed. K.C. Chilman, pp. 85-95. Atlanta, GA: USDA National Park Service, Southeast Region.

Driver, B.L. and N.E. Koch. 1981. "Conditions which nurture the application of forest research results." *Journal of Technology Transfer 6:* 33-40.

Driver, B.L., P.J. Brown, G.H. Stankey, and T.G. Gregoire. 1987. "The ROS planning system: evolution and basic concepts." *Leisure Sciences 9:* 203-214.

Driver, B.L. and W.R. Burch, Jr. 1988. "A framework for more comprehensive valuations of public amenity goods and services." In *Amenity Resource Valuation: Integrating Economics with Other Disciplines,* eds. G.L. Peterson, B.L. Driver, and R. Gregory, pp. 31-45. State College, PA: Venture Publishing.

Freeman, D.M. and R.S. Frey. 1986. "A method for assessing the social impacts of natural resource policies." *Journal of Environmental Management 23:* 229-245.

Ross, D.M. and B.L. Driver. 1986. "Importance of appraising response of subgroups in evaluations: Youth Conservation Corps." *Journal of Environmental Education 17 (3):* 16-23.

Scott, J.C., B.L. Driver, and R.W. Marans. 1973. *Toward Environmental Understanding: An Evaluation of the 1972 Youth Conservation Corps.* Ann Arbor, MI: Institute for Social Research, Survey Research Center, The University of Michigan.

The World Publishing Company. 1968. *Webster's New World Dictionary of the American Language, College Edition.* New York, NY.

PART FIVE

The Future

There are two pressing questions facing research in the field of recreation and leisure studies as we move into the final decade of the twentieth century. Is it reliable? And is it relevant? There are no easy answers to either question, for the very notions of reliability and relevance are themselves uncertain and changing. Nevertheless, these are questions which cannot be avoided. The two chapters in this fifth and final part of the book address them.

Is recreation and leisure research *reliable*? By this we mean, is it sound conceptually and methodologically, such that one can have reasonable confidence in its findings? If it is not — or if it is only partly so — what must be done to improve this condition? The issue is addressed directly in the concluding chapter, which we ourselves have written. It is our contention that while considerable progress has been made in the field during the past two decades — both in the development of concepts and theories and in the enhancement of methods and techniques — there is still much to be accomplished. The weaknesses that exist in conceptualization and the building of theory stem, we believe, from inadequate cross-disciplinary fertilization in recreation and leisure studies. We also contend that methodological inadequacies arise not so much from a preponderance of any one methodology currently in use in the field (although this is, in fact, the case) as from an apparent unwillingness among many leisure researchers to experiment with and employ multiple methods. It is the quality and appropriateness of the *bundle* of research methods and techniques currently in use which is in question. The solution to both concerns, we suggest, lies in the willingness and ability of leisure scholars from each and all of the pertinent disciplines and fields of study to communicate with, learn from, and respect the contributions of those whose disciplinary background and training do not match their own.

Godbey, too, touches upon the issue of reliability when he remarks upon the almost total absence of replication in recreation and leisure research, without which it has been virtually impossible to establish trends. He also notes that an overwhelming dependence upon quantitative research within a logical positivist framework, most of which is cross-sectional, atheoretical, and ahistorical, has contributed significantly to the non-cumulative character of recreation and leisure research.

The principal concern of Godbey's chapter, however, is with the question of *relevance*. Is recreation and leisure research relevant, not only to the problems faced by professionals in recreation practice, but also to the broader society in which we live? The answer appears to be, "partly." The lack of dissemination of the findings of much research beyond the confines of the scholarly journals; the inability of many practitioners to make effective use of much of the research that they do receive; the lack of an appropriate value framework within which research findings can be interpreted for practitioners; patronage and management by policy which ignores research findings — all have combined to undermine the effectiveness with which recreation and leisure research has contributed to practice. A priority for both leisure scholars and recreation practitioners during the next decade must be to break down these barriers on as many fronts as possible.

Looking at the wider society, Godbey contends that leisure and recreation are emerging as the center of the economy in the rapidly postindustrializing world; that recreation and leisure behavior cannot be a central concern of any one government agency, but, equally, cannot be ignored by any; that recreation and leisure are learned experiences; and, finally, that recreation and leisure form an increasingly important component of individual identity.

These trends and conditions have significant implications for future themes and emphases in recreation and leisure research. We, ourselves, would go further, for it is our contention that these changes within the domain of recreation and leisure are important but not sufficient indicators of research needs in the field. Leisure scholars need to be able to relate leisure (and leisure research) to social change. They must pay more attention than heretofore to social trends and changes, and place and interpret the results of their research in this broad social context.

E. L. J.
T. L. B.

IMPLICATIONS OF RECREATION AND LEISURE RESEARCH FOR PROFESSIONALS

Geoffrey Godbey

As recreation and leisure research has grown in quality and quantity, it has begun to have an impact on both the education of recreation, park, and leisure service professionals and on the operation of their agencies. The influence of such research has been incremental; it has not revolutionized the field. Nevertheless, it would appear that tomorrow's professional will know more about, have more respect for, and will use research to a greater extent than now occurs. This chapter attempts to identify some reasons for the limitations on the use of recreation and leisure research by professionals, some professional implications of such research, and some broader (societal) implications.

Research will be considered here in a broad sense, that is "a systematic and objective attempt to study a problem for the purpose of deriving general principles. The investigation is guided by previously collected information and aims to add to the body of knowledge on the subject" (Theodorson and Theodorson 1969: 347). Using such a definition, many books and monographs qualify as research, while some information-gathering projects of leisure service agencies do not. In the following discussion, the reader will be referred to a single example of the type of research in question, rather than be bombarded with several hundred references.

SOME LIMITATIONS

The factors limiting the use of recreation and leisure research by the professional are critical. It would appear that some of these limitations will be minimized within the next few decades; others may not.

Lack of Dissemination and Ability to Use Research

Perhaps the biggest limitation of recreation and leisure research, in terms of its ability to shape the profession, is the lack of appropriate dissemination and lack of use. There are certainly many avenues for the dissemination of such research in North America, including journals such as the *Journal of Leisure Research, Leisure Sciences, Recreation Research Review, Journal of Park and Recreation Administration, Journal of Therapeutic Recreation, Journal of Leisurability*, and (from Britain) *Leisure Studies*. While these journals (and others) certainly disseminate research, there are two major problems preventing them from shaping the profession. First, the vast majority of practitioners do not read them. *Leisure Studies*, for instance, has fewer than 150 subscribers in North America. While the *Journal of Leisure Research* has a few thousand subscribers, the vast majority are libraries and professors.

Second, and more important, is the fact that almost all of the articles in such journals are written by academics who are writing for other academics. The often ponderous language, stultifying style, and heavy reliance on statistics assure that such writing will not or cannot be read by most practitioners. There is, of course, a great need for academics to communicate their research to each other, and journals fill this need. Perhaps because of this, however, the level of writing in most such journals presumes that the reader has at least a Master's Degree, yet a decade ago a national study of public recreation and park professionals found that fewer than four percent of all public sector employees in recreation, park, and leisure service agencies had such educational credentials (Henkel and Godbey 1977). While the situation may have changed since the time of that study, the vast majority of practitioners are not prepared to read research journals and most research journals are not designed for practitioners.

This, of course, is not to say that practitioners do not read research. Some become involved in studies of their own agencies' operations, undertaken either by consultants or by agency staff. Such research varies greatly in quality and complexity, ranging from ill-conceived surveys to highly sophisticated, scientifically valid studies. Much of this research, however, has either limited generalizability or is never disseminated to other professionals.

Some of the more interesting research to the practitioner is currently being done by private-sector research and marketing companies (see, for example, Simmons Market Research Bureau 1984). In some cases, such studies find their way into the public domain, but usually they remain privileged information.

Lack of a Value Framework Necessary for Interpretation

To implement research findings in the management of a recreation, park, or leisure service agency, it is necessary to have not only access to, interest in, and an understanding of the research in question, but also a value framework through which it can be implemented. As Cranz (1982) and others have argued, public recreation, park, and leisure service agencies have evolved through several stages of management, in which there were identifiable organizational values enunciated to a stage at which management has attempted to operate "scientifically" and to react passively to "demand" from the public. For instance, the process of designing a park becomes one of "technology" rather than "cultural discovery." Nothing can be undertaken, however, regardless of the sophistication of the scientific research and technology, until some values are established, some vision enunciated.

How does an agency act upon the research finding that establishing a fee for the use of public tennis courts will result in a drop-out of only 19 percent of all users, most of whom are minority group teenagers? What should be done about a finding that the majority of visitors to a given national park never get out of their cars or that they want a cocktail lounge established on a scenic overlook? How should the agency react to a study which shows negative environmental impact from crowding on a hiking trail but high levels of satisfaction among hikers? What should be done about the finding that the majority of swimmers at a public pool don't want a physically handicapped group integrated with them?

None of these research findings leads to any necessary conclusion until some system of goals based upon ethics is established. Even the marketing concepts of "demand" are highly value-loaded and must be understood as such. In effect, the leisure service system always has some values at work in decision-making, but such values may not be systematic or may not even be recognized. In either case, research cannot be brought to bear on practical problems with any systematic effect.

Patronage and Management by Policy Which Ignores Research

There is a great myth that most public recreation, park, and leisure service agencies have "professional" staff. The previously mentioned study by Henkel and Godbey found that only about 40 percent of such employees had specialized, post-secondary degrees in recreation and parks curricula. These statistics probably have not changed much. In some large urban governments in the United States, such as those in Philadelphia, New York, Boston, Chicago and others, as well as countless county and state park systems, recreation, park, and leisure services are staffed largely by political appointees. Such individuals are not only unlikely to be researchers, but are often politically hindered from using research in their operations even if they wish to, since the agency must be managed in accordance with the wishes of some political boss higher up in the system. This phenomenon occurs to varying extents in many other countries.

In the United States, the Department of the Interior has not been able even to replicate a national survey of outdoor recreation every five years (under administrations previous to the Reagan Administration, which quit doing the survey) in the development of the Nationwide Outdoor Recreation Plan. In Canada, during the 1970s, the Local Initiatives Program, launched by the

Federal Government to create temporary employment and, hence, political support, resulted in a large number of ill-conceived projects, such as counting every gymnasium in the country.

While many recreation, park, and leisure service agencies use research, many more cannot, or will not, because of political exigencies.

Some Limitations of the Research

Not only has recreation and leisure research been limited in its usefulness for the above reasons, but also because of several of the characteristics of the research itself. One of the primary problems with the research is the almost total absence of replications. Because of this, it has been almost impossible to establish trends. Trend analysis should be understood as one form of aggregation. Aggregation accomplishes two purposes: it reduces errors of measurement, and it establishes a range of generalization.

Perhaps the most common form of aggregation is aggregation over individuals to reduce errors associated with individual differences (Epstein 1981). This, of course, is done by leisure researchers. Another form of aggregation is aggregation over stimuli, or situations, to reduce the error variance associated with the unique contributions of specific stimuli or situations and determine the class of stimuli or situations to which results can be generalized. This is sometimes done by leisure researchers.

Third, we may aggregate over different research measures to minimize variance associated with a single research method rather than true variance. This is rarely done by leisure researchers. When an existing research study is "replicated," the research is aggregating over trials or occasions, not only because there may be error in measurement, but also because, otherwise, there is no way of determining whether the results can be generalized over time. Such replication is almost unheard of among leisure researchers for a number of reasons: replications of studies often do not get published in journals; funding for leisure research is tenuous (as is academic tenure for young professors), so that the researcher is encouraged to "do something quick"; research done in-house by government agencies is politically sensitive and subject to change without notice, so there is never any assurance that a study can be replicated for a period in the future longer than the next election. There is also often no adequate storage of past research so that results can be compared to replicated studies. All of this means that we know precious little about trends in participation in leisure activities, trends in satisfaction with an agency's services, trends in almost anything except, perhaps, attendance.

Recreation and leisure research has also relied almost exclusively on quantitative research within a logical positivistic framework. The debate raging within several social sciences concerning the use of quantitative versus the so-called qualitative methods appears to have by-passed leisure research, although a few qualitative studies are beginning to be undertaken (see, for instance, Howe 1985). Most recreation and leisure research uses one of the survey techniques (Riddick *et al.* 1984, found that 94 percent of the research reported in the *Journal of Leisure Research* from 1978 to 1982 used survey methodologies). Most is also cross-sectional, quantitative, atheoretical and ahistorical. This means, to some extent, that much of the body of research has a "non-cumulative effect." As Zuzanek (1982: 12) stated, much of the effort of leisure researchers "is still of an ad hoc and eclectic nature, and lacks broader theoretical conceptualization." Our researchers are often what the poet Theodore Roethke called "perpetual beginners." Research findings often lack context, historical perspective, or an appreciation of the flavor, meaning, or styles involved in what is studied. How ironic that the methods used to study leisure tend to standardize it, even though it is the primary arena for individual expression within the Western world.

SOME PROFESSIONAL IMPLICATIONS

In spite of the many limitations previously mentioned, recreation and leisure research implies much to the recreation, park, and leisure service professional. Some of the more important implications are outlined here.

The Central Importance of Qualities and Style of Recreation and Leisure Experience

Several research findings imply that the specific qualities, or style, of a recreation or leisure experience are of central importance in determining an individual's interest in and satisfaction derived from a specific activity (see Kelly, this volume). A number of studies show that individuals attain a wide range of differing satisfactions from the same leisure experience. Further, it appears that, in many cases, it is possible to substitute one leisure activity for another in ways which satisfy an individual's motives for participation (see, for example, Tinsley 1986). The style of participation (or qualities of the leisure activity) is a key determinant in satisfying these differing motives or sources of satisfactions (see, for example, Heywood 1987). Research by the Rapoports (1975), and many others, shows how central life interests vary at differing life stages, producing preoccupations which lead to specific interests, including interests in specific leisure activities. Such preoccupations lead to interests in leisure activities which are thought to be satisfying because of the qualities associated with the activity or the style of participation. Thus, preoccupation with socialization with members of the opposite sex will lead to different swimming programs and swimming pool design than would be appropriate where the desire is for demonstrated competence at what one has chosen. (Wave pools have excellent potential for the former, but not the latter).

Style and qualities of a leisure experience will also vary with levels of specialization in given leisure activities (see, for example, Donnelly, Vaske, and Graefe 1986). As Bryan (1979) and others have shown, the highly specialized fisherman differs from the novice in desired fishing environment, equipment used, and desired companions.

In short, the activity labels used by recreation and park practitioners (e.g. softball, hiking, dancing, crafts) do not really convey much about the meaning of the behaviors that will take place. Desired style of participation in leisure experience is often recognized by the commercial sector as a key determinant in whether individuals will stay in a hotel, eat at a restaurant, or join a fitness club. The importance of style and quality of participation does not apply only to the commercial sector; it applies to all forms of leisure expression and to all those who help provide such experiences.

The Recognition of Serving Partial Publics Who Are Partially Informed

Research has played a major role in developing an understanding of how the "public" or "consumers" use or do not use recreation, park, and leisure services. A number of studies have developed typologies such as "core" and "fringe" to describe the portion of the public which uses such services (see, for example, Howard and Crompton 1984). Others have documented the extent to which potential users are aware of such services and, among those who are aware, their information levels (see, for example, Spotts and Styne 1985)

Additionally, several studies have addressed the issue of barriers to participation, sometimes merely identifying the frequency of responses to "laundry lists" of barriers and, at other times, attempting to deal with the subject conceptually (see Goodale and Witt's chapter in this volume, and Crawford and Godbey 1987). All of this research has made it clear that the "full information assumption" which many practitioners make concerning their publics is patently false. Further, there is a heightened understanding that leisure service agencies, in reality, serve "partial publics," as do most social service organizations. Additionally, segments of the public simply are not interested in such services, and the barriers which keep other interested segments from participating cover a range of social and psychological factors as well as ones pertaining to the logistics and structure of the services offered. The cumulative effect of such research has been to begin stripping away the rhetoric of recreation, park, and leisure service agencies and to provide a basis upon which to understand and realistically plan such services.

The Link Between Individual Statuses and Recreation and Leisure Attitudes, Desires, and Participation

While much has been made of the "democratization" of leisure, there continues to be a strong relationship between a whole array of individual statuses and leisure attitudes and behavior (see, for example, Spreitzer and Snyder 1987). Such individual statuses do not operate in a causal way, nor do they operate in isolation from each other. Nevertheless, they are of critical importance in predicting and (perhaps more importantly) explaining leisure attitudes and behavior. Take, for example, the impact of generational effects. Today's older people are different from the next generation of the elderly because of the life events which shaped their generation. The three adult generations in American society today have been described by Masnick and Banes (1980). The oldest generation, born before 1920, survived the Great Depression. Most have been through two world wars. They were often immigrants, or sons and daughters of immigrants, who were brought up in an era when half the country was rural. They married late and had small families. They were exposed to a very limited range of leisure behaviors and were taught that leisure was suspect. Their levels of formal education are considerably lower than those of the other two generations. Many of them moved from rural areas to cities.

A second generation, born between 1920 and 1940, entered adulthood during a period of unparalleled affluence and optimism about the future. They married early, had large families, bought large houses and cars, and often moved from cities to suburbs. This "Baby Boom" generation obtained higher levels of formal education than their parents and advocated civil rights and environmental issues. Today, many of them are divorced. Leisure, for this generation, is viewed as legitimate when earned by work. It is accompanied by much specialized equipment and facilities.

The third and youngest generation, born during the "boom" years that began during World War II, began to settle in central cities and small towns, the areas deserted by their parents. More women in this generation have put independence, formal education, and work before marriage and childbearing. Leisure, for this generation, is viewed as a right and an important part of self expression. Many in this generation are marrying late, or not at all.

From this very terse description, it is clear that the effects of one's generation are of fundamental importance in regard to leisure. A recreation and park practitioner with an understanding of such effects would not be surprised that the very recreation program or facility which was successful with one generation was not (or will not be) with another.

The Increased Need for Knowledge in Determining Management Practices

Recreation and leisure research both implies and has responded to the increasing need for knowledge to establish management practices. While research has not yet been pivotal in shaping management, due partially to some of the limitations mentioned earlier, it helps increasingly to shape management practices. In short, current research, with all its serious limitations, has been increasingly helpful in influencing the ways in which specific programs and facilities are managed and operated. Perhaps because of its limitations, however, it has failed to affect significantly the underlying concepts and tenets of management itself.

Such research has dealt with a number of topics. First, it has investigated what people actually do while visiting areas and facilities managed for recreation purposes and the impacts that their behavior has on the environment (see, for example, Jubenville 1986), as well as a host of subjects dealing with management practices. One recent concern of such research has been the emergence of marketing practices in public leisure services (see, for example, Crompton and Lamb 1986). As recreation, park, and leisure service agencies have increasingly been required to generate their own revenues and to reduce costs, there has also been more attention paid to methods of doing this, including case studies of successful approaches (see, for example, Crompton 1987).

For many land managing agencies who, traditionally, have not considered recreation to be a legitimate use of the land in question, research has helped open the door to new styles of management and new management concerns. Managers of agencies involved in leisure services are slowly becoming information users and, as they do, the importance of research in their operations will increase.

The Connectedness of Recreation and Leisure Services to the Rest of Life

As the previous discussion implies, leisure services do not operate in a vacuum (or at least not for long). Leisure research can help provide information about the tenor of the times, the condition of the national or local psyche, or the demographic profile which will shape not only what people are likely to do during leisure but, more fundamentally, the values and conditions which will shape what leisure means.

A single case of leisure research will provide an example of this perspective. Research by Yankelovich, Skelly, and White (1986) found that the American public, during the 1980s, had begun to adapt to a variety of negative economic and social conditions: "the move to adaptation results in tempering the felt need to pursue a wide variety of leisure time activities, which had been a dominant approach of the 1960s and 1970s" (p. 5). Instead, individuals are more likely to seek advanced skills in a smaller range of leisure behaviors. Such a finding, when combined with research by Stebbins (1979), which identified the rise of the amateur whose leisure interests revolve around a single activity about which the individual is serious, knowledgeable, and specialized, would seem to have profound implications for public (and private) leisure services.

Not only are the qualitative aspects of an experience sponsored by a leisure service agency likely to assume additional importance, but there is also the need to plan for participants who are highly specialized in a leisure activity. This will affect almost all aspects of leisure services: planning leisure areas and facilities for use by the skilled and knowledgeable participant as well as the novice; leisure skills courses which continue far past the introductory stage; special events which are planned with the recognition that, for many, the event is of primary importance; and so on. There is also the clear implication that public recreation, park, and leisure service agencies may have to provide fewer services but of a much higher quality — a difficult feat to accomplish. "Quality," of course, is a subjective concept. Quality implies values and any research which addresses the qualitative aspects of leisure experience must have some value system specified to make it useful.

Recreation, park, and leisure services are connected to the rest of life and countless examples from research could help make, or re-establish, this connection.

SOME BROADER IMPLICATIONS

Not only does recreation and leisure research have a number of implications for the professional, it also contains a number of implications for the general academic community and the informed public. Among such implications are the following.

The Incompleteness of Science As A Method of Studying Recreation and Leisure

Science alone cannot provide all the models for the management or explanation of leisure behavior. As Cranz (1982) concluded after an extraordinary study of urban recreation and park systems undertaken from an historical perspective, the creation of recreation and park services in urban areas is not a matter of technology but rather one of cultural discovery. Similarly, as Kelly (1987, p. 235) concluded in a recent analysis of leisure from a theoretical perspective, leisure is best understood in terms of its dialectic nature: "a dialectic formulation can serve as the basis for many varieties of research but makes the sequential propositions of logical positivism impossible." This rather astounding proposition by America's foremost sociologist of leisure should be heeded. Leisure behavior — and, hence, leisure services — cannot be satisfactorily conceived or completely understood through the techniques of science, although science has much to contribute to our understanding of the subject. The nature of leisure is subjective and dialectic. It is both idea and ideal, involving complex concepts such as "freedom" and "pleasure" which are not directly observable or capable of being made operational for research. Recreation and leisure behavior is ultimately infinite, non-rational, and full of meaning which is, or can be, spiritual. It is dependent upon human imagination and, if those in recreation, park, and leisure services, as well as those within the university, are to benefit from recreation and leisure research, it must be understood that such research can never, in its present form, substitute for vision, intuition, historical knowledge, or feeling. All are necessary to manage organizations concerned with leisure behavior. All are necessary to grasp the subject intellectually.

The Inherently Interdisciplinary Nature of Recreation and Leisure Research

It follows from the previous point that recreation and leisure research is inherently interdisciplinary. It is the province of geographers, historians, theologians, psychologists, sociologists, recreation and park educators, and many, many others. The lack of interdisciplinary involvement has meant that what research tells us is often incomplete, out of context, or even incorrect. Take, for example, the belief that the "recreation and park movement" in the early part of the twentieth century in North America was somehow a beginning point for urban recreation and park reform. In reality, the Rational Recreation Movement, which began more than a century earlier in Britain, was concerned with most of the same reform agendas (Cunningham 1980), but it took research by a social historian to demonstrate this.

Recreation and leisure, as it has become a more central and distinct part of life, is more complex to understand and, at the same time, more important to be understood. It cuts across academic boundaries and competencies such that its study cannot be relegated to one curriculum or intellectual base. This reality is increasingly reflected in the diverse academic backgrounds of those who contribute to the recreation and leisure research literature, but many academic areas have yet to contribute in any substantial way (see the first and second chapters in this volume for further discussion).

Recreation and Leisure As the Emerging Center of the Economy

One of the emerging implications from recreation and leisure research is that what people choose to do during leisure is an important and, increasingly, a critical element of our economy. There are several indicators of this phenomenon. Direct expenditures for recreation and leisure account for almost 13 percent of household spending in the United States (Tierney 1982), and if indirect and illegal expenditures were considered, the percentage would increase dramatically. Travel and tourism is currently the largest industry in the world and the second or third most important sector of many country's economies. The transition in the economies of most major North American cities is from a manufacturing base to a base of leisure services: shopping, dining, tourism, theater, professional sports, high culture, parks, historic re-development, and other forms of leisure expression are critical to the economy of many cities. Conferences and conventions may be pivotal in determining whether or not a city can pay its bills.

Because of the increasingly large economic impact of recreation and leisure services, there has been a growing tendency to conduct impact studies of various recreation and tourism phenomena (see, for example, Walsh 1986), sometimes undertaken as though the significance of such phenomena were exclusively in the economic realm. Recreation and leisure professionals need to understand that economic impact studies provide insight into a by-product of the efforts of leisure service professionals, not the product. Recreation economists and other researchers, however, have begun to help the public develop an understanding of the increasingly huge economic impact of leisure behavior.

Recreation and Leisure Behavior, Broadly Defined, Cannot be a Central Purpose of any One Government Agency

It is clear from research dealing with recreation and leisure behavior that a fundamental change has occurred in the very meaning of such behavior and in the range of recreation and leisure experience. The extraordinary restrictions put on such behavior in the early stages of the industrial revolutions of modern nations have been, to an amazing extent, lifted. Leisure has moved from the realm of mere catharsis to pleasure to meaning and self-identity (see, for example, Goodale and Godbey 1988). As this has happened, it makes increasingly less sense to charge a single government agency with responsibility for "leisure." Leisure, which is experienced in individual terms in modern society, is essentially infinite in terms of meaning and forms of expression. It is not a phenomenon which a single government agency can deal with in a meaningful way. It would be like establishing a department of "self-actualization."

Further, the technical skills needed for the employees of such a department or agency would encompass an extraordinary range of human endeavor. In reality, recreation, park, and leisure service agencies select some aspect of leisure behavior (such as certain forms of sport, outdoor recreation, or hobbies) and provide services related to these. The study by Burton and Kyllo (1974) of the Canadian system offers a case in point. Providing for leisure in any comprehensive manner would not only be beyond the capacity of any single government (or non-government) agency, but it would also give that agency tremendous influence over the population in question. This can be seen in the changing names of government agencies in the United States, Canada, and elsewhere, names that change periodically to include sport, youth, tourism, heritage conservation, fitness, environment, parks, community services, culture, and other concerns.

Recreation and Leisure Behavior Cannot Be Ignored by Any Government Agency

While no government agency can provide "leisure" services comprehensively, the increased importance of recreation and leisure and the broadening of its functions means that no agency of government can afford to ignore it entirely. Leisure behavior is an important consideration in the design of schools and public housing, in the development of highway systems, in the well-being of the armed forces, in the incarceration and rehabilitation of criminals, in the management of public institutions for various special populations, and, to some capacity, in almost every function of government. Because of this, we are beginning to see a recognition of recreation and leisure as a legitimate concern of personnel in government agencies who previously would have had no interest in the subject or in recreation and leisure research. Those involved in functions as diverse as land management, transportation systems, housing, health, public water supply, and others will be more closely concerned with leisure-related issues. As this changes, the cutting edge of future research may shift to those in extremely diverse sectors of government, where new research questions may be asked and answered.

Recreation and Leisure As Learned Experience

A broad range of research implies that, increasingly, recreation and leisure are learned experiences into which the individual is socialized and that such learning is often necessary for enjoyment to take place. This learning is also, often, enjoyable (Kelly 1974). It is axiomatic among leisure researchers that people prefer doing something in their leisure which they do well. While some forms of leisure which do not involve skill, such as, perhaps, television viewing, may be exempted from this observation, the importance of learning in leisure expression has become central. Individuals are socialized into various forms of leisure expression, by friends, family, school, the mass media, and otherwise. This involves learning not only skills, but also how to appreciate and enjoy the experience. People with higher levels of formal education tend to have a larger range of leisure experiences than those with lower education levels, partly because the process of education exposes the individual to various leisure alternatives and takes some first, imperfect steps toward socializing them into the activity. The rise of non-vocational adult education, the central roles of highly acquired skills in many forms of currently popular leisure expression — such as high risk and adventure activities, sports pursued at high skill levels, historic and natural interpretation, computer play, and many other forms of leisure expression — are increasingly being combined with learning, or necessitate learning. This is not to argue that such activities are becoming most prevalent in terms of time spent; they are not. What can be claimed, however, is that they are becoming increasingly prevalent and that learning is an increasingly critical part of the experience.

Recreation and Leisure as Identity

Last, and perhaps most important, is the implication from the literature that recreation and leisure form an increasingly important component of individual identity. While such a conclusion is certainly judgmental, it seems warranted from the findings of a number of diverse types of research: research which shows the increasingly important link between satisfaction with the use of leisure and life satisfaction; research which shows that monetary spending for leisure has increased in recent years even when discretionary spending has not; and research which implies the frankly spiritual meaning of many behaviors, such as some forms of running, which the public often thinks of in terms of "physical" rather than spiritual fitness. Again, there is research which shows the increasing leisure use made of environments, from bathrooms to tours of abandoned coal mines to visits to the Arctic (and soon the moon) which were never thought of or used for such. Finally, there is research which implies that the ability to use leisure is an increasingly critical variable in the adjustment of the retired, various disability groups, and, in fact, all of us.

While these implications are broad in nature, they speak, or can speak, to the recreation, park, and leisure service practitioner at the most fundamental level, since such research defines the area of life to which the practitioner devotes his or her energies, in the hope of making it better.

References

Bryan, H. 1979. *Conflict in the Great Outdoors*. University of Alabama: University of Alabama Press.

Burton, T.L. and L.T. Kyllo. 1974. *Federal-Provincial Responsibilities for Leisure Services in Alberta and Ontario*. Ottawa.

Cranz, G. 1982. *The Politics of Park Design*. Cambridge, MA: MIT Press.

Crawford, D. and G. Godbey. 1987. "Reconceptualizing barriers to family recreation." *Leisure Sciences 9:* 119-127.

Crompton, J. 1987. *Doing More With Less in Parks and Recreation Services*. State College, PA: Venture Publishing.

Crompton, J. and C. Lamb. 1986. "The marketing audit: A starting point for strategic planning." *Journal of Park and Recreation Administration 4:* 19-34.

Cunningham, H. 1980. *Leisure in the Industrial Revolution*. London: Croom Helm.

Donnelly, M., J.J. Vaske, and A.R. Graefe. 1986. "Degree and range of leisure specialization: Toward a typology of boating related activities." *Journal of Leisure Research 18:* 81-96.

Epstein, S. 1981. "The stability of behavior: Implications for research." *American Psychologist 18:* 33-51.

Goodale, T. and G. Godbey. 1988. *The Evolution of Leisure: Historical and Philosophical Perspectives*. State College, PA: Venture Publishing.

Henkel, D. and G. Godbey. 1977. *Recreation and Parks in the Public Sector - Employemnt Statuses and Trends*. Arlington, VA: National Recreation and Park Association.

Heywood, J. 1987. "Experience preferences of participants in different types of river recreation groups." *Journal of Leisure Research 19:* 1-13.

Howard, D.R. and J.L. Crompton. 1984. "Who are the consumers of public park and recreation services? An analysis of the users and non-users of three municipal leisure service organizations." *Journal of Park and Recreation Administration 2:* 33-49.

Howe, C.Z. 1985. "Possibilities for using a qualitative research approach in the sociological study of leisure." *Journal of Leisure Research 17:* 212-224.

Jubenville, A. 1986. "Recreational use of public lands." *Journal of Park and Recreation Administration 4:* 53-61.

Kelly, J.R. 1974. "Socialization toward leisure: A developmental approach." *Journal of Leisure Research 6:*3:181-193.

Kelly, J.R. 1987. *Freedom to Be: A New Sociology of Leisure.* New York: Macmillan.

Masnick, G. and M.J. Banes. 1980. *The Nation's Families: 1960-1990.* Cambridge: Center for Urban Studies of MIT and Harvard.

Rapoport, R. and R.N. Rapoport. 1975. *Leisure and The Family Life Cycle.* Boston: Routledge and Kegan Paul.

Riddick, C., M. De Schriver, and F. Weissinger. 1984. "A methodological review of research in Journal of Leisure Research from 1978 to 1982." *Journal of Leisure Research 16:* 136-149.

Simmons Market Research Bureau. 1984. *Study of Media and Markets. Volume P-10, Sports and Leisure.* New York.

Spotts, D. and T. Styne. 1985. "Measuring the public's familiarity with recreation areas." *Journal of Leisure Research 17:* 253-265.

Spreitzer, E. and E.E. Snyder. 1987. "Educational-occupational fit and leisure orientation as related to life satisfaction." *Journal of Leisure Research 19:* 149-158.

Stebbins, R. 1979. *Amateurs: On the Margin Between Work and Leisure.* Beverly Hills: Sage Publications.

Theodorson, G.A. and A.G. Theodorson. 1969. *Modern Dictionary of Sociology.* New York: Thomas Y. Crowell.

Tierney, V. 1982. *The Economic Significance of Recreation in Pennsylvania.* Harrisburg, PA: Department of Environmental Resources.

Tinsley, H.E.A.. 1986. "Motivations to participate in recreation: Their identification and measurement. A Literature Review." Washington, DC: President's Commission on Americans Outdoors.

Walsh, R.G. 1986. *Recreation Economic Decisions: Comparing Benefits and Costs.* State College, PA: Venture Publishing.

Yankelovich, Skelly, and White, Inc. 1982. *The Impact of Changing Values on Leisure.*

Zuzanek, J. 1982. "Leisure research in North America from a socio-historical perspective." Paper presented at the NRPA Leisure Research Symposium, Louisville, KY.

CHARTING THE FUTURE

Thomas L. Burton and Edgar L. Jackson

DESCRIPTION AND PRESCRIPTION

The intent in the opening chapter of this book was to offer an overview of the development of leisure and recreation research during the past twenty years. The purpose was to *describe*, in some detail, what has occurred in the two decades that have passed since the publication of the inaugural edition of the *Journal of Leisure Research* in 1969. The title, "Mapping The Past," was intended to indicate the kind of detail that was envisaged. Maps typically illustrate the primary features of an area: roads, rivers, rail-lines, principal geological characteristics, and major urban concentrations. Depending on their scale, they may also include the secondary features: minor roads, streams, footpaths, lesser geological characteristics, and small towns and villages. Their principal purpose is to represent, cartographically, what actually exists on the ground.

In mapping the past development of leisure and recreation research, the purpose was to describe the principal features in sufficient detail to provide a base from which the reader could view the specialized themes that were addressed in the score or so of chapters that were to follow. Thus, it drew upon past reviews of the state of leisure and recreation research and upon the findings of an international survey of active scholars in the field, in order to assess the growth in the quantity of research during the past twenty years, the varying contributions that have been made by a wide range of scholarly disciplines, and the particular issues and topics that have been most prevalent in this research effort. It also assessed the views of active scholars concerning the quality of the progress that has been made during this time. While limited, the level of detail in our opening chapter was specific and focused.

The purpose in this closing chapter is considerably different. The intent in charting the future of leisure and recreation research is to offer a prescription for future research efforts *in broad terms*. Only a few major concerns will be addressed, and these in outline only. The object is to provide a skeletal framework which emphasizes the principal issues and themes that, we believe, must be addressed by the scholarly community in recreation and leisure studies during the coming decade and beyond.

The basis for our observations is threefold: first, comments and suggestions in the various reviews of the state of leisure and recreation research that were cited in our opening chapter; second, the proposals put forward by the respondents to the international survey of active research scholars in recreation and leisure studies; and third, the recommendations made by the authors of the other chapters in this volume. All of these have been filtered through our own perceptions and are colored by our own backgrounds and experiences. What has emerged is a series of observations and comments on a limited number of themes which, collectively, reflect a broad prescription for future research in recreation and leisure studies. Though they may have varying degrees of support within the scholarly (and professional) community in the field, these observations are, in the final analysis, personal.

THE DEVELOPMENT OF CONCEPTS AND THEORIES

One of the six questions that was included in the international survey of active research scholars in recreation and leisure studies asked respondents to identify the three principal issues or needs that must be addressed during the next decade or so. The question was open-ended (the only one of this type in the survey), and requested the respondents to state these issues in their own words and at any length. The responses consisted of a mix of conceptual, theoretical, and methodological needs, as well as calls for research on specific substantive questions (Table 1). The strongest plea, however, was for the development of stable concepts and theories about leisure and recreation. Almost one-third (30.8 percent) of the respondents gave this as one of the three principal issues to be addressed. Furthermore, in doing so, many respondents offered comments and opinions. One Canadian respondent remarked: "If we do not understand why people choose to participate or not to participate in various forms of leisure, how can we hope to proceed to questions of how, with whom, and so on? We need a stable theory explaining why people recreate." An American respondent commented on "the imperative need to integrate explanations of leisure behavior with the dominant theories in psychology and sociology." Yet another called for "the development of a sound theoretical base unique to leisure and recreation." Finally, there was the cry from the heart of one respondent who pleaded that "we look at theory — from anywhere and wherever — and try to apply it to leisure and recreation!" The same call for the development of stable concepts and theories has also been made in many of the state-of-the-art reviews of recreation and leisure studies carried out during the past decade or so, notably those by Bregha (1979), Burton (1979, 1980, 1981), D'Amours (1984), Harper (1981), Rojek (1985), and Stockdale (1987).

Table 1
The Principal Issues for Research During the Next Decade
(n = 143)

Issues	Times Mentioned		Respondents Mentioning
	n	%	%
Development of concepts and theories	44	11.4	30.8
Research methods and techniques	33	8.6	23.1
Forecasting models and futures methods	9	2.3	6.3
Leisure, socialization, and social change	32	8.3	22.4
Leisure, lifestyles, and quality of life	27	7.0	18.9
Education for leisure	14	3.6	9.8
Leisure opportunities for special groups	29	7.5	20.3
Political economy of leisure	16	4.2	11.2
Policy studies	17	4.4	11.9
Planning and management	21	5.5	14.7
Delivery system	18	4.7	12.6
Professionalism and practice	17	4.4	11.9
Leisure values, attitudes, experiences	20	5.2	14.0
Leisure demand, consumption, behavior	16	4.2	11.2
Environmental impacts and issues	14	3.6	9.8
Economic and social impacts	13	3.4	9.1
Leisure and tourism	15	3.9	10.5
Historical studies	9	2.3	6.3
Other issues	21	5.5	14.7
TOTAL	385	100.0	-

Note:
Each respondent was invited to mention up to three issues. The **n** for the
number of respondents is 143. The **n** for times mentioned is 385, an average of
2.7 responses per respondent.

It is important to understand that this call for the development of stable concepts and theories does *not* imply that no such concepts and theories currently exist. Concepts (in the sense of generalized notions) abound in the literature about the nature, character, and meaning of leisure — as Godbey and Goodale have demonstrated in their recent book, *The Evolution of Leisure: Historical and Philosophical Perspectives* (1988). At a more specific level, various researchers have developed concepts that seek to explain sources of constraints on leisure behavior (e.g., Godbey 1985; Iso-Ahola and Mannell 1985); the relationships between values, societal types, and characteristics of leisure and recreation (Jackson 1986, and this volume); the seeking and escaping dimensions of leisure behavior (Iso-Ahola 1984); the nature and characteristics of leisure planning (Burton 1976, and this volume); and so on.

Theories, in the sense of specific (testable) principles that hypothesize explanations of the nature, character, and meaning of leisure also have a considerable history. Wilensky (1960), for example, developed the spillover-compensation theory of the relationship between work and leisure. Parker (1971, 1983) refined this notion to produce a theory of extension, opposition, and neutrality between the two. Rojek (1985, and this volume) has demonstrated how sociological theories of agency and structure have been engaged in a long-running battle to explain the nature and meaning of leisure, to both the individual and society. Stockdale (this volume) notes how the theory of social representations, deriving from social psychology, offers a powerful basis for developing an understanding of leisure as an integral component of the experience and behavior of individuals caught up in an increasingly complex web of personal and societal situations and expectations. And the list, of course, goes on.

Several points emerge from this brief review. First, there is evidence of a considerable preoccupation with concepts and theory among those currently engaged in leisure and recreation research — and, indeed, among many practitioners as well (see, for example, "Search Into Research," *Recreation Alberta*, July-August, 1988). Second, evident from the literature and studies that have illustrated this preoccupation is a search, by some scholars, for a unique theory. We noted earlier the comment of one respondent to the international survey of active leisure scholars which argued for "the development of a sound theoretical base *unique* to leisure and recreation" (our italics). This merely echoes similar comments that have been made elsewhere (see, for example, Burton and Taylor 1984). Third, there are some in the field who go even further, and who appear to be in search of nothing less than a Holy Grail — an all-encompassing, universal, and grand theory capable of expounding upon the laws and dynamics of leisure, for both society (in all its complex and different forms) and the individual within it. Finally, and perhaps most important, this misguided search for the unique and universal fails to recognize that abundant concepts and theories *do*, in fact, already exist — principally, if not exclusively, within the primary social science disciplines that have contributed to the development of leisure and recreation research during the past two decades.

What, then, do we make of all this? It is, perhaps, as well to note unequivocally that we do not oppose or look askance upon the general concern within the leisure and recreation field for the development of a relatively stable set of concepts and theories. The term "relatively stable" is used advisedly, since it is a mark of vibrancy in many fields and disciplines for concepts and theories to evolve on the basis of both argument and empirical observation. A pertinent example would be the evolution of theories about the work-leisure relationship during the past two decades alone: from compensation-spillover, to extension-opposition-neutrality, to ways in which the theory of social representations might view the two life spheres, to the notion of relationality, with its implicit rejection of a constant and objective interaction between the two. None of these theories necessarily claims to be the correct or dominant explanation. Rather, each offers (often radically) alternate explanations. The preoccupation with concepts and theories in leisure and recreation is not, then, in itself, a worrisome matter.

What *does* give us cause for concern, however, is the preoccupation among some leisure scholars and practitioners with the search for a single, dominant, or unique theory. Leisure and recreation, like other aspects of social life, such as education, religion, family, and crime, are phenomena which are readily amenable to examination through the theories of a wide array of the social sciences (a point which should be obvious, if only from the contributions to this volume), as well as through the growing collection of multidisciplinary and interdisciplinary approaches that have been developed in recent years. One of the significant findings to emerge from the international survey of active research scholars was the general perception that virtually all of the social science disciplines and professional fields of study have contributed to the development of leisure studies during the past two decades. This reassuring discovery was tempered, however, by the disconcerting finding that most respondents tended to perceive their own disciplines as having made the first or second most significant contributions, and that the detailed findings on this topic, when taken as a surrogate indicator of communication among disciplines, provided little indication of a "two-way street." The picture is not a stark one: there are indications of effective and important cross-disciplinary communications in leisure studies, not only from the findings of the survey, but also from the state-of-the-art reviews and several of the chapters in this volume (see especially those by Rojek, Kelly, Jackson, Goodale and Witt, and Wall).

This cross-disciplinarity has also been sustained by the establishment and growth of organizations of scholars (and some practitioners), which have been designed to embrace many disciplines. The (British) Leisure Studies Association has succeeded in attracting members from a wide variety of disciplinary backgrounds, as well as those studying in such multidisciplinary fields as environmental studies, health and nutrition, and education. (Unfortunately, because there are few academic departments or units of recreation and leisure studies as such, there are few members from this milieu). The Canadian Association for Leisure Studies has a membership which is almost equally divided between scholars from many social science disciplines and those studying within multidisciplinary contexts: and, in this case, there is significant representation from the academic departments of recreation and leisure studies. (Regrettably, there is no parallel in the United States to these two organizations). But, notwithstanding these positive indicators, the principal impression is one of insufficient communication or cross-fertilization among the disciplines.

It is our contention, then, that researchers in recreation and leisure studies should be considerably more active in exploring concepts and theories (as well as methods and applications) beyond the confines of their own disciplines. That this is currently happening cannot be denied. There is also some basis for believing that it is happening more frequently today than it did a decade ago — thanks, in no small measure, to the various conferences of the Leisure Studies Association, as well as the triennial Canadian Congress on Leisure Research. Nevertheless, the dominant impression that we have gained is that cross-disciplinary fertilization is still the exception rather than the rule. This, we suggest, is the real issue underlying the current preoccupation with the development of concepts and theories in the field.

THE ENHANCEMENT OF METHODS AND TECHNIQUES

If the most pressing concern of respondents to the international survey of active leisure scholars was for the development of stable concepts and theories, second in importance was a concern for the methodological state of the field. About one-quarter (23.1 percent) of the respondents called for the enhancement of research methods and techniques in recreation and leisure studies (Table 1). We noted in our opening chapter that many of the state-of-the-art reviews had chastised scholars in the field for their general reluctance to employ research methods and techniques other than the relatively simplistic questionnaire survey (e.g. Burton 1980; Iso-Ahola 1984; Patmore and Collins 1980; Riddick *et al* 1984; Social Science Research Council/Sports Council 1978; Stockdale 1987). Several of the authors in this book have also remarked upon this general aura of methodological rigidity. Rojek, noting that empiricism has been the dominant approach to the study of recreation and leisure during the past two decades or so, observes that the principal methods have been questionnaires, surveys and statistical analysis (Rojek, this volume). Stockdale, citing Riddick *et al.* (1984), notes that leisure research suffers not only from chronic problems of measurement, but is also strongly biased toward survey research methods (Stockdale, this volume). Similar kinds of observations, both direct and indirect, are to be found in the contributions of Bella, Godbey, Goodale and Witt, and Kelly.

Several of the respondents to the international survey of active leisure scholars amplified their statements about a perceived deficiency in, and an urgent need for the improvement of, methods and techniques employed in recreation and leisure research. One noted that: "There is a major over-emphasis upon survey techniques and statistical analysis — and the fault lies squarely at the feet of the major journals which are obsessed with 'observable facts' (only *Leisure Studies* has fully avoided this mould)." Another, citing the same condition, saw its cause in the growth of multidisciplinary academic departments, such as recreation and leisure studies, in which "the methodological rigor associated with the principal social science departments is rarely demanded or attained. As a result, researchers in our field are loath to go beyond the tried and trusted methods of surveys and bivariate analysis." Yet another noted that "our methodological poverty is directly related to our persistent failure to be cumulative in our theoretical development."

The principal point to be gleaned from all of this is not the attribution of blame, nor even the overriding preponderance of survey methods, *per se*, in the field as a whole. It is, as we noted in our opening chapter, the general sense of concern and disquiet among scholars in the field about the quality and appropriateness of the bundle of research methods and techniques currently being employed in recreation and leisure studies, especially the heavy dependence upon quantitative methods that are tied very closely to those that dominate our parent disciplines. And, surely, the solution to this can be found only within the body of active research scholars itself. No matter what may be our own particular disciplinary training, we should strive to make ourselves — and, even more important, our research students — familiar with methodological approaches to the study of leisure beyond the confines of our own disciplines. We need to gain an understanding of (and, yes, even a tolerance for) methods of accumulating knowledge that are not empirical and quantitative in character: the philosophical discourse so aptly demonstrated by Cooper's contribution to this volume; phenomenology; historiography; ethnography; and, not least, theorizing. We are led, then, back to the comment we made earlier when discussing the development of concepts and theories. We contend that concepts, theories, methods, and techniques are not discrete entities, but are closely interwoven. Their development in an inherently multidisciplinary field such as recreation and leisure studies depends, in the final analysis, upon the ability of leisure scholars from each and all of the pertinent disciplines to communicate with, learn from, and respect the contributions of those whose disciplinary backgrounds and training do not match their own.

TOPICS AND ISSUES

As befits a many-sided domain of human behavior, recreation and leisure have thrown up a large array of diverse topics for researchers. As we noted in the opening chapter of this book, the dominant themes in research in the field have included such divergent issues as attitudes and motivations, demand analyses, carrying capacity, parks and reserves, sport, recreation delivery systems, and many more. In looking to the future, the respondents to the international survey of active leisure scholars suggested that priority should be given to the development of concepts and theories and to the enhancement of research methods and approaches. But following these overriding developmental concerns was a series of suggestions for research on particular topics and issues.

Chief among these was the call for increased (and improved) research into the relationships between leisure and social change, with more than one-fifth (22.4 percent) citing this (Table 1). One respondent suggested that: "We must examine and understand how leisure is affected by larger social and economic changes in society, such as aging, unemployment, drug abuse, and so on." Several cited the importance of studies of leisure and gender, with one echoing some of the points developed in Bella's chapter (this volume): "The field of the sociology of sport has an extensive literature on gender and feminist theory. This is absent in recreation and leisure (except for gender comparisons in survey data)". Yet another comment had to do with deviant leisure, an issue which has been explored in Rojek's chapter (this volume): "We must give greater attention to the relationships between leisure and delinquency, to 'negative recreation' and to progressive alternatives for youth."

Finally, within this broad notion of leisure and social change, was a series of calls for improved international and cross-cultural leisure research. Indeed, one respondent took us to task by noting: "I would have wished to see some scope [in the questionnaire] for national issues and emphases. I fear you have been in North America too long!" Another simply noted an important need for "comparative leisure studies, particularly across dominant language barriers and between the 'First' and 'Third' Worlds."

In addition to this strong call for research on issues relating to leisure and social change were suggestions for research on leisure opportunities for special populations (20.3 percent of the respondents), the relationships between leisure, lifestyle, and quality of life (18.9 percent), planning and management issues (14.7 percent), and leisure values, attitudes, and experiences (14.0 percent). At the other extreme, there seemed to be little support for research into forecasting models and futures methods (only 6.3 percent), notwithstanding the fact that this topic has been a major concern in the past.

Many of the themes that emerged from the international survey of active leisure scholars have been addressed, in great detail, in the various chapters in this book. We have noted that Bella's chapter has confronted the issue of gender in leisure research, in a far-reaching and soul-searching manner, and that Rojek has addressed the need for studies of deviant leisure. He has also suggested that there is an urgent need to consider the implications of the collapse of the work-leisure dichotomy and the place of fantasy in people's perceptions and experiences of leisure. Glyptis has discussed the relationships between leisure and unemployment, and has charted some directions for research. Kelly, Iso-Ahola, and Mannell, each in their own way, have tackled issues of the meaning of leisure to individuals and its place in lifestyles and the quality of life. Burton has reviewed approaches to leisure forecasting, policymaking, and planning, and has suggested a preferred way of addressing these. And so the list goes on.

It seems to us, however, that among all of these perfectly legitimate research topics is one which, in some ways, supersedes them all and, in fact, provides a foundation for the majority of them. This was recognized by a significant proportion of the survey respondents and has been addressed, explicitly or implicitly, by many of the writers in the book. It was the specific concern of Jackson's chapter. It has to do with the values ascribed to leisure and recreation by people engaged in leisure and recreation activities. We need to investigate the values that underlie leisure and recreation behavior. For it is these values that determine so much else: motivation, satisfaction, behavior (deviant or otherwise), perceived quality of life, cross-national and cross-cultural differences, forecasts, policies, plans, gender differences, and much more. Moreover, examining the values of the leisure participant also forces the researcher to recognize, consider, and question the value framework within which he or she is conducting research. In the final analysis, nothing that we do as leisure researchers and scholars is entirely value-free, no matter how much we strive to be objective. What we *must* be aware of, and willing to acknowledge, are the particular value frameworks that we choose to employ. One sure way of reminding ourselves of this is through research which examines the values that people ascribe to their own leisure behaviors and experiences.

FRAGMENTATION OR PLURALITY?

A major outcome of the international survey of active leisure scholars was the realization that almost two-thirds (61.5 percent) of the respondents considered that recreation and leisure research is characterized by fragmentation — "consisting of disparate, and even conflicting, conceptual and methodological development, inconsistent terminology, disconnected themes, and intellectual disharmony." This view was reinforced further, of course, by the dominant pleas for future research to be directed at the development of stable concepts and theories, and the enhancement of research methods and techniques. Yet, as we noted in the opening chapter, there were a few respondents who *welcomed* this sense of fragmentation. One remarked that: "Fragmented approaches are not unhealthy for a field of study." Another commented that: "There is no absolute truth: the debate, discussion and differences of opinion that derive from fragmentation are healthy." Yet another noted that: "Fragmented approaches and conflict are not unhealthy. It is the parochial and controlling influences of a dominant paradigm that may prohibit a deeper understanding of leisure as a meaningful part of life. There is a (mistaken) belief that data from the scientific methodological paradigm are more important than insights obtained from phenomenology, heuristics, ethnography, and the like, because they are 'hard' data."

We believe that there is a confusion here between the notions of fragmentation and pluralism. Fragmentation, as it was defined in the survey (and reproduced above), implies a lack of any commonality in the field: the absence of a common language, conflicting concepts at the most fundamental level, discord and disharmony in comprehending the very nature of the field. Pluralism, on the other hand, reflects the view that there is more than one principle, concept, or theory capable of explaining leisure in its many manifestations. The quotations noted above appear to be referring to pluralism rather than fragmentation. And, as we argued earlier, in the section on the development of concepts and theories, it is a mark of vibrancy in many fields and disciplines for concepts and theories to evolve on the basis of both argument and empirical observation. We believe that the leisure studies field *is* overly fragmented at this time; but we also believe that there is room in the field for a wide diversity of concepts and theories. All may be legitimate, depending on the purpose of the investigation. When it comes to the question of the future development of the field, we are unashamed pluralists.

LEISURE RESEARCH AND THE SOCIAL SCIENCES

In the opening chapter to this volume, we introduced a model as an organizational framework against which to examine past changes in leisure studies. This model, which illustrates three sets of factors that effect change in leisure studies, is reproduced here (Figure 1). The two key components of leisure studies shown

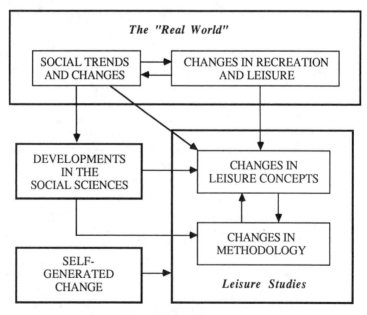

Figure 1
Components of and Influences upon Leisure Studies

in the model are concepts and methodologies. (We argue that specific substantive topics are best excluded at this level of commentary). The three main influences on the development of leisure studies are identified in the model as: the "real world," made up of changes in recreation and leisure, and broader social trends and changes; developments in the social sciences; and self-generated change. These three influences are not mutually exclusive: they overlap. Nor are they of equal strength. The interaction among them is especially evident for the relative effects of social trends and changes, changes in recreation and leisure, and developments in the social sciences. As we argued in the opening chapter, to try to separate out specific effects would be pointless: the model is a matter of convenience that enables us to suggest what have been some of the principal influences on the field of study.

In the opening chapter, we employed the model as a descriptive device to show what, we believe, have been the relative strengths of the various components in the development of leisure research in the recent past. We contended that changes in leisure and recreation have been the most powerful influence on the past evolution of leisure studies, followed, in rank-order, by self-generated change, social trends and changes, and developments in the social sciences.

In this concluding chapter, we wish to employ the model in a prescriptive manner. We suggest that there is a pressing need within the community of leisure scholars for a greater recognition of, and closer ties to, those influences on the development of leisure studies that have been relatively neglected in the past. In particular, leisure researchers must be much more aware of developments in the social sciences generally. We need to know what is happening on the frontiers of social science research: in sociology, psychology, economics, geography, political science, and the many other disciplines and fields of study that contribute to leisure research. Moreover, this interest should extend to both theoretical and applied research.

Leisure scholars also need to pay more attention to social trends and changes, and to place and interpret the results of their own research in this broad societal context. We need to be able to relate leisure research to social change. It is our belief that relatively less emphasis should be placed upon changes in recreation and leisure and upon self-generated change. Not that these should be ignored: far from it. What we advocate, instead, is an *improved balance* among the various influences upon the content and direction of leisure studies.

We cannot prescribe an ideal balance among these influences. In fact, we doubt that such a prescription would be sensible or realistic. Moreover, the balance will invariably shift over time and differ among countries. Of one thing, however, we are sure. If leisure studies continues to be guided in its research efforts primarily by changes in recreation and leisure *per se* and by self-generated change from leisure scholars, to the virtual exclusion of the broader social changes in the "real world" and developments in the social sciences generally, the field will run the grave risk of becoming cut off, both from the "real world" and from the most up-to-date thinking on human behavior. Leisure studies will face the threat of being dismissed as, at best, tangential and, more likely, irrelevant! To return to our opening metaphor, leisure studies will run the risk of exploring ever more isolated peninsulas.

To conclude on a more positive note, let us emphasize, once more, the need for plurality in leisure studies — a theme common to each of the broad recommendations that we have made earlier in this chapter. Plurality is required in the development of concepts and theories (and in the concepts and theories themselves), in methods and approaches, in the topics and issues addressed by researchers, and in the sources of ideas that will fuel future developments in leisure studies. (And to ensure that plurality does not lead to fragmentation, it is also essential that leisure studies build cumulatively upon this work). Furthermore, as is surely evident from much of the material in this book, and especially in comments taken from the international survey of leisure scholars, plurality, like beauty, is in the eye of the beholder. In the final analysis, then, what is most needed in leisure studies is a perceptual shift among those in the field, based on mutual understanding, tolerance, and above all, increased communication.

References

Alberta Recreation and Parks Association. 1988. "Search into research." *Recreation Alberta 7(3):* 4-16.

Bregha, F.J. 1979. "Future directions of leisure research." In *Contemporary Leisure Research: Proceedings of the Second Canadian Congress on Leisure Research*, pp. 578-581. Toronto: Ontario Research Council on Leisure.

Burton, T.L. 1976. *Making Man's Environment: Leisure.* Toronto: Van Nostrand Reinhold.

Burton, T.L. 1979. "The development of leisure research in Canada: An analogical tale." *Loisir et Société 2:* 13-34.

Burton, T.L. 1980. "The maturation of leisure research." In *Recreation and Leisure: Issues in an Era of Change* eds. T.L. Goodale and P.A. Witt, pp. 373-385. State College, PA: Venture Publishing.

Burton, T.L. 1981. "You can't get there from here: A personal perspective on recreation forecasting in Canada." *Recreation Research Review 9:* 38-43.

Burton, T.L. and J. Taylor (eds.). 1984. *Proceedings of the Third Canadian Congress on Leisure Research.* Edmonton: Canadian Association for Leisure Studies.

D'Amours, M.C. 1984. "Leisure sciences and leisure studies: Indicators of interdisciplinarity?" *Leisure Sciences 6:* 359-373.

Godbey, G. 1985. "Non-participation in public leisure services: A model." *Journal of Park and Recreation Administration 3:* 1-13.

Godbey, G. and T.L. Goodale. 1988. *The Evolution of Leisure: Historical and Philosophical Perspectives.* State College, PA: Venture Publishing.

Harper, W. 1981. "The experience of leisure." *Leisure Sciences 4:* 113-126.

Iso-Ahola, S.E. 1984. "What is appropriate for publication?" *Journal of Leisure Research 16(4):* iv-v.

Iso-Ahola, S.E. and R.C. Mannell. 1985. "Social and psychological constraints on leisure." In *Constraints on Leisure*, ed. M.G. Wade, pp. 111-154. Springfield, IL: Charles C. Thomas.

Jackson, E.L. 1986. "Outdoor recreation participation and attitudes to the environment." *Leisure Studies 5:* 1-23.

Parker, S. 1971. *The Future of Work and Leisure*. London: MacGibbon and Kee.

Parker, S. 1983. *Leisure and Work*. London: George Allen and Unwin.

Patmore, J.A. and M.F. Collins. 1980. "Recreation and leisure." *Progress in Human Geography 4:* 91-97.

Riddick, C., M. De Schriver, and E. Weissinger. 1984. "A methodological review of research in the Journal of Leisure Research from 1978 to 1982." *Journal of Leisure Research 16:* 136-149.

Rojek, C. 1985. *Capitalism and Leisure Theory*. London: Tavistock.

Social Science Research Council/Sports Council. 1978. "Report of the Joint Working Party on Recreation Research." London.

Stockdale, J.E. 1987. *Methodological Techniques in Leisure Research*. London: Sports Council/Economic and Social Research Council Joint Panel on Leisure and Recreation Research.

Wilensky, H.L. 1960. "Work, careers and social integration." *International Social Science Journal 12:* 543-560.

THE EDITORS AND CONTRIBUTORS

The Editors

Edgar L. Jackson took a First Class Honors degree in Geography at the London School of Economics, University of London, in 1967. He continued his education in Canada, completing the M.A. degree in Geography at the University of Calgary in 1970 and the Ph.D. degree in Geography at the University of Toronto in 1974, where his research focussed on environmental perception and behavior. After a year as Visiting Assistant Professor at the University of Toronto, he joined the Department of Geography at the University of Alberta, where he is now Professor.

 Dr. Jackson has conducted numerous studies of public participation in recreation, both in the academic environment and as a consultant to business firms and government departments. He has published some twenty research-based papers related to recreation in the major international recreation research journals, as well as many other papers and articles on social science research and resource management (especially energy and natural hazards). His current research deals with several aspects of recreation, including the influence of environmental attitudes on outdoor recreation participation, and leisure non-participation and constraints. His teaching responsibilities include senior undergraduate and graduate courses on Recreation Geography. Dr. Jackson is Secretary of the Canadian Association for Leisure Studies, an Associate Editor of the *Journal of Leisure Research*, and a Fellow of the Academy of Leisure Sciences.

Thomas L. Burton took a B.Sc. (Economics) degree at University College, London, in 1963, and a Ph.D. degree in Land Economics at Wye College, London, in 1967. He has held appointments as Assistant Lecturer at Wye College, London, from 1963 to 1966; Lecturer in the Centre for Urban and Regional Studies, University of Birmingham, from 1966 to 1969; Assistant Professor in the Department of Parks and Recreation at Michigan State University from 1969 to 1970; Associate Professor and Graduate Chairman in the School of Urban and Regional Planning, University of Waterloo, from 1970 to 1973; and Consultant to the Ministry of State for Urban Affairs, Government of Canada, from 1973 to 1976. Since 1976 he has been a Professor in the Department of Recreation and Leisure Studies (formerly Recreation Administration), University of Alberta, and was Department Chairman from 1979 to 1988. He has been a Visiting Professor at the University of British Columbia and at the Phillip Institute of Technology in Melbourne, Australia.

 Dr. Burton is the author of seven books in the recreation, resource, planning, and research fields, as well as more than fifty reports, articles, and papers. He was founding President of the Canadian Association for Leisure Studies from 1981 to 1984, and is again President for 1987-1990. He is also a member of the Board of Directors of the World Leisure and Recreation Association, and a Fellow of the Academy of Leisure Sciences. Dr. Burton teaches leisure services policy and planning at the graduate level and is currently conducting research in the area of professional education and professionalization in recreation.

The Contributors

Leslie Bella took an honors degree in Architectural Studies from the University of Newcastle-upon-Tyne in 1966, and then emigrated to Canada. In 1969 she completed a Master's in Social Work at the University of British Columbia, winning both the University Prize in Social Work and the British Columbia Association of Social Workers' Prize. In 1981 she completed a Ph.D. in Political Science at the University of Alberta.

She has been employed as a community worker in Winnipeg and Edmonton. In 1975 she was appointed as Lecturer in the Department of Recreation and Leisure Studies (then Recreation Administration) at the University of Alberta. From 1982 to 1984, she served as Associate Dean of Physical Education and Recreation, and from 1983 to 1985 chaired the President's Advisory Committee on Sexual Harassment. In 1986, she joined the University of Regina as Dean of Social Work, and in 1989 moved to Memorial University, St. John's, Newfoundland.

Her more than seventy publications include a detailed study of Alberta social policy under the Social Credit Governments, and *Parks for Profit*, a history of Canada's national parks. Her current research includes investigation of the source of the "Christmas imperative" and a study of power and the professions.

Rabel J. Burdge is Professor in the Institute for Environmental Studies, Department of Agricultural Economics (Rural Sociology), and Department of Leisure Studies (Parks and Recreation) at the University of Illinois at Urbana-Champaign, and is a member of the graduate faculty in Urban and Regional Planning. He has also served on the faculties of the University of Kentucky (Lexington), University of Washington (Seattle), and the U.S. Air Force Academy in Colorado Springs.

Educated at Penn State and Ohio State Universities, he is the author of *Coping with Change: An Interdisciplinary Assessment of the Lake Shelbyville Reservoir*, co-author of *Social Change in Rural Societies: A Rural Sociology Textbook*, former editor of the *Journal of Leisure Research*, and founding co-editor of both *Leisure Sciences* and *Society and Natural Resources*. He has written over two hundred scholarly articles and papers on natural resource issues, needs assessment surveys, the use of public involvement in the resource decision making process, the social impacts of development on rural communities, and outdoor leisure behavior.

Dr. Burdge has served as Vice-President of the Rural Sociological Society and was the 1988 recipient of the Society's Natural Resources Research Award for contributions to the sociology of natural resources. He received the 1982 Theodore and Franklin Roosevelt Award for Excellence in Recreation, Park and Conservation Research given by the National Recreation and Park Association.

Richard W. Butler is Professor of Geography at the University of Western Ontario. He was educated at Nottingham University (B.A., 1964) and Glasgow University (Ph.D., 1973). He has been a faculty member at Western Ontario since 1967, with leave periods at Glasgow School of Art (1975), St. Andrews University (1982-1983), and Edinburgh University (1983). His research interests are in the development and evolution of tourist destination areas, the effects of tourism and recreation on visitor and visited populations, links between literature, geography and tourism, and, in a regional sense, the Pleasure Periphery, Canada and Scotland. A forward-looking lapsed historian, he is working on a special issue of the *Annals of Tourism Research*, on "Tourism in the Twenty-First Century".

W.E. Cooper took a B.A. (Philosophy) degree at Occidental College, Los Angeles, in 1966, a B.Litt. degree at the University of Oxford in 1971, and a Ph.D. degree in Philosophy at the University of Calgary in 1976. He has taught at the University of Alberta as Sessional Lecturer (1971-72), Assistant Professor (1972-78), and Associate Professor (since 1978). He has also taught at the University of Maryland (1970-71).

Dr. Cooper has published extensively in philosophical journals on topics in the areas of Philosophy of Mind and Social Philosophy. Currently he is preparing a book on philosophical aspects of leisure and recreation theory. Among his other research interests is the philosophical psychology of William James.

B.L. Driver took a B.S. degree in Forestry from the Virginia Polytechnic Institute in 1957, and two M.S. degrees (Natural Resource Administration in 1964 and Environmental Health Planning in 1965) and an interdisciplinary Ph.D. (Public Policy Analysis and Resource Planning — with a heavy dose of economics — in 1967) from the University of Michigan. He worked in a management position with the U.S. Department of Agriculture (USDA) Forest Service from 1957 to 1961; as an Assistant and Associate Professor at the University of Michigan from 1967 to 1973, with an appointment in Michigan's Survey Research Center from 1971 to 1973; as Recreation Research project leader with the USDA Forest Service's Rocky Mountain Forest and Range Experiment Station from 1973 to 1981; and as Visiting Lecturer at Yale University in 1982 and 1983. He is currently a research social scientist at the Rocky Mountain Station and a faculty affiliate at Colorado State University.

Dr. Driver has published over eighty scientific articles, edited two texts, and co-authored about fifty reports — mostly empirical — to public agencies. He was a lead scientist on a long-term program of research evaluating the U.S. Youth Conservation Corps Program, took the lead role in developing the 45 Recreation Experience Scales and has applied them in over eighty studies with which he has been associated, has done conceptual and empirical work on recreation user fees, and for the past several years has been working in the area of recreation benefits. He has been active in applied as well as basic research and has helped in the application of several widely-used recreation resource planning and management technologies based on his research.

Jack B. Ellis graduated from the University of Toronto with a B.A.Sc. degree in 1958. He then studied in London on an Athlone Fellowship, completing an M.Sc. degree in 1961 at Imperial College, University of London. His Ph.D. degree was taken at Michigan State University in 1965, where part of his research focussed on the application of systems theory to large-scale computer models of recreation behavior. He held academic positions at the University of Waterloo from 1961 to 1970, starting in the Faculty of Engineering and later serving as chair of the first Executive Committee which set up the current Faculty of Environmental Studies at Waterloo. In 1970, he was appointed as Professor in Environmental Studies at York University in Toronto, where he is currently Professor and Associate Dean.

Dr. Ellis is the author of over 60 reports, papers, monographs and book chapters on recreation and its economic aspects. He has served as a consultant to a wide range of government and private clients on recreation and tourism. He served as President of the Ontario Research Council on Leisure from 1972 to 1984, and as a founding Director of the Canadian Association for Leisure Studies, being President from 1984-87. Dr. Ellis teaches at the graduate level on topics in environmental planning and modelling.

Sue Glyptis took a B.A. (Honors) degree in Geography at the University College of Wales, Aberystwyth, in 1974, followed by a Ph.D. in Geography at the University of Hull, in 1979, for research entitled "Countryside visitors: site use and leisure lifestyles". From 1977 to 1981 she was a Research Officer at the Sports Council in London, involved in designing, commissioning and managing many research projects, particularly on countryside sport, sports participation, and facility management. In 1981, she received the British Travel Educational Trust's Travelling Research Fellowship, to produce a report on sport and tourism in Western Europe. Later that year she was appointed Lecturer in Recreation Management and Leisure Studies in the Department of Physical Education and Sports Science at Loughborough University of Technology, and in 1987 she was promoted to Senior Lecturer.

Dr. Glyptis is involved in four main areas of teaching and research: countryside recreation; inner city recreation; leisure lifestyles, with particular reference to home-based leisure; and providing for the recreation needs of different sectors of the population. She has undertaken research funded by a wide range of organizations in the UK, including the Economic and Social Research Council, the Sports Council, the Department of the Environment, and numerous local authorities, and has published some 50 reports, papers, and monographs. She has presented papers at many national and international conferences. From 1980 to 1983 she was Secretary of the Leisure Studies Association, and she is currently an Examiner and a member of the Training Board of the Institute of Leisure and Amenity Management.

Geoffrey Godbey is Professor of Leisure Studies at the Pennsylvania State University. He is the author of five books concerning leisure and leisure services: *Leisure Studies and Services: An Overview*, with Stanley Parker; *Recreation, Park and Leisure Services: Foundations, Organization, Administration*; *Leisure in Your Life: An Exploration*; *The Evolution of Leisure: Historical and Philosophical Perspectives*, with Tom Goodale; and *The Future of Leisure Services: Thriving on Change*. Godbey has written for a wide variety of academic, practitioner, and mass market publications, including the *Journal of Leisure Research*, *The Nation*, *Public Opinion*, *World Tennis*, and *Parks and Recreation*. He has served as associate editor and reviewer for several journals and is the Editor of Venture Publishing Inc., a publishing house specializing in leisure-related literature.

Formerly, Dr. Godbey was Acting Chairman, Department of Recreation, University of Waterloo; Instructor-in-Charge of the Recreation Leadership Curriculum at the Ogontz Campus of the Pennsylvania State University, near Philadelphia; and a Research Intern with the Philadelphia Department of Recreation. He was a consultant to the U.S. Department of the Interior for three years in the development of the Third Nationwide Outdoor Recreation Plan. Dr. Godbey is Past President of the Academy of Leisure Sciences and President of the Society of Park and Recreation Educators. A member of the Board of Directors of the World Leisure and Recreation Association, he has given invited presentations in sixteen countries.

Thomas L. Goodale received undergraduate degrees at the State University of New York at Alfred and at Cortland and received the M.Sc. and Ph.D. degrees from the University of Illinois. Currently Professor of Leisure Studies at George Mason University in Virginia, he previously taught at the State University of New York at Cortland, the University of Wisconsin at Green Bay, and the University of Ottawa, where he served one term as Department Chairman.

Dr. Goodale has authored many articles and chapters in research, scholarly, and professional publications, a number of reports for government and professional associations, and has edited, authored, or co-authored four books. In addition to his interest in the history and philosophy of leisure, he also engages in research and writing about the social psychology of leisure and recreation.

Seppo E. Iso-Ahola received his B.S. from the University of Jyväskylä, Finland, in 1971, an M.S. from the University of Illinois in 1972, an M.S. from the University of Jyväskylä in 1973, and the Ph.D. from the University of Illinois in 1976. He was Assistant and Associate Professor at the University of Iowa from 1976 to 1981, and Associate Professor (1981 to 1984) and Professor (since 1984) at the University of Maryland. He has published over fifty research articles in various psychological and recreation journals, and has authored three books dealing with the social psychology of leisure, recreation, and sports. He was Editor of the *Journal of Leisure Research* between 1983 and 1986. In 1987, he received the prestigious Theodore and Franklin Roosevelt Award for Excellence in Recreation and Park Research.

John R. Kelly is Professor in the Institute for Research on Human Development and in the Department of Leisure Studies at the University of Illinois at Urbana-Champaign, where he has been on the faculty since 1975. He is also Director of the Office of Gerontology and Aging Studies. His Ph.D. in Sociology is from the University of Oregon, and he has received Master's degrees from Oregon, Yale, and the University of Southern California.

He is the author of six published books: *Leisure* (an introduction to leisure studies); *Leisure Identities and Interactions* (a study of personal development and expression through the life course); *Recreation Business* (an introduction to market-sector leisure provisions); *Freedom to Be: A New Sociology of Leisure* (a critical analysis of theory and research); *Peoria Winter: Styles and Resources in Later Life* (a study of coping with later life changes); and *Recreation Trends Toward the Year 2000* (an analysis of national participation in recreation activities).

Dr. Kelly has published fifteen chapters in edited books, nine technical reports for federal agencies and business consultants, and over forty journal articles. In a study of citations in leisure research between 1972 and 1982, he was cited more than any other author. He was the founding Chair of the Commission on Research of the World Leisure and Recreation Association and is a member of the Academy of Leisure Sciences.

Roger C. Mannell is a social psychologist and Associate Professor in the Department of Recreation and Leisure Studies, University of Waterloo. He is currently the Associate Chairman of Graduate Affairs for the Department and Director of the Leisure Studies Data Bank. Before coming to the University of Waterloo in 1979, Dr. Mannell was Director of the Centre of Leisure Studies at Acadia University.

Dr. Mannell's research and writing focus on the personality and social factors that influence what people do in their free time and, in turn, the impact of this structuring of leisure on psychological well-being and adjustment. With the use of psychological laboratory and experiential sampling methods, Dr. Mannell has studied topics such as personality differences in the ability to cope with free time, the role of intrinsic motivation and satisfaction in leisure, leisure and coping with life crises, and the integration of work and leisure in daily life.

Stephen F. McCool is Professor of Wildland Recreation Management and Director of the Institute for Tourism and Recreation Research at the University of Montana in Missoula. Dr. McCool holds a B.Sc. degree in Forest Resource Management from the University of Idaho and M.Sc. and Ph.D. degrees, specializing in outdoor recreation management, from the University of Minnesota.

His research interests include social aspects of managing wilderness resources, the role of information as a visitor management tool, and developing linkages between wilderness-like resources, tourism, and economic development.

Chris Rojek gained a B.A. Honors degree in Sociology from Leicester University in 1976 and an M.Phil. in Sociology from the same university in 1979. He held a fixed-term one-year appointment as Lecturer in Sociology at the College of St. Mark & St. John, Plymouth, in 1981-1982. From 1982 to 1986 he was Lecturer in Sociology at the Queen's College, Glasgow. In 1986, he foresook the groves of academe to embroil himself in the "enterprise culture." He is currently Senior Editor in Social and Behavioral Science at Routledge Publishers, London.

Chris Rojek is currently preparing his Ph.D. thesis for presentation to the Department of Sociology at the University of Glasgow. He is the author of numerous articles. His books include *Capitalism and Leisure Theory* and *Ways of Escape: Leisure and Travel in the Modern World*, as well as *Leisure for Leisure: Critical Essays* (edited), *Social Work and Received Ideas* (co-authored with G. Peacock and S. Collins), and *The Haunt of Misery: Critical Essays in Social Work and Helping* (co-edited with G. Peacock and S. Collins). His research interests include leisure, travel, and hyperreality.

Richard Schreyer is Professor of Recreation Resources in the Department of Forest Resources, College of Natural Resources, at Utah State University. His principal professional interests are studying human perceptions of natural environments and seeking applications of social science knowledge in natural resource management. Dr. Schreyer received his Ph.D. from the University of Michigan in Resource Planning and Conservation. He also holds degrees in Natural Resource Administration and Forest Recreation Management.

Dr. Schreyer has been involved in teaching courses in outdoor recreation behavior, environmental interpretation, principles of wildland recreation, human dimensions of natural resource management, and human-environment relations. He has also taught on principles of recreation behavior to natural resource managers, in a number of short courses and workshops across the U.S.A. His research in the area of environmental perception has included studying the mental images of wilderness recreationists, the psychology of high-risk recreation, non-traditional uses of national parks, the preservation of unique natural environments, and the subjective nature of the recreation experience. In the area of social science applications to resource management, he has carried out research on recreational conflict, the impact of change in recreation environments, succession and displacement in recreation, and the determination of recreational carrying capacity. He has also studied the impact of information on the behavior of recreationists, problems in the application of recreation research, and potential impacts of major federal projects to recreation and tourism, such as the construction of a high-level nuclear waste repository.

Stephen L.J. Smith received his B.A. in Geography from Wright State University, Dayton, Ohio, in 1968, and his M.A. from Ohio State University in 1970. He also holds a Ph.D. in Recreation and Resources Development, Texas A&M University, class of 1973. His first professorial position was with the Department of Park and Recreation Resources, Michigan State University. He joined the Department of Recreation and Leisure Studies at the University of Waterloo in 1976. He is currently Professor and Chairman in that Department.

Dr. Smith is the author of numerous scholarly articles on various aspects of recreation, tourism, and leisure, and was editor of the *Recreation Research Review*. He has written two texts, *Recreation Geography* and *Tourism Analysis*. He has served on the National Task Force on Tourism data, administered by Statistics Canada. He is also co-founder of the Tourism Research and Education Centre, an inter-university consortium of tourism researchers and educators.

He teaches courses in the economics of recreation, an introductory course on leisure concepts, and research methods. A current project is the development of a concepts dictionary for the field of recreation and leisure studies.

George H. Stankey obtained his B.S. and M.S. degrees in Geography at Oregon State University in 1965 and 1966 respectively, and his Ph.D. degree, also in Geography, from Michigan State University, in 1970. From 1968 until 1987 he was a Research Social Scientist with the USDA Forest Service's Wilderness Management Research Unit. He also held an appointment as a Faculty Affiliate in the School of Forestry and the Department of Geography at the University of Montana. In 1981-82, while on a leave of absence from the

Forest Service, he was a Senior Lecturer in the School of Applied Science at Canberra College of Advanced Education, Canberra, Australia. In 1987, he moved to Sydney, Australia, to take up a joint appointment between the Department of Leisure and Tourism Studies, Kuring-gai College of Advanced Education and the New South Wales National Parks and Wildlife Service.

Dr. Stankey has published widely in the recreation and wilderness management field. He is a co-author of the text *Wilderness Management*. He is also a member of the Commission on National Parks and Protected Areas of the International Union for the Conservation of Nature.

Janet E. Stockdale took a First Class Honors degree in Psychology at University College London in 1967, and was awarded a Ph.D. degree from the University of London in 1971. She was appointed Lecturer in Social Psychology at the London School of Economics and Political Science in 1970, and was promoted to Senior Lecturer in 1987. Currently, Dr. Stockdale also holds the post of Adviser to Women Students at the School, and she acts as a consultant on training to the Metropolitan Police Force. Dr. Stockdale has held visiting appointments at the University of California, Berkeley, in 1973, and at the University of North Carolina, Chapel Hill, in 1976 and 1977.

Dr. Stockdale's teaching responsibilities include undergraduate and postgraduate courses in Psychology, Statistics, and Research Methods. She has published reports and articles in a variety of research areas, including leisure, crowding, equal opportunities, and social research methodology. She was commissioned to contribute two projects to the initiative funded by the Sports Council and the Economic and Social Research Council Joint Panel on Leisure and Recreation Research. The first of these, which focused on the perception and meaning of leisure, was published in 1985; the second, an evaluation of research methods in leisure and recreation, was published in 1987. Her current research includes the application of the theory of social representations to a range of social issues.

Guy S. Swinnerton obtained a B.A. Honors degree in Geography from the London School of Economics and Political Science, University of London, in 1965. He then continued his education in Canada, completing an M.A. degree in Geography at the University of British Columbia in 1969. Between 1967 and 1969 he was a Research Officer with the Canada Land Inventory Program in Victoria, B.C. He then returned to Britain to the Countryside Planning Unit at Wye College, University of London, and received a Ph.D. degree in Land Use Studies in 1974. From 1973 to 1978 he was Principal Lecturer in Land Use Studies and Director of the Natural Resources and Rural Economy Program at Seale-Hayne College in south-west England. In 1978 he joined the Department of Recreation and Leisure Studies (then Recreation Administration) at the University of Alberta and is currently Professor and Chairman.

Dr. Swinnerton teaches senior undergraduate and graduate courses in the areas of the planning and management of outdoor recreation resources and parks and conservation. His research interests include countryside recreation, conservation policies and practices, and provincial parks policy and planning. He has served as a consultant to a number of government departments on issues dealing with integrated resource management, conservation policies, and water-based recreation.

R.W. Vickerman graduated in Economics from Clare College, Cambridge in 1968 and obtained a D.Phil. in Transport Economics from the University of Sussex in 1972. After a short period as a Research Fellow at the University of Sussex he became Lecturer in Economics at the University of Hull from 1972 to 1976, moving to the University of Kent at Canterbury in 1977 as Lecturer in Economics, becoming Senior Lecturer in 1979 and Reader in 1987. He has held visiting appointments at the University of Münster, West Germany and the University of Guelph, Canada.

He has undertaken research in transport economics and urban and regional economics as well as leisure and recreation. His work on the economics of leisure and recreation has been based on the premise of the need to develop rigorous economic models of behavior; this has included work on issues in the pricing and allocation of recreational resources. Dr. Vickerman is the author of *The Economics of Leisure and Recreation* as well as numerous articles on the economics of leisure. He was a member of the Sports Council and Economic and Social Research Council Joint Panel on Recreation and Leisure Research in the UK from 1979 to 1986, and has been an economic consultant to the U.K. Sports Council.

Geoffrey Wall took a B.A. degree (Geography) at Leeds University in 1966, a Certificate of Education at Cambridge University in 1967, an M.A. (Geography) at the University of Toronto in 1968, and a Ph.D. in Geography at Hull University in 1970. He has held appointments as Junior Research Fellow at Sheffield University, Assistant Professor at the University of Kentucky, and has been a faculty member in Geography at the University of Waterloo since 1974, where he is currently Professor and Associate Chairman for Graduate Studies in Geography, and is cross-appointed with the Department of Recreation and Leisure Studies. He has also been a Visiting Professor at the Universities of Madras, Kent, and South Carolina.

Dr. Wall has undertaken research, both as an academic and as a consultant, on a wide variety of aspects of tourism and recreation. He is the author of six books, ten chapters in books, and more than forty papers in refereed journals, as well as numerous consulting reports and other papers. Dr. Wall teaches an undergraduate course on recreational geography and a graduate course on recreational land use. His current research projects include studies of the economic impacts of tourism, the development of economic impact models, implications of the greenhouse effect for tourism and recreation, and the development of a strategic plan for Bali.

Peter A. Witt has been a member of the faculty at the University of North Texas since 1979. He is currently the Associate Dean of the Graduate School and Professor of Recreation and Leisure Studies. He has also served as the Associate Vice-President for Research, Acting Dean of the Graduate School, and Chair of the Division of Recreation and Leisure Studies at the same institution.

A native of Los Angeles, Dr. Witt received his Doctorate in leisure studies from the University of Illinois. He holds Bachelor's and Master's degrees from the University of California at Los Angeles. After completing his doctorate, he held a faculty position in the Department of Leisure Studies at the University of Ottawa from 1969 to 1979.

He has written or edited four books and authored or co-authored more than 75 articles on the social psychology of leisure and recreation and on leisure services for the handicapped. In addition, he has prepared over 50 reports for government, university, or private organizations. In 1980-81, he was recognized as the most published author in recreation and leisure. Among his major works are *Recreation and Leisure: Issues in an Era of Change* (with Tom Goodale), and *The Leisure Diagnostic Battery* (with Gary Ellis). Witt was also the author of a major study of recreation services for the handicapped which served as the basis for the development of federal and provincial policy and services in Canada during the 1970s.

Dr. Witt is the editor of the *Therapeutic Recreation Journal* and was recently selected to be the editor of the *Journal of Leisure Research* when his *TRJ* editorship expires. He has been an editor or associate editor for almost every major journal in the leisure studies field in North America. He is a fellow of the Academy of Leisure Sciences and in 1988 received the Theodore and Franklin Roosevelt Award for Excellence in Park and Recreation Research from the National Recreation and Park Association. He has also received the Outstanding Achievement Award from the American Association for Leisure and Recreation.

OTHER BOOKS FROM
VENTURE PUBLISHING, INC.

Acquiring Parks and Recreation Facilities through Mandatory Dedication: A Comprehensive Guide, by Ronald A. Kaiser and James D. Mertes

Amenity Resource Valuation, edited by George L. Peterson, B.L. Driver and Robin Gregory

Behavior Modification in Therapeutic Recreation: An Introductory Learning Manual, by John Dattilo and William D. Murphy

Being at Leisure—Playing at Life: A Guide to Health and Joyful Living, by Bruno Hans Geba

Beyond the Bake Sale: A Fund Raising Handbook for Public Agencies, (Distributed for City of Sacramento, Department of Recreation and Parks)

Community Tourism Industry Imperative—The Necessity, The Opportunities, Its Potential, by Uel Blank

Doing More with Less in the Delivery of Recreation and Park Services: A Book of Case Studies, by John L. Crompton

Evaluation of Therapeutic Recreation through Quality Assurance, edited by Bob Riley

The Evolution of Leisure: Historical and Philosophical Perspectives, by Thomas L. Goodale and Geoffrey C. Godbey

The Future of Leisure Services: Thriving on Change, by Geoffrey Godbey

Gifts to Share: A Gifts Catalogue How-To Manual for Public Agencies, (Distributed for City of Sacramento, Department of Recreation and Parks)

International Directory of Academic Institutions in Leisure, Recreation and Related Fields (Distributed for WLRA)

Leadership Administration of Outdoor Pursuits, by Phyllis Ford and James Blanchard

The *Leisure Diagnostic Battery—Users Manual and Sample Forms,* by
Peter A. Witt and Gary D. Ellis

Leisure Education: A Manual of Activities and Resources, by Norma J.
Stumbo and Steven R. Thompson

*Leisure Education: Program Materials for Persons with Developmental
Disabilities, by Kenneth Joswiak*

Leisure in Your Life: An Exploration, Revised Edition, by Geoffrey Godbey

*Leisure of One's Own: A Feminist Perspective on Women's Leisure, by Karla
Henderson, Deborah Bialeschki, Susan Shaw and Valeria Freysinger*

Outdoor Recreation Management: Theory and Application, Revised and
Enlarged, by Alan Jubenville, Ben W. Twight and Robert H. Becker

Park Ranger Handbook, by J. W. Shiner

Planning Parks for People, by John Hultsman, Richard L. Cottrell and
Wendy Zales-Hultsman

*Playing, Living, Learning—A Worldwide Perspective on Children's
Opportunities to Play,* by Cor Westland and Jane Knight

Private and Commercial Recreation, edited by Arlin Epperson

Recreation and Leisure: An Introductory Handbook, edited by Alan Graefe
and Stan Parker

Recreation and Leisure: Issues in an Era of Change, Revised Edition, edited
by Thomas L. Goodale and Peter A. Witt

Recreation Economic Decisions: Comparing Benefits and Costs, by
Richard G. Walsh

*Risk Management in Therapeutic Recreation: A Component of Quality
Assurance,* by Judith Voelkl

Wilderness in America:Personal Perspectives, edited by Daniel Dustin

Venture Publishing, Inc.
1640 Oxford Circle
State College, PA 16803
(814) 234-4561